core
JavaServer™ Faces

Second Edition

core
JavaServer™ Faces

Second Edition

DAVID GEARY
CAY HORSTMANN

PRENTICE
HALL

Upper Saddle River, NJ • Boston • Indianapolis • San Francisco
New York • Toronto • Montreal • London • Munich • Paris • Madrid
Capetown • Sydney • Tokyo • Singapore • Mexico City

The publisher offers excellent discounts on this book when ordered in quantity for bulk purchases or special sales, which may include electronic versions and/or custom covers and content particular to your business, training goals, marketing focus, and branding interests. For more information, please contact: U.S. Corporate and Government Sales, (800) 382-3419, corpsales@pearsontechgroup.com. For sales outside the United States, please contact: International Sales, international@pearsoned.com.

This Book Is Safari Enabled

The Safari® Enabled icon on the cover of your favorite technology book means the book is available through Safari Bookshelf. When you buy this book, you get free access to the online edition for 45 days.

Safari Bookshelf is an electronic reference library that lets you easily search thousands of technical books, find code samples, download chapters, and access technical information whenever and wherever you need it.

To gain 45-day Safari Enabled access to this book:

- Go to http://www.prenhallprofessional.com/safarienabled
- Complete the brief registration form
- Enter the coupon code UTDI-44NC-JP3B-7ZC5-NAIG

If you have difficulty registering on Safari Bookshelf or accessing the online edition, please e-mail customer-service@safaribooksonline.com.

Visit us on the Web: www.prenhallprofessional.com

Library of Congress Cataloging-in-Publication Data

Geary, David M.
  Core JavaServer faces / David Geary, Cay Horstmann.—2nd ed.
    p. cm.
  Includes bibliographical references and index.
  ISBN-13: 978-0-13-173886-7 (pbk. : alk. paper)
  ISBN-10: 0-13-173886-0 (pbk. : alk. paper) 1. JavaServer pages. 2.
Web site development. 3. Web sites—Design. I. Horstmann, Cay S.,
1959- II. Title.

TK5105.8885.J38G433 2007
005.2'768—dc22
                                    2007006830

ISBN 0-13-173886-0

Text printed in the United States on recycled paper at RR Donnelley in Crawfordsville, Indiana.
First printing, April 2007

Contents

Preface

When we heard about JavaServer Faces (JSF) at the 2002 JavaOne conference, we were very excited. Both of us had extensive experience with client-side Java programming, and had lived to tell the tale—David in *Graphic Java™*, and Cay in *Core Java™*, both published by Sun Microsystems Press. When we first tried web programming with servlets and JavaServer Pages (JSP), we found it to be rather unintuitive and tedious. JavaServer *Faces* promised to put a friendly face in front of a web application, allowing programmers to think about text fields and menus instead of fretting over page flips and request parameters. Each of us proposed a book project to the publisher, who promptly suggested that we should jointly write the Sun Microsystems Press book on this technology.

It took the JSF Expert Group (of which David was a member) until 2004 to release the JSF 1.0 specification and reference implementation. A bug fix 1.1 release emerged shortly afterwards, and an incremental 1.2 release added a number of cleanups and convenience features in 2006.

JSF is now the preeminent server-side Java web framework, and it has fulfilled most of its promises. You really can design web user interfaces by putting components on a form and linking them to Java objects, without having to mix code and markup. A strong point of JSF is its extensible component model, and a large number of third-party components have become available. The flexible design of the framework has allowed it to grow well and accommodate new technologies such as Ajax. The framework was designed for tool support, and usable drag-and-drop GUI builders have finally emerged. And finally, unlike competing technologies that let you tumble down a deep cliff once you step beyond the glitz, JSF supports the hard stuff—separation of presentation and business logic, navigation, connections with external services, and configuration management.

We are still excited about JSF, and we hope you will share this excitement when you learn how this technology makes you a more effective web application developer.

About This Book

This book is suitable for web developers whose main focus is user interface design, as well as for programmers who implement reusable components for web applications. This is in stark contrast to the official JSF specification, a dense and pompously worded document whose principal audience is framework implementors, as well as long-suffering book authors.

The first half of the book, extending through Chapter 6, focuses on the JSF *tags*. These tags are similar to HTML form tags. They are the basic building blocks for JSF user interfaces. No programming is required for use of the tags. We assume only basic HTML skills for web pages and standard Java programming for the business logic.

The first part of the book covers these topics:

- Setting up your programming environment (Chapter 1)
- Connecting JSF tags to application logic (Chapter 2)
- Navigating between pages (Chapter 3)
- Using the standard JSF tags (Chapters 4 and 5)
- Converting and validating input (Chapter 6)

Starting with Chapter 7, we begin JSF programming in earnest. You will learn how to perform advanced tasks, and how to extend the JSF framework. Here are the main topics of the second part:

- Event handling (Chapter 7)
- Including common content among multiple pages (Chapter 8)
- Implementing custom components, converters, and validators (Chapter 9)
- Connecting to databases and other external services (Chapter 10)
- Ajax (Chapter 11)
- Open source technologies, with a focus on Facelets, Seam, and Shale (Chapter 12)

We end the book with a chapter that aims to answer common questions of the form "How do I . . . ?" (see Chapter 13). We encourage you to have a peek at that chapter as soon as you become comfortable with the basics of JSF. There are helpful notes on debugging and logging, and we also give you implementation details and working code for features that are missing from JSF, such as file uploads, pop-up menus, and a pager component for long tables.

JSF is built on top of servlets and JSP, but from the point of view of the JSF developer, these technologies merely form the low-level plumbing. While it can't hurt to be familiar with other web technologies such as servlets, JSP, or Struts, we do not assume any such knowledge.

Required Software

All software that you need for this book is freely available. You need the Java Software Development Kit from Sun Microsystems and an application server that supports JSF, such as the excellent open source GlassFish project. The software runs identically on Linux, Mac OS X, Solaris, and Windows. We used Java 5 and GlassFish on both Linux and Mac OS X to develop the code examples in the book.

If you are looking for a development environment that supports JSF development, we can heartily recommend the freely available NetBeans IDE. Good JSF support for Eclipse is available from several vendors that sell Eclipse enhancements.

Web Support

The web page for this book is http://corejsf.com. It contains

- The source code for all examples in this book
- Useful reference material that we felt is more effective in browseable form than in print
- A list of known errors in the book and the code
- A form for submitting corrections and suggestions

Acknowledgments

First and foremost, we'd like to thank Greg Doench, our editor at Prentice Hall, who has shepherded us through this project, never losing his nerve in spite of numerous delays and complications.

We very much appreciate our reviewers for both editions who have done a splendid job, finding errors and suggesting improvements in various drafts of the manuscript. They are:

- Gail Anderson, Anderson Software Group, Inc.
- Larry Brown, LMBrown.com, Inc.
- Frank Cohen, PushToTest
- Brian Goetz, Sun Microsystems, Inc.
- Rob Gordon, Crooked Furrow Farm
- Marty Hall, author of *Core Java Servlets and JavaServer Pages*
- Charlie Hunt, Sun Microsystems, Inc.
- Jeff Langr, Langr Software Solutions
- Bill Lewis, Tufts University
- Jeff Markham, Markham Software Company
- Angus McIntyre, IBM Corporation
- John Muchow, author of *Core J2ME*
- Dan Shellman, BearingPoint

- Sergei Smirnov, principal architect of Exadel JSF Studio
- Roman Smolgovsky, Flytecomm
- Stephen Stelting, Sun Microsystems, Inc.
- Christopher Taylor, Nanshu Densetsu
- Kim Topley, Keyboard Edge Limited
- Michael Yuan, co-author of *JBoss Seam: Simplicity and Power Beyond Java EE*

Finally, thanks to our families and friends who have supported us through this project and who share our relief that it is finally completed.

core
JavaServer™ Faces

Second Edition

GETTING STARTED

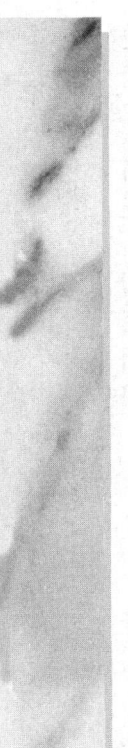

Topics in This Chapter

1

Why JavaServer Faces?

Judging from the job advertisements at employment web sites, there are two popular techniques for developing web applications:

*   The "rapid development" style, in which you use a visual development environment, such as Microsoft ASP.NET
*   The "hard-core coding" style, in which you write lots of code to support a high-performance backend, such as Java EE (Java Enterprise Edition)

Development teams face a difficult choice. Java EE is an attractive platform. It is highly scalable, portable to multiple platforms, and supported by many vendors. On the other hand, ASP.NET makes it easy to create attractive user interfaces without tedious programming. Of course, programmers want both: a high-performance backend and easy user interface programming. The promise of JSF (JavaServer Faces) is to bring rapid user interface development to server-side Java.

If you are familiar with client-side Java development, you can think of JSF as "Swing for server-side applications." If you have experience with JSP (JavaServer Pages), you will find that JSF provides much of the plumbing that JSP developers have to implement by hand, such as page navigation and validation. You can think of servlets and JSP as the "assembly language" under the hood of the high-level JSF framework. If you already know a server-side framework such as Struts, you will find that JSF uses a similar architecture but provides many additional services.

 NOTE: You need *not* know anything about Swing, JSP, or Struts to use this book. We assume basic familiarity only with Java and HTML.

JSF has these parts:

- A set of prefabricated UI (user interface) components
- An event-driven programming model
- A component model that enables third-party developers to supply additional components

Some JSF components are simple, such as input fields and buttons. Others are quite sophisticated—for example, data tables and trees.

JSF contains all the necessary code for event handling and component organization. Application programmers can be blissfully ignorant of these details and spend their effort on the application logic.

Perhaps most important, JSF is part of the Java EE standard. JSF is included in every Java EE application server, and it can be easily added to a standalone web container such as Tomcat.

For additional details, see "JSF Framework Services" on page 28. Many IDEs (integrated development environments) support JSF, with features that range from code completion to visual page designers. See "Development Environments for JSF" on page 21 for more information. In the following sections, we show you how to compose a JSF application by hand, so that you understand what your IDE does under the hood and you can troubleshoot problems effectively.

Software Installation

You need the following software packages to get started:

- JDK (Java SE Development Kit) 5.0 or higher (http://java.sun.com/j2se)
- JSF 1.2
- The sample code for this book, available at http://corejsf.com

We assume that you have already installed the JDK and that you are familiar with the JDK tools. For more information on the JDK, see Horstmann, Cay, and Cornell, Gary, 2004, 2005. *Core Java™ 2, vol. 2—Advanced Features (7th ed.)*. Santa Clara, CA: Sun Microsystems Press/Prentice Hall.

Since JSF 1.2 is part of the Java EE 5 specification, the easiest way to try out JSF is to use an application server that is compatible with Java EE 5. In this section, we describe the GlassFish application server (http://glassfish.dev.java.net). You will find instructions for other application servers on the companion web site (http://corejsf.com).

 NOTE: As this book is published, there are two major versions of JSF. The most recent version, JSF 1.2, was released as part of Java EE 5 in 2006. The original version, JSF 1.0, was released in 2004, and a bug-fix release, named JSF 1.1, was issued shortly thereafter. This book covers both versions 1.1 and 1.2, but the main focus is on version 1.2.

 NOTE: If you do not want to install a complete application server, you can also use Tomcat (http://tomcat.apache.org), together with the JSF libraries from Sun Microsystems (http://javaserverfaces.dev.java.net). See the book's companion web site (http://corejsf.com) for installation instructions.

Install GlassFish, following the directions on the web site. Then start the application server. On Unix/Linux, you use the command

    glassfish/bin/asadmin start-domain

(See Figure 1–1.) Here, *glassfish* is the directory into which you installed the GlassFish software.

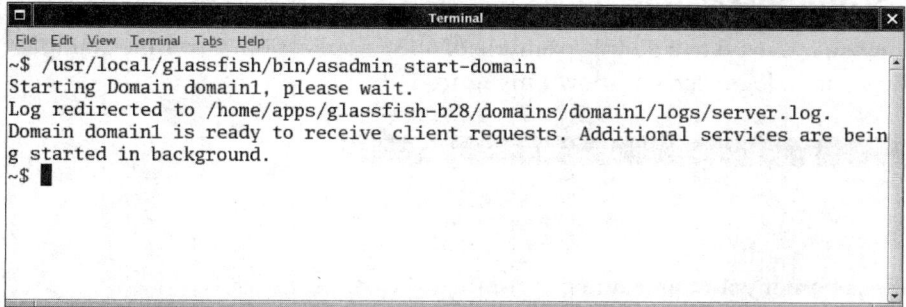

Figure 1–1   Starting GlassFish

On Windows, launch

    glassfish\bin\asadmin start-domain

To test that GlassFish runs properly, point your browser to http://localhost:8080. You should see a welcome page (see Figure 1–2).

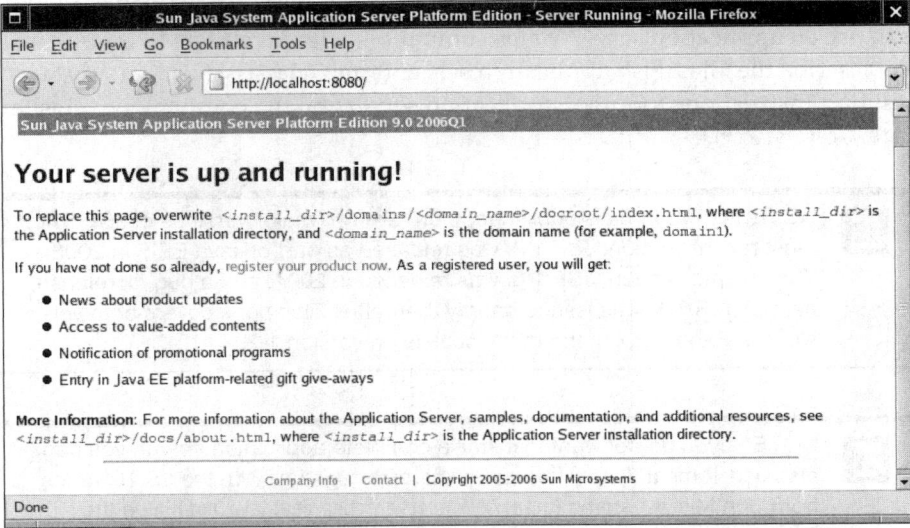

Figure 1–2   GlassFish welcome page

You shut down GlassFish with the command

   glassfish/bin/asadmin stop-domain

or, on Windows,

   glassfish\bin\asadmin stop-domain

A Simple Example

Now we move on to a simple example of a JSF application. Our first example starts with a login screen, shown in Figure 1–3.

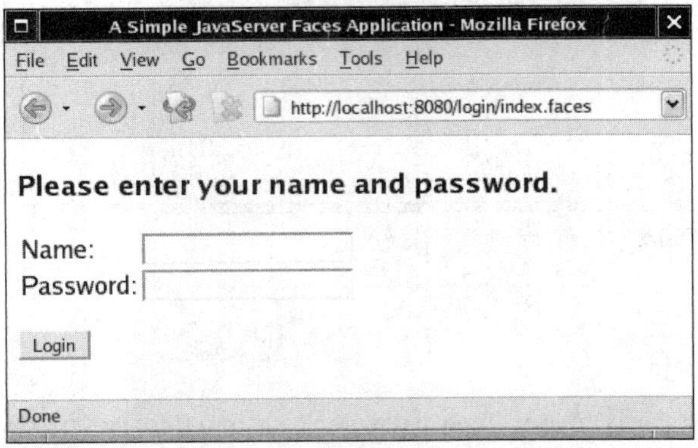

Figure 1–3   A login screen

Of course, in a real web application, this screen would be beautified by a skilled graphic artist.

The file that describes the login screen is essentially an HTML file with a few additional tags (see Listing 1–1). Its visual appearance can be easily improved by a graphic artist who need not have any programming skills.

Listing 1–1   login/web/index.jsp

```
1.  <html>
2.     <%@ taglib uri="http://java.sun.com/jsf/core" prefix="f" %>
3.     <%@ taglib uri="http://java.sun.com/jsf/html" prefix="h" %>
4.     <f:view>
5.        <head>
6.           <title>A Simple JavaServer Faces Application</title>
7.        </head>
8.        <body>
9.           <h:form>
10.             <h3>Please enter your name and password.</h3>
11.             <table>
12.                <tr>
13.                   <td>Name:</td>
14.                   <td>
15.                      <h:inputText value="#{user.name}"/>
16.                   </td>
17.                </tr>
18.                <tr>
19.                   <td>Password:</td>
20.                   <td>
21.                      <h:inputSecret value="#{user.password}"/>
22.                   </td>
23.                </tr>
24.             </table>
25.             <p>
26.                <h:commandButton value="Login" action="login"/>
27.             </p>
28.          </h:form>
29.       </body>
30.    </f:view>
31. </html>
```

We discuss the contents of this file in detail later in this chapter, in the section "JSF Pages" on page 13. For now, note the following points:

- A number of the tags are standard HTML tags: body, table, and so on.
- Some tags have *prefixes*, such as f:view and h:inputText. These are JSF tags. The two taglib declarations declare the JSF tag libraries.

- The h:inputText, h:inputSecret, and h:commandButton tags correspond to the text field, password field, and submit button in Figure 1–3.
- The input fields are linked to object properties. For example, the attribute value="#{user.name}" tells the JSF implementation to link the text field with the name property of a user object. We discuss this linkage in more detail later in this chapter, in the section "Beans" on page 12.

When the user enters the name and password, and clicks the "Login" button, a welcome screen appears (see Figure 1–4). Listing 1–3 on page 14 shows the source code for this screen. The section "Navigation" on page 16 explains how the application navigates from the login screen and the welcome screen.

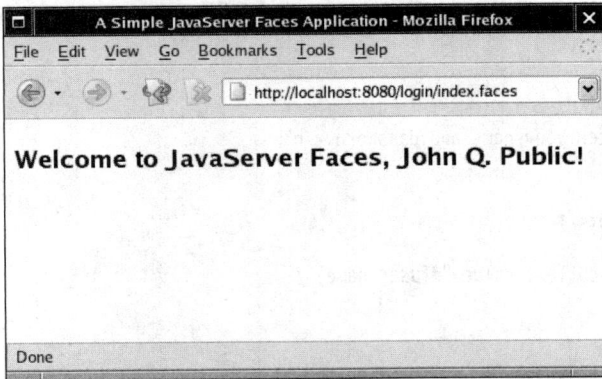

Figure 1–4   A welcome screen

The welcome message contains the username. The password is ignored for now.

The purpose of this application is, of course, not to impress anyone but to illustrate the various pieces that are necessary to produce a JSF application.

Ingredients

Our sample application consists of the following ingredients:

- Pages that define the login and welcome screens. We call them index.jsp and welcome.jsp.
- A bean that manages the user data (in our case, username and password). A *bean* is a Java class that exposes properties, usually by following a simple naming convention for the getter and setter methods. The code is in the file UserBean.java (see Listing 1–2). Note that the class is contained in the com.corejsf package.

- A configuration file for the application that lists bean resources and navigation rules. By default, this file is called faces-config.xml.

- Miscellaneous files that are needed to keep the servlet container happy: the web.xml file, and an index.html file that redirects the user to the correct URL for the login page.

More advanced JSF applications have the same structure, but they can contain additional Java classes, such as event handlers, validators, and custom components.

Listing 1–2 login/src/java/com/corejsf/UserBean.java

```
1. package com.corejsf;
2.
3. public class UserBean {
4.    private String name;
5.    private String password;
6.
7.    // PROPERTY: name
8.    public String getName() { return name; }
9.    public void setName(String newValue) { name = newValue; }
10.
11.    // PROPERTY: password
12.    public String getPassword() { return password; }
13.    public void setPassword(String newValue) { password = newValue; }
14. }
```

Directory Structure

A JSF application is deployed as a *WAR file*: a zipped file with extension .war and a directory structure that follows a standardized layout:

```
HTML and JSP files
WEB-INF/
    ├── configuration files
    ├── classes/
    │      └── class files
    └── lib/
           └──library files
```

For example, the WAR file of our sample application has the directory structure shown in Figure 1–5. Note that the UserBean class is in the package com.corejsf.

The META-INF directory is automatically produced by the jar program when the WAR file is created.

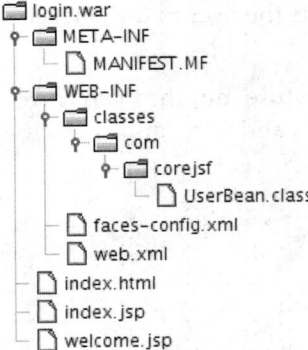

Figure 1–5   Directory structure of the sample WAR file

We package our application source in a slightly different directory structure, following the Java Blueprints conventions (http://java.sun.com/blueprints/code/projectconventions.html). The source code is contained in an src/java directory, and the JSF pages and configuration files are contained in a web directory (see Figure 1–6).

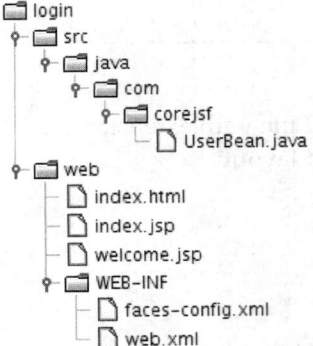

Figure 1–6   Directory structure of the sample application

Build Instructions

We now walk you through the steps required for building JSF applications with your bare hands. At the end of this chapter, we show you how to automate this process.

1. Launch a command shell.

2. Change to the *corejsf-examples* directory—that is, the directory that contains the sample code for this book.

3. Run the following commands:

```
cd ch1/login/src/java
mkdir ../../web/WEB-INF/classes
javac -d ../../web/WEB-INF/classes com/corejsf/UserBean.java
```

On Windows, use backslashes instead:

```
cd ch1\login\web
mkdir WEB-INF\classes
javac -d ..\..\web\WEB-INF\classes com\corejsf\UserBean.java
```

4. Change to the ch1/login/web directory.

5. Run the following command:

```
jar cvf login.war .
```

(Note the period at the end of the command, indicating the current directory.)

6. Copy the login.war file to the directory *glassfish*/domains/domain1/autodeploy.

7. Make sure that GlassFish has been started. Point your browser to

```
http://localhost:8080/login
```

The application should start up at this point.

The bean classes in more complex programs may need to interact with the JSF framework. In that case, the compilation step is more complex. Your class path must include the JSF libraries. With the GlassFish application server, add a single JAR file:

glassfish/lib/javaee.jar

With other systems, you may need multiple JAR files.

A typical compilation command would look like this:

```
javac -classpath .:glassfish/lib/javaee.jar
    -d ../../web/WEB-INF/classes com/corejsf/*.java
```

On Windows, use semicolons to separate the path elements:

```
javac -classpath .;glassfish\lib\javaee.jar
    -d ..\..\web\WEB-INF\classes com\corejsf\*.java
```

Be sure to include the current directory (denoted by a period) in the class path.

Sample Application Analysis

Web applications have two parts: the *presentation layer* and the *business logic*. The presentation layer is concerned with the look of the application. In the context of a browser-based application, the look is determined by the HTML tags that specify layout, fonts, images, and so on. The business logic is implemented in the Java code that determines the behavior of the application.

Some web technologies intermingle HTML and code. That approach is seductive since it is easy to produce simple applications in a single file. But for serious applications, mixing markup and code poses considerable problems.

Professional web designers know about graphic design, but they typically rely on tools that translate their vision into HTML. They would certainly not want to deal with embedded code. On the other hand, programmers are notoriously unqualified when it comes to graphic design. (The example programs in this book bear ample evidence.)

Thus, for designing professional web applications, it is important to *separate* the presentation from the business logic. This allows both web designers and programmers to focus on their core competences.

In the context of JSF, the application code is contained in beans, and the design is contained in web pages. We look at beans first.

Beans

A Java *bean* is a class that exposes properties and events to an environment such as JSF. A *property* is a named value of a given type that can be read and/or written. The simplest way to define a property is to use a standard naming convention for the reader and writer methods, namely, the familiar get/set convention. The first letter of the property name is changed to upper case in the method names.

For example, the UserBean class has two properties, name and password, both of type String:

```
public class UserBean {
    public String getName() { . . . }
    public void setName(String newValue) {. . . }
    public String getPassword() { . . . }
    public void setPassword(String newValue) { . . . }
    . . .
}
```

The get/set methods can carry out arbitrary actions. In many cases, they simply get or set an instance field. But they might also access a database or a JNDI (Java Naming and Directory Interface) directory.

 NOTE: According to the bean specification, it is legal to omit a read or write method. For example, if getPassword is omitted, then password is a write-only property. That might indeed be desirable for security reasons. However, JSF deals poorly with this situation and throws an exception instead of taking a default action when a read or write method is absent. Therefore, it is best to give read/write access to all bean properties.

In JSF applications, you use beans for all data that needs to be accessible from a page. The beans are the conduits between the user interface and the backend of the application.

JSF Pages

You need a JSF page for each browser screen. Depending on your development environment, JSF pages typically have the extension .jsp or .jsf. At the time of this writing, the extension .jsp requires less configuration effort. For that reason, we use the .jsp extension in the examples of this book.

 NOTE: The extension of the page *files* is .jsp or .jsf, whereas in the preferred configuration, the extension of the page *URLs* is .faces. For example, when the browser requests the URL http://localhost:8080/login/index.faces, the URL extension .faces is *mapped* to the file extension .jsp and the servlet container loads the file index.jsp. This process sounds rather byzantine, but it is a consequence of implementing JSF on top of the servlet technology.

Now we take another look at the first page of our sample application in Listing 1–1.

The page starts out with the tag library declarations:

```
<%@ taglib uri="http://java.sun.com/jsf/core" prefix="f" %>
<%@ taglib uri="http://java.sun.com/jsf/html" prefix="h" %>
```

The JSF implementation defines two sets of tags. The HTML tags generate HTML-specific markup. If you want your web application to render pages for an alternative client technology, you must use a different tag library. The core tags are independent of the rendering technology. For example, you need the f:view tag both for HTML pages and for pages that are rendered by a cell phone.

NOTE: You can choose any prefixes for tags, such as faces:view and html:inputText. In this book, we use f for the core tags and h for the HTML tags.

Much of the page is similar to an HTML form. Note the following differences:

- All JSF tags are contained in an f:view tag.
- Instead of using an HTML form tag, you enclose all the JSF components in an h:form tag.
- Instead of using the familiar input HTML tags, use h:inputText, h:inputSecret, and h:commandButton.

We discuss all standard JSF tags and their attributes in Chapters 4 and 5. In the first three chapters, we can get by with input fields and command buttons.

The input field values are bound to properties of the bean with name user:

```
<h:inputText value="#{user.name}"/>
```

You will see the declaration of the user variable in "Navigation" on page 16. The #{...} delimiters are explained in "The Syntax of Value Expressions" on page 64 of Chapter 2.

When the page is displayed, the framework calls the getName method to obtain the current property value. When the page is submitted, the framework invokes the setName method to set the value that the user entered.

The h:commandButton tag has an action attribute whose value is used when specifying navigation rules:

```
<h:commandButton value="Login" action="login"/>
```

We discuss navigation rules in "Navigation" on page 16. The value attribute is the string that is displayed on the button.

The second JSF page of our application is even simpler than the first. It uses the h:outputText tag to display the username (see Listing 1–3).

Listing 1–3   login/web/welcome.jsp

```
1. <html>
2.    <%@ taglib uri="http://java.sun.com/jsf/core" prefix="f" %>
3.    <%@ taglib uri="http://java.sun.com/jsf/html" prefix="h" %>
4.
5.    <f:view>
6.       <head>
7.          <title>A Simple JavaServer Faces Application</title>
8.       </head>
```

Listing 1–3   login/web/welcome.jsp (cont.)

```
9.      <body>
10.         <h:form>
11.             <h3>
12.                 Welcome to JavaServer Faces,
13.                 <h:outputText value="#{user.name}"/>!
14.             </h3>
15.         </h:form>
16.     </body>
17. </f:view>
18. </html>
```

 NOTE: We use a plain and old-fashioned format for our JSF pages so that they are as easy to read as possible.

XML-savvy readers will want to do a better job. First, it is desirable to use proper XML for the tag library declarations, eliminating the <%...%> tags. Moreover, you will want to emit a proper DOCTYPE declaration for the generated HTML document.

The following format solves both issues:

```
<?xml version="1.0" ?>
<jsp:root version="2.0"
      xmlns:jsp="http://java.sun.com/JSP/Page"
      xmlns:f="http://java.sun.com/jsf/core"
      xmlns:h="http://java.sun.com/jsf/html">
   <jsp:directive.page contentType="text/html"/>
   <jsp:output omit-xml-declaration="no"
         doctype-root-element="html"
         doctype-public="-//W3C//DTD XHTML 1.0 Transitional//EN"
         doctype-system="http://www.w3.org/TR/xhtml1/DTD/xhtml1-transitional.dtd"/>
   <f:view>
      <html xmlns="http://www.w3.org/1999/xhtml">
         <head>
            <title>A Simple Java Server Faces Application</title>
         </head>
         <body>
            <h:form>
            . . .
            </h:form>
         </body>
      </html>
   </f:view>
</jsp:root>
```

If you use an XML-aware editor, you should seriously consider this form.

CAUTION: You sometimes see naive page authors produce documents that start with an HTML DOCTYPE declaration, like this:

```
<!DOCTYPE HTML PUBLIC "-//W3C//DTD HTML 4.01 Transitional//EN">
<html>
    <%@ taglib uri="http://java.sun.com/jsf/html" prefix="h" %>
    <%@ taglib uri="http://java.sun.com/jsf/core" prefix="f" %>
    <f:view>
    . . .
```

This may have been acceptable at one time, but nowadays, it is quite reprehensible. Plainly, this document is *not* an "HTML 4.01 Transitional" document. It merely aims to produce such a document. Many XML editors and tools do not take it kindly when you lie about the document type. Therefore, either omit the DOCTYPE altogether or follow the outline given in the preceding note.

Navigation

To complete our JSF application, we need to specify the navigation rules. A navigation rule tells the JSF implementation which page to send back to the browser after a form has been submitted.

In this case, navigation is simple. When the user clicks the login button, we want to navigate from the index.jsp page to welcome.jsp. You specify this navigation rule in the faces-config.xml file:

```
<navigation-rule>
    <from-view-id>/index.jsp</from-view-id>
    <navigation-case>
        <from-outcome>login</from-outcome>
        <to-view-id>/welcome.jsp</to-view-id>
    </navigation-case>
</navigation-rule>
```

The from-outcome value matches the action attribute of the command button of the index.jsp page:

```
<h:commandButton value="Login" action="login"/>
```

In addition to the navigation rules, the faces-config.xml file contains the bean definitions. Here is the definition of the user bean:

```
<managed-bean>
    <managed-bean-name>user</managed-bean-name>
    <managed-bean-class>
        com.corejsf.UserBean
```

```
    </managed-bean-class>
    <managed-bean-scope>session</managed-bean-scope>
  </managed-bean>
```

You can use the bean name, user, in the attributes of the user interface components. For example, index.jsp contains the tag

```
<h:inputText value="#{user.name}"/>
```

The value attribute refers to the name property of the user bean.

The managed-bean-class tag specifies the bean class, in our case, com.corejsf.UserBean.
Finally, the scope is set to session. This means that the bean object is available
for one user across multiple pages. Different users who use the web application
are given different instances of the bean object.

Listing 1–4 shows the complete faces-config.xml file.

 NOTE: JSF 1.2 uses a schema declaration to define the syntax of a configuration file. The configuration tags are enclosed in

```
<faces-config xmlns="http://java.sun.com/xml/ns/javaee"
    xmlns:xsi="http://www.w3.org/2001/XMLSchema-instance"
    xsi:schemaLocation="http://java.sun.com/xml/ns/javaee
        http://java.sun.com/xml/ns/javaee/web-facesconfig_1_2.xsd"
    version="1.2">
    . . .
</faces-config>
```

JSF 1.1 uses a DOCTYPE declaration instead:

```
<!DOCTYPE faces-config PUBLIC
    "-//Sun Microsystems, Inc.//DTD JavaServer Faces Config 1.0//EN"
    "http://java.sun.com/dtd/web-facesconfig_1_0.dtd">
<faces-config>
    . . .
</faces-config>
```

We recommend that you use an XML editor that understands XML Schema
declarations. If you use Eclipse, a good choice is the XMLBuddy plugin
(http://xmlbuddy.com).

Listing 1–4   login/web/WEB-INF/faces-config.xml

```
1. <?xml version="1.0"?>
2. <faces-config xmlns="http://java.sun.com/xml/ns/javaee"
3.    xmlns:xsi="http://www.w3.org/2001/XMLSchema-instance"
4.    xsi:schemaLocation="http://java.sun.com/xml/ns/javaee
5.        http://java.sun.com/xml/ns/javaee/web-facesconfig_1_2.xsd"
6.    version="1.2">
7.    <navigation-rule>
8.        <from-view-id>/index.jsp</from-view-id>
9.        <navigation-case>
10.           <from-outcome>login</from-outcome>
11.           <to-view-id>/welcome.jsp</to-view-id>
12.        </navigation-case>
13.    </navigation-rule>
14.
15.    <managed-bean>
16.        <managed-bean-name>user</managed-bean-name>
17.        <managed-bean-class>com.corejsf.UserBean</managed-bean-class>
18.        <managed-bean-scope>session</managed-bean-scope>
19.    </managed-bean>
20. </faces-config>
```

Servlet Configuration

When you deploy a JSF application inside an application server, you need to supply a configuration file named web.xml. Fortunately, you can use the same web.xml file for most JSF applications. Listing 1–5 shows the file.

Listing 1–5   login/web/WEB-INF/web.xml

```
1. <?xml version="1.0"?>
2. <web-app xmlns="http://java.sun.com/xml/ns/javaee"
3.    xmlns:xsi="http://www.w3.org/2001/XMLSchema-instance"
4.    xsi:schemaLocation="http://java.sun.com/xml/ns/javaee
5.        http://java.sun.com/xml/ns/javaee/web-app_2_5.xsd"
6.    version="2.5">
7.    <servlet>
8.        <servlet-name>Faces Servlet</servlet-name>
9.        <servlet-class>javax.faces.webapp.FacesServlet</servlet-class>
10.       <load-on-startup>1</load-on-startup>
11.    </servlet>
12.
```

Listing 1–5 login/web/WEB-INF/web.xml (cont.)

```
13.    <servlet-mapping>
14.       <servlet-name>Faces Servlet</servlet-name>
15.       <url-pattern>*.faces</url-pattern>
16.    </servlet-mapping>
17.
18.    <welcome-file-list>
19.       <welcome-file>index.html</welcome-file>
20.    </welcome-file-list>
21. </web-app>
```

The only remarkable aspect of this file is the *servlet mapping*. All JSF pages are processed by a special servlet that is a part of the JSF implementation code. To ensure that the correct servlet is activated when a JSF page is requested, the JSF URLs have a special format. In our configuration, they have an extension .faces.

For example, you cannot simply point your browser to http://localhost:8080/login/index.jsp. The URL has to be http://localhost:8080/login/index.faces. The servlet container uses the servlet mapping rule to activate the JSF servlet, which strips off the faces suffix and loads the index.jsp page.

 NOTE: You can also define a *prefix mapping* instead of the .faces extension mapping. Use the following directive in your web.xml file:

```
<servlet-mapping>
   <servlet-name>Faces Servlet</servlet-name>
   <url-pattern>/faces/*</url-pattern>
</servlet-mapping>
```

Then use the URL http://localhost:8080/login/faces/index.jsp. That URL activates the JSF servlet, which then strips off the faces prefix and loads the file /login/index.jsp.

 NOTE: If you want to use a .jsf extension for JSF page files, then you need to configure your web application so that it invokes the JSP servlet for files with that extension. Use the following mapping in the web.xml file:

```
<servlet-mapping>
   <servlet-name>jsp</servlet-name>
   <url-pattern>*.jsf</url-pattern>
</servlet-mapping>
```

You now need to tell the JSF implementation to map the .faces extension of the URLs to the .jsf extension of the associated files.

```
<context-param>
    <param-name>javax.faces.DEFAULT_SUFFIX</param-name>
    <param-value>.jsf</param-value>
</context-param>
```

Note that this configuration affects only the web developers, not the users of your web application. The URLs still have a .faces extension or /faces prefix.

 NOTE: If you use an older application server that supports version 2.3 of the servlet specification, you use a DTD (DOCTYPE declaration) instead of a schema declaration in the web.xml file. The DTD is as follows:

```
<!DOCTYPE web-app PUBLIC
    "-//Sun Microsystems, Inc.//DTD Web Application 2.3//EN"
    "http://java.sun.com/dtd/web-app_2_3.dtd">
```

The Welcome File

When a user enters a directory URL such as http://localhost:8080/login, the application server automatically loads the index.jsp page when it is present. Unfortunately, that mechanism does not work smoothly with JSF pages because the JSF processing phase is skipped.

To overcome this issue, you can supply an index.html file that automatically redirects the user to the proper faces URL. Listing 1–6 shows such an index file.

Listing 1–6 login/web/index.html

```
1. <html>
2.    <head>
3.       <meta http-equiv="Refresh" content= "0; URL=index.faces"/>
4.       <title>Start Web Application</title>
5.    </head>
6.    <body>
7.       <p>Please wait for the web application to start.</p>
8.    </body>
9. </html>
```

Finally, it is a good idea to specify index.html as the welcome file in web.xml. See the welcome-file tag in Listing 1–5 on page 18.

NOTE: The index.html file redirects the browser to the index.faces URL. It is slightly more efficient to use a JSP forward action instead. Create a page, say, start.jsp, that contains the line

`<jsp:forward page="/index.faces"/>`

Then set this page as the welcome-file in the web.xml configuration file.

Development Environments for JSF

You can produce the pages and configuration files for a simple JSF application with a text editor. However, as your applications become more complex, you will want to use more sophisticated tools. In the next three sections, we discuss JSF support in integrated development environments, visual builder tools, and build automation with Ant.

Integrated Development Environments

IDEs, such as Eclipse or NetBeans, are deservedly popular with programmers. Support for autocompletion, refactoring, debugging, and so on, can dramatically increase programmer productivity, particularly for large projects.

As this book is written, Eclipse has an experimental JSF plug-in that plainly needs more work. Several commercial Eclipse derivatives (such as MyEclipse, Exadel Studio, BEA Workshop Studio, and Rational Application Developer) have better JSF support, but some of them are expensive. They all have trial versions that you can download.

NetBeans, on the other hand, is free and has very good JSF support out of the box. If you are not satisfied with the JSF support in your favorite IDE, we suggest that you give NetBeans a try.

NetBeans gives you autocompletion in JSF pages and configuration files. With NetBeans, it is very easy to launch or debug JSF applications just by clicking toolbar buttons. Figure 1–7 shows the NetBeans debugger, stopped at a breakpoint in the UserBean class.

 NOTE: Since the user interfaces for IDEs can change quite a bit between versions, we put a guide for getting started with NetBeans on the web (http://corejsf.com) rather than in the printed book.

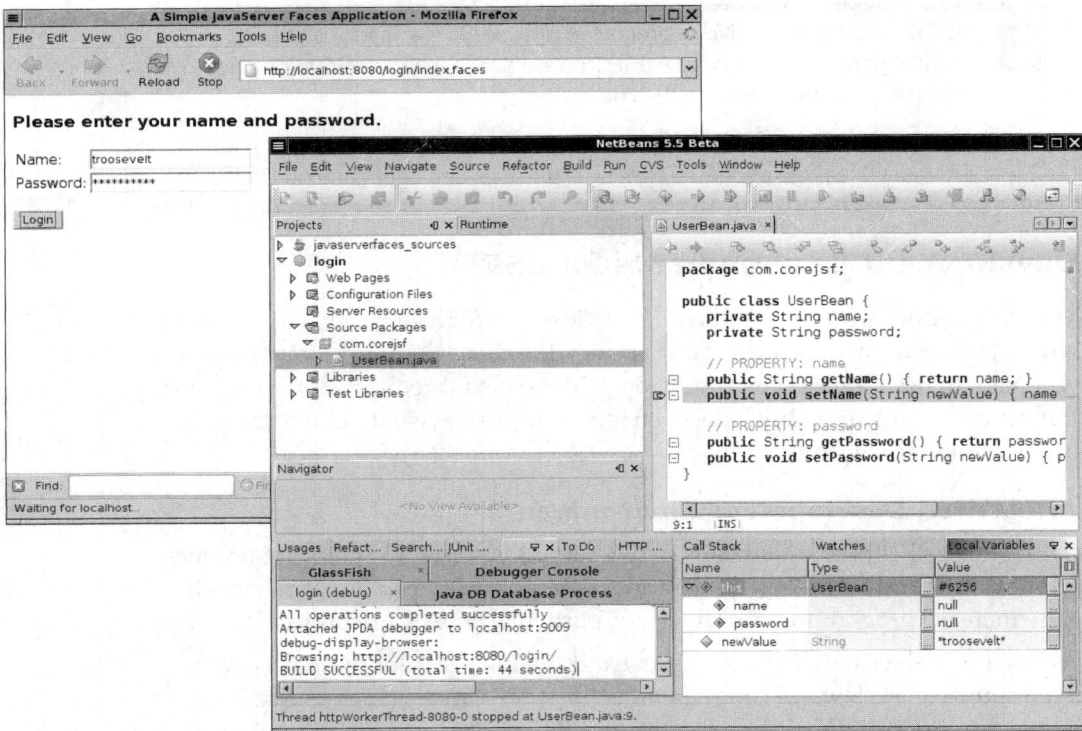

Figure 1–7   Using NetBeans for JSF debugging

Visual Builder Tools

A visual builder tool displays a graphical representation of the components and allows a designer to drag and drop components from a palette. Builder tools can be standalone programs such as Sun Java Studio Creator, or they can be modules of integrated development environments.

Figure 1–8 shows Sun Java Studio Creator (http://www.sun.com/software/products/ jscreator). The component palette is in the lower-left corner. You drag the components onto the center of the window and customize them with the property sheet in the upper-right corner. The environment produces the corresponding JSF tags automatically (see Figure 1–9).

Moreover, visual builders give you graphical interfaces for specifying the navigation rules and beans (see Figure 1–10). The faces-config.xml file is produced automatically.

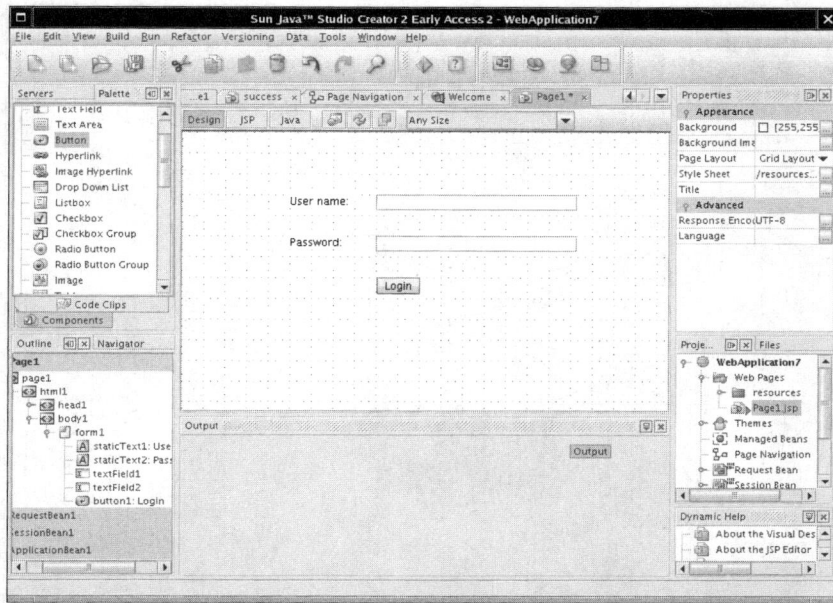

Figure 1–8   Visual JSF development environment

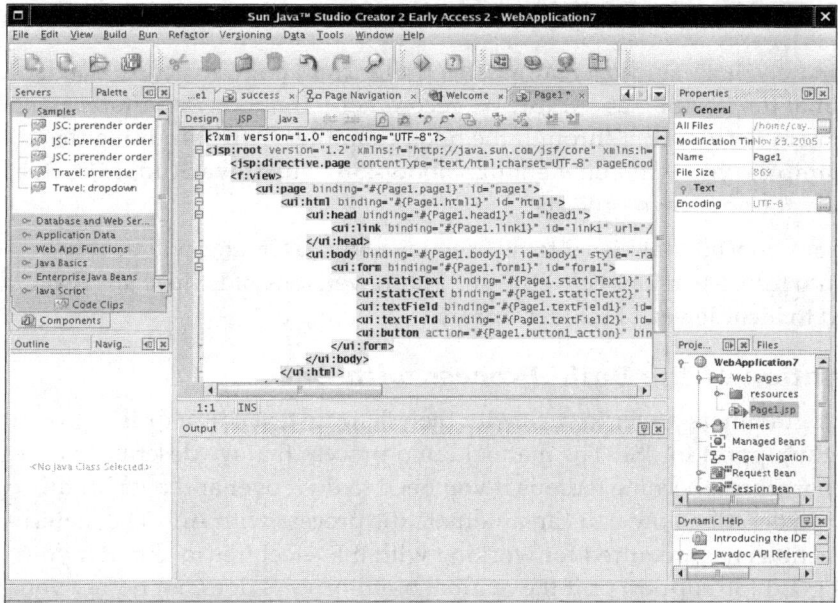

Figure 1–9   Automatically generated JSF markup

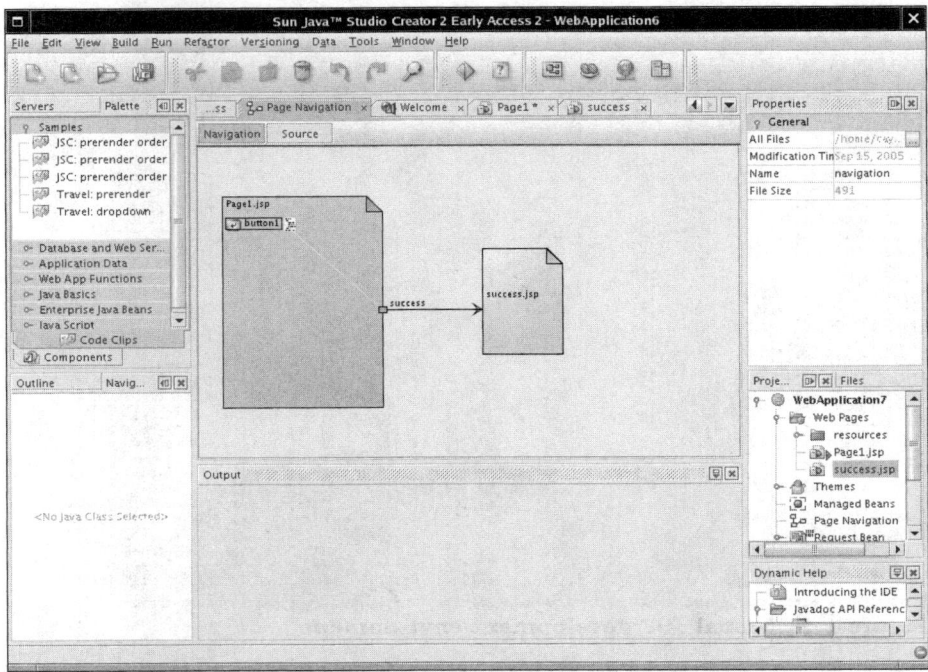

Figure 1–10   Visually specifying navigation rules

Unfortunately, Java Studio Creator has a rather rigid page structure that is not optimal for learning about JSF. We recommend that you use another environment for working through the book examples. After studying the book examples, you will know enough about JSF to use Java Studio Creator effectively for your own projects.

Sun has announced that visual tools from Java Studio Creator will be integrated into future versions of NetBeans. Future versions of Eclipse are also expected to include visual builder features.

Automation of the Build Process with Ant

Many programmers prefer to stick with their favorite text editor or IDE, even if it has little support for JSF. The manual build process that we described earlier in this chapter can become tedious if you need to do it over and over. In this section, we describe how you can automate the process with Ant. The material in this section is not required for working with JSF—feel free to skip it if your IDE has good JSF support or if the manual build process does not bother you.

Fortunately, you need not know much about Ant if you want to use the build script that we prepared. Start by downloading Ant from http://ant.apache.org and install it in a directory of your choice. Or, if you use GlassFish, use the asant tool that is included in the *glassfish*/bin directory.

Ant takes directions from a *build file*. By default, the build file is named build.xml. We provide a build.xml file for building JSF applications. This file is contained in the root of the *corejsf-examples* directory. The build.xml file contains the instructions for compiling, copying, zipping, and deploying to an application server, described in XML syntax (see Listing 1–7).

Listing 1–7   build.xml

```
 1. <project default="install">
 2.
 3.     <property environment="env"/>
 4.     <property file="build.properties"/>
 5.     <property name="appdir" value="${basedir}/${app}"/>
 6.     <basename property="appname" file="${appdir}"/>
 7.     <property name="builddir" value="${appdir}/build"/>
 8.     <property name="warfile" value="${builddir}/${appname}.war"/>
 9.
10.     <path id="classpath">
11.         <pathelement location="${javaee.api.jar}"/>
12.         <fileset dir="${appdir}">
13.           <include name="web/WEB-INF/**/*.jar"/>
14.         </fileset>
15.     </path>
16.
17.     <target name="init">
18.         <fail unless="app" message="Run ant -Dapp=..."/>
19.     </target>
20.
21.     <target name="prepare" depends="init"
22.           description="Create build directory.">
23.         <mkdir dir="${builddir}"/>
24.         <mkdir dir="${builddir}/WEB-INF"/>
25.         <mkdir dir="${builddir}/WEB-INF/classes"/>
26.     </target>
27.
28.     <target name="copy" depends="prepare"
29.           description="Copy files to build directory.">
30.         <copy todir="${builddir}" failonerror="false" verbose="true">
31.             <fileset dir="${appdir}/web"/>
32.         </copy>
33.         <copy todir="${builddir}/WEB-INF/classes"
34.             failonerror="false" verbose="true">
```

Listing 1–7   build.xml (cont.)

```
35.          <fileset dir="${appdir}/src/java">
36.              <exclude name="**/*.java"/>
37.          </fileset>
38.      </copy>
39.      <copy todir="${builddir}/WEB-INF" failonerror="false" verbose="true">
40.          <fileset dir="${appdir}">
41.              <include name="lib/**"/>
42.          </fileset>
43.      </copy>
44.  </target>
45.
46.  <target name="compile" depends="copy"
47.          description="Compile source files.">
48.      <javac
49.          srcdir="${appdir}/src/java"
50.          destdir="${builddir}/WEB-INF/classes"
51.          debug="true"
52.          deprecation="true">
53.          <compilerarg value="-Xlint:unchecked"/>
54.          <include name="**/*.java"/>
55.          <classpath refid="classpath"/>
56.      </javac>
57.  </target>
58.
59.  <target name="war" depends="compile"
60.          description="Build WAR file.">
61.      <delete file="${warfile}"/>
62.      <jar jarfile="${warfile}" basedir="${builddir}"/>
63.  </target>
64.
65.  <target name="install" depends="war"
66.          description="Deploy web application.">
67.      <copy file="${warfile}" todir="${deploy.dir}"/>
68.  </target>
69.
70.  <target name="clean" depends="init"
71.          description="Clean everything.">
72.      <delete dir="${builddir}"/>
73.  </target>
74. </project>
```

To use this build file, you must customize the build.properties file that is contained in the same directory. The default file looks like what is shown in Listing 1–8.

Listing 1–8 `build.properties`

```
1. appserver.dir=${env.GLASSFISH_HOME}
2. javaee.api.jar=${appserver.dir}/lib/javaee.jar
3. deploy.dir=${appserver.dir}/domains/domain1/autodeploy
```

You need to change the directory for the application server to match your local installation. Edit the first line of `build.properties`.

Now you are ready to build the sample application (see Figure 1–11).

1. Open a command shell and change into the *corejsf-examples* directory.

2. Run the command

    apache-ant/bin/ant -Dapp=ch1/login

    Here, *apache-ant* is the directory into which you installed Ant, such as c:\apache-ant-1.6.5. With GlassFish, you can also use

    glassfish/bin/asant -Dapp=ch1/login

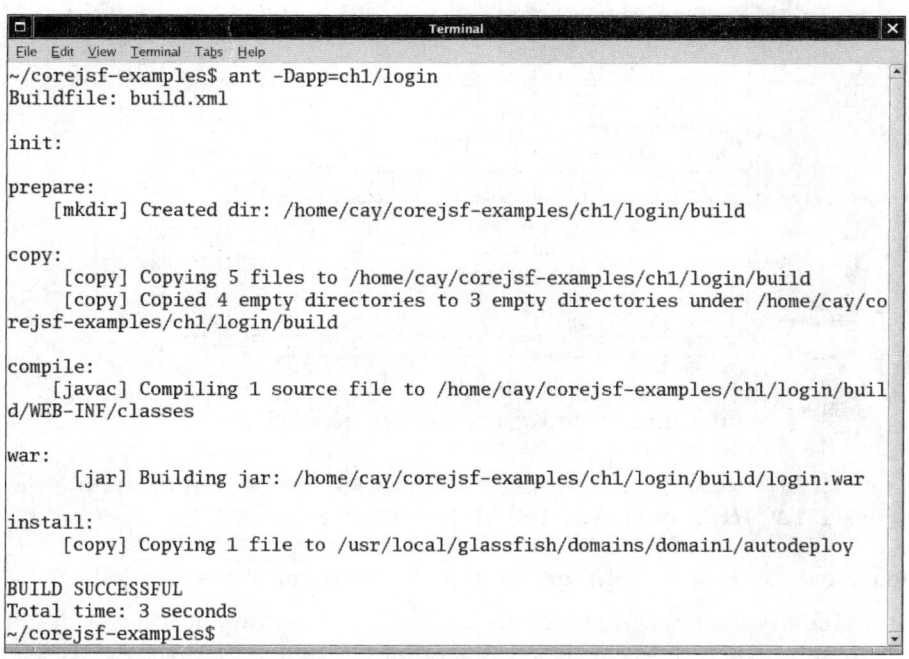

```
~/corejsf-examples$ ant -Dapp=ch1/login
Buildfile: build.xml

init:

prepare:
    [mkdir] Created dir: /home/cay/corejsf-examples/ch1/login/build

copy:
     [copy] Copying 5 files to /home/cay/corejsf-examples/ch1/login/build
     [copy] Copied 4 empty directories to 3 empty directories under /home/cay/co
rejsf-examples/ch1/login/build

compile:
    [javac] Compiling 1 source file to /home/cay/corejsf-examples/ch1/login/buil
d/WEB-INF/classes

war:
      [jar] Building jar: /home/cay/corejsf-examples/ch1/login/build/login.war

install:
     [copy] Copying 1 file to /usr/local/glassfish/domains/domain1/autodeploy

BUILD SUCCESSFUL
Total time: 3 seconds
~/corejsf-examples$
```

Figure 1–11 Installing a web application with Ant

NOTE: Our Ant script is a bit different from the scripts that you often find with sample applications. We use a single script that can build all applications in the book. You use the -Dapp=... flag to specify the name of the application that you want to build. We think that approach is better than supplying lots of nearly identical scripts. Note that you call the script from the *corejsf-examples* directory, not the directory of the application.

JSF Framework Services

Now that you have seen your first JSF application, it is easier to explain the services that the JSF framework offers to developers. Figure 1–12 gives a high-level overview of the JSF architecture. As you can see, the JSF framework is responsible for interacting with client devices, and it provides tools for tying together the visual presentation, application logic, and business logic of a web application. However, the scope of JSF is restricted to the presentation tier. Database persistence, web services, and other backend connections are outside the scope of JSF.

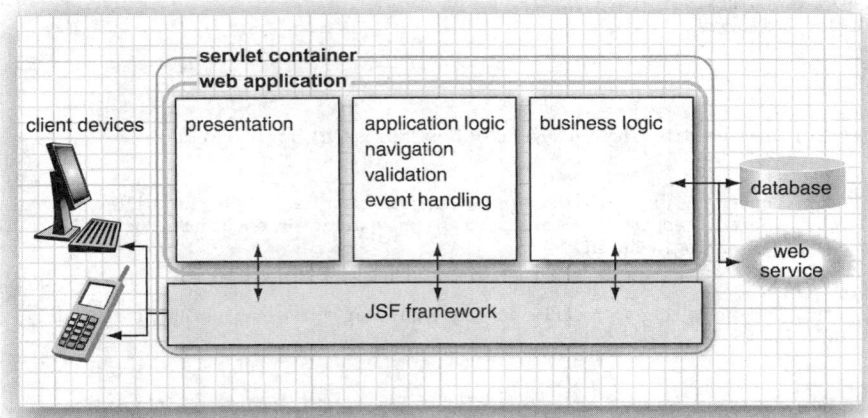

Figure 1–12   High-level overview of the JSF framework

Here are the most important services that the JSF framework provides:

> **Model-view-controller architecture**—All software applications let users manipulate certain data, such as shopping carts, travel itineraries, or whatever data is required in a particular problem domain. This data is called the *model*. Just as an artist creates a painting of a model in a studio,

a software developer produces *views* of the data model. In a web application, HTML (or a similar rendering technology) is used to paint these views.

JSF connects the view and the model. As you have seen, a view component can be wired to a bean property of a model object, such as

```
<h:inputText value="#{user.name}"/>
```

Moreover, JSF operates as the *controller* that reacts to the user by processing action and value change events, routing them to code that updates the model or the view. For example, you may want to invoke a method to check whether a user is allowed to log on. Use the following JSF tag:

```
<h:commandButton value="Login" action="#{user.check}"/>
```

When the user clicks the button and the form is submitted to the server, the JSF implementation invokes the check method of the user bean. That method can take arbitrary actions to update the model, and it returns the navigation ID of the next page to be displayed. We discuss this mechanism further in "Dynamic Navigation" on page 73 of Chapter 3.

Thus, JSF implements the classical model-view-controller architecture.

Data conversion—Users enter data into web forms as text. Business objects want data as numbers, dates, or other data types. As explained in Chapter 6, JSF makes it easy to specify and customize conversion rules.

Validation and error handling—JSF makes it easy to attach validation rules for fields such as "this field is required" or "this field must be a number". Of course, when users enter invalid data, you need to display appropriate error messages. JSF takes away much of the tedium of this programming task. We cover validation in Chapter 6.

Internationalization—JSF manages internationalization issues such as character encodings and the selection of resource bundles. We cover resource bundles in "Message Bundles" on page 42 of Chapter 2.

Custom components—Component developers can develop sophisticated components that page designers simply drop into their pages. For example, suppose a component developer produces a calendar component with all the usual bells and whistles. You just use it in your page, with a command such as

```
<acme:calendar value="#{flight.departure}" startOfWeek="Mon"/>
```

Chapter 9 covers custom components in detail.

Alternative renderers—By default, JSF generates markup for HTML pages. But it is easy to extend the JSF framework to produce markup for another page description language such as WML or XUL. The book's companion site contains a chapter that shows you how to use JSF to communicate with Java ME-powered cell phones.

Tool support—JSF is optimized for use with automated tools. As these tools mature in the coming years, we believe that JSF will be the must-have framework for developing web interfaces with Java.

Behind the Scenes

Now that you have read about the "what" and the "why" of JSF, you may be curious about just how the JSF framework does its job.

Next, we look behind the scenes of our sample application. We start at the point when the browser first connects to http://localhost:8080/login/index.faces. The JSF servlet initializes the JSF code and reads the index.jsp page. That page contains tags such as f:form and h:inputText. Each tag has an associated *tag handler* class. When the page is read, the tag handlers are executed. The JSF tag handlers collaborate with each other to build a *component tree* (see Figure 1–13).

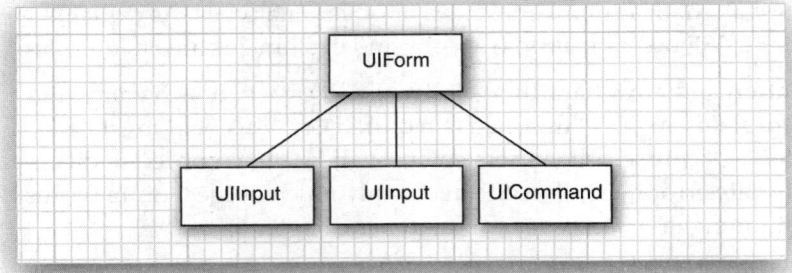

Figure 1–13   Component tree of the sample application

The component tree is a data structure that contains Java objects for all user interface elements on the JSF page. For example, the two UIInput objects correspond to the h:inputText and h:inputSecret fields in the JSF file.

Rendering Pages

Next, the HTML page is *rendered*. All text that is not a JSF tag is passed through. The h:form, h:inputText, h:inputSecret, and h:commandButton tags are converted to HTML.

As we just discussed, each of these tags gives rise to an associated component. Each component has a *renderer* that produces HTML output, reflecting the component state. For example, the renderer for the component that corresponds to the h:inputText tag produces the following output:

```
<input type="text" name="unique ID" value="current value"/>
```

This process is called *encoding*. The renderer of the UIInput object asks the framework to look up the unique ID and the current value of the expression user.name. By default, ID strings are assigned by the framework. The IDs can look rather random, such as _id_id12:_id_id21.

The encoded page is sent to the browser, and the browser displays it in the usual way (see Figure 1–14).

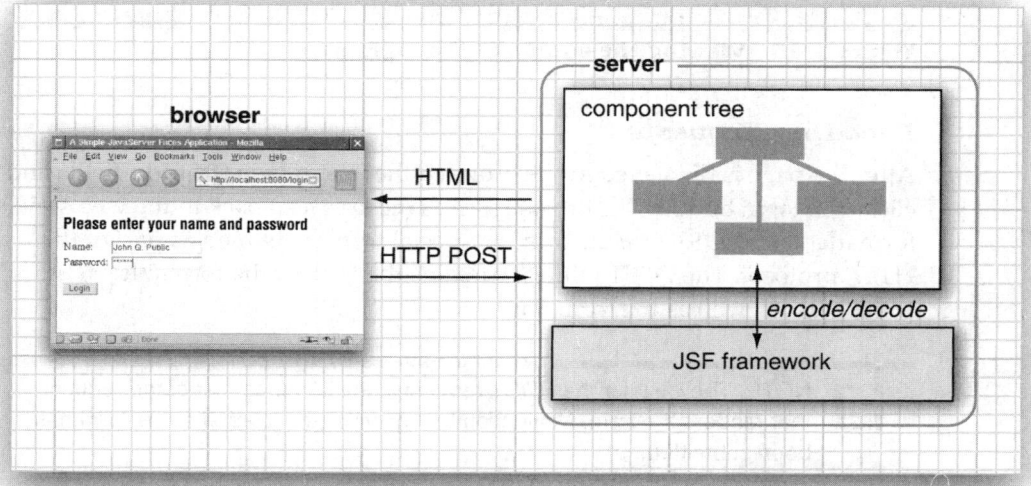

Figure 1–14   Encoding and decoding JSF pages

 TIP: Select "View->Page source" from the browser menu to see the HTML output of the rendering process. Figure 1–15 shows a typical output. This is useful for debugging JSF problems.

```
view-source: - Source of: http://localhost:8080/login/index.faces - Mozilla Firefox

File  Edit  View
        <head>
          <title>A Simple JavaServer Faces Application</title>
        </head>
        <body>
          <form id="_id_id12" name="_id_id12" method="post" action="/login/index.faces;jsessionid

            <h3>Please enter your name and password.</h3>
            <table>
              <tr>
                <td>Name:</td>
                <td>
                  <input type="text" name="_id_id12:_id_id21" />
                </td>
              </tr>
              <tr>
                <td>Password:</td>
                <td>
                  <input type="password" name="_id_id12:_id_id29" value="" />
                </td>
              </tr>
            </table>
```

Figure 1–15   Viewing the source of the login page

Decoding Requests

After the page is displayed in the browser, the user fills in the form fields and clicks the login button. The browser sends the *form data* back to the web server, formatted as a *POST request*. This is a special format, defined as part of the HTTP protocol. The POST request contains the URL of the form (/login/ index.faces), as well as the form data.

> NOTE: The URL for the POST request is the same as that of the request that renders the form. Navigation to a new page occurs after the form has been submitted.

The form data is a string of ID/value pairs, such as

id1=me&*id2*=secret&*id3*=Login

As part of the normal servlet processing, the form data is placed in a hash table that all components can access.

Next, the JSF framework gives each component a chance to inspect that hash table, a process called *decoding*. Each component decides on its own how to interpret the form data.

The login form has three component objects: two UIInput objects that correspond to the text fields on the form and a UICommand object that corresponds to the submit button.

- The UIInput components update the bean properties referenced in the value attributes: they invoke the setter methods with the values that the user supplied.

- The UICommand component checks whether the button was clicked. If so, it fires an *action event* to launch the login action referenced in the action attribute. That event tells the navigation handler to look up the successor page, welcome.jsp.

Now the cycle repeats.

You have just seen the two most important processing steps of the JSF framework: encoding and decoding. However, the processing sequence (also called the *life cycle*) is a bit more intricate. If everything goes well, you do not need to worry about the intricacies of the life cycle. However, when an error occurs, you will definitely want to understand what the framework does. In the next section, we look at the life cycle in greater detail.

The Life Cycle

The JSF specification defines six distinct *phases*, as shown in Figure 1–16. The normal flow of control is shown with solid lines; alternative flows are shown with dashed lines.

The *Restore View* phase retrieves the component tree for the requested page if it was displayed previously or constructs a new component tree if it is displayed for the first time. If the page was displayed previously, all components are set to their prior state. This means that JSF automatically retains form information. For example, when a user posts illegal data that is rejected during decoding, the inputs are redisplayed so that the user can correct them.

If the request has no query data, the JSF implementation skips ahead to the *Render Response* phase. This happens when a page is displayed for the first time.

Otherwise, the next phase is the *Apply Request Values* phase. In this phase, the JSF implementation iterates over the component objects in the component tree. Each component object checks which request values belong to it and stores them.

 NOTE: In addition to extracting request information, the Apply Request Values phase adds events to an event queue when a command button or link has been clicked. We discuss event handling in detail in Chapter 7. As you can see in Figure 1–16, events can be executed after each phase. In specialized situations, an event handler can "bail out" and skip to the Render Response phase or even terminate request processing altogether.

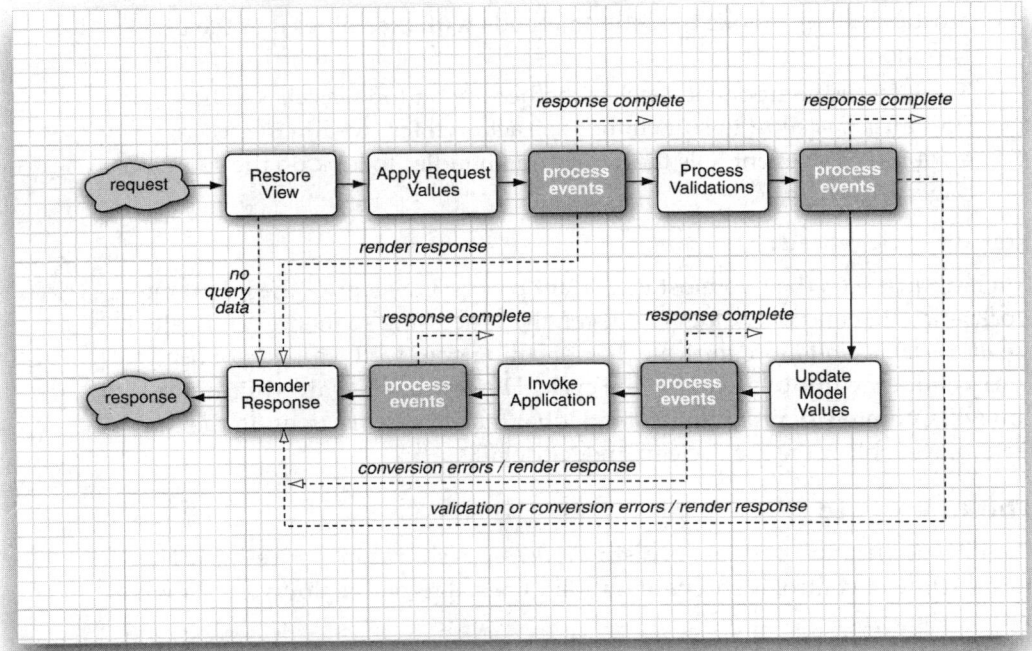

Figure 1–16   The JSF life cycle

In the *Process Validations* phase, the submitted string values are first converted to "local values," which can be objects of any type. When you design a JSF page, you can attach *validators* that perform correctness checks on the local values. If validation passes, the JSF life cycle proceeds normally. However, when conversion or validation errors occur, the JSF implementation invokes the Render Response phase directly, redisplaying the current page so that the user has another chance to provide correct inputs.

 NOTE: To many programmers, this is the most surprising aspect of the JSF life cycle. If a converter or validator fails, the current page is redisplayed. You should add tags to display the validation errors so that your users know why they see the old page again. See Chapter 6 for details.

After the converters and validators have done their work, it is assumed that it is safe to update the model data. During the *Update Model Values* phase, the local values are used to update the beans that are wired to the components.

In the *Invoke Application* phase, the action method of the button or link component that caused the form submission is executed. That method can carry out arbitrary application processing. It returns an outcome string that is passed to the navigation handler. The navigation handler looks up the next page.

Finally, the Render Response phase encodes the response and sends it to the browser. When a user submits a form, clicks a link, or otherwise generates a new request, the cycle starts anew.

You have now seen the basic mechanisms that make the JSF magic possible. In the following chapters, we examine the various parts of the life cycle in more detail.

MANAGED BEANS

Topics in This Chapter

Chapter 2

A central theme of web application design is the separation of presentation and business logic. JSF uses *beans* to achieve this separation. JSF pages refer to bean properties, and the program logic is contained in the bean implementation code. Because beans are so fundamental to JSF programming, we discuss them in detail in this chapter.

The first half of the chapter discusses the essential features of beans that every JSF developer needs to know. We then present an example program that puts these essentials to work. The remaining sections cover more technical aspects about bean configuration and value expressions. You can safely skip these sections when you first read this book and return to them when the need arises.

Definition of a Bean

According to the JavaBeans specification (available at http://java.sun.com/products/javabeans/), a Java bean is "a reusable software component that can be manipulated in a builder tool." That is a pretty broad definition and indeed, as you will see in this chapter, beans are used for a variety of purposes.

At first glance, a bean seems to be similar to an object. However, beans serve a different purpose. Objects are created and manipulated inside a Java program when the program calls constructors and invokes methods. Yet, beans can be configured and manipulated *without programming*.

NOTE: You may wonder where the term "bean" comes from. Well, Java is a synonym for coffee (at least in the United States), and coffee is made from beans that encapsulate its flavor. You may find the analogy cute or annoying, but the term has stuck.

The "classic" application for JavaBeans is a user interface builder. A palette window in the builder tool contains component beans such as text fields, sliders, checkboxes, and so on. Instead of writing Swing code, you use a user interface designer to drag and drop component beans from the palette into a form. Then you can customize the components by selecting property values from a *property sheet* dialog (see Figure 2–1).

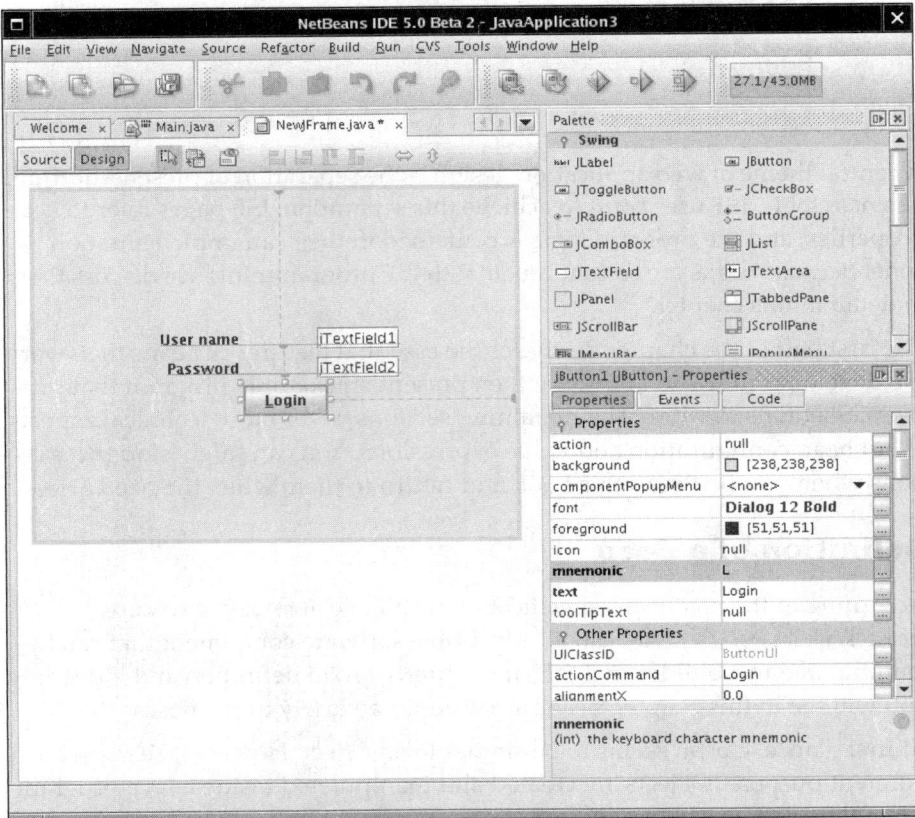

Figure 2–1 Customizing a bean in a GUI builder

In the context of JSF, beans go beyond user interface components. You use beans whenever you need to wire up Java classes with web pages or configuration files.

Consider the `login` application in Chapter 1, shown in "A Simple Example" on page 6. A `UserBean` instance is configured in the `faces-config.xml` file:

```
<managed-bean>
   <managed-bean-name>user</managed-bean-name>
   <managed-bean-class>com.corejsf.UserBean</managed-bean-class>
   <managed-bean-scope>session</managed-bean-scope>
</managed-bean>
```

This means: Construct an object of the class `com.corejsf.UserBean`, give it the name user, and keep it alive for the duration of the *session*—that is, for all requests that originate from the same client.

Once the bean has been defined, it can be accessed by JSF components. For example, this input field reads and updates the `password` property of the `user` bean:

```
<h:inputSecret value="#{user.password}"/>
```

As you can see, the JSF developer does not need to write any code to construct and manipulate the `user` bean. The JSF implementation constructs the beans according to the `managed-bean` elements in the configuration file.

In a JSF application, beans are commonly used for the following purposes:

- User interface components (traditional user interface beans)
- Tying together the behavior of a web form (called "backing beans")
- Business objects whose properties are displayed on web pages
- Services such as external data sources that need to be configured when an application is assembled

Because beans are so ubiquitous, we now turn to a review of those parts of the JavaBeans specification that are relevant to JSF programmers.

Bean Properties

Bean classes need to follow specific programming conventions to expose features that tools can use. We discuss these conventions in this section.

The most important features of a bean are the properties that it exposes. A *property* is any attribute of a bean that has

- A name
- A type
- Methods for getting and/or setting the property value

For example, the UserBean class of the preceding chapter has a property with name password and type String. The methods getPassword and setPassword access the property value.

Some programming languages, in particular Visual Basic and C#, have direct support for properties. However, in Java, a bean is simply a class that follows certain coding conventions.

The JavaBeans specification puts a single demand on a bean class: It must have a public default constructor—that is, a constructor without parameters. However, to define properties, a bean must either use a *naming pattern* for property getters and setters, or it must define property descriptors. The latter approach is quite tedious and not commonly used, and we will not discuss it here. See Horstmann and Cornell, 2004, 2005. *Core Java™ 2*, vol. 2, chap. 8, for more information.

Defining properties with naming patterns is straightforward. Consider the following pair of methods:

```
public T getFoo()
public void setFoo(T newValue)
```

The pair corresponds to a read-write property with type *T* and name foo. If you have only the first method, then the property is read-only. If you have only the second method, then the property is write-only.

The method names and signatures must match the pattern precisely. The method name must start with get or set. A get method must have no parameters. A set method must have one parameter and no return value. A bean class can have other methods, but the methods do not yield bean properties.

Note that the name of the property is the "decapitalized" form of the part of the method name that follows the get or set prefix. For example, getFoo gives rise to a property named foo, with the first letter turned into lower case. However, if the first *two* letters after the prefix are upper case, then the first letter stays unchanged. For example, the method name getURL defines a property URL and not uRL.

For properties of type boolean, you have a choice of prefixes for the method that reads the property. Both

```
public boolean isConnected()
```

and

```
public boolean getConnected()
```

are valid names for the reader of the connected property.

NOTE: The JavaBeans specification also defines indexed properties, specified by method sets such as the following:

```
public T[] getFoo()
public T getFoo(int index)
public void setFoo(T[] newArray)
public void setFoo(int index, T newValue)
```

However, JSF provides no support for accessing the indexed values.

The JavaBeans specification is silent on the *behavior* of the getter and setter methods. In many situations, these methods simply manipulate an instance field. But they may equally well carry out more sophisticated operations, such as database lookups, data conversion, validation, and so on.

A bean class may have other methods beyond property getters and setters. Of course, those methods do not give rise to bean properties.

Value Expressions

Many JSF user interface components have an attribute value that lets you specify either a value or a *binding* to a value that is obtained from a bean property. For example, you can specify a direct value:

```
<h:outputText value="Hello, World!"/>
```

Or you can specify a value expression:

```
<h:outputText value="#{user.name}"/>
```

In most situations, a value expression such as #{user.name} describes a property. Note that the expression can be used both for reading and writing when it is used in an input component, such as

```
<h:inputText value="#{user.name}"/>
```

The property getter is invoked when the component is rendered. The property setter is invoked when the user response is processed.

We will discuss the syntax of value expressions in detail under "The Syntax of Value Expressions" on page 64.

NOTE: JSF value expressions are related to the expression language used in JSP. Those expressions are delimited by ${...} instead of #{...}. As of JSF 1.2 and JSP 2.1, the syntax of both expression languages has been unified. (See "The Syntax of Value Expressions" on page 64 for a complete description of the syntax.)

The ${...} delimiter denotes *immediate* evaluation of expressions, at the time that the application server processes the page. The #{...} delimiter denotes *deferred* evaluation. With deferred evaluation, the application server retains the expression and evaluates it whenever a value is needed.

As a rule of thumb, you always use deferred expressions for JSF component properties, and you use immediate expressions in plain JSP or JSTL (JavaServer Pages Standard Template Library) constructs. (These constructs are rarely needed in JSF pages.)

Message Bundles

When you implement a web application, it is a good idea to collect all message strings in a central location. This process makes it easier to keep messages consistent and, crucially, makes it easier to localize your application for other locales. In this section, we show you how JSF makes it simple to organize messages. In the section "A Sample Application" on page 46, we put managed beans and message bundles to work.

You collect your message strings in a file in the time-honored *properties* format:

```
guessNext=Guess the next number in the sequence!
answer=Your answer:
```

 NOTE: Look into the API documentation of the load method of the java.util.Properties class for a precise description of the file format.

Save the file together with your classes—for example, insrc/java/com/corejsf/messages.properties. You can choose any directory path and file name, but you must use the extension .properties.

You can declare the message bundle in two ways. The simplest way is to include the following elements in your faces-config.xml file:

```
<application>
   <resource-bundle>
      <base-name>com.corejsf.messages</base-name>
      <var>msgs</var>
   </resource-bundle>
</application>
```

Alternatively, you can add the f:loadBundle element to each JSF page that needs access to the bundle, like this:

```
<f:loadBundle basename="com.corejsf.messages" var="msgs"/>
```

In either case, the messages in the bundle are accessible through a map variable with the name msgs. (The base name com.corejsf.messages looks like a class name, and indeed the properties file is loaded by the class loader.)

You can now use value expressions to access the message strings:

```
<h:outputText value="#{msgs.guessNext}"/>
```

That is all there is to it! When you are ready to localize your application for another locale, you simply supply localized bundle files.

 NOTE: The resource-bundle element is more efficient than the f:loadBundle action since the bundle can be created once for the entire application. However, it is a JSF 1.2 feature. If you want your application to be compatible with JSF 1.1, you must use f:loadBundle.

When you localize a bundle file, you need to add a locale suffix to the file name: an underscore followed by the lower case, two-letter ISO-639 language code. For example, German strings would be in com/corejsf/messages_de.properties.

 NOTE: You can find a listing of all two- and three-letter ISO-639 language codes at http://www.loc.gov/standards/iso639-2/.

As part of the internationalization support in Java, the bundle that matches the current locale is automatically loaded. The default bundle without a locale prefix is used as a fallback when the appropriate localized bundle is not available. See Horstmann and Cornell, 2004, 2005. *Core Java™ 2*, vol. 2, chap. 10, for a detailed description of Java internationalization.

 NOTE: When you prepare translations, keep one oddity in mind: Message bundle files are not encoded in UTF-8. Instead, Unicode characters beyond 127 are encoded as \uxxxx escape sequences. The Java SDK utility native2ascii can create these files.

You can have multiple bundles for a particular locale. For example, you may want to have separate bundles for commonly used error messages.

Messages with Variable Parts

Often, messages have variable parts that need to be filled. For example, suppose we want to display the sentence "You have *n* points.", where *n* is a value that is retrieved from a bean. Make a resource string with a placeholder:

```
currentScore=Your current score is {0}.
```

Placeholders are numbered {0}, {1}, {2}, and so on. In your JSF page, use the h:outputFormat tag and supply the values for the placeholders as f:param child elements, like this:

```
<h:outputFormat value="#{msgs.currentScore}">
  <f:param value="#{quiz.score}"/>
</h:outputFormat>
```

The h:outputFormat tag uses the MessageFormat class from the standard library to format the message string. That class has several features for locale-aware formatting.

You can format numbers as currency amounts by adding a suffix number,currency to the placeholder, like this:

```
currentTotal=Your current total is {0,number,currency}.
```

In the United States, a value of 1023.95 would be formatted as $1,023.95. The same value would be displayed as €1.023,95 in Germany, using the local currency symbol and decimal separator convention.

The choice format lets you format a number in different ways, such as "zero points", "one point", "2 points", "3 points", and so on. Here is the format string that achieves this effect:

```
currentScore=Your current score is {0,choice,0#zero points|1#one point|2#{0} points}.
```

There are three cases: 0, 1, and ≥ 2. Each case defines a separate message string.

Note that the 0 placeholder appears twice, once to select a choice, and again in the third choice, to produce a result such as "3 points".

Listings 2–5 and 2–6 on page 53 illustrate the choice format in our sample application. The English locale does not require a choice for the message, "Your score is . . . ". However, in German, this is expressed as "Sie haben . . . punkte" (You have . . . points). Now the choice format is required to deal with the singular form "einen punkt" (one point).

For more information on the MessageFormat class, see the API documentation or Horstmann and Cornell, 2004, 2005. *Core Java™ 2*, vol. 2, chap. 10.

Setting the Application Locale

Once you have prepared your message bundles, you need to decide how to set the locale of your application. You have three choices:

1. You can let the browser choose the locale. Set the default and supported locales in WEB-INF/faces-config.xml (or another application configuration resource):

```
<faces-config>
  <application>
    <locale-config>
      <default-locale>en</default-locale>
      <supported-locale>de</supported-locale>
    </locale-config>
  </application>
</faces-config>
```

   When a browser connects to your application, it usually includes an Accept-Language value in the HTTP header (see http://www.w3.org/International/questions/qa-accept-lang-locales.html). The JSF implementation reads the header and finds the best match among the supported locales. You can test this feature by setting the preferred language in your browser (see Figure 2–2).

2. You can add a locale attribute to the f:view element—for example,

```
<f:view locale="de">
```

   The locale can be dynamically set:

```
<f:view locale="#{user.locale}"/>>
```

   Now the locale is set to the string that the getLocale method returns. This is useful in applications that let the user pick a preferred locale.

3. You can set the locale programatically. Call the setLocale method of the UIViewRoot object:

```
UIViewRoot viewRoot = FacesContext.getCurrentInstance().getViewRoot();
viewRoot.setLocale(new Locale("de"));
```

   See "Using Command Links" on page 125 of Chapter 4 for an example.

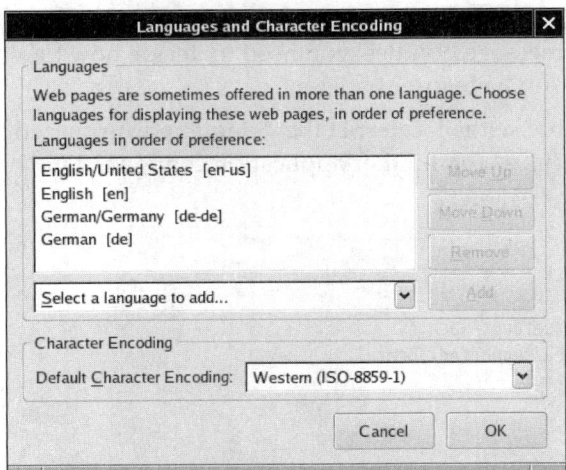

Figure 2–2   Selecting the preferred language

A Sample Application

After all these rather abstract rules and regulations, it is time for a concrete example. The application presents a series of quiz questions. Each question displays a sequence of numbers and asks the participant to guess the next number of the sequence.

For example, Figure 2–3 asks for the next number in the sequence

    3 1 4 1 5

You often find puzzles of this kind in tests that purport to measure intelligence. To solve the puzzle, you need to find the pattern. In this case, we have the first digits of π.

Type in the next number in the sequence (9), and the score goes up by one.

 NOTE: There is a Java-compatible mnemonic for the digits of π: "Can I have a small container of coffee?" Count the letters in each word, and you get 3 1 4 1 5 9 2 6. See http://dir.yahoo.com/Science/Mathematics/Numerical_Analysis/ Numbers/Specific_Numbers/Pi/Mnemonics/ for more elaborate memorization aids.

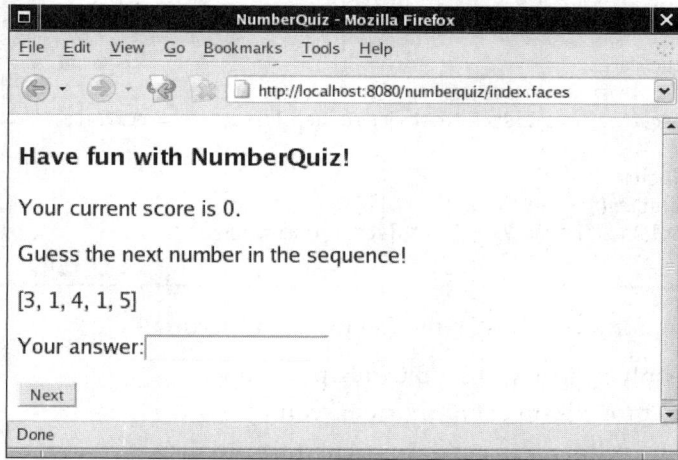

Figure 2–3   The number quiz

In this example, we place the quiz questions in the QuizBean class. Of course, in a real application, you would be more likely to store this information in a database. But the purpose of the example is to demonstrate how to use beans that have complex structure.

We start out with a ProblemBean class. A ProblemBean has two properties: solution, of type int, and sequence, of type ArrayList (see Listing 2–1).

Listing 2–1   numberquiz/src/java/com/corejsf/ProblemBean.java

```
1. package com.corejsf;
2. import java.util.ArrayList;
3.
4. public class ProblemBean {
5.    private ArrayList<Integer> sequence;
6.    private int solution;
7.
8.    public ProblemBean() {}
9.
10.    public ProblemBean(int[] values, int solution) {
11.       sequence = new ArrayList<Integer>();
12.       for (int i = 0; i < values.length; i++)
13.          sequence.add(values[i]);
14.       this.solution = solution;
15.    }
16.
```

Listing 2–1 numberquiz/src/java/com/corejsf/ProblemBean.java (cont.)

```
17.    // PROPERTY: sequence
18.    public ArrayList<Integer> getSequence() { return sequence; }
19.    public void setSequence(ArrayList<Integer> newValue) { sequence = newValue; }
20.
21.    // PROPERTY: solution
22.    public int getSolution() { return solution; }
23.    public void setSolution(int newValue) { solution = newValue; }
24. }
```

Next, we define a bean for the quiz with the following properties:

- problems: a write-only property to set the quiz problems
- score: a read-only property to get the current score
- current: a read-only property to get the current quiz problem
- answer: a property to get and set the answer that the user provides

The problems property is unused in this sample program—we initialize the problem set in the QuizBean constructor. However, under "Chaining Bean Definitions" on page 61, you will see how to set up the problem set inside faces-config.xml, without having to write any code.

The current property is used to display the current problem. However, the value of the current property is a ProblemBean object, and we cannot directly display that object in a text field. We make a second property access to get the number sequence:

```
<h:outputText value="#{quiz.current.sequence}"/>
```

The value of the sequence property is an ArrayList. When it is displayed, it is converted to a string by a call to the toString method. The result is a string of the form

```
[3, 1, 4, 1, 5]
```

Finally, we do a bit of dirty work with the answer property. We tie the answer property to the input field:

```
<h:inputText value="#{quiz.answer}"/>
```

When the input field is displayed, the getter is called, and we define the getAnswer method to return an empty string.

When the form is submitted, the setter is called with the value that the user typed into the input field. We define setAnswer to check the answer, update the score for a correct answer, and advance to the next problem.

```
public void setAnswer(String newValue) {
   try {
      int answer = Integer.parseInt(newValue.trim());
      if (getCurrent().getSolution() == answer) score++;
      currentIndex = (currentIndex + 1) % problems.size();
   }
   catch (NumberFormatException ex) {
   }
}
```

Strictly speaking, it is a bad idea to put code into a property setter that is unrelated to the task of setting the property. Updating the score and advancing to the next problem should really be contained in a handler for the button action. However, we have not yet discussed how to react to button actions, so we use the flexibility of the setter method to our advantage.

Another weakness of our sample application is that we have not yet covered how to stop at the end of the quiz. Instead, we just wrap around to the beginning, letting the user rack up a higher score. You will learn in the next chapter how to do a better job. Remember—the point of this application is to show you how to configure and use beans.

Finally, note that we use message bundles for internationalization. Try switching your browser language to German, and the program will appear as in Figure 2–4.

This finishes our sample application. Figure 2–5 shows the directory structure. The remaining code is in Listings 2–2 through 2–6.

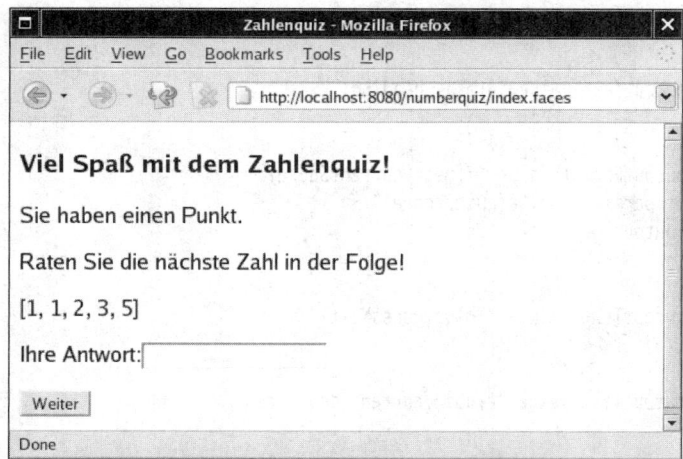

Figure 2–4   Viel Spaß mit dem Zahlenquiz!

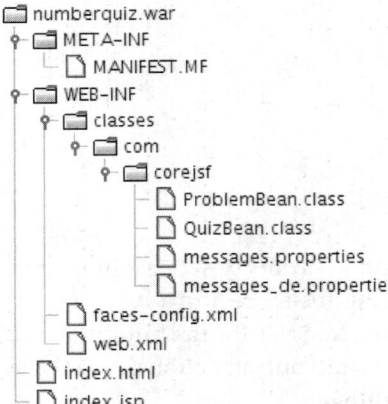

numberquiz.war
  META-INF
    MANIFEST.MF
  WEB-INF
    classes
      com
        corejsf
          ProblemBean.class
          QuizBean.class
          messages.properties
          messages_de.properties
    faces-config.xml
    web.xml
  index.html
  index.jsp

Figure 2–5   The directory structure of the number quiz example

Listing 2–2   `numberquiz/web/index.jsp`

```
1.  <html>
2.  <%@ taglib uri="http://java.sun.com/jsf/html" prefix="h" %>
3.  <%@ taglib uri="http://java.sun.com/jsf/core" prefix="f" %>
4.
5.  <f:view>
6.     <head>
7.        <title><h:outputText value="#{msgs.title}"/></title>
8.     </head>
9.     <body>
10.       <h:form>
11.          <h3>
12.             <h:outputText value="#{msgs.heading}"/>
13.          </h3>
14.          <p>
15.             <h:outputFormat value="#{msgs.currentScore}">
16.                <f:param value="#{quiz.score}"/>
17.             </h:outputFormat>
18.          </p>
19.          <p>
20.             <h:outputText value="#{msgs.guessNext}"/>
21.          </p>
22.          <p>
23.             <h:outputText value="#{quiz.current.sequence}"/>
24.          </p>
```

Listing 2–2　numberquiz/web/index.jsp (cont.)

```
25.            <p>
26.               <h:outputText value="#{msgs.answer}"/>
27.               <h:inputText value="#{quiz.answer}"/></p>
28.            <p>
29.               <h:commandButton value="#{msgs.next}" action="next"/>
30.            </p>
31.         </h:form>
32.      </body>
33.   </f:view>
34. </html>
```

Listing 2–3　numberquiz/src/java/com/corejsf/QuizBean.java

```
1. package com.corejsf;
2. import java.util.ArrayList;
3.
4. public class QuizBean {
5.    private ArrayList<ProblemBean> problems = new ArrayList<ProblemBean>();
6.    private int currentIndex;
7.    private int score;
8.
9.    public QuizBean() {
10.      problems.add(
11.        new ProblemBean(new int[] { 3, 1, 4, 1, 5 }, 9)); // pi
12.      problems.add(
13.        new ProblemBean(new int[] { 1, 1, 2, 3, 5 }, 8)); // fibonacci
14.      problems.add(
15.        new ProblemBean(new int[] { 1, 4, 9, 16, 25 }, 36)); // squares
16.      problems.add(
17.        new ProblemBean(new int[] { 2, 3, 5, 7, 11 }, 13)); // primes
18.      problems.add(
19.        new ProblemBean(new int[] { 1, 2, 4, 8, 16 }, 32)); // powers of 2
20.    }
21.
22.    // PROPERTY: problems
23.    public void setProblems(ArrayList<ProblemBean> newValue) {
24.      problems = newValue;
25.      currentIndex = 0;
26.      score = 0;
27.    }
28.
29.    // PROPERTY: score
30.    public int getScore() { return score; }
```

Listing 2–3   numberquiz/src/java/com/corejsf/QuizBean.java (cont.)

```
31.
32.    // PROPERTY: current
33.    public ProblemBean getCurrent() {
34.       return problems.get(currentIndex);
35.    }
36.
37.    // PROPERTY: answer
38.    public String getAnswer() { return ""; }
39.    public void setAnswer(String newValue) {
40.       try {
41.          int answer = Integer.parseInt(newValue.trim());
42.          if (getCurrent().getSolution() == answer) score++;
43.          currentIndex = (currentIndex + 1) % problems.size();
44.       }
45.       catch (NumberFormatException ex) {
46.       }
47.    }
48. }
```

Listing 2–4   numberquiz/web/WEB-INF/faces-config.xml

```
 1. <?xml version="1.0"?>
 2. <faces-config xmlns="http://java.sun.com/xml/ns/javaee"
 3.    xmlns:xsi="http://www.w3.org/2001/XMLSchema-instance"
 4.    xsi:schemaLocation="http://java.sun.com/xml/ns/javaee
 5.       http://java.sun.com/xml/ns/javaee/web-facesconfig_1_2.xsd"
 6.    version="1.2">
 7.    <application>
 8.       <locale-config>
 9.          <default-locale>en</default-locale>
10.          <supported-locale>de</supported-locale>
11.       </locale-config>
12.    </application>
13.
14.    <navigation-rule>
15.       <from-view-id>/index.jsp</from-view-id>
16.       <navigation-case>
17.          <from-outcome>next</from-outcome>
18.          <to-view-id>/index.jsp</to-view-id>
19.       </navigation-case>
20.    </navigation-rule>
21.
```

Listing 2–4	numberquiz/web/WEB-INF/faces-config.xml (cont.)

```
22.    <managed-bean>
23.        <managed-bean-name>quiz</managed-bean-name>
24.        <managed-bean-class>com.corejsf.QuizBean</managed-bean-class>
25.        <managed-bean-scope>session</managed-bean-scope>
26.    </managed-bean>
27.
28.    <application>
29.        <resource-bundle>
30.            <base-name>com.corejsf.messages</base-name>
31.            <var>msgs</var>
32.        </resource-bundle>
33.    </application>
34. </faces-config>
```

Listing 2–5	numberquiz/src/java/com/corejsf/messages.properties

```
1. title=NumberQuiz
2. heading=Have fun with NumberQuiz!
3. currentScore=Your current score is {0}.
4. guessNext=Guess the next number in the sequence!
5. answer=Your answer:
6. next=Next
```

Listing 2–6	numberquiz/src/java/com/corejsf/messsages_de.properties

```
1. title=Zahlenquiz
2. heading=Viel Spa\u00df mit dem Zahlenquiz!
3. currentScore=Sie haben {0,choice,0#0 Punkte|1#einen Punkt|2#{0} Punkte}.
4. guessNext=Raten Sie die n\u00e4chste Zahl in der Folge!
5. answer=Ihre Antwort:
6. next=Weiter
```

Backing Beans

Sometimes it is convenient to design a bean that contains some or all component objects of a web form. Such a bean is called a *backing bean* for the web form.

For example, we can define a backing bean for the quiz form by adding properties for the form component:

```
public class QuizFormBean {
    private UIOutput scoreComponent;
    private UIInput answerComponent;
```

```
// PROPERTY: scoreComponent
public UIOutput getScoreComponent() { return scoreComponent; }
public void setScoreComponent(UIOutput newValue) { scoreComponent = newValue; }

// PROPERTY: answerComponent
public UIInput getAnswerComponent() { return answerComponent; }
public void setAnswerComponent(UIInput newValue) { answerComponent = newValue; }
...
}
```

Output components belong to the UIOutput class and input components belong to the UIInput class. We discuss these classes in greater detail in "The Custom Component Developer's Toolbox" on page 360 of Chapter 9.

Why would you want such a bean? As we show in "Validating Relationships Between Multiple Components" on page 260 of Chapter 6, it is sometimes necessary for validators and event handlers to have access to the actual components on a form. Moreover, visual JSF development environments generally use backing beans (called *page beans* in Java Studio Creator because a bean is added for every page). These environments automatically generate the property getters and setters for all components that are dragged onto a form.

When you use a backing bean, you need to wire up the components on the form to those on the bean. You use the binding attribute for this purpose:

```
<h:outputText binding="#{quizForm.scoreComponent}"/>
```

When the component tree for the form is built, the getScoreComponent method of the backing bean is called, but it returns null. As a result, an output component is constructed and installed into the backing bean with a call to setScoreComponent.

Backing beans have their uses, but they can also be abused. You should not mix form components and business data in the same bean. If you use backing beans for your presentation data, use a different set of beans for business objects.

Bean Scopes

For the convenience of the web application programmer, a servlet container provides separate scopes, each of which manages a table of name/value bindings.

These scopes typically hold beans and other objects that need to be available in different components of a web application.

Session Scope

Recall that the HTTP protocol is *stateless*. The browser sends a request to the server, the server returns a response, and then neither the browser nor the server has any obligation to keep any memory of the transaction. This simple arrangement works well for retrieving basic information, but it is unsatisfactory for server-side applications. For example, in a shopping application, you want the server to remember the contents of the shopping cart.

For that reason, servlet containers augment the HTTP protocol to keep track of a *session*—that is, repeated connections by the same client. There are various methods for session tracking. The simplest method uses *cookies*: name/value pairs that a server sends to a client, hoping to have them returned in subsequent requests (see Figure 2–6).

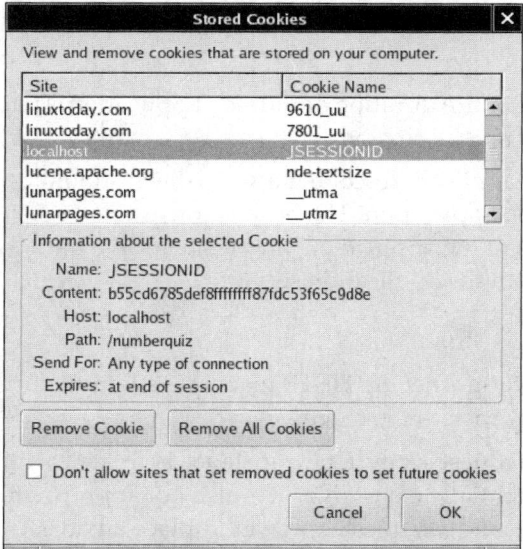

Figure 2–6   The cookie sent by a JSF application

As long as the client does not deactivate cookies, the server receives a session identifier with each subsequent request.

Application servers use fallback strategies, such as *URL rewriting*, for dealing with those clients that do not return cookies. URL rewriting adds a session identifier to a URL, which looks somewhat like this:

```
http://corejsf.com/login/index.jsp;jsessionid=b55cd6...d8e
```

 NOTE: To see this behavior, tell your browser to reject cookies from the `localhost`, then restart the web application and submit a page. The next page will have a `jsessionid` attribute.

Session tracking with cookies is completely transparent to the web developer, and the standard JSF tags automatically perform URL rewriting if a client does not use cookies.

The *session scope* persists from the time that a session is established until session termination. A session terminates if the web application invokes the invalidate method on the HttpSession object, or if it times out.

Web applications typically place most of their beans into session scope.

For example, a UserBean can contain information about users that is accessible throughout the entire session. A ShoppingCartBean can be filled up gradually during the requests that make up a session.

Application Scope

The *application scope* persists for the entire duration of the web application. That scope is shared among all requests and all sessions.

You place managed beans into the application scope if a single bean should be shared among all instances of a web application. The bean is constructed when it is first requested by any instance of the application, and it stays alive until the web application is removed from the application server.

Request Scope

The *request scope* is short-lived. It starts when an HTTP request is submitted and ends when the response is sent back to the client.

If you place a managed bean into request scope, a new instance is created with each request. Not only is this is potentially expensive, it is also not appropriate if you want your data to persist beyond a request. You would place an object into request scope only if you wanted to forward it to another processing phase inside the current request.

For example, the f:loadBundle tag places the bundle variable in request scope. The variable is needed only during the *Render Response* phase in the same request.

 CAUTION: Only request scope beans are single-threaded and, therefore, inherently threadsafe. Perhaps surprisingly, session beans are *not* single-threaded. For example, a user can simultaneously submit responses from multiple browser windows. Each response is processed by a separate request thread. If you need thread safety in your session beans, you should provide locking mechanisms.

Life Cycle Annotations

Starting with JSF 1.2, you can specify managed bean methods that are automatically called just after the bean has been constructed and just before the bean goes out of scope. This is particularly convenient for beans that establish connections to external resources such as databases.

Annotate the methods with @PostConstruct or @PreDestroy, like this:

```
public class MyBean {
   @PostConstruct
   public void initialize() {
      // initialization code
   }
   @PreDestroy
   public void shutdown() {
      // shutdown code
   }

   // other bean methods
}
```

These methods will be automatically called, provided the web application is deployed in a container that supports the annotations of JSR (Java Specification Request) 250 (see http://www.jcp.org/en/jsr/detail?id=250). In particular, Java EE 5-compliant application servers such as GlassFish support these annotations. It is expected that standalone containers such as Tomcat will also provide support in the future.

Configuring Beans

This section describes how you can configure a bean in a configuration file. The details are rather technical. You may want to have a glance at this section and return to it when you need to configure beans with complex properties.

The most commonly used configuration file is WEB-INF/faces-config.xml. However, you can also place configuration information inside the following locations:

- Files named META-INF/faces-config.xml inside any JAR files loaded by the external context's class loader. (You use this mechanism if you deliver reusable components in a JAR file.)
- Files listed in the javax.faces.CONFIG_FILES initialization parameter inside WEB-INF/web.xml. For example,

```
<web-app>
   <context-param>
      <param-name>javax.faces.CONFIG_FILES</param-name>
```

```
        <param-value>WEB-INF/navigation.xml,WEB-INF/beans.xml</param-value>
      </context-param>
      ...
   </web-app>
```

(This mechanism is attractive for builder tools because it separates navigation, beans, etc.)

For simplicity, we use WEB-INF/faces-config.xml in this chapter.

A bean is defined with a managed-bean element inside the top-level faces-config element. Minimally, you must specify the name, class, and scope of the bean.

```
<faces-config>
   <managed-bean>
      <managed-bean-name>user</managed-bean-name>
      <managed-bean-class>com.corejsf.UserBean</managed-bean-class>
      <managed-bean-scope>session</managed-bean-scope>
   </managed-bean>
</faces-config>
```

The scope can be request, session, application, or none. The none scope denotes an object that is not kept in one of the three scope maps. You use objects with scope none as building blocks when wiring up complex beans. You will see an example in the section "Chaining Bean Definitions" on page 61.

Setting Property Values

We start with a simple example. Here we customize a UserBean instance:

```
<managed-bean>
   <managed-bean-name>user</managed-bean-name>
   <managed-bean-class>com.corejsf.UserBean</managed-bean-class>
   <managed-bean-scope>session</managed-bean-scope>
   <managed-property>
      <property-name>name</property-name>
      <value>me</value>
   </managed-property>
   <managed-property>
      <property-name>password</property-name>
      <value>secret</value>
   </managed-property>
</managed-bean>
```

When the user bean is first looked up, it is constructed with the UserBean() default constructor. Then the setName and setPassword methods are executed.

To initialize a property with null, use a null-value element. For example,

```
<managed-property>
    <property-name>password</property-name>
    <null-value/>
</managed-property>
```

Initializing Lists and Maps

A special syntax initializes values that are of type List or Map. Here is an example of a list:

```
<list-entries>
    <value-class>java.lang.Integer</value.class>
    <value>3</value>
    <value>1</value>
    <value>4</value>
    <value>1</value>
    <value>5</value>
</list-entries>
```

Here we use the java.lang.Integer wrapper type since a List cannot hold values of primitive type.

The list can contain a mixture of value and null-value elements. The value-class is optional. If it is omitted, a list of java.lang.String objects is produced.

A map is more complex. You specify optional key-class and value-class elements (again, with a default of java.lang.String). Then you provide a sequence of map-entry elements, each of which has a key element, followed by a value or null-value element.

Here is an example:

```
<map-entries>
    <key-class>java.lang.Integer</key-class>
    <map-entry>
        <key>1</key>
        <value>George Washington</value>
    </map-entry>
    <map-entry>
        <key>3</key>
        <value>Thomas Jefferson</value>
    </map-entry>
    <map-entry>
        <key>16</key>
        <value>Abraham Lincoln</value>
    </map-entry>
    <map-entry>
```

```
        <key>26</key>
        <value>Theodore Roosevelt</value>
      </map-entry>
   </map-entries>
```

You can use list-entries and map-entries elements to initialize either a managed-bean or a managed-property, provided that the bean or property type is a List or Map.

Figure 2–7 shows a *syntax diagram* for the managed-bean element and all of its child elements. Follow the arrows to see which constructs are legal inside a managed-bean element. For example, the second graph tells you that a managed-property element starts with zero or more description elements, followed by zero or more display-name elements, zero or more icons, then a mandatory property-name, an optional property-class, and exactly one of the elements value, null-value, map-entries, or list-entries.

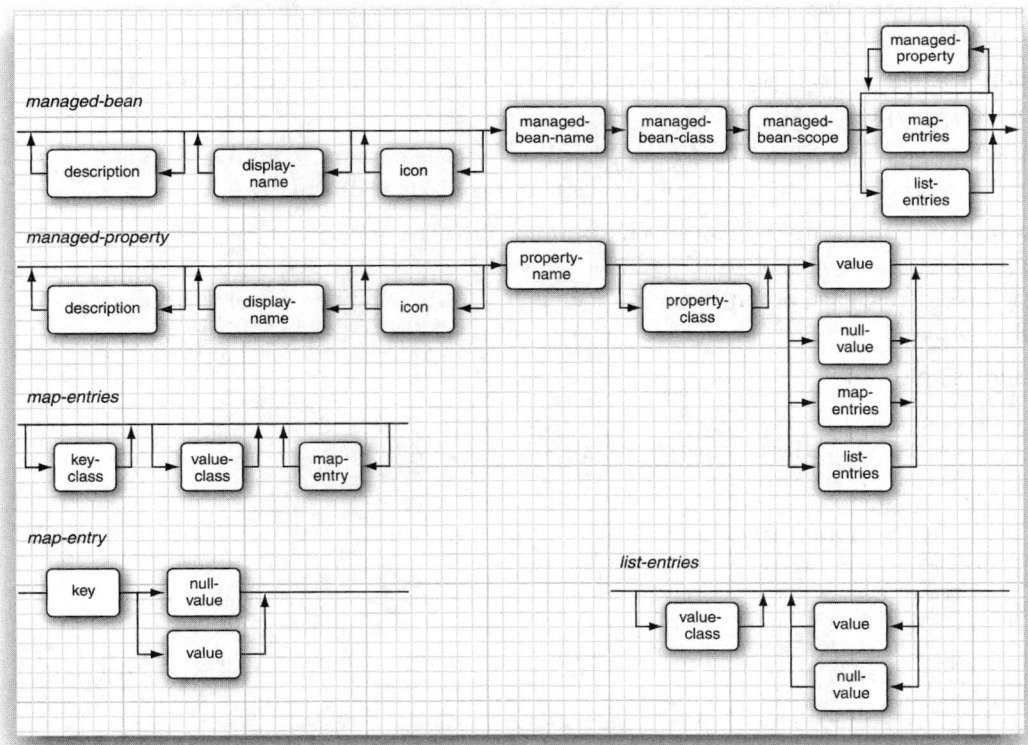

Figure 2–7   Syntax diagram for managed-bean **elements**

Chaining Bean Definitions

You can achieve more complex arrangements by using value expressions inside the value element to chain beans together. Consider the quiz bean in the number-quiz application.

The quiz contains a collection of problems, represented as the write-only problems property. You can configure it with the following instructions:

```
<managed-bean>
   <managed-bean-name>quiz</managed-bean-name>
   <managed-bean-class>com.corejsf.QuizBean</managed-bean-class>
   <managed-bean-scope>session</managed-bean-scope>
   <managed-property>
      <property-name>problems</property-name>
      <list-entries>
         <value-class>com.corejsf.ProblemBean</value-class>
         <value>#{problem1}</value>
         <value>#{problem2}</value>
         <value>#{problem3}</value>
         <value>#{problem4}</value>
         <value>#{problem5}</value>
      </list-entries>
   </managed-property>
</managed-bean>
```

Of course, now we must define beans with names problem1 through problem5, like this:

```
<managed-bean>
   <managed-bean-name>problem1</managed-bean-name>
   <managed-bean-class>
      com.corejsf.ProblemBean
   </managed-bean-class>
   <managed-bean-scope>none</managed-bean-scope>
      <managed-property>
         <property-name>sequence</property-name>
         <list-entries>
            <value-class>java.lang.Integer</value-class>
            <value>3</value>
            <value>1</value>
            <value>4</value>
            <value>1</value>
            <value>5</value>
         </list-entries>
      </managed-property>
```

```
<managed-property>
    <property-name>solution</property-name>
    <value>9</value>
</managed-property>
</managed-bean>
```

When the `quiz` bean is requested, then the creation of the beans `problem1` through `problem5` is triggered automatically. You need not worry about the order in which you specify managed beans.

Note that the problem beans have scope `none` since they are never requested from a JSF page but are instantiated when the `quiz` bean is requested.

When you wire beans together, make sure that their scopes are compatible. Table 2–1 lists the permissible combinations.

Table 2–1   Compatible Bean Scopes

When defining a bean of this scope . . .	. . . you can use beans of these scopes
none	none
application	none, application
session	none, application, session
request	none, application, session, request

String Conversions

You specify property values and elements of lists or maps with a `value` element that contains a string. The enclosed string needs to be converted to the type of the property or element. For primitive types, this conversion is straightforward. For example, you can specify a `boolean` value with the string `true` or `false`.

Starting with JSF 1.2, values of enumerated types are supported as well. The conversion is performed by calling `Enum.valueOf(`*propertyClass*, *valueText*`)`.

For other property types, the JSF implementation attempts to locate a matching `PropertyEditor`. If a property editor exists, its `setAsText` method is invoked to convert strings to property values. Property editors are heavily used for client-side beans, to convert between property values and a textual or graphical representation that can be displayed in a property sheet (see Figure 2–8).

Defining a property editor is somewhat involved, and we refer the interested reader to Horstmann and Cornell, 2004, 2005. *Core Java™ 2,* vol. 2, chap. 8.

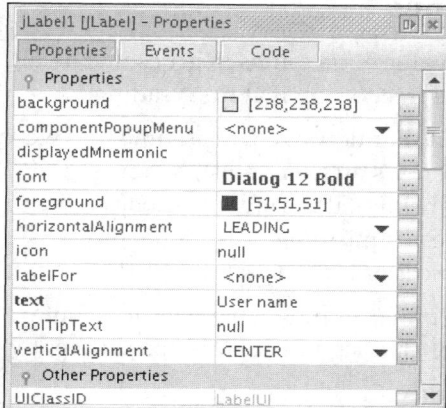

Figure 2–8   A property sheet in a GUI builder

Note that the rules are fairly restrictive. For example, if you have a property of type URL, you cannot simply specify the URL as a string, even though there is a constructor URL(String). You would need to supply a property editor for the URL type or reimplement the property type as String.

Table 2–2 summarizes these conversion rules. They are identical to the rules for the jsp:setProperty action of the JSP specification.

Table 2–2   String Conversions

Target Type	Conversion
int, byte, short, long, float, double, or the corresponding wrapper type	The valueOf method of the wrapper type, or 0 if the string is empty.
boolean or Boolean	The result of Boolean.valueOf, or false if the string is empty.
char or Character	The first character of the string, or (char) 0 if the string is empty.
String or Object	A copy of the string; new String("") if the string is empty.
bean property	A type that calls the setAsText method of the property editor if it exists. If the property editor does not exist or it throws an exception, the property is set to null if the string is empty. Otherwise, an error occurs.

The Syntax of Value Expressions

In this section, we discuss the syntax for value expressions in gruesome detail. This section is intended for reference. Feel free to skip it at first reading.

We start with an expression of the form a.b. For now, we will assume that we already know the object to which a refers. If a is an array, a list, or a map, then special rules apply (see "Using Brackets" below). If a is any other object, then b must be the name of a property of a. The exact meaning of a.b depends on whether the expression is used in *rvalue mode* or *lvalue mode*.

This terminology is used in the theory of programming languages to denote that an expression on the *right-hand side* of an assignment is treated differently from an expression on the *left-hand side*.

Consider the assignment

```
left = right;
```

A compiler generates different code for the left and right expressions. The right expression is evaluated in rvalue mode and yields a value. The left expression is evaluated in lvalue mode and stores a value in a location.

The same phenomenon happens when you use a value expression in a user interface component:

```
<h:inputText value="#{user.name}"/>
```

When the text field is rendered, the expression user.name is evaluated in rvalue mode, and the getName method is called. During decoding, the same expression is evaluated in lvalue mode and the setName method is called.

In general, the expression a.b in rvalue mode is evaluated by calling the property getter, whereas a.b in lvalue mode calls the property setter.

Using Brackets

Just as in JavaScript, you can use brackets instead of the dot notation. That is, the following three expressions all have the same meaning:

```
a.b
a["b"]
a['b']
```

For example, user.password, user["password"], and user['password'] are equivalent expressions.

Why would anyone write user["password"] when user.password is much easier to type? There are a number of reasons:

- When you access an array or map, the [] notation is more intuitive.
- You can use the [] notation with strings that contain periods or dashes— for example, msgs["error.password"].
- The [] notation allows you to dynamically compute a property: a[b.propname].

 TIP: Use single quotes in value expressions if you delimit attributes with double quotes: value="#{user['password']}". Alternatively, you can switch single and double quotes: value='#{user["password"]}'.

Map and List Expressions

The value expression language goes beyond bean property access. For example, let m be an object of any class that implements the Map interface. Then m["key"] (or the equivalent m.key) is a binding to the associated value. In rvalue mode, the value

```
m.get("key")
```

is fetched. In lvalue mode, the statement

```
m.put("key", right);
```

is executed. Here, right is the *right-hand side* value that is assigned to m.key.

You can also access a value of any object of a class that implements the List interface (such as an ArrayList). You specify an integer index for the list position. For example, a[i] (or, if you prefer, a.i) binds the ith element of the list a. Here i can be an integer, or a string that can be converted to an integer. The same rule applies for array types. As always, index values start at zero.

Table 2–3 summarizes these evaluation rules.

Table 2–3   Evaluating the Value Expression a.b

Type of a	Type of b	lvalue Mode	rvalue Mode
null	any	error	null
any	null	error	null
Map	any	a.put(b, right)	a.get(b)

Table 2–3   Evaluating the Value Expression a.b **(cont.)**

Type of a	Type of b	lvalue Mode	rvalue Mode
List	convertible to int	a.set(b, right)	a.get(b)
array	convertible to int	a[b] = right	a[b]
bean	any	call setter of property with name b.toString()	call getter of property with name b.toString()

 CAUTION: Unfortunately, value expressions do not work for indexed properties. If p is an indexed property of a bean b, and i is an integer, then b.p[i] does not access the ith value of the property. It is simply a syntax error. This deficiency is inherited from the JSP expression language.

Resolving the Initial Term

Now you know how an expression of the form a.b is resolved. The rules can be applied repetitively to expressions such as a.b.c.d (or, of course, a['b'].c["d"]). We still need to discuss the meaning of the initial term a.

In the examples you have seen so far, the initial term referred to a bean that was configured in the faces-config.xml file or to a message bundle map. Those are indeed the most common situations. But it is also possible to specify other names.

There are a number of predefined objects. Table 2–4 shows the complete list. For example,

```
header['User-Agent']
```

is the value of the User-Agent parameter of the HTTP request that identifies the user's browser.

If the initial term is not one of the predefined objects, the JSF implementation looks for it in the *request, session,* and *application scopes,* in that order. Those scopes are map objects that are managed by the servlet container. For example, when you define a managed bean, its name and value are added to the appropriate scope map.

Table 2–4   Predefined Objects in the Value Expression Language

Variable Name	Meaning
header	A Map of HTTP header parameters, containing only the first value for each name.
headerValues	A Map of HTTP header parameters, yielding a String[]array of all values for a given name.
param	A Map of HTTP request parameters, containing only the first value for each name.
paramValues	A Map of HTTP request parameters, yielding a String[]array of all values for a given name.
cookie	A Map of the cookie names and values of the current request.
initParam	A Map of the initialization parameters of this web application. Initialization parameters are discussed in Chapter 10.
requestScope	A Map of all request scope attributes.
sessionScope	A Map of all session scope attributes.
applicationScope	A Map of all application scope attributes.
facesContext	The FacesContext instance of this request. This class is discussed in Chapter 6.
view	The UIViewRoot instance of this request. This class is discussed in Chapter 7.

Finally, if the name is still not found, it is passed to the VariableResolver of the JSF application. The default variable resolver looks up managed-bean elements in a configuration resource, typically the faces-config.xml file.

Consider, for example, the expression

```
#{user.password}
```

The term user is not one of the predefined objects. When it is encountered for the first time, it is not an attribute name in request, session, or application scope.

Therefore, the variable resolver processes the faces-config.xml entry:

```
<managed-bean>
   <managed-bean-name>user</managed-bean-name>
   <managed-bean-class>com.corejsf.UserBean</managed-bean-class>
   <managed-bean-scope>session</managed-bean-scope>
</managed-bean>
```

The variable resolver calls the default constructor of the class `com.corejsf.User-Bean`. Next, it adds an association to the `sessionScope` map. Finally, it returns the object as the result of the lookup.

When the term user needs to be resolved again in the same session, it is located in the session scope.

Composite Expressions

You can use a limited set of operators inside value expressions:

- Arithmetic operators + - * / %. The last two operators have alphabetic variants `div` and `mod`.
- Relational operators < <= > >= == != and their alphabetic variants `lt le gt ge eq ne`. The first four variants are required for XML safety.
- Logical operators && || ! and their alphabetic variants `and or not`. The first variant is required for XML safety.
- The `empty` operator. The expression `empty a` is `true` if `a` is `null`, an array or `String` of length 0, or a `Collection` or `Map` of size 0.
- The ternary ?: selection operator.

Operator precedence follows the same rules as in Java. The `empty` operator has the same precedence as the unary - and ! operators.

Generally, you do not want to do a lot of expression computation in web pages—that would violate the separation of presentation and business logic. However, occasionally, the presentation layer can benefit from operators. For example, suppose you want to hide a component when the `hide` property of a bean is true. To hide a component, you set its `rendered` attribute to `false`. Inverting the bean value requires the ! (or not) operator:

```
<h:inputText rendered="#{!bean.hide}" ... />
```

Finally, you can concatenate plain strings and value expressions by placing them next to each other. Consider, for example,

```
<h:outputText value="#{messages.greeting}, #{user.name}!"/>
```

The statement concatenates four strings: the string returned from `#{messages.greeting}`, the string consisting of a comma and a space, the string returned from `#{user.name}`, and the string consisting of an exclamation mark.

You have now seen all the rules that are applied to resolve value expressions. Of course, in practice, most expressions are of the form #{bean.property}. Just come back to this section when you need to tackle a more complex expression.

Method Expressions

A *method expression* denotes an object, together with a method that can be applied to it.

For example, here is a typical use of a method expression:

```
<h:commandButton action="#{user.checkPassword}"/>
```

We assume that user is a value of type UserBean and checkPassword is a method of that class. The method expression is a convenient way of describing a method invocation that needs to be carried out at some future time.

When the expression is evaluated, the method is applied to the object.

In our example, the command button component will call user.checkPassword() and pass the returned string to the navigation handler.

Syntax rules for method expressions are similar to those of value expressions. All but the last component are used to determine an object. The last component must be the name of a method that can be applied to that object.

Four component attributes can take a method expression:

- action (see "Dynamic Navigation" on page 73 of Chapter 3)
- validator (see "Validating with Bean Methods" on page 259 of Chapter 6)
- valueChangeListener ("Value Change Events" on page 269 of see Chapter 7)
- actionListener (see "Action Events" on page 275 of Chapter 7)

The parameter and return types of the method depend on the context in which the method expression is used. For example, an action must be bound to a method with no parameters and return type String, whereas an actionListener is bound to a method with one parameter of type ActionEvent and return type void. The code that invokes the method expression is responsible for supplying parameter values and processing the return value.

NAVIGATION

Topics in This Chapter

Chapter 3

In this short chapter, we discuss how you configure the navigation of your web application. In particular, you will learn how your application can move from one page to the next, depending on user actions and the outcomes of decisions in the business logic.

Static Navigation

Consider what happens when the user of a web application fills out a web page. The user might fill in text fields, click radio buttons, or select list entries.

All these edits happen inside the user's browser. When the user clicks a button that posts the form data, the changes are transmitted to the server.

At that time, the web application analyzes the user input and must decide which JSF page to use for rendering the response. The *navigation handler* is responsible for selecting the next JSF page.

In a simple web application, page navigation is static. That is, clicking a particular button always selects a fixed JSF page for rendering the response. In "A Simple Example" on page 6 of Chapter 1, you saw how to wire up static navigation between JSF pages in the `faces-config.xml` file.

You give each button an `action` attribute—for example,

```
<h:commandButton label="Login" action="login"/>
```

NOTE: As you will see in Chapter 4, navigation actions can also be attached to hyperlinks.

The action must match an *outcome* in a navigation rule:

```
<navigation-rule>
    <from-view-id>/index.jsp</from-view-id>
    <navigation-case>
        <from-outcome>login</from-outcome>
        <to-view-id>/welcome.jsp</to-view-id>
    </navigation-case>
</navigation-rule>
```

This rule states that the login action navigates to /welcome.jsp if it occurred inside /index.jsp.

Note that the view ID strings must start with a /. The extension should match the file extension (.jsp), not the URL extension. For example, if you use a from-view-id of /index.faces, then the rule will not work.

If you pick the action strings carefully, you can group multiple navigation rules together. For example, you may have buttons with action logout sprinkled throughout your application's pages. You can have all these buttons navigate to the logout.jsp page with the single rule

```
<navigation-rule>
    <navigation-case>
        <from-outcome>logout</from-outcome>
        <to-view-id>/logout.jsp</to-view-id>
    </navigation-case>
</navigation-rule>
```

This rule applies to all pages because no from-view-id element was specified.

You can merge navigation rules with the same from-view-id—for example,

```
<navigation-rule>
    <from-view-id>/index.jsp</from-view-id>
    <navigation-case>
        <from-outcome>login</from-outcome>
        <to-view-id>/welcome.jsp</to-view-id>
    </navigation-case>
    <navigation-case>
        <from-outcome>signup</from-outcome>
        <to-view-id>/newuser.jsp</to-view-id>
    </navigation-case>
</navigation-rule>
```

This merging seems like a good idea, even though it is not required.

 CAUTION: If no navigation rule matches a given action, then the current page is redisplayed.

Dynamic Navigation

In most web applications, navigation is not static. The page flow does not just depend on which button you click but also on the inputs that you provide. For example, submitting a login page may have two outcomes: success or failure. The outcome depends on a computation—namely, whether the username and password are legitimate.

To implement dynamic navigation, the submit button must have a *method expression*, such as

```
<h:commandButton label="Login" action="#{loginController.verifyUser}"/>
```

In our example, loginController references a bean of some class, and that class must have a method named verifyUser.

A method expression in an action attribute has no parameters. It can have any return type. The return value is converted to a string by calling toString.

 NOTE: In JSF 1.1, an action method was required to have return type String. In JSF 1.2, you can use any return type. In particular, using enumerations is a useful alternative since the compiler can catch typos in the action names.

Here is an example of an action method:

```
String verifyUser() {
    if (...)
        return "success";
    else
        return "failure";
}
```

The method returns an outcome string such as "success" or "failure". The navigation handler uses the returned string to look up a matching navigation rule.

NOTE: An action method may return `null` to indicate that the same page should be redisplayed.

In summary, here are the steps that are carried out whenever the user clicks a command button whose `action` attribute is a method expression:

- The specified bean is retrieved.
- The referenced method is called.
- The resulting string is passed to the navigation handler. (As explained under "The Navigation Algorithm" on page 87, the navigation handler also receives the method expression string.)
- The navigation handler looks up the next page.

Thus, to implement branching behavior, you supply a reference to a method in an appropriate bean class. You have wide latitude about where to place that method. The best approach is to find a class that has all the data that you need for decision making.

Next, we work through this process in an actual application. Our sample program presents the user with a sequence of quiz questions (see Figure 3–1).

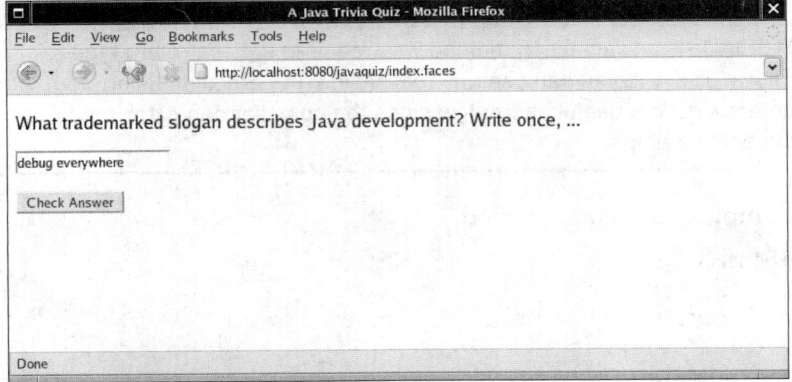

Figure 3–1   A quiz question

When the user clicks the "Check Answer" button, the application checks whether the user provided the correct answer. If not, the user has one additional chance to answer the same problem (see Figure 3–2).

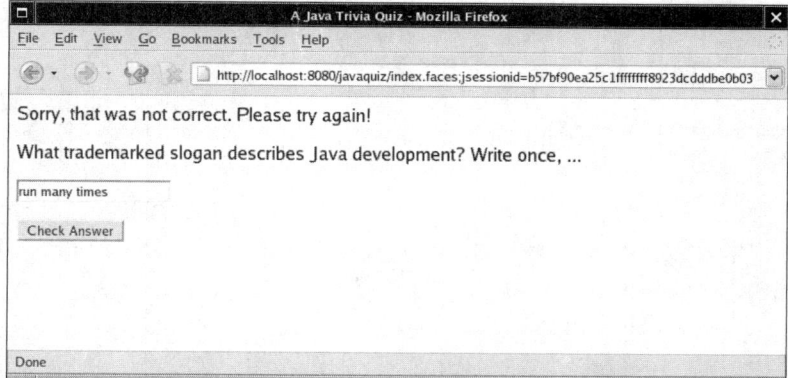

Figure 3–2   One wrong answer: Try again

After two wrong answers, the next problem is presented (see Figure 3–3).

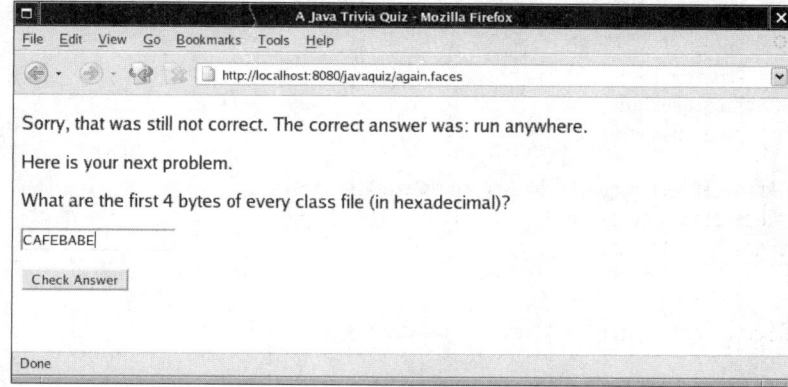

Figure 3–3   Two wrong answers: Move on

And, of course, after a correct answer, the next problem is presented as well. Finally, after the last problem, a summary page displays the score and invites the user to start over (see Figure 3–4).

Our application has two classes. The Problem class, shown in Listing 3–1, describes a single problem, with a question, an answer, and a method to check whether a given response is correct.

The QuizBean class describes a quiz that consists of a number of problems. A QuizBean instance also keeps track of the current problem and the total score of a user. You will find the complete code in Listing 3–2.

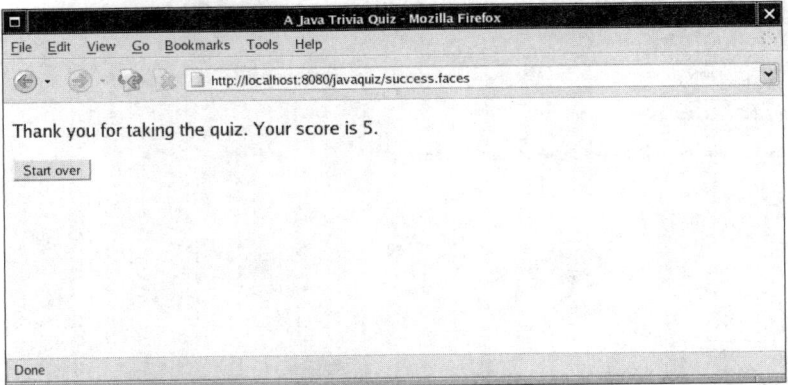

Figure 3–4 Done with the quiz

Listing 3–1   javaquiz/src/java/com/corejsf/Problem.java

```java
 1. package com.corejsf;
 2.
 3. public class Problem {
 4.     private String question;
 5.     private String answer;
 6.
 7.     public Problem(String question, String answer) {
 8.         this.question = question;
 9.         this.answer = answer;
10.     }
11.
12.     public String getQuestion() { return question; }
13.
14.     public String getAnswer() { return answer; }
15.
16.     // override for more sophisticated checking
17.     public boolean isCorrect(String response) {
18.         return response.trim().equalsIgnoreCase(answer);
19.     }
20. }
```

In this example, the QuizBean is the appropriate class for holding the navigation methods. That bean has all the knowledge about the user's actions, and it can determine which page should be displayed next.

Listing 3–2 javaquiz/src/java/com/corejsf/QuizBean.java

```java
1. package com.corejsf;
2.
3. public class QuizBean {
4.    private int currentProblem;
5.    private int tries;
6.    private int score;
7.    private String response;
8.    private String correctAnswer;
9.
10.    // here, we hardwire the problems. In a real application,
11.    // they would come from a database
12.    private Problem[] problems = {
13.       new Problem(
14.          "What trademarked slogan describes Java development? Write once, ...",
15.          "run anywhere"),
16.       new Problem(
17.          "What are the first 4 bytes of every class file (in hexadecimal)?",
18.          "CAFEBABE"),
19.       new Problem(
20.          "What does this statement print? System.out.println(1+\"2\");",
21.          "12"),
22.       new Problem(
23.          "Which Java keyword is used to define a subclass?",
24.          "extends"),
25.       new Problem(
26.          "What was the original name of the Java programming language?",
27.          "Oak"),
28.       new Problem(
29.          "Which java.util class describes a point in time?",
30.          "Date")
31.    };
32.
33.    public QuizBean() { startOver(); }
34.
35.    // PROPERTY: question
36.    public String getQuestion() {
37.       return problems[currentProblem].getQuestion();
38.    }
39.
40.    // PROPERTY: answer
41.    public String getAnswer() { return correctAnswer; }
42.
43.    // PROPERTY: score
44.    public int getScore() { return score; }
45.
```

Hitesh

Listing 3–2   javaquiz/src/java/com/corejsf/QuizBean.java (cont.)

```
46.    // PROPERTY: response
47.    public String getResponse() { return response; }
48.    public void setResponse(String newValue) { response = newValue; }
49.
50.    public String answerAction() {
51.       tries++;
52.       if (problems[currentProblem].isCorrect(response)) {
53.          score++;
54.          nextProblem();
55.          if (currentProblem == problems.length) return "done";
56.          else return "success";
57.       }
58.       else if (tries == 1) {
59.          return "again";
60.       }
61.       else {
62.          nextProblem();
63.          if (currentProblem == problems.length) return "done";
64.          else return "failure";
65.       }
66.    }
67.
68.    public String startOverAction() {
69.       startOver();
70.       return "startOver";
71.    }
72.
73.    private void startOver() {
74.       currentProblem = 0;
75.       score = 0;
76.       tries = 0;
77.       response = "";
78.    }
79.
80.    private void nextProblem() {
81.       correctAnswer = problems[currentProblem].getAnswer();
82.       currentProblem++;
83.       tries = 0;
84.       response = "";
85.    }
86. }
```

Have a glance at the code inside the answerAction method of the QuizBean class. The
method returns one of the strings "success" or "done" if the user answered the
question correctly, "again" after the first wrong answer, and "failure" or "done"
after the second wrong try.

```
public String answerAction() {
    tries++;
    if (problems[currentProblem].isCorrect(response)) {
        score++;
        if (currentProblem == problems.length - 1) {
            return "done";
        }
        else {
            nextProblem();
            return "success";
        }
    }
    else if (tries == 1) {
        return "again";
    }
    else {
        if (currentProblem == problems.length - 1) {
            return "done";
        }
        else {
            nextProblem();
            return "failure";
        }
    }
}
```

We attach the answerAction method expression to the buttons on each of the
pages. For example, the index.jsp page contains the following element:

```
<h:commandButton value="Check answer" action="#{quiz.answerAction}"/>
```

Here, quiz is the QuizBean instance that is defined in faces-config.xml.

Figure 3–5 shows the directory structure of the application. Listing 3–3 shows
the main quiz page index.jsp. The success.jsp and failure.jsp pages are omitted.
They differ from index.jsp only in the message at the top of the page.

The done.jsp page in Listing 3–4 shows the final score and invites the user to
play again. Pay attention to the command button on that page. It looks as if we
could use static navigation, since clicking the "Start over" button always
returns to the index.jsp page. However, we use a method expression:

```
<h:commandButton value="Start over" action="#{quiz.startOverAction}"/>
```

The startOverAction method carries out useful work that needs to take place to reset the game. It resets the score and reshuffles the response items:

```
public String startOverAction() {
    startOver();
    return "startOver";
}
```

In general, action methods have two roles:

- To carry out the model updates that are a consequence of the user action
- To tell the navigation handler where to go next

 NOTE: As you will see in Chapter 7, you can also attach action listeners to buttons. When the user clicks the button, the code in the processAction method of the action listener is executed. However, action listeners do not interact with the navigation handler.

Listing 3–5 shows the application configuration file with the navigation rules.

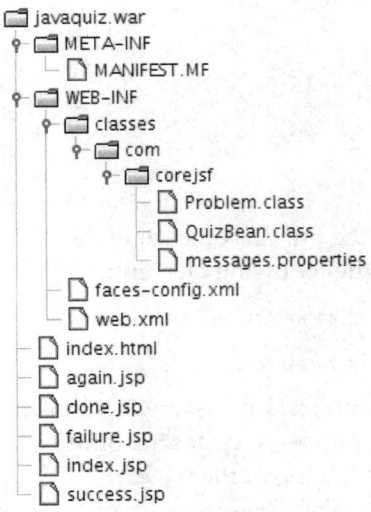

```
javaquiz.war
  META-INF
    MANIFEST.MF
  WEB-INF
    classes
      com
        corejsf
          Problem.class
          QuizBean.class
          messages.properties
    faces-config.xml
    web.xml
  index.html
  again.jsp
  done.jsp
  failure.jsp
  index.jsp
  success.jsp
```

Figure 3–5   Directory structure of the Java Quiz application

Because we selected our outcome strings so that they uniquely determine the successor web page, we can use a single navigation rule:

```
<navigation-rule>
  <navigation-case>
     <from-outcome>success</from-outcome>
     <to-view-id>/success.jsp</to-view-id>
  </navigation-case>
  <navigation-case>
     <from-outcome>again</from-outcome>
     <to-view-id>/again.jsp</to-view-id>
  </navigation-case>
  ...
</navigation-rule>
```

Figure 3–6 shows the transition diagram.

Finally, Listing 3–6 shows the message strings.

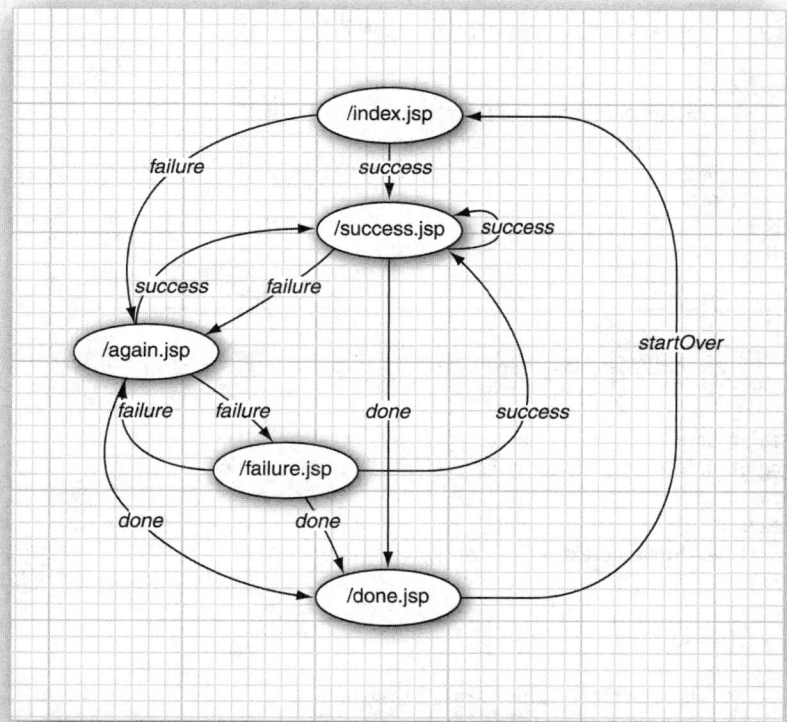

Figure 3–6   The transition diagram of the Java Quiz application

Listing 3–3   javaquiz/web/index.jsp

```
1.  <html>
2.  <%@ taglib uri="http://java.sun.com/jsf/core" prefix="f" %>
3.  <%@ taglib uri="http://java.sun.com/jsf/html" prefix="h" %>
4.
5.  <f:view>
6.     <head>
7.       <title><h:outputText value="#{msgs.title}"/></title>
8.     </head>
9.     <body>
10.       <h:form>
11.         <p>
12.           <h:outputText value="#{quiz.question}"/>
13.         </p>
14.         <p>
15.           <h:inputText value="#{quiz.response}"/>
16.         </p>
17.         <p>
18.           <h:commandButton value="#{msgs.answerButton}"
19.               action="#{quiz.answerAction}"/>
20.         </p>
21.       </h:form>
22.     </body>
23.  </f:view>
24. </html>
```

Listing 3–4   javaquiz/web/done.jsp

```
1.  <html>
2.  <%@ taglib uri="http://java.sun.com/jsf/core" prefix="f" %>
3.  <%@ taglib uri="http://java.sun.com/jsf/html" prefix="h" %>
4.  <f:view>
5.     <head>
6.       <title><h:outputText value="#{msgs.title}"/></title>
7.     </head>
8.     <body>
9.       <h:form>
10.         <p>
11.           <h:outputText value="#{msgs.thankYou}"/>
12.           <h:outputFormat value="#{msgs.score}">
13.             <f:param value="#{quiz.score}"/>
14.           </h:outputFormat>
15.         </p>
```

Listing 3–4 javaquiz/web/done.jsp (cont.)

```
16.            <p>
17.                <h:commandButton value="#{msgs.startOverButton}"
18.                    action="#{quiz.startOverAction}"/>
19.            </p>
20.        </h:form>
21.    </body>
22.  </f:view>
23. </html>
```

Listing 3–5 javaquiz/web/WEB-INF/faces-config.xml

```
1. <?xml version="1.0"?>
2. <faces-config xmlns="http://java.sun.com/xml/ns/javaee"
3.    xmlns:xsi="http://www.w3.org/2001/XMLSchema-instance"
4.    xsi:schemaLocation="http://java.sun.com/xml/ns/javaee
5.        http://java.sun.com/xml/ns/javaee/web-facesconfig_1_2.xsd"
6.    version="1.2">
7.    <navigation-rule>
8.        <navigation-case>
9.            <from-outcome>success</from-outcome>
10.            <to-view-id>/success.jsp</to-view-id>
11.            <redirect/>
12.        </navigation-case>
13.        <navigation-case>
14.            <from-outcome>again</from-outcome>
15.            <to-view-id>/again.jsp</to-view-id>
16.        </navigation-case>
17.        <navigation-case>
18.            <from-outcome>failure</from-outcome>
19.            <to-view-id>/failure.jsp</to-view-id>
20.        </navigation-case>
21.        <navigation-case>
22.            <from-outcome>done</from-outcome>
23.            <to-view-id>/done.jsp</to-view-id>
24.        </navigation-case>
25.        <navigation-case>
26.            <from-outcome>startOver</from-outcome>
27.            <to-view-id>/index.jsp</to-view-id>
28.        </navigation-case>
29.    </navigation-rule>
```

Listing 3–5   javaquiz/web/WEB-INF/faces-config.xml (cont.)

```
30.    <managed-bean>
31.        <managed-bean-name>quiz</managed-bean-name>
32.        <managed-bean-class>com.corejsf.QuizBean</managed-bean-class>
33.        <managed-bean-scope>session</managed-bean-scope>
34.    </managed-bean>
35.
36.    <application>
37.        <resource-bundle>
38.            <base-name>com.corejsf.messages</base-name>
39.            <var>msgs</var>
40.        </resource-bundle>
41.    </application>
42. </faces-config>
```

Listing 3–6   javaquiz/src/java/com/corejsf/messages.properties

```
1. title=A Java Trivia Quiz
2. answerButton=Check Answer
3. startOverButton=Start over
4. correct=Congratulations, that is correct.
5. notCorrect=Sorry, that was not correct. Please try again!
6. stillNotCorrect=Sorry, that was still not correct.
7. correctAnswer=The correct answer was: {0}.
8. score=Your score is {0}.
9. thankYou=Thank you for taking the quiz.
```

Advanced Navigation Issues

The techniques of the preceding sections should be sufficient for most practical navigation needs. In this section, we describe the remaining rules for the navigation elements that can appear in the faces-config.xml file. Figure 3–7 shows a syntax diagram of the valid elements.

 NOTE: As you saw in "Configuring Beans" on page 57 of Chapter 2, it is also possible to place the navigation information into configuration files other than the standard faces-config.xml file.

As you can see from the syntax diagram, each navigation-rule and navigation-case element can have an arbitrary description, a display-name, and icon elements. These elements are intended for use in builder tools, and we do not discuss them further.

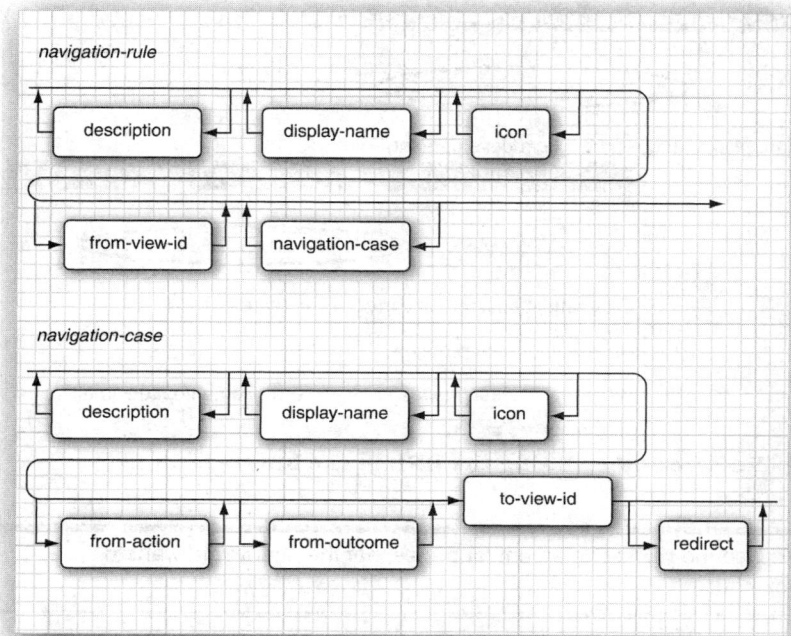

Figure 3–7   Syntax diagram for navigation elements

Redirection

If you add a redirect element after to-view-id, then the JSP container terminates the current request and sends an HTTP redirect to the client. The redirect response tells the client which URL to use for the next page.

Redirecting the page is slower than forwarding because another round trip to the browser is involved. However, the redirection gives the browser a chance to update its address field.

Figure 3–8 shows how the address field changes when you add a redirection element, as follows:

```
<navigation-case>
    <from-outcome>success</from-outcome>
    <to-view-id>/success.jsp</to-view-id>
    <redirect/>
</navigation-case>
```

Without redirection, the original URL (localhost:8080/javaquiz/index.faces) is unchanged when the user moves from the /index.jsp page to the /success.jsp face. With redirection, the browser displays the new URL (localhost:8080/javaquiz/success.faces).

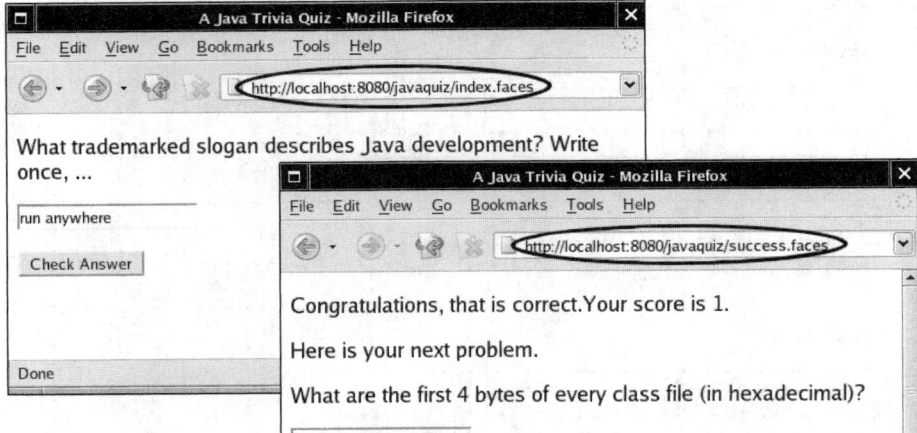

Figure 3–8 Redirection updating the URL in the browser

 TIP: Use the `redirect` element for pages that the user might want to bookmark.

 CAUTION: Without the `redirect` element, the navigation handler forwards the current request to the next page, and all name/value pairs stored in the request scope are carried over to the new page. However, with the `redirect` element, the request scope data is lost.

Wildcards

You can use *wildcards* in the `from-view-id` element of a navigation rule, for example:

```
<navigation-rule>
   <from-view-id>/secure/*</from-view-id>
   <navigation-case>
      . . .
   </navigation-case>
</navigation-rule>
```

This rule applies to all pages that start with the prefix /secure/. Only a single * is allowed, and it must be at the end of the ID string.

If there are multiple matching wildcard rules, the longest match is taken.

NOTE: Instead of leaving out a `from-view-id` element, you can also use one of the following to specify a rule that applies to all pages:

`<from-view-id>/*</from-view-id>`

or

`<from-view-id>*</from-view-id>`

Using from-action

The structure of the `navigation-case` element is more complex than we previously discussed. In addition to the `from-outcome` element, there is also a `from-action` element. That flexibility can be useful if you have two separate actions with the same action string or two action method expressions that return the same action string.

For example, suppose that in our quiz application, the `startOverAction` returns the string "again" instead of "startOver". The same string can be returned by the `answerAction`. To differentiate between the two navigation cases, you can use a `from-action` element. The contents of the element must be identical to the method expression string of the `action` attribute:

```
<navigation-case>
    <from-action>#{quiz.answerAction}</from-action>
    <from-outcome>again</from-outcome>
    <to-view-id>/again.jsp</to-view-id>
</navigation-case>
<navigation-case>
    <from-action>#{quiz.startOverAction}</from-action>
    <from-outcome>again</from-outcome>
    <to-view-id>/index.jsp</to-view-id>
</navigation-case>
```

 NOTE: The navigation handler does *not* invoke the method inside the #{...} delimiters. The method has been invoked before the navigation handler kicks in. The navigation handler merely uses the `from-action` string as a key to find a matching navigation case.

The Navigation Algorithm

We finish this chapter with a description of the precise algorithm that the navigation handler uses to resolve ambiguous situations. Feel free to skip this section for now and come back when you have to decipher rules produced by other programmers or by automated tools.

The algorithm has three inputs:

1. The *outcome*—that is, the value of an action attribute or the string resulting from the invocation of a method expression
2. The *view ID* of the current view
3. The *action*—that is, the literal value of the action attribute in the component that triggered the navigation

The first of two phases is to find the matching navigation-rule, following these steps:

1. If the outcome is null, return immediately and redisplay the current page.
2. Merge all navigation rules with the same from-view-id value.
3. Try to find a navigation rule whose from-view-id value matches the view ID exactly. If such a rule exists, take it.
4. Consider all navigation rules whose from-view-id values end with a wildcard suffix, such as secure. For each such rule, check whether the prefix (after removing the *) is identical to the corresponding prefix of the view ID. If there are matching rules, take the one with the longest matching prefix.
5. If there is a rule without a from-view-id, take it.
6. If there is no match at all, redisplay the current page.

The second of two phases is to consider all navigation-case elements in the matching navigation rule (which may consist of several merged navigation-rule elements with matching from-view-id.values).

Follow these steps to find the matching case:

1. If a case has both matching from-outcome and from-action, take it.
2. Otherwise, if a case has matching from-outcome and no from-action, take it.
3. Otherwise, if a case has matching from-action and no from-outcome, take it.
4. Otherwise, if there is a case with neither from-outcome nor from-action, take it.
5. If there is no match at all, redisplay the current page.

Naturally, we recommend that you do not create tricky navigation rules in your own programs. As long as you stay away from wildcards and from-action elements, you will not need to know about the gory details of the navigation algorithm.

Standard JSF Tags

Topics in This Chapter

Chapter 4

Development of compelling JSF applications requires a good grasp of the JSF tag libraries—core and HTML—that represent a combined total of 45 tags. Because of the prominence of those tags in the JSF framework, this chapter and Chapter 5, "Data Tables," provide in-depth coverage of tags, their attributes, and how you can best use them.

Even simple JSF pages use tags from both libraries. Many JSF pages have a structure similar to this:

```
<%@ taglib uri="http://java.sun.com/jsf/core" prefix="f" %>
<%@ taglib uri="http://java.sun.com/jsf/html" prefix="h" %>

<f:view>
   <h:form>
      ...
   </h:form>
</f:view>
```

To use the JSF tag libraries, you must import them with `taglib` directives, as in the preceding code fragment. You can choose any name you want for the prefixes. The convention is `f` and `h`, for the core and HTML libraries, respectively.

This chapter starts with a brief look at the core library. That library, with 18 tags, is smaller than its HTML sibling, which has 25. It is also considerably simpler than the HTML library. Because of that simplicity and because most of the core tags are discussed elsewhere in this book, the majority of this chapter focuses on the HTML library.

We then move to the HTML library with a look at common attributes shared by most JSF HTML tags. Finally, we discuss each tag individually with attribute tables for reference and useful code examples that you can adapt to your own applications.

 NOTE: The core library has an average of 3.5 attributes per tag; the HTML library has 28.9.

An Overview of the JSF Core Tags

The core library contains the tags that are independent of the rendering technology. The core tags are listed in Table 4–1.

Table 4–1   JSF Core Tags

Tag	Description	See Chapter
view	Creates the top-level view	1
subview	Creates a subview of a view	8
attribute	Sets an attribute (key/value) in its parent component	4
param	Adds a parameter child component to its parent component	4
facet	Adds a facet to a component	4
actionListener	Adds an action listener to a component	7
setPropertyActionListener (JSF 1.2)	Adds an action listener that sets a property	7
valueChangeListener	Adds a value change listener to a component	7
phaseListener (JSF 1.2)	Adds a phase listener to the parent view	7
converter	Adds an arbitrary converter to a component	6
convertDateTime	Adds a datetime converter to a component	6
convertNumber	Adds a number converter to a component	6
validator	Adds a validator to a component	6
validateDoubleRange	Validates a double range for a component's value	6
validateLength	Validates the length of a component's value	6

Table 4–1   JSF Core Tags (cont.)

Tag	Description	See Chapter
validateLongRange	Validates a long range for a component's value	6
loadBundle	Loads a resource bundle, stores properties as a Map	2
selectitems	Specifies items for a select one or select many component	4
selectitem	Specifies an item for a select one or select many component	4
verbatim	Turns text containing markup into a component	4

Most of the core tags represent *objects you add to components:*

- Attributes
- Listeners
- Converters
- Validators
- Facets
- Parameters
- Select items

The core library also contains tags for defining views and subviews, loading resource bundles, and adding arbitrary text to a page.

All of the core tags are discussed at length elsewhere in this book, as shown in Table 4–1.

We briefly describe the f:attribute, f:param, and f:facet tags here. Any component can store artibrary name/value pairs in its *attribute map.* You can set an attribute in a page and later retrieve it programatically. For example, in "Supplying Attributes to Converters" on page 260 of Chapter 6, we set the separator character for credit card digit groups like this:

```
<h:outputText value = "#{payment.card}">
    <f:attribute name = "separator" vlude = "-" />
</h:outputText>
```

The converter that formats the output retrieves the attribute from the component.

The f:param tag also lets you define a name/value pair, but the value is placed in a separate child component, a much bulkier storage mechanism. However, the child components form a list, not a map. You use f:param if you need to supply a number of values with the same name (or no name at all). You saw an example in "Messages with Variable Parts" on page 44 of Chapter 2, where the h:output-Format component contains a list of f:param children.

 NOTE: the h:commandlink component turns its f:param children into HTTP request name/value pairs. The event listener that is activated when the user clicks the link can then retrieve the name/value pairs from the request map. We demonstrate this technique in Chapter 7.

Finally, f:facet adds a named component to a component's *facet map*. A facet is not a child component; each component has *both* a list of child components and a map of named facet components. The facet components are usually rendered in a special place. You will see in "Headers, Footers, and Captions" on page 178 of Chapter 5 how to use facets named "header" and "footer" in data tables.

Table 4–2 shows the attributes for the f:attribute, f:param, and f:facet tags.

Table 4–2   Attributes for f:attribute, f:param, **and** f:facet

Attribute	Description
name	The attribute, parameter component, or facet name
value	The attribute or parameter component value (does not apply to f:facet)
binding, id	See Table 4–4 on page 97 (f:param only)

 NOTE: All tag attributes, except for var and id, accept value or method expressions. The var attribute must be a string. The id attribute can be a string or an immediate ${...} expression.

An Overview of the JSF HTML Tags

JSF HTML tags represent the following kinds of components:

- Inputs
- Outputs
- Commands

- Selection
- Others

The "others" category includes forms, messages, and components that lay out other components. Table 4–3 lists all the HTML tags.

Table 4–3   JSF HTML Tags

Tag	Description
form	HTML form
inputText	Single-line text input control
inputTextarea	Multiline text input control
inputSecret	Password input control
inputHidden	Hidden field
outputLabel	Label for another component for accessibility
outputLink	HTML anchor
outputFormat	Like outputText, but formats compound messages
outputText	Single-line text output
commandButton	Button: submit, reset, or pushbutton
commandLink	Link that acts like a pushbutton
message	Displays the most recent message for a component
messages	Displays all messages
graphicImage	Displays an image
selectOneListbox	Single-select listbox
selectOneMenu	Single-select menu
selectOneRadio	Set of radio buttons
selectBooleanCheckbox	Checkbox
selectManyCheckbox	Set of checkboxes
selectManyListbox	Multiselect listbox
selectManyMenu	Multiselect menu

Table 4–3 JSF HTML Tags (cont.)

Tag	Description
panelGrid	HTML table
panelGroup	Two or more components that are laid out as one
dataTable	A feature-rich table control
column	Column in a dataTable

We can group the HTML tags in the following categories:

- Inputs (input...)
- Outputs (output...)
- Commands (commandButton and commandLink)
- Selections (checkbox, listbox, menu, radio)
- Layouts (panelGrid)
- Data table (dataTable); see Chapter 5
- Errors and messages (message, messages)

The JSF HTML tags share common attributes, HTML pass-through attributes, and attributes that support dynamic HTML.

 NOTE: The HTML tags may seem overly verbose—for example, selectManyListbox could be more efficiently expressed as multiList. But those verbose names correspond to a component/renderer combination, so selectManyListbox represents a selectMany component paired with a listbox renderer. Knowing the type of component a tag represents is crucial if you want to access components programmatically.

 NOTE: Both JSF and Struts developers implement web pages with JSP custom tags. But Struts tags generate HTML directly, whereas JSF tags represent a component that is independent of the markup technology, and a renderer that generates HTML. That key difference makes it easy to adapt JSF applications to alternative display technologies. For an example, see the chapter on wireless JSF applications that is available on the book's companion web site (http://corejsf.com).

Common Attributes

Three types of tag attributes are shared among multiple HTML component tags:

- Basic
- HTML 4.0
- DHTML events

Next, we look at each type.

Basic Attributes

As you can see from Table 4–4, basic attributes are shared by the majority of JSF HTML tags.

Table 4–4   Basic HTML Tag Attributes[a]

Attribute	Component Types	Description
id	A (*25*)	Identifier for a component
binding	A (*25*)	Links this component with a backing bean property
rendered	A (*25*)	A Boolean; false suppresses rendering
styleClass	A (*23*)	CSS (Cascading Style Sheet) class name
value	I, O, C (*19*)	A component's value, typically a value expression
valueChangeListener	I (*11*)	A method expression to a method that responds to value changes
converter	I, O (*15*)	Converter class name
validator	I (*11*)	Class name of a validator that is created and attached to a component
required	I (*11*)	A Boolean; if true, requires a value to be entered in the associated field
converterMessage, validatorMessage, requiredMessage (JSF 1.2)	I (*11*)	A custom message to be displayed when a conversion or validation error occurs, or when required input is missing

a. A = all, I = input, O = output, C = commands, (*n*) = number of tags with attribute

The id and binding attributes, applicable to all HTML tags, reference a component—the former is used primarily by page authors and the latter is used by Java developers.

The value and converter attributes let you specify a component value and a means to convert it from a string to an object, or vice versa.

The validator, required, and valueChangeListener attributes are available for input components so that you can validate values and react to changes to those values. See Chapter 6 for more information about validators and converters.

The ubiquitous rendered and styleClass attributes affect how a component is rendered.

Now we take a brief look at these important attributes.

IDs and Bindings

The versatile id attribute lets you do the following:

- Access JSF components from other JSF tags
- Obtain component references in Java code
- Access HTML elements with scripts

In this section, we discuss the first two tasks listed above. See "Form Elements and JavaScript" on page 105 for more about the last task.

The id attribute lets page authors reference a component from another tag. For example, an error message for a component can be displayed like this:

```
<h:inputText id="name" .../>
<h:message for="name"/>
```

You can also use component identifiers to get a component reference in your Java code. For example, you could access the name component in a listener like this:

```
UIComponent component = event.getComponent().findComponent("name");
```

The preceding call to findComponent has a caveat: The component that generated the event and the name component must be in the same form (or data table). There is a better way to access a component in your Java code. Define the component as an instance field of a class. Provide property getters and setters for the component. Then use the binding attribute, which you specify in a JSF page, like this:

```
<h:outputText binding="#{form.statePrompt}" .../>
```

The binding attribute is specified with a value expression. That expression refers to a read-write bean property. See "Backing Beans" on page 53 of Chapter 2 for more information about the binding attribute. The JSF implementation sets the property to the component, so you can programatically manipulate components.

You can also *programmatically create a component* that will be used in lieu of the component specified in the JSF page. For example, the form bean's statePrompt property could be implemented like this:

```
private UIComponent statePrompt = new UIOutput();
public UIComponent getStatePrompt() { return statePrompt; }
public void setStatePrompt(UIComponent statePrompt) {...}
```

When the #{form.statePrompt} value expression is first encountered, the JSF framework calls Form.getStatePrompt(). If that method returns null—as is typically the case—the JSF implementation creates the component specified in the JSF page. But *if that method returns a reference to a component*—as is the case in the preceding code fragment—*that component is used instead.*

Values, Converters, and Validators

Inputs, outputs, commands, and data tables all have values. Associated tags in the HTML library, such as h:inputText and h:dataTable, come with a value attribute. You can specify values with a string, like this:

```
<h:outputText value="William"/>
```

Most of the time you will use a value expression—for example:

```
<h:outputText value="#{customer.name}"/>
```

The converter attribute, shared by inputs and outputs, lets you attach a converter to a component. Input tags also have a validator attribute that you can use to attach a validator to a component. Converters and validators are discussed at length in Chapter 6.

Styles

You can use CSS styles, either inline (style) or classes (styleClass), to influence how components are rendered. Most of the time you will specify string constants instead of value expressions for the style and styleClass attributes—for example:

```
<h:outputText value="#{customer.name}" styleClass="emphasis"/>
<h:outputText value="#{customer.id}" style="border: thin solid blue"/>
```

Value expressions are useful when you need programmatic control over styles. You can also control whether components are rendered at all with the rendered attribute. That attribute comes in handy in all sorts of situations—for example, an optional table column.

TIP: Instead of using a hardwired style, it is better to use a style sheet. Define a CSS style such as

```
.prompts {
    color:red;
}
```

Place it in a style sheet, say, `styles.css`. Add a `link` element inside the head element in your JSF page:

```
<link href="styles.css" rel="stylesheet" type="text/css"/>
```

Then use the `styleClass` attribute:

```
<h:outputText value="#{msgs.namePrompt}" styleClass="prompts"/>
```

Now you can change the appearance of all prompts by updating the style sheet.

Conditional Rendering

You use the rendered attribute to include or exclude a component, depending on a condition. For example, you may want to render a "Logout" button only if the user is currently logged in:

```
<h:commandButton ... rendered = "#{user.loggedIn}"/>
```

To conditionally include a group of components, include them in an `h:panelGrid` with a rendered attribute. See "Panels" on page 163 for more information.

TIP: Remember, you can use operators in value expressions. For example, you might have a view that acts as a tabbed pane by optionally rendering a panel depending on the selected tab. In that case, you could use `h:panelGrid` like this:

```
<h:panelGrid rendered='#{bean.selectedTab == "Movies"}'/>
```

The preceding code renders the movies panel when the user selects the `Movies` tab.

NOTE: Sometimes, you will see the JSTL `c:if` construct used for conditional rendering. However, that is less efficient than the `rendered` attribute.

HTML 4.0 Attributes

JSF HTML tags have appropriate HTML 4.0 pass-through attributes. Those attribute values are passed through to the generated HTML element. For example, `<h:inputText value="#{form.name.last}" size="25".../>` generates this HTML: `<input type="text" size="25".../>`. Notice that the size attribute is passed through to HTML.

The HTML 4.0 attributes are listed in Table 4–5.

Table 4–5   HTML 4.0 Pass-Through Attributes[a]

Attribute	Description
accesskey (*14*)	A key, typically combined with a system-defined metakey, that gives focus to an element.
accept (*1*)	Comma-separated list of content types for a form.
acceptcharset (*1*)	Comma- or space-separated list of character encodings for a form. The HTML accept-charset attribute is specified with the JSF attribute named acceptcharset.
alt (*4*)	Alternative text for nontextual elements such as images or applets.
border (*4*)	Pixel value for an element's border width.
charset (*2*)	Character encoding for a linked resource.
coords (*2*)	Coordinates for an element whose shape is a rectangle, circle, or polygon.
dir (*22*)	Direction for text. Valid values are "ltr" (left to right) and "rtl" (right to left).
disabled (*13*)	Disabled state of an input element or button.
hreflang (*2*)	Base language of a resource specified with the href attribute; hreflang may only be used with href.
lang (*22*)	Base language of an element's attributes and text.
maxlength (*2*)	Maximum number of characters for text fields.
readonly (*11*)	Read-only state of an input field; text can be selected in a read-only field but not edited.
rel (*2*)	Relationship between the current document and a link specified with the href attribute.

Table 4–5   HTML 4.0 Pass-Through Attributes[a] (cont.)

Attribute	Description
rev (2)	Reverse link from the anchor specified with href to the current document. The value of the attribute is a space-separated list of link types.
rows (1)	Number of visible rows in a text area. h:dataTable has a rows attribute, but it is not an HTML pass-through attribute.
shape (2)	Shape of a region. Valid values: default, rect, circle, poly (default signifies the entire region).
size (4)	Size of an input field.
style (23)	Inline style information.
tabindex (14)	Numerical value specifying a tab index.
target (3)	The name of a frame in which a document is opened.
title (22)	A title, used for accessibility, that describes an element. Visual browsers typically create tooltips for the title's value.
type (3)	Type of a link—for example, "stylesheet".
width (3)	Width of an element.

a. (*n*) = number of tags with attribute

The attributes listed in Table 4–5 are defined in the HTML specification, which you can access online at http://www.w3.org/TR/REC-html40. That web site is an excellent resource for deep digging into HTML.

DHTML Events

Client-side scripting is useful for all sorts of tasks, such as syntax validation or rollover images, and it is easy to use with JSF. HTML attributes that support scripting, such as onclick and onchange are called *DHTML (dynamic HTML) event attributes*. JSF supports DHTML event attributes for nearly all of the JSF HTML tags. Those attributes are listed in Table 4–6.

Table 4–6   DHTML Event Attributes[a]

Attribute	Description
onblur (14)	Element loses focus
onchange (11)	Element's value changes

Table 4–6   DHTML Event Attributes[a] (cont.)

Attribute	Description
onclick (17)	Mouse button is clicked over the element
ondblclick (18)	Mouse button is double-clicked over the element
onfocus (14)	Element receives focus
onkeydown (18)	Key is pressed
onkeypress (18)	Key is pressed and subsequently released
onkeyup (18)	Key is released
onmousedown (18)	Mouse button is pressed over the element
onmousemove (18)	Mouse moves over the element
onmouseout (18)	Mouse leaves the element's area
onmouseover (18)	Mouse moves onto an element
onmouseup (18)	Mouse button is released
onreset (1)	Form is reset
onselect (11)	Text is selected in an input field
onsubmit (1)	Form is submitted

a. (n) = number of tags with attribute

The DHTML event attributes listed in Table 4–6 let you associate client-side scripts with events. Typically, JavaScript is used as a scripting language, but you can use any scripting language you like. See the HTML specification for more details.

 TIP: You will probably add client-side scripts to your JSF pages soon after you start using JSF. One common use is to submit a request when an input's value is changed so that value change listeners are immediately notified of the change, like this: <h:selectOneMenu onchange="submit()"...>

Forms

Web applications run on form submissions, and JSF applications are no exception. Table 4–7 lists all h:form attributes.

Table 4–7   **Attributes for** h:form

Attributes	Description
prependId (JSF 1.2)	true (default) if the ID of this form is prepended to the IDs of its components; false to suppress prepending the form ID (useful if the ID is used in JavaScript code)
binding, id, rendered, styleClass	Basic attributes[a]
accept, acceptcharset, dir, enctype, lang, style, target, title	HTML 4.0[b] attributes
onclick, ondblclick, onfocus, onkeydown, onkeypress, onkeyup, onmousedown, onmousemove, onmouseout, onmouseover, onmouseup, onreset, onsubmit	DHTML events[c]

a. See Table 4–4 on page 97 for information about basic attributes.
b. See Table 4–5 on page 101 for information about HTML 4.0 attributes.
c. See Table 4–6 on page 102 for information about DHTML event attributes.

Although the HTML form tag has method and action attributes, h:form does not. Because you can save state in the client—an option that is implemented as a hidden field—posting forms with the GET method is disallowed. The contents of that hidden field can be quite large and may overrun the buffer for request parameters, so all JSF form submissions are implemented with the POST method.

There is no need for an anchor attribute since JSF form submissions always post to the current page. (Navigation to a new page happens after the form data have been posted.)

The h:form tag generates an HTML form element. For example, if, in a JSF page named /index.jsp, you use an h:form tag with no attributes, the Form renderer generates HTML like this:

```
<form id="_id0" method="post" action="/forms/faces/index.jsp"
    enctype="application/x-www-form-urlencoded">
```

h:form comes with a full complement of DHTML event attributes. You can also specify the style or styleClass attributes for h:form. Those styles will then be applied to all output elements contained in the form.

Finally, the id attribute is passed through to the HTML form element. If you do not specify the id attribute explicitly, a value is generated by the JSF implementation, as is the case for all generated HTML elements. The id attribute is often explicitly specified for forms so that it can be referenced from style sheets or scripts.

Form Elements and JavaScript

Java*Server* Faces is all about *server*-side components, but it is also designed to work with scripting languages, such as JavaScript. For example, the application shown in Figure 4–1 uses JavaScript to confirm that a password field matches a password confirm field. If the fields do not match, a JavaScript dialog is displayed. If they do match, the form is submitted.

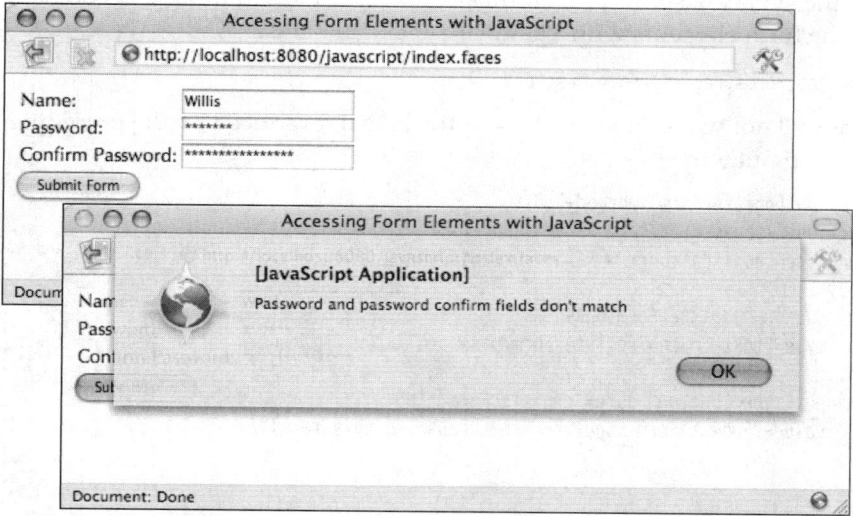

Figure 4–1 Using JavaScript to access form elements

We use the id attribute to assign names to the relevant HTML elements so that we can access them with JavaScript:

```
<h:form id="registerForm">
  ...
  <h:inputText id="password" .../>
  <h:inputText id="passwordConfirm" .../>
  ...
  <h:commandButton type="button"
    onclick="checkPassword(this.form)"/>
  ...
</h:form>
```

When the user clicks the button, a JavaScript function—checkPassword—is invoked, as follows:

```
function checkPassword(form) {
    var password = form["registerForm:password"].value;
    var passwordConfirm = form["registerForm:passwordConfirm"].value;

    if (password == passwordConfirm)
        form.submit();
    else
        alert("Password and password confirm fields don't match");
}
```

Notice the syntax used to access form elements. You might think you could access the form elements with a simpler syntax, like this:

```
documents.forms.registerForm.password
```

But that will not work. Now we look at the HTML produced by the preceding code to find out why:

```
<form id="registerForm" method="post"
    action="/javascript/faces/index.jsp"
    enctype="application/x-www-form-urlencoded">
    ...
    <input id="registerForm:password"
        type="text" name="registerForm:password"/>
    ...
    <input type="button" name="registerForm:_id5"
        value="Submit Form" onclick="checkPassword(this.form)"/>
    ...
</form>
```

All form controls generated by JSF have names that conform to

formName:componentName

where *formName* represents the name of the control's form and *componentName* represents the control's name. If you do not specify id attributes, the JSF framework creates identifiers for you, as you can see from the button in the preceding HTML fragment. Therefore, to access the password field in the preceding example, you must do this instead:

```
documents.forms.registerForm["registerForm:password"].value
```

The directory structure for the application shown in Figure 4–1 is shown in Figure 4–2. The JSF page is listed in Listing 4–1 and the English resource bundle is listed in Listing 4–2.

```
javascript.war
 META-INF
    MANIFEST.MF
 WEB-INF
    classes
       com
          corejsf
             messages.properties
    faces-config.xml
    web.xml
 styles.css
 index.html
 index.jsp
```

Figure 4–2   The JavaScript example directory structure

Listing 4–1   javascript/web/index.jsp

```jsp
1. <html>
2.   <%@ taglib uri="http://java.sun.com/jsf/core" prefix="f" %>
3.   <%@ taglib uri="http://java.sun.com/jsf/html" prefix="h" %>
4.   <f:view>
5.     <head>
6.       <title>
7.         <h:outputText value="#{msgs.windowTitle}"/>
8.       </title>
9.     </head>
10.    <body>
11.      <h:form id="registerForm">
12.        <table>
13.          <tr>
14.            <td>
15.              <h:outputText value="#{msgs.namePrompt}"/>
16.            </td>
17.            <td>
18.              <h:inputText/>
19.            </td>
20.          </tr>
21.          <tr>
22.            <td>
23.              <h:outputText value="#{msgs.passwordPrompt}"/>
24.            </td>
25.            <td>
26.              <h:inputSecret id="password"/>
27.            </td>
28.          </tr>
```

Listing 4–1   javascript/web/index.jsp (cont.)

```
29.              <tr>
30.                <td>
31.                  <h:outputText value="#{msgs.confirmPasswordPrompt}"/>
32.                </td>
33.                <td>
34.                  <h:inputSecret id="passwordConfirm"/>
35.                </td>
36.              </tr>
37.            </table>
38.            <h:commandButton type="button" value="Submit Form"
39.                onclick="checkPassword(this.form)"/>
40.          </h:form>
41.        </body>
42.        <script type="text/javascript">
43.        <!--
44.          function checkPassword(form) {
45.              var password = form["registerForm:password"].value;
46.              var passwordConfirm = form["registerForm:passwordConfirm"].value;
47.
48.              if(password == passwordConfirm)
49.                  form.submit();
50.              else
51.                  alert("Password and password confirm fields don't match");
52.          }
53.        -->
54.        </script>
55.      </f:view>
56. </html>
```

Listing 4–2   javascript/src/java/com/corejsf/messages.properties

```
1. windowTitle=Accessing Form Elements with JavaScript
2. namePrompt=Name:
3. passwordPrompt=Password:
4. confirmPasswordPrompt=Confirm Password:
```

Text Fields and Text Areas

Text inputs are the mainstay of most web applications. JSF supports three varieties represented by the following tags:

- h:inputText
- h:inputSecret
- h:inputTextarea

Since the three tags use similar attributes, Table 4–8 lists attributes for all three.

Table 4–8 Attributes for h:inputText, h:inputSecret, h:inputTextarea, **and** h:inputHidden

Attributes	Description
cols	For h:inputTextarea only—number of columns.
immediate	Process validation early in the life cycle.
redisplay	For h:inputSecret only—when true, the input field's value is redisplayed when the web page is reloaded.
required	Require input in the component when the form is submitted.
rows	For h:inputTextarea only—number of rows.
valueChangeListener	A specified listener that is notified of value changes.
label (JSF 1.2)	A description of the component for use in error messages. Does not apply to h:inputHidden.
binding, converter, converterMessage (JSF 1.2), id, rendered, required, requiredMessage (JSF 1.2), styleClass, value, validator, validatorMessage (JSF 1.2)	Basic attributes[a]. styleClass does not apply to h:inputHidden.
accesskey, alt, dir, disabled, lang, maxlength, readonly, size, style, tabindex, title	HTML 4.0 pass-through attributes[b]—alt, maxlength, and size do not apply to h:inputTextarea. None apply to h:inputHidden.
autocomplete	If the value is "off", render the nonstandard HTML attribute autocomplete="off" (h:inputText and h:inputSecret only).
onblur, onchange, onclick, ondblclick, onfocus, onkeydown, onkeypress, onkeyup, onmousedown, onmousemove, onmouseout, onmouseover, onmouseup, onselect	DHTML events. None apply to h:inputHidden.[c]

a. See Table 4–4 on page 97 for information about basic attributes.
b. See Table 4–5 on page 101 for information about HTML 4.0 attributes.
c. See Table 4–6 on page 102 for information about DHTML event attributes.

All three tags have immediate, required, value, and valueChangeListener attributes. The immediate attribute is used primarily for value changes that affect the user interface and is rarely used by these three tags. Instead, it is more commonly used by other input components such as menus and listboxes. See "Immediate Components" on page 287 of Chapter 7 for more information about the immediate attribute.

Three attributes in Table 4–8 are each applicable to only one tag: cols, rows, and redisplay. The rows and cols attributes are used with h:inputTextarea to specify the number of rows and columns, respectively, for the text area. The redisplay attribute, used with h:inputSecret, is a boolean that determines whether a secret field retains its value—and therefore redisplays it—when the field's form is resubmitted.

Table 4–9 shows sample uses of the h:inputText and h:inputSecret tags.

Table 4–9   h:inputText **and** h:inputSecret **Examples**

Example	Result
<h:inputText value="#{form.testString}" readonly="true"/>	12345678901234567890
<h:inputSecret value="#{form.passwd}" redisplay="true"/>	********** (shown after an unsuccessful form submit)
<h:inputSecret value="#{form.passwd}" redisplay="false"/>	(shown after an unsuccessful form submit)
<h:inputText value="inputText" style="color: Yellow; background: Teal;"/>	inputText
<h:inputText value="1234567" size="5"/>	123456
<h:inputText value="1234567890" maxlength="6" size="10"/>	123456

The first example in Table 4–9 produces the following HTML:

```
<input type="text" name="_id0:_id4" value="12345678901234567890"
    readonly="readonly"/>
```

The input field is read-only, so our form bean defines only a getter method:

```
private String testString = "12345678901234567890";
public String getTestString() {
    return testString;
}
```

The h:inputSecret examples illustrate the use of the redisplay attribute. If that attribute is true, the text field stores its value between requests and, therefore, the value is redisplayed when the page reloads. If redisplay is false, the value is discarded and is not redisplayed.

The size attribute specifies the number of visible characters in a text field. But because most fonts are variable width, the size attribute is not precise, as you can see from the fifth example in Table 4–9, which specifies a size of 5 but displays six characters. The maxlength attribute specifies the maximum number of characters a text field will display. That attribute is precise. Both size and maxlength are HTML pass-through attributes.

Table 4–10 shows examples of the h:inputTextarea tag.

Table 4–10 h:inputTextarea **Examples**

Example	Result
<h:inputTextarea rows="5"/>	
<h:inputTextarea cols="5"/>	
<h:inputTextarea value="123456789012345" rows="3" cols="10"/>	456789012345
<h:inputTextarea value="#{form.dataInRows}" rows="2" cols="15"/>	line one line two line three

The h:inputTextarea has cols and rows attributes to specify the number of columns and rows, respectively, in the text area. The cols attribute is analogous to the size attribute for h:inputText and is also imprecise.

If you specify one long string for h:inputTextarea's value, the string will be placed in its entirety in one line, as you can see from the third example in Table 4–10. If you want to put data on separate lines, you can insert newline characters (\n) to force a line break. For example, the last example in Table 4–10 accesses the dataInRows property of a backing bean. That property is implemented like this:

```
private String dataInRows = "line one\nline two\nline three";
public void setDataInRows(String newValue) {
    dataInRows = newValue;
}
public String getDataInRows() {
    return dataInRows;
}
```

Hidden Fields

JSF provides support for hidden fields with h:inputHidden. Hidden fields are often used with JavaScript actions to send data back to the server. The h:inputHidden tag has the same attributes as the other input tags, except that it does not support the standard HTML and DHTML tags.

Using Text Fields and Text Areas

Next, we take a look at a complete example that uses text fields and text areas. The application shown in Figure 4–3 uses h:inputText, h:inputSecret, and h:inputTextarea to collect personal information from a user. The values of those components are wired to bean properties, which are accessed in a Thank You page that redisplays the information the user entered.

Three things are noteworthy about the following application. First, the JSF pages reference a user bean (com.corejsf.UserBean). Second, the h:inputTextarea tag transfers the text entered in a text area to the model (in this case, the user bean) as one string with embedded newlines (\n). We display that string by using the HTML <pre> element to preserve that formatting. Third, for illustration, we use the style attribute to format output. A more industrial-strength application would presumably use style sheets exclusively to make global style changes easier to manage.

○ ○ ○   Using Textfields and Textareas

Please enter the following personal information

Name: William

Password: ●●●●●

Please tell us about yourself: I like to do these things:

                                  Read good books
                                  Program Web user interfaces with JSF
                                  Play with my dog

Submit your information

⊖ ○ ○   Thank you for submitting your information

Name: William

Some information about you:

I like to do these things:

Read good books
Program Web user interfaces with JSF
Play with my dog

Figure 4–3   Using text fields and text areas

Figure 4–4 shows the directory structure for the application shown in Figure 4–3. Listing 4–3 through Listing 4–7 show the pertinent JSF pages, managed beans, faces configuration file, and resource bundle.

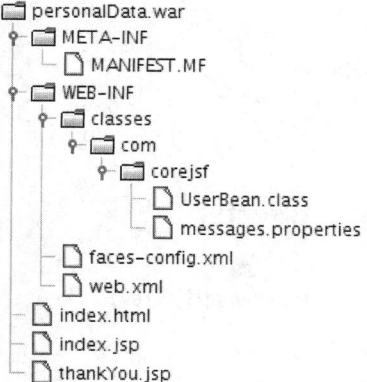

```
personalData.war
├── META-INF
│   └── MANIFEST.MF
├── WEB-INF
│   ├── classes
│   │   └── com
│   │       └── corejsf
│   │           ├── UserBean.class
│   │           └── messages.properties
│   ├── faces-config.xml
│   └── web.xml
├── index.html
├── index.jsp
└── thankYou.jsp
```

Figure 4–4   Directory structure of the text fields and text areas example

Listing 4–3   personalData/web/index.jsp

```
1.  <html>
2.    <%@ taglib uri="http://java.sun.com/jsf/core" prefix="f" %>
3.    <%@ taglib uri="http://java.sun.com/jsf/html" prefix="h" %>
4.    <f:view>
5.      <head>
6.        <title>
7.          <h:outputText value="#{msgs.indexWindowTitle}"/>
8.        </title>
9.      </head>
10.     <body>
11.       <h:outputText value="#{msgs.indexPageTitle}"
12.         style="font-style: italic; font-size: 1.5em"/>
13.       <h:form>
14.         <table>
15.           <tr>
16.             <td>
17.               <h:outputText value="#{msgs.namePrompt}"/>
18.             </td>
19.             <td>
20.               <h:inputText value="#{user.name}"/>
21.             </td>
22.           </tr>
23.           <tr>
24.             <td>
25.               <h:outputText value="#{msgs.passwordPrompt}"/>
26.             </td>
27.             <td>
28.               <h:inputSecret value="#{user.password}"/>
29.             </td>
30.           </tr>
31.           <tr>
32.             <td>
33.               <h:outputText value="#{msgs.tellUsPrompt}"/>
34.             </td>
35.             <td>
36.               <h:inputTextarea value="#{user.aboutYourself}" rows="5"
37.                 cols="35"/>
38.             </td>
39.           </tr>
40.         </table>
41.         <h:commandButton value="#{msgs.submitPrompt}" action="thankYou"/>
42.       </h:form>
43.     </body>
44.   </f:view>
45. </html>
```

Listing 4–4   personalData/web/thankYou.jsp

```
1. <html>
2.    <%@ taglib uri="http://java.sun.com/jsf/core" prefix="f" %>
3.    <%@ taglib uri="http://java.sun.com/jsf/html" prefix="h" %>
4.    <f:view>
5.       <head>
6.          <title>
7.             <h:outputText value="#{msgs.thankYouWindowTitle}"/>
8.          </title>
9.       </head>
10.      <body>
11.         <h:outputText value="#{msgs.namePrompt}" style="font-style: italic"/>
12.         <h:outputText value="#{user.name}"/>
13.         <br/>
14.         <h:outputText value="#{msgs.aboutYourselfPrompt}"
15.            style="font-style: italic"/>
16.         <br/>
17.         <pre><h:outputText value="#{user.aboutYourself}"/></pre>
18.      </body>
19.   </f:view>
20. </html>
```

Listing 4–5   personalData/src/java/com/corejsf/UserBean.java

```
1. package com.corejsf;
2.
3. public class UserBean {
4.    private String name;
5.    private String password;
6.    private String aboutYourself;
7.
8.    // PROPERTY: name
9.    public String getName() { return name; }
10.   public void setName(String newValue) { name = newValue; }
11.
12.   // PROPERTY: password
13.   public String getPassword() { return password; }
14.   public void setPassword(String newValue) { password = newValue; }
15.
16.   // PROPERTY: aboutYourself
17.   public String getAboutYourself() { return aboutYourself; }
18.   public void setAboutYourself(String newValue) { aboutYourself = newValue; }
19. }
```

Listing 4–6   personalData/web/WEB-INF/faces-config.xml

```
 1. <?xml version="1.0"?>
 2. <faces-config xmlns="http://java.sun.com/xml/ns/javaee"
 3.     xmlns:xsi="http://www.w3.org/2001/XMLSchema-instance"
 4.     xsi:schemaLocation="http://java.sun.com/xml/ns/javaee
 5.         http://java.sun.com/xml/ns/javaee/web-facesconfig_1_2.xsd"
 6.     version="1.2">
 7.     <navigation-rule>
 8.         <from-view-id>/index.jsp</from-view-id>
 9.         <navigation-case>
10.             <from-outcome>thankYou</from-outcome>
11.             <to-view-id>/thankYou.jsp</to-view-id>
12.         </navigation-case>
13.     </navigation-rule>
14.     <managed-bean>
15.         <managed-bean-name>user</managed-bean-name>
16.         <managed-bean-class>com.corejsf.UserBean</managed-bean-class>
17.         <managed-bean-scope>session</managed-bean-scope>
18.     </managed-bean>
19.     <application>
20.         <resource-bundle>
21.             <base-name>com.corejsf.messages</base-name>
22.             <var>msgs</var>
23.         </resource-bundle>
24.     </application>
25. </faces-config>
```

Listing 4–7   personalData/src/java/com/corejsf/messages.properties

```
1. indexWindowTitle=Using Textfields and Textareas
2. thankYouWindowTitle=Thank you for submitting your information
3. thankYouPageTitle=Thank you!
4. indexPageTitle=Please enter the following personal information
5. namePrompt=Name:
6. passwordPrompt=Password:
7. tellUsPrompt=Please tell us about yourself:
8. aboutYourselfPrompt=Some information about you:
9. submitPrompt=Submit your information
```

Displaying Text and Images

JSF applications use the following tags to display text and images:

- h:outputText
- h:outputFormat
- h:graphicImage

The h:outputText tag is one of JSF's simplest tags. With only a handful of attributes, it does not typically generate an HTML element. Instead, it generates mere text—with one exception: If you specify the style or styleClass attributes, h:outputText will generate an HTML span element. Also, h:outputText and h:outputFormat have one attribute that is unique among all JSF HTML tags: escape.

By default, the escape attribute is false, but if you set it to true, the following characters < > & are converted to < > and & respectively. Changing those characters helps prevent cross-site scripting attacks. See http://www.cert.org/advisories/CA-2000-02.html for more information about cross-site scripting attacks. Table 4–11 lists all h:outputText attributes.

Table 4–11   Attributes for h:outputText **and** h:outputFormat

Attributes	Description
escape	If set to true, escapes <, >, and & characters. Default value is false.
binding, converter, id, rendered, styleClass, value	Basic attributes.[a]
style, title, dir (JSF 1.2), lang (JSF 1.2)	HTML 4.0.[b]

a. See Table 4–4 on page 97 for information about basic attributes.
b. See Table 4–5 on page 101 for information about HTML 4.0 attributes.

The h:outputFormat tag formats a compound message with parameters specified in the body of the tag—for example:

```
<h:outputFormat value="{0} is {1} years old">
   <f:param value="Bill"/>
   <f:param value="38"/>
</h:outputFormat>
```

In the preceding code fragment, the compound message is {0} is {1} years old and the parameters, specified with f:param tags, are Bill and 38. The output of the preceding code fragment is: Bill is 38 years old. The h:outputFormat tag uses a java.text.MessageFormat instance to format its output.

Table 4–11 lists all the attributes for h:outputFormat.

The h:graphicImage tag lets you use a context-relative path—meaning relative to the web application's top-level directory—to display images. h:graphicImage generates an HTML img element.

Table 4–12 shows all the attributes for h:graphicImage.

Table 4–12   Attributes for h:graphicImage

Attributes	Description
binding, id, rendered, styleClass, value	Basic attributes[a]
alt, dir, height, ismap, lang, longdesc, style, title, url, usemap, width	HTML 4.0[b]
onclick, ondblclick, onkeydown, onkeypress, onkeyup, onmousedown, onmousemove, onmouseout, onmouseover, onmouseup	DHTML events[c]

a. See Table 4–4 on page 97 for information about basic attributes.
b. See Table 4–5 on page 101 for information about HTML 4.0 attributes.
c. See Table 4–6 on page 102 for information about DHTML event attributes.

Table 4–13 shows some examples of using h:outputText and h:graphicImage.

Table 4–13   h:outputText and h:graphicImage Examples

Example	Result
`<h:outputText value="#{form.testString}"/>`	12345678901234567890
`<h:outputText value="Number #{form.number}"/>`	Number 1000
`<h:outputText value="<input type='text' value='hello'/>"/>`	hello
`<h:outputText escape="true" value='<input type="text" value="hello"/>'/>`	`<input type="text" value="hello">`
`<h:graphicImage value="/tjefferson.jpg"/>`	
`<h:graphicImage value="/tjefferson.jpg" style="border: thin solid black"/>`	

The third and fourth examples in Table 4–13 illustrate use of the escape attribute. If the value for h:outputText is <input type='text' value='hello'/>, and the escape attribute is false—as is the case for the third example in Table 4–13—the h:outputText tag generates an HTML input element. Unintentional generation of HTML elements is exactly the sort of mischief that enables miscreants to carry out cross-site scripting attacks. With the escape attribute set to true—as in the fourth example in Table 4–13—that output is transformed to harmless text, thereby thwarting a potential attack.

The final two examples in Table 4–13 show you how to use h:graphicImage.

Buttons and Links

Buttons and links are ubiquitous among web applications, and JSF provides the following tags to support them:

- h:commandButton
- h:commandLink
- h:outputLink

The h:commandButton and h:commandLink actions both represent JSF command components—the JSF framework fires action events and invokes actions when a button or link is activated. See "Action Events" on page 275 of Chapter 7 for more information about event handling for command components.

The h:outputLink tag generates an HTML anchor element that points to a resource such as an image or a web page. Clicking the generated link takes you to the designated resource without further involving the JSF framework.

Table 4–14 lists the attributes shared by h:commandButton and h:commandLink.

Table 4–14 Attributes for h:commandButton **and** h:commandLink

Attribute	Description
action	*If specified as a string:* Directly specifies an outcome used by the navigation handler to determine the JSF page to load next as a result of activating the button or link.
	If specified as a method expression: The method has this signature: String methodName(); the string represents the outcome.
actionListener	A method expression that refers to a method with this signature: void methodName(ActionEvent).
charset	For h:commandLink only—The character encoding of the linked reference.
image	For h:commandButton only—The path to an image displayed in a button. If you specify this attribute, the HTML input's type will be image.

Table 4–14   Attributes for h:commandButton **and** h:commandLink **(cont.)**

Attribute	Description
immediate	A Boolean. If false (the default), actions and action listeners are invoked at the end of the request life cycle; if true, actions and action listeners are invoked at the beginning of the life cycle. See Chapter 6 for more information about the immediate attribute.
type	For h:commandButton—The type of the generated input element: button, submit, or reset. The default, unless you specify the image attribute, is submit. For h:commandLink—The content type of the linked resource; for example, text/html, image/gif, or audio/basic.
value	The label displayed by the button or link. You can specify a string or a value expression.
binding, id, rendered, styleClass	Basic attributes.[a]
accesskey, alt (h:commandLink only), coords (h:commandLink only), dir (in JSF 1.1), disabled (h:commandButton only in JSF 1.1), hreflang (h:commandLink only), lang, readonly (h:commandLink only), rel (h:commandLink only), rev (h:commandLink only), shape (h:commandLink only), style, tabindex, target (h:commandLink only), title	HTML 4.0.[b]
onblur, onchange (h:commandLink only), onclick, ondblclick, onfocus, onkeydown, onkeypress, onkeyup, onmousedown, onmousemove, onmouseout, onmouseover, onmouseup, onselect (h:commandLink only)	DHTML events.[c]

a. See Table 4–4 on page 97 for information about basic attributes.
b. See Table 4–5 on page 101 for information about HTML 4.0 attributes.
c. See Table 4–6 on page 102 for information about DHTML event attributes.

Using Command Buttons

The h:commandButton tag generates an HTML input element whose type is button, image, submit, or reset, depending on the attributes you specify. Table 4–15 illustrates some uses of h:commandButton.

Table 4–15   h:commandButton **Examples**

Example	Result
`<h:commandButton value="submit" type="submit"/>`	submit
`<h:commandButton value="reset"` `    type="reset"/>`	reset

`<h:commandButton value="click this button..."`
`    onclick="alert('button clicked')"`
`    type="button"/>`
	click this button to execute JavaScript

`<h:commandButton value="disabled"` `    disabled="#{not form.buttonEnabled}"/>`	disabled
`<h:commandButton value="#{form.buttonText}"` `    type="reset"/>`	press me

The third example in Table 4–15 generates a push button—an HTML input element whose type is button—that does not result in a form submit. The only way to attach behavior to a push button is to specify a script for one of the DHTML event attributes, as we did for onclick in the example.

CAUTION: h:graphicImage and h:commandButton can both display images, but in JSF 1.1, the way in which you specify the image was not consistent between the two tags. h:commandButton required a context path, whereas the context path was added automatically by h:graphicImage. For example, for an application named myApp, here is how you specified the same image for each tag:

```
<h:commandButton image="/myApp/imageFile.jpg"/> <!-- JSF 1.1 -->
<h:graphicImage value="/imageFile.jpg"/>
```

In JSF 1.2, you do not add the context path for either attribute. If the path is absolute (starting with a /), the context path is automatically added. If the path is relative to the enclosing page (i.e., not starting with a /), it is used without change.

The h:commandLink tag generates an HTML anchor element that acts like a form submit button. Table 4–16 shows some h:commandLink examples.

Table 4–16   h:commandLink **Examples**

Example	Result

```<h:commandLink>```
```   <h:outputText value="register"/>```
```</h:commandLink>```
	register

```<h:commandLink style="font-style: italic">```
```   <h:outputText value="#{msgs.linkText}"/>```
```</h:commandLink>```
	click here to register

```<h:commandLink>```
```   <h:outputText value="#{msgs.linkText}"/>```
```   <h:graphicImage value="/registration.jpg"/>```
```</h:commandLink>```
	
	click here to register

```<h:commandLink value="welcome"```
```   actionListener="#{form.useLinkValue}"```
```   action="#{form.followLink}">```
	welcome

```<h:commandLink>```
```   <h:outputText value="welcome"/>```
```   <f:param name="outcome" value="welcome"/>```
```</h:commandLink>```
	welcome

h:commandLink generates JavaScript to make links act like buttons. For example, here is the HTML generated by the first example in Table 4–16:

```
<a href="#" onclick="document.forms['_id0']['_id0:_id2'].value='_id0:_id2';
    document.forms['_id0'].submit()">register</a>
```

When the user clicks the link, the anchor element's value is set to the h:commandLink's client ID, and the enclosing form is submitted. That submission sets the JSF life cycle in motion and, because the href attribute is "#", the current page will be reloaded unless an action associated with the link returns a non-null outcome. See Chapter 3 for more information about JSF navigation.

You can place as many JSF HTML tags as you want in the body of an
h:commandLink tag—each corresponding HTML element is part of the link. So,
for example, if you click on either the text or image in the third example in
Table 4–16, the link's form will be submitted.

The next-to-last example in Table 4–16 attaches an action listener, in addition to
an action, to a link. Action listeners are discussed in "Action Events" on
page 275 of Chapter 7.

The last example in Table 4–16 embeds an f:param tag in the body of the
h:commandLink tag. When you click the link, a request parameter with the name
and value specified with the f:param tag is created by the link. You can use that
request parameter any way you like. See "Passing Data from the UI to the
Server" on page 291 of Chapter 7 for an example.

Both h:commandButton and h:commandLink submit requests and subsequently invoke
the JSF life cycle. Although those tags are useful, sometimes you just need a link
that loads a resource without invoking the JSF life cycle. In that case, you can
use the h:outputLink tag. Table 4–17 lists all attributes for h:outputLink.

Table 4–17 Attributes for h:outputLink

Attributes	Description
binding, converter, id, lang, rendered, styleClass, value	Basic attributes[a]
accesskey, charset, coords, dir, disabled (JSF 1.2), hreflang, lang, rel, rev, shape, style, tabindex, target, title, type	HTML 4.0[b]
onblur, onclick, ondblclick, onfocus, onkeydown, onkeypress, onkeyup, onmousedown, onmousemove, onmouseout, onmouseover, onmouseup	DHTML events[c]

a. See Table 4–4 on page 97 for information about basic attributes.
b. See Table 4–5 on page 101 for information about HTML 4.0 attributes.
c. See Table 4–6 on page 102 for information about DHTML event attributes.

Like h:commandLink, h:outputLink generates an HTML anchor element. But unlike
h:commandLink, h:outputLink does not generate JavaScript to make the link act like a
submit button. The value of the h:outputLink value attribute is used for the anchor's
href attribute, and the contents of the h:outputLink body are used to populate the
body of the anchor element. Table 4–18 shows some h:outputLink examples.

Table 4–18   h:outputLink **Examples**

Example	Result

`<h:outputLink value="http://java.net">`
  `<h:graphicImage value="java-dot-net.jpg"/>`
  `<h:outputText value="java.net"/>`
`</h:outputLink>`	

`<h:outputLink value="#{form.welcomeURL}">`
  `<h:outputText value="#{form.welcomeLinkText}"/>`
`</h:outputLink>`
	go to welcome page

`<h:outputLink value="#introduction">`
  `<h:outputText value="Introduction"`
    `style="font-style: italic"/>`
`</h:outputLink>`
	Introduction

`<h:outputLink value="#conclusion"`
    `title="Go to the conclusion">`
  `<h:outputText value="Conclusion"/>`
`</h:outputLink>`
	Conclusion
	Go to the conclusion

`<h:outputLink value="#toc"`
    `title="Go to the table of contents">`
  `<h2>Table of Contents</h2>`
`</h:outputLink>`
	Table of Contents

The first example in Table 4–18 is a link to http://java.net. The second example uses properties stored in a bean for the link's URL and text. Those properties are implemented like this:

```
private String welcomeURL = "/outputLinks/faces/welcome.jsp";
public String getWelcomeURL() {
    return welcomeURL;
}
private String welcomeLinkText = "go to welcome page";
public String getWelcomeLinkText() {
    return welcomeLinkText;
}
```

The last three examples in Table 4–18 are links to named anchors in the same JSF page. Those anchors look like this:

```
<a name="introduction">Introduction</a>
...
<a name="conclusion">Conclusion</a>
...
```

```
<a name="toc">Table of Contents</a>
...
```

 CAUTION: If you use JSF 1.1, you need to use the f:verbatim tag for the last example in Table 4–18:

`<h:outputLink...><f:verbatim>Table of Contents</f:verbatim></h:outputLink>`

You cannot simply place text inside the h:outputLink tag—the text would appear outside the link. In JSF 1.1, children of a component had to be another component, such as h:outputText or f:verbatim. This problem has been fixed in JSF 1.2.

Using Command Links

Now that we have discussed the details of JSF tags for buttons and links, we take a look at a complete example. Figure 4–5 shows the application discussed in "Using Text Fields and Text Areas" on page 112, with two links that let you select either English or German locales. When a link is activated, an action changes the view's locale and the JSF implementation reloads the current page.

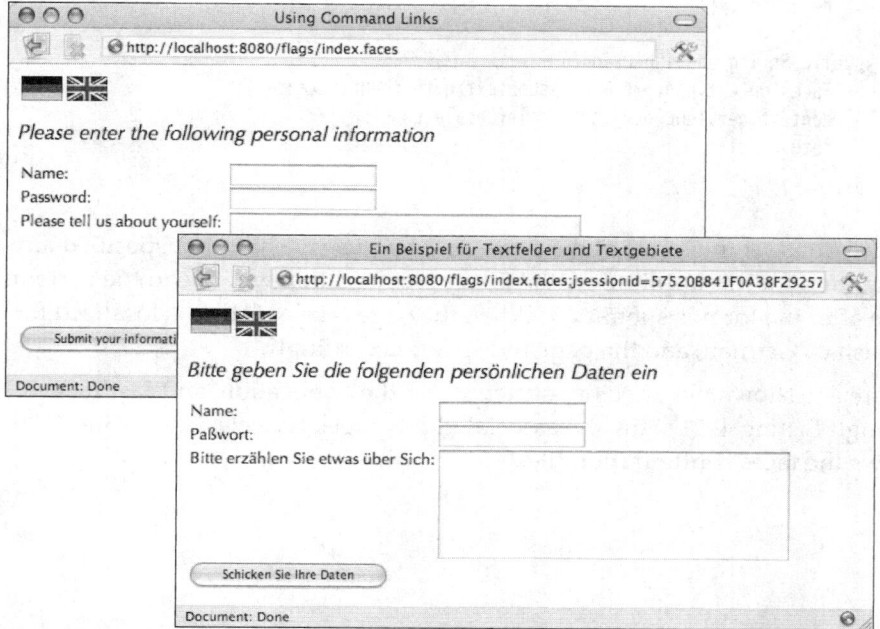

Figure 4–5 Using command links to change locales

The two links are implemented like this:

```
<h:form>
    ...
    <h:commandLink action="#{localeChanger.germanAction}">
        <h:graphicImage value="/german_flag.gif"
            style="border: 0px"/>
    </h:commandLink>

    <h:commandLink action="#{localeChanger.englishAction}">
        <h:graphicImage value="/britain_flag.gif"
            style="border: 0px"/>
    </h:commandLink>
    ...
</h:form>
```

Both links specify an image, a request parameter, and an action method. Those methods look like this:

```
public class ChangeLocaleBean {
    public String germanAction() {
        FacesContext context = FacesContext.getCurrentInstance();
        context.getViewRoot().setLocale(Locale.GERMAN);
        return null;
    }
    public String englishAction() {
        FacesContext context = FacesContext.getCurrentInstance();
        context.getViewRoot().setLocale(Locale.ENGLISH);
        return null;
    }
}
```

Both actions set the locale of the view. And because we have not specified any navigation for this application, the JSF implementation will reload the current page after the form is submitted. When the page is reloaded, it is localized for English or German, and the page redisplays accordingly.

Figure 4–6 shows the directory structure for the application, and Listing 4–8 through Listing 4–11 show the associated JSF pages Java classes. Listing 4-11 shows the faces configuration file.

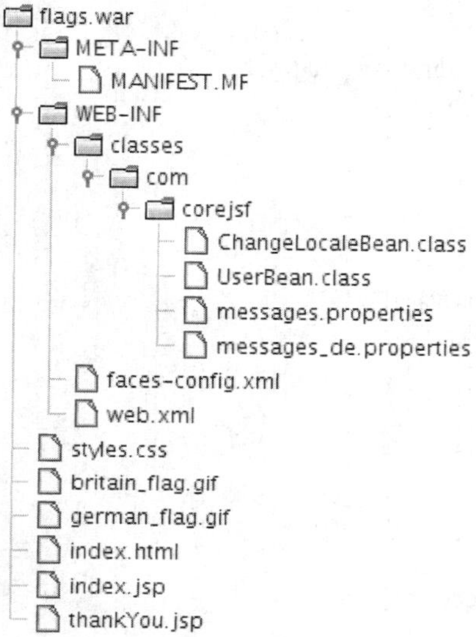

```
flags.war
├── META-INF
│    └── MANIFEST.MF
├── WEB-INF
│    ├── classes
│    │    └── com
│    │         └── corejsf
│    │              ├── ChangeLocaleBean.class
│    │              ├── UserBean.class
│    │              ├── messages.properties
│    │              └── messages_de.properties
│    ├── faces-config.xml
│    └── web.xml
├── styles.css
├── britain_flag.gif
├── german_flag.gif
├── index.html
├── index.jsp
└── thankYou.jsp
```

Figure 4–6   Directory structure of the flags example

Listing 4–8   flags/web/index.jsp

```
1.  <html>
2.     <%@ taglib uri="http://java.sun.com/jsf/core" prefix="f" %>
3.     <%@ taglib uri="http://java.sun.com/jsf/html" prefix="h" %>
4.     <f:view>
5.        <head>
6.           <link href="styles.css" rel="stylesheet" type="text/css"/>
7.           <title>
8.              <h:outputText value="#{msgs.indexWindowTitle}"/>
9.           </title>
10.       </head>
11.       <body>
12.          <h:form>
13.             <table>
14.                <tr>
15.                   <td>
16.                      <h:commandLink immediate="true"
17.                         action="#{localeChanger.germanAction}">
18.                         <h:graphicImage value="/german_flag.gif"
19.                            style="border: 0px"/>
20.                      </h:commandLink>
21.                   </td>
22.                   <td>
23.                      <h:commandLink immediate="true"
24.                         action="#{localeChanger.englishAction}">
```

Listing 4–8   flags/web/index.jsp (cont.)

```
25.                         <h:graphicImage value="/britain_flag.gif"
26.                             style="border: 0px"/>
27.                     </h:commandLink>
28.                 </td>
29.             </tr>
30.         </table>
31.         <p>
32.             <h:outputText value="#{msgs.indexPageTitle}"
33.                 style="font-style: italic; font-size: 1.3em"/>
34.         </p>
35.         <table>
36.             <tr>
37.                 <td>
38.                     <h:outputText value="#{msgs.namePrompt}"/>
39.                 </td>
40.                 <td>
41.                     <h:inputText value="#{user.name}"/>
42.                 </td>
43.             </tr>
44.             <tr>
45.                 <td>
46.                     <h:outputText value="#{msgs.passwordPrompt}"/>
47.                 </td>
48.                 <td>
49.                     <h:inputSecret value="#{user.password}"/>
50.                 </td>
51.             </tr>
52.             <tr>
53.                 <td style="vertical-align: top">
54.                     <h:outputText value="#{msgs.tellUsPrompt}"/>
55.                 </td>
56.                 <td>
57.                     <h:inputTextarea value="#{user.aboutYourself}" rows="5"
58.                         cols="35"/>
59.                 </td>
60.             </tr>
61.             <tr>
62.                 <td>
63.                     <h:commandButton value="#{msgs.submitPrompt}"
64.                         action="thankYou"/>
65.                 </td>
66.             </tr>
67.         </table>
68.         </h:form>
69.     </body>
70. </f:view>
71. </html>
```

Listing 4–9   flags/src/java/com/corejsf/UserBean.java

```
1. package com.corejsf;
2.
3. public class UserBean {
4.    private String name;
5.    private String password;
6.    private String aboutYourself;
7.
8.    // PROPERTY: name
9.    public String getName() { return name; }
10.   public void setName(String newValue) { name = newValue; }
11.
12.   // PROPERTY: password
13.   public String getPassword() { return password; }
14.   public void setPassword(String newValue) { password = newValue; }
15.
16.   // PROPERTY: aboutYourself
17.   public String getAboutYourself() { return aboutYourself; }
18.   public void setAboutYourself(String newValue) { aboutYourself = newValue; }
19. }
```

Listing 4–10   flags/src/java/com/corejsf/ChangeLocaleBean.java

```
1. package com.corejsf;
2.
3. import java.util.Locale;
4. import javax.faces.context.FacesContext;
5.
6. public class ChangeLocaleBean {
7.    public String germanAction() {
8.       FacesContext context = FacesContext.getCurrentInstance();
9.       context.getViewRoot().setLocale(Locale.GERMAN);
10.      return null;
11.   }
12.
13.   public String englishAction() {
14.      FacesContext context = FacesContext.getCurrentInstance();
15.      context.getViewRoot().setLocale(Locale.ENGLISH);
16.      return null;
17.   }
18. }
```

Listing 4–11   flags/web/WEB-INF/faces-config.xml

```xml
1. <?xml version="1.0"?>
2. <faces-config xmlns="http://java.sun.com/xml/ns/javaee"
3.    xmlns:xsi="http://www.w3.org/2001/XMLSchema-instance"
4.    xsi:schemaLocation="http://java.sun.com/xml/ns/javaee
5.        http://java.sun.com/xml/ns/javaee/web-facesconfig_1_2.xsd"
6.    version="1.2">
7.    <navigation-rule>
8.       <from-view-id>/index.jsp</from-view-id>
9.       <navigation-case>
10.          <from-outcome>thankYou</from-outcome>
11.          <to-view-id>/thankYou.jsp</to-view-id>
12.       </navigation-case>
13.    </navigation-rule>
14.
15.    <managed-bean>
16.       <managed-bean-name>localeChanger</managed-bean-name>
17.       <managed-bean-class>com.corejsf.ChangeLocaleBean</managed-bean-class>
18.       <managed-bean-scope>session</managed-bean-scope>
19.    </managed-bean>
20.
21.    <managed-bean>
22.       <managed-bean-name>user</managed-bean-name>
23.       <managed-bean-class>com.corejsf.UserBean</managed-bean-class>
24.       <managed-bean-scope>session</managed-bean-scope>
25.    </managed-bean>
26.
27.    <application>
28.       <resource-bundle>
29.          <base-name>com.corejsf.messages</base-name>
30.          <var>msgs</var>
31.       </resource-bundle>
32.    </application>
33. </faces-config>
```

Selection Tags

JSF has seven tags for making selections:

- h:selectBooleanCheckbox
- h:selectManyCheckbox
- h:selectOneRadio
- h:selectOneListbox
- h:selectManyListbox
- h:selectOneMenu
- h:selectManyMenu

Table 4–19 shows examples of each tag.

Table 4–19   Selection Tag Examples

Tag	Generated HTML	Examples
h:selectBooleanCheckbox	`<input type="checkbox">`	Receive email: ☑

h:selectManyCheckbox	`<table>`
	`...`
	`<label>`
	`<input type="checkbox"/>`
	`</label>`
	`...`
	`</table>`
		☐ Red ☑ Blue ☐ Yellow

h:selectOneRadio	`<table>`
	`...`
	`<label>`
	`<input type="radio"/>`
	`</label>`
	`...`
	`</table>`
		○ High School
		◉ Bachelor's
		○ Master's
		○ Doctorate

h:selectOneListbox	`<select>`
	`<option value="Cheese">`
	`Cheese`
	`</option>`
	`...`
	`</select>`
		Cheese
		Pickle
		Mustard
		Lettuce

h:selectManyListbox	`<select multiple>`
	`<option value="Cheese">`
	`Cheese`
	`</option>`
	`...`
	`</select>`
		Cheese
		Pickle
		Mustard
		Lettuce
		Onions

h:selectOneMenu	`<select size="1">`
	`<option value="Cheese">`
	`Cheese`
	`</option>`
	`...`
	`</select>`
		Pickle ▼
		Cheese
		Pickle
		Mustard
		Lettuce
		Onions

h:selectManyMenu	`<select multiple size="1">`
	`<option value="Sunday">`
	`Sunday`
	`</option>`
	`...`
	`</select>`
		Sunday
		Monday
		Tuesday
		Wednesday

The h:selectBooleanCheckbox is the simplest selection tag—it renders a checkbox you can wire to a boolean bean property. You can also render a set of checkboxes with h:selectManyCheckbox.

Tags whose names begin with selectOne let you select one item from a collection. The selectOne tags render sets of radio buttons, single-select menus, or listboxes. The selectMany tags render sets of checkboxes, multiselect menus, or listboxes.

All selection tags share an almost identical set of attributes, listed in Table 4–20.

Table 4–20   Attributes for h:selectBooleanCheckbox, h:selectManyCheckbox, h:selectOneRadio, h:selectOneListbox, h:selectManyListbox, h:selectOneMenu, **and** h:selectManyMenu

Attributes	Description
disabledClass	CSS class for disabled elements—for h:selectOneRadio and h:selectManyCheckbox only.
enabledClass	CSS class for enabled elements—for h:selectOneRadio and h:selectManyCheckbox only.
layout	Specification for how elements are laid out: lineDirection (horizontal) or pageDirection (vertical)—for h:selectOneRadio and h:selectManyCheckbox only.
label (JSF 1.2)	A description of the component for use in error messages.
binding, converter, converterMessage (JSF 1.2), requiredMessage (JSF 1.2), id, immediate, styleClass, required, rendered, validator, validatorMessage (JSF 1.2), value, valueChangeListener	Basic attributes.[a]
accesskey, border, dir, disabled, lang, readonly, style, size, tabindex, title	HTML 4.0[b]—border is applicable to h:selectOneRadio and h:selectManyCheckbox only. size is applicable to h:selectOneListbox and h:selectManyListbox only.
onblur, onchange, onclick, ondblclick, onfocus, onkeydown, onkeypress, onkeyup, onmousedown, onmousemove, onmouseout, onmouseover, onmouseup, onselect	DHTML events.[c]

a. See Table 4–4 on page 97 for information about basic attributes.
b. See Table 4–5 on page 101 for information about HTML 4.0 attributes.
c. See Table 4–6 on page 102 for information about DHTML event attributes.

Checkboxes and Radio Buttons

Two JSF tags represent checkboxes:

- `h:selectBooleanCheckbox`
- `h:selectManyCheckbox`

`h:selectBooleanCheckbox` represents a single checkbox that you can wire to a `boolean` bean property. Here is an example:

Contact me ☑

In your JSF page, you do this:

```
<h:selectBooleanCheckbox value="#{form.contactMe}"/>
```

In your backing bean, provide a read-write property:

```
private boolean contactMe;
public void setContactMe(boolean newValue) {
   contactMe = newValue;
}
public boolean getContactMe() {
   return contactMe;
}
```

The generated HTML looks something like this:

```
<input type="checkbox" name="_id2:_id7"/>
```

You can create a group of checkboxes with `h:selectManyCheckbox`. As the tag name implies, you can select one or more of the checkboxes in the group. You specify that group within the body of `h:selectManyCheckbox`, either with one or more `f:selectItem` tags or one `f:selectItems` tag. See "Items" on page 138 for more information about those core tags. For example, here is a group of checkboxes for selecting colors:

☐ Red ☑ Blue ☐ Yellow ☐ Green ☑ Orange

The `h:selectManyCheckbox` tag looks like this:

```
<h:selectManyCheckbox value="#{form.colors}">
   <f:selectItem itemValue="Red" itemLabel="Red"/>
   <f:selectItem itemValue="Blue" itemLabel="Blue"/>
   <f:selectItem itemValue="Yellow" itemLabel="Yellow"/>
   <f:selectItem itemValue="Green" itemLabel="Green"/>
   <f:selectItem itemValue="Orange" itemLabel="Orange"/>
</h:selectManyCheckbox>
```

The checkboxes are specified with f:selectItem (page 138) or f:selectItems (page 140).

The h:selectManyCheckbox tag generates an HTML table element; for example, here is the generated HTML for our color example:

```
<table>
  <tr>
    <td>
      <label for="_id2:_id14">
        <input name="_id2:_id14" value="Red" type="checkbox"> Red</input>
      </label>
    </td>
  </tr>
  ...
</table>
```

Each color is an input element, wrapped in a label for accessibility. That label is placed in a td element.

Radio buttons are implemented with h:selectOneRadio. Here is an example:

○ High School ○ Bachelor's ◉ Master's ○ Doctorate

The value attribute of the h:selectOneRadio tag specifies the currently selected item. Once again, we use multiple f:selectItem tags to populate the radio buttons:

```
<h:selectOneRadio value="#{form.education}">
  <f:selectItem itemValue="High School" itemLabel="High School"/>
  <f:selectItem itemValue="Bachelor's" itemLabel="Bachelor's"/>
  <f:selectItem itemValue="Master's" itemLabel="Master's"/>
  <f:selectItem itemValue="Doctorate" itemLabel=Doctorate"/>
</h:selectOneRadio>
```

Like h:selectManyCheckbox, h:selectOneRadio generates an HTML table. Here is the table generated by the preceding tag:

```
<table>
  <tr>
    <td>
      <label for="_id2:_id14">
        <input name="_id2:_id14" value="High School" type="radio">
          High School
        </input>
      </label>
    </td>
  </tr>
  ...
</table>
```

Besides generating HTML tables, h:selectOneRadio and h:selectManyCheckbox have something else in common—a handful of attributes unique to those two tags:

- border
- enabledClass
- disabledClass
- layout

The border attribute specifies the width of the border. For example, here are radio buttons and checkboxes with borders of 1 and 2, respectively:

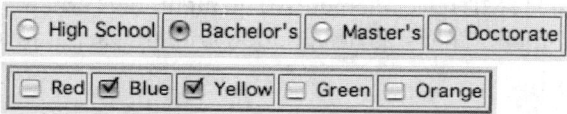

enabledClass and disabledClass specify CSS classes used when the checkboxes or radio buttons are enabled or disabled, respectively. For example, the following picture shows an enabled class with an italic font style, blue color, and yellow background:

The layout attribute can be either lineDirection (horizontal) or pageDirection (vertical). For example, the following checkboxes on the left have a pageDirection layout and the checkboxes on the right are lineDirection.

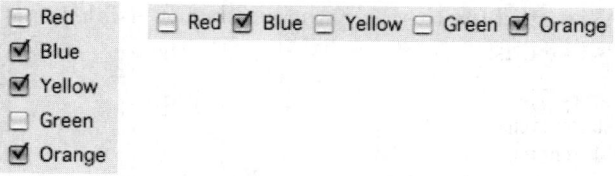

 NOTE: You might wonder why layout attribute values are not horizontal and vertical, instead of lineDirection and pageDirection, respectively. Although lineDirection and pageDirection are indeed horizontal and vertical for Latin-based languages, that is not always the case for other languages. For example, a Chinese browser that displays text top to bottom could regard lineDirection as vertical and pageDirection as horizontal.

Menus and Listboxes

Menus and listboxes are represented by the following tags:

- `h:selectOneListbox`
- `h:selectManyListbox`
- `h:selectOneMenu`
- `h:selectManyMenu`

The attributes for the preceding tags are listed in Table 4–20 on page 132, so that discussion is not repeated here.

Menu and listbox tags generate HTML `select` elements. The menu tags add a `size="1"` attribute to the `select` element. That size designation is all that separates menus and listboxes.

Here is a single-select listbox:

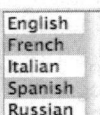

The corresponding listbox tag looks like this:

```
<h:selectOneListbox value="#{form.year}" size="5">
  <f:selectItem itemValue="1900" itemLabel="1900"/>
  <f:selectItem itemValue="1901" itemLabel="1901"/>
  ...
</h:selectOneListbox>
```

Notice that we've used the `size` attribute to specify the number of visible items. The generated HTML looks like this:

```
<select name="_id2:_id11" size="5">
  <option value="1900">1900</option>
  <option value="1901">1901</option>
  ...
</select>
```

Use `h:selectManyListbox` for multiselect listboxes like this one:

The listbox tag looks like this:

```
<h:selectManyListbox value="#{form.languages}">
    <f:selectItem itemValue="English" itemLabel="English"/>
    <f:selectItem itemValue="French" itemLabel="French"/>
    <f:selectItem itemValue="Italian" itemLabel="Italian"/>
    <f:selectItem itemValue="Spanish" itemLabel="Spanish"/>
    <f:selectItem itemValue="Russian" itemLabel="Russian"/>
</h:selectManyListbox>
```

This time we do not specify the size attribute, so the listbox grows to accommodate all its items. The generated HTML looks like this:

```
<select name="_id2:_id11" multiple>
    <option value="English">English</option>
    <option value="French">French</option>
    ...
</select>
```

Use h:selectOneMenu and h:selectManyMenu for menus. A single-select menu looks like this:

```
Wednesday ⬍
```

h:selectOneMenu created the preceding menu:

```
<h:selectOneMenu value="#{form.day}">
    <f:selectItem itemValue="Sunday" itemLabel="Sunday"/>
    <f:selectItem itemValue="Monday" itemLabel="Monday"/>
    <f:selectItem itemValue="Tuesday" itemLabel="Tuesday"/>
    <f:selectItem itemValue="Wednesday" itemLabel="Wednesday"/>
    <f:selectItem itemValue="Thursday" itemLabel="Thursday"/>
    <f:selectItem itemValue="Friday" itemLabel="Friday"/>
    <f:selectItem itemValue="Saturday" itemLabel="Saturday"/>
</h:selectOneMenu>
```

Here is the generated HTML:

```
<select name="_id2:_id17" size="1">
    <option value="Sunday">Sunday</option>
    ...
</select>
```

h:selectManyMenu is used for multiselect menus. That tag generates HTML, which looks like this:

```
<select name="_id2:_id17" multiple size="1">
    <option value="Sunday">Sunday</option>
    ...
</select>
```

That HTML does not yield consistent results among browsers. For example, here is h:selectManyMenu on Internet Explorer (left) and Netscape (right):

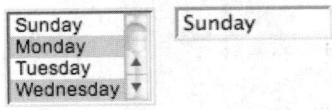

 NOTE: In HTML, the distinction between menus and listboxes is artificial. Menus and listboxes are both HTML select elements. The only distinction: Menus always have a size="1" attribute.

Browsers consistently render single-select menus as drop-down lists, as expected. But they do not consistently render multiple select menus, specified with size="1" and multiple attributes. Instead of rendering a drop-down list with multiple selection, as you might expect, some browsers render absurdities such as tiny scrollbars that are nearly impossible to manipulate (Windows IE 6) or no scrollbar at all, leaving you to navigate with arrow keys (Firefox 1.5).

Starting with "Selection Tags" on page 130, we have consistently used multiple f:selectItem to populate select components. Now that we are familiar with the fundamentals of selection tags, we take a closer look at f:selectItem and the related f:selectItems tags.

Items

All selection tags except h:selectBooleanCheckbox use f:selectItem or f:selectItems to specify their items. Next, we look at those core tags, starting with f:selectItem.

The f:selectItem *Tag*

You use f:selectItem to specify single selection items, like this:

```
<h:selectOneMenu value="#{form.condiments}">
    <f:selectItem itemValue="Cheese" itemLabel="Cheese"/>
    <f:selectItem itemValue="Pickle" itemLabel="Pickle"/>
    <f:selectItem itemValue="Mustard" itemLabel="Mustard"/>
    <f:selectItem itemValue="Lettuce" itemLabel="Lettuce"/>
    <f:selectItem itemValue="Onions" itemLabel="Onions"/>
</h:selectOneMenu>
```

The values—Cheese, Pickle, etc.—are transmitted as request parameter values when a selection is made from the menu and the menu's form is subsequently submitted. The itemLabel values are used as labels for the menu items. Sometimes you want to specify different values for request parameter values and item labels:

```
<h:selectOneMenu value="#{form.condiments}">
    <f:selectItem itemValue="1" itemLabel="Cheese"/>
    <f:selectItem itemValue="2" itemLabel="Pickle"/>
    <f:selectItem itemValue="3" itemLabel="Mustard"/>
    <f:selectItem itemValue="4" itemLabel="Lettuce"/>
    <f:selectItem itemValue="5" itemLabel="Onions"/>
</h:selectOneMenu>
```

In the preceding code, the item values are strings. "Binding the value Attribute" on page 145 shows you how to use different data types for item values.

In addition to labels and values, you can also supply item descriptions and specify an item's disabled state:

```
<f:selectItem itemLabel="Cheese" itemValue="#{form.cheeseValue}"
        itemDescription="used to be milk"
        itemDisabled="true"/>
```

Item descriptions are for tools only—they do not affect the generated HTML. The itemDisabled attribute, however, is passed to HTML. The f:selectItem tag has the attributes shown in Table 4–21.

Table 4–21   Attributes for f:selectItem

Attribute	Description
binding	Component binding—see Chapter 2 for more information about component bindings
id	Component ID
itemDescription	Description used by tools only
itemDisabled	Boolean value that sets the item's disabled HTML attribute
itemLabel	Text shown by the item
itemValue	Item's value, which is passed to the server as a request parameter
value	Value expression that points to a SelectItem instance
escape (JSF 1.2)	true if special characters in the value should be converted to character entities (default), false if the value should be emitted without change

You can use f:selectItem's value attribute to access SelectItem instances created in a bean:

```
<f:selectItem value="#{form.cheeseItem}"/>
```

The value expression for the value attribute points to a method that returns a javax.faces.model.SelectItem instance:

```
public SelectItem getCheeseItem() {
    return new SelectItem("Cheese");
}
```

API | **javax.faces.model.SelectItem**

- SelectItem(Object value)
  Creates a SelectItem with a value. The item label is obtained by applying toString() to the value.
- SelectItem(Object value, String label)
  Creates a SelectItem with a value and a label.
- SelectItem(Object value, String label, String description)
  Creates a SelectItem with a value, label, and description.
- SelectItem(Object value, String label, String description, boolean disabled)
  Creates a SelectItem with a value, label, description, and disabled state.

The f:selectItems Tag

As we saw in "The f:selectItem Tag" on page 138, f:selectItem is versatile, but it is tedious for specifying more than a few items. The first code fragment shown in that section can be reduced to the following with f:selectItems:

```
<h:selectOneRadio value="#{form.condiments}>
    <f:selectItems value="#{form.condimentItems}"/>
</h:selectOneRadio>
```

The value expression #{form.condimentItems} could point to an array of SelectItem instances:

```
private static SelectItem[] condimentItems = {
    new SelectItem(1, "Cheese"),
    new SelectItem(2, "Pickle"),
    new SelectItem(3, "Mustard"),
    new SelectItem(4, "Lettuce"),
    new SelectItem(5, "Onions")
};
```

```
public SelectItem[] getCondimentItems() {
   return condimentItems;
}
```

The f:selectItems value attribute must be a value expression that points to one of the following:

- A single SelectItem instance
- A collection of SelectItem instances
- An array of SelectItem instances
- A map whose entries represent SelectItem labels and values

 NOTE: Can't remember what you can specify for the f:selectItems value attribute? It's a SCAM: Single select item; Collection of select items; Array of select items; Map.

 NOTE: A single f:selectItems tag is usually better than multiple f:selectItem tags. If the number of items changes, you have to modify only Java code if you use f:selectItems, whereas f:selectItem may require you to modify both Java code and JSF pages.

If you specify a map, the JSF implementation creates a SelectItem instance for every entry in the map. The entry's key is used as the item's label, and the entry's value is used as the item's value. For example, here are condiments specified with a map:

```
private Map<String, Object> condimentItem = null;

public Map<String, Object> getCondimentItems() {
   if (condimentItem == null) {
      condimentItem = new LinkedHashMap<String, Object>();
      condimentItem.put("Cheese",  1);  // label, value
      condimentItem.put("Pickle",  2);
      condimentItem.put("Mustard", 3);
      condimentItem.put("Lettuce", 4);
      condimentItem.put("Onions",  5);
   }
   return condimentItem;
}
```

Note that you cannot specify item descriptions or disabled status when you use a map.

If you use SelectItem, you couple your code to the JSF API. You avoid that coupling when you use a Map, which makes it an attractive alternative. However, pay attention to these issues.

1. You will generally want to use a LinkedHashMap, not a TreeMap or HashMap. In a LinkedHashMap, you can control the order of the items because items are visited in the order in which they were inserted. If you use a TreeMap, the labels that are presented to the user (which are the keys of the map) are sorted alphabetically. That may or may not be what you want. For example, days of the week would be neatly arranged as Friday Monday Saturday Sunday Thursday Tuesday Wednesday. If you use a HashMap, the items are ordered randomly.

2. Map keys are turned into item labels and map values into item values. When a user selects an item, your backing bean receives a value in your map, not a key. For example, in the example above, if the backing bean receives a value of 5, you would need to iterate through the entries if you wanted to find the matching "Onions". Since the value is probably more meaningful to your application than the label, this is usually not a problem, just something to be aware of.

Item Groups

You can group menu or listbox items together, like this:

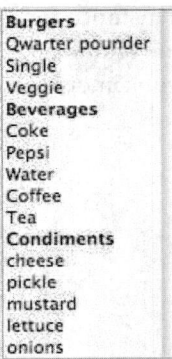

Here are the JSF tags that define the listbox:

```
<h:selectManyListbox>
    <f:selectItems value="#{form.menuItems}"/>
</h:selectManyListbox>
```

The menuItems property is a SelectItem array:

```
public SelectItem[] getMenuItems() { return menuItems; }
```

The menuItems array is instantiated like this:

```
private static SelectItem[] menuItems = { burgers, beverages, condiments };
```

The burgers, beverages, and condiments variables are SelectItemGroup instances that are instantiated like this:

```
private SelectItemGroup burgers =
    new SelectItemGroup("Burgers",    // value
        "burgers on the menu",        // description
        false,                        // disabled
        burgerItems);                 // select items

private SelectItemGroup beverages =
    new SelectItemGroup("Beverages",  // value
        "beverages on the menu",      // description
        false,                        // disabled
        beverageItems);               // select items

private SelectItemGroup condiments =
    new SelectItemGroup("Condiments", // value
        "condiments on the menu",     // description
        false,                        // disabled
        condimentItems);              // select items
```

Notice that we are using SelectItemGroups to populate an array of SelectItems. We can do that because SelectItemGroup extends SelectItem. The groups are created and initialized like this:

```
private SelectItem[] burgerItems = {
    new SelectItem("Qwarter pounder"),
    new SelectItem("Single"),
    new SelectItem("Veggie"),
};
private SelectItem[] beverageItems = {
    new SelectItem("Coke"),
    new SelectItem("Pepsi"),
    new SelectItem("Water"),
    new SelectItem("Coffee"),
    new SelectItem("Tea"),
};
private SelectItem[] condimentItems = {
    new SelectItem("cheese"),
    new SelectItem("pickle"),
    new SelectItem("mustard"),
    new SelectItem("lettuce"),
    new SelectItem("onions"),
};
```

SelectItemGroup instances encode HTML optgroup elements. For example, the preceding code generates the following HTML:

```
<select name="_id0:_id1" multiple size="16">
    <optgroup label="Burgers">
        <option value="1"  selected>Qwarter pounder</option>
        <option value="2">Single</option>
        <option value="3">Veggie</option>
    </optgroup>

    <optgroup label="Beverages">
        <option value="4"  selected>Coke</option>
        <option value="5">Pepsi</option>
        <option value="6">Water</option>
        <option value="7">Coffee</option>
        <option value="8">Tea</option>
    </optgroup>

    <optgroup label="Condiments">
        <option value="9">cheese</option>
        <option value="10">pickle</option>
        <option value="11">mustard</option>
        <option value="12">lettuce</option>
        <option value="13">onions</option>
    </optgroup>
</select>
```

 NOTE: The HTML 4.01 specification does not allow nested optgroup elements, which would be useful for things like cascading menus. The specification does mention that future HTML versions may support that behavior.

javax.faces.model.SelectItemGroup

- SelectItemGroup(String label)
  Creates a group with a label but no selection items.

- SelectItemGroup(String label, String description, boolean disabled, SelectItem[] items)
  Creates a group with a label, a description (which is ignored by the JSF Reference Implementation), a boolean that disables all the items when true, and an array of select items used to populate the group.

- setSelectItems(SelectItem[] items)
  Sets a group's array of SelectItems.

Binding the value *Attribute*

In all likelihood, whether you are using a set of checkboxes, a menu, or a listbox, you will want to keep track of selected items. For that purpose, you can exploit selectOne and selectMany tags, which have value attributes that represent selected items. For example, you can specify a selected item with the h:selectOneRadio value attribute, like this:

```
<h:selectOneRadio value="#{form.beverage}">
   <f:selectItems value="#{form.beverageItems}"/>
</h:selectOneRadio>
```

The #{form.beverage} value expression refers to the beverage property of a bean named form. That property is implemented like this:

```
private Integer beverage;
public Integer getBeverage() {
   return beverage;
}
public void setBeverage(Integer newValue) {
   beverage = newValue;
}
```

Notice that the beverage property type is Integer. That means the radio buttons must have Integer values. Those radio buttons are specified with f:selectItems, with a value attribute that points to the beverageItems property of the form bean:

```
private static SelectItem[] beverageItems = {
   new SelectItem(1, "Water"),    // value, label
   new SelectItem(2, "Cola"),
   new SelectItem(3, "Orange Juice")
};
public SelectItem[] getBeverageItems() {
   return beverage;
}
```

In the preceding example, we chose the Integer type to represent beverages. You can choose any type you like as long as the properties for items and selected item have matching types. An enumerated type would be a better choice in this case (see Listing 4–14 for an example).

You can keep track of multiple selections with a selectMany tag. These tags also have a value attribute that lets you specify one or more selected items. That attribute's value must be an array or list of convertible types.

Now we take a look at some different data types. We will use h:selectManyListbox to let a user choose multiple condiments:

```
<h:selectManyListbox value="#{form.condiments}">
   <f:selectItems value="#{form.condimentItems}"/>
</h:selectManyListbox>
```

Here are the condimentItems and condiments properties:

```
private static SelectItem[] condimentItems = {
   new SelectItem(1, "Cheese"),
   new SelectItem(2, "Pickle"),
   new SelectItem(3, "Mustard"),
   new SelectItem(4, "Lettuce"),
   new SelectItem(5, "Onions"),
};
public SelectItem[] getCondimentItems() {
   return condimentItems;
}

private Integer[] condiments;
public void setCondiments(Integer[] newValue) {
   condiments = newValue;
}
public Integer[] getCondiments() {
   return condiments;
}
```

Instead of an Integer array for the condiments property, we could have used the corresponding primitive type, int:

```
private int[] condiments;
public void setCondiments(int[] newValue) {
   condiments = newValue;
}
public int[] getCondiments() {
   return condiments;
}
```

If you use strings for item values, you can use a string array or list of strings for your selected items property:

```
private static SelectItem[] condimentItems = {
   new SelectItem("cheese", "Cheese"),
   new SelectItem("pickle", "Pickle"),
   new SelectItem("mustard", "Mustard"),
   new SelectItem("lettuce", "Lettuce"),
   new SelectItem("onions", "Onions"),
};
public SelectItem[] getCondimentItems() {
   return condimentItems;
}
```

```
private String[] condiments;
public void setCondiments(String[] newValue) {
   condiments = newValue;
}
public String[] getCondiments() {
   return condiments;
}
```

The preceding condiments property is an array of strings. You could use a collection instead:

```
private static Collection<SelectItem> condiments;
static {
   condiments = new ArrayListList<SelectItem>();
   condiments.add(new SelectItem("cheese", "Cheese"));
   condiments.add(new SelectItem("pickle", "Pickle"));
   condiments.add(new SelectItem("mustard", "Mustard"));
   condiments.add(new SelectItem("lettuce", "Lettuce"));
   condiments.add(new SelectItem("onions", "Onions"));
}
public List getCondiments() { return condiments; }
```

All Together: Checkboxes, Radio Buttons, Menus, and Listboxes

We close out our section on selection tags with an example that exercises nearly all those tags. That example, shown in Figure 4–7, implements a form requesting personal information. We use an h:selectBooleanCheckbox to determine whether the user wants to receive email, and h:selectOneMenu lets the user select the best day of the week for us to call.

The year listbox is implemented with h:selectOneListbox; the language checkboxes are implemented with h:selectManyCheckbox; the education level is implemented with h:selectOneRadio.

When the user submits the form, JSF navigation takes us to a JSF page that shows the data the user entered.

The directory structure for the application shown in Figure 4–7 is shown in Figure 4–8. The JSF pages, RegisterForm bean, faces configuration file, and resource bundle are shown in Listing 4–12 through Listing 4–16.

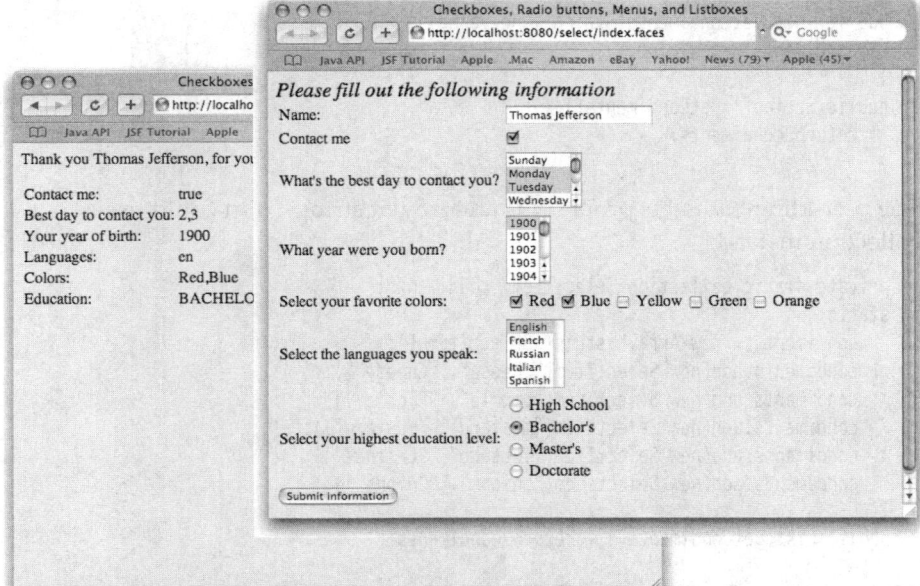

Figure 4–7   Using checkboxes, radio buttons, menus, and listboxes

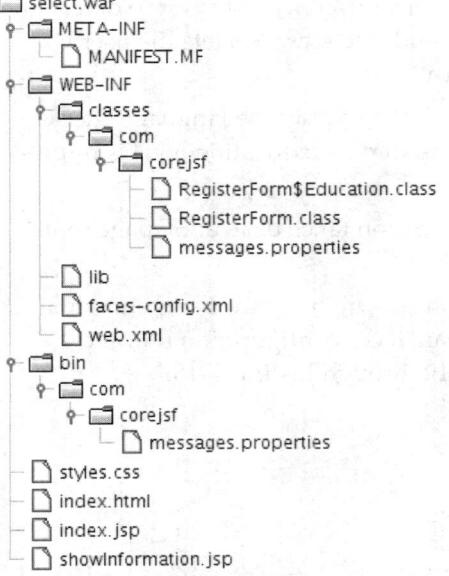

Figure 4–8   The directory structure of the personal information example

Listing 4–12 select/web/index.jsp

```
1.  <html>
2.    <%@ taglib uri="http://java.sun.com/jsf/core" prefix="f" %>
3.    <%@ taglib uri="http://java.sun.com/jsf/html" prefix="h" %>
4.    <f:view>
5.       <head>
6.          <link href="styles.css" rel="stylesheet" type="text/css"/>
7.          <title>
8.             <h:outputText value="#{msgs.indexWindowTitle}"/>
9.          </title>
10.      </head>
11.
12.      <body>
13.         <h:outputText value="#{msgs.indexPageTitle}" styleClass="emphasis"/>
14.         <h:form>
15.            <table>
16.               <tr>
17.                  <td>
18.                     <h:outputText value="#{msgs.namePrompt}"/>
19.                  </td>
20.                  <td>
21.                     <h:inputText value="#{form.name}"/>
22.                  </td>
23.               </tr>
24.               <tr>
25.                  <td>
26.                     <h:outputText value="#{msgs.contactMePrompt}"/>
27.                  </td>
28.                  <td>
29.                     <h:selectBooleanCheckbox value="#{form.contactMe}"/>
30.                  </td>
31.               </tr>
32.               <tr>
33.                  <td>
34.                     <h:outputText value="#{msgs.bestDayPrompt}"/>
35.                  </td>
36.                  <td>
37.                     <h:selectManyMenu value="#{form.bestDaysToContact}">
38.                        <f:selectItems value="#{form.daysOfTheWeekItems}"/>
39.                     </h:selectManyMenu>
40.                  </td>
41.               </tr>
42.               <tr>
43.                  <td>
44.                     <h:outputText value="#{msgs.yearOfBirthPrompt}"/>
45.                  </td>
```

Listing 4–12   select/web/index.jsp (cont.)

```
46.                    <td>
47.                       <h:selectOneListbox size="5" value="#{form.yearOfBirth}">
48.                          <f:selectItems value="#{form.yearItems}"/>
49.                       </h:selectOneListbox>
50.                    </td>
51.                 </tr>
52.                 <tr>
53.                    <td>
54.                       <h:outputText value="#{msgs.colorPrompt}"/>
55.                    </td>
56.                    <td>
57.                       <h:selectManyCheckbox value="#{form.colors}">
58.                          <f:selectItems value="#{form.colorItems}"/>
59.                       </h:selectManyCheckbox>
60.                    </td>
61.                 </tr>
62.                 <tr>
63.                    <td>
64.                       <h:outputText value="#{msgs.languagePrompt}"/>
65.                    </td>
66.                    <td>
67.                       <h:selectManyListbox value="#{form.languages}">
68.                          <f:selectItems value="#{form.languageItems}"/>
69.                       </h:selectManyListbox>
70.                    </td>
71.                 </tr>
72.                 <tr>
73.                    <td>
74.                       <h:outputText value="#{msgs.educationPrompt}"/>
75.                    </td>
76.                    <td>
77.                       <h:selectOneRadio value="#{form.education}"
78.                          layout="pageDirection">
79.                          <f:selectItems value="#{form.educationItems}"/>
80.                       </h:selectOneRadio>
81.                    </td>
82.                 </tr>
83.              </table>
84.              <h:commandButton value="#{msgs.buttonPrompt}"
85.                 action="showInformation"/>
86.           </h:form>
87.           <h:messages/>
88.        </body>
89.     </f:view>
90. </html>
```

Listing 4–13   select/web/showInformation.jsp

```
1.  <html>
2.    <%@ taglib uri="http://java.sun.com/jsf/core" prefix="f" %>
3.    <%@ taglib uri="http://java.sun.com/jsf/html" prefix="h" %>
4.    <f:view>
5.      <head>
6.        <link href="styles.css" rel="stylesheet" type="text/css"/>
7.        <title>
8.          <h:outputText value="#{msgs.indexWindowTitle}"/>
9.        </title>
10.     </head>
11.
12.     <body>
13.       <h:outputFormat value="#{msgs.thankYouLabel}">
14.         <f:param value="#{form.name}"/>
15.       </h:outputFormat>
16.       <p>
17.       <table>
18.         <tr>
19.           <td><h:outputText value="#{msgs.contactMeLabel}"/></td>
20.           <td><h:outputText value="#{form.contactMe}"/></td>
21.         </tr>
22.
23.         <tr>
24.           <td><h:outputText value="#{msgs.bestDayLabel}"/></td>
25.           <td><h:outputText value="#{form.bestDaysConcatenated}"/></td>
26.         </tr>
27.
28.         <tr>
29.           <td><h:outputText value="#{msgs.yearOfBirthLabel}"/></td>
30.           <td><h:outputText value="#{form.yearOfBirth}"/></td>
31.         </tr>
32.
33.         <tr>
34.           <td><h:outputText value="#{msgs.languageLabel}"/></td>
35.           <td><h:outputText value="#{form.languagesConcatenated}"/></td>
36.         </tr>
37.
38.         <tr>
39.           <td><h:outputText value="#{msgs.colorLabel}"/></td>
40.           <td><h:outputText value="#{form.colorsConcatenated}"/></td>
41.         </tr>
42.
```

Listing 4–13   select/web/showInformation.jsp (cont.)

```
43.            <tr>
44.                <td><h:outputText value="#{msgs.educationLabel}"/></td>
45.                <td><h:outputText value="#{form.education}"/></td>
46.            </tr>
47.          </table>
48.        </body>
49.    </f:view>
50. </html>
```

Listing 4–14   select/src/java/com/corejsf/RegisterForm.java

```
1. package com.corejsf;
2.
3. import java.text.DateFormatSymbols;
4. import java.util.ArrayList;
5. import java.util.Calendar;
6. import java.util.Collection;
7. import java.util.HashMap;
8. import java.util.LinkedHashMap;
9. import java.util.Map;
10.
11. import javax.faces.model.SelectItem;
12.
13. public class RegisterForm {
14.    enum Education { HIGH_SCHOOL, BACHELOR, MASTER, DOCTOR };
15.
16.    private String name;
17.    private boolean contactMe;
18.    private Integer[] bestDaysToContact;
19.    private Integer yearOfBirth;
20.    private String[] colors;
21.    private String[] languages;
22.    private Education education;
23.
24.    // PROPERTY: name
25.    public String getName() {
26.       return name;
27.    }
28.    public void setName(String newValue) {
29.       name = newValue;
30.    }
31.
32.    // PROPERTY: contactMe
33.    public boolean getContactMe() {
34.       return contactMe;
35.    }
```

Listing 4–14   `select/src/java/com/corejsf/RegisterForm.java (cont.)`

```
36.    public void setContactMe(boolean newValue) {
37.        contactMe = newValue;
38.    }
39.
40.    // PROPERTY: bestDaysToContact
41.    public Integer[] getBestDaysToContact() {
42.        return bestDaysToContact;
43.    }
44.    public void setBestDaysToContact(Integer[] newValue) {
45.        bestDaysToContact = newValue;
46.    }
47.
48.    // PROPERTY: yearOfBirth
49.    public Integer getYearOfBirth() {
50.        return yearOfBirth;
51.    }
52.    public void setYearOfBirth(Integer newValue) {
53.        yearOfBirth = newValue;
54.    }
55.
56.    // PROPERTY: colors
57.    public String[] getColors() {
58.        return colors;
59.    }
60.    public void setColors(String[] newValue) {
61.        colors = newValue;
62.    }
63.
64.    // PROPERTY: languages
65.    public String[] getLanguages() {
66.        return languages;
67.    }
68.    public void setLanguages(String[] newValue) {
69.        languages = newValue;
70.    }
71.
72.    // PROPERTY: education
73.    public Education getEducation() {
74.        return education;
75.    }
76.
77.    public void setEducation(Education newValue) {
78.        education = newValue;
79.    }
80.
81.    // PROPERTY: yearItems
```

Listing 4–14   select/src/java/com/corejsf/RegisterForm.java (cont.)

```
82.    public Collection<SelectItem> getYearItems() {
83.       return birthYears;
84.    }
85.
86.    // PROPERTY: daysOfTheWeekItems
87.    public SelectItem[] getDaysOfTheWeekItems() {
88.       return daysOfTheWeek;
89.    }
90.
91.    // PROPERTY: languageItems
92.    public Map<String, Object> getLanguageItems() {
93.       return languageItems;
94.    }
95.
96.    // PROPERTY: colorItems
97.    public SelectItem[] getColorItems() {
98.       return colorItems;
99.    }
100.
101.   // PROPERTY: educationItems
102.   public SelectItem[] getEducationItems() {
103.      return educationItems;
104.   }
105.
106.   // PROPERTY: bestDaysConcatenated
107.   public String getBestDaysConcatenated() {
108.      return concatenate(bestDaysToContact);
109.   }
110.
111.   // PROPERTY: languagesConcatenated
112.   public String getLanguagesConcatenated() {
113.      return concatenate(languages);
114.   }
115.
116.   // PROPERTY: colorsConcatenated
117.   public String getColorsConcatenated() {
118.      return concatenate(colors);
119.   }
120.
121.   private static String concatenate(Object[] values) {
122.      if (values == null)
123.         return "";
124.      StringBuilder r = new StringBuilder();
125.      for (Object value : values) {
126.         if (r.length()> 0)
127.            r.append(',');
```

Listing 4–14 select/src/java/com/corejsf/RegisterForm.java (cont.)

```
128.         r.append(value.toString());
129.       }
130.       return r.toString();
131.     }
132.
133.     private static SelectItem[] colorItems = {
134.       new SelectItem("Red"),
135.       new SelectItem("Blue"),
136.       new SelectItem("Yellow"),
137.       new SelectItem("Green"),
138.       new SelectItem("Orange")
139.     };
140.
141.     private static SelectItem[] educationItems = {
142.       new SelectItem(Education.HIGH_SCHOOL, "High School"),
143.       new SelectItem(Education.BACHELOR, "Bachelor's"),
144.       new SelectItem(Education.MASTER, "Master's"),
145.       new SelectItem(Education.DOCTOR, "Doctorate") };
146.
147.     private static Map<String, Object> languageItems;
148.     static {
149.       languageItems = new LinkedHashMap<String, Object>();
150.       languageItems.put("English", "en"); // item, value
151.       languageItems.put("French", "fr");
152.       languageItems.put("Russian", "ru");
153.       languageItems.put("Italian", "it");
154.       languageItems.put("Spanish", "es");
155.     }
156.
157.     private static Collection<SelectItem> birthYears;
158.     static {
159.       birthYears = new ArrayList<SelectItem>();
160.       for (int i = 1900; i < 2000; ++i) {
161.         birthYears.add(new SelectItem(i));
162.       }
163.     }
164.
165.     private static SelectItem[] daysOfTheWeek;
166.     static {
167.       DateFormatSymbols symbols = new DateFormatSymbols();
168.       String[] weekdays = symbols.getWeekdays();
169.       daysOfTheWeek = new SelectItem[7];
170.       for (int i = Calendar.SUNDAY; i <= Calendar.SATURDAY; i++) {
171.         daysOfTheWeek[i - 1] = new SelectItem(new Integer(i), weekdays[i]);
172.       }
173.     }
174.   }
```

Listing 4–15 select/src/java/com/corejsf/messages.properties

```
 1. indexWindowTitle=Checkboxes, Radio buttons, Menus, and Listboxes
 2. indexPageTitle=Please fill out the following information
 3.
 4. namePrompt=Name:
 5. contactMePrompt=Contact me
 6. bestDayPrompt=What's the best day to contact you?
 7. yearOfBirthPrompt=What year were you born?
 8. buttonPrompt=Submit information
 9. languagePrompt=Select the languages you speak:
10. educationPrompt=Select your highest education level:
11. emailAppPrompt=Select your email application:
12. colorPrompt=Select your favorite colors:
13.
14. thankYouLabel=Thank you {0}, for your information
15. contactMeLabel=Contact me:
16. bestDayLabel=Best day to contact you:
17. yearOfBirthLabel=Your year of birth:
18. colorLabel=Colors:
19. languageLabel=Languages:
20. educationLabel=Education:
```

Listing 4–16 select/web/WEB-INF/faces-config.xml

```
 1. <?xml version="1.0"?>
 2. <faces-config xmlns="http://java.sun.com/xml/ns/javaee"
 3.     xmlns:xsi="http://www.w3.org/2001/XMLSchema-instance"
 4.     xsi:schemaLocation="http://java.sun.com/xml/ns/javaee
 5.         http://java.sun.com/xml/ns/javaee/web-facesconfig_1_2.xsd"
 6.     version="1.2">
 7.     <navigation-rule>
 8.         <navigation-case>
 9.             <from-outcome>showInformation</from-outcome>
10.             <to-view-id>/showInformation.jsp</to-view-id>
11.         </navigation-case>
12.     </navigation-rule>
13.     <managed-bean>
14.         <managed-bean-name>form</managed-bean-name>
15.         <managed-bean-class>com.corejsf.RegisterForm</managed-bean-class>
16.         <managed-bean-scope>session</managed-bean-scope>
17.     </managed-bean>
18.     <application>
19.         <resource-bundle>
20.             <base-name>com.corejsf.messages</base-name>
21.             <var>msgs</var>
22.         </resource-bundle>
23.     </application>
24. </faces-config>
```

Messages

During the JSF life cycle, any object can create a message and add it to a queue of messages maintained by the faces context. At the end of the life cycle—in the Render Response phase—you can display those messages in a view. Typically, messages are associated with a particular component and indicate either conversion or validation errors.

Although error messages are usually the most prevalent message type in a JSF application, messages come in four varieties:

- Information
- Warning
- Error
- Fatal

All messages can contain a summary and a detail. For example, a summary might be Invalid Entry and a detail might be The number entered was greater than the maximum.

JSF applications use two tags to display messages in JSF pages: h:messages and h:message.

The h:messages tag displays all messages that were stored in the faces context during the course of the JSF life cycle. You can restrict those messages to global messages—meaning messages not associated with a component—by setting h:message's globalOnly attribute to true. By default, that attribute is false.

The h:message tag displays a single message for a particular component. That component is designated with h:message's mandatory for attribute. If more than one message has been generated for a component, h:message shows only the last one.

h:message and h:messages share many attributes. Table 4–22 lists all attributes for both tags.

Table 4–22   Attributes for h:message **and** h:messages

Attributes	Description
errorClass	CSS class applied to error messages.
errorStyle	CSS style applied to error messages.
fatalClass	CSS class applied to fatal messages.

Table 4–22 Attributes for h:message **and** h:messages **(cont.)**

Attributes	Description
fatalStyle	CSS style applied to fatal messages.
for	The id of the component for which to display the message (h:message only).
globalOnly	Instruction to display only global messages—applicable only to h:messages. Default is false.
infoClass	CSS class applied to information messages.
infoStyle	CSS style applied to information messages.
layout	Specification for message layout: "table" or "list"—applicable only to h:messages.
showDetail	A Boolean that determines whether message details are shown. Defaults are false for h:messages, true for h:message.
showSummary	A Boolean that determines whether message summaries are shown. Defaults are true for h:messages, false for h:message.
tooltip	A Boolean that determines whether message details are rendered in a tooltip; the tooltip is only rendered if showDetail and showSummary are true.
warnClass	CSS class for warning messages.
warnStyle	CSS style for warning messages.
binding, id, rendered, styleClass	Basic attributes.[a]
style, title, dir (JSF 1.2), lang (JSF 1.2)	HTML 4.0.[b]

a. See Table 4–4 on page 97 for information about basic attributes.
b. See Table 4–5 on page 101 for information about HTML 4.0 attributes.

The majority of the attributes in Table 4–22 represent CSS classes or styles that h:message and h:messages apply to particular types of messages.

You can also specify whether you want to display a message's summary or detail, or both, with the showSummary and showDetail attributes, respectively.

The h:messages layout attribute can be used to specify how messages are laid out, either as a list or a table. If you specify true for the tooltip attribute and you have also set showDetail and showSummary to true, the message's detail will be wrapped in a tooltip that is shown when the mouse hovers over the error message.

Now that we have a grasp of message fundamentals, we take a look at an application that uses the h:message and h:messages tags. The application shown in Figure 4–9 contains a simple form with two text fields. Both text fields have required attributes.

Moreover, the Age text field is wired to an integer property, so its value is converted automatically by the JSF framework. Figure 4–9 shows the error messages generated by the JSF framework when we neglect to specify a value for the Name field and provide the wrong type of value for the Age field.

Figure 4–9   Displaying messages

At the top of the JSF page, we use h:messages to display all messages. We use h:message to display messages for each input field:

```
<h:form>
<h:messages layout="table" errorClass="errors"/>
   ...
<h:inputText id="name"
   value="#{user.name}" required="true" label="#{msgs.namePrompt}"/>
<h:message for="name" errorClass="errors"/>
   ...
<h:inputText id="age"
   value="#{form.age}" required="true" label="#{msgs.agePrompt}"/>
<h:message for="age" errorClass="errors"/>
   ...
</h:form>
```

Note that the input fields have `label` attributes that describe the fields. These labels are used in the error messages—for example, the Age: label (generated by #{msgs.agePrompt}) in this message:

Age: old must be a number between -2147483648 and 2147483647 Example: 9346

Generally, you will want to use the same expression for the `label` attribute as for the value of the `h:outputText` tag that labels the input field. For example, the age field as preceded by

```
<h:outputText value = "#{msgs.agePrompt}"/>
```

Both message tags in our example specify a CSS class named `errors`, which is defined in `styles.css`. That class definition looks like this:

```
.errors {
    font-style: italic;
}
```

We have also specified `layout="table"` for the `h:messages` tag. If we had omitted that attribute (or alternatively specified `layout="list"`), the output would look like this:

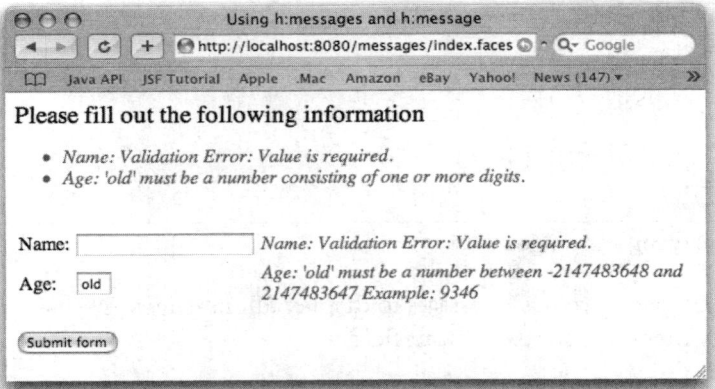

The `list` layout encodes the error messages in an unnumbered list (whose appearance you can control through styles).

 CAUTION: In JSF 1.1, the "list" style placed the messages one after the other, without any separators, which was not very useful.

Figure 4–10 shows the directory structure for the application shown in Figure 4–9. Listing 4–17 through Listing 4–19 list the JSP page, resource bundle, and style sheet for the application.

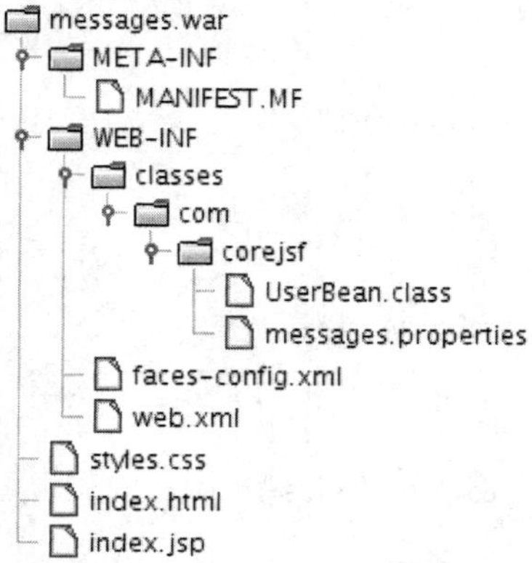

Figure 4–10 Directory structure for the messages example

Listing 4–17 messages/web/index.jsp

```
1.  <html>
2.  <%@ taglib uri="http://java.sun.com/jsf/core" prefix="f" %>
3.  <%@ taglib uri="http://java.sun.com/jsf/html" prefix="h" %>
4.  <f:view>
5.     <head>
6.        <link href="styles.css" rel="stylesheet" type="text/css"/>
7.        <title>
8.           <h:outputText value="#{msgs.windowTitle}"/>
9.        </title>
10.     </head>
11.     <body>
12.        <h:form>
13.           <h:outputText value="#{msgs.greeting}" styleClass="emphasis"/>
14.           <br/>
15.           <h:messages errorClass="errors" layout="table"/>
16.           <br/>
17.           <table>
18.              <tr>
19.                 <td>
20.                    <h:outputText value="#{msgs.namePrompt}:"/>
21.                 </td>
22.                 <td>
23.                    <h:inputText id="name"
24.                       value="#{user.name}" required="true"
25.                       label="#{msgs.namePrompt}"/>
26.                 </td>
```

Listing 4–17   messages/web/index.jsp (cont.)

```
27.                    <td>
28.                        <h:message for="name" errorClass="errors"/>
29.                    </td>
30.                </tr>
31.                <tr>
32.                    <td>
33.                        <h:outputText value="#{msgs.agePrompt}:"/>
34.                    </td>
35.                    <td>
36.                        <h:inputText id="age"
37.                            value="#{user.age}" required="true" size="3"
38.                            label="#{msgs.agePrompt}"/>
39.                    </td>
40.                    <td>
41.                        <h:message for="age" errorClass="errors"/>
42.                    </td>
43.                </tr>
44.            </table>
45.            <br/>
46.            <h:commandButton value="#{msgs.submitPrompt}"/>
47.        </h:form>
48.    </body>
49. </f:view>
50. </html>
```

Listing 4–18   messages/src/java/com/corejsf/messages.properties

```
1. windowTitle=Using h:messages and h:message
2. greeting=Please fill out the following information
3. namePrompt=Name
4. agePrompt=Age
5. submitPrompt=Submit form
```

Listing 4–19   messages/web/styles.css

```
1. .errors {
2.    font-style: italic;
3.    color: red;
4. }
5. .emphasis {
6.    font-size: 1.3em;
7. }
```

NOTE: By default, h:messages shows message summaries but not details. h:message, on the other hand, shows details but not summaries. If you use h:messages and h:message together, as we did in the preceding example, summaries will appear at the top of the page, with details next to the appropriate input field.

Panels

Throughout this chapter we have used HTML tables to align form prompts and input fields. Creating table markup by hand is tedious and error prone, so now we'll look at alleviating some of that tediousness with h:panelGrid, which generates an HTML table element. You can specify the number of columns in the table with the columns attribute, like this:

```
<h:panelGrid columns="3">
    ...
</h:panelGrid>
```

The columns attribute is not mandatory—if you do not specify it, the number of columns defaults to 1. h:panelGrid places components in columns from left to right and top to bottom. For example, if you have a panel grid with three columns and nine components, you will wind up with three rows, each containing three columns. If you specify three columns and ten components, you will have four rows, and in the last row only the first column will contain a component—the tenth component.

Table 4–23 lists h:panelGrid attributes.

Table 4–23   Attributes for h:panelGrid

Attributes	Description
bgcolor	Background color for the table
border	Width of the table's border
cellpadding	Padding around table cells
cellspacing	Spacing between table cells
columnClasses	Comma-separated list of CSS classes for columns
columns	Number of columns in the table
footerClass	CSS class for the table footer

Table 4–23   Attributes for h:panelGrid **(cont.)**

Attributes	Description
frame	Specification for sides of the frame surrounding the table that are to be drawn; valid values: none, above, below, hsides, vsides, lhs, rhs, box, border
headerClass	CSS class for the table header
rowClasses	Comma-separated list of CSS classes for rows
rules	Specification for lines drawn between cells; valid values: groups, rows, columns, all
summary	Summary of the table's purpose and structure used for nonvisual feedback such as speech
captionClass (JSF 1.2), captionStyle (JSF 1.2)	CSS class or style for the caption; a panel caption is optionally supplied by a facet named "caption"
binding, id, rendered, styleClass, value	Basic attributes[a]
dir, lang, style, title, width	HTML 4.0[b]
onclick, ondblclick, onkeydown, onkeypress, onkeyup, onmousedown, onmousemove, onmouseout, onmouseover, onmouseup	DHTML events[c]

a. See Table 4–4 on page 97 for information about basic attributes.
b. See Table 4–5 on page 101 for information about HTML 4.0 attributes.
c. See Table 4–6 on page 102 for information about DHTML event attributes.

You can specify CSS classes for different parts of the table: header, footer, rows, and columns. The columnClasses and rowClasses specify lists of CSS classes that are applied to columns and rows, respectively. If those lists contain fewer class names than rows or columns, the CSS classes are reused. That makes it possible to specify classes, like this: rowClasses="evenRows, oddRows" and columnClasses="evenColumns, oddColumns".

The cellpadding, cellspacing, frame, rules, and summary attributes are HTML pass-through attributes that apply only to tables. See the HTML 4.0 specification for more information.

h:panelGrid is often used with h:panelGroup, which groups two or more components so they are treated as one. For example, you might group an input field and its error message, like this:

```
<h:panelGrid columns="2">
    ...
    <h:panelGroup>
        <h:inputText id="name" value="#{user.name}">
        <h:message for="name"/>
    </h:panelGroup>
    ...
</h:panelGrid>
```

Grouping the text field and error message puts them in the same table cell. Without that grouping, the error message component would occupy its own cell. In the absence of an error message, the error message component produces no output but still takes up a cell, so you wind up with an empty cell.

h:panelGroup is a simple tag with only a handful of attributes. Those attributes are listed in Table 4–24.

Table 4–24 Attributes for h:panelGroup

Attributes	Description
layout (JSF 1.2)	If the value is "block", use an HTML div to lay out the children. Otherwise, use a span.
binding, id, rendered, styleClass	Basic attributes.[a]
style	HTML 4.0.[b]

a. See Table 4–4 on page 97 for information about basic attributes.
b. See Table 4–5 on page 101 for information about HTML 4.0 attributes.

Figure 4–11 shows a simple example that uses h:panelGrid and h:panelGroup. The application contains a form that asks for the user's name and age. We have added a required validator—with h:inputText's required attribute—to the name field and used an h:message tag to display the corresponding error when that constraint is violated. We have placed no restrictions on the Age text field.

Notice that those constraints require three columns in the first row—one each for the name prompt, text field, and error message—but only two in the second: the age prompt and text field. Since h:panelGrid allows only one value for its columns attribute, we can resolve this column quandary by placing the name text field and error message in a panel group, and because those two components will be treated as one, we actually have only two columns in each row.

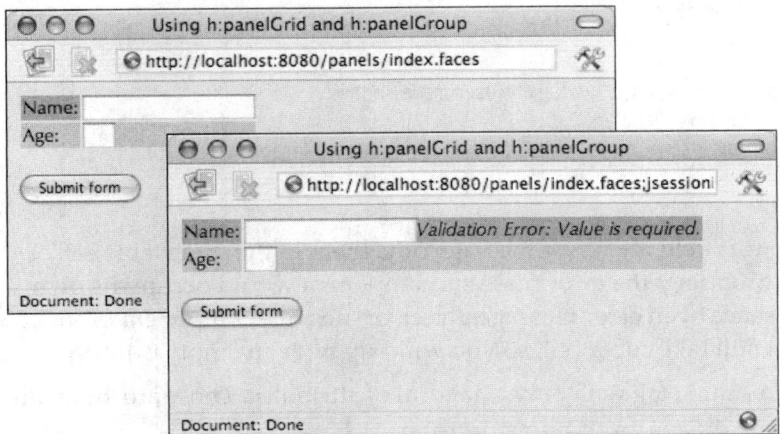

Figure 4–11   Using h:panelGrid **and** h:panelGroup

The directory structure for the application shown in Figure 4–11 is shown in Figure 4–12. Listings 4–20 through 4–22 contain the code of the JSF page and related files.

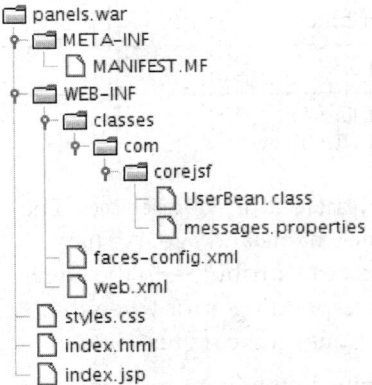

Figure 4–12   Directory structure for the panels example

Listing 4–20   panels/web/index.jsp

```jsp
1.  <html>
2.     <%@ taglib uri="http://java.sun.com/jsf/core" prefix="f" %>
3.     <%@ taglib uri="http://java.sun.com/jsf/html" prefix="h" %>
4.     <f:view>
5.        <head>
6.           <link href="styles.css" rel="stylesheet" type="text/css"/>
7.           <title>
8.              <h:outputText value="#{msgs.windowTitle}"/>
9.           </title>
10.       </head>
11.
12.       <body>
13.          <h:form>
14.             <h:panelGrid columns="2" rowClasses="oddRows,evenRows">
15.                <h:outputText value="#{msgs.namePrompt}:"/>
16.                <h:panelGroup>
17.                   <h:inputText id="name"
18.                      value="#{user.name}" required="true"
19.                      label="#{msgs.namePrompt}"/>
20.                   <h:message for="name" errorClass="errors"/>
21.                </h:panelGroup>
22.                <h:outputText value="#{msgs.agePrompt}:"/>
23.                <h:inputText size="3" value="#{user.age}"
24.                   label="#{msgs.agePrompt}"/>
25.             </h:panelGrid>
26.             <br/>
27.             <h:commandButton value="#{msgs.submitPrompt}"/>
28.          </h:form>
29.       </body>
30.    </f:view>
31. </html>
```

Listing 4–21   panels/src/java/com/corejsf/messages.properties

```
1. windowTitle=Using h:panelGrid and h:panelGroup
2. namePrompt=Name
3. agePrompt=Age
4. submitPrompt=Submit form
```

Listing 4–22   panels/web/styles.css

```
1. body {
2.    background: #eee;
3. }
4. .errors {
5.    font-style: italic;
6. }
7. .evenRows {
8.    background: PowderBlue;
9. }
10. .oddRows {
11.    background: MediumTurquoise;
12. }
```

DATA TABLES

Chapter **5**

Classic web applications deal extensively in tabular data. In the days of old, HTML tables were preferred for that task, in addition to acting as page layout managers. That latter task has, for the most part, been subsequently rendered to CSS, but displaying tabular data is still big business.

This chapter discusses the h:dataTable tag, a capable but limited component that lets you manipulate tabular data.

 NOTE: The h:dataTable tag represents a capable component/renderer pair. For example, you can easily display JSF components in table cells, add headers and footers to tables, and manipulate the look and feel of your tables with CSS classes. However, h:dataTable is missing some high-end features that you might expect out of the box. For example, if you want to sort table columns, you will have to write some code to do that. See "Sorting and Filtering" on page 203 for more details on how to do that.

The Data Table Tag—h:dataTable

The h:dataTable tag iterates over *data* to create an HTML *table*. Here is how you use it:

```
<h:dataTable value='#{items}' var='item'>
   <h:column>
```

```
        <%-- left column components --%>
        <h:output_text value='#{item.propertyName}'/>
    </h:column>

    <h:column>
        <%-- next column components --%>
        <h:output_text value='#{item.anotherPropertyName}'/>
    </h:column>

    <%-- add more columns, as desired --%>
    </h:dataTable>
```

The value attribute represents the data over which h:dataTable iterates; that data must be one of the following:

- A Java object
- An array
- An instance of java.util.List
- An instance of java.sql.ResultSet
- An instance of javax.servlet.jsp.jstl.sql.Result
- An instance of javax.faces.model.DataModel

As h:dataTable iterates, it makes each item in the array, list, result set, etc., available within the body of the tag. The name of the item is specified with h:dataTable's var attribute. In the preceding code fragment, each item (item) of a collection (items) is made available, in turn, as h:dataTable iterates through the collection. You use properties from the current item to populate columns for the current row.

You can also specify any Java object for h:dataTable's value attribute, although the usefulness of doing so is questionable. If that object is a scalar (meaning it is not a collection of some sort), h:dataTable iterates once, making the object available in the body of the tag.

The body of h:dataTable tags can contain only h:column tags; h:dataTable ignores all other component tags. Each column can contain an unlimited number of components in addition to optional header and footer components.

h:dataTable pairs a UIData component with a Table renderer. That combination provides robust table generation that includes support for CSS styles, database access, custom table models, and more. We start our h:dataTable exploration with a simple table.

A Simple Table

Figure 5–1 shows a table of names.

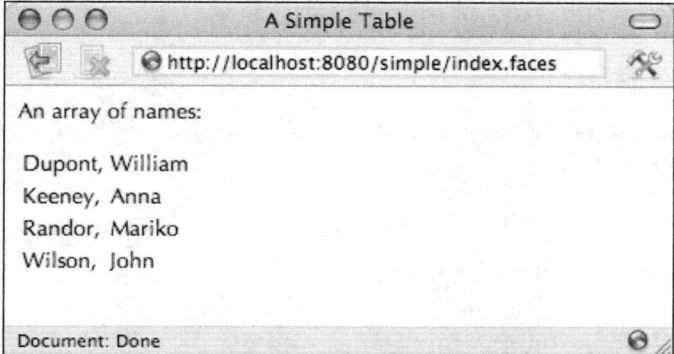

Figure 5–1   A simple table

The directory structure for the application shown in Figure 5–1 is shown in Figure 5–2. The application's JSF page is given in Listing 5–1.

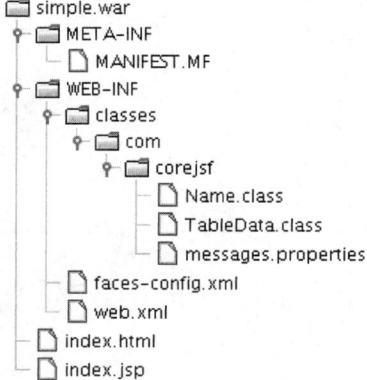

Figure 5–2   The directory structure for the simple table

In Listing 5–1, we use h:dataTable to iterate over an array of names. The last name followed by a comma is placed in the left column and the first name is placed in the right column.

The array of names in this example is instantiated by a bean, which is managed by JSF. That bean is an instance of com.corejsf.TableData, which is shown in Listing 5–3. Listing 5–2 shows the Name class. The faces configuration file and message resource bundle are shown in Listing 5–4 and Listing 5–5, respectively.

Listing 5–1 simple/web/index.jsp

```
1. <html>
2.   <%@ taglib uri="http://java.sun.com/jsf/core"  prefix="f" %>
3.   <%@ taglib uri="http://java.sun.com/jsf/html"  prefix="h" %>
4.   <f:view>
5.     <head>
6.       <title>
7.         <h:outputText value="#{msgs.windowTitle}"/>
8.       </title>
9.     </head>
10.
11.     <body>
12.       <h:outputText value="#{msgs.pageTitle}"/>
13.       <p>
14.       <h:form>
15.         <h:dataTable value="#{tableData.names}"
16.                          var="name">
17.           <h:column>
18.             <h:outputText value="#{name.last}, "/>
19.           </h:column>
20.
21.           <h:column>
22.             <h:outputText value="#{name.first}"/>
23.           </h:column>
24.         </h:dataTable>
25.       </h:form>
26.     </body>
27.   </f:view>
28. </html>
```

Listing 5–2 simple/src/java/com/corejsf/Name.java

```
1. package com.corejsf;
2.
3. public class Name {
4.   private String first;
5.   private String last;
6.
7.   public Name(String first, String last) {
8.     this.first = first;
9.     this.last = last;
10.  }
11.
```

Listing 5–2 simple/src/java/com/corejsf/Name.java (cont.)

```
12.    public void setFirst(String newValue) { first = newValue; }
13.    public String getFirst() { return first; }
14.
15.    public void setLast(String newValue) { last = newValue; }
16.    public String getLast() { return last; }
17. }
```

Listing 5–3 simple/src/java/com/corejsf/TableData.java

```
1. package com.corejsf;
2.
3. public class TableData {
4.    private static final Name[] names = new Name[] {
5.        new Name("William", "Dupont"),
6.        new Name("Anna", "Keeney"),
7.        new Name("Mariko", "Randor"),
8.        new Name("John", "Wilson")
9.    };
10.
11.    public Name[] getNames() { return names;}
12. }
```

Listing 5–4 simple/web/WEB-INF/faces-config.xml

```
1. <?xml version="1.0"?>
2. <faces-config xmlns="http://java.sun.com/xml/ns/javaee"
3.    xmlns:xsi="http://www.w3.org/2001/XMLSchema-instance"
4.    xsi:schemaLocation="http://java.sun.com/xml/ns/javaee
5.        http://java.sun.com/xml/ns/javaee/web-facesconfig_1_2.xsd"
6.    version="1.2">
7.    <application>
8.        <resource-bundle>
9.            <base-name>com.corejsf.messages</base-name>
10.           <var>msgs</var>
11.       </resource-bundle>
12.   </application>
13.
14.   <managed-bean>
15.       <managed-bean-name>tableData</managed-bean-name>
16.       <managed-bean-class>com.corejsf.TableData</managed-bean-class>
17.       <managed-bean-scope>session</managed-bean-scope>
18.   </managed-bean>
19. </faces-config>
```

Listing 5–5   simple/src/java/com/corejsf/messages.properties

1. windowTitle=A Simple Table
2. pageTitle=An array of names:

The table in Figure 5–1 is intentionally vanilla. Throughout this chapter we will see how to add bells and whistles, such as CSS styles and column headers, to tables. But first we take a short tour of h:dataTable attributes.

 CAUTION: h:dataTable data is row oriented—for example, the names in Listing 5–3 correspond to table rows, but the names say nothing about what is stored in each column—it is up to the page author to specify column content. Row-oriented data might be different from what you are used to; Swing table models, for example, keep track of what is in each row *and* column.

h:dataTable *Attributes*

h:dataTable attributes are listed in Table 5–1.

Table 5–1   Attributes for h:dataTable

Attribute	Description
bgcolor	Background color for the table
border	Width of the table's border
captionClass (JSF 1.2)	The CSS class for the table caption
captionStyle (JSF 1.2)	A CSS style for the table caption
cellpadding	Padding around table cells
cellspacing	Spacing between table cells
columnClasses	Comma-separated list of CSS classes for columns
dir	Text direction for text that does not inherit directionality; valid values: LTR (left to right) and RTL (right to left)
first	A zero-relative index of the first row shown in the table
footerClass	CSS class for the table footer

Table 5–1 Attributes for h:dataTable **(cont.)**

Attribute	Description
frame	Specification for sides of the frame surrounding the table; valid values: none, above, below, hsides, vsides, lhs, rhs, box, border
headerClass	CSS class for the table header
rowClasses	Comma-separated list of CSS classes for columns
rows	The number of rows displayed in the table, starting with the row specified with the first attribute; if you set this value to zero, all table rows will be displayed
rules	Specification for lines drawn between cells; valid values: groups, rows, columns, all
summary	Summary of the table's purpose and structure used for nonvisual feedback such as speech
var	The name of the variable created by the data table that represents the current item in the value
binding, id, rendered, styleClass, value	Basic
lang, style, title, width	HTML 4.0
onclick, ondblclick, onkeydown, onkeypress, onkeyup, onmousedown, onmousemove, onmouseout, onmouseover, onmouseup	DHTML events

The binding and id attributes are discussed in "IDs and Bindings" on page 98 of Chapter 4, and rendered attributes are discussed in "An Overview of the JSF HTML Tags" on page 94 of Chapter 4.

h:dataTable also comes with a full complement of DHTML event and HTML 4.0 pass-through attributes. You can read more about those attributes in Chapter 4.

The first attribute specifies a zero-relative index of the first visible row in the table. The value attribute points to the data over which h:dataTable iterates. At the start of each iteration, h:dataTable creates a request-scoped variable that you name with h:dataTable's var attribute. Within the body of the h:dataTable tag, you can reference the current item with that name.

h:column *Attributes*

h:column attributes are listed in Table 5–2.

Table 5–2   Attributes for h:column

Attribute	Description
footerClass (JSF 1.2)	The CSS class for the column's footer
headerClass (JSF 1.2)	The CSS class for the column's header
binding, id, rendered, styleClass, value	Basic

Headers, Footers, and Captions

If you display a list of names as we did in "A Simple Table" on page 173, you need to distinguish last names from first names. You can do that with a column header, as shown in Figure 5–3.

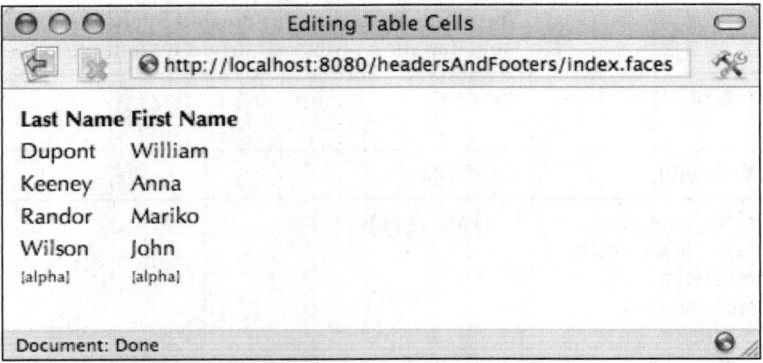

Figure 5–3   Specifying column headers and footers

Besides headers, the table columns in Figure 5–3 also contain footers that indicate the data type of their respective columns; in this case, both columns are [alpha], for alphanumeric.

Column headers and footers are specified with facets, as shown below:

```
<h:dataTable>
    ...
    <h:column headerClass="columnHeader"
            footerClass="columnFooter">
        <f:facet name="header">
```

```
        <%-- header components go here --%>
      </f:facet>

      <%-- column components go here --%>

      <f:facet name="footer">
         <%-- footer components go here --%>
      </f:facet>
   </h:column>
   ...
</h:dataTable>
```

h:dataTable places the components specified for the header and footer facets in the HTML table's header and footer, respectively. Notice that we use the h:column headerClass and footerClass attributes to specify CSS styles for column headers and footers, respectively. Those attributes are new for JSF 1.2.

JSF 1.2 adds table captions to h:dataTable. You add a caption facet to your h:dataTable tag, like this:

```
<h:dataTable ...>
   <f:facet name="caption">
      An array of names:
   </f:facet>
</h:dataTable>
```

If you add this facet to the table shown in Figure 5–3, this is what you will see:

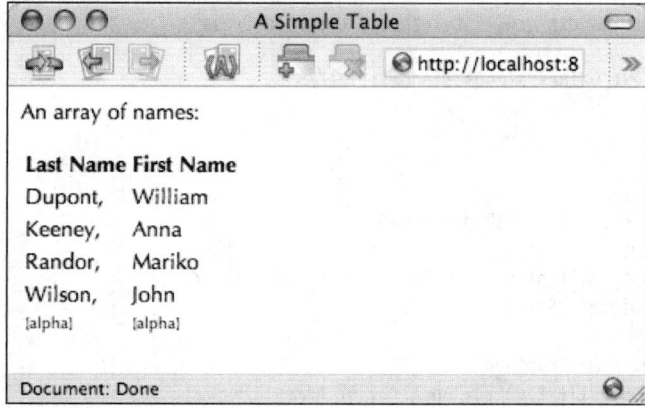

Figure 5–4   A table caption

You can use captionStyle and captionClass to specify a style or CSS class, respectively, for the caption:

```
<h:dataTable ... captionClass="caption">
   <f:facet name="caption">
      An array of names:
   </f:facet>
</h:dataTable>
```

In the preceding code snippet, we used some plain text for the facet, but like any facet, you can specify a JSF component instead.

The full code for the JSF page shown in Figure 5–4 is given in Listing 5–6. The application's resource bundle is shown in Listing 5–7. The directory structure for the application is identical to the one shown in Figure 5–2 on page 173.

You will notice we have used the style attribute for output components to format column headers and footers. See "HTML 4.0 Attributes" on page 101 of Chapter 4 for more information on the style attribute in general, and "Styles" on page 189 for more about CSS style classes and JSF tables.

Listing 5–6   headersAndFooters/web/index.jsp

```
1.  <html>
2.     <%@ taglib uri="http://java.sun.com/jsf/core"  prefix="f" %>
3.     <%@ taglib uri="http://java.sun.com/jsf/html"  prefix="h" %>
4.     <f:view>
5.        <head>
6.           <link href="styles.css" rel="stylesheet" type="text/css"/>
7.           <title>
8.              <h:outputText value="#{msgs.windowTitle}"/>
9.           </title>
10.       </head>
11.       <body>
12.          <h:form>
13.             <h:dataTable value="#{tableData.names}"
14.                var="name"
15.                captionStyle="font-size: 0.95em; font-style:italic"
16.                style="width: 250px;">
17.
18.                <f:facet name="caption">
19.                   <h:outputText value="An array of names:"/>
20.                </f:facet>
21.
22.                <h:column headerClass="columnHeader"
23.                   footerClass="columnFooter">
```

Listing 5–6 headersAndFooters/web/index.jsp (cont.)

```
24.                    <f:facet name="header">
25.                        <h:outputText value="#{msgs.lastnameColumn}"/>
26.                    </f:facet>
27.
28.                    <h:outputText value="#{name.last}"/>
29.
30.                    <f:facet name="footer">
31.                        <h:outputText value="#{msgs.alphanumeric}"/>
32.                    </f:facet>
33.                 </h:column>
34.
35.                 <h:column headerClass="columnHeader"
36.                     footerClass="columnFooter">
37.                    <f:facet name="header">
38.                        <h:outputText value="#{msgs.firstnameColumn}"/>
39.                    </f:facet>
40.
41.                    <h:outputText value="#{name.first}"/>
42.
43.                    <f:facet name="footer">
44.                        <h:outputText value="#{msgs.alphanumeric}"/>
45.                    </f:facet>
46.                 </h:column>
47.              </h:dataTable>
48.           </h:form>
49.        </body>
50.     </f:view>
51. </html>
```

Listing 5–7 headersAndFooters/src/java/corejsf/messages.properties

```
1. windowTitle=Headers, Footers, and Captions
2. lastnameColumn=Last Name
3. firstnameColumn=First Name
4. editColumn=Edit
5. alphanumeric=[alpha]
```

 TIP: To place multiple components in a table header or footer, you must group them in an h:panelGroup tag or place them in a container component with h:panelGrid or h:dataTable. If you place multiple components in a facet, only the first component will be displayed.

JSF Components

To this point, we have used only output components in table columns, but you can place any JSF component in a table cell. Figure 5–5 shows an application that uses a variety of components in a table.

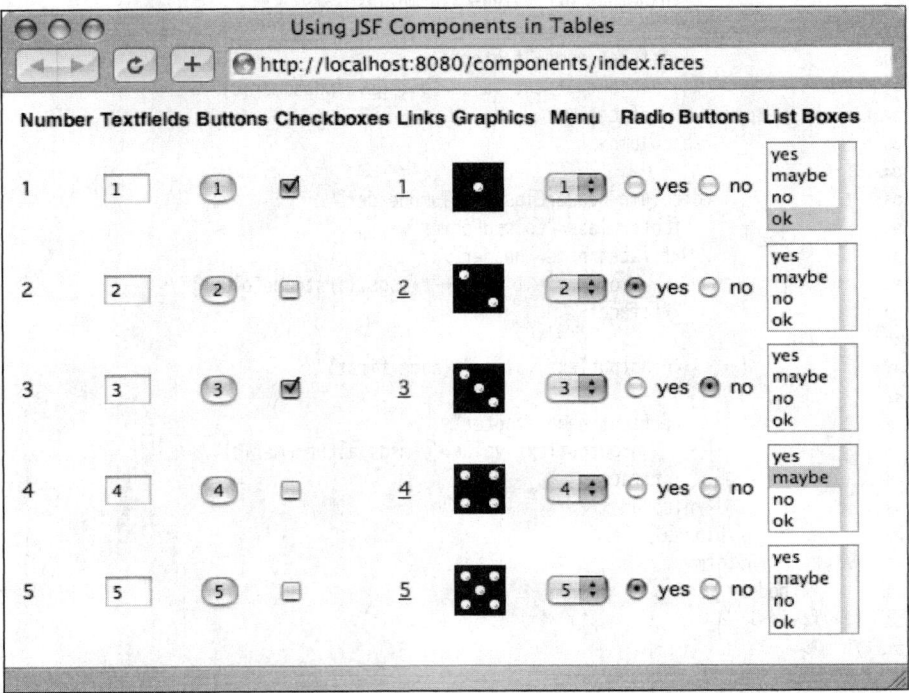

Figure 5–5   JSF components in table cells

h:dataTable iterates over data, so the table shown in Figure 5–5 provides a list of integers for that purpose. We use the current integer to configure components in the "Number", "Textfields", "Buttons", and "Menu" columns.

Components in a table are no different than components outside a table; you can manipulate them in any manner you desire, including conditional rendering with the rendered attribute, handling events, and the like.

The directory structure for the application shown in Figure 5–5 is shown in Figure 5–6. The JSF page, faces configuration file, and property resource bundle are given in Listings 5–8 through 5–10.

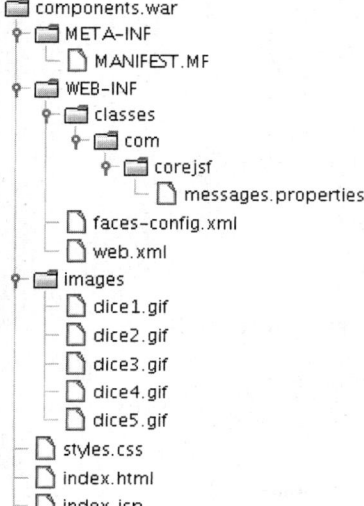

```
components.war
    META-INF
        MANIFEST.MF
    WEB-INF
        classes
            com
                corejsf
                    messages.properties
        faces-config.xml
        web.xml
    images
        dice1.gif
        dice2.gif
        dice3.gif
        dice4.gif
        dice5.gif
    styles.css
    index.html
    index.jsp
```

Figure 5–6   Directory structure for the components example

Listing 5–8 components/web/index.jsp

```jsp
1.  <html>
2.     <%@ taglib uri="http://java.sun.com/jsf/core"  prefix="f" %>
3.     <%@ taglib uri="http://java.sun.com/jsf/html"  prefix="h" %>
4.     <f:view>
5.        <head>
6.           <link href="styles.css" rel="stylesheet" type="text/css"/>
7.           <title>
8.              <h:outputText value="#{msgs.windowTitle}"/>
9.           </title>
10.       </head>
11.       <body style="background: #eee">
12.          <h:form>
13.             <h:dataTable value="#{numberList}" var="number">
14.                <h:column>
15.                   <f:facet name="header">
16.                      <h:outputText value="#{msgs.numberHeader}"/>
17.                   </f:facet>
18.                   <h:outputText value="#{number}"/>
19.                </h:column>
20.                <h:column>
21.                   <f:facet name="header">
22.                      <h:outputText value="#{msgs.textfieldHeader}"/>
23.                   </f:facet>
```

Listing 5–8   components/web/index.jsp (cont.)

```
24.                    <h:inputText value="#{number}" size="3"/>
25.                </h:column>
26.                <h:column>
27.                    <f:facet name="header">
28.                        <h:outputText value="#{msgs.buttonHeader}"/>
29.                    </f:facet>
30.                    <h:commandButton value="#{number}"/>
31.                </h:column>
32.                <h:column>
33.                    <f:facet name="header">
34.                        <h:outputText value="#{msgs.checkboxHeader}"/>
35.                    </f:facet>
36.                    <h:selectBooleanCheckbox value="false"/>
37.                </h:column>
38.                <h:column>
39.                    <f:facet name="header">
40.                        <h:outputText value="#{msgs.linkHeader}"/>
41.                    </f:facet>
42.                    <h:commandLink>
43.                        <h:outputText value="#{number}"/>
44.                    </h:commandLink>
45.                </h:column>
46.                <h:column>
47.                    <f:facet name="header">
48.                        <h:outputText value="#{msgs.graphicHeader}"/>
49.                    </f:facet>
50.                    <h:graphicImage value="images/dice#{number}.gif"
51.                        style="border: 0px"/>
52.                </h:column>
53.                <h:column>
54.                    <f:facet name="header">
55.                        <h:outputText value="#{msgs.menuHeader}"/>
56.                    </f:facet>
57.                    <h:selectOneMenu>
58.                        <f:selectItem itemLabel="#{number}" itemValue="#{number}"/>
59.                    </h:selectOneMenu>
60.                </h:column>
61.                <h:column>
62.                    <f:facet name="header">
63.                        <h:outputText value="#{msgs.radioHeader}"/>
64.                    </f:facet>
65.                    <h:selectOneRadio layout="LINE_DIRECTION" value="nextMonth">
66.                        <f:selectItem itemValue="yes" itemLabel="yes"/>
67.                        <f:selectItem itemValue="no" itemLabel="no" />
68.                    </h:selectOneRadio>
69.                </h:column>
```

Listing 5–8   components/web/index.jsp (cont.)

```
70.                    <h:column>
71.                      <f:facet name="header">
72.                        <h:outputText value="#{msgs.listboxHeader}"/>
73.                      </f:facet>
74.                      <h:selectOneListbox size="3">
75.                        <f:selectItem itemValue="yes" itemLabel="yes"/>
76.                        <f:selectItem itemValue="maybe" itemLabel="maybe"/>
77.                        <f:selectItem itemValue="no" itemLabel="no" />
78.                        <f:selectItem itemValue="ok" itemLabel="ok" />
79.                      </h:selectOneListbox>
80.                    </h:column>
81.                  </h:dataTable>
82.                </h:form>
83.            </body>
84.        </f:view>
85.    </html>
```

Listing 5–9   components/web/WEB-INF/faces-config.xml

```
1.  <?xml version="1.0"?>
2.  <faces-config xmlns="http://java.sun.com/xml/ns/javaee"
3.      xmlns:xsi="http://www.w3.org/2001/XMLSchema-instance"
4.      xsi:schemaLocation="http://java.sun.com/xml/ns/javaee
5.          http://java.sun.com/xml/ns/javaee/web-facesconfig_1_2.xsd"
6.      version="1.2">
7.      <application>
8.          <resource-bundle>
9.              <base-name>com.corejsf.messages</base-name>
10.             <var>msgs</var>
11.         </resource-bundle>
12.     </application>
13.
14.     <managed-bean>
15.         <managed-bean-name>numberList</managed-bean-name>
16.         <managed-bean-class>java.util.ArrayList</managed-bean-class>
17.         <managed-bean-scope>session</managed-bean-scope>
18.         <list-entries>
19.             <value>1</value>
20.             <value>2</value>
21.             <value>3</value>
22.             <value>4</value>
23.             <value>5</value>
24.         </list-entries>
25.     </managed-bean>
26.  </faces-config>
```

Listing 5-10   components/src/java/com/corejsf/messages.properties

```
 1. windowTitle=Using JSF Components in Tables
 2.
 3. numberHeader=Number
 4. textfieldHeader=Textfields
 5. buttonHeader=Buttons
 6. checkboxHeader=Checkboxes
 7. linkHeader=Links
 8. menuHeader=Menu
 9. graphicHeader=Graphics
10. radioHeader=Radio Buttons
11. listboxHeader=List Boxes
```

Editing Table Cells

To edit table cells, you provide an input component for the cell you want to edit. The application shown in Figure 5–7 allows editing of all its cells. You click a checkbox to edit a row and then click the "Save Changes" button to save your changes. From top to bottom, Figure 5–7 shows a cell being edited.

Figure 5–7   Editing table cells

The table cells in Figure 5–7 use an input component when the cell is being edited and an output component when it is not. Here is how that is implemented:

```
...
<h:dataTable value='#{tableData.names}' var='name'>
   <!-- checkbox column -->
   <h:column>
      <f:facet name='header'>
         <h:output_text value='#{msgs.editColumn}'
            style='font-weight: bold'/>
      </f:facet>

      <h:selectBooleanCheckbox value='#{name.editable}'
         onclick='submit()'/>
   </h:column>

   <!-- last name column -->
   <h:column>
      ...
      <h:inputText value='#{name.last}'
         rendered='#{name.editable}'
         size='10'/>

      <h:outputText value='#{name.last}'
         rendered='#{not name.editable}'/>
   </h:column>
   ...
</h:dataTable>
<p>
<h:commandButton value="#{msgs.saveChangesButtonText}"/>
...
```

The preceding code fragment lists only the code for the checkbox and last name columns. The value of the checkbox corresponds to whether the current name is editable; if so, the checkbox is checked. Two components are specified for the last name column: an h:inputText and an h:outputText. If the name is editable, the input component is rendered. If the name is not editable, the output component is rendered.

The full listing for the JSF page shown in Figure 5–7 is given in Listing 5–11. The messages resource bundle for the application is shown in Listing 5–12. The directory structure for the application is the same as the one shown in Figure 5–2 on page 173.

Listing 5–11   editing/web/index.jsp

```
1.  <html>
2.    <%@ taglib uri="http://java.sun.com/jsf/core"  prefix="f" %>
3.    <%@ taglib uri="http://java.sun.com/jsf/html"  prefix="h" %>
4.    <f:view>
5.      <head>
6.        <title>
7.          <h:outputText value="#{msgs.windowTitle}"/>
8.        </title>
9.      </head>
10.     <body>
11.       <h:form>
12.         <h:dataTable value="#{tableData.names}" var="name">
13.           <h:column>
14.             <f:facet name="header">
15.               <h:outputText value="#{msgs.editColumn}"
16.                 style="font-weight: bold"/>
17.             </f:facet>
18.             <h:selectBooleanCheckbox value="#{name.editable}"
19.               onclick="submit()"/>
20.           </h:column>
21.           <h:column>
22.             <f:facet name="header">
23.               <h:outputText value="#{msgs.lastnameColumn}"
24.                 style="font-weight: bold"/>
25.             </f:facet>
26.             <h:inputText value="#{name.last}" rendered="#{name.editable}"
27.               size="10"/>
28.             <h:outputText value="#{name.last}"
29.               rendered="#{not name.editable}"/>
30.           </h:column>
31.           <h:column>
32.             <f:facet name="header">
33.               <h:outputText value="#{msgs.firstnameColumn}"
34.                 style="font-weight: bold"/>
35.             </f:facet>
36.             <h:inputText value="#{name.first}"
37.               rendered="#{name.editable}" size="10"/>
38.             <h:outputText value="#{name.first}"
39.               rendered="#{not name.editable}"/>
40.           </h:column>
41.         </h:dataTable>
42.         <h:commandButton value="#{msgs.saveChangesButtonText}"/>
43.       </h:form>
44.     </body>
45.   </f:view>
46. </html>
```

Listing 5–12 editing/src/java/com/corejsf/messages.properties

```
1. windowTitle=Editing Table Cells
2. lastnameColumn=Last Name
3. firstnameColumn=First Name
4. editColumn=Edit
5. alphanumeric=[alpha]
6. saveChangesButtonText=Save changes
```

 NOTE: Table cell editing, as illustrated in "Editing Table Cells" on page 186, works for all valid types of table data: Java objects, arrays, lists, result sets, and results. However, for database tables, the *result set* associated with a table must be *updatable* for the JSF implementation to update the database.

Styles

h:dataTable has attributes that specify CSS classes for the following:

* The table as a whole (styleClass)
* Column headers and footers (headerClass and footerClass)
* Individual columns (columnClasses)
* Individual rows (rowClasses)

The table shown in Figure 5–8 uses styleClass, headerClass, and columnClasses.

Order Number	Order Date	Customer ID	Amount	Description
1	2002-05-20	1	129.99	Wristwatch
2	2002-05-21	1	19.95	Coffee grinder
3	2002-05-24	1	29.76	Bath towel
4	2002-05-23	1	39.34	Deluxe cheese grater
5	2002-05-22	2	56.75	Champagne glass set
6	2002-05-20	2	28.11	Instamatic camera
7	2002-05-22	2	38.77	Walkman
8	2002-05-21	2	56.76	Coffee maker
9	2002-05-23	2	21.47	Car wax
10	2002-05-21	2	16.8	Tape recorder
11	2002-05-24	2	25.44	Art brush set
12	2002-05-22	3	47.63	Game software

Figure 5–8   Applying styles to columns and headers

NOTE: The `h:dataTable` `rowClasses` and `columnClasses` attributes are mutually exclusive. If you specify both, `columnClasses` has priority.

Styles by Column

Here is how the CSS classes in Figure 5–8 are specified:

```
<link href='styles.css' rel='stylesheet' type='text/css'/>
...
<h:dataTable value="#{order.all}" var="order"
    styleClass="orders"
    headerClass="ordersHeader"
    columnClasses="oddColumn,evenColumn">
```

Those CSS classes are listed below.

```
.orders {
    border: thin solid black;
}
.ordersHeader {
    text-align: center;
    font-style: italic;
    color: Snow;
    background: Teal;
}
.oddColumn {
    height: 25px;
    text-align: center;
    background: MediumTurquoise;
}
.evenColumn {
    text-align: center;
    background: PowderBlue;
}
```

We specified only two column classes, but notice that we have five columns. In this case, `h:dataTable` reuses the column classes, starting with the first. By specifying only the first two column classes, we can set the CSS classes for even and odd columns (1-based counting).

Styles by Row

You can use the `rowClasses` attribute to specify CSS classes by rows instead of columns, as illustrated in Figure 5–9. That data table is implemented like this:

```
<link href='styles.css' rel='stylesheet' type='text/css'/>
...
<h:dataTable value="#{order.all}" var="order"
   styleClass="orders"
   headerClass="ordersHeader"
   rowClasses="oddRow,evenRow">
```

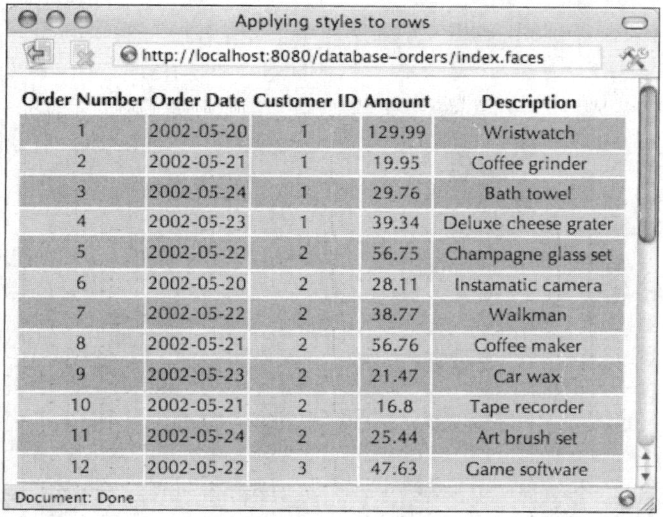

Order Number	Order Date	Customer ID	Amount	Description
1	2002-05-20	1	129.99	Wristwatch
2	2002-05-21	1	19.95	Coffee grinder
3	2002-05-24	1	29.76	Bath towel
4	2002-05-23	1	39.34	Deluxe cheese grater
5	2002-05-22	2	56.75	Champagne glass set
6	2002-05-20	2	28.11	Instamatic camera
7	2002-05-22	2	38.77	Walkman
8	2002-05-21	2	56.76	Coffee maker
9	2002-05-23	2	21.47	Car wax
10	2002-05-21	2	16.8	Tape recorder
11	2002-05-24	2	25.44	Art brush set
12	2002-05-22	3	47.63	Game software

Figure 5–9 Applying styles to rows

Like column classes, `h:dataTable` reuses row classes when the number of classes is less than the number of rows. In the preceding code fragment, we have taken advantage of this feature to specify CSS classes for even and odd rows.

> CAUTION: We use color names, such as PowderBlue and Medium-Turquoise, in our style classes for the sake of illustration. You should prefer the equivalent hex constants because they are portable, whereas color names are not.

Database Tables

Databases store information in tables, so the JSF data table component is a good fit for showing data stored in a database. In this section, we show you how to display the results of a database query.

Figure 5–10 shows a JSF application that displays a database table.

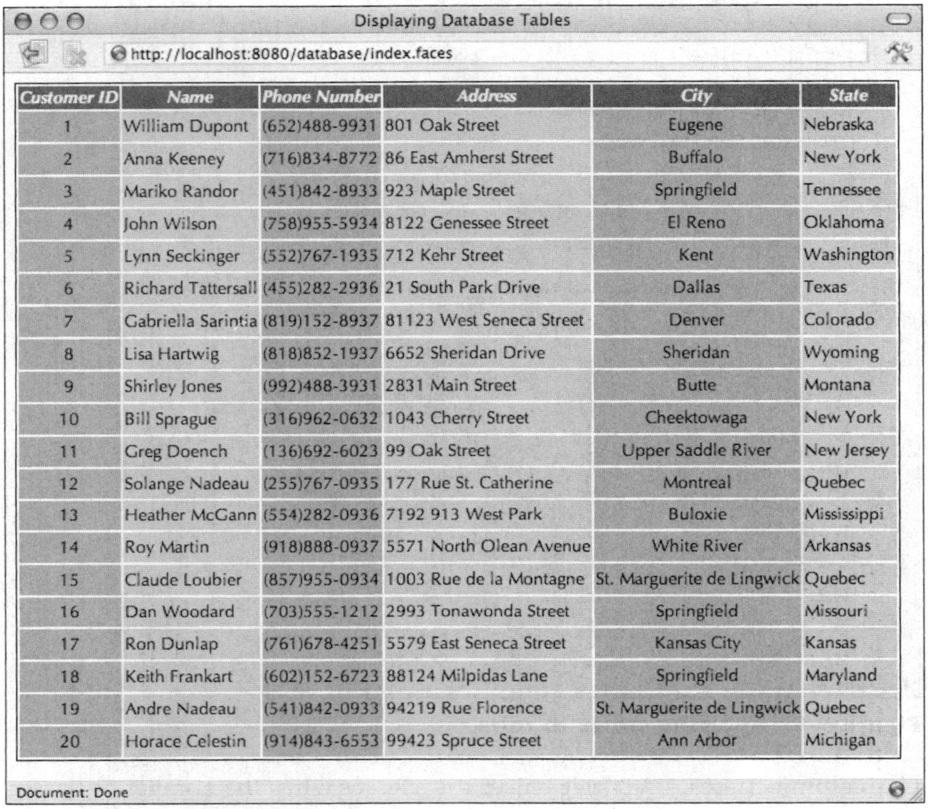

Customer ID	Name	Phone Number	Address	City	State
1	William Dupont	(652)488-9931	801 Oak Street	Eugene	Nebraska
2	Anna Keeney	(716)834-8772	86 East Amherst Street	Buffalo	New York
3	Mariko Randor	(451)842-8933	923 Maple Street	Springfield	Tennessee
4	John Wilson	(758)955-5934	8122 Genessee Street	El Reno	Oklahoma
5	Lynn Seckinger	(552)767-1935	712 Kehr Street	Kent	Washington
6	Richard Tattersall	(455)282-2936	21 South Park Drive	Dallas	Texas
7	Gabriella Sarintia	(819)152-8937	81123 West Seneca Street	Denver	Colorado
8	Lisa Hartwig	(818)852-1937	6652 Sheridan Drive	Sheridan	Wyoming
9	Shirley Jones	(992)488-3931	2831 Main Street	Butte	Montana
10	Bill Sprague	(316)962-0632	1043 Cherry Street	Cheektowaga	New York
11	Greg Doench	(136)692-6023	99 Oak Street	Upper Saddle River	New Jersey
12	Solange Nadeau	(255)767-0935	177 Rue St. Catherine	Montreal	Quebec
13	Heather McGann	(554)282-0936	7192 913 West Park	Buloxie	Mississippi
14	Roy Martin	(918)888-0937	5571 North Olean Avenue	White River	Arkansas
15	Claude Loubier	(857)955-0934	1003 Rue de la Montagne	St. Marguerite de Lingwick	Quebec
16	Dan Woodard	(703)555-1212	2993 Tonawonda Street	Springfield	Missouri
17	Ron Dunlap	(761)678-4251	5579 East Seneca Street	Kansas City	Kansas
18	Keith Frankart	(602)152-6723	88124 Milpidas Lane	Springfield	Maryland
19	Andre Nadeau	(541)842-0933	94219 Rue Florence	St. Marguerite de Lingwick	Quebec
20	Horace Celestin	(914)843-6553	99423 Spruce Street	Ann Arbor	Michigan

Figure 5–10 Displaying database tables

The JSF page shown in Figure 5–10 uses `h:dataTable`, like this:

```
<h:dataTable value="#{customer.all}" var="currentCustomer"
   styleClass="customers"
   headerClass="customersHeader"
   columnClasses="custid,name">
      <h:column>
      <f:facet name="header">
         <h:outputText value="#{msgs.customerIdHeader}"/>
      </f:facet>
      <h:outputText value="#{currentCustomer.Cust_ID}"/>
   </h:column>
```

```
      <h:column>
        <f:facet name="header">
          <h:outputText value="#{msgs.nameHeader}"/>
        </f:facet>
          <h:outputText value="#{currentCustomer.Name}"/>
      </h:column>
      ...
    </h:dataTable>
```

The customer bean is a managed bean that knows how to connect to a database and perform a query of all customers in the database. The CustomerBean.all method performs that query.

The preceding JSF page accesses column data by referencing column names—for example, #{customer.Cust_ID} references the Cust_ID column.

The directory structure for the database example is shown in Figure 5–11. Listings for the application are given in Listing 5–13 through Listing 5–16.

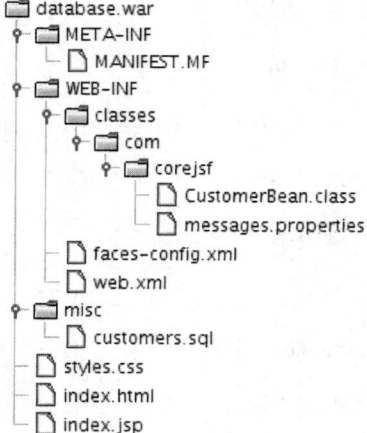

```
📁 database.war
├─📁 META-INF
│  └─📄 MANIFEST.MF
├─📁 WEB-INF
│  ├─📁 classes
│  │  └─📁 com
│  │     └─📁 corejsf
│  │        ├─📄 CustomerBean.class
│  │        └─📄 messages.properties
│  ├─📄 faces-config.xml
│  └─📄 web.xml
├─📁 misc
│  └─📄 customers.sql
├─📄 styles.css
├─📄 index.html
└─📄 index.jsp
```

Figure 5–11   Directory structure for the database example

Listing 5–13   database/web/index.jsp

```
1.  <html>
2.    <%@ taglib uri="http://java.sun.com/jsf/core"  prefix="f" %>
3.    <%@ taglib uri="http://java.sun.com/jsf/html"  prefix="h" %>
4.    <f:view>
5.      <head>
6.        <link href="styles.css" rel="stylesheet" type="text/css"/>
7.        <title>
8.          <h:outputText value="#{msgs.pageTitle}"/>
9.        </title>
10.     </head>
11.     <body>
12.       <h:form>
13.         <h:dataTable value="#{customer.all}" var="customer"
14.           styleClass="customers"
15.           headerClass="customersHeader" columnClasses="custid,name">
16.           <h:column>
17.             <f:facet name="header">
18.               <h:outputText value="#{msgs.customerIdHeader}"/>
19.             </f:facet>
20.             <h:outputText value="#{customer.Cust_ID}"/>
21.           </h:column>
22.           <h:column>
23.             <f:facet name="header">
24.               <h:outputText value="#{msgs.nameHeader}"/>
25.             </f:facet>
26.             <h:outputText value="#{customer.Name}"/>
27.           </h:column>
28.           <h:column>
29.             <f:facet name="header">
30.               <h:outputText value="#{msgs.phoneHeader}"/>
31.             </f:facet>
32.             <h:outputText value="#{customer.Phone_Number}"/>
33.           </h:column>
34.           <h:column>
35.             <f:facet name="header">
36.               <h:outputText value="#{msgs.addressHeader}"/>
37.             </f:facet>
38.             <h:outputText value="#{customer.Street_Address}"/>
39.           </h:column>
40.           <h:column>
41.             <f:facet name="header">
42.               <h:outputText value="#{msgs.cityHeader}"/>
43.             </f:facet>
44.             <h:outputText value="#{customer.City}"/>
45.           </h:column>
```

Listing 5–13	database/web/index.jsp (cont.)

```
46.                 <h:column>
47.                   <f:facet name="header">
48.                     <h:outputText value="#{msgs.stateHeader}"/>
49.                   </f:facet>
50.                   <h:outputText value="#{customer.State}"/>
51.                 </h:column>
52.               </h:dataTable>
53.             </h:form>
54.           </body>
55.         </f:view>
56. </html>
```

Listing 5–14	database/src/java/com/corejsf/CustomerBean.java

```
 1. package com.corejsf;
 2.
 3. import java.sql.Connection;
 4. import java.sql.ResultSet;
 5. import java.sql.SQLException;
 6. import java.sql.Statement;
 7. import javax.naming.Context;
 8. import javax.naming.InitialContext;
 9. import javax.naming.NamingException;
10. import javax.servlet.jsp.jstl.sql.Result;
11. import javax.servlet.jsp.jstl.sql.ResultSupport;
12. import javax.sql.DataSource;
13.
14. public class CustomerBean {
15.    private Connection conn;
16.
17.    public void open() throws SQLException, NamingException {
18.       if (conn != null) return;
19.       Context ctx = new InitialContext();
20.       DataSource ds = (DataSource) ctx.lookup("java:comp/env/jdbc/mydb");
21.       conn = ds.getConnection();
22.    }
23.
24.    public Result getAll() throws SQLException, NamingException {
25.       try {
26.          open();
27.          Statement stmt = conn.createStatement();
28.          ResultSet result = stmt.executeQuery("SELECT * FROM Customers");
29.          return ResultSupport.toResult(result);
```

Listing 5-14 database/src/java/com/corejsf/CustomerBean.java (cont.)

```
30.        } finally {
31.            close();
32.        }
33.    }
34.
35.    public void close() throws SQLException {
36.        if (conn == null) return;
37.        conn.close();
38.        conn = null;
39.    }
40. }
```

Listing 5-15 database/web/WEB-INF/web.xml

```
1. <?xml version="1.0"?>
2. <web-app xmlns="http://java.sun.com/xml/ns/javaee"
3.     xmlns:xsi="http://www.w3.org/2001/XMLSchema-instance"
4.     xsi:schemaLocation="http://java.sun.com/xml/ns/javaee
5.         http://java.sun.com/xml/ns/javaee/web-app_2_5.xsd"
6.     version="2.5">
7.     <servlet>
8.         <servlet-name>Faces Servlet</servlet-name>
9.         <servlet-class>javax.faces.webapp.FacesServlet</servlet-class>
10.        <load-on-startup>1</load-on-startup>
11.    </servlet>
12.
13.    <servlet-mapping>
14.        <servlet-name>Faces Servlet</servlet-name>
15.        <url-pattern>*.faces</url-pattern>
16.    </servlet-mapping>
17.
18.    <welcome-file-list>
19.        <welcome-file>index.html</welcome-file>
20.    </welcome-file-list>
21.
22.    <resource-ref>
23.        <res-ref-name>jdbc/mydb</res-ref-name>
24.        <res-type>javax.sql.DataSource</res-type>
25.        <res-auth>Container</res-auth>
26.    </resource-ref>
27. </web-app>
```

| Listing 5–16 | database/src/java/com/corejsf/messages.properties |

```
1. pageTitle=Displaying Database Tables
2. customerIdHeader=Customer ID
3. nameHeader=Name
4. phoneHeader=Phone Number
5. addressHeader=Address
6. cityHeader=City
7. stateHeader=State
8. refreshFromDB=Read from database
```

JSTL Result Versus Result Sets

The value you specify for h:dataTable can be, among other things, an instance of javax.servlet.jsp.jstl.Result or an instance of java.sql.ResultSet—as was the case in "Database Tables" on page 191. h:dataTable wraps instances of those objects in instances of ResultDataModel and ResultSetDataModel, respectively. So how do the models differ? And which should you prefer?

If you have worked with result sets, you know they are fragile objects that require a good deal of programmatic control. The JSTL Result class is a bean that wraps a result set and implements that programmatic control for you; results are thus easier to deal with than are result sets.

On the other hand, wrapping a result set in a result involves some overhead in creating the Result object; your application may not be able to afford the performance penalty.

In the application discussed in "Database Tables" on page 191, we follow our own advice and return a JSTL Result object from the CustomerBean.all method.

Table Models

When you use a Java object, array, list, result set, or JSTL result object to represent table data, h:dataTable wraps those objects in a model that extends the javax.faces.model.DataModel class. All of those model classes, listed below, reside in the javax.faces.model package:

- ArrayDataModel
- ListDataModel
- ResultDataModel
- ResultSetDataModel
- ScalarDataModel

h:dataTable deals with the models listed above; it never directly accesses the object—array, list, etc.—you specify with the value attribute. You can, however, access those objects yourself with the `DataModel.getWrappedData` method. That method comes in handy for adding and removing table rows.

Editing Table Models

It is easy to add and delete table rows with two methods provided by all data models: `getWrappedData()` and `setWrappedData()`. Now we see how it works with an application, shown in Figure 5–12, that allows users to delete rows from a table.

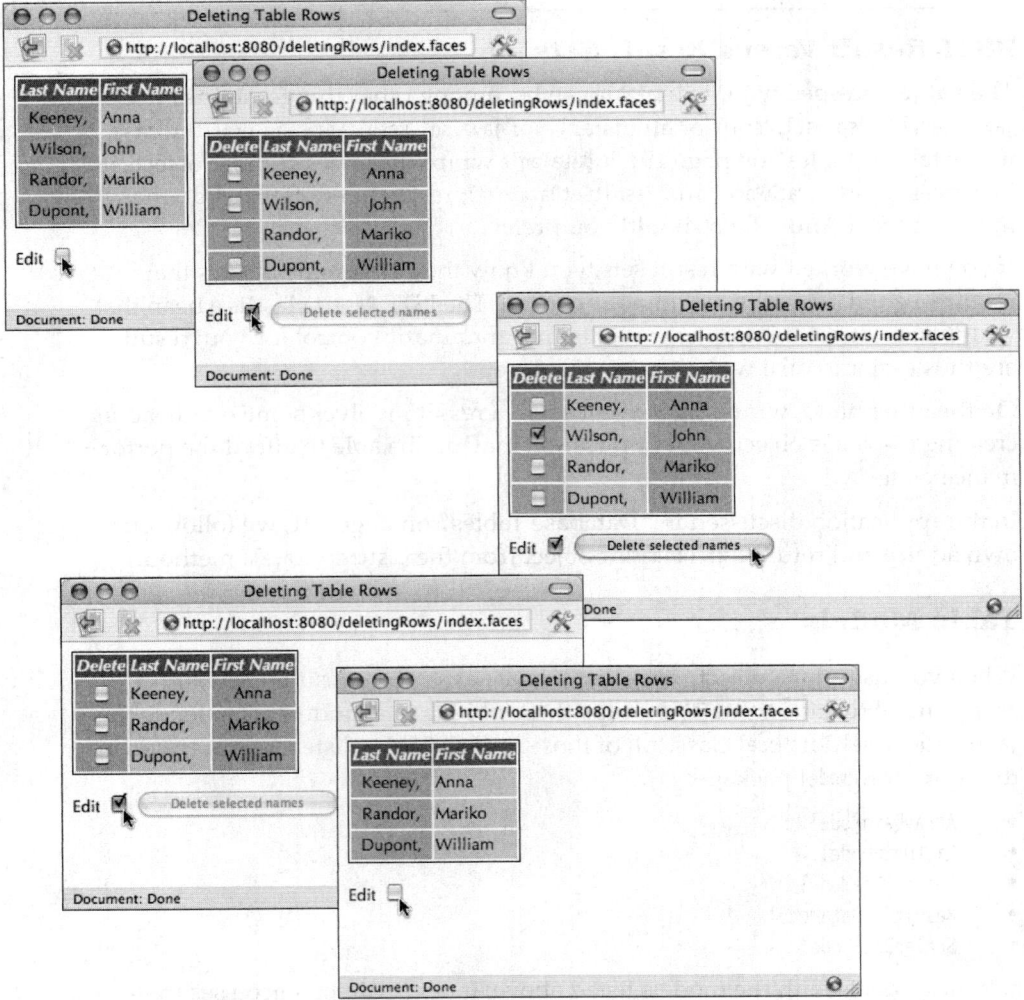

Figure 5–12 Deleting table rows

From top to bottom, Figure 5–12 shows the deletion of a single row. When a
user activates the "Delete selected names" button, the JSF implementation
invokes an action listener method that deletes the selected rows. That method
looks like this:

```
public String deleteNames() {
    if (!getAnyNamesMarkedForDeletion())
        return null;

    Name[] currentNames = (Name[]) model.getWrappedData();
    Name[] newNames = new Name[currentNames.length -
        getNumberOfNamesMarkedForDeletion()];

    int i=0;
    for (Name name : currentNames) {
        if (!name.isMarkedForDeletion()) {
            newNames[i++] = name;
        }
    }
    model.setWrappedData(newNames);
    return null;
    }
}
```

The deleteNames method obtains a reference to the current set of names by calling
the model's getWrappedData method. Then it creates a new array whose size is the
size of the current array, minus the number of names that have been marked
for deletion. Subsequently, the method adds each of the current names to the
new array, leaving out names that were marked for deletion. Finally, the
method calls the model's setWrappedData method to reset the model with the new
array of names.

The JSF implementation invokes the TableData.deleteNames method when the
"Delete selected names" button is activated. The deleteNames method obtains a
reference to the current array of names by invoking the data model's
getWrappedData method. The deleteNames method subsequently creates a new
array—without the names marked for deletion—that it pushes to the model
with the setWrappedData method.

Although the preceding example does not illustrate adding rows, it does
illustrate the principle: Get the current object wrapped by the model with
getWrappedData(), modify it (by adding or deleting rows), and then reset the
wrapped object with setWrappedData().

Figure 5–13 shows the directory structure for the application. Listing 5–17 through
Listing 5–19 list the pertinent files from the application shown in Figure 5–12.

NOTE: Calling the model's setWrappedData() to reset the model's data is one way to delete rows. We could have also reset the model itself, like this:

```
model = new ArrayDataModel(newNames);
```

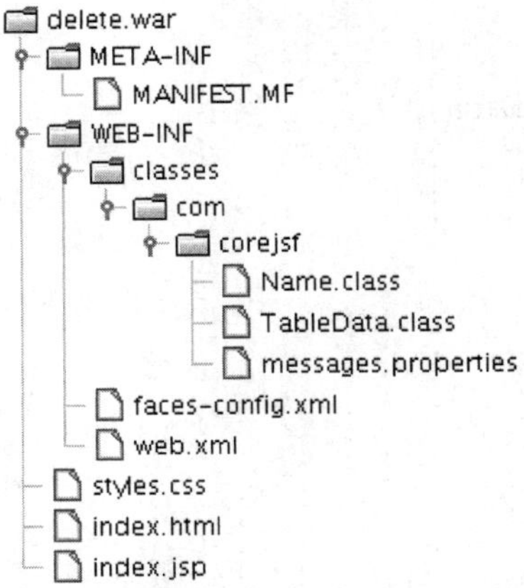

```
delete.war
├── META-INF
│   └── MANIFEST.MF
├── WEB-INF
│   ├── classes
│   │   └── com
│   │       └── corejsf
│   │           ├── Name.class
│   │           ├── TableData.class
│   │           └── messages.properties
│   ├── faces-config.xml
│   └── web.xml
├── styles.css
├── index.html
└── index.jsp
```

Figure 5–13   The directory structure for the delete example

Listing 5–17   delete/web/index.jsp

```
1.  <html>
2.    <%@ taglib uri="http://java.sun.com/jsf/core"  prefix="f" %>
3.    <%@ taglib uri="http://java.sun.com/jsf/html"  prefix="h" %>
4.    <f:view>
5.      <head>
6.        <link href="styles.css" rel="stylesheet" type="text/css"/>
7.        <title>
8.          <h:outputText value="#{msgs.windowTitle}"/>
9.        </title>
10.     </head>
11.     <body>
12.       <h:form>
13.         <h:dataTable value="#{tableData.names}" var="name"
14.           styleClass="names" headerClass="namesHeader"
15.           columnClasses="last,first">
16.           <h:column rendered="#{tableData.editable}">
17.             <f:facet name="header">
18.               <h:outputText value="#{msgs.deleteColumnHeader}"/>
19.             </f:facet>
```

Listing 5–17	delete/web/index.jsp (cont.)

```
20.              <h:selectBooleanCheckbox value="#{name.markedForDeletion}"
21.                 onchange="submit()"/>
22.            </h:column>
23.            <h:column>
24.              <f:facet name="header">
25.                <h:outputText value="#{msgs.lastColumnHeader}"/>
26.              </f:facet>
27.              <h:outputText value="#{name.last},"/>
28.            </h:column>
29.            <h:column>
30.              <f:facet name="header">
31.                <h:outputText value="#{msgs.firstColumnHeader}"/>
32.              </f:facet>
33.              <h:outputText value="#{name.first}"/>
34.            </h:column>
35.          </h:dataTable>
36.          <h:outputText value="#{msgs.editPrompt}"/>
37.          <h:selectBooleanCheckbox onchange="submit()"
38.             value="#{tableData.editable}"/>
39.          <h:commandButton value="#{msgs.deleteButtonText}"
40.             rendered="#{tableData.editable}"
41.             action="#{tableData.deleteNames}"
42.             disabled="#{not tableData.anyNamesMarkedForDeletion}"/>
43.        </h:form>
44.      </body>
45.    </f:view>
46. </html>
```

Listing 5–18	delete/src/java/com/corejsf/Name.java

```
1. package com.corejsf;
2.
3. public class Name {
4.    private String first;
5.    private String last;
6.    private boolean markedForDeletion = false;
7.
8.    public Name(String first, String last) {
9.       this.first = first;
10.      this.last = last;
11.   }
12.
13.   public void setFirst(String newValue) { first = newValue; }
14.   public String getFirst() { return first; }
```

Listing 5–18   delete/src/java/com/corejsf/Name.java (cont.)

```
15.
16.    public void setLast(String newValue) { last = newValue; }
17.    public String getLast() { return last; }
18.
19.    public boolean isMarkedForDeletion() { return markedForDeletion; }
20.    public void setMarkedForDeletion(boolean newValue) {
21.       markedForDeletion = newValue;
22.    }
23. }
```

Listing 5–19   delete/src/java/com/corejsf/TableData.java

```
 1. package com.corejsf;
 2.
 3. import javax.faces.model.DataModel;
 4. import javax.faces.model.ArrayDataModel;
 5.
 6. public class TableData {
 7.    private boolean editable = false;
 8.    private ArrayDataModel model = null;
 9.
10.    private static final Name[] names = {
11.       new Name("Anna", "Keeney"),
12.       new Name("John", "Wilson"),
13.       new Name("Mariko", "Randor"),
14.       new Name("William", "Dupont"),
15.    };
16.
17.    public TableData() { model = new ArrayDataModel(names); }
18.
19.    public DataModel getNames() { return model; }
20.
21.    public boolean isEditable() { return editable; }
22.    public void setEditable(boolean newValue) { editable = newValue; }
23.
24.    public String deleteNames() {
25.       if (!getAnyNamesMarkedForDeletion())
26.          return null;
27.
28.       Name[] currentNames = (Name[]) model.getWrappedData();
29.       Name[] newNames = new Name[currentNames.length
30.          - getNumberOfNamesMarkedForDeletion()];
```

Listing 5–19   delete/src/java/com/corejsf/TableData.java (cont.)

```
31.
32.        for(int i = 0, j = 0; i < currentNames.length; ++i) {
33.            Name name = (Name) currentNames[i];
34.            if (!name.isMarkedForDeletion()) {
35.                newNames[j++] = name;
36.            }
37.        }
38.        model.setWrappedData(newNames);
39.        return null;
40.    }
41.
42.    public int getNumberOfNamesMarkedForDeletion() {
43.        Name[] currentNames = (Name[]) model.getWrappedData();
44.        int cnt = 0;
45.
46.        for(int i = 0; i < currentNames.length; ++i) {
47.            Name name = (Name) currentNames[i];
48.            if (name.isMarkedForDeletion())
49.                ++cnt;
50.        }
51.        return cnt;
52.    }
53.
54.    public boolean getAnyNamesMarkedForDeletion() {
55.        Name[] currentNames = (Name[]) model.getWrappedData();
56.        for(int i = 0; i < currentNames.length; ++i) {
57.            Name name = (Name) currentNames[i];
58.            if (name.isMarkedForDeletion())
59.                return true;
60.        }
61.        return false;
62.    }
63. }
```

We have seen how to perform simple manipulation of a data model. Sometimes, a little more sophistication is required—for example, when you sort or filter a model's data.

Sorting and Filtering

To sort or filter tables with h:dataTable, you need to implement a table model that decorates one of the table models listed on page 197. Figure 5–14 shows what it means to decorate a table model.

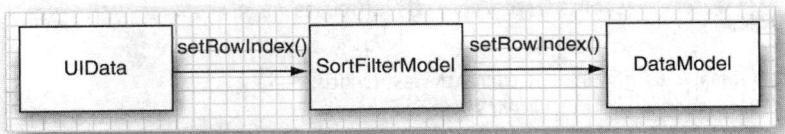

Figure 5–14   Data model filter

Instances of UIData—the component associated with h:dataTable—invoke methods on their model. When you decorate that model, your model intercepts those method calls. Your decorator model forwards method calls to the original model, except for the setRowIndex method, which returns a sorted index instead of the original model's index. Next, we see how that works.

Figure 5–15 shows the application discussed in "Editing Table Cells" on page 186, rewritten to support sortable table columns.

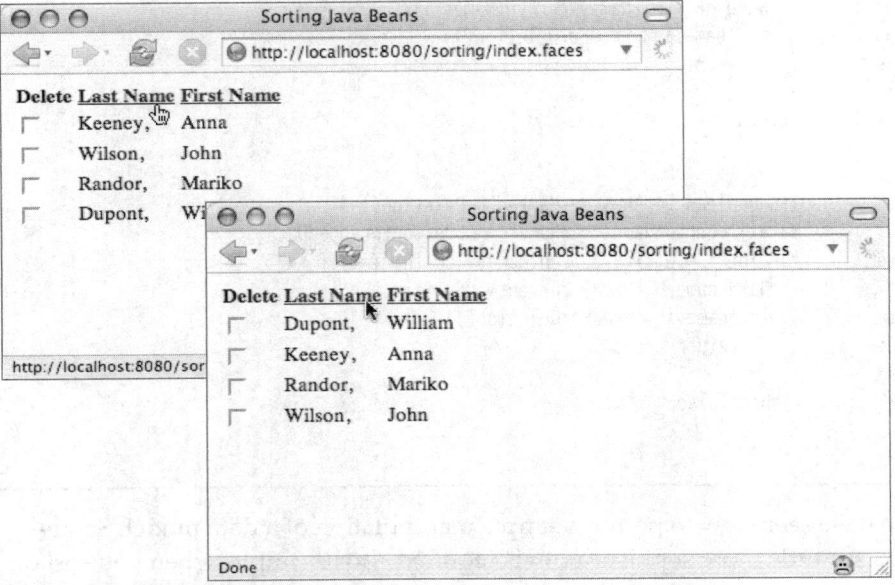

Figure 5–15   Sorting table columns

The application shown in Figure 5–15 sorts table columns by decorating a table data model. First, we specify the h:dataTable's value attribute, like this:

```
<h:dataTable value="#{tableData.names}" var="name" ...>
    ...
```

The TableData.names method returns a data model:

```java
public class TableData {
    private DataModel filterModel= null;
    private static final Name[] names = {
        new Name("Anna", "Keeney"),
        new Name("John", "Wilson"),
        new Name("Mariko", "Randor"),
        new Name("William", "Dupont"),
    };

    public TableData() {
        ArrayDataModel model = new ArrayDataModel(names);
        filterModel = new SortFilterModel(model);
    }
    public DataModel getNames() {
        return filterModel;
    }
}
```

When the tableData object is created, it creates an ArrayDataModel instance, passing it the array of names. That is the *original* model. Then the TableData constructor wraps that model in a *sorting* model. When the getNames method is subsequently called to populate the data table, that method returns the sorting model. The sorting model is implemented like this:

```java
public class SortFilterModel extends DataModel {
    private DataModel model;
    private Row[] rows;
    ...
    public SortFilterModel(DataModel model) {
        this.model = model;
        int rowCnt = model.getRowCount();
        if (rowCnt != -1) {
            rows = new Row[rowCnt];
            for (int i=0; i < rowCnt; ++i) {
            rows[i] = new Row(i);
        }
    }
    public void setRowIndex(int rowIndex) {
        if (rowIndex == -1 || rowIndex >= model.getRowCount()) {
        model.setRowIndex(rowIndex);
    }
    else {
        model.setRowIndex(rows[rowIndex].row);
        }
    }
```

```
        . . .
    }
```

Notice that we create an array of indices that represent sorted indices. We return a sorted index from the setRowIndex method when the indicated index is in range.

So how does the sorting happen? The SortFilterModel class provides two methods, sortByFirst() and sortByLast():

```
    public String sortByLast() {
        Arrays.sort(rows, byLast);
        return null;
    }

    public String sortByFirst() {
        Arrays.sort(rows, byFirst);
        return null;
    }
```

The byLast and byFirst variables are comparators. The former compares last names and the latter compares first names. You can see the implementation of the comparators in Listing 5–21 on page 208.

The directory structure for the sorting example is shown in Figure 5–16. Listing 5–20 through Listing 5–26 provide full listings of the application.

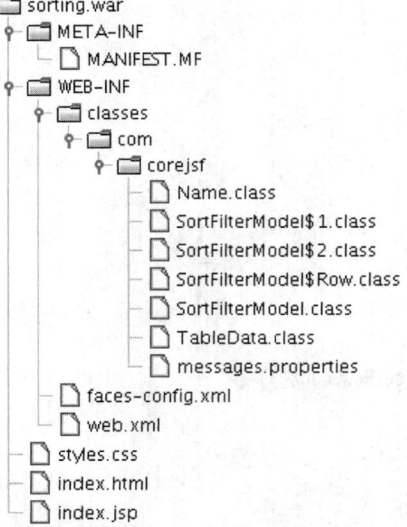

```
📁 sorting.war
├─📁 META-INF
│   └─📄 MANIFEST.MF
├─📁 WEB-INF
│   ├─📁 classes
│   │   └─📁 com
│   │       └─📁 corejsf
│   │           ├─📄 Name.class
│   │           ├─📄 SortFilterModel$1.class
│   │           ├─📄 SortFilterModel$2.class
│   │           ├─📄 SortFilterModel$Row.class
│   │           ├─📄 SortFilterModel.class
│   │           ├─📄 TableData.class
│   │           └─📄 messages.properties
│   ├─📄 faces-config.xml
│   └─📄 web.xml
├─📄 styles.css
├─📄 index.html
└─📄 index.jsp
```

Figure 5–16   The directory structure for the sorting example

NOTE: The JSF 1.2 specification recommends that concrete `DataModel` classes provide at least two constructors: a no-argument constructor that calls `setWrappedData(null)` and a constructor that passes wrapped data to `setWrappedData()`. See Listing 5–21 on page 208 for an example of those constructors.

Listing 5–20 sorting/web/index.jsp

```
1.  <html>
2.    <%@ taglib uri="http://java.sun.com/jsf/core"  prefix="f" %>
3.    <%@ taglib uri="http://java.sun.com/jsf/html"  prefix="h" %>
4.    <f:view>
5.      <head>
6.        <link href="site.css" rel="stylesheet" type="text/css"/>
7.        <title>
8.          <h:outputText value="#{msgs.windowTitle}"/>
9.        </title>
10.     </head>
11.     <body>
12.       <h:form>
13.         <h:dataTable value="#{tableData.names}" var="name"
14.           styleClass="names" headerClass="namesHeader"
15.           columnClasses="last,first">
16.           <h:column>
17.             <f:facet name="header">
18.               <h:outputText value="#{msgs.deleteColumnHeader}"/>
19.             </f:facet>
20.             <h:selectBooleanCheckbox
21.               value="#{name.markedForDeletion}"
22.               onchange="submit()"/>
23.           </h:column>
24.
25.           <h:column>
26.             <f:facet name="header">
27.               <h:commandLink action="#{tableData.names.sortByLast}">
28.                 <h:outputText value="#{msgs.lastColumnHeader}"/>
29.               </h:commandLink>
30.             </f:facet>
31.             <h:outputText value="#{name.last}, "/>
32.           </h:column>
33.           <h:column>
34.             <f:facet name="header">
35.               <h:commandLink action="#{tableData.names.sortByFirst}">
36.                 <h:outputText value="#{msgs.firstColumnHeader}"/>
```

Listing 5–20   sorting/web/index.jsp (cont.)

```
37.                    </h:commandLink>
38.                </f:facet>
39.                <h:outputText value="#{name.first}"/>
40.            </h:column>
41.        </h:dataTable>
42.        <h:commandButton value="#{msgs.deleteButtonText}"
43.            action="#{tableData.deleteNames}"
44.            rendered="#{tableData.anyNamesMarkedForDeletion}"/>
45.        </h:form>
46.    </body>
47.  </f:view>
48. </html>
```

Listing 5–21   sorting/src/java/com/corejsf/SortFilterModel.java

```
1. package com.corejsf;
2.
3. import java.util.Arrays;
4. import java.util.Comparator;
5. import javax.faces.model.DataModel;
6. import javax.faces.model.DataModelEvent;
7. import javax.faces.model.DataModelListener;
8.
9. public class SortFilterModel extends DataModel {
10.    private DataModel model;
11.    private Row[] rows;
12.
13.    private static Comparator<Row> byLast = new
14.        Comparator<Row>() {
15.            public int compare(Row r1, Row r2) {
16.                Name n1 = (Name) r1.getData();
17.                Name n2 = (Name) r2.getData();
18.                return n1.getLast().compareTo(n2.getLast());
19.            }
20.        };
21.
22.    private static Comparator<Row> byFirst = new
23.        Comparator<Row>() {
24.            public int compare(Row r1, Row r2) {
25.                Name n1 = (Name) r1.getData();
26.                Name n2 = (Name) r2.getData();
27.                return n1.getFirst().compareTo(n2.getFirst());
28.            }
29.        };
```

Listing 5–21 sorting/src/java/com/corejsf/SortFilterModel.java (cont.)

```
30.
31.     private class Row {
32.         private int row;
33.         public Row(int row) {
34.             this.row = row;
35.         }
36.         public Object getData() {
37.             int originalIndex = model.getRowIndex();
38.             model.setRowIndex(row);
39.             Object thisRowData = model.getRowData();
40.             model.setRowIndex(originalIndex);
41.             return thisRowData;
42.         }
43.     }
44.
45.     public SortFilterModel() { // mandated by JSF spec
46.         this((Name[])null);
47.     }
48.     public SortFilterModel(Name[] names) { // recommended by JSF spec
49.         setWrappedData(names);
50.     }
51.     public SortFilterModel(DataModel model) {
52.         this.model = model;
53.         initializeRows();
54.     }
55.
56.     public String sortByLast() {
57.         Arrays.sort(rows, byLast);
58.         return null;
59.     }
60.
61.     public String sortByFirst() {
62.         Arrays.sort(rows, byFirst);
63.         return null;
64.     }
65.
66.     public void setRowIndex(int rowIndex) {
67.         if(rowIndex == -1 || rowIndex >= model.getRowCount()) {
68.             model.setRowIndex(rowIndex);
69.         }
70.         else {
71.             model.setRowIndex(rows[rowIndex].row);
72.         }
73.     }
```

Listing 5–21   sorting/src/java/com/corejsf/SortFilterModel.java (cont.)

```
74.
75.    // The following methods delegate directly to the
76.    // decorated model
77.
78.    public boolean isRowAvailable() {
79.        return model.isRowAvailable();
80.    }
81.    public int getRowCount() {
82.        return model.getRowCount();
83.    }
84.    public Object getRowData() {
85.        return model.getRowData();
86.    }
87.    public int getRowIndex() {
88.        return model.getRowIndex();
89.    }
90.    public Object getWrappedData() {
91.        return model.getWrappedData();
92.    }
93.    public void setWrappedData(Object data) {
94.        model.setWrappedData(data);
95.        initializeRows();
96.    }
97.    public void addDataModelListener(DataModelListener listener) {
98.        model.addDataModelListener(listener);
99.    }
100.   public DataModelListener[] getDataModelListeners() {
101.       return model.getDataModelListeners();
102.   }
103.   public void removeDataModelListener(DataModelListener listener) {
104.       model.removeDataModelListener(listener);
105.   }
106.   private void initializeRows() {
107.       int rowCnt = model.getRowCount();
108.       if(rowCnt != -1) {
109.           rows = new Row[rowCnt];
110.           for(int i=0; i < rowCnt; ++i) {
111.               rows[i] = new Row(i);
112.           }
113.       }
114.   }
115. }
```

Listing 5–22　sorting/src/java/com/corejsf/Name.java

```
1. package com.corejsf;
2.
3. public class Name {
4.    private String first;
5.    private String last;
6.    private boolean markedForDeletion = false;
7.
8.    public Name(String first, String last) {
9.       this.first = first;
10.      this.last = last;
11.   }
12.
13.   public void setFirst(String newValue) { first = newValue; }
14.   public String getFirst() { return first; }
15.
16.   public void setLast(String newValue) { last = newValue; }
17.   public String getLast() { return last; }
18.
19.   public boolean isMarkedForDeletion() { return markedForDeletion; }
20.   public void setMarkedForDeletion(boolean newValue) {
21.      markedForDeletion = newValue;
22.   }
23. }
```

Listing 5–23　sorting/src/java/com/corejsf/TableData.java

```
1. package com.corejsf;
2.
3. import javax.faces.model.DataModel;
4. import javax.faces.model.ArrayDataModel;
5.
6. public class TableData {
7.    private DataModel filterModel = null;
8.    private static final Name[] names = {
9.       new Name("Anna", "Keeney"),
10.      new Name("John", "Wilson"),
11.      new Name("Mariko", "Randor"),
12.      new Name("William", "Dupont"),
13.   };
14.
15.   public TableData() {
16.      filterModel = new SortFilterModel(new ArrayDataModel(names));
17.   }
```

Listing 5–23 sorting/src/java/com/corejsf/TableData.java (cont.)

```
18.   public DataModel getNames() {
19.      return filterModel;
20.   }
21.   public String deleteNames() {
22.      if (!getAnyNamesMarkedForDeletion())
23.         return null;
24.
25.      Name[] currentNames = (Name[]) filterModel.getWrappedData();
26.      Name[] newNames = new Name[currentNames.length
27.         - getNumberOfNamesMarkedForDeletion()];
28.
29.      for(int i = 0, j = 0; i < currentNames.length; ++i) {
30.         Name name = (Name) currentNames[i];
31.         if (!name.isMarkedForDeletion()) {
32.            newNames[j++] = name;
33.         }
34.      }
35.      filterModel.setWrappedData(newNames);
36.      return null;
37.   }
38.
39.   public int getNumberOfNamesMarkedForDeletion() {
40.      Name[] currentNames = (Name[]) filterModel.getWrappedData();
41.      int cnt = 0;
42.
43.      for(int i = 0; i < currentNames.length; ++i) {
44.         Name name = (Name) currentNames[i];
45.         if (name.isMarkedForDeletion())
46.            ++cnt;
47.      }
48.      return cnt;
49.   }
50.
51.   public boolean getAnyNamesMarkedForDeletion() {
52.      Name[] currentNames = (Name[]) filterModel.getWrappedData();
53.      for(int i = 0; i < currentNames.length; ++i) {
54.         Name name = (Name) currertNames[i];
55.         if (name.isMarkedForDeletion())
56.            return true;
57.      }
58.      return false;
59.   }
60. }
```

Listing 5–24 sorting/web/WEB-INF/faces-config.xml

```
1. <?xml version="1.0"?>
2. <faces-config xmlns="http://java.sun.com/xml/ns/javaee"
3.    xmlns:xsi="http://www.w3.org/2001/XMLSchema-instance"
4.    xsi:schemaLocation="http://java.sun.com/xml/ns/javaee
5.        http://java.sun.com/xml/ns/javaee/web-facesconfig_1_2.xsd"
6.    version="1.2">
7.    <application>
8.      <resource-bundle>
9.        <base-name>com.corejsf.messages</base-name>
10.       <var>msgs</var>
11.     </resource-bundle>
12.   </application>
13.
14.   <managed-bean>
15.     <managed-bean-name>tableData</managed-bean-name>
16.     <managed-bean-class>com.corejsf.TableData</managed-bean-class>
17.     <managed-bean-scope>session</managed-bean-scope>
18.   </managed-bean>
19. </faces-config>
```

Listing 5–25 sorting/web/styles.css

```
1. .names {
2.    border: thin solid black;
3. }
4. .namesHeader {
5.    text-align: center;
6.    font-style: italic;
7.    color: Snow;
8.    background: Teal;
9. }
10. .last {
11.    height: 25px;
12.    text-align: center;
13.    background: MediumTurquoise;
14. }
15. .first {
16.    text-align: left;
17.    background: PowderBlue;
18. }
19. .caption {
20.    font-size: 0.9em;
21.    font-style: italic;
22. }
```

Listing 5–26   sorting/src/java/com/corejsf/messages.properties

```
1. windowTitle=Sorting Java Beans
2. pageTitle=An array of names:
3. firstColumnHeader=First Name
4. lastColumnHeader=Last Name
5. deleteColumnHeader=Delete
6. deleteButtonText=Delete selected names
```

API   **javax.faces.model.DataModel**

- int getRowCount()

  Returns the total number of rows, if known; otherwise, it returns –1. The ResultSetDataModel always returns –1 from this method.

- Object getRowData()

  Returns the data associated with the current row.

- boolean isRowAvailable()

  Returns true if there is valid data at the current row index.

- int getRowIndex()

  Returns the index of the current row.

- void setRowIndex(int index)

  Sets the current row index and updates the scoped variable representing the current item in the collection (that variable is specified with the var attribute of h:dataTable).

- void addDataModelListener(DataModelListener listener)

  Adds a data model listener that is notified when the row index changes.

- void removeDataModelListener(DataModelListener listener)

  Removes a data model listener.

- void setWrappedData(Object obj)

  Sets the object that a data model wraps.

- Object getWrappedData()

  Returns a data model's wrapped data.

Scrolling Techniques

There are two ways to scroll through tables with lots of rows: with a scrollbar or with some other type of control that moves through the rows. We explore both techniques in this section.

Scrolling with a Scrollbar

Scrolling with a scrollbar is the simplest solution. Wrap your h:dataTable in an HTML div, like this:

```
<div style="overflow:auto; width:100%; height:200px;">
    <h:dataTable...>
        <h:column>
            ...
        </h:column>
        ...
    </h:dataTable>
</div>
```

The application shown in Figure 5–17 is identical to the application discussed in "Database Tables" on page 191, except that the data table is placed in a scrollable div, as shown above.

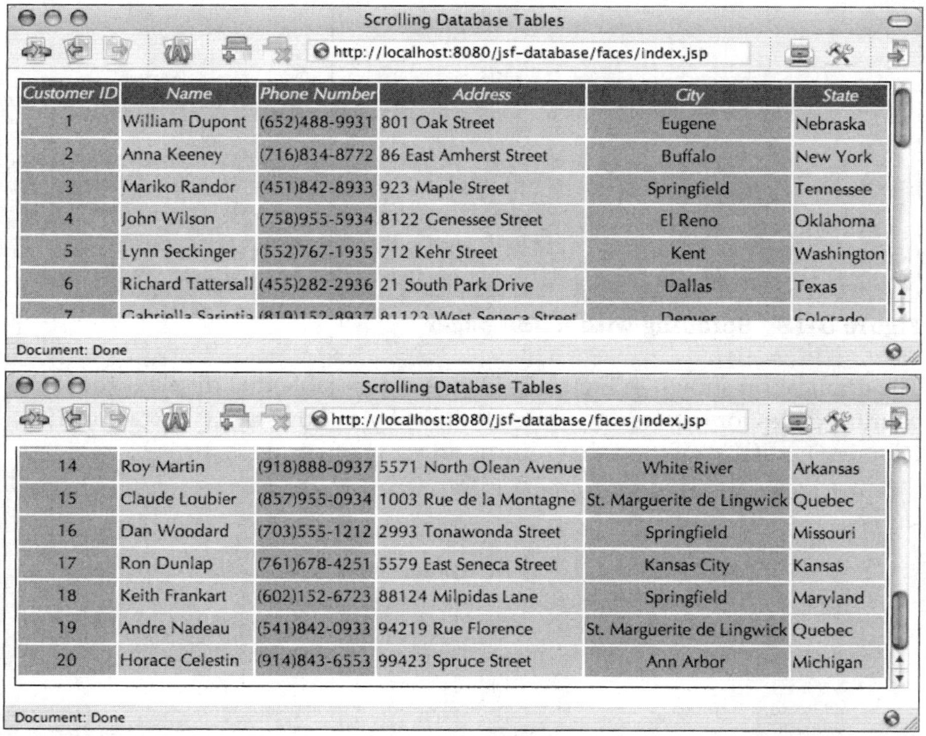

Figure 5–17   Scrolling a table with a scrollable div

Scrollbars are nice from a usability standpoint, but they can be expensive for large tables because all the table data is loaded at once. A less resource-intensive alternative is to scroll through tables with page widgets, an approach that requires only one page of data at a time.

Scrolling with Pager Widgets

Scrolling with pager widgets is more efficient than scrolling with a scrollable DIV, but it is also considerably more complex. In Chapter 13, we show you how to implement a pager widget that you can use with any table created with h:dataTable (see "How do I show a large data set, one page at a time?" on page 638 of Chapter 13). Figure 5–18 shows an example of that pager.

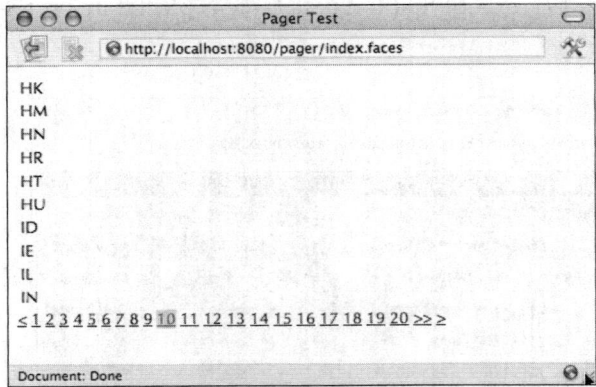

Figure 5–18   Scrolling with a JSF pager

The application shown in Figure 5–18 uses a data table that displays the ISO country codes for locales. We obtain that list by calling java.util.Locale.getISO-Countries(), a static method that returns an array of strings.

CONVERSION AND VALIDATION

Chapter 6

In this chapter, we discuss how form data is converted to Java objects and how the conversion results are checked for correctness. The JSF container carries out these steps before updating the model, so you can rest assured that invalid inputs will never end up in the business logic.

We first look at the concepts behind the conversion and validation process. Then we discuss the standard tags that JSF provides for conversion and validation. These tags suffice for the most common needs. Next, you see how to supply your own conversion and validation code for more complex scenarios.

It is also possible to implement custom tags—reusable converters and validators that can be configured by page authors. However, implementing custom tags requires significantly more programming. The details are covered in "Implementing Custom Converters and Validators" on page 432 of Chapter 9.

Overview of the Conversion and Validation Process

Now we look at user input in slow motion as it travels from the browser form to the beans that make up the business logic.

First, the user fills in a field of a web form. When the user clicks the submit button, the browser sends the form data to the server. We call this value the *request value*.

In the Apply Request Values phase, the request values are stored in component objects. (Recall that each input tag of the JSF page has a corresponding component object.) The value stored in the component object is called the *submitted value*.

Of course, all request values are *strings*—after all, the client browser sends the strings that the user supplies. On the other hand, the web application deals with arbitrary types, such as int, Date, or even more sophisticated types. A *conversion* process transforms the incoming strings to those types. In the next section, we discuss conversion in detail.

The converted values are not immediately transmitted to the beans that make up the business logic. Instead, they are first stored inside the component objects as *local values*. After conversion, the local values are *validated*. Page designers can specify validation conditions—for example, that certain fields should have a minimum or maximum length. We begin our discussion of validation under "Using Standard Validators" on page 233. After all local values have been validated, the Update Model Values phase starts, and the local values are stored in beans, as specified by their value references.

You may wonder why JSF bothers with local values at all. Could not one simply store the request values directly in the model?

JSF uses a two-step approach to make it easier to preserve model integrity. As all programmers know only too well, users enter wrong information with distressing regularity. Suppose some of the model values had been updated before the first user error was detected. The model might then be in an inconsistent state, and it would be tedious to bring it back to its old state.

For that reason, JSF first converts and validates all user input. If errors are found, the page is redisplayed with the values that the user entered so that the user can try again. The Update Model Values phase starts only if all validations are successful.

Figure 6–1 shows the journey of a field value from the browser to the server-side component object and finally to the model bean.

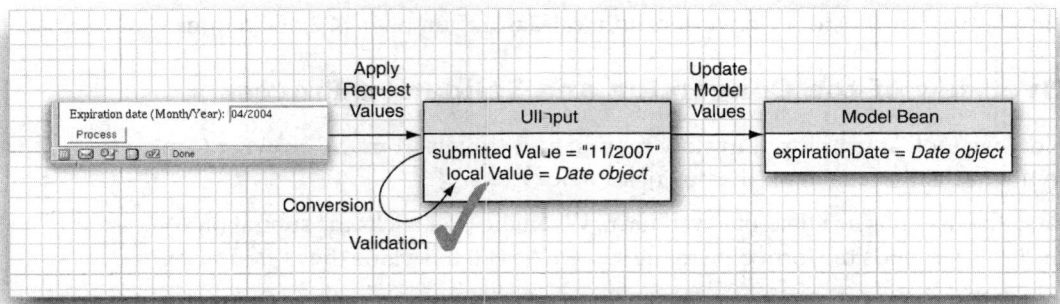

Figure 6–1   A value travels from the browser to the model

Using Standard Converters

In the following sections, we cover the converters and validators that are part of the JSF library. Later in this chapter, you learn how to supply your own validation code if your needs go beyond the basics.

Conversion of Numbers and Dates

A web application stores data of many types, but the web user interface deals exclusively with strings. For example, suppose the user needs to edit a Date object that is stored in the business logic. First, the Date object is converted to a string that is sent to the client browser to be displayed inside a text field. The user then edits the text field. The resulting string is returned to the server and must be converted back to a Date object.

The same situation holds, of course, for primitive types such as int, double, or boolean. The user of the web application edits strings, and the JSF container needs to convert the string to the type required by the application.

To see a typical use of a built-in converter, imagine a web application that is used to process payments (see Figure 6–2). The payment data includes

- The amount to be charged
- The credit card number
- The credit card expiration date

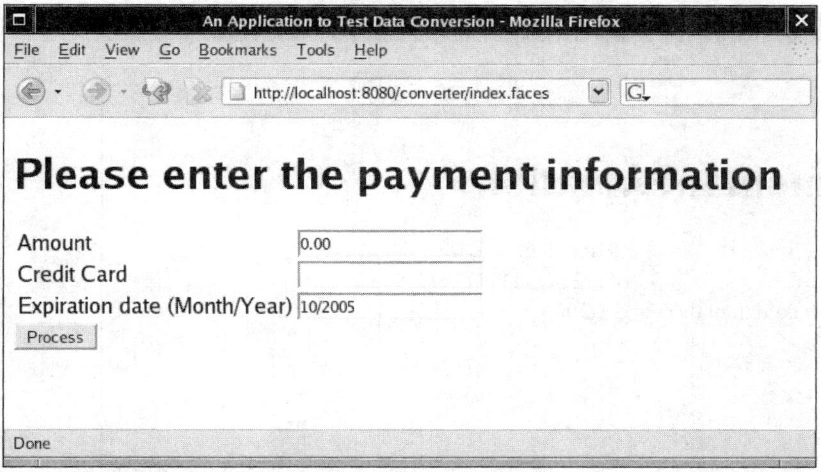

Figure 6–2   Processing payments

We attach a converter to the text field and tell it to format the current value with at least two digits after the decimal point:

```
<h:inputText value="#{payment.amount}">
    <f:convertNumber minFractionDigits="2"/>
</h:inputText>
```

The f:convertNumber converter is one of the standard converters supplied by the JSF implementation.

The second field in this screen does not use a converter. (Later in this chapter, we attach a custom converter.) The third field uses an f:convertDateTime converter whose pattern attribute is set to the string MM/yyyy. (The pattern string format is documented in the API documentation for the java.text.SimpleDateFormat class.)

```
<h:inputText value="#{payment.date}">
    <f:convertDateTime pattern="MM/yyyy"/>
</h:inputText>
```

In the result.jsp page, we show the inputs that the user provided, using a different converter for the payment amount:

```
<h:outputText value="#{payment.amount}">
    <f:convertNumber type="currency"/>
</h:outputText>
```

This converter automatically supplies a currency symbol and decimal separators (see Figure 6–3).

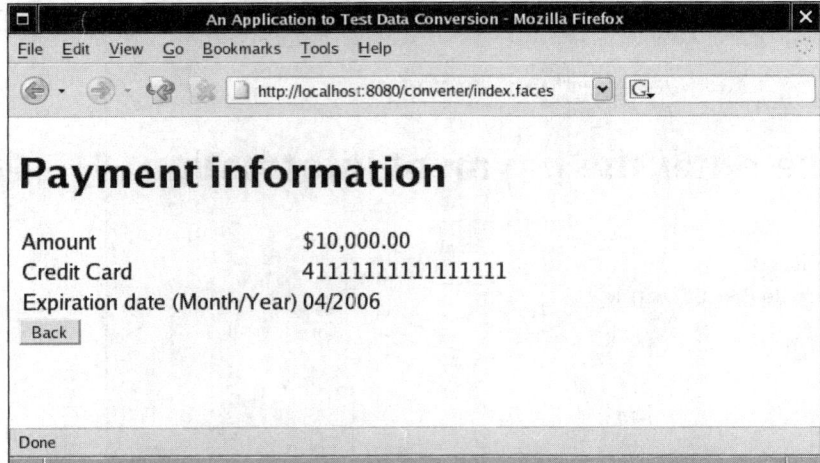

Figure 6–3 Displaying the payment information

Converters and Attributes

Tables 6–1 and 6–2 show the standard converters and their attributes.

 NOTE: If you use a value expression whose type is either a primitive type, or, starting with JSF 1.2, an enumerated type or `BigInteger/BigDecimal`, then you do not need to specify any converter. The JSF implementation automatically picks a standard converter. However, you need to specify an explicit converter for `Date` values.

Table 6–1   Attributes of the `f:convertNumber` **Tag**

Attribute	Type	Value
type	String	number (default), currency, or percent
pattern	String	Formatting pattern, as defined in java.text.DecimalFormat
maxFractionDigits	int	Maximum number of digits in the fractional part
minFractionDigits	int	Minimum number of digits in the fractional part
maxIntegerDigits	int	Maximum number of digits in the integer part
minIntegerDigits	int	Minimum number of digits in the integer part
integerOnly	boolean	True if only the integer part is parsed (default: false)
groupingUsed	boolean	True if grouping separators are used (default: true)
locale	java.util.Locale	Locale whose preferences are to be used for parsing and formatting
currencyCode	String	ISO 4217 currency code to use when converting currency values
currencySymbol	String	Currency symbol to use when converting currency values

Table 6–2   Attributes of the `f:convertDateTime` **Tag**

Attribute	Type	Value
type	String	date (default), time, or both
dateStyle	String	default, short, medium, long, or full
timeStyle	String	default, short, medium, long, or full
pattern	String	Formatting pattern, as defined in java.text.SimpleDateFormat
locale	java.util.Locale	Locale whose preferences are to be used for parsing and formatting
timeZone	java.util.TimeZone	Time zone to use for parsing and formatting

The converter *Attribute*

An alternate syntax for attaching a converter to a component is to add the converter attribute to the component tag. You specify the ID of the converter like this:

```
<h:outputText value="#{payment.date}" converter="javax.faces.DateTime"/>
```

This is equivalent to using `f:convertDateTime` with no attributes:

```
<h:outputText value="#{payment.date}">
   <f:convertDateTime/>
</h:outputText>
```

A third way of specifying the converter would be as follows:

```
<h:outputText value="#{payment.date}">
   <f:converter converterId="javax.faces.DateTime"/>
</h:outputText>
```

All JSF implementations must define a set of converters with predefined IDs:

- `javax.faces.DateTime` (used by `f:convertDateTime`)
- `javax.faces.Number` (used by `f:convertNumber`)
- `javax.faces.Boolean`, `javax.faces.Byte`, `javax.faces.Character`, `javax.faces.Double`, `javax.faces.Float`, `javax.faces.Integer`, `javax.faces.Long`, `javax.faces.Short` (automatically used for primitive types and their wrapper classes)
- `javax.faces.BigDecimal`, `javax.faces.BigInteger` (automatically used for BigDecimal/BigInteger)

Additional converter IDs can be configured in an application configuration file (see "Specifying Converters" on page 243 for details).

CAUTION: When the value of the `converter` attribute is a string, then the value indicates the ID of a converter. However, if it is a value expression, then its value must be a *converter object*—an object of a class that implements the `Converter` interface. That interface is introduced under "Programming with Custom Converters and Validators" on page 240.

 NOTE: As of JSF 1.2, the `f:convertNumber`, `f:convertDateTime`, and `f:converter` tags have an optional `binding` attribute. This allows you to tie a converter instance to a backing bean property of type `javax.faces.convert.Converter`.

Conversion Errors

When a conversion error occurs, the following actions are the result:

- The component whose conversion failed posts a *message* and declares itself invalid. (You will see in the following sections how to display the message.)
- The JSF implementation redisplays the current page immediately after the Process Validations phase has completed. The redisplayed page contains all values that the user provided—no user input is lost.

This behavior is generally desirable. If a user provides an illegal input for, say, a field that requires an integer, then the web application should not try to use that illegal input. The JSF implementation automatically redisplays the current page, giving the user another chance to enter the value correctly.

However, you should avoid overly restrictive conversion options for *input* fields. For example, consider the "Amount" field in our example. Had we used a currency format, then the current value would have been nicely formatted. But suppose a user enters 100 (without a leading $ sign). The currency formatter will complain that the input is not a legal currency value. That is too strict for human use.

To overcome this problem, you can program a custom converter. A custom converter can format a value prettily, yet be lenient when interpreting human input. Custom converters are described later in this chapter under "Programming with Custom Converters and Validators" on page 240.

TIP: When gathering input from the user, you should either use a lenient converter or redesign your form to be more user friendly. For example, rather than forcing users to format the expiration date as MM/yyyy, you can supply two input fields, one for the month and another for the year.

Displaying Error Messages

Of course, it is important that the user be able to see the messages that are caused by conversion and validation errors. You should add h:message tags whenever you use converters and validators.

Normally, you want to show the error messages next to the components that reported them (see Figure 6–4). Give an ID to the component and reference that ID in the h:message tag. As of JSF 1.2, you also need to supply a component label that is displayed in the error message.

```
<h:inputText id="amount" label="#{msgs.amount}" value="#{payment.amount}"/>
<h:message for="amount"/>
```

For JSF 1.1, omit the label attribute.

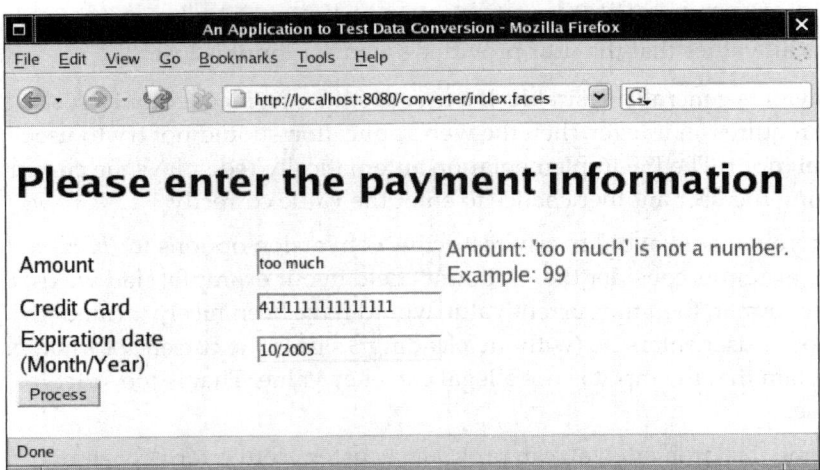

Figure 6–4   Displaying a conversion error message

The h:message tag takes a number of attributes to describe the appearance of the message (see "Messages" on page 157 of Chapter 4 for details). Here, we discuss only the attributes that are of particular interest for error reporting.

A message has two versions: *summary* and *detail*.

For the number converter, the detail error message shows the label of the component, the offending value, and a sample of a correct value, like this:

Amount: 'too much' is not a number. Example: 99

The summary message omits the example.

 NOTE: In JSF 1.1, the converters displayed a generic message "Conversion error occurred."

By default, the h:message tag shows the detail and hides the summary. If you want to show the summary message instead, use these attributes:

```
<h:message for="amount" showSummary="true" showDetail="false"/>
```

 CAUTION: If you use a standard converter, display either the summary message or the detail message, but not both—the messages are nearly identical. You do not want your users to ponder an error message that reads "...is not a number ... is not a number. Example: 99".

 TIP: If you do not use an explicit f:convertNumber converter but instead rely on the standard converters for numeric types, use the summary message and not the detail message. The detail messages give *far too much* detail. For example, the standard converter for double values has this detail message: "... must be a number between 4.9E-324 and 1.7976931348623157E308 Example: 1999999".

Usually, you will want to show error messages in a different color. You use the styleClass or style attribute to change the appearance of the error message:

```
<h:messages styleClass="errorMessage"/>
```

or

```
<h:message for="amount" style="color:red"/>
```

We recommend that you use styleClass and a style sheet instead of a hardcoded style.

Displaying All Error Messages

It is uncommon to have multiple messages for one component, but it can happen. The h:message tag produces only the *first* message. Unfortunately, you do not know whether the first message is the most useful one for the user. While no tag shows all messages for a particular component, you can show a listing of all messages from all components with the h:messages tag.

By default, the h:messages tag shows the message summary instead of the message detail. This behavior is opposite from that of the h:message tag.

For h:messages, you usually want to set the layout attribute to "table" so that the messages are lined up vertically. Otherwise they are concatenated.

```
<h:messages layout="table"/>
```

 TIP: Whenever you create a message, make sure it ends with a period and a space, to ensure a neat appearance when messages are concatenated.

 TIP: The h:messages tag is useful for debugging. Whenever your JSF application stalls at a particular page and is unwilling to move on, add a <h:messages/> tag to see if a failed conversion or validation is the culprit.

 CAUTION: In JSF 1.1, the error messages did not include the message label. That made the h:messages tag far less useful because users were left wondering which of their inputs caused an error.

Using a Custom Error Message

Starting with JSF 1.2, you can provide a custom converter error message for a component. Set the converterMessage attribute of the component whose value is being converted. For example,

```
<h:inputText ... converterMessage="Not a valid number."/>
```

 CAUTION: Unlike the message strings of the next section, these message attributes are taken literally. Placeholders such as {0} are not replaced.

Changing the Text of Standard Error Messages

Sometimes, you may want to change the standard conversion messages for your entire web application. Table 6–3 shows the most useful standard messages. Note that all detail message keys end in _detail. To save space, the table does not list separate summary and detail strings when the summary string is a substring of the detail string. Instead, the additional detail phrase is set in italics. In most messages, {0} is the invalid value, {1} is a sample valid value, and {2} is the component label; however, for the Boolean converter, {1} is the component label.

To replace a standard message, set up a message bundle, as explained in Chapter 2. Add the replacement message, using the appropriate key from Table 6–3.

Suppose you do not want to fuss with input labels or example values when the f:convertNumber converter reports an error. Add the following definition to a message bundle:

```
javax.faces.converter.NumberConverter.NUMBER_detail=''{0}'' is not a number.
```

Then set the base name of the bundle in a configuration file (such as faces-config.xml):

```
<faces-config>
  <application>
    <message-bundle>com.corejsf.messages</message-bundle>
  </application>
  ...
</faces-config>
```

You need only specify the messages that you want to override.

Table 6–3 Standard Conversion Error Messages

Resource ID	Default Text
javax.faces.converter.IntegerConverter. INTEGER	{2}: "{0}" must be a number consisting of one or more digits.
javax.faces.converter.IntegerConverter. INTEGER_detail	{2}: "{0}" must be a number between -2147483648 and 2147483647. Example: {1}
javax.faces.converter.DoubleConverter. DOUBLE	{2}: "{0}" must be a number consisting of one or more digits.
javax.faces.converter.DoubleConverter. DOUBLE_detail	{2}: "{0}" must be a number between 4.9E-324 and 1.7976931348623157E308. Example: {1}
javax.faces.converter.BooleanConverter. BOOLEAN_detail	{1}: "{0}" must be 'true' or 'false'. Any value other than 'true' will evaluate to 'false'.
javax.faces.converter.NumberConverter. NUMBER_detail	{2}: "{0}" is not a number. Example: {1}

Table 6–3 Standard Conversion Error Messages (cont.)

Resource ID	Default Text
javax.faces.converter.NumberConverter.CURRENCY_detail	{2}: "{0}" could not be understood as a currency value. Example: {1}
javax.faces.converter.NumberConverter.PERCENT_detail	{2}: "{0}" could not be understood as a percentage. Example: {1}
javax.faces.converter.DateTimeConverter.DATE_detail	{2}: "{0}" could not be understood as a date. Example: {1}
javax.faces.converter.DateTimeConverter.TIME_detail	{2}: "{0}" could not be understood as a time. Example: {1}
javax.faces.converter.DateTimeConverter.PATTERN_TYPE	{1}: A 'pattern' or 'type' attribute must be specified to convert the value "{0}".
javax.faces.converter.EnumConverter.ENUM	{2}: "{0}" must be convertible to an enum.
javax.faces.converter.EnumConverter.ENUM_detail	{2}: "{0}" must be convertible to an enum from the enum that contains the constant "{1}".
javax.faces.converter.EnumConverter.ENUM_NO_CLASS	{1}: "{0}" must be convertible to an enum from the enum, but no enum class provided.
javax.faces.converter.EnumConverter.ENUM_NO_CLASS_detail	{1}: "{0}" must be convertible to an enum from the enum, but no enum class provided.

 NOTE: In JSF 1.1, the generic message "Conversion error occurred" has key javax.faces.component.UIInput.Conversion.

A Complete Converter Example

We are now ready for our first complete example. Figure 6–5 shows the directory structure of the application. This web application asks the user to supply payment information (Listing 6–1) and then displays the formatted information on a confirmation screen (Listing 6–2). The messages are in Listing 6–3 and the bean class is in Listing 6–4.

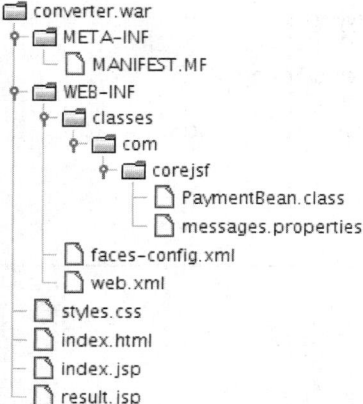

```
converter.war
├── META-INF
│   └── MANIFEST.MF
├── WEB-INF
│   ├── classes
│   │   └── com
│   │       └── corejsf
│   │           ├── PaymentBean.class
│   │           └── messages.properties
│   ├── faces-config.xml
│   └── web.xml
├── styles.css
├── index.html
├── index.jsp
└── result.jsp
```

Figure 6–5   Directory structure of the converter sample

Listing 6–1   converter/web/index.jsp

```jsp
 1. <html>
 2.   <%@ taglib uri="http://java.sun.com/jsf/core" prefix="f" %>
 3.   <%@ taglib uri="http://java.sun.com/jsf/html" prefix="h" %>
 4.   <f:view>
 5.     <head>
 6.       <link href="styles.css" rel="stylesheet" type="text/css"/>
 7.       <title><h:outputText value="#{msgs.title}"/></title>
 8.     </head>
 9.     <body>
10.       <h:form>
11.         <h1><h:outputText value="#{msgs.enterPayment}"/></h1>
12.         <h:panelGrid columns="3">
13.           <h:outputText value="#{msgs.amount}"/>
14.           <h:inputText id="amount" label="#{msgs.amount}"
15.               value="#{payment.amount}">
16.             <f:convertNumber minFractionDigits="2"/>
17.           </h:inputText>
18.           <h:message for="amount" styleClass="errorMessage"/>
19.
20.           <h:outputText value="#{msgs.creditCard}"/>
21.           <h:inputText id="card" label="#{msgs.creditCard}"
22.               value="#{payment.card}"/>
23.           <h:panelGroup/>
24.
```

Listing 6–1   converter/web/index.jsp (cont.)

```
25.              <h:outputText value="#{msgs.expirationDate}"/>
26.              <h:inputText id="date" label="#{msgs.expirationDate}"
27.                  value="#{payment.date}">
28.                <f:convertDateTime pattern="MM/yyyy"/>
29.              </h:inputText>
30.              <h:message for="date" styleClass="errorMessage"/>
31.            </h:panelGrid>
32.            <h:commandButton value="#{msgs.process}" action="process"/>
33.          </h:form>
34.        </body>
35.      </f:view>
36. </html>
```

Listing 6–2   converter/web/result.jsp

```
1. <html>
2.    <%@ taglib uri="http://java.sun.com/jsf/core" prefix="f" %>
3.    <%@ taglib uri="http://java.sun.com/jsf/html" prefix="h" %>
4.    <f:view>
5.      <head>
6.        <link href="styles.css" rel="stylesheet" type="text/css"/>
7.        <title><h:outputText value="#{msgs.title}"/></title>
8.      </head>
9.      <body>
10.       <h:form>
11.         <h1><h:outputText value="#{msgs.paymentInformation}"/></h1>
12.         <h:panelGrid columns="2">
13.           <h:outputText value="#{msgs.amount}"/>
14.           <h:outputText value="#{payment.amount}">
15.             <f:convertNumber type="currency"/>
16.           </h:outputText>
17.
18.           <h:outputText value="#{msgs.creditCard}"/>
19.           <h:outputText value="#{payment.card}"/>
20.
21.           <h:outputText value="#{msgs.expirationDate}"/>
22.           <h:outputText value="#{payment.date}">
23.             <f:convertDateTime pattern="MM/yyyy"/>
24.           </h:outputText>
25.         </h:panelGrid>
26.         <h:commandButton value="Back" action="back"/>
27.       </h:form>
28.     </body>
29.   </f:view>
30. </html>
```

Listing 6–3   converter/src/java/com/corejsf/messages.properties

```
1. title=An Application to Test Data Conversion
2. enterPayment=Please enter the payment information
3. amount=Amount
4. creditCard=Credit Card
5. expirationDate=Expiration date (Month/Year)
6. process=Process
7. paymentInformation=Payment information
```

Listing 6–4   converter/src/java/com/corejsf/PaymentBean.java

```java
1.  package com.corejsf;
2.
3.  import java.util.Date;
4.
5.  public class PaymentBean {
6.     private double amount;
7.     private String card = "";
8.     private Date date = new Date();
9.
10.    // PROPERTY: amount
11.    public void setAmount(double newValue) { amount = newValue; }
12.    public double getAmount() { return amount; }
13.
14.    // PROPERTY: card
15.    public void setCard(String newValue) { card = newValue; }
16.    public String getCard() { return card; }
17.
18.    // PROPERTY: date
19.    public void setDate(Date newValue) { date = newValue; }
20.    public Date getDate() { return date; }
21. }
```

Using Standard Validators

It is difficult to imagine a web application that should not perform a healthy dose of data validation. Since validation is so pervasive, you want it to be easy to use and extend. JSF fits the bill in both respects by providing a handful of standard validators and affording you a simple mechanism for implementing your own validators.

A key role of validation is to protect the model. Because JSF uses separate phases for processing validations and updating model values, you can be assured that the model is not put into an inconsistent state if some of the inputs cannot be validated.

Validating String Lengths and Numeric Ranges

It is easy to use JSF validators within JSF pages—add validator tags to the body of a component tag, like this:

```
<h:inputText id="card" value="#{payment.card}">
   <f:validateLength minimum="13"/>
</h:inputText>
```

The preceding code fragment adds a validator to a text field; when the text field's form is submitted, the validator makes sure that the string contains at least 13 characters. When validation fails (in this case, when the string has 12 or fewer characters), validators generate error messages associated with the guilty component. These messages can later be displayed in a JSF page by the h:message or h:messages tag.

 NOTE: JavaServer Faces 1.x does not explicitly support client-side validation. All validation occurs on the server after the user has submitted the form data. If you want validation to occur inside the browser, you need to supply custom tags that contain the appropriate JavaScript commands. See Chapter 13 for details.

JavaServer Faces has built-in mechanisms that let you carry out the following validations:

- Checking the length of a string
- Checking limits for a numerical value (for example, > 0 or ≤ 100)
- Checking that a value has been supplied

Table 6–4 lists the standard validators that are provided with JSF. You saw the string length validator in the preceding section. To validate numerical input, you use a range validator. For example,

```
<h:inputText id="amount" value="#{payment.amount}">
   <f:validateLongRange minimum="10" maximum="10000"/>
</h:inputText>
```

The validator checks that the supplied value is ≥ 10 and ≤ 10000.

All the standard validator tags have minimum and maximum attributes. You need to supply one or both of these attributes.

Table 6–4   Standard Validators

JSP Tag	Validator Class	Attributes	Validates
f:validateDoubleRange	DoubleRangeValidator	minimum, maximum	A double value within an optional range
f:validateLongRange	LongRangeValidator	minimum, maximum	A long value within an optional range
f:validateLength	LengthValidator	minimum, maximum	A String with a minimum and maximum number of characters

Checking for Required Values

To check that a value is supplied, you do not nest a validator inside the input component tag. Instead, you supply the attribute required="true":

```
<h:inputText id="date" value="#{payment.date}" required="true"/>
```

All JSF input tags support the required attribute. You can combine the required attribute with a nested validator:

```
<h:inputText id="card" value="#{payment.card}" required="true">
   <f:validateLength minimum="13"/>
</h:inputText>
```

 CAUTION: If the required attribute is not set and a user supplies a blank input, then no validation occurs at all! Instead, the blank input is interpreted as a request to leave the existing value unchanged.

An alternate syntax for attaching a validator to a component is to use the f:validator tag. You specify the ID of the validator and the validator parameters like this:

```
<h:inputText id="card" value="#{payment.card}">
   <f:validator validatorId="javax.faces.validator.LengthValidator">
      <f:attribute name="minimum" value="13"/>
   </f:validator>
</h:inputText>
```

Yet another way of specifying the validator is with a `validator` attribute to the component tag (see "Validating with Bean Methods" on page 259).

 NOTE: As of JSF 1.2, the `f:validateLength`, `f:validateLongRange`, `f:validate-DoubleRange`, and `f:validator` tags have an optional `binding` attribute. This allows you to tie a validator instance to a backing bean property of type `javax.faces.validator.Validator`.

Displaying Validation Errors

Validation errors are handled in the same way as conversion errors. A message is added to the component that failed validation, the component is invalidated, and the current page is redisplayed immediately after the Process Validations phase has completed.

You use the `h:message` or `h:messages` tag to display the validation errors. For details, see "Displaying Error Messages" on page 226.

As of JSF 1.2, you can supply a custom message for a component by setting the `requiredMessage` or `validatorMessage` attribute, like this:

```
<h:inputText id="card" value="#{payment.card}" required="true">
    requiredMessage="#{msgs.cardRequired}"
    validatorMessage="#{msgs.cardInvalid}">
  <f:validateLength minimum="13"/>
</h:inputText>
```

You can also globally override the default validator messages shown in Table 6–5. Define a message bundle for your application and supply messages with the appropriate keys, as shown under "Changing the Text of Standard Error Messages" on page 228.

Table 6–5   Standard Validation Error Messages

Resource ID	Default Text	Reported By
`javax.faces.component.` `UIInput.REQUIRED`	{0}: Validation Error: Value is required.	`UIInput` with `required` attribute when value is missing

`javax.faces.validator.`
`DoubleRangeValidator.NOT_IN_RANGE`
`javax.faces.validator.`
`LongRangeValidator.NOT_IN_RANGE`
	{2}: Validation Error:
	Specified attribute is not between the expected values of {0} and {1}.
		`DoubleRangeValidator` and `LongRange-`
		`Validator` when value is out of range and both `minimum` and `maximum` are specified

Table 6–5   Standard Validation Error Messages (cont.)

Resource ID	Default Text	Reported By
javax.faces.validator.DoubleRangeValidator.MAXIMUM javax.faces.validator.LongRangeValidator.MAXIMUM	{1}: Validation Error: Value is greater than allowable maximum of "{0}".	DoubleRangeValidator or LongRangeValidator when value is out of range and only maximum is specified
javax.faces.validator.DoubleRangeValidator.MINIMUM javax.faces.validator.LongRangeValidator.MINIMUM	{1}: Validation Error: Value is less than allowable minimum of "{0}".	DoubleRangeValidator or LongRangeValidator when value is out of range and only minimum is specified
javax.faces.validator.DoubleRangeValidator.TYPE javax.faces.validator.LongRangeValidator.TYPE	{0}: Validation Error: Value is not of the correct type.	DoubleRangeValidator or LongRangeValidator when value cannot be converted to double or long
javax.faces.validator.LengthValidator.MAXIMUM	{1}: Validation Error: Value is greater than allowable maximum of "{0}".	LengthValidator when string length is greater than maximum
javax.faces.validator.LengthValidator.MINIMUM	{1}: Validation Error: Value is less than allowable minimum of "{0}".	LengthValidator when string length is less than minimum

 NOTE: In JSF 1.1, the input label was not included in the validation messages. The key for the "not in range" messages was javax.faces.validator.NOT_IN_RANGE.

Bypassing Validation

As you saw in the preceding examples, validation errors (as well as conversion errors) force a redisplay of the current page. This behavior can be problematic with certain navigation actions. Suppose, for example, you add a "Cancel" button to a page that contains required fields. If the user clicks "Cancel", leaving a required field blank, then the validation mechanism kicks in and forces the current page to be redisplayed.

It would be unreasonable to expect your users to fill in required fields before they are allowed to cancel their input. Fortunately, a bypass mechanism is available. If a command has the immediate attribute set, then the command is executed during the Apply Request Values phase.

Thus, you would implement a "Cancel" button like this:

```
<h:commandButton value="Cancel" action="cancel" immediate="true"/>
```

A Complete Validation Example

The following sample application shows a form that employs all the standard JSF validation checks: required fields, string length, and numeric limits. The application makes sure that values are entered in all fields, the amount is between $10 and $10,000, the credit card number has at least 13 characters, and the PIN is a number between 1000 and 9999. Figure 6–6 shows typical validation error messages. A "Cancel" button is also provided to demonstrate the validation bypass.

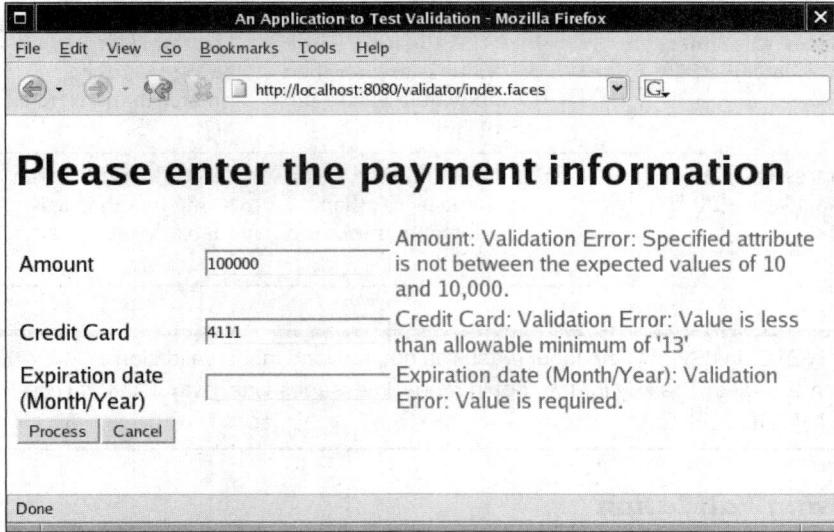

Figure 6–6   Typical validation error messages

Figure 6–7 shows the directory structure of the application. Listing 6–5 contains the JSF page with the validators.

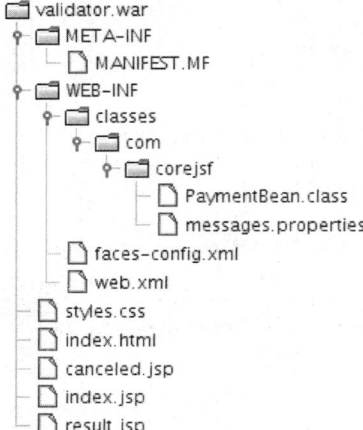

```
validator.war
  META-INF
    MANIFEST.MF
  WEB-INF
    classes
      com
        corejsf
          PaymentBean.class
          messages.properties
    faces-config.xml
    web.xml
  styles.css
  index.html
  canceled.jsp
  index.jsp
  result.jsp
```

Figure 6–7 Directory structure of the validation example

Listing 6–5 validator/web/index.jsp

```
1.  <html>
2.    <%@ taglib uri="http://java.sun.com/jsf/core" prefix="f" %>
3.    <%@ taglib uri="http://java.sun.com/jsf/html" prefix="h" %>
4.    <f:view>
5.      <head>
6.        <link href="styles.css" rel="stylesheet" type="text/css"/>
7.        <title><h:outputText value="#{msgs.title}"/></title>
8.      </head>
9.      <body>
10.       <h:form>
11.         <h1><h:outputText value="#{msgs.enterPayment}"/></h1>
12.         <h:panelGrid columns="3">
13.           <h:outputText value="#{msgs.amount}"/>
14.           <h:inputText id="amount" label="#{msgs.amount}"
15.               value="#{payment.amount}" required="true">
16.             <f:convertNumber minFractionDigits="2"/>
17.             <f:validateDoubleRange minimum="10" maximum="10000"/>
18.           </h:inputText>
19.           <h:message for="amount" styleClass="errorMessage"/>
20.
21.           <h:outputText value="#{msgs.creditCard}"/>
22.           <h:inputText id="card" label="#{msgs.creditCard}"
23.               value="#{payment.card}" required="true">
24.             <f:validateLength minimum="13"/>
25.           <f:attribute name="requiredMessage" value="#{msgs.cardRequired}"/>
26.           </h:inputText>
```

Listing 6–5   validator/web/index.jsp (cont.)

```
27.                <h:message for="card" styleClass="errorMessage"/>
28.
29.                <h:outputText value="#{msgs.expirationDate}"/>
30.                <h:inputText id="date" label="#{msgs.expirationDate}"
31.                   value="#{payment.date}" required="true">
32.                   <f:convertDateTime pattern="MM/yyyy"/>
33.                </h:inputText>
34.                <h:message for="date" styleClass="errorMessage"/>
35.             </h:panelGrid>
36.             <h:commandButton value="Process" action="process"/>
37.             <h:commandButton value="Cancel" action="cancel" immediate="true"/>
38.          </h:form>
39.       </body>
40.    </f:view>
41. </html>
```

Programming with Custom Converters and Validators

JSF standard converters and validators cover a lot of bases, but many web applications must go further. For example, you may need to convert to types other than numbers and dates or perform application-specific validation, such as checking a credit card.

In the following sections, we show you how to implement application-specific converters and validators. These implementations require a moderate amount of programming.

Implementing Custom Converter Classes

A *converter* is a class that converts between strings and objects. A converter must implement the Converter interface, which has the following two methods:

```
Object getAsObject(FacesContext context, UIComponent component, String newValue)
String getAsString(FacesContext context, UIComponent component, Object value)
```

The first method converts a string into an object of the desired type, throwing a ConverterException if the conversion cannot be carried out. This method is called when a string is submitted from the client, typically in a text field. The second method converts an object into a string representation to be displayed in the client interface.

To illustrate these methods, we develop a custom converter for credit card numbers. Our converter allows users to enter a credit card number with or without spaces. That is, we accept inputs of the following forms:

```
1234567890123456
1234 5678 9012 3456
```

Listing 6–6 shows the code for the custom converter. The getAsObject method of the converter strips out all characters that are not digits. It then creates an object of type CreditCard. If an error is found, then we generate a FacesMessage object and throw a ConverterException. We will discuss these steps in the next section, "Reporting Conversion Errors," on page 245.

The getAsString method of our converter makes an effort to format the credit card number in a way that is pleasing to the eye of the user. The digits are separated into the familiar patterns, depending on the credit card type. Table 6–6 shows the most common credit card formats.

Table 6–6 Credit Card Formats

Card Type	Digits	Format
MasterCard	16	5xxx xxxx xxxx xxxx
Visa	16	4xxx xxxx xxxx xxxx
Visa	13	4xxx xxx xxx xxx
Discover	16	6xxx xxxx xxxx xxxx
American Express	15	37xx xxxxxx xxxxx
American Express	22	3xxxxx xxxxxxxx xxxxxxxx
Diners Club, Carte Blanche	14	3xxxx xxxx xxxxx

In this example, the CreditCard class is minor; it contains just the credit card number (see Listing 6–7). We could have left the credit card number as a String object, reducing the converter to a formatter. However, most converters have a target type other than String. To make it easier for you to reuse this example, we use a distinct target type.

Listing 6–6   converter2/src/java/com/coresjf/CreditCardConverter.java

```java
1. package com.corejsf;
2.
3. import javax.faces.application.FacesMessage;
4. import javax.faces.component.UIComponent;
5. import javax.faces.context.FacesContext;
6. import javax.faces.convert.Converter;
7. import javax.faces.convert.ConverterException;
8.
```

Listing 6–6　converter2/src/java/com/coresjf/CreditCardConverter.java (cont.)

```
 9.  public class CreditCardConverter implements Converter {
10.     public Object getAsObject(FacesContext context, UIComponent component,
11.         String newValue) throws ConverterException {
12.        StringBuilder builder = new StringBuilder(newValue);
13.        boolean foundInvalidCharacter = false;
14.        char invalidCharacter = '\0';
15.        int i = 0;
16.        while (i < builder.length() && !foundInvalidCharacter) {
17.           char ch = builder.charAt(i);
18.           if (Character.isDigit(ch))
19.              i++;
20.           else if (Character.isWhitespace(ch))
21.              builder.deleteCharAt(i);
22.           else {
23.              foundInvalidCharacter = true;
24.              invalidCharacter = ch;
25.           }
26.        }
27.
28.        if (foundInvalidCharacter) {
29.           FacesMessage message = com.corejsf.util.Messages.getMessage(
30.              "com.corejsf.messages", "badCreditCardCharacter",
31.              new Object[]{ new Character(invalidCharacter) });
32.           message.setSeverity(FacesMessage.SEVERITY_ERROR);
33.           throw new ConverterException(message);
34.        }
35.
36.        return new CreditCard(builder.toString());
37.     }
38.
39.     public String getAsString(FacesContext context, UIComponent component,
40.         Object value) throws ConverterException {
41.        // length 13: xxxx xxx xxx xxx
42.        // length 14: xxxxx xxxx xxxxx
43.        // length 15: xxxx xxxxxx xxxxx
44.        // length 16: xxxx xxxx xxxx xxxx
45.        // length 22: xxxxxx xxxxxxxx xxxxxxxx
46.        String v = value.toString();
47.        int[] boundaries = null;
48.        int length = v.length();
49.        if (length == 13)
50.           boundaries = new int[]{ 4, 7, 10 };
51.        else if (length == 14)
52.           boundaries = new int[]{ 5, 9 };
```

Listing 6–6 converter2/src/java/com/coresjf/CreditCardConverter.java (cont.)

```
53.     else if (length == 15)
54.         boundaries = new int[]{ 4, 10 };
55.     else if (length == 16)
56.         boundaries = new int[]{ 4, 8, 12 };
57.     else if (length == 22)
58.         boundaries = new int[]{ 6, 14 };
59.     else
60.         return v;
61.     StringBuilder result = new StringBuilder();
62.     int start = 0;
63.     for (int i = 0; i < boundaries.length; i++) {
64.         int end = boundaries[i];
65.         result.append(v.substring(start, end));
66.         result.append(" ");
67.         start = end;
68.     }
69.     result.append(v.substring(start));
70.     return result.toString();
71.     }
72. }
```

Listing 6–7 converter2/src/java/com/corejsf/CreditCard.java

```
1. package com.corejsf;
2.
3. public class CreditCard {
4.     private String number;
5.
6.     public CreditCard(String number) { this.number = number; }
7.     public String toString() { return number; }
8. }
```

Specifying Converters

One mechanism for specifying converters involves a symbolic ID that you register with the JSF application. We will use the ID com.corejsf.CreditCard for our credit card converter. The following entry to faces-config.xml associates the converter ID with the class that implements the converter:

```
<converter>
    <converter-id>com.corejsf.CreditCard</converter-id>
    <converter-class>com.corejsf.CreditCardConverter</converter-class>
</converter>
```

In the following examples, we will assume that the card property of the Payment-Bean has type CreditCard, as shown in Listing 6–13 on page 254. Now we can use the f:converter tag and specify the converter ID:

```
<h:inputText value="#{payment.card}">
  <f:converter converterId="com.corejsf.CreditCard"/>
</h:inputText>
```

Or, more succinctly, we can use the converter attribute:

```
<h:inputText value="#{payment.card}" converter="com.corejsf.CreditCard"/>
```

You can also access a converter without defining it in a configuration file. Use the converter attribute with a value expression that yields the converter object:

```
<h:outputText value="#{payment.card}" converter="#{bb.convert}"/>
```

Here, the bb bean must have a convert property of type Converter.

If you like, you can implement the property getter so that it returns an inner class object:

```
public class BackingBean {
    ...
    public Converter getConvert() {
        return new Converter() {
            public Object getAsObject(FacesContext context, UIComponent component,
                String newValue) throws ConverterException { ... }
            public String getAsString(FacesContext context, UIComponent component,
                Object value) throws ConverterException { ... }
        };
    }
}
```

This approach is convenient because the conversion methods can access the bean's private data.

Alternatively, if you are confident that your converter is appropriate for all conversions between String and CreditCard objects, then you can register it as the default converter for the CreditCard class:

```
<converter>
  <converter-for-class>com.corejsf.CreditCard</converter-for-class>
  <converter-class>com.corejsf.CreditCardConverter</converter-class>
</converter>
```

Now you do not have to mention the converter any longer. It is automatically used whenever a value reference has the type CreditCard. For example, consider the tag

```
<h:inputText value="#{payment.card}"/>
```

When the JSF implementation converts the request value, it notices that the target type is CreditCard, and it locates the converter for that class. This is the ultimate in converter convenience for the page author!

API *javax.faces.convert.Converter*

- Object getAsObject(FacesContext context, UIComponent component, String value)
  Converts the given string value into an object that is appropriate for storage in the given component.

- String getAsString(FacesContext context, UIComponent component, Object value)
  Converts the given object, which is stored in the given component, into a string representation.

Reporting Conversion Errors

When a converter detects an error, it should throw a ConverterException. For example, the getAsObject method of our credit card converter checks whether the credit card contains characters other than digits or separators. If it finds an invalid character, it signals an error:

```
if (foundInvalidCharacter) {
    FacesMessage message = new FacesMessage(
        "Conversion error occurred. ", "Invalid card number. ");
    message.setSeverity(FacesMessage.SEVERITY_ERROR);
    throw new ConverterException(message);
}
```

The FacesMessage object contains the summary and detail messages that can be displayed with message tags.

API **javax.faces.application.FacesMessage**

- FacesMessage(FacesMessage.Severity severity, String summary, String detail)
  Constructs a message with the given severity, summary, and detail. The severity is one of the constants SEVERITY_ERROR, SEVERITY_FATAL, SEVERITY_INFO, or SEVERITY_WARN in the FacesMessage class.

- FacesMessage(String summary, String detail)
  Constructs a message with severity SEVERITY_INFO and the given summary and detail.

- void setSeverity(FacesMessage.Severity severity)
  Sets the severity to the given level. The severity is one of the constants SEVERITY_ERROR, SEVERITY_FATAL, SEVERITY_INFO, or SEVERITY_WARN in the FacesMessage class.

API   `javax.faces.convert.ConverterException`

- `ConverterException(FacesMessage message)`
- `ConverterException(FacesMessage message, Throwable cause)`

  These constructors create exceptions whose getMessage method returns the summary of the given message and whose getFacesMessage method returns the given message.

- `ConverterException()`
- `ConverterException(String detailMessage)`
- `ConverterException(Throwable cause)`
- `ConverterException(String detailMessage, Throwable cause)`

  These constructors create exceptions whose getMessage method returns the given detail message and whose getFacesMessage method returns null.

- `FacesMessage getFacesMessage()`

  Returns the FacesMessage with which this exception object was constructed or returns null if none was supplied.

Getting Error Messages from Resource Bundles

Of course, for proper localization, you will want to retrieve the error messages from a message bundle.

Doing that involves some busywork with locales and class loaders:

1. Get the current locale.

   ```
   FacesContext context = FacesContext.getCurrentInstance();
   UIViewRoot viewRoot = context.getViewRoot();
   Locale locale = viewRoot.getLocale();
   ```

2. Get the current class loader. You need it to locate the resource bundle.

   ```
   ClassLoader loader = Thread.currentThread().getContextClassLoader();
   ```

3. Get the resource bundle with the given name, locale, and class loader.

   ```
   ResourceBundle bundle = ResourceBundle.getBundle(bundleName, locale, loader);
   ```

4. Get the resource string with the given ID from the bundle.

   ```
   String resource = bundle.getString(resourceId);
   ```

However, there are several wrinkles in the process. We actually need two message strings: one for the summary and one for the detail messages. By convention, the resource ID of a detail message is obtained by addition of the string _detail to the summary key. For example,

```
badCreditCardCharacter=Invalid card number.
badCreditCardCharacter_detail=The card number contains invalid characters.
```

Moreover, converters are usually part of a reusable library. It is a good idea to allow a specific application to override messages. (You saw in "Changing the Text of Standard Error Messages" on page 228 how to override the standard converter messages.) Therefore, you should first attempt to locate the messages in the application-specific message bundle before retrieving the default messages.

Recall that an application can supply a bundle name in a configuration file, such as

```
<faces-config>
   <application>
      <message-bundle>com.mycompany.myapp.messages</message-bundle>
   </application>
   ...
</faces-config>
```

The following code snippet retrieves that bundle name:

```
Application app = context.getApplication();
String appBundleName = app.getResourceBundle();
```

Look up your resources in this bundle before going to the library default.

Finally, you may want some messages to provide detailed information about the nature of the error. For example, you want to tell the user which character in the credit card number was objectionable. Message strings can contain place-holders {0}, {1}, and so on—for example:

```
The card number contains the invalid character {0}.
```

The java.text.MessageFormat class can substitute values for the placeholders:

```
Object[] params = ...;
MessageFormat formatter = new MessageFormat(resource, locale);
String message = formatter.format(params);
```

Here, the params array contains the values that should be substituted. (For more information about the MessageFormat class, see Horstmann and Cornell, 2004, 2005. *Core Java™ 2*, vol. 2, chap. 10.)

Ideally, much of this busywork should have been handled by the JSF framework. Of course, you can find the relevant code in the innards of the reference implementation, but the framework designers chose not to make it available to JSF programmers.

We provide the package com.corejsf.util with convenience classes that implement these missing pieces. Feel free to use these classes in your own code.

The com.corejsf.util.Messages class has a static method, getMessage, that returns a FacesMessage with a given bundle name, resource ID, and parameters:

```
FacesMessage message
    = com.corejsf.util.Messages.getMessage(
        "com.corejsf.messages", "badCreditCardCharacter",
        new Object[] { new Character(invalidCharacter) });
```

You can pass null for the parameter array if the message does not contain placeholders.

Our implementation follows the JSF convention of displaying missing resources as ???*resourceId*???. See Listing 6–8 for the source code.

NOTE: If you prefer to reuse the standard JSF message for conversion errors, call

```
FacesMessage message = com.corejsf.util.Messages.getMessage(
    "javax.faces.Messages",
    "javax.faces.component.UIInput.CONVERSION",
    null);
```

---

javax.faces.context.FacesContext

- static FacesContext getCurrentInstance()
  Gets the context for the request that is being handled by the current thread, or null if the current thread does not handle a request.

- UIViewRoot getViewRoot()
  Gets the root component for the request described by this context.

javax.faces.component.UIViewRoot

- Locale getLocale()
  Gets the locale for rendering this view.

Listing 6–8 converter2/src/java/com/corejsf/util/Messages.java

```
1. package com.corejsf.util;
2.
3. import java.text.MessageFormat;
4. import java.util.Locale;
5. import java.util.MissingResourceException;
6. import java.util.ResourceBundle;
7. import javax.faces.application.Application;
```

Listing 6–8   converter2/src/java/com/corejsf/util/Messages.java (cont.)

```
 8. import javax.faces.application.FacesMessage;
 9. import javax.faces.component.UIViewRoot;
10. import javax.faces.context.FacesContext;
11.
12. public class Messages {
13.    public static FacesMessage getMessage(String bundleName, String resourceId,
14.       Object[] params) {
15.       FacesContext context = FacesContext.getCurrentInstance();
16.       Application app = context.getApplication();
17.       String appBundle = app.getMessageBundle();
18.       Locale locale = getLocale(context);
19.       ClassLoader loader = getClassLoader();
20.       String summary = getString(appBundle, bundleName, resourceId,
21.          locale, loader, params);
22.       if (summary == null) summary = "???" + resourceId + "???";
23.       String detail = getString(appBundle, bundleName, resourceId + "_detail",
24.          locale, loader, params);
25.       return new FacesMessage(summary, detail);
26.    }
27.
28.    public static String getString(String bundle, String resourceId,
29.          Object[] params) {
30.       FacesContext context = FacesContext.getCurrentInstance();
31.       Application app = context.getApplication();
32.       String appBundle = app.getMessageBundle();
33.       Locale locale = getLocale(context);
34.       ClassLoader loader = getClassLoader();
35.       return getString(appBundle, bundle, resourceId, locale, loader, params);
36.    }
37.
38.    public static String getString(String bundle1, String bundle2,
39.          String resourceId, Locale locale, ClassLoader loader,
40.          Object[] params) {
41.       String resource = null;
42.       ResourceBundle bundle;
43.
44.       if (bundle1 != null) {
45.          bundle = ResourceBundle.getBundle(bundle1, locale, loader);
46.          if (bundle != null)
47.             try {
48.                resource = bundle.getString(resourceId);
49.             } catch (MissingResourceException ex) {
50.             }
51.       }
52.
```

Listing 6–8	converter2/src/java/com/corejsf/util/Messages.java (cont.)

```
53.         if (resource == null) {
54.             bundle = ResourceBundle.getBundle(bundle2, locale, loader);
55.             if (bundle != null)
56.                 try {
57.                     resource = bundle.getString(resourceId);
58.                 } catch (MissingResourceException ex) {
59.                 }
60.         }
61.
62.         if (resource == null) return null; // no match
63.         if (params == null) return resource;
64.
65.         MessageFormat formatter = new MessageFormat(resource, locale);
66.         return formatter.format(params);
67.     }
68.
69.     public static Locale getLocale(FacesContext context) {
70.         Locale locale = null;
71.         UIViewRoot viewRoot = context.getViewRoot();
72.         if (viewRoot != null) locale = viewRoot.getLocale();
73.         if (locale == null) locale = Locale.getDefault();
74.         return locale;
75.     }
76.
77.     public static ClassLoader getClassLoader() {
78.         ClassLoader loader = Thread.currentThread().getContextClassLoader();
79.         if (loader == null) loader = ClassLoader.getSystemClassLoader();
80.         return loader;
81.     }
82. }
```

The Custom Converter Sample Application

Here are the remaining pieces of our next sample application. Figure 6–8 shows the directory structure. Listings 6–9 and 6–10 show the input and result pages. Look at the inputText and outputText tags for the credit card numbers to see the two styles of specifying a custom converter. (Both converter specifications could have been omitted if the converter had been registered to be the default for the CreditCard type.)

The custom converter is defined in the faces-config.xml file (Listing 6–11). The messages.properties file (shown in Listing 6–12) contains the error message for the credit card converter. Finally, Listing 6–13 shows the payment bean with three properties of type double, Date, and CreditCard.

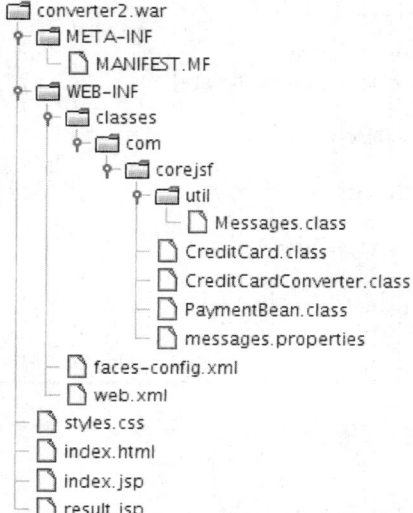

Figure 6–8   Directory structure of the custom converter example

Listing 6–9	converter2/web/index.jsp

```
1.  <html>
2.     <%@ taglib uri="http://java.sun.com/jsf/core" prefix="f" %>
3.     <%@ taglib uri="http://java.sun.com/jsf/html" prefix="h" %>
4.     <f:view>
5.        <head>
6.           <link href="styles.css" rel="stylesheet" type="text/css"/>
7.           <title><h:outputText value="#{msgs.title}"/></title>
8.        </head>
9.        <body>
10.          <h:form>
11.             <h1><h:outputText value="#{msgs.enterPayment}"/></h1>
12.             <h:panelGrid columns="3">
13.                <h:outputText value="#{msgs.amount}"/>
14.                <h:inputText id="amount" label="#{msgs.amount}"
15.                      value="#{payment.amount}">
16.                   <f:convertNumber minFractionDigits="2"/>
17.                </h:inputText>
18.                <h:message for="amount" styleClass="errorMessage"/>
19.
20.                <h:outputText value="#{msgs.creditCard}"/>
21.                <h:inputText id="card" label="#{msgs.creditCard}"
22.                      value="#{payment.card}">
23.                   <f:converter converterId="com.corejsf.CreditCard"/>
24.                </h:inputText>
25.                <h:message for="card" styleClass="errorMessage"/>
26.
```

Listing 6–9   converter2/web/index.jsp (cont.)

```
27.                    <h:outputText value="#{msgs.expirationDate}"/>
28.                    <h:inputText id="date" label="#{msgs.expirationDate}"
29.                        value="#{payment.date}">
30.                      <f:convertDateTime pattern="MM/yyyy"/>
31.                    </h:inputText>
32.                    <h:message for="date" styleClass="errorMessage"/>
33.                  </h:panelGrid>
34.                  <h:commandButton value="Process" action="process"/>
35.                </h:form>
36.              </body>
37.            </f:view>
38.          </html>
```

Listing 6–10   converter2/web/result.jsp

```
 1. <html>
 2.    <%@ taglib uri="http://java.sun.com/jsf/core" prefix="f" %>
 3.    <%@ taglib uri="http://java.sun.com/jsf/html" prefix="h" %>
 4.    <f:view>
 5.      <head>
 6.        <link href="styles.css" rel="stylesheet" type="text/css"/>
 7.        <title><h:outputText value="#{msgs.title}"/></title>
 8.      </head>
 9.      <body>
10.        <h:form>
11.          <h1><h:outputText value="#{msgs.paymentInformation}"/></h1>
12.          <h:panelGrid columns="2">
13.            <h:outputText value="#{msgs.amount}"/>
14.            <h:outputText value="#{payment.amount}">
15.              <f:convertNumber type="currency"/>
16.            </h:outputText>
17.
18.            <h:outputText value="#{msgs.creditCard}"/>
19.            <h:outputText value="#{payment.card}"
20.              converter="com.corejsf.CreditCard"/>
21.
22.            <h:outputText value="#{msgs.expirationDate}"/>
23.            <h:outputText value="#{payment.date}">
24.              <f:convertDateTime pattern="MM/yyyy"/>
25.            </h:outputText>
26.          </h:panelGrid>
27.          <h:commandButton value="Back" action="back"/>
28.        </h:form>
29.      </body>
30.    </f:view>
31. </html>
```

Listing 6–11 converter2/web/WEB-INF/faces-config.xml

```
1. <?xml version="1.0"?>
2. <faces-config xmlns="http://java.sun.com/xml/ns/javaee"
3.    xmlns:xsi="http://www.w3.org/2001/XMLSchema-instance"
4.    xsi:schemaLocation="http://java.sun.com/xml/ns/javaee
5.        http://java.sun.com/xml/ns/javaee/web-facesconfig_1_2.xsd"
6.    version="1.2">
7.    <application>
8.       <message-bundle>com.corejsf.messages</message-bundle>
9.    </application>
10.
11.    <navigation-rule>
12.       <from-view-id>/index.jsp</from-view-id>
13.       <navigation-case>
14.          <from-outcome>process</from-outcome>
15.          <to-view-id>/result.jsp</to-view-id>
16.       </navigation-case>
17.    </navigation-rule>
18.
19.    <navigation-rule>
20.       <from-view-id>/result.jsp</from-view-id>
21.       <navigation-case>
22.          <from-outcome>back</from-outcome>
23.          <to-view-id>/index.jsp</to-view-id>
24.       </navigation-case>
25.    </navigation-rule>
26.
27.    <converter>
28.       <converter-id>com.corejsf.CreditCard</converter-id>
29.       <converter-class>com.corejsf.CreditCardConverter</converter-class>
30.    </converter>
31.
32.    <managed-bean>
33.       <managed-bean-name>payment</managed-bean-name>
34.       <managed-bean-class>com.corejsf.PaymentBean</managed-bean-class>
35.       <managed-bean-scope>session</managed-bean-scope>
36.    </managed-bean>
37.
38.    <application>
39.       <resource-bundle>
40.          <base-name>com.corejsf.messages</base-name>
41.          <var>msgs</var>
42.       </resource-bundle>
43.    </application>
44. </faces-config>
```

Listing 6–12   converter2/src/java/com/corejsf/messages.properties

```
1. badCreditCardCharacter=Invalid card number.
2. badCreditCardCharacter_detail=The card number contains the invalid character {0}.
3. title=An Application to Test Data Conversion
4. enterPayment=Please enter the payment information
5. amount=Amount
6. creditCard=Credit Card
7. expirationDate=Expiration date (Month/Year)
8. process=Process
9. paymentInformation=Payment information
```

Listing 6–13   converter2/src/java/com/corejsf/PaymentBean.java

```
1. package com.corejsf;
2. import java.util.Date;
3.
4. public class PaymentBean {
5.     private double amount;
6.     private CreditCard card = new CreditCard("");
7.     private Date date = new Date();
8.
9.     // PROPERTY: amount
10.    public void setAmount(double newValue) { amount = newValue; }
11.    public double getAmount() { return amount; }
12.
13.    // PROPERTY: card
14.    public void setCard(CreditCard newValue) { card = newValue; }
15.    public CreditCard getCard() { return card; }
16.
17.    // PROPERTY: date
18.    public void setDate(Date newValue) { date = newValue; }
19.    public Date getDate() { return date; }
20. }
```

Implementing Custom Validator Classes

Implementing custom validator classes is a two-step process, similar to the process you saw in the preceding section:

1.   Implement a validator by implementing the javax.faces.validator.Validator interface.

2.   Register your validator in a configuration file (such as faces-config.xml).

The Validator interface defines only one method:

```
void validate(FacesContext context, UIComponent component, Object value)
```

If validation fails, generate a FacesMessage that describes the error, construct a ValidatorException from the message, and throw it:

```
if (validation fails) {
    FacesMessage message = ...;
    message.setSeverity(FacesMessage.SEVERITY_ERROR);
    throw new ValidatorException(message);
}
```

The process is analogous to the reporting of conversion errors, except that you throw a ValidatorException instead of a ConverterException.

For example, Listing 6–14 shows a validator that checks the digits of a credit card, using the Luhn formula. Figure 6–9 shows the application at work. As described under "Getting Error Messages from Resource Bundles" on page 246, we use the convenience class com.corejsf.util.Messages to locate the message strings in a resource bundle.

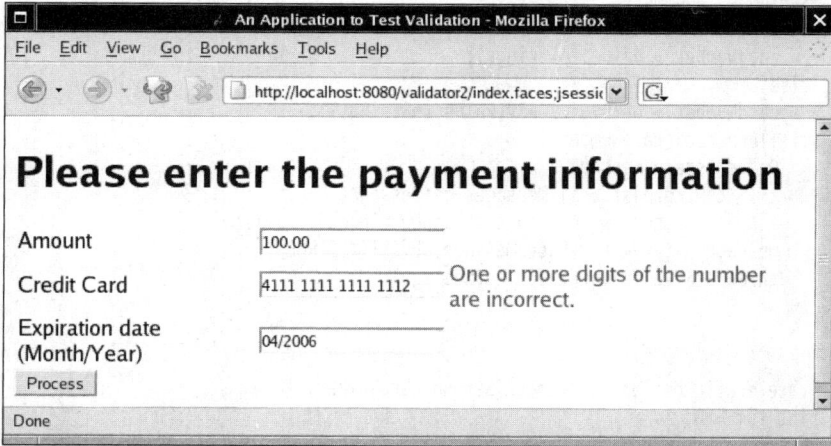

Figure 6–9   Luhn check failed

 NOTE: The Luhn formula—developed by a group of mathematicians in the late 1960s—verifies and generates credit card numbers, as well as Social Insurance numbers for the Canadian government. The formula can detect whether a digit is entered wrongly or whether two digits were transposed. See the web site http://www.merriampark.com/anatomycc.htm for more information about the Luhn formula. For debugging, it is handy to know that the number 4111 1111 1111 1111 passes the Luhn check.

API   *javax.faces.validator.Validator*

- void validate(FacesContext context, UIComponent component, Object value)

  Validates the component to which this validator is attached. If there is a validation error, throw a ValidatorException.

Listing 6–14   validator2/src/java/com/corejsf/CreditCardValidator.java

```java
 1. package com.corejsf;
 2.
 3. import javax.faces.application.FacesMessage;
 4. import javax.faces.component.UIComponent;
 5. import javax.faces.context.FacesContext;
 6. import javax.faces.validator.Validator;
 7. import javax.faces.validator.ValidatorException;
 8.
 9. public class CreditCardValidator implements Validator {
10.    public void validate(FacesContext context, UIComponent component,
11.          Object value) {
12.       if(value == null) return;
13.       String cardNumber;
14.       if (value instanceof CreditCard)
15.          cardNumber = value.toString();
16.       else
17.          cardNumber = getDigitsOnly(value.toString());
18.       if(!luhnCheck(cardNumber)) {
19.          FacesMessage message
20.             = com.corejsf.util.Messages.getMessage(
21.                "com.corejsf.messages", "badLuhnCheck", null);
22.          message.setSeverity(FacesMessage.SEVERITY_ERROR);
23.          throw new ValidatorException(message);
24.       }
25.    }
26.
27.    private static boolean luhnCheck(String cardNumber) {
28.       int sum = 0;
29.
30.       for(int i = cardNumber.length() - 1; i >= 0; i -= 2) {
31.          sum += Integer.parseInt(cardNumber.substring(i, i + 1));
32.          if(i > 0) {
33.             int d = 2 * Integer.parseInt(cardNumber.substring(i - 1, i));
34.             if(d > 9) d -= 9;
35.             sum += d;
36.          }
37.       }
38.
39.       return sum % 10 == 0;
40.    }
```

| Listing 6–14 | validator2/src/java/com/corejsf/CreditCardValidator.java (cont.) |

```
41.
42.    private static String getDigitsOnly(String s) {
43.        StringBuilder digitsOnly = new StringBuilder ();
44.        char c;
45.        for(int i = 0; i < s.length (); i++) {
46.            c = s.charAt (i);
47.            if (Character.isDigit(c)) {
48.                digitsOnly.append(c);
49.            }
50.        }
51.        return digitsOnly.toString ();
52.    }
53. }
```

Registering Custom Validators

Now that we have created a validator, we need to register it in a configuration file (such as faces-config.xml), like this:

```
<validator>
    <validator-id>com.corejsf.CreditCard</validator-id>
    <validator-class>com.corejsf.CreditCardValidator</validator-class>
</validator>
```

You can use custom validators with the f:validator tag—for example, the following code fragment uses the credit card validator discussed above:

```
<h:inputText id="card" value="#{payment.card}" required="true">
    <f:converter converterId="com.corejsf.CreditCard"/>
    <f:validator validatorId="com.corejsf.CreditCard"/>
</h:inputText>
```

The validatorId specified for f:validator must correspond to a validator ID specified in the configuration file. The f:validator tag uses the validator ID to look up the corresponding class, creates an instance of that class if necessary, and invokes its validate method.

NOTE: JSF uses separate name spaces for converter and validator IDs. Thus, it is okay to have both a converter and a validator with the ID com.corejsf.CreditCard.

NOTE: JSF registers its three standard validators with IDs javax.faces.LongRange, javax.faces.DoubleRange, and javax.faces.Length.

The remainder of the sample application is straightforward. Figure 6–10 shows the directory structure, and Listing 6–15 contains the JSF page.

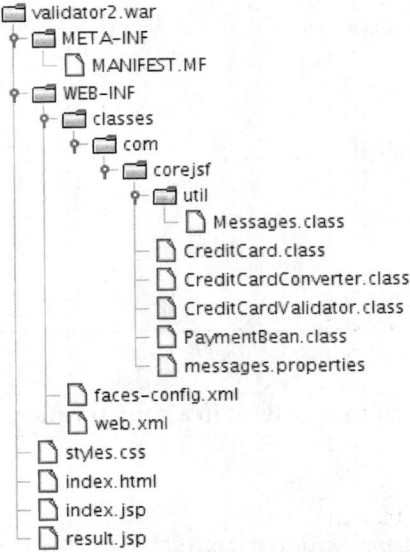

Figure 6–10   **The directory structure of the Luhn check example**

Listing 6–15   validator2/web/index.jsp

```
1.  <html>
2.    <%@ taglib uri="http://java.sun.com/jsf/core" prefix="f" %>
3.    <%@ taglib uri="http://java.sun.com/jsf/html" prefix="h" %>
4.    <f:view>
5.      <head>
6.        <link href="styles.css" rel="stylesheet" type="text/css"/>
7.        <title><h:outputText value="#{msgs.title}"/></title>
8.      </head>
9.      <body>
10.       <h:form>
11.         <h1><h:outputText value="#{msgs.enterPayment}"/></h1>
12.         <h:panelGrid columns="3">
13.           <h:outputText value="#{msgs.amount}"/>
14.           <h:inputText id="amount" label="#{msgs.amount}"
15.               value="#{payment.amount}">
16.             <f:convertNumber minFractionDigits="2"/>
17.           </h:inputText>
18.           <h:message for="amount" styleClass="errorMessage"/>
```

Listing 6–15	`validator2/web/index.jsp (cont.)`

```
19.
20.              <h:outputText value="#{msgs.creditCard}"/>
21.              <h:inputText id="card" label="#{msgs.creditCard}"
22.                   value="#{payment.card}" required="true">
23.                <f:converter converterId="com.corejsf.CreditCard"/>
24.                <f:validator validatorId="com.corejsf.CreditCard"/>
25.              </h:inputText>
26.              <h:message for="card" styleClass="errorMessage"/>
27.
28.              <h:outputText value="#{msgs.expirationDate}"/>
29.              <h:inputText id="date" label="#{msgs.expirationDate}"
30.                   value="#{payment.date}">
31.                <f:convertDateTime pattern="MM/yyyy"/>
32.              </h:inputText>
33.              <h:message for="date" styleClass="errorMessage"/>
34.            </h:panelGrid>
35.            <h:commandButton value="Process" action="process"/>
36.          </h:form>
37.        </body>
38.      </f:view>
39. </html>
```

The f:validator tag is useful for simple validators that do not have parameters, such as the credit validator discussed above. If you need a validator with properties that can be specified in a JSF page, you should implement a custom tag for your validator. You will see how to do that in "Implementing Custom Converters and Validators" on page 432 of Chapter 9.

Validating with Bean Methods

In the preceding section, you saw how to implement a validation class. However, you can also add the validation method to an existing class and invoke it through a method expression, like this:

```
<h:inputText id="card" value="#{payment.card}"
   required="true" validator="#{payment.luhnCheck}"/>
```

The payment bean must then have a method with the exact same signature as the validate method of the Validator interface:

```
public class PaymentBean {
    ...
    public void luhnCheck(FacesContext context, UIComponent component, Object value) {
        ... // same code as in the preceding example
    }
}
```

Why would you want to do this? There is one major advantage. The validation method can access other instance fields of the class. You will see an example in the next section, "Supplying Attributes to Converters."

On the downside, this approach makes it more difficult to move a validator to a new web application, so you would probably only use it for application-specific scenarios.

 CAUTION: The value of the `validator` attribute is a *method expression*, whereas the seemingly similar `converter` attribute specifies a *converter ID* (if it is a string) or a *converter object* (if it is a value expression). As Emerson said, "A foolish consistency is the hobgoblin of little minds."

Supplying Attributes to Converters

Every JSF component can store arbitrary attributes. You can set an attribute of the component to which you attach a converter; use the `f:attribute` tag. Your converter can then retrieve the attribute from its component. Here is how that technique would work to set the separator string for the credit card converter.

When attaching the converter, also nest an `f:attribute` tag inside the component:

```
<h:outputText value="#{payment.card}">
    <f:converter converterId="CreditCard"/>
    <f:attribute name="separator" value="-"/>
</h:outputText>
```

In the converter, retrieve the attribute as follows:

```
separator = (String) component.getAttributes().get("separator");
```

In Chapter 9, you will see a more elegant mechanism for passing attributes to a converter—writing your own converter tag.

   `javax.faces.component.UIComponent`

- `Map getAttributes()`
  Returns a mutable map of all attributes and properties of this component.

Validating Relationships Between Multiple Components

The validation mechanism in JSF was designed to validate a *single* component. However, in practice, you often need to ensure that related components have reasonable values before letting the values propagate into the model. For example, as we noted earlier, it is not a good idea to ask users to enter a date into a single text field. Instead, you would use three different text fields, for the day, month, and year, as in Figure 6–11.

Figure 6–11   Validating a relationship involving three components

If the user enters an illegal date, such as February 30, you would want to show a validation error and prevent the illegal data from entering the model.

The trick is to attach the validator to the last of the components. By the time its validator is called, the preceding components have passed validation and had their local values set. The last component has passed conversion, and the converted value is passed as the Object parameter of the validation method.

Of course, you need to have access to the other components. You can easily achieve that access by using a backing bean that contains all components of the current form (see Listing 6–16). Attach the validation method to the backing bean:

```
public class BackingBean {
    private UIInput dayInput;
    private UIInput monthInput;
    ...
    public void validateDate(FacesContext context, UIComponent component,
        Object value) {
        int d = ((Integer) dayInput.getLocalValue()).intValue();
        int m = ((Integer) monthInput.getLocalValue()).intValue();
        int y = ((Integer) value).intValue();

        if (!isValidDate(d, m, y)) {
            FacesMessage message = ...;
```

```
            throw new ValidatorException(message);
        }
    }
    ...
}
```

Note that the value lookup is a bit asymmetric. The last component does not yet have the local value set because it has not passed validation.

Figure 6–12 shows the application's directory structure. Listing 6–17 shows the JSF page. Note the converter property of the last input field. Also note the use of the binding attributes that bind the input components to the backing bean.

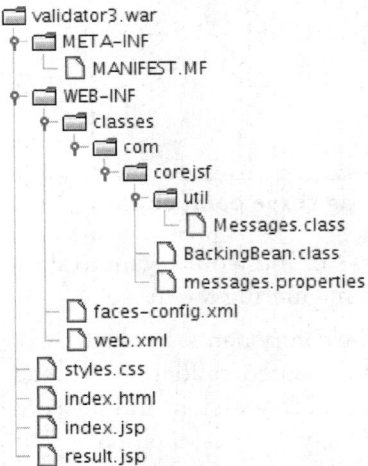

Figure 6–12   Directory structure of the date validation example

Listing 6–16   validator3/src/java/com/corejsf/BackingBean.java

```java
 1. package com.corejsf;
 2.
 3. import javax.faces.application.FacesMessage;
 4. import javax.faces.component.UIComponent;
 5. import javax.faces.component.UIInput;
 6. import javax.faces.context.FacesContext;
 7. import javax.faces.validator.ValidatorException;
 8.
 9. public class BackingBean {
10.    private int day;
11.    private int month;
12.    private int year;
13.    private UIInput dayInput;
14.    private UIInput monthInput;
15.    private UIInput yearInput;
```

Listing 6–16 validator3/src/java/com/corejsf/BackingBean.java (cont.)

```
16.
17.    // PROPERTY: day
18.    public int getDay() { return day; }
19.    public void setDay(int newValue) { day = newValue; }
20.
21.    // PROPERTY: month
22.    public int getMonth() { return month; }
23.    public void setMonth(int newValue) { month = newValue; }
24.
25.    // PROPERTY: year
26.    public int getYear() { return year; }
27.    public void setYear(int newValue) { year = newValue; }
28.
29.    // PROPERTY: dayInput
30.    public UIInput getDayInput() { return dayInput; }
31.    public void setDayInput(UIInput newValue) { dayInput = newValue; }
32.
33.    // PROPERTY: monthInput
34.    public UIInput getMonthInput() { return monthInput; }
35.    public void setMonthInput(UIInput newValue) { monthInput = newValue; }
36.
37.    // PROPERTY: yearInput
38.    public UIInput getYearInput() { return yearInput; }
39.    public void setYearInput(UIInput newValue) { yearInput = newValue; }
40.
41.    public void validateDate(FacesContext context, UIComponent component,
42.       Object value) {
43.       int d = ((Integer) dayInput.getLocalValue()).intValue();
44.       int m = ((Integer) monthInput.getLocalValue()).intValue();
45.       int y = ((Integer) value).intValue();
46.
47.       if (!isValidDate(d, m, y)) {
48.          FacesMessage message
49.             = com.corejsf.util.Messages.getMessage(
50.                "com.corejsf.messages", "invalidDate", null);
51.          message.setSeverity(FacesMessage.SEVERITY_ERROR);
52.          throw new ValidatorException(message);
53.       }
54.    }
55.
56.    private static boolean isValidDate(int d, int m, int y) {
57.       if (d < 1 || m < 1 || m > 12) return false;
58.       if (m == 2) {
59.          if (isLeapYear(y)) return d <= 29;
60.          else return d <= 28;
61.       }
```

Listing 6–16   validator3/src/java/com/corejsf/BackingBean.java (cont.)

```java
62.        else if (m == 4 || m == 6 || m == 9 || m == 11)
63.            return d <= 30;
64.        else
65.            return d <= 31;
66.    }
67.
68.    private static boolean isLeapYear(int y) {
69.        return y % 4 == 0 && (y % 400 == 0 || y % 100 != 0);
70.    }
71. }
```

Listing 6–17   validator3/web/index.jsp

```jsp
1. <html>
2.    <%@ taglib uri="http://java.sun.com/jsf/core" prefix="f" %>
3.    <%@ taglib uri="http://java.sun.com/jsf/html" prefix="h" %>
4.    <f:view>
5.        <head>
6.          <link href="styles.css" rel="stylesheet" type="text/css"/>
7.          <title><h:outputText value="#{msgs.title}"/></title>
8.        </head>
9.        <body>
10.          <h:form>
11.            <h1><h:outputText value="#{msgs.enterDate}"/></h1>
12.            <h:panelGrid columns="3">
13.              <h:outputText value="#{msgs.day}"/>
14.              <h:inputText value="#{bb.day}" binding="#{bb.dayInput}"
15.                  size="2" required="true"/>
16.              <h:panelGroup/>
17.
18.              <h:outputText value="#{msgs.month}"/>
19.              <h:inputText value="#{bb.month}" binding="#{bb.monthInput}"
20.                  size="2" required="true"/>
21.              <h:panelGroup/>
22.
23.              <h:outputText value="#{msgs.year}"/>
24.              <h:inputText id="year" value="#{bb.year}"
25.                  binding="#{bb.yearInput}" size="4" required="true"
26.                  validator="#{bb.validateDate}"/>
27.              <h:message for="year" styleClass="errorMessage"/>
28.            </h:panelGrid>
29.            <h:commandButton value="#{msgs.submit}" action="submit"/>
30.          </h:form>
31.        </body>
32.    </f:view>
33. </html>
```

An alternative approach is to attach the validator to a *hidden input field* that comes after all other fields on the form:

```
<h:inputHidden id="datecheck" validator="#{bb.validateDate}"
   value="needed"/>
```

The hidden field is rendered as a hidden HTML input field. When the field value is posted back, the validator kicks in. (It is essential that you supply some field value. Otherwise, the component value is never updated.) With this approach, the validation function is more symmetrical since all other form components already have their local values set.

 NOTE: It would actually be worthwhile to write a custom date component that renders three input fields and has a single value of type Date. That single component could then be validated easily. However, the technique of this section is useful for any form that needs validation across fields.

As you have seen, JSF provides extensive and extensible support for conversion and validation. You can use the JSF standard converter and validators with one line of code in your JSF pages, or you can supply your own logic if more complex conversions or validations are needed. Finally, as you will see in Chapter 9, you can define your own conversion and validation tags.

EVENT HANDLING

Chapter 7

Web applications often need to respond to user events, such as selecting items from a menu or clicking a button. For example, you might want to respond to the selection of a country in an address form by changing the locale and reloading the current page to better accommodate your users.

Typically, you register event handlers with components—for example, you might register a value change listener with a menu in a JSF page, like this:

```
<h:selectOneMenu valueChangeListener="#{form.countryChanged}"...>
    ...
</h:selectOneMenu>
```

In the preceding code, the method binding #{form.countryChanged} references the countryChanged method of a bean named form. That method is invoked by the JSF implementation after the user makes a selection from the menu. Exactly when that method is invoked is one topic of discussion in this chapter.

JSF supports three kinds of events:

- Value change events
- Action events
- Phase events

Value change events are fired by input components—such as h:inputText, h:selectOneRadio, and h:selectManyMenu—when the component's value changes.

Action events are fired by command components—for example, h:commandButton and h:commandLink, when the button or link is activated. Phase events are routinely fired by the JSF life cycle. If you want to handle events, you need to have a basic understanding of that life cycle. Next, we see how the life cycle works.

Life Cycle Events

Requests in JSF applications are processed by the JSF implementation with a controller servlet, which in turn executes the JSF life cycle. The JSF life cycle is shown in Figure 7–1.

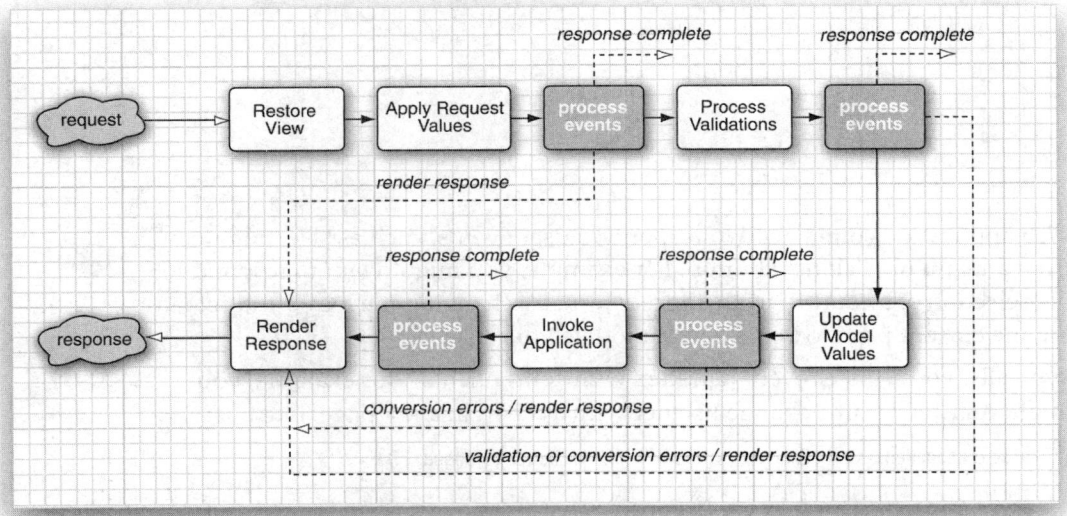

Figure 7–1   The JSF life cycle

The JSF life cycle consists of the following phases:

- Restore View
- Apply Request Values
- Process Validations
- Update Model Values
- Invoke Application
- Render Response

Starting with the Apply Request Values phase, the JSF implementation may create events and add them to an event queue during each life cycle phase. After those phases, the JSF implementation broadcasts queued events to registered listeners. Those events and their associated listeners are the focus of this chapter.

NOTE: Event listeners can affect the JSF life cycle in one of three ways:

1. Let the life cycle proceed normally.
2. Call `FacesContext.renderResponse()` to skip the rest of the life cycle up to Render Response.
3. Call `FacesContext.responseComplete()` to skip the rest of the life cycle entirely.

See "Immediate Components" on page 287 for an example of using `FacesContext.renderResponse()`.

Value Change Events

Components in a web application often depend on each other. For example, in the application shown in Figure 7–2, the value of the "State" prompt depends on the "Country" menu's value. You can keep dependent components in synch with value change events, which are fired by input components after their new value has been validated.

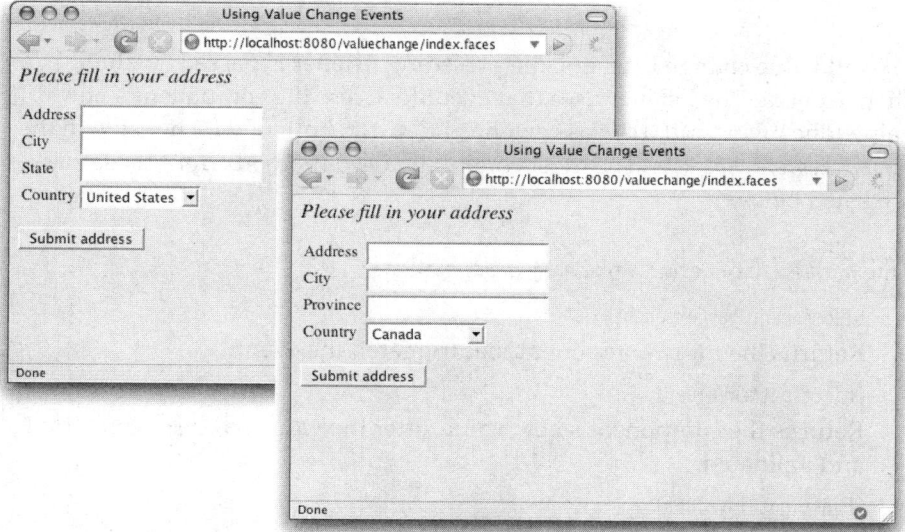

Figure 7–2   Using value change events

The application in Figure 7–2 attaches a value change listener to the "Country" menu and uses the onchange attribute to force a form submit after the menu's value is changed:

```
<h:selectOneMenu value="#{form.country}" onchange="submit()"
   valueChangeListener="#{form.countryChanged}">
   <f:selectItems value="#{form.countryNames}"/>
</h:selectOneMenu>
```

When a user selects a country from the menu, the JavaScript submit function is invoked to submit the menu's form, which subsequently invokes the JSF life cycle. After the Process Validations phase, the JSF implementation invokes the form bean's countryChanged method. That method changes the view root's locale, according to the new country value:

```
private static String US = "United States";
...
public void countryChanged(ValueChangeEvent event) {
   FacesContext context = FacesContext.getCurrentInstance();

   if (US.equals((String) event.getNewValue()))
      context.getViewRoot().setLocale(Locale.US);
   else
      context.getViewRoot().setLocale(Locale.CANADA);
   }
}
```

Like all value change listeners, the preceding listener is passed a value change event. The listener uses that event to access the component's new value. The ValueChangeEvent class extends FacesEvent, both of which reside in the javax.faces.event package. The most commonly used methods from those classes are listed below.

| API | **javax.faces.event.ValueChangeEvent** |

- UIComponent getComponent()
  Returns the input component that triggered the event.

- Object getNewValue()
  Returns the component's new value, after the value has been converted and validated.

- Object getOldValue()
  Returns the component's previous value.

| API | **javax.faces.event.FacesEvent** |

- void queue()
  Queues the event for delivery at the end of the current life cycle phase.

- `PhaseId getPhaseId()`

  Returns the phase identifier corresponding to the phase during which the event is delivered.

- `void setPhaseId(PhaseId)`

  Sets the phase identifier corresponding to the phase during which the event is delivered.

The directory structure for the application in Figure 7–2 is shown in Figure 7–3 and the application is shown in Listing 7–1 through Listing 7–5.

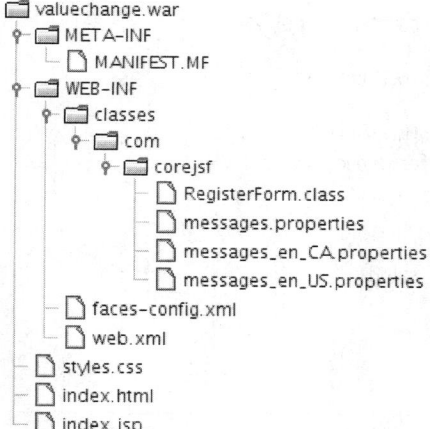

Figure 7–3 Directory structure for the value change example

Listing 7–1   `valuechange/web/index.jsp`

```
1.  <html>
2.     <%@ taglib uri="http://java.sun.com/jsf/core" prefix="f" %>
3.     <%@ taglib uri="http://java.sun.com/jsf/html" prefix="h" %>
4.     <f:view>
5.        <head>
6.           <link href="styles.css" rel="stylesheet" type="text/css"/>
7.           <title>
8.              <h:outputText value="#{msgs.windowTitle}"/>
9.           </title>
10.       </head>
11.
12.       <body>
13.          <h:outputText value="#{msgs.pageTitle}" styleClass="emphasis"/>
14.          <p/>
15.          <h:form>
16.             <h:panelGrid columns="2">
```

Listing 7–1   valuechange/web/index.jsp (cont.)

```
17.          <h:outputText value="#{msgs.streetAddressPrompt}"/>
18.          <h:inputText id="streetAddress" value="#{form.streetAddress}"
19.             required="true"/>
20.
21.          <h:outputText id="cityPrompt" value="#{msgs.cityPrompt}"/>
22.          <h:inputText value="#{form.city}"/>
23.
24.          <h:outputText id="statePrompt" value="#{msgs.statePrompt}"/>
25.          <h:inputText value="#{form.state}"/>
26.
27.          <h:outputText value="#{msgs.countryPrompt}"/>
28.
29.          <h:selectOneMenu value="#{form.country}"
30.             onchange="submit()"
31.             valueChangeListener="#{form.countryChanged}">
32.             <f:selectItems value="#{form.countryNames}"/>
33.          </h:selectOneMenu>
34.       </h:panelGrid>
35.       <p/>
36.       <h:commandButton value="#{msgs.submit}"/>
37.    </h:form>
38.  </body>
39.  </f:view>
40. </html>
```

Listing 7–2   valuechange/src/java/com/corejsf/RegisterForm.java

```
1. package com.corejsf;
2.
3. import java.util.ArrayList;
4. import java.util.Collection;
5. import java.util.Locale;
6. import javax.faces.context.FacesContext;
7. import javax.faces.event.ValueChangeEvent;
8. import javax.faces.model.SelectItem;
9.
10. public class RegisterForm {
11.    private String streetAddress;
12.    private String city;
13.    private String state;
14.    private String country;
15.
16.    private static final String US = "United States";
17.    private static final String CANADA = "Canada";
```

Listing 7–2   valuechange/src/java/com/corejsf/RegisterForm.java (cont.)

```
18.    private static final String[] COUNTRY_NAMES = { US, CANADA };
19.    private static ArrayList<SelectItem> countryItems = null;
20.
21.    // PROPERTY: countryNames
22.    public Collection getCountryNames() {
23.       if (countryItems == null) {
24.          countryItems = new ArrayList<SelectItem>();
25.          for (int i = 0; i < COUNTRY_NAMES.length; i++) {
26.             countryItems.add(new SelectItem(COUNTRY_NAMES[i]));
27.          }
28.       }
29.       return countryItems;
30.    }
31.
32.    // PROPERTY: streetAddress
33.    public void setStreetAddress(String newValue) { streetAddress = newValue; }
34.    public String getStreetAddress() { return streetAddress; }
35.
36.    // PROPERTY: city
37.    public void setCity(String newValue) { city = newValue; }
38.    public String getCity() { return city; }
39.
40.    // PROPERTY: state
41.    public void setState(String newValue) { state = newValue; }
42.    public String getState() { return state; }
43.
44.    // PROPERTY: country
45.    public void setCountry(String newValue) { country = newValue; }
46.    public String getCountry() { return country; }
47.
48.    public void countryChanged(ValueChangeEvent event) {
49.       FacesContext context = FacesContext.getCurrentInstance();
50.
51.       if (US.equals((String) event.getNewValue()))
52.          context.getViewRoot().setLocale(Locale.US);
53.       else
54.          context.getViewRoot().setLocale(Locale.CANADA);
55.    }
56. }
```

Listing 7–3   valuechange/web/WEB-INF/faces-config.xml

```
1. <?xml version="1.0"?>
2. <faces-config xmlns="http://java.sun.com/xml/ns/javaee"
3.    xmlns:xsi="http://www.w3.org/2001/XMLSchema-instance"
4.    xsi:schemaLocation="http://java.sun.com/xml/ns/javaee
5.        http://java.sun.com/xml/ns/javaee/web-facesconfig_1_2.xsd"
6.    version="1.2">
7.    <application>
8.       <resource-bundle>
9.          <base-name>com.corejsf.messages</base-name>
10.         <var>msgs</var>
11.      </resource-bundle>
12.   </application>
13.
14.   <managed-bean>
15.      <managed-bean-name>form</managed-bean-name>
16.      <managed-bean-class>com.corejsf.RegisterForm</managed-bean-class>
17.      <managed-bean-scope>session</managed-bean-scope>
18.   </managed-bean>
19. </faces-config>
```

Listing 7–4   valuechange/src/java/com/corejsf/messages_en_US.properties

```
1. windowTitle=Using Value Change Events
2. pageTitle=Please fill in your address
3.
4. streetAddressPrompt=Address
5. cityPrompt=City
6. statePrompt=State
7. countryPrompt=Country
8. submit=Submit address
```

Listing 7–5   valuechange/src/java/com/corejsf/messages_en_CA.properties

```
1. windowTitle=Using Value Change Events
2. pageTitle=Please fill in your address
3.
4. streetAddressPrompt=Address
5. cityPrompt=City
6. statePrompt=Province
7. countryPrompt=Country
8. submit=Submit address
```

Action Events

Action events are fired by command components—buttons, links, etc.—when the component is activated. As we saw in "Life Cycle Events" on page 268, action events are fired during the Invoke Application phase, near the end of the life cycle.

You typically attach action listeners to command components in JSP. For example, you can add an action listener to a link, like this:

```
<h:commandLink actionListener="#{bean.linkActivated}">
   ...
</h:commandLink>
```

Command components submit requests when they are activated, so there is no need to use onchange to force form submits as we did with value change events in "Value Change Events" on page 269. When you activate a command or link, the surrounding form is submitted and the JSF implementation subsequently fires action events.

It is important to distinguish between *action listeners* and *actions*. In a nutshell, actions are designed for business logic and participate in navigation handling, whereas action listeners typically perform user interface logic and do not participate in navigation handling.

Action listeners sometimes work in concert with actions when an action needs information about the user interface. For example, the application shown in Figure 7–4 uses an action and an action listener to react to mouse clicks by forwarding to a JSP page.

If you click on a president's face, the application forwards to a JSF page with information about that president. Note that an action alone cannot implement that behavior—an action can *navigate* to the appropriate page, but it cannot *determine* the appropriate page because it knows nothing about the image button in the user interface or the mouse click.

The application shown in Figure 7–4 uses a button with an image, like this:

```
<h:commandButton image="mountrushmore.jpg"
   actionListener="#{rushmore.listen}"
   action="#{rushmore.act}"/>
```

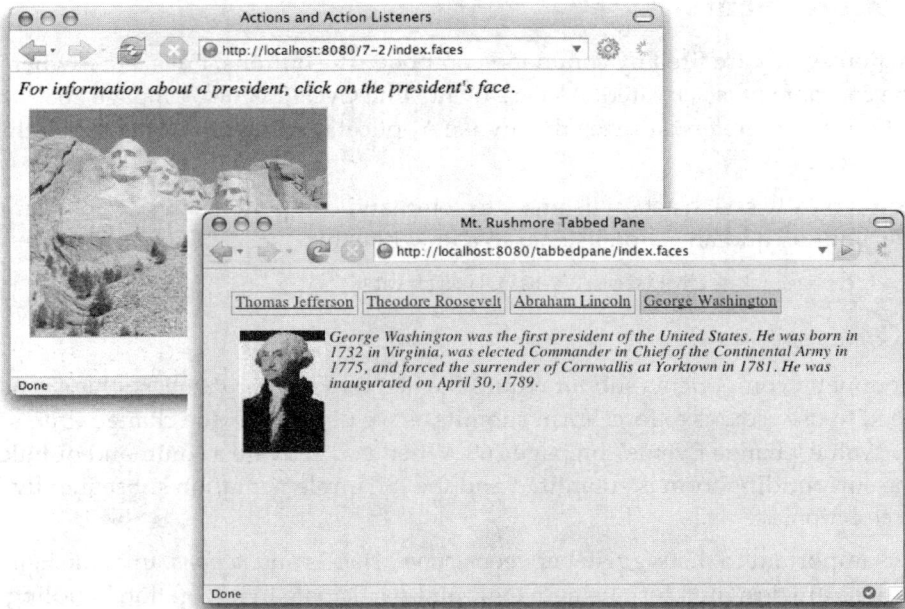

Figure 7–4 The Rushmore application

When you click a president, a listener—which has access to the mouse click coordinates—determines which president was selected. But the listener cannot affect navigation, so it stores an outcome corresponding to the selected president in an instance field:

```
public class Rushmore {
   private String outcome;
   private Rectangle washingtonRect = new Rectangle(70,30,40,40);
   private Rectangle jeffersonRect  = new Rectangle(115,45,40,40);
   private Rectangle rooseveltRect  = new Rectangle(135,65,40,40);
   private Rectangle lincolnRect    = new Rectangle(175,62,40,40);

   public void listen(ActionEvent e) {
      FacesContext context = FacesContext.getCurrentInstance();
      String clientId = e.getComponent().getClientId(context);
      Map requestParams = context.getExternalContext().
         getRequestParameterMap();

      int x = new Integer((String) requestParams.get(clientId + ".x")).intValue();
      int y = new Integer((String) requestParams.get(clientId + ".y")).intValue();
```

```
    outcome = null;

    if (washingtonRect.contains(new Point(x,y)))
        outcome = "washington";

    if (jeffersonRect.contains(new Point(x,y)))
        outcome = "jefferson";

    if (rooseveltRect.contains(new Point(x,y)))
        outcome = "roosevelt";

    if (lincolnRect.contains(new Point(x,y)))
        outcome = "lincoln";

    }
}
```

The action associated with the button uses the outcome to affect navigation:

```
public String act() {
    return outcome;
}
```

Note that the JSF implementation always invokes action listeners before actions.

 NOTE: JSF insists that you separate user interface logic and business logic by refusing to give actions access to events or the components that fire them. In the preceding example, the action cannot access the client ID of the component that fired the event, information that is necessary for extraction of mouse coordinates from the request parameters. Because the action knows nothing about the user interface, we must add an action listener to the mix to implement the required behavior.

The directory structure for the application shown in Figure 7–4 is shown in Figure 7–5. The application is shown in Listing 7–6 through Listing 7–13.

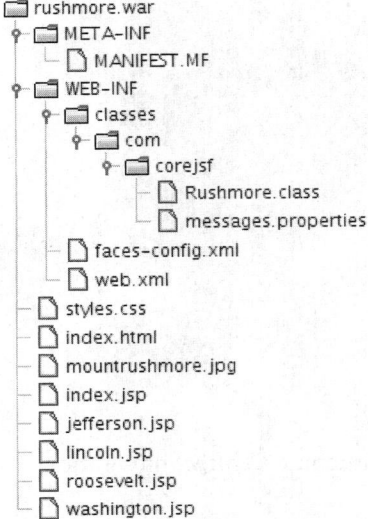

Figure 7–5   Directory structure for the Rushmore example

Listing 7–6   rushmore/web/index.jsp

```
 1. <html>
 2.    <%@ taglib uri="http://java.sun.com/jsf/core" prefix="f" %>
 3.    <%@ taglib uri="http://java.sun.com/jsf/html" prefix="h" %>
 4.    <f:view>
 5.       <head>
 6.          <link href="styles.css" rel="stylesheet" type="text/css"/>
 7.          <title>
 8.             <h:outputText value="#{msgs.indexWindowTitle}"/>
 9.          </title>
10.       </head>
11.
12.       <body>
13.          <h:outputText value="#{msgs.instructions}"
14.             styleClass="instructions"/>
15.          <h:form>
16.             <h:commandButton image="mountrushmore.jpg"
17.                styleClass="imageButton"
18.                actionListener="#{rushmore.handleMouseClick}"
19.                action="#{rushmore.navigate}"/>
20.          </h:form>
21.       </body>
22.    </f:view>
23. </html>
```

Listing 7–7   rushmore/web/lincoln.jsp

```
1.  <<html>
2.    <%@ taglib uri="http://java.sun.com/jsf/core" prefix="f" %>
3.    <%@ taglib uri="http://java.sun.com/jsf/html" prefix="h" %>
4.    <f:view>
5.      <head>
6.        <link href="styles.css" rel="stylesheet" type="text/css"/>
7.        <title>
8.          <h:outputText value="#{msgs.lincolnWindowTitle}"/>
9.        </title>
10.     </head>
11.
12.     <body>
13.       <h:form>
14.         <h:outputText value="#{msgs.lincolnPageTitle}"
15.           styleClass="presidentPageTitle"/>
16.         <p/>
17.         <h:outputText value="#{msgs.lincolnDiscussion}"
18.           styleClass="presidentDiscussion"/>
19.         <p>
20.           <h:commandLink action="index"
21.             styleClass="backLink">
22.             ${msgs.indexLinkText}
23.           </h:commandLink>
24.         </p>
25.       </h:form>
26.     </body>
27.   </f:view>
28. </html>
```

Listing 7–8   rushmore/web/jefferson.jsp

```
1.  <html>
2.    <%@ taglib uri="http://java.sun.com/jsf/core" prefix="f" %>
3.    <%@ taglib uri="http://java.sun.com/jsf/html" prefix="h" %>
4.    <f:view>
5.      <head>
6.        <link href="styles.css" rel="stylesheet" type="text/css"/>
7.        <title>${msgs.jeffersonWindowTitle}</title>
8.      </head>
9.
10.     <body>
11.       <h:form>
12.         <h:outputText value="#{msgs.jeffersonPageTitle}"
13.           styleClass="presidentPageTitle"/>
14.         <p/>
```

Listing 7-8   rushmore/web/jefferson.jsp (cont.)

```
15.            <h:outputText value="#{msgs.jeffersonDiscussion}"
16.              styleClass="presidentDiscussion"/>
17.            <p>
18.              <h:commandLink action="index"
19.                styleClass="backLink">
20.                ${msgs.indexLinkText}
21.              </h:commandLink>
22.            </p>
23.          </h:form>
24.        </body>
25.      </f:view>
26. </html>
```

Listing 7-9   rushmore/web/roosevelt.jsp

```
1. <html>
2.    <%@ taglib uri="http://java.sun.com/jsf/core" prefix="f" %>
3.    <%@ taglib uri="http://java.sun.com/jsf/html" prefix="h" %>
4.    <f:view>
5.      <head>
6.        <link href="styles.css" rel="stylesheet" type="text/css"/>
7.        <title>
8.          <h:outputText value="#{msgs.rooseveltWindowTitle}"/>
9.        </title>
10.      </head>
11.
12.      <body>
13.        <h:form>
14.          <h:outputText value="#{msgs.rooseveltPageTitle}"
15.            styleClass="presidentPageTitle"/>
16.          <p/>
17.          <h:outputText value="#{msgs.rooseveltDiscussion}"
18.            styleClass="presidentDiscussion"/>
19.          <p>
20.            <h:commandLink action="index"
21.              styleClass="backLink">
22.              ${msgs.indexLinkText}
23.            </h:commandLink>
24.          </p>
25.        </h:form>
26.      </body>
27.    </f:view>
28. </html>
```

Listing 7–10 rushmore/web/washington.jsp

```
1. <html>
2.   <%@ taglib uri="http://java.sun.com/jsf/core" prefix="f" %>
3.   <%@ taglib uri="http://java.sun.com/jsf/html" prefix="h" %>
4.   <f:view>
5.     <head>
6.       <link href="styles.css" rel="stylesheet" type="text/css"/>
7.       <title>
8.         <h:outputText value="#{msgs.washingtonWindowTitle}"/>
9.       </title>
10.    </head>
11.
12.    <body>
13.      <h:form>
14.        <h:outputText value="#{msgs.washingtonPageTitle}"
15.          styleClass="presidentPageTitle"/>
16.        <p/>
17.        <h:outputText value="#{msgs.washingtonDiscussion}"
18.          styleClass="presidentDiscussion"/>
19.        <p>
20.          <h:commandLink action="index"
21.            styleClass="backLink">
22.            ${msgs.indexLinkText}
23.          </h:commandLink>
24.        </p>
25.      </h:form>
26.    </body>
27.  </f:view>
28. </html>
```

Listing 7–11 rushmore/src/java/com/corejsf/Rushmore.java

```
1. package com.corejsf;
2.
3. import java.awt.Point;
4. import java.awt.Rectangle;
5. import java.util.Map;
6. import javax.faces.context.FacesContext;
7. import javax.faces.event.ActionEvent;
8.
9. public class Rushmore {
10.    private String outcome = null;
11.    private Rectangle washingtonRect = new Rectangle(70, 30, 40, 40);
12.    private Rectangle jeffersonRect = new Rectangle(115, 45, 40, 40);
```

Listing 7–11   `rushmore/src/java/com/corejsf/Rushmore.java (cont.)`

```java
13.    private Rectangle rooseveltRect = new Rectangle(135, 65, 40, 40);
14.    private Rectangle lincolnRect = new Rectangle(175, 62, 40, 40);
15.
16.    public void handleMouseClick(ActionEvent e) {
17.       FacesContext context = FacesContext.getCurrentInstance();
18.       String clientId = e.getComponent().getClientId(context);
19.       Map requestParams = context.getExternalContext().getRequestParameterMap();
20.
21.       int x = new Integer((String) requestParams.get(clientId + ".x"))
22.          .intValue();
23.       int y = new Integer((String) requestParams.get(clientId + ".y"))
24.          .intValue();
25.
26.       outcome = null;
27.
28.       if (washingtonRect.contains(new Point(x, y)))
29.          outcome = "washington";
30.
31.       if (jeffersonRect.contains(new Point(x, y)))
32.          outcome = "jefferson";
33.
34.       if (rooseveltRect.contains(new Point(x, y)))
35.          outcome = "roosevelt";
36.
37.       if (lincolnRect.contains(new Point(x, y)))
38.          outcome = "lincoln";
39.    }
40.
41.    public String navigate() {
42.       return outcome;
43.    }
44. }
```

Listing 7–12   `rushmore/web/WEB-INF/faces-config.xml`

```xml
1. <?xml version="1.0"?>
2. <faces-config xmlns="http://java.sun.com/xml/ns/javaee"
3.    xmlns:xsi="http://www.w3.org/2001/XMLSchema-instance"
4.    xsi:schemaLocation="http://java.sun.com/xml/ns/javaee
5.    http://java.sun.com/xml/ns/javaee/web-facesconfig_1_2.xsd"
6.    version="1.2">
7.    <application>
```

Listing 7–12   rushmore/web/WEB-INF/faces-config.xml (cont.)

```
 8.        <resource-bundle>
 9.            <base-name>com.corejsf.messages</base-name>
10.            <var>msgs</var>
11.        </resource-bundle>
12.    </application>
13.
14.    <navigation-rule>
15.        <navigation-case>
16.            <from-outcome>index</from-outcome>
17.            <to-view-id>/index.jsp</to-view-id>
18.        </navigation-case>
19.    </navigation-rule>
20.
21.    <navigation-rule>
22.        <from-view-id>/index.jsp</from-view-id>
23.        <navigation-case>
24.            <from-outcome>washington</from-outcome>
25.            <to-view-id>/washington.jsp</to-view-id>
26.        </navigation-case>
27.        <navigation-case>
28.            <from-outcome>jefferson</from-outcome>
29.            <to-view-id>/jefferson.jsp</to-view-id>
30.        </navigation-case>
31.        <navigation-case>
32.            <from-outcome>roosevelt</from-outcome>
33.            <to-view-id>/roosevelt.jsp</to-view-id>
34.        </navigation-case>
35.        <navigation-case>
36.            <from-outcome>lincoln</from-outcome>
37.            <to-view-id>/lincoln.jsp</to-view-id>
38.        </navigation-case>
39.    </navigation-rule>
40.
41.    <managed-bean>
42.        <managed-bean-name>rushmore</managed-bean-name>
43.        <managed-bean-class>com.corejsf.Rushmore</managed-bean-class>
44.        <managed-bean-scope>session</managed-bean-scope>
45.    </managed-bean>
46.
47. </faces-config>
```

Listing 7–13   rushmore/src/java/com/corejsf/messages.properties

```
 1. instructions=For information about a president, click on the president's face.
 2.
 3. indexWindowTitle=Actions and Action Listeners
 4. indexLinkText=Back...
 5. jeffersonWindowTitle=President Jefferson
 6. rooseveltWindowTitle=President Roosevelt
 7. lincolnWindowTitle=President Lincoln
 8. washingtonWindowTitle=President Washington
 9.
10. jeffersonPageTitle=Thomas Jefferson
11. rooseveltPageTitle=Theodore Roosevelt
12. lincolnPageTitle=Abraham Lincoln
13. washingtonPageTitle=George Washington
14.
15. jeffersonTabText=Jefferson
16. rooseveltTabText=Roosevelt
17. lincolnTabText=Lincoln
18. washingtonTabText=Washington
19.
20. lincolnDiscussion=President Lincoln was known as the Great Emancipator because \
21.   he was instrumental in abolishing slavery in the United States. He was born \
22.   into a poor family in Kentucky in 1809, elected president in 1860, and \
23.   assassinated by John Wilkes Booth in 1865.
24.
25. washingtonDiscussion=George Washington was the first president of the United \
26.   States. He was born in 1732 in Virginia, was elected Commander in Chief of \
27.   the Continental Army in 1775, and forced the surrender of Cornwallis at Yorktown \
28.   in 1781. He was inaugurated on April 30, 1789.
29.
30. rooseveltDiscussion=Theodore Roosevelt was the 26th president of the United \
31.   States. In 1901 he became president after the assassination of President \
32.   McKinley. At only 42, he was the youngest president in U.S. history.
33.
34. jeffersonDiscussion=Thomas Jefferson, the 3rd U.S. president, was born in \
35.   1743 in Virginia. Jefferson was tall and awkward, and was not known as a \
36.   great public speaker. Jefferson became minister to France in 1785, after \
37.   Benjamin Franklin held that post. In 1796, Jefferson was a reluctant \
38.   presidential candidate, and missed winning the election by a mere three votes. \
39.   He served as president from 1801 to 1809.
```

Event Listener Tags

Up to now, we have added action and value change listeners to components with the actionListener and valueChangeListener *attributes*, respectively. However, you can also add action and value change listeners to a component with the following tags:

- f:actionListener
- f:valueChangeListener

The f:actionListener *and* f:valueChangeListener *Tags*

The f:actionListener and f:valueChangeListener tags are analogous to the actionListener and valueChangeListener attributes. For example, in Listing 7–1 on page 271, we defined a menu like this:

```
<h:selectOneMenu value="#{form.country}" onchange="submit()"
   valueChangeListener="#{form.countryChanged}">
   <f:selectItems value="#{form.countryNames}"/>
</h:selectOneMenu>
```

Alternatively, we could use f:valueChangeListener, like this:

```
<h:selectOneMenu value="#{form.country}" onchange="submit()">
   <f:valueChangeListener type="com.corejsf.CountryListener"/>
   <f:selectItems value="#{form.countryNames}"/>
</h:selectOneMenu>
```

The tags have one advantage over the attributes: Tags let you attach multiple listeners to a single component.

Notice the difference between the values specified for the valueChangeListener attribute and the f:valueChangeListener tag in the preceding code. The former specifies a method binding, whereas the latter specifies a Java class. For example, the class referred to in the previous code fragment looks like this:

```
public class CountryListener implements ValueChangeListener {
   private static final String US = "United States";

   public void processValueChange(ValueChangeEvent event) {
      FacesContext context = FacesContext.getCurrentInstance();

      if (US.equals((String) event.getNewValue()))
         context.getViewRoot().setLocale(Locale.US);
      else
         context.getViewRoot().setLocale(Locale.CANADA);
   }
}
```

Like all listeners specified with f:valueChangeListener, the preceding class implements the ValueChangeListener interface. That class defines a single method: void processValueChange(ValueChangeEvent).

The f:actionListener tag is analogous to f:valueChangeListener—the former also has a type attribute that specifies a class name; the class must implement the ActionListener interface. For example, in Listing 7–6 on page 278, we defined a button like this:

```
<h:commandButton image="mountrushmore.jpg"
    styleClass="imageButton"
    actionListener="#{rushmore.handleMouseClick}"
    action="#{rushmore.navigate}"/>
```

Instead of using the actionListener attribute to define our listener, we could have used the f:actionListener tag instead:

```
<h:commandButton image="mountrushmore.jpg" action="#{rushmore.navigate}">
    <f:actionListener type="com.corejsf.RushmoreListener"/>
</h:commandButton>
```

Action listener classes must implement the ActionListener interface, which defines a processAction method, so in the preceding code fragment, JSF will call RushmoreListener.processAction after the image button is activated.

You can also specify multiple listeners with multiple f:actionListener or f:valueChangeListener tags per component. For example, we could add another action listener to our previous example, like this:

```
<h:commandButton image="mountrushmore.jpg" action="#{rushmore.navigate}">
    <f:actionListener type="com.corejsf.RushmoreListener"/>
    <f:actionListener type="com.corejsf.ActionLogger"/>
</h:commandButton>
```

In the preceding code fragment, the ActionLogger class is a simple action listener that logs action events.

If you specify multiple listeners for a component, as we did in the preceding code fragment, the listeners are invoked in the following order:

1.   The listener specified by the listener attribute

2.   Listeners specified by listener tags, in the order in which they are declared

 NOTE: You may wonder why you must specify a method binding for listeners when you use the actionListener and valueChangeListener attributes, and why you must use a class name for listeners specified with f:actionListener and f:valueChangeListener tags. The truth is that the mismatch between listener attributes and tags was an oversight on the part of the JSF expert group.

Immediate Components

In "Life Cycle Events" on page 268, we saw that value change events are normally fired after the Process Validations phase, and action events are normally fired after the Invoke Application phase. Typically, that is the preferred behavior. You usually want to be notified of value changes only when they are valid, and actions should be invoked after all submitted values have been transmitted to the model.

But sometimes you want value change events or action events to fire at the beginning of the life cycle to bypass validation for one or more components. In "Using Immediate Input Components" on page 288 and "Bypassing Validation" on page 237, we make compelling arguments for such behavior. For now, we will look at the mechanics of how immediate events are delivered, as illustrated by Figure 7–6.

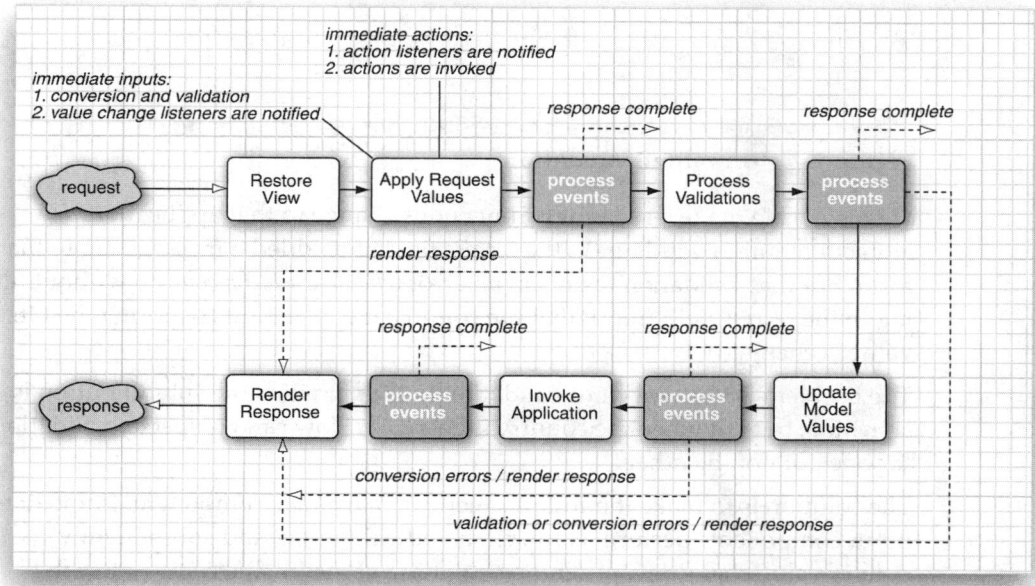

Figure 7–6   Immediate components

Immediate events are fired after the Apply Request Values phase. For input components, conversion and validation are performed after the Apply Request Values phase, and value change events are subsequently fired. For command components, action listeners are invoked, followed by actions; that process kicks in the navigation handler and circumvents the rest of the life cycle up to Render Response.

Using Immediate Input Components

Figure 7–7 shows the value change example discussed in "Value Change Events" on page 269. Recall that the application uses a value change listener to change the view's locale, which in turn changes the localized state prompt according to the selected locale.

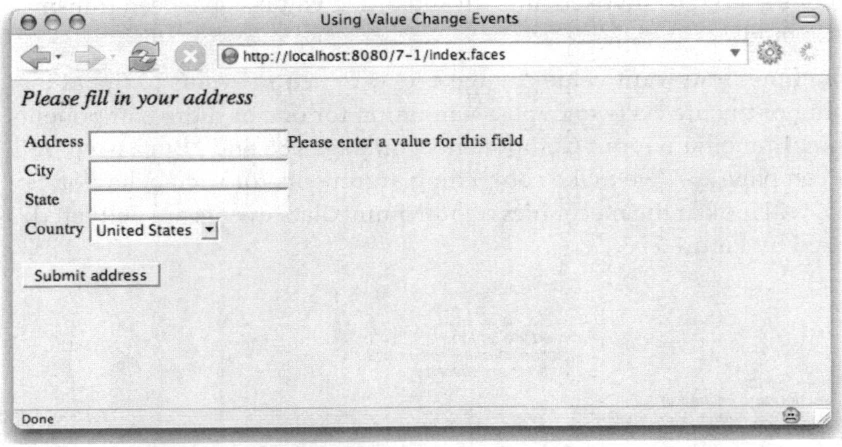

Figure 7–7 Unwanted validation

Here we have made a seemingly innocuous change to that application: We added a required validator to the Address field and added a message tag to the form. But that validation results in an error *when we select a country* without filling in the Address field (recall that the country menu submits its form when its value is changed).

The problem is this: We want validation to kick in when the submit button is activated, but not when the country is changed. How can we specify validation for one but not the other?

The solution is to make the country menu an *immediate* component. Immediate input components perform conversion and validation, and subsequently deliver value change events at the beginning of the JSF life cycle—after the Apply Request Values—instead of after Process Validations.

We specify immediate components with the immediate attribute, which is available to all input and command components:

```
<h:selectOneMenu value="#{form.country}" onchange="submit()" immediate="true"
    valueChangeListener="#{form.countryChanged}">
    <f:selectItems value="#{form.countryNames}"/>
</h:selectOneMenu>
```

With the immediate attribute set to true, our menu fires value change events after Apply Request Values, well before any other input components are validated. You may wonder what good that does us if the other validations happen later instead of sooner—after all, the validations will still be performed and the validation error will still be displayed. To prevent validations for the other components in the form, we have one more thing to do, which is to call the faces context renderResponse method at the end of our value change listener, like this:

```
private static final String US = "United States";
...
public void countryChanged(ValueChangeEvent event) {
   FacesContext context = FacesContext.getCurrentInstance();

   if (US.equals((String) event.getNewValue()))
      context.getViewRoot().setLocale(Locale.US);
   else
      context.getViewRoot().setLocale(Locale.CANADA);

   context.renderResponse();
}
```

The call to renderResponse() skips the rest of the life cycle—including validation of the rest of the input components in the form—up to Render Response. Thus, the other validations are skipped and the response is rendered normally (in this case, the current page is redisplayed).

To summarize, you can skip validation when a value change event fires by doing the following:

1. Adding an immediate attribute to your input tag
2. Calling FacesContext.renderResponse() at the end of your listener

One more thing is noteworthy about this example. Notice that we add an onchange attribute whose value is submit() to our h:selectOneMenu tag. Setting that attribute means that the JavaScript submit function will be invoked whenever someone changes the selected value of the menu, which causes the surrounding form to be submitted.

That form submit is crucial because *the JSF implementation handles all events on the server.* If you take out the onchange attribute, the form will not be submitted when the selected menu item is changed, meaning that the JSF life cycle will never be invoked, our value change listener will never be called, and the locale will never be changed.

You may find it odd that JSF handles all events on the server, but remember that *you* can handle events on the client if you wish by attaching JavaScript to components with attributes such as onblur, onfocus, onclick, etc. Also, client-side event handling is on the table for the next version of JSF.

Using Immediate Command Components

In Chapter 4 we discussed an application, shown in Figure 7–8, that uses command links to change locales.

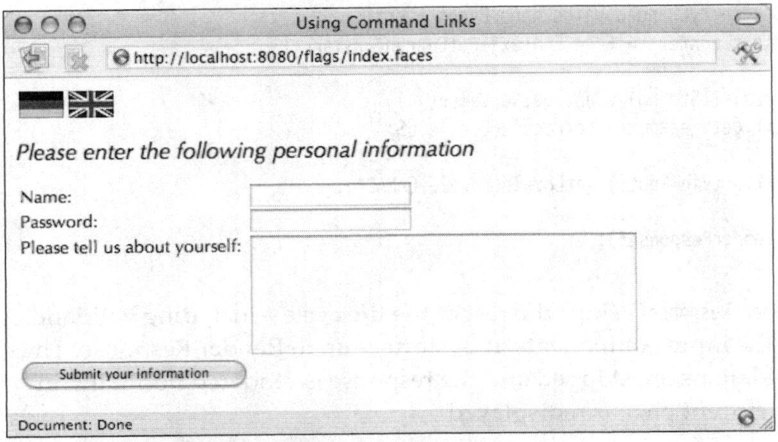

Figure 7–8   Changing locales with links

If we add a required validator to one of the input fields in the form, we will have the same problem we had with the application discussed in "Using Immediate Input Components" on page 288: The validation error will appear when we just want to change the locale by clicking a link. This time, however, we need an immediate *command* component instead of an immediate *input* component. All we need to do is add an immediate attribute to our h:commandLink tag, like this:

```
<h:commandLink action="#{localeChanger.germanAction}" immediate="true">
    <h:graphicImage value="/german_flag.gif" style="border: 0px"/>
</h:commandLink>
```

Unlike value change events, we do not need to modify our listener to invoke FacesContext.renderResponse() because all actions, immediate or not, proceed directly to the Render Response phase, regardless of when they are fired.

Passing Data from the UI to the Server

The two flags in the application shown in Figure 7–8 are implemented with links. The link for the German flag is listed in the previous section. Here is the link for the British flag:

```
<h:commandLink action="#{localeChanger.englishAction}" immediate="true">
   <h:graphicImage value="/british_flag.gif" style="border: 0px"/>
</h:commandLink>
```

Notice that each link has a different action: localeChanger.englishAction for the British flag and localeChanger.germanAction for the German flag. The implementations of those actions are minor:

```
public class ChangeLocaleBean {
   public String germanAction() {
      FacesContext context = FacesContext.getCurrentInstance();
      context.getViewRoot().setLocale(Locale.GERMAN);
      return null;
   }

   public String englishAction() {
      FacesContext context = FacesContext.getCurrentInstance();
      context.getViewRoot().setLocale(Locale.ENGLISH);
      return null;
   }
}
```

Each listener sets the locale of the view root and returns null to indicate that the JSF implementation should reload the same page. Pretty simple.

But imagine if we supported many languages—for example, if we supported 100 languages, we would have to implement 100 actions, and each action would be identical to all the others except for the locale that it would set. Not so simple.

To reduce redundant code that we must write and maintain, it's better to pass the language code from the UI to the server. That way, we can write a single action or action listener to change the view root's locale. JSF gives us three convenient mechanisms to pass information from the UI to the server, in the form of JSP tags:

- f:param
- f:setPropertyActionListener
- f:attribute

Now we take a look at each tag in turn to see how we can eliminate redundant code.

The f:param *Tag*

The f:param tag lets you attach a parameter to a component. Interestingly enough, the f:param tag behaves differently depending upon the type of component to which it is attached. For example, if you attach an f:param tag to an h:outputText, the JSF implementation uses the parameter to fill in placeholders, such as {0}, {1}, etc. If you attach an f:param tag to a command component, such as a button or a link, the JSF implementation passes the parameter's value to the server as a request parameter. Here is how we can use the f:param tag for our flag example:

```
<h:commandLink immediate="true"
    action="#{localeChanger.changeLocale}">
    <f:param name="languageCode" value="de"/>
    <h:graphicImage value="/german_flag.gif" style="border: 0px"/>
</h:commandLink>
...
<h:commandLink immediate="true"
    action="#{localeChanger.changeLocale}">
    <f:param name="languageCode" value="en"/>
    <h:graphicImage value="/british_flag.gif" style="border: 0px"/>
</h:commandLink>
```

On the server, we access the languageCode request parameter to set the locale:

```
public class ChangeLocaleBean {
    public String changeLocale() {
        FacesContext context = FacesContext.getCurrentInstance();
        String languageCode = getLanguageCode(context);
        context.getViewRoot().setLocale(new Locale(languageCode));
        return null;
    }
    private String getLanguageCode(FacesContext context) {
        Map<String, String> params = context.getExternalContext().
            getRequestParameterMap();
        return params.get("languageCode");
    }
}
```

No matter how many flags links we add to our JSP page, our ChangeLocaleBean is finished. No more redundant code.

The f:attribute *Tag*

Another way to pass information from the UI to the server is to set a component's attribute with the f:attribute tag. Here is how we do that with our flag example:

```
<h:commandLink immediate="true"
    actionListener="#{localeChanger.changeLocale}">
    <f:attribute name="languageCode" value="de"/>
    <h:graphicImage value="/german_flag.gif" style="border: 0px"/>
</h:commandLink>
...

<h:commandLink immediate="true"
    actionListener="#{localeChanger.changeLocale}">
    <f:attribute name="languageCode" value="en"/>
    <h:graphicImage value="/british_flag.gif" style="border: 0px"/>
</h:commandLink>
```

There are two things to notice here. First, we are using f:attribute to set an attribute on the link. That attribute's name is languageCode and its value is either en or de.

Second, we have switched from an action to an action listener. That is because action listeners are passed an event object that gives us access to the component that triggered the event; of course, that is one of our links. We need that component to access its languageCode attribute. Here is how it all hangs together on the server:

```
public class ChangeLocaleBean {
    public void changeLocale(ActionEvent event) {
        UIComponent component = event.getComponent();
        String languageCode = getLanguageCode(component);
        FacesContext.getCurrentInstance()
            .getViewRoot().setLocale(new Locale(languageCode));
    }
    private String getLanguageCode(UIComponent component) {
        Map<String, Object> attrs = component.getAttributes();
        return (String) attrs.get("languageCode");
    }
}
```

This time, instead of pulling the language code out of a request parameter, we pull it out of a component attribute. Either way, the ChangeLocaleBean's implementation is finished, no matter how many locales we support.

The f:setPropertyActionListener *Tag*

As we have seen, f:param and f:attribute are handy for passing information from the UI to the server, but those tags require us to manually dig the information out from a request parameter or component attribute, respectively.

The f:setPropertyActionListener tag, new for JSF 1.2, puts an end to that digging. With f:setPropertyActionListener, the JSF implementation sets a property in your backing bean for you. Here is how it works for our flags example:

```
<h:commandLink immediate="true"
   action="#{localeChanger.changeLocale}">
   <f:setPropertyActionListener target="#{localeChanger.languageCode}"
      value="de"/>
   <h:graphicImage value="/german_flag.gif" style="border: 0px"/>
</h:commandLink>
...
<h:commandLink immediate="true"
   action="#{localeChanger.changeLocale}">
   <f:setPropertyActionListener target="#{localeChanger.languageCode}"
      value="en"/>
   <h:graphicImage value="/british_flag.gif" style="border: 0px"/>
</h:commandLink>
```

In the preceding JSP code, we tell the JSF implementation to set the languageCode property of the localeChanger bean with either de or en. Here is the corresponding implementation of the localeChanger bean:

```
public class ChangeLocaleBean {
   private String languageCode;

   public String changeLocale() {
      FacesContext context = FacesContext.getCurrentInstance();
      context.getViewRoot().setLocale(new Locale(languageCode));
      return null;
   }
   public void setLanguageCode(String newValue) {
      languageCode = newValue;
   }
}
```

For this implementation of the ChangeLocaleBean, we provide a languageCode read-only property that is set by the JSF implementation.

In the context of this example, f:setPropertyActionListener is ostensibly the best choice for setting the localeChanger bean's languageCode property because it results in the simplest implementation of the ChangeLocaleBean class. However, f:param and f:attribute have their place in other contexts, to set request parameters or component attributes, respectively.

So far in this chapter, we have seen how to attach event handling to component instances. JSF also lets you specify global event handlers that are invoked at different points in the JSF life cycle. Those events are the focus of the next section.

Phase Events

The JSF implementation fires events, called *phase events*, before and after each life cycle phase. Those events are handled by phase listeners. Unlike value change and action listeners that you attach to individual components, you specify phase listeners in a faces configuration file, like this:

```
<faces-config>
   <lifecycle>
      <phase-listener>com.corejsf.PhaseTracker</phase-listener>
   </lifecycle>
</faces-config>
```

The preceding code fragment specifies only one listener, but you can specify as many as you want. Listeners are invoked in the order in which they are specified in the configuration file.

You implement phase listeners by means of the PhaseListener interface from the javax.faces.event package. That interface defines three methods:

- PhaseId getPhaseId()
- void afterPhase(PhaseEvent)
- void beforePhase(PhaseEvent)

The getPhaseId method tells the JSF implementation when to deliver phase events to the listener—for example, getPhaseId() could return PhaseId.APPLY_REQUEST_VALUES. In that case, beforePhase() and afterPhase() would be called once per life cycle: before and after the Apply Request Values phase. You could also specify PhaseId.ANY_PHASE, which really means *all phases*. Your phase listener's beforePhase and afterPhase methods will be called six times per life cycle: once each for each life cycle phase.

Phase listeners are useful for debugging and for highly specialized behavior. For example, if you use JSF components in another web application framework such as Struts, you might want to update that framework's locale after the Apply Request Values phase, when JSF internally sets its locale. Phase listeners are also useful for applications that use Ajax to provide a rich user experience, as discussed in Chapter 11.

The application shown in Figure 7–9 illustrates the use of phase listeners. This application has a single phase listener that logs messages with a logger, like this:

```
public class PhaseTracker implements PhaseListener {
   ...
   private static final Logger logger = Logger.getLogger("com.corejsf.phases");
```

```
...
public void beforePhase(PhaseEvent e) {
   logger.info("BEFORE " + e.getPhaseId());
}
public void afterPhase(PhaseEvent e) {
   logger.info("AFTER " + e.getPhaseId());
}
}
```

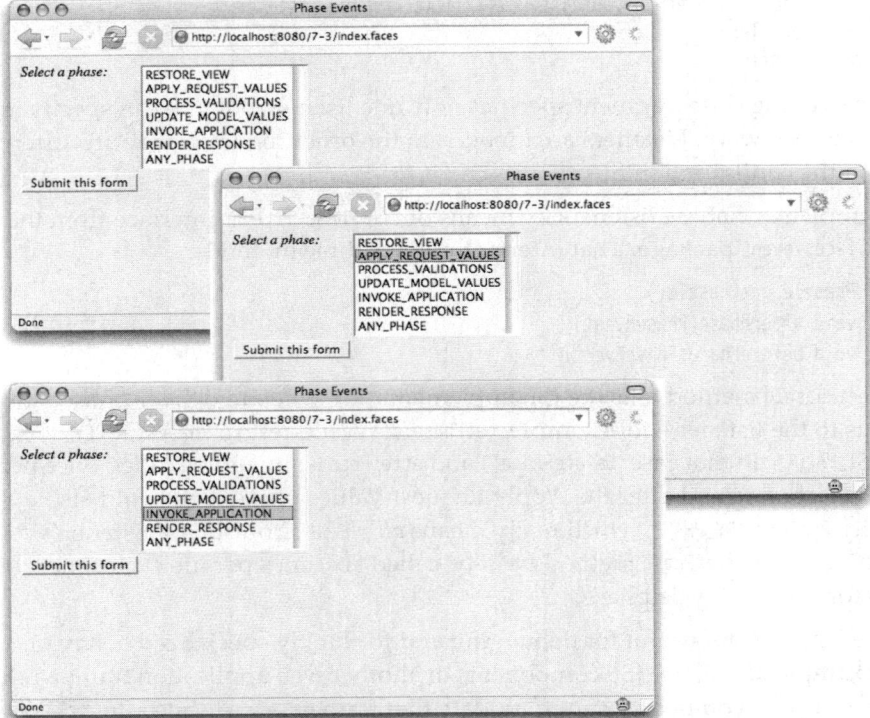

Figure 7–9 Using phase listeners

The phase ID for the listener is set with a listbox that is defined like this:

```
<h:selectOneListbox onchange="submit()"
   valueChangeListener="#{form.phaseChange}">
   <f:selectItems value="#{form.phases}"/>
</h:selectOneListbox>
```

When you select a phase and activate the submit button, the phase listener's phase ID is set by a value change listener:

```
public class FormBean {
    ...
    // VALUE CHANGE LISTENER: phaseChange
    public void phaseChange(ValueChangeEvent e) {
        // get a reference to the current lifecycle
        ...
        PhaseListener[] listeners = lifecycle.getPhaseListeners();
        for (int i=0; i < listeners.length; i++) {
            PhaseListener listener = listeners[i];
            if (listener instanceof com.corejsf.PhaseTracker)
                ((com.corejsf.PhaseTracker) listener).setPhase((String)
                                                  e.getNewValue());
        }
    }
}
```

The top picture in Figure 7–9 shows the application at startup—nothing is selected in the listbox. Because we set the listener's default phase to PhaseId.ANY_PHASE, the listener will be invoked before and after every phase until something is selected in the listbox and the form is submitted. Now we see what output the listener writes to the servlet container log file at application startup:

```
INFO: BEFORE RESTORE_VIEW 1
INFO: AFTER RESTORE_VIEW 1
INFO: BEFORE RENDER_RESPONSE 6
INFO: AFTER RENDER_RESPONSE 6
```

Why was the listener not notified of phases two (Apply Request Values) through five (Invoke Application)? When the application is started, there is no view to restore because the JSF page has not been loaded before. Without a component tree, there is no sense in processing validations, updating model values, or invoking actions, so the JSF life cycle skips directly to rendering the response. That is the last time this will happen for the application until it is reloaded by the servlet container. If you activate the submit button without selecting a phase, you will see this output:

```
INFO: BEFORE RESTORE_VIEW 1
INFO: AFTER RESTORE_VIEW 1
INFO: BEFORE APPLY_REQUEST_VALUES 2
INFO: AFTER APPLY_REQUEST_VALUES 2
INFO: BEFORE PROCESS_VALIDATIONS 3
INFO: AFTER PROCESS_VALIDATIONS 3
INFO: BEFORE UPDATE_MODEL_VALUES 4
INFO: AFTER UPDATE_MODEL_VALUES 4
INFO: BEFORE INVOKE_APPLICATION 5
INFO: AFTER INVOKE_APPLICATION 5
```

```
INFO: BEFORE RENDER_RESPONSE 6
INFO: AFTER RENDER_RESPONSE 6
```

Now you can see that the listener is notified of all phases because we have set the default phase to PhaseId.ANY_PHASE.

Next, we select Apply Request Values from the listbox and activate the submit button, as shown in the middle picture in Figure 7–9. Here's the listener's output for that form submit:

```
INFO: BEFORE RESTORE_VIEW 1
INFO: AFTER RESTORE_VIEW 1
INFO: BEFORE APPLY_REQUEST_VALUES 2
INFO: AFTER APPLY_REQUEST_VALUES 2
INFO: BEFORE PROCESS_VALIDATIONS 3
```

You might have expected only the Apply Request Values output. Why was our listener notified before and after Restore View and before Process Validations? First, when the form was submitted, the listener's phase was still ANY_PHASE. So when the life cycle began, our listener was interested in all phases and was notified accordingly.

Second, remember that the phase ID for our listener is set with a value change listener, and recall from Figure 7–1 on page 268 that value change listeners are invoked after the Process Validations phase. At the end of Process Validations, the value change listener set the phase listener's phase to APPLY_REQUEST_VALUES.

Since Apply Request Values has already executed, our listener was not notified for the remainder of the life cycle. If you click the submit button once again, you will see the output you expect because the listener's phase ID was set to Apply Request Values from the beginning of the life cycle:

```
INFO: BEFORE APPLY_REQUEST_VALUES 2
INFO: AFTER APPLY_REQUEST_VALUES 2
```

Finally, we select Invoke Application and submit the form. That produces the following output:

```
INFO: BEFORE APPLY_REQUEST_VALUES 2
INFO: AFTER APPLY_REQUEST_VALUES 2
INFO: BEFORE INVOKE_APPLICATION 5
INFO: AFTER INVOKE_APPLICATION 5
```

Does the output make sense this time? When the life cycle starts, the listener's phase ID is Apply Request Values, so the listener is notified of that phase. Later in the life cycle—after Process Validation—the value change listener changes the listener's phase ID to INVOKE_APPLICATION. Subsequently, the listener is notified of the Invoke Application phase. If you click the submit button again, you will see this output:

```
INFO: BEFORE INVOKE_APPLICATION 5
INFO: AFTER INVOKE_APPLICATION 5
```

The directory structure for the phase listener example is shown in Figure
7–10. The application shown in Figure 7–9 is listed in Listing 7–14 through
Listing 7–19.

 TIP: You can use the phase tracker in your own applications to see when
events are fired: Any log messages you generate will be mixed with the
phase tracker messages. To use the phase tracker, make sure the class file
is in your WAR file and you have declared the listener in faces-config.xml as
we did in Listing 7–17. For more industrial-strength JSF tracing, see "How
do I debug a stuck page?" on page 696 of Chapter 13.

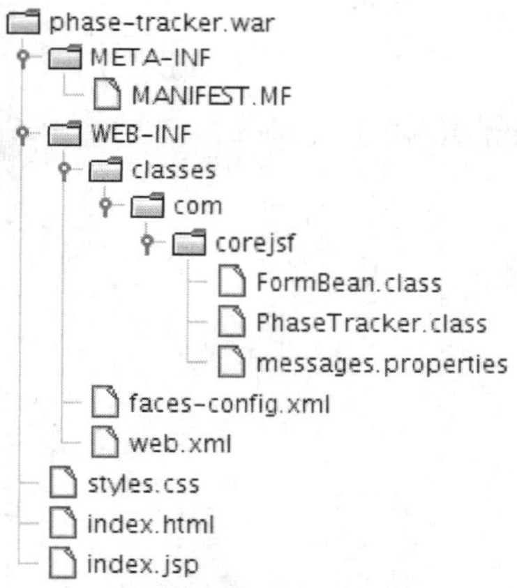

```
📁 phase-tracker.war
  📁 META-INF
    📄 MANIFEST.MF
  📁 WEB-INF
    📁 classes
      📁 com
        📁 corejsf
          📄 FormBean.class
          📄 PhaseTracker.class
          📄 messages.properties
    📄 faces-config.xml
    📄 web.xml
  📄 styles.css
  📄 index.html
  📄 index.jsp
```

Figure 7–10   Directory structure for the phase listener example

---

Listing 7–14 phase-tracker/web/index.jsp

```
 1. <html>
 2.    <%@ taglib uri="http://java.sun.com/jsf/core" prefix="f" %>
 3.    <%@ taglib uri="http://java.sun.com/jsf/html" prefix="h" %>
 4.    <f:view beforePhase="#{form.beforePhase}"
 5.       afterPhase="#{form.afterPhase}">
 6.       <head>
 7.          <link href="styles.css" rel="stylesheet" type="text/css"/>
 8.          <title>
 9.             <h:outputText value="#{msgs.indexWindowTitle}"/>
10.          </title>
11.       </head>
```

Listing 7–14 phase-tracker/web/index.jsp (cont.)

```
12.
13.        <body>
14.          <h:form>
15.            <h:panelGrid columns="2" columnClasses="phaseFormColumns">
16.              <h:outputText value="#{msgs.phasePrompt}"/>
17.
18.              <h:selectOneListbox valueChangeListener="#{form.phaseChange}">
19.                <f:selectItems value="#{form.phases}"/>
20.              </h:selectOneListbox>
21.
22.              <h:commandButton value="#{msgs.submitPrompt}"/>
23.            </h:panelGrid>
24.          </h:form>
25.        </body>
26.      </f:view>
27. </html>
```

Listing 7–15 phase-tracker/src/java/com/corejsf/FormBean.java

```
 1. package com.corejsf;
 2.
 3. import javax.faces.FactoryFinder;
 4. import javax.faces.event.PhaseEvent;
 5. import javax.faces.event.PhaseListener;
 6. import javax.faces.event.ValueChangeEvent;
 7. import javax.faces.lifecycle.Lifecycle;
 8. import javax.faces.lifecycle.LifecycleFactory;
 9. import javax.faces.model.SelectItem;
10.
11. public class FormBean {
12.    private SelectItem[] phases = {
13.      new SelectItem("RESTORE_VIEW"),
14.      new SelectItem("APPLY_REQUEST_VALUES"),
15.      new SelectItem("PROCESS_VALIDATIONS"),
16.      new SelectItem("UPDATE_MODEL_VALUES"),
17.      new SelectItem("INVOKE_APPLICATION"),
18.      new SelectItem("RENDER_RESPONSE"),
19.      new SelectItem("ANY_PHASE"),
20.    };
21.
22.    public SelectItem[] getPhases() { return phases; }
23.
24.    public void phaseChange(ValueChangeEvent e) {
25.      LifecycleFactory factory = (LifecycleFactory) FactoryFinder.getFactory(
26.          FactoryFinder.LIFECYCLE_FACTORY);
```

Listing 7–15 phase-tracker/src/java/com/corejsf/FormBean.java (cont.)

```
27.        Lifecycle lifecycle = factory.getLifecycle(LifecycleFactory.
28.            DEFAULT_LIFECYCLE);
29.
30.        PhaseListener[] listeners = lifecycle.getPhaseListeners();
31.        for (int i = 0; i < listeners.length; i++) {
32.          PhaseListener listener = listeners[i];
33.          if (listener instanceof com.corejsf.PhaseTracker)
34.            ((com.corejsf.PhaseTracker) listener).setPhase(
35.                (String) e.getNewValue());
36.        }
37.      }
38.      public void afterPhase(PhaseEvent event) {
39.        System.out.println("AFTER PHASE " + showEvent(event));
40.      }
41.      public void beforePhase(PhaseEvent event) {
42.        System.out.println("BEFORE PHASE " + showEvent(event));
43.      }
44.      private String showEvent(PhaseEvent event) {
45.        return "Phase Event: " + event.getPhaseId();
46.      }
47. }
```

Listing 7–16 phase-tracker/src/java/com/corejsf/PhaseTracker.java

```
1. package com.corejsf;
2.
3. import java.util.logging.Logger;
4. import javax.faces.context.FacesContext;
5. import javax.faces.event.PhaseEvent;
6. import javax.faces.event.PhaseListener;
7. import javax.faces.event.PhaseId;
8.
9. public class PhaseTracker implements PhaseListener {
10.    private static final String PHASE_PARAMETER ="com.corejsf.phaseTracker.phase";
11.    private static final Logger logger = Logger.getLogger("com.corejsf.phases");
12.    private static String phase = null;
13.
14.    public void setPhase(String newValue) { phase = newValue; }
15.
16.    public PhaseId getPhaseId() {
17.      if (phase == null) {
18.        FacesContext context = FacesContext.getCurrentInstance();
19.        phase = (String) context.getExternalContext().getInitParameter(
20.                                            PHASE_PARAMETER);
21.      }
22.      PhaseId phaseId = PhaseId.ANY_PHASE;
```

Listing 7–16 phase-tracker/src/java/com/corejsf/PhaseTracker.java (cont.)

```java
23.
24.        if (phase != null) {
25.            if ("RESTORE_VIEW".equals(phase))
26.                phaseId = PhaseId.RESTORE_VIEW;
27.            else if ("APPLY_REQUEST_VALUES".equals(phase))
28.                phaseId = PhaseId.APPLY_REQUEST_VALUES;
29.            else if ("PROCESS_VALIDATIONS".equals(phase))
30.                phaseId = PhaseId.PROCESS_VALIDATIONS;
31.            else if ("UPDATE_MODEL_VALUES".equals(phase))
32.                phaseId = PhaseId.UPDATE_MODEL_VALUES;
33.            else if ("INVOKE_APPLICATION".equals(phase))
34.                phaseId = PhaseId.INVOKE_APPLICATION;
35.            else if ("RENDER_RESPONSE".equals(phase))
36.                phaseId = PhaseId.RENDER_RESPONSE;
37.            else if ("ANY_PHASE".equals(phase))
38.                phaseId = PhaseId.ANY_PHASE;
39.        }
40.        return phaseId;
41.    }
42.    public void beforePhase(PhaseEvent e) {
43.        logger.info("BEFORE " + e.getPhaseId());
44.    }
45.    public void afterPhase(PhaseEvent e) {
46.        logger.info("AFTER " + e.getPhaseId());
47.    }
48. }
```

Listing 7–17 phase-tracker/web/WEB-INF/faces-config.xml

```xml
1. <?xml version="1.0"?>
2. <faces-config xmlns="http://java.sun.com/xml/ns/javaee"
3.     xmlns:xsi="http://www.w3.org/2001/XMLSchema-instance"
4.     xsi:schemaLocation="http://java.sun.com/xml/ns/javaee
5.     http://java.sun.com/xml/ns/javaee/web-facesconfig_1_2.xsd"
6.     version="1.2">
7.     <application>
8.         <resource-bundle>
9.             <base-name>com.corejsf.messages</base-name>
10.            <var>msgs</var>
11.        </resource-bundle>
12.    </application>
13.
```

Listing 7–17   phase-tracker/web/WEB-INF/faces-config.xml (cont.)

```
14.    <managed-bean>
15.        <managed-bean-name>form</managed-bean-name>
16.        <managed-bean-class>com.corejsf.FormBean</managed-bean-class>
17.        <managed-bean-scope>session</managed-bean-scope>
18.    </managed-bean>
19.
20.    <lifecycle>
21.        <phase-listener>com.corejsf.PhaseTracker</phase-listener>
22.    </lifecycle>
23. </faces-config>
```

Listing 7–18   phase-tracker/src/java/com/corejsf/messages.properties

```
1. indexWindowTitle=Phase Events
2. phasePrompt=Select a phase:
3. submitPrompt=Submit this form
```

Listing 7–19   phase-tracker/web/styles.css

```
1. body {
2.     background: #eee;
3. }
4. .phaseFormColumns {
5.     vertical-align: top;
6.     font-style: italic;
7.     font-size: 1.1em;
8. }
9. .columns {
10.     vertical-align: top;
11. }
```

Putting It All Together

We close out this chapter with an example of a poor man's implementation of a tabbed pane. That example demonstrates event handling and advanced aspects of using JSF HTML tags. Those advanced uses include the following:

- Nesting h:panelGrid tags
- Using facets
- Specifying tab indexing
- Adding tooltips to components with the title attribute
- Dynamically determining style classes

- Using action listeners
- Optional rendering
- Statically including JSF pages

JSF 1.2 does not have a tabbed pane component, so if you want a tabbed pane in your application, you have two choices: implement a custom component or use existing tags—with a backing bean—to create an ad hoc tabbed pane. Figure 7–11 shows the latter. The former is discussed in "Using Child Components and Facets" on page 408 of Chapter 9.

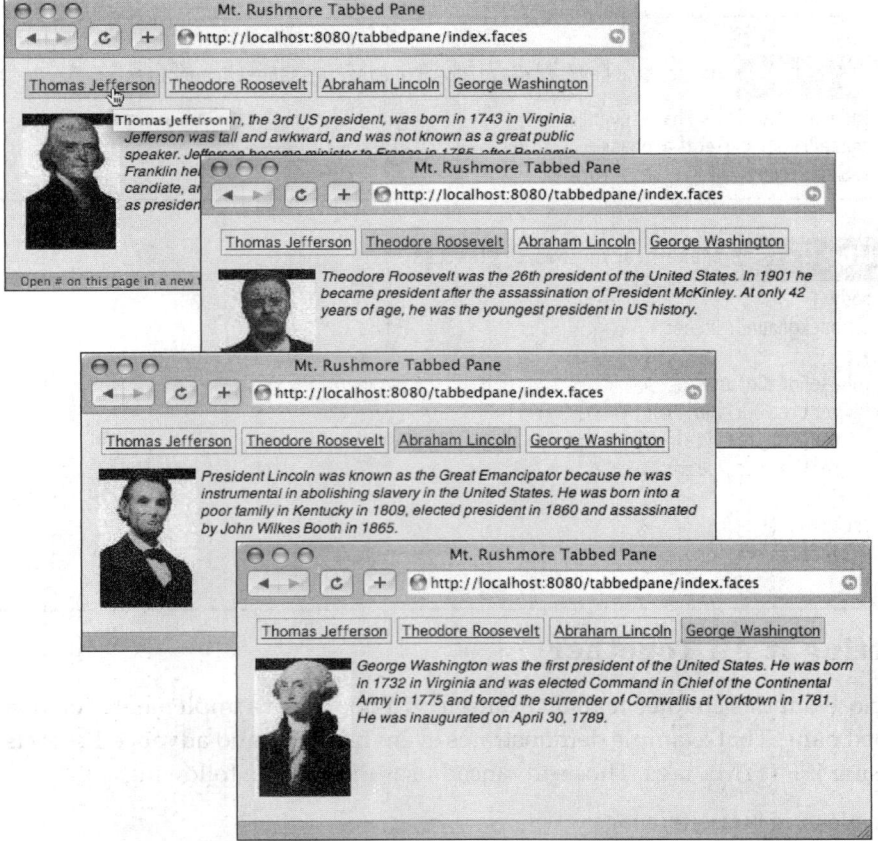

Figure 7–11   A poor man's tabbed pane

The tabbed pane shown in Figure 7–11 is implemented entirely with existing JSF HTML tags and a backing bean; no custom renderers or components are used. The JSF page for the tabbed pane looks like this:

```
...
<h:form>
    <%-- Tabs --%>
    <h:panelGrid styleClass="tabbedPane" columnClasses="displayPanel">
        <f:facet name="header">
            <h:panelGrid columns="4" styleClass="tabbedPaneHeader">
                <h:commandLink tabindex="1"
                    title="#{tp.jeffersonTooltip}"
                    styleClass="#{tp.jeffersonStyle}"
                    actionListener="#{tp.jeffersonAction}">
                    <h:outputText value="#{msgs.jeffersonTab}"/>
                </h:commandLink>
                ...
            </h:panelGrid>
        </f:facet>

    <%-- Main panel --%>
    <%@ include file="jefferson.jsp" %>
    <%@ include file="roosevelt.jsp" %>
    <%@ include file="lincoln.jsp" %>
    <%@ include file="washington.jsp" %>
    </h:panelGrid>
</h:form>
...
```

The tabbed pane is implemented with h:panelGrid. Because we do not specify the columns attribute, the panel has one column. The panel's header—defined with an f:facet tag—contains the tabs, which are implemented with another h:panelGrid that contains h:commandLink tags for each tab. The only row in the panel contains the content associated with the selected tab.

When a user selects a tab, the associated action listener for the command link is invoked and modifies the data stored in the backing bean. Because we use a different CSS style for the selected tab, the styleClass attribute of each h:commandLink tag is pulled from the backing bean with a value reference expression.

As you can see from the top picture in Figure 7–11, we have used the title attribute to associate a tooltip with each tab. Another accessibility feature is the ability to move from one tab to another with the keyboard instead of the mouse. We implemented that feature by specifying the tabindex attribute for each h:commandLink.

The content associated with each tab is statically included with the JSP include directive. For our application, that content is a picture and some text, but you could modify the included JSF pages to contain any set of appropriate components. Notice that even though all the JSF pages representing content are included, only the content associated with the current tab is rendered. That is achieved with the rendered attribute—for example, jefferson.jsp looks like this:

```
<h:panelGrid columns="2" columnClasses="presidentDiscussionColumn"
    rendered="#{tp.jeffersonCurrent}">
    <h:graphicImage value="/images/jefferson.jpg"/>
    <h:outputText value="#{msgs.jeffersonDiscussion}" styleClass="tabbedPaneContent"/>
</h:panelGrid>
```

Figure 7–12 shows the directory structure for the tabbed pane application and Listing 7–20 through Listing 7–28 show those files.

 NOTE: The JSF reference implementation contains a samples directory that holds a handful of sample applications. One of those applications, contained in jsf-components.war, is a tabbed pane component. Although the sample components are provided largely as proof-of-concept, you may find them useful as a starting point for your own custom components.

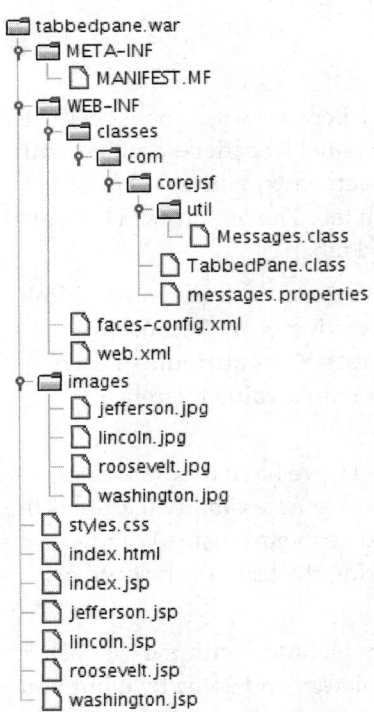

Figure 7–12   Directory structure for the tabbed pane example

Listing 7–20	tabbedpane/web/index.jsp

```
1.  <html>
2.     <%@ taglib uri="http://java.sun.com/jsf/core"  prefix="f" %>
3.     <%@ taglib uri="http://java.sun.com/jsf/html"  prefix="h" %>
4.
5.     <f:view>
6.        <head>
7.           <link href="styles.css" rel="stylesheet" type="text/css"/>
8.           <title>
9.              <h:outputText value="#{msgs.windowTitle}"/>
10.          </title>
11.       </head>
12.
13.       <body>
14.          <h:form>
15.             <h:panelGrid styleClass="tabbedPane" columnClasses="displayPanel">
16.                <%-- Tabs --%>
17.
18.                <f:facet name="header">
19.                   <h:panelGrid columns="5" styleClass="tabbedPaneHeader">
20.
21.                      <h:commandLink tabindex="1"
22.                         title="#{tp.jeffersonTooltip}"
23.                         styleClass="#{tp.jeffersonStyle}"
24.                         actionListener="#{tp.jeffersonAction}">
25.
26.                         <h:outputText value="#{msgs.jeffersonTabText}"/>
27.                      </h:commandLink>
28.
29.                      <h:commandLink tabindex="2"
30.                         title="#{tp.rooseveltTooltip}"
31.                         styleClass="#{tp.rooseveltStyle}"
32.                         actionListener="#{tp.rooseveltAction}">
33.
34.                         <h:outputText value="#{msgs.rooseveltTabText}"/>
35.                      </h:commandLink>
36.
37.                      <h:commandLink tabindex="3"
38.                         title="#{tp.lincolnTooltip}"
39.                         styleClass="#{tp.lincolnStyle}"
40.                         actionListener="#{tp.lincolnAction}">
41.
42.                         <h:outputText value="#{msgs.lincolnTabText}"/>
43.                      </h:commandLink>
44.
```

Listing 7–20   tabbedpane/web/index.jsp (cont.)

```
45.                    <h:commandLink tabindex="4"
46.                         title="#{tp.washingtonTooltip}"
47.                      styleClass="#{tp.washingtonStyle}"
48.                  actionListener="#{tp.washingtonAction}">
49.
50.                  <h:outputText value="#{msgs.washingtonTabText}"/>
51.                </h:commandLink>
52.             </h:panelGrid>
53.          </f:facet>
54.
55.          <%-- Tabbed pane content --%>
56.
57.          <%@ include file="washington.jsp" %>
58.          <%@ include file="roosevelt.jsp" %>
59.          <%@ include file="lincoln.jsp" %>
60.          <%@ include file="jefferson.jsp" %>
61.       </h:panelGrid>
62.     </h:form>
63.   </body>
64.  </f:view>
65. </html>
```

Listing 7–21   tabbedpane/web/jefferson.jsp

```
1. <h:panelGrid columns="2" columnClasses="presidentDiscussionColumn"
2.     rendered="#{tp.jeffersonCurrent}">
3.
4.    <h:graphicImage value="/images/jefferson.jpg"/>
5.    <h:outputText value="#{msgs.jeffersonDiscussion}"
6.       styleClass="tabbedPaneContent"/>
7.
8. </h:panelGrid>
```

Listing 7–22   tabbedpane/web/roosevelt.jsp

```
1. <h:panelGrid columns="2" columnClasses="presidentDiscussionColumn"
2.     rendered="#{tp.rooseveltCurrent}">
3.
4.    <h:graphicImage value="/images/roosevelt.jpg"/>
5.    <h:outputText value="#{msgs.rooseveltDiscussion}"
6.       styleClass="tabbedPaneContent"/>
7.
8. </h:panelGrid>
```

Listing 7-23   tabbedpane/web/lincoln.jsp

```
1. <h:panelGrid columns="2" columnClasses="presidentDiscussionColumn"
2.    rendered="#{tp.lincolnCurrent}">
3.
4.    <h:graphicImage value="/images/lincoln.jpg"/>
5.    <h:outputText value="#{msgs.lincolnDiscussion}"
6.       styleClass="tabbedPaneContent"/>
7.
8. </h:panelGrid>
```

Listing 7-24   tabbedpane/web/washington.jsp

```
1. <h:panelGrid columns="2" columnClasses="presidentDiscussionColumn"
2.    rendered="#{tp.washingtonCurrent}">
3.
4.    <h:graphicImage value="/images/washington.jpg"/>
5.    <h:outputText value="#{msgs.washingtonDiscussion}"
6.       styleClass="tabbedPaneContent"/>
7.
8. </h:panelGrid>
```

Listing 7-25   tabbedpane/src/java/com/corejsf/messages.properties

```
1. windowTitle=Mt. Rushmore Tabbed Pane
2. lincolnTooltip=Abraham Lincoln
3. lincolnTabText=Abraham Lincoln
4. lincolnDiscussion=President Lincoln was known as the Great Emancipator because \
5. he was instrumental in abolishing slavery in the United States. He was born \
6. into a poor family in Kentucky in 1809, elected president in 1860, and \
7. assassinated by John Wilkes Booth in 1865.
8.
9. washingtonTooltip=George Washington
10. washingtonTabText=George Washington
11. washingtonDiscussion=George Washington was the first president of the United \
12. States. He was born in 1732 in Virginia, was elected Commander in Chief of \
13. the Continental Army in 1775, and forced the surrender of Cornwallis at Yorktown \
14. in 1781. He was inaugurated on April 30, 1789.
15.
16. rooseveltTooltip=Theodore Roosevelt
17. rooseveltTabText=Theodore Roosevelt
18. rooseveltDiscussion=Theodore Roosevelt was the 26th president of the United \
19. States. In 1901 he became president after the assassination of President \
20. McKinley. At only 42, he was the youngest president in U.S. history.
```

Listing 7–25 tabbedpane/src/java/com/corejsf/messages.properties (cont.)

```
21.
22. jeffersonTooltip=Thomas Jefferson
23. jeffersonTabText=Thomas Jefferson
24. jeffersonDiscussion=Thomas Jefferson, the 3rd U.S. president, was born in \
25. 1743 in Virginia. Jefferson was tall and awkward, and was not known as a \
26. great public speaker. Jefferson became minister to France in 1785, after \
27. Benjamin Franklin held that post. In 1796, Jefferson was a reluctant \
28. presidential candiate, and missed winning the election by a mere three votes. \
29. He served as president from 1801 to 1809.
```

Listing 7–26 tabbedpane/web/styles.css

```
1. body {
2.     background: #eee;
3. }
4. .tabbedPaneHeader {
5.     vertical-align: top;
6.     text-align: left;
7.     padding: 2px 2px 0px 2px;
8. }
9. .tabbedPaneText {
10.     font-size: 1.0em;
11.     font-style: regular;
12.     padding: 3px;
13.     border: thin solid CornflowerBlue;
14. }
15. .tabbedPaneTextSelected {
16.     font-size: 1.0em;
17.     font-style: regular;
18.     padding: 3px;
19.     background: PowderBlue;
20.     border: thin solid CornflowerBlue;
21. }
22. .tabbedPane {
23.     vertical-align: top;
24.     text-align: left;
25.     padding: 10px;
26. }
27. .displayPanel {
28.     vertical-align: top;
29.     text-align: left;
30.     padding: 10px;
31. }
```

Listing 7–26 tabbedpane/web/styles.css (cont.)

```
32. .tabbedPaneContent {
33.     width: 100%;
34.     height: 100%;
35.     font-style: italic;
36.     vertical-align: top;
37.     text-align: left;
38.     font-size: 1.2m;
39. }
40. .presidentDiscussionColumn {
41.     vertical-align: top;
42.     text-align: left;
43. }
```

Listing 7–27 tabbedpane/web/WEB-INF/faces-config.xml

```
1.  <?xml version="1.0"?>
2.  <faces-config xmlns="http://java.sun.com/xml/ns/javaee"
3.      xmlns:xsi="http://www.w3.org/2001/XMLSchema-instance"
4.      xsi:schemaLocation="http://java.sun.com/xml/ns/javaee
5.      http://java.sun.com/xml/ns/javaee/web-facesconfig_1_2.xsd"
6.      version="1.2">
7.      <application>
8.          <resource-bundle>
9.              <base-name>com.corejsf.messages</base-name>
10.             <var>msgs</var>
11.         </resource-bundle>
12.     </application>
13.
14.     <managed-bean>
15.         <managed-bean-name>tp</managed-bean-name>
16.         <managed-bean-class>com.corejsf.TabbedPane</managed-bean-class>
17.         <managed-bean-scope>session</managed-bean-scope>
18.     </managed-bean>
19. </faces-config>
```

Listing 7–28 tabbedpane/src/java/com/corejsf/TabbedPane.java

```java
1. package com.corejsf;
2.
3. import javax.faces.event.ActionEvent;
4.
5. public class TabbedPane {
6.    private int index;
7.    private static final int JEFFERSON_INDEX = 0;
8.    private static final int ROOSEVELT_INDEX = 1;
9.    private static final int LINCOLN_INDEX = 2;
10.   private static final int WASHINGTON_INDEX = 3;
11.
12.   private String[] tabs = { "jeffersonTabText", "rooseveltTabText",
13.       "lincolnTabText", "washingtonTabText", };
14.
15.   private String[] tabTooltips = { "jeffersonTooltip", "rooseveltTooltip",
16.       "lincolnTooltip", "washingtonTooltip" };
17.
18.   public TabbedPane() {
19.       index = JEFFERSON_INDEX;
20.   }
21.
22.   // action listeners that set the current tab
23.
24.   public void jeffersonAction(ActionEvent e) { index = JEFFERSON_INDEX;   }
25.   public void rooseveltAction(ActionEvent e) { index = ROOSEVELT_INDEX;   }
26.   public void lincolnAction(ActionEvent e) { index = LINCOLN_INDEX;       }
27.   public void washingtonAction(ActionEvent e) { index = WASHINGTON_INDEX; }
28.
29.   // CSS styles
30.
31.   public String getJeffersonStyle() { return getCSS(JEFFERSON_INDEX);   }
32.   public String getRooseveltStyle() { return getCSS(ROOSEVELT_INDEX);   }
33.   public String getLincolnStyle() { return getCSS(LINCOLN_INDEX);       }
34.   public String getWashingtonStyle() { return getCSS(WASHINGTON_INDEX); }
35.
36.   private String getCSS(int forIndex) {
37.       return forIndex == index ? "tabbedPaneTextSelected" : "tabbedPaneText";
38.   }
39.
40.   // methods for determining the current tab
41.
42.   public boolean isJeffersonCurrent() { return index == JEFFERSON_INDEX;   }
43.   public boolean isRooseveltCurrent() { return index == ROOSEVELT_INDEX;   }
44.   public boolean isLincolnCurrent() { return index == LINCOLN_INDEX;       }
45.   public boolean isWashingtonCurrent() { return index == WASHINGTON_INDEX; }
```

Listing 7–28 tabbedpane/src/java/com/corejsf/TabbedPane.java (cont.)

```
46.
47.    // methods that get tooltips for titles
48.
49.    public String getJeffersonTooltip() {
50.        return com.corejsf.util.Messages.getString(
51.            "com.corejsf.messages", tabTooltips[JEFFERSON_INDEX], null);
52.    }
53.    public String getRooseveltTooltip() {
54.        return com.corejsf.util.Messages.getString(
55.            "com.corejsf.messages", tabTooltips[ROOSEVELT_INDEX], null);
56.    }
57.    public String getLincolnTooltip() {
58.        return com.corejsf.util.Messages.getString(
59.            "com.corejsf.messages", tabTooltips[LINCOLN_INDEX], null);
60.    }
61.    public String getWashingtonTooltip() {
62.        return com.corejsf.util.Messages.getString(
63.            "com.corejsf.messages", tabTooltips[WASHINGTON_INDEX], null);
64.    }
65. }
```

SUBVIEWS
AND TILES

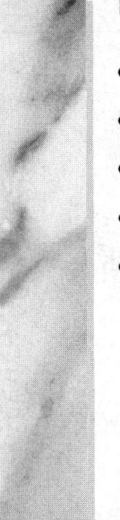

Topics in This Chapter

Chapter 8

User interfaces are typically the most volatile aspect of web applications during development, so it is crucial to create flexible and extensible interfaces. This chapter shows you how to achieve that flexibility and extensibility by including common content. First we discuss standard JSP mechanisms—JSP includes and JSTL imports—that you can use to include common content in a JSF application. Next, we explore the use of the Apache Tiles package—which lets you encapsulate layout in addition to content, among other handy features—with JSF.

Common Layouts

Many popular web sites, such as `nytimes.com`, `java.sun.com`, or `amazon.com`, use a common layout for their web pages. For example, all three of the web sites listed above use a header-menu-content layout, as depicted in Figure 8–1.

You can use HTML frames to achieve the layout shown in Figure 8–1, but frames are undesirable for several reasons. For example, frames make it hard for users to bookmark pages. Frames also generate separate requests, which can be problematic for web applications. Including content, which is the focus of this chapter, is generally preferred over frames.

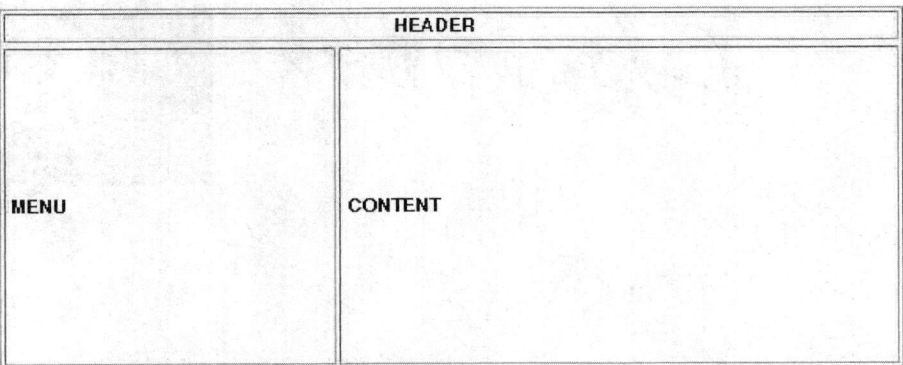

Figure 8–1 A typical web page layout

A Book Viewer and a Library

To illustrate implementing layouts, including common content, and using Tiles, we discuss two applications in this chapter: a book viewer and a library. Those applications are shown in Figure 8–2 and Figure 8–3, respectively.

The book viewer is intuitive. If you click a chapter link, that chapter is shown in the content region of the web page. The library is an extension of the book viewer that lets you view more than one book. You can select books from the menu at the top of the web page.

The book viewer addresses the following topics:

- "Monolithic JSF Pages" on page 320
- "Common Content Inclusion" on page 326
- "Looking at Tiles" on page 331
- "Parameterizing Tiles" on page 334
- "Extending Tiles" on page 335

The library illustrates these Tiles features:

- "Nested Tiles" on page 339
- "Tile Controllers" on page 341

Coverage of the book viewer begins in the next section, "The Book Viewer" on page 318. The library is discussed in "The Library" on page 339.

NOTE: For the examples in this chapter, we downloaded *Alice in Wonderland* and *Peter Pan* from the Project Gutenberg web site (`http://promo.net/pg/`), chopped them up into chapters, and converted them to HTML.

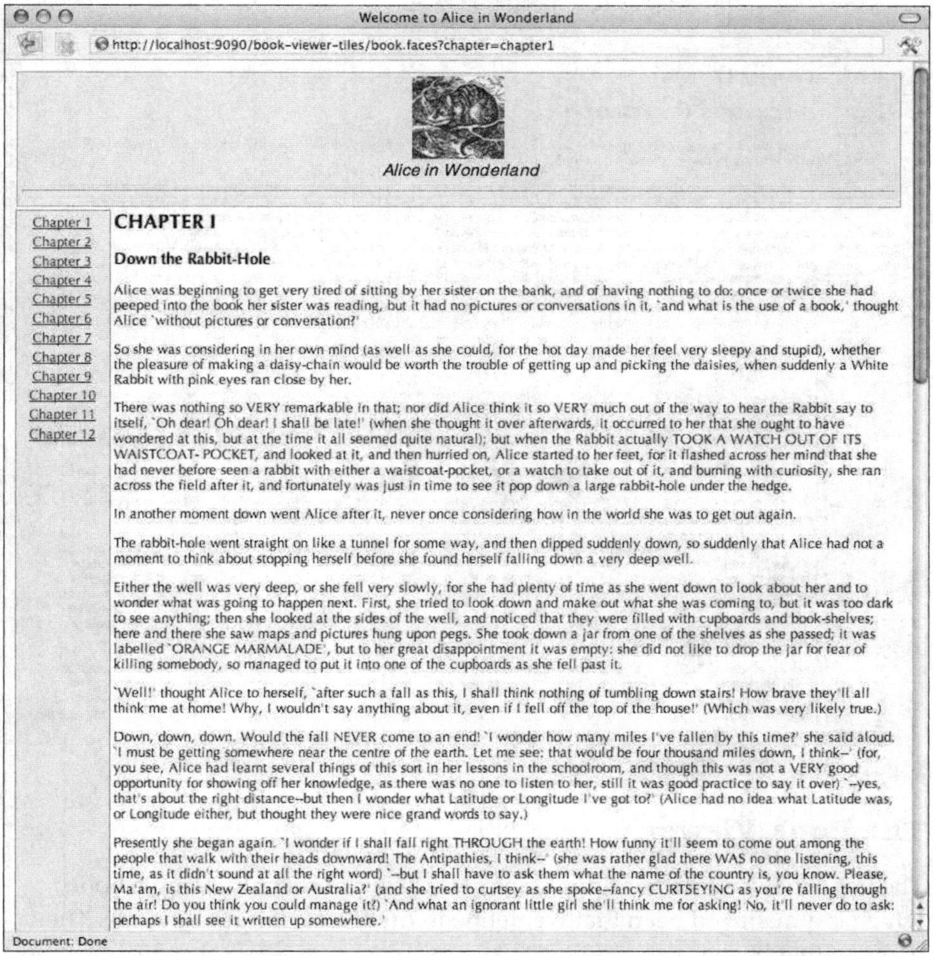

```
000                    Welcome to Alice in Wonderland
        http://localhost:9090/book-viewer-tiles/book.faces?chapter=chapter1
```

Alice in Wonderland

	CHAPTER I
Chapter 1	
Chapter 2	**Down the Rabbit-Hole**
Chapter 3	
Chapter 4	Alice was beginning to get very tired of sitting by her sister on the bank, and of having nothing to do: once or twice she had
Chapter 5	peeped into the book her sister was reading, but it had no pictures or conversations in it, `and what is the use of a book,` thought
Chapter 6	Alice `without pictures or conversation?`
Chapter 7	
Chapter 8	So she was considering in her own mind (as well as she could, for the hot day made her feel very sleepy and stupid), whether
Chapter 9	the pleasure of making a daisy-chain would be worth the trouble of getting up and picking the daisies, when suddenly a White
Chapter 10	Rabbit with pink eyes ran close by her.
Chapter 11	
Chapter 12	There was nothing so VERY remarkable in that; nor did Alice think it so VERY much out of the way to hear the Rabbit say to

itself, `Oh dear! Oh dear! I shall be late!` (when she thought it over afterwards, it occurred to her that she ought to have wondered at this, but at the time it all seemed quite natural); but when the Rabbit actually TOOK A WATCH OUT OF ITS WAISTCOAT- POCKET, and looked at it, and then hurried on, Alice started to her feet, for it flashed across her mind that she had never before seen a rabbit with either a waistcoat-pocket, or a watch to take out of it, and burning with curiosity, she ran across the field after it, and fortunately was just in time to see it pop down a large rabbit-hole under the hedge.

In another moment down went Alice after it, never once considering how in the world she was to get out again.

The rabbit-hole went straight on like a tunnel for some way, and then dipped suddenly down, so suddenly that Alice had not a moment to think about stopping herself before she found herself falling down a very deep well.

Either the well was very deep, or she fell very slowly, for she had plenty of time as she went down to look about her and to wonder what was going to happen next. First, she tried to look down and make out what she was coming to, but it was too dark to see anything; then she looked at the sides of the well, and noticed that they were filled with cupboards and book-shelves; here and there she saw maps and pictures hung upon pegs. She took down a jar from one of the shelves as she passed; it was labelled `ORANGE MARMALADE`, but to her great disappointment it was empty: she did not like to drop the jar for fear of killing somebody, so managed to put it into one of the cupboards as she fell past it.

`Well!` thought Alice to herself, `after such a fall as this, I shall think nothing of tumbling down stairs! How brave they'll all think me at home! Why, I wouldn't say anything about it, even if I fell off the top of the house!` (Which was very likely true.)

Down, down, down. Would the fall NEVER come to an end! `I wonder how many miles I've fallen by this time?` she said aloud. `I must be getting somewhere near the centre of the earth. Let me see: that would be four thousand miles down, I think--` (for, you see, Alice had learnt several things of this sort in her lessons in the schoolroom, and though this was not a VERY good opportunity for showing off her knowledge, as there was no one to listen to her, still it was good practice to say it over) `--yes, that's about the right distance--but then I wonder what Latitude or Longitude I've got to?` (Alice had no idea what Latitude was, or Longitude either, but thought they were nice grand words to say.)

Presently she began again. `I wonder if I shall fall right THROUGH the earth! How funny it'll seem to come out among the people that walk with their heads downward! The Antipathies, I think--` (she was rather glad there WAS no one listening, this time, as it didn't sound at all the right word) `--but I shall have to ask them what the name of the country is, you know. Please, Ma'am, is this New Zealand or Australia?` (and she tried to curtsey as she spoke--fancy CURTSEYING as you're falling through the air! Do you think you could manage it?) `And what an ignorant little girl she'll think me for asking! No, it'll never do to ask: perhaps I shall see it written up somewhere.`

```
Document: Done
```

Figure 8–2   The book viewer

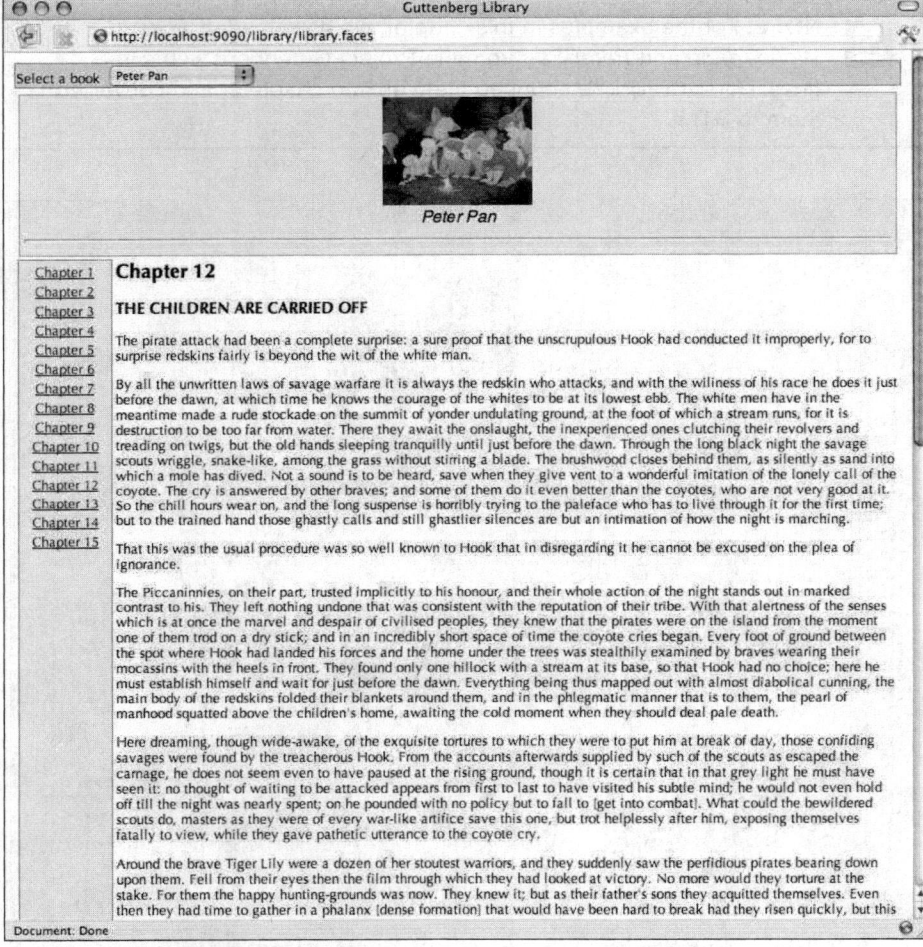

Figure 8–3   The library

The Book Viewer

The book viewer is rather limited in scope. It supports only a single book, which is a managed bean that we define in the faces configuration file. The name of that bean is book.

The book bean has these properties:

- titleKey
- image

- numChapters
- chapterKeys

The titleKey property represents a key in a resource bundle for the book's title. In the book viewer's properties file we have the key/value pair titleKey=Alice in Wonderland. When we display the book's title, we use the titleKey property, like this:

```
<h:outputText value="#{msgs[book.titleKey]}"/>
```

The image property is a string. The application interprets that string as a URL and loads it in the book viewer's header like this:

```
<h:graphicImage url="#{book.image}"/>
```

The chapterKeys property is a read-only list of keys, one for each chapter. The book viewer populates the book viewer's menu with corresponding values from a resource bundle:

```
<h:dataTable value="#{book.chapterKeys}" var="chapterKey">
    <h:commandLink>
        <h:outputText value="#{msgs[chapterKey]}"/>
        ...
    </h:commandLink>
</h:dataTable>
```

The Book class uses the numChapters property to compute the chapter keys.

The implementation of the Book class is rather mundane. You can see it in Listing 8–3 on page 324. Here is how we define an instance of the Book class in faces-config.xml:

```
<faces-config>
    <!-- The book -->
    <managed-bean>
    <managed-bean-name>book</managed-bean-name>
    <managed-bean-class>com.corejsf.Book</managed-bean-class>
    <managed-bean-scope>request</managed-bean-scope>

    <managed-property>
        <property-name>titleKey</property-name>
        <value>aliceInWonderland</value>
    </managed-property>

    <managed-property>
        <property-name>image</property-name>
        <value>cheshire.jpg</value>
    </managed-property>
```

```
<managed-property>
    <property-name>numChapters</property-name>
    <property-class>java.lang.Integer</property-class>
    <value>12</value>
</managed-property>
    </managed-bean>
</faces-config>
```

There are many ways to implement page layout. In this section, we look at three options: a monolithic JSF page, inclusion of common content, and Tiles.

 NOTE: We do not set the book's chapterKeys property in faces-config.xml. This is because the Book class creates that list of chapter keys for us. All we have to do is define the numChapters property.

Monolithic JSF Pages

A monolithic JSF page is perhaps the quickest way to implement the book viewer, shown in Figure 8–2. For example, here is a naive implementation:

```
<!-- A panel grid, which resides in a form, for the entire page --%>
<h:panelGrid columns="2" styleClass="book"
    columnClasses="menuColumn, chapterColumn">

    <!-- The header, containing an image, title, and horizontal rule --%>
    <f:facet name="header">
        <h:panelGrid columns="1" styleClass="bookHeader">
            <h:graphicImage value="#{book.image}"/>
            <h:outputText value="#{msgs[book.titleKey]}" styleClass='bookTitle'/>
            <hr>
        </h:panelGrid>
    </f:facet>

    <!-- Column 1 of the panel grid: The menu, which consists of chapter links --%>
    <h:dataTable value="#{book.chapterKeys}" var="chapterKey"
            styleClass="links" columnClasses="linksColumn">
        <h:column>
            <h:commandLink>
                <h:outputText value="#{msgs[chapterKey]}"/>
                <f:param name="chapter" value="#{chapterKey}"/>
            </h:commandLink>
        </h:column>
    </h:dataTable>

    <!-- Column 2 of the panel grid: The chapter content --%>
    <c:import url="${param.chapter}.html"/>
</h:panelGrid>
```

The book viewer is implemented with a panel grid with two columns. The header region is populated with an image, text, and HTML horizontal rule. Besides the header, the panel grid has only one row—the menu occupies the left column and the current chapter is displayed in the right column.

The menu is composed of chapter links. By default, `Book.getChapterKeys()` returns a list of strings that looks like this:

```
chapter1
chapter2
...
chapterN
```

`ChapterN` represents the last chapter in the book. In the book viewer's resource bundle, we define values for those keys:

```
chapter1=Chapter 1
chapter2=Chapter 2
...
```

To create chapter links, we use `h:dataTable` to iterate over the book's chapter keys. For every chapter, we create a link whose text corresponds to the chapter key's value with this expression: `#{msgs[chapterKey]}`. So, for example, we wind up with "Chapter 1" ... "Chapter 12" displayed in the menu when the number of chapters is 12.

The right column is reserved for chapter content. That content is included with JSTL's `c:import` tag.

The directory structure for the book viewer is shown in Figure 8–4. The monolithic JSF version of the book viewer is shown in Listing 8–1 through Listing 8–5.

 NOTE: Notice the `f:param` tag inside `h:commandLink`. The JSF framework turns that parameter into a request parameter—named `chapter`—when the link is activated. When the page is reloaded, that request parameter is used to load the chapter's content, like this:

```
<c:import url="${param.chapter}"/>
```

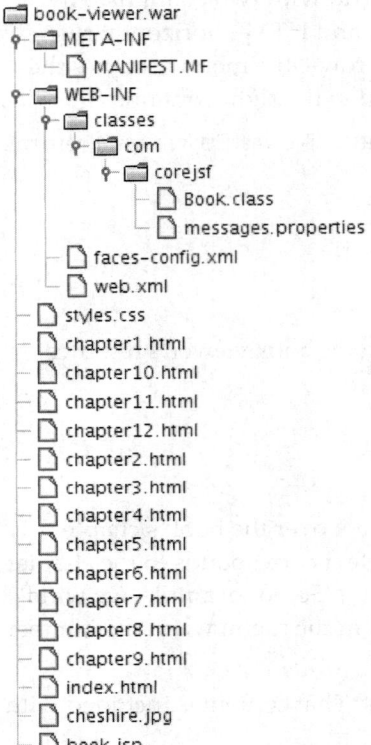

```
book-viewer.war
├── META-INF
│   └── MANIFEST.MF
├── WEB-INF
│   ├── classes
│   │   └── com
│   │       └── corejsf
│   │           ├── Book.class
│   │           └── messages.properties
│   ├── faces-config.xml
│   └── web.xml
├── styles.css
├── chapter1.html
├── chapter10.html
├── chapter11.html
├── chapter12.html
├── chapter2.html
├── chapter3.html
├── chapter4.html
├── chapter5.html
├── chapter6.html
├── chapter7.html
├── chapter8.html
├── chapter9.html
├── index.html
├── cheshire.jpg
└── book.jsp
```

Figure 8–4   The directory structure of the book viewer

Listing 8–1   book-viewer/web/book.jsp

```
1.  <html>
2.     <%@ taglib uri="http://java.sun.com/jsp/jstl/core" prefix="c" %>
3.     <%@ taglib uri="http://java.sun.com/jsf/core"  prefix="f" %>
4.     <%@ taglib uri="http://java.sun.com/jsf/html"  prefix="h" %>
5.
6.     <f:view>
7.        <f:loadBundle basename="com.corejsf.messages" var="msgs"/>
8.        <head>
9.           <link href="styles.css" rel="stylesheet" type="text/css"/>
10.          <title><h:outputText value="#{msgs.bookWindowTitle}"/></title>
11.       </head>
12.
13.       <body>
14.          <h:form>
```

Listing 8–1   book-viewer/web/book.jsp (cont.)

```
15.              <h:panelGrid columns="2" styleClass="book"
16.                  columnClasses="menuColumn, chapterColumn">
17.                <f:facet name="header">
18.                  <h:panelGrid columns="1" styleClass="bookHeader">
19.                    <h:graphicImage value="#{book.image}"/>
20.                    <h:outputText value="#{msgs[book.titleKey]}"
21.                            styleClass='bookTitle'/>
22.                    <hr/>
23.                  </h:panelGrid>
24.                </f:facet>
25.
26.                <h:dataTable value="#{book.chapterKeys}" var="chapterKey"
27.                        styleClass="links" columnClasses="linksColumn">
28.                  <h:column>
29.                    <h:commandLink>
30.                      <h:outputText value="#{msgs[chapterKey]}"/>
31.                      <f:param name="chapter" value="#{chapterKey}"/>
32.                    </h:commandLink>
33.                  </h:column>
34.                </h:dataTable>
35.
36.                <c:import url="${param.chapter}.html"/>
37.              </h:panelGrid>
38.            </h:form>
39.          </body>
40.        </f:view>
41.      </html>
```

Listing 8–2   book-viewer/web/WEB-INF/faces-config.xml

```
1.  <?xml version="1.0"?>
2.  <faces-config xmlns="http://java.sun.com/xml/ns/javaee"
3.      xmlns:xsi="http://www.w3.org/2001/XMLSchema-instance"
4.      xsi:schemaLocation="http://java.sun.com/xml/ns/javaee
5.          http://java.sun.com/xml/ns/javaee/web-facesconfig_1_2.xsd"
6.      version="1.2">
7.      <managed-bean>
8.        <managed-bean-name>book</managed-bean-name>
9.        <managed-bean-class>com.corejsf.Book</managed-bean-class>
10.       <managed-bean-scope>request</managed-bean-scope>
11.
```

Listing 8–2 book-viewer/web/WEB-INF/faces-config.xml (cont.)

```
12.          <managed-property>
13.             <property-name>titleKey</property-name>
14.             <value>aliceInWonderland</value>
15.          </managed-property>
16.
17.          <managed-property>
18.             <property-name>image</property-name>
19.             <value>cheshire.jpg</value>
20.          </managed-property>
21.
22.          <managed-property>
23.             <property-name>numChapters</property-name>
24.             <property-class>java.lang.Integer</property-class>
25.             <value>12</value>
26.          </managed-property>
27.       </managed-bean>
28.    </faces-config>
```

Listing 8–3 book-viewer/src/java/com/corejsf/Book.java

```
1.  package com.corejsf;
2.
3.  import java.util.LinkedList;
4.  import java.util.List;
5.
6.  public class Book {
7.     private String titleKey;
8.     private String image;
9.     private int numChapters;
10.    private List<String> chapterKeys = null;
11.
12.    // PROPERTY: titleKey
13.    public void setTitleKey(String titleKey) { this.titleKey = titleKey; }
14.    public String getTitleKey() { return titleKey; }
15.
16.    // PROPERTY: image
17.    public void setImage(String image) { this.image = image; }
18.    public String getImage() { return image; }
19.
20.    // PROPERTY: numChapters
21.    public void setNumChapters(int numChapters) { this.numChapters = numChapters;}
22.    public int getNumChapters() { return numChapters; }
23.
```

Listing 8–3 book-viewer/src/java/com/corejsf/Book.java (cont.)

```
24.    // PROPERTY: chapterKeys
25.    public List<String> getChapterKeys() {
26.       if(chapterKeys == null) {
27.          chapterKeys = new LinkedList<String>();
28.          for(int i=1; i <= numChapters; ++i)
29.             chapterKeys.add("chapter" + i);
30.       }
31.       return chapterKeys;
32.    }
33. }
```

Listing 8–4 book-viewer/src/java/com/corejsf/messages.properties

```
1. bookWindowTitle=Welcome to Alice in Wonderland
2. aliceInWonderland=Alice in Wonderland
3.
4. chapter1=Chapter 1
5. chapter2=Chapter 2
6. chapter3=Chapter 3
7. chapter4=Chapter 4
8. chapter5=Chapter 5
9. chapter6=Chapter 6
10. chapter7=Chapter 7
11. chapter8=Chapter 8
12. chapter9=Chapter 9
13. chapter10=Chapter 10
14. chapter11=Chapter 11
15. chapter12=Chapter 12
16. chapter13=Chapter 13
17. chapter14=Chapter 14
18. chapter15=Chapter 15
```

Listing 8–5 book-viewer/web/styles.css

```
1. .bookHeader {
2.    width: 100%;
3.    text-align: center;
4.    background-color: #eee;
5.    padding: 0 px;
6.    border: thin solid CornflowerBlue;
7. }
```

```
8.  .bookTitle {
9.      text-align: center;
10.     font-style: italic;
11.     font-size: 1.3em;
12.     font-family: Helvetica;
13. }
14. .book {
15.     vertical-align: top;
16.     width: 100%;
17.     height: 100%;
18. }
19. .menuColumn {
20.     vertical-align: top;
21.     background-color: #eee;
22.     width: 100px;
23.     border: thin solid #777;
24. }
25. .chapterColumn {
26.     vertical-align: top;
27.     text-align: left;
28.     width: *;
29. }
```

Common Content Inclusion

A monolithic JSF page is a poor choice for the book viewer because the JSF page is difficult to modify. Also, realize that our monolithic JSF page represents two things: layout and content.

Layout is implemented with an h:panelGrid tag, and content is represented by various JSF tags, such as h:graphicImage, h:outputText, h:commandLink, and the book chapters. Realize that *with a monolithic JSF page, we cannot reuse content or layout*.

In the next section, we concentrate on including content. In "Looking at Tiles" on page 331, we discuss including layout.

Content Inclusion in JSP-Based Applications

Instead of cramming a bunch of code into a monolithic JSF page, as we did in Listing 8–1 on page 322, it is better to include common content so you can reuse that content in other JSF pages. With JSP, you have three choices for including content:

- `<%@ include file="header.jsp"% >`
- `<jsp:include page="header.jsp"/>`
- `<c:import url="header.jsp"/>`

The first choice listed above—the JSP include directive—includes the specified file before the enclosing JSF page is compiled to a servlet. However, the include directive suffers from an important limitation: If the included file's content changes after the enclosing page was first processed, those changes are not reflected in the enclosing page. That means you must manually update the enclosing pages—whether the including pages changed or not—whenever included content changes.

The last two choices listed above include the content of a page at runtime and merge the included content with the including JSF page. Because the inclusion happens at runtime, changes to included pages are always reflected when the enclosing page is redisplayed. For that reason, jsp:include and c:import are usually preferred to the include directive.

The c:import tag works just like jsp:include, but it has more features—for example, c:import can import resources from another web application, whereas jsp:include cannot. Also, prior to JSP 2.0, you cannot use JSP expressions for jsp:include attributes, whereas you can with c:import. Remember that you must import the JSTL core tag library to use c:import.

Throughout this chapter, we use c:import for consistency. You can use either jsp:include or c:import to dynamically include content. If you do not need c:import's extra features, then it is ever-so-slightly easier to use jsp:include because you do not need to import the JSTL core tag library.

JSF-Specific Considerations

Regardless of whether you include content with the include directive, jsp:include, or c:import, you must take into account two special considerations when you include content in a JavaServer Faces application:

1. You must wrap included JSF tags in an f:subview tag.
2. Included JSF tags cannot contain f:view tags.

The first rule applies to included content that contains JSF tags. For example, the book viewer should encapsulate header content in its own JSF page so that we can reuse that content:

```
<%-- this is header.jsp --%>
<%@ taglib uri="http://java.sun.com/jsf/core" prefix="f" %>
<%@ taglib uri="http://java.sun.com/jsf/html" prefix="h" %>
```

```
<h:panelGrid columns="1" styleClass="header">
   <h:graphicImage value="books/book/cheshire.jpg"/>
   <h:outputText value="#{msgs.bookTitle}" styleClass="bookTitle"/>
   ...
</h:panelGrid>
```

Now we can include that content from the original JSF page:

```
<%-- This is from the original JSF page --%>
<f:view>
   ...
   <f:subview id="header">
      <c:import url="header.jsp"/>
   </f:subview>
   ...
</f:view>
```

You must assign an ID to each subview. The standard convention for including content is to name the subview after the imported JSF page.

JSF views, which are normally web pages, can contain an unlimited number of subviews. But there can be only one view. Because of that restriction, included JSF tags—which must be wrapped in a subview—cannot contain f:view tags.

 CAUTION: The book-viewer-include application maps the Faces servlet to *.faces. That means you can start the application with this URL: http://www.localhost:8080/book-viewer-include/book.faces. The Faces servlet maps books.faces to books.jsp. However, you cannot use the faces suffix when you use c:import. If you use c:import, you must use the jsp suffix.

Content Inclusion in the Book Viewer

To include content in the book viewer, we split our monolithic JSF page into four files: the original JSF page, /header.jsp, /menu.jsp, and /content.jsp. We include the header, menu, and content in the original JSF page:

```
<h:panelGrid columns="2" styleClass="book"
   columnClasses="menuColumn, contentColumn">

   <f:facet name="header">
      <f:subview id="header">
         <c:import url="header.jsp"/>
      </f:subview>
   </f:facet>

   <f:subview id="menu">
```

```
        <c:import url="menu.jsp"/>
    </f:subview>

        <c:import url="content.jsp"/>
    </h:panelGrid>
    ...
```

This code is much cleaner than the original JSF page listed in Listing 8–1, so it is easier to understand, maintain, and modify. But more important, we are now free to reuse the header, menu, and content for other views.

The directory structure for the book viewer with includes example is shown in Figure 8–5. Listing 8–6 through Listing 8–9 show the JSF pages for the book, its header, menu, and content.

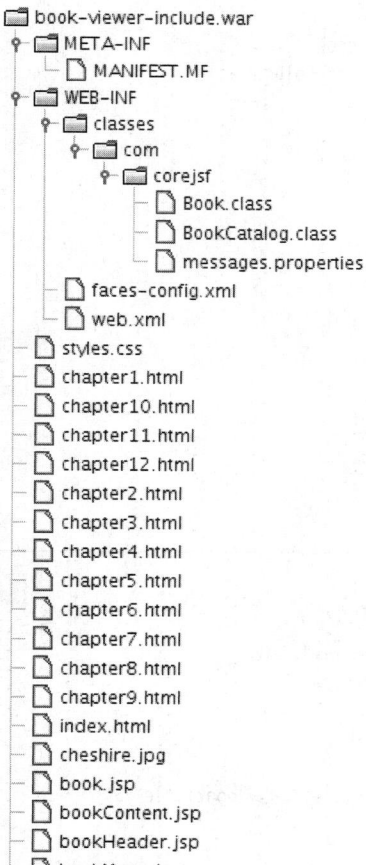

```
book-viewer-include.war
   META-INF
      MANIFEST.MF
   WEB-INF
      classes
         com
            corejsf
               Book.class
               BookCatalog.class
               messages.properties
      faces-config.xml
      web.xml
   styles.css
   chapter1.html
   chapter10.html
   chapter11.html
   chapter12.html
   chapter2.html
   chapter3.html
   chapter4.html
   chapter5.html
   chapter6.html
   chapter7.html
   chapter8.html
   chapter9.html
   index.html
   cheshire.jpg
   book.jsp
   bookContent.jsp
   bookHeader.jsp
   bookMenu.jsp
```

Figure 8–5   The directory structure of the book viewer with includes

Listing 8–6 `book-viewer-include/web/book.jsp`

```
1. <html>
2.    <%@ taglib uri="http://java.sun.com/jsp/jstl/core" prefix="c" %>
3.    <%@ taglib uri="http://java.sun.com/jsf/core"  prefix="f" %>
4.    <%@ taglib uri="http://java.sun.com/jsf/html"  prefix="h" %>
5.
6.    <f:view>
7.       <f:loadBundle basename="com.corejsf.messages" var="msgs"/>
8.       <head>
9.          <link href="styles.css" rel="stylesheet" type="text/css"/>
10.          <title><h:outputText value="#{msgs.bookWindowTitle}"/></title>
11.       </head>
12.
13.       <body>
14.          <h:form>
15.             <h:panelGrid columns="2" styleClass="book"
16.                   columnClasses="menuColumn, chapterColumn">
17.                <f:facet name="header">
18.                   <f:subview id="header">
19.                      <c:import url="/bookHeader.jsp"/>
20.                   </f:subview>
21.                </f:facet>
22.
23.                <f:subview id="menu">
24.                   <c:import url="/bookMenu.jsp"/>
25.                </f:subview>
26.
27.                <c:import url="/bookContent.jsp"/>
28.             </h:panelGrid>
29.          </h:form>
30.       </body>
31.    </f:view>
32. </html>
```

Listing 8–7 `book-viewer-include/web/bookHeader.jsp`

```
1. <%@ taglib uri="http://java.sun.com/jsf/core" prefix="f" %>
2. <%@ taglib uri="http://java.sun.com/jsf/html" prefix="h" %>
3.
4. <h:panelGrid columns="1" styleClass="bookHeader">
5.    <h:graphicImage value="#{book.image}"/>
6.    <h:outputText value="#{msgs[book.titleKey]}" styleClass="bookTitle"/>
7.    <hr>
8. </h:panelGrid>
```

Listing 8-8 book-viewer-include/web/bookMenu.jsp

```
1. <%@ taglib uri="http://java.sun.com/jsf/core" prefix="f" %>
2. <%@ taglib uri="http://java.sun.com/jsf/html" prefix="h" %>
3.
4. <h:dataTable value="#{book.chapterKeys}" var="chapterKey"
5.       styleClass="links" columnClasses="linksColumn">
6.    <h:column>
7.       <h:commandLink>
8.          <h:outputText value="#{msgs[chapterKey]}"/>
9.          <f:param name="chapter" value="#{chapterKey}"/>
10.      </h:commandLink>
11.   </h:column>
12. </h:dataTable>
```

Listing 8-9 book-viewer-include/web/bookContent.jsp

```
1. <%@ taglib uri="http://java.sun.com/jsp/jstl/core" prefix="c" %>
2.
3. <c:import url="${param.chapter}.html"/>
```

Looking at Tiles

We have seen how to encapsulate and include content and how that strategy increases flexibility—it is much easier to reuse content if you include it rather than mixing it all in one file. Now that you can create user interfaces with pluggable content, you may be satisfied with that level of flexibility and reuse—but wait, there's more.

In addition to *encapsulating content*, you can use Tiles to *encapsulate layout*. For the application shown in Figure 8–2 on page 317, encapsulating layout means making the layout code—the h:panelGrid and its contents listed in Listing 8–6 on page 330—available for reuse. As it stands in Listing 8–6, that layout code can only be used by the JSF page shown in Figure 8–2. If you implement JSF pages with identical layouts, you must *replicate that layout code for every page*.

With Tiles, you define a single layout that can be reused by multiple *tiles*, which are nothing more mysterious than imported JSP pages. *Tiles lets you implement layout code once and reuse it among many pages*.

But reusing layout is just the beginning of the Tiles bag of tricks. You can do more:

- Nest tiles
- Extend tiles

- Restrict tiles to users of a particular role
- Attach controllers (Java objects) to tiles that are invoked just before their tile is displayed

Those are the core features that Tiles offers in the pursuit of the ultimate flexibility in crafting web-based user interfaces.

Installing Tiles

To use Tiles, you need the standalone Tiles JAR file. That JAR file can be found in the source code for this book.

Once you have the Tiles JAR file, follow these steps to install Tiles in your application:

1. Copy the Tiles JAR file to your application's WEB-INF/lib directory.
2. Add the Tiles servlet to your deployment descriptor (web.xml). Use the load-on-startup element to ensure that the Tiles servlet is loaded when your application starts.

Your deployment descriptor should look similar to the following:

```xml
<?xml version="1.0"?>

<web-app xmlns="http://java.sun.com/xml/ns/j2ee"
      xmlns:xsi="http://www.w3.org/2001/XMLSchema-instance"
      xsi:schemaLocation="http://java.sun.com/xml/ns/j2ee
         http://java.sun.com/xml/ns/j2ee/web-app_2_4.xsd"
      version="2.4">
   ...
   <servlet>
      <servlet-name>Faces Servlet</servlet-name>
      <servlet-class>javax.faces.webapp.FacesServlet</servlet-class>
      <load-on-startup>1</load-on-startup>
   </servlet>

   <servlet>
      <servlet-name>Tiles Servlet</servlet-name>
      <servlet-class>org.apache.tiles.servlets.TilesServlet</servlet-class>
      <load-on-startup>2</load-on-startup>
   </servlet>
   ...
</web-app>
```

Using Tiles with the Book Viewer

Using Tiles with JSF is a three-step process:

1. Use `tiles:insert` to insert a tile definition in a JSF page.
2. Define the tile in your Tiles configuration file.
3. Implement the tile's layout.

For the book viewer, we start in `book.jsp`, where we insert a tile named book:

```
...
<%@ taglib uri="http://jakarta.apache.org/tiles" prefix="tiles" %>
...
<h:form>
   <tiles:insert definition="book" flush="false"/>
</h:form>
...
```

We define the book tile in `/WEB-INF/tiles.xml`:

```
<definition name="book" path="/headerMenuContentLayout.jsp">
    <put name="header" value="/bookHeader.jsp"/>
    <put name="menu" value="/bookMenu.jsp"/>
    <put name="content" value="/bookContent.jsp"/>
</definition>
```

The previous snippet of XML defines a tile. The tile's layout is specified with the definition element's path attribute. The tile attributes, specified with put elements, are used by the layout. That layout looks like this:

```
<%-- this is /headerMenuContentLayout.jsp --%>

<%@ taglib uri="http://java.sun.com/jsf/html" prefix="h"%>
<%@ taglib uri="http://java.sun.com/jsf/core" prefix="f"%>
<%@ taglib uri="http://jakarta.apache.org/tiles" prefix="tiles" %>

<h:panelGrid columns="2" styleClass="gridClass"
   headerClass="headerClass"
   columnClasses="menuClass, contentClass">

   <f:facet name="header">
      <f:subview id="header">
         <tiles:insert attribute="header" flush="false"/>
      </f:subview>
   </f:facet>

   <f:subview id="menu">
      <tiles:insert attribute="menu" flush="false"/>
   </f:subview>
```

```
<f:subview id="content">
    <tiles:insert attribute="content" flush="false"/>
</f:subview>
</h:panelGrid>
```

The `tiles:insert` tag dynamically includes content. That content is the value of the `attribute` tag of `tiles:insert`. For example, the preceding code inserts the `header` attribute. That attribute's value is `/bookHeader.jsp`, so `tiles:insert` dynamically includes that file.

Notice that we specified a `flush="false"` attribute for the `tiles:insert` tag. That is necessary for most modern servlet containers because those containers disallow buffer flushing inside custom tags. If your servlet container throws an exception stating that you cannot flush from a custom tag, then you know you have forgotten to specify that attribute, which is true by default.

What have we gained by using Tiles in this example? *We have encapsulated layout so that we can reuse it in other tiles, instead of replicating that layout code from one JSF page to another.* For example, you could reuse the book viewer's layout, implemented in `/headerMenuContentLayout.jsp`, for other pages in the application that have the same layout.

Parameterizing Tiles

There is one flaw to the layout listed in the previous section: It hardcodes CSS classes, namely `gridClass`, `headerClass`, `menuClass`, and `contentClass`. This means that every web page using the header-menu-content layout will have the same look and feel. It would be better if we could parameterize the CSS class names. That way, other tiles with a header-menu-content layout could define their own look and feel.

Next, we look at how we can do that. First, we add three attributes to the `book` tile:

```
<definition name="book" path="/headerMenuContentLayout.jsp">
    <put name="headerClass"  value="headerClass"/>
    <put name="menuClass" value="menuClass"/>
    <put name="contentClass" value="contentClass"/>

    <put name="header" value="/bookHeader.jsp"/>
    <put name="menu" value="/bookMenu.jsp"/>
    <put name="content" value="/bookContent.jsp"/>
</definition>
```

Then we use those attributes in the layout:

```
<%-- this is an excerpt of /headerMenuContentLayout.jsp --%>
...
<tiles:importAttribute scope="request"/>

<h:panelGrid columns="2" styleClass="#{gridClass}"
   headerClass="#{headerClass}"
   columnClasses="#{menuClass}, #{contentClass}">
   ...
</h:panelGrid>
```

Tile attributes, such as headerClass, menuClass, etc., in the preceding code, exist in *tiles scope*, which is inaccessible to JSF. To make our attributes accessible to the layout JSF page listed above, we use the tiles:importAttribute tag. That tag imports all tile attributes to the scope you specify with the scope attribute. In the preceding code, we imported them to request scope.

Now we can specify different CSS classes for other tiles:

```
<definition name="anotherTile" path="/headerMenuContentLayout.jsp">
   <put name="headerClass" value="aDifferentHeaderClass"/>
   ...
</definition>
```

NOTE: The tiles:importAttribute tag also lets you import one attribute at a time—for example: <tiles:importAttribute name="headerClass" scope="..."/>.

Extending Tiles

In "Parameterizing Tiles" on page 334 we defined a tile that looked like this:

```
<definition name="book" path="/headerMenuContentLayout.jsp">
   <put name="headerClass"  value="headerClass"/>
   <put name="menuClass" value="menuClass"/>
   <put name="contentClass" value="contentClass"/>

   <put name="header" value="/bookHeader.jsp"/>
   <put name="menu" value="/bookMenu.jsp"/>
   <put name="content" value="/bookContent.jsp"/>
</definition>
```

There are two distinct types of attributes in that tile: CSS classes and included content. Although the latter is specific to the book tile, the former can be used by tiles that represent something other than books. Because of that generality, we split the book tile into two:

```
<definition name="header-menu-content" path="/headerMenuContentLayout.jsp">
    <put name="headerClass" value="headerClass"/>
    <put name="menuClass" value="menuClass"/>
    <put name="contentClass" value="contentClass"/>
</definition

<definition name="book" extends="header-menu-content">
    <put name="header" value="/bookHeader.jsp"/>
    <put name="menu" value="/bookMenu.jsp"/>
    <put name="content" value="/bookContent.jsp"/>
</definition>
```

Now the book tile *extends* the header-menu-content tile. When you extend a tile, you inherit its layout and attributes, much the same as Java subclasses inherit methods and variables from their base classes. Because we have split the original tile in two, the CSS class attributes are available for reuse by other tiles that extend the header-menu-content tile.

 NOTE: Here is one more thing to consider about Tiles. Imagine the book viewer has been a huge success and Project Gutenberg has commissioned you to implement a library that can display all 6,000+ of their books. You define more than 6,000 tiles that reuse the same layout—one tile for each book—and present your finished product to the folks at Gutenberg. They think it's great, but they want you to add a footer to the bottom of every page. Since you have used Tiles, you only need to change the single layout used by all your tiles. Imagine the difficulty you would encounter making that change if you had replicated the layout code more than 6,000 times!

Figure 8–6 shows the directory structure for the "tileized" version of the book viewer. That directory structure is the same as the previous version of the book viewer, except that we have added a layout—headerMenuContentLayout.jsp—and the tiles definition file, /WEB-INF/tiles.xml.

Listing 8–10 through Listing 8–12 show the Tiles definition file, the book layout, and the JSF page that displays *Alice in Wonderland*. We left out the listings of the other files in the application because they are unchanged from the application discussed in "Content Inclusion in JSP-Based Applications" on page 326.

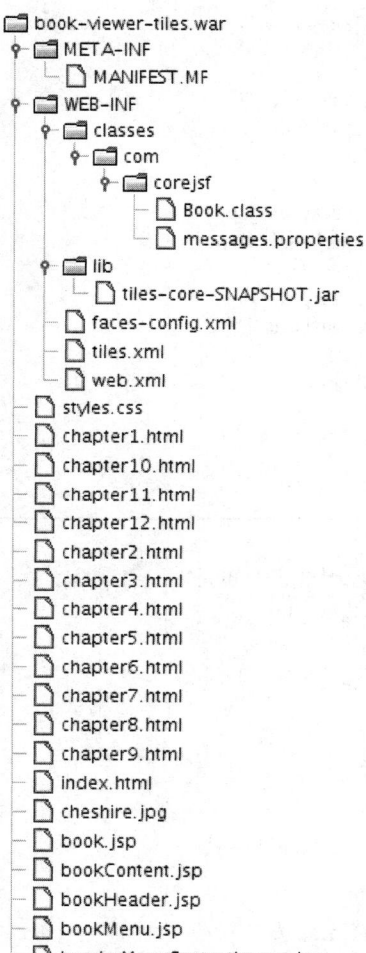

Figure 8–6   Book viewer with extended tile directory structure

Listing 8–10   book-viewer-tiles/web/WEB-INF/tiles.xml

```
1.  <!DOCTYPE tiles-definitions PUBLIC
2.    "-//Apache Software Foundation//DTD Tiles Configuration//EN"
3.    "http://jakarta.apache.org/struts/dtds/tiles-config.dtd">
4.
5.  <tiles-definitions>
6.    <definition name="book" path="/headerMenuContentLayout.jsp">
7.        <put name="gridClass"          value="headerMenuContent"/>
8.        <put name="headerClass"        value="header"/>
9.        <put name="menuColumnClass"    value="menuColumn"/>
10.       <put name="contentColumnClass" value="contentColumn"/>
11.
12.       <put name="header"  value="/bookHeader.jsp"/>
13.       <put name="menu"    value="/bookMenu.jsp"/>
14.       <put name="content" value="/bookContent.jsp"/>
15.    </definition>
16. </tiles-definitions>
```

Listing 8–11   book-viewer-tiles/web/headerMenuContentLayout.jsp

```
1.  <%@ taglib uri="http://java.sun.com/jsf/core"  prefix="f" %>
2.  <%@ taglib uri="http://java.sun.com/jsf/html"  prefix="h" %>
3.  <%@ taglib uri="http://jakarta.apache.org/tiles" prefix="tiles" %>
4.
5.  <tiles:importAttribute scope="request"/>
6.
7.  <h:panelGrid columns="2" styleClass="#{gridClass}"
8.      headerClass="#{headerClass}"
9.      columnClasses="#{menuColumnClass}, #{contentColumnClass}">
10.    <f:facet name="header">
11.      <f:subview id="header">
12.        <tiles:insert attribute="header" flush="false"/>
13.      </f:subview>
14.    </f:facet>
15.
16.    <f:subview id="menu">
17.      <tiles:insert attribute="menu" flush="false"/>
18.    </f:subview>
19.
20.    <f:subview id="content">
21.      <tiles:insert attribute="content" flush="false"/>
22.    </f:subview>
23. </h:panelGrid>
```

| Listing 8–12 | `book-viewer-tiles/web/book.jsp` |

```
1. <html>
2.    <%@ taglib uri="http://java.sun.com/jsp/jstl/core" prefix="c" %>
3.    <%@ taglib uri="http://java.sun.com/jsf/core"  prefix="f" %>
4.    <%@ taglib uri="http://java.sun.com/jsf/html"  prefix="h" %>
5.    <%@ taglib uri="http://jakarta.apache.org/tiles" prefix="tiles" %>
6.
7.    <f:view>
8.       <f:loadBundle basename="com.corejsf.messages" var="msgs"/>
9.       <head>
10.         <link href="styles.css" rel="stylesheet" type="text/css"/>
11.         <title><h:outputText value="#{msgs.bookWindowTitle}"/></title>
12.      </head>
13.
14.      <body>
15.         <f:subview id="book">
16.            <h:form>
17.               <tiles:insert definition="book" flush="false"/>
18.            </h:form>
19.         </f:subview>
20.      </body>
21.   </f:view>
22. </html>
```

The Library

In this section, we turn the book viewer into a library, as shown in Figure 8–7.

The library application shown in Figure 8–7 contains a menu at the top of the page that lets you select a book, either *Alice in Wonderland* or *Peter Pan*. The rest of the application works like the book viewer we have discussed throughout this chapter.

The library employs two Tiles techniques that are of interest to us: nesting tiles and using tile controllers.

Nested Tiles

The library shown in Figure 8–7 contains a book viewer. So does the library tile:

```
<definition name="book">
   ...
</definition>

<definition name="library" path="/libraryLayout.jsp"
    controllerClass="com.corejsf.LibraryTileController">
```

```
<put name="header" value="/bookSelector.jsp"/>
<put name="book" value="book"/>
</definition>
```

Notice the value for the book attribute—it is a tile, not a JSP page. Using a tile name instead of a JSP page lets you nest tiles, as we did by nesting the book tile in the library.

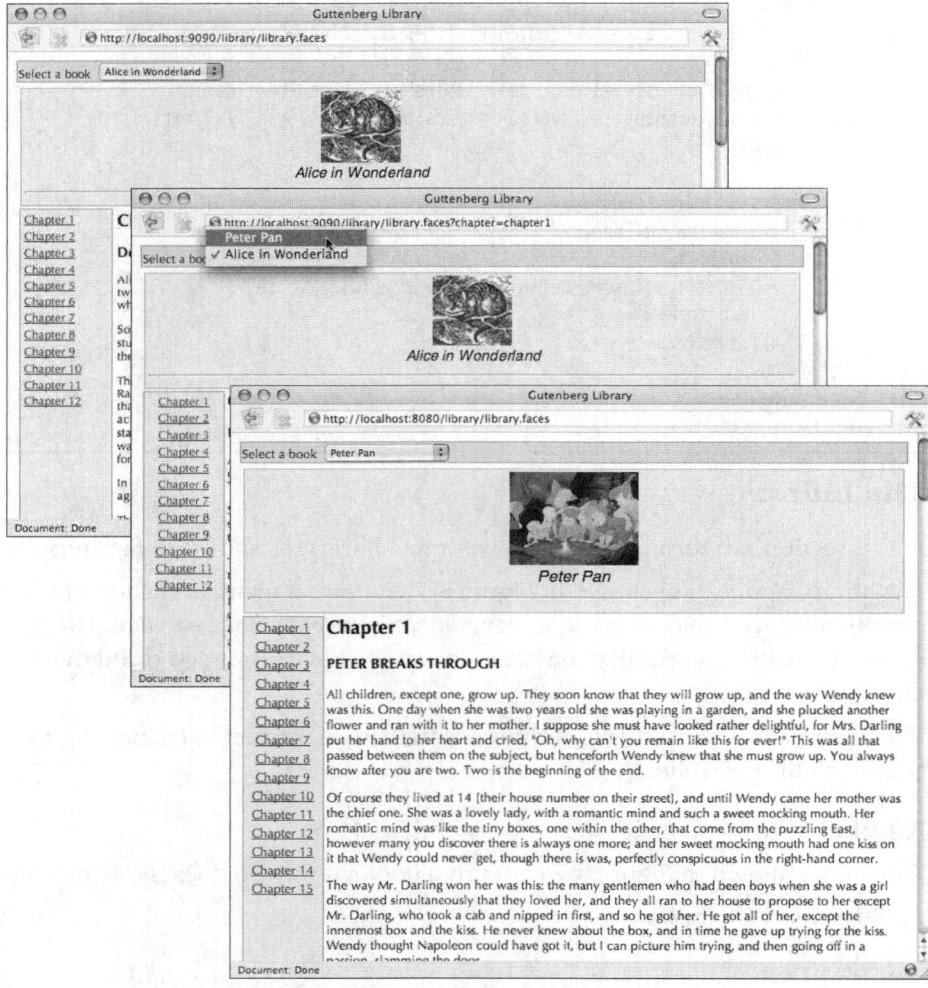

Figure 8–7 Library implemented with JSF and tiles

Tile Controllers

In our book viewer application, we had one managed bean named book (see "The Book Viewer" on page 318 for more information about the book bean). The library, on the other hand, must be aware of more than one book.

In this section—with a sleight of hand—we show you how to support multiple books without having to change the book viewer. The book viewer will continue to manipulate a book bean, but that bean will no longer be a managed bean. Instead, it will be the book that was last selected in the library's pulldown menu at the top of the page.

We accomplish that sleight of hand with a Tiles controller. Tiles lets you attach a Java object, called a *tile controller*, to a tile. That object's class must implement the org.apache.struts.tiles.Controller interface, which defines a single perform method. Tiles invokes that method just before it loads the controller's associated tile. Tile controllers have access to their tile's context, which lets the controller access the tile's attributes or create new attributes.

We attach a controller to the library tile. The controller looks for a library attribute in session scope. If the library is not there, the controller creates a library and stores it in session scope. The controller then consults the library's selectedBook property to see if a book has been selected. If so, the controller sets the value of the book session attribute to the selected book. If there is no selected book, the controller sets the book attribute to that for *Peter Pan*. Subsequently, when the library tile is loaded, the book viewer accesses the selected book. The controller is listed in Listing 8–20 on page 348.

Figure 8–8 shows the directory structure for the library application. For brevity, we left out the book HTML files.

The files shown in Figure 8–8 are shown in Listing 8–13 through Listing 8–28, with the exception of the HTML files. As you look through those listings, note the effort required to add a new book. All you have to do is modify the constructor in Library.java—see Listing 8–19 on page 346—to create your book and add it to the book map.

You could even implement the Library class so that it reads XML book definitions. That way, you could add books without any programming. Digesting XML is an easy task with Tiles's distant cousin, the Apache Commons Digester. See http://jakarta.apache.org/commons/digester/ for more information about the Digester.

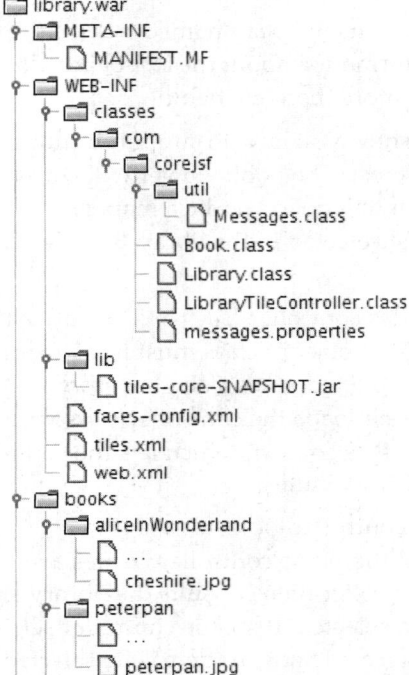

Figure 8–8 Library directory structure

Listing 8–13 library/web/library.jsp

```
1. <html>
2.    <%@ taglib uri="http://java.sun.com/jsf/core"  prefix="f" %>
3.    <%@ taglib uri="http://java.sun.com/jsf/html"  prefix="h" %>
4.    <%@ taglib uri="http://jakarta.apache.org/tiles" prefix="tiles" %>
5.
6.    <f:view>
7.       <f:loadBundle basename="com.corejsf.messages" var="msgs"/>
8.       <head>
9.         <link href="styles.css" rel="stylesheet" type="text/css"/>
10.        <title><h:outputText value="#{msgs.libraryWindowTitle}"/></title>
11.      </head>
12.
```

Listing 8–13 `library/web/library.jsp (cont.)`

```
13.      <body>
14.          <f:subview id="library">
15.              <h:form>
16.                  <tiles:insert definition="library" flush="false"/>
17.              </h:form>
18.          </f:subview>
19.      </body>
20.    </f:view>
21. </html>
```

Listing 8–14 `library/web/WEB-INF/tiles.xml`

```
1. <?xml version="1.0" encoding="ISO-8859-1" ?>
2.
3. <!DOCTYPE tiles-definitions PUBLIC
4. "-//Apache Software Foundation//DTD Tiles Configuration 1.1//EN"
5. "http://struts.apache.org/dtds/tiles-config_1_1.dtd">
6.
7. <tiles-definitions>
8.    <definition name="menu-header-content" path="/headerMenuContentLayout.jsp">
9.        <put name="gridClass"          value="headerMenuContent"/>
10.       <put name="headerClass"         value="header"/>
11.       <put name="menuColumnClass"     value="menuColumn"/>
12.       <put name="contentColumnClass"  value="contentColumn"/>
13.   </definition>
14.
15.   <definition name="book" extends="menu-header-content">
16.       <put name="header"  value="/bookHeader.jsp"/>
17.       <put name="menu"    value="/bookMenu.jsp"/>
18.       <put name="content" value="/bookContent.jsp"/>
19.   </definition>
20.
21.   <definition name="library" path="/libraryLayout.jsp"
22.          controllerClass="com.corejsf.LibraryTileController">
23.       <put name="header" value="/bookSelector.jsp"/>
24.       <put name="book" value="book"/>
25.   </definition>
26. </tiles-definitions>
```

Listing 8–15　library/web/libraryLayout.jsp

```
1. <%@ taglib uri="http://java.sun.com/jsf/core"  prefix="f" %>
2. <%@ taglib uri="http://java.sun.com/jsf/html"  prefix="h" %>
3. <%@ taglib uri="http://jakarta.apache.org/tiles" prefix="tiles" %>
4.
5. <h:panelGrid columns="1" styleClass="book" headerClass="libraryHeader">
6.    <f:facet name="header">
7.       <f:subview id="header">
8.          <tiles:insert attribute="header" flush="false"/>
9.       </f:subview>
10.    </f:facet>
11.
12.    <f:subview id="book">
13.       <tiles:insert attribute="book" flush="false"/>
14.    </f:subview>
15. </h:panelGrid>
```

Listing 8–16　library/web/bookSelector.jsp

```
1. <%@ taglib uri="http://java.sun.com/jsf/core" prefix="f" %>
2. <%@ taglib uri="http://java.sun.com/jsf/html" prefix="h" %>
3.
4. <h:outputText value="#{msgs.selectABookPrompt}"/>
5.
6.   
7.
8. <h:selectOneMenu onchange="submit()" value="#{library.book}"
9.       valueChangeListener="#{library.bookSelected}">
10.    <f:selectItems value="#{library.bookItems}"/>
11. </h:selectOneMenu>
```

Listing 8–17　library/src/java/com/corejsf/Library.java

```
1. package com.corejsf;
2.
3. import java.util.*;
4. import javax.faces.model.SelectItem;
5. import javax.faces.event.ValueChangeEvent;
6.
7. public class Library {
8.    private Map<String,Book> bookMap = new HashMap<String,Book>();
9.    private Book initialBook = null;
10.    private List bookItems = null;
```

Listing 8-17 library/src/java/com/corejsf/Library.java (cont.)

```
11.   private String book = null;
12.   private String selectedBook = null;
13.
14.   public Library() {
15.      Book peterpan = new Book();
16.      Book aliceInWonderland = new Book();
17.
18.      initialBook = peterpan;
19.
20.      aliceInWonderland.setDirectory("books/aliceInWonderland");
21.      aliceInWonderland.setTitleKey("aliceInWonderland");
22.      aliceInWonderland.setImage("books/aliceInWonderland/cheshire.jpg");
23.      aliceInWonderland.setNumChapters(12);
24.
25.      peterpan.setDirectory("books/peterpan");
26.      peterpan.setTitleKey("peterpan");
27.      peterpan.setImage("books/peterpan/peterpan.jpg");
28.      peterpan.setNumChapters(15);
29.
30.      bookMap.put("aliceInWonderland", aliceInWonderland);
31.      bookMap.put("peterpan", peterpan);
32.   }
33.   public void setBook(String book) { this.book = book; }
34.   public String getBook() { return book; }
35.
36.   public Map<String,Book> getBooks() {
37.      return bookMap;
38.   }
39.   public void bookSelected(ValueChangeEvent e) {
40.      selectedBook = (String) e.getNewValue();
41.   }
42.   public Book getSelectedBook() {
43.      return selectedBook != null ? bookMap.get(selectedBook) : initialBook;
44.   }
45.   public List getBookItems() {
46.      if(bookItems == null) {
47.         bookItems = new LinkedList();
48.         Iterator<Book> it = bookMap.values().iterator();
49.         while(it.hasNext()) {
50.            Book book = it.next();
51.            bookItems.add(new SelectItem(book.getTitleKey(),
52.                                     getBookTitle(book.getTitleKey())));
53.         }
54.      }
55.      return bookItems;
```

Listing 8–17   library/src/java/com/corejsf/Library.java (cont.)

```
56.    }
57.    private String getBookTitle(String key) {
58.       return com.corejsf.util.Messages.
59.                    getString("com.corejsf.messages", key, null);
60.    }
61. }
```

Listing 8–18   library/web/bookSelector.jsp

```
1. <%@ taglib uri="http://java.sun.com/jsf/core" prefix="f" %>
2. <%@ taglib uri="http://java.sun.com/jsf/html" prefix="h" %>
3.
4. <h:outputText value="#{msgs.selectABookPrompt}"/>
5.
6.   
7.
8. <h:selectOneMenu onchange="submit()" value="#{library.book}"
9.      valueChangeListener="#{library.bookSelected}">
10.   <f:selectItems value="#{library.bookItems}"/>
11. </h:selectOneMenu>
```

Listing 8–19   library/src/java/com/corejsf/Library.java

```
1. package com.corejsf;
2.
3. import java.util.*;
4. import javax.faces.model.SelectItem;
5. import javax.faces.event.ValueChangeEvent;
6.
7. public class Library {
8.    private Map<String,Book> bookMap = new HashMap<String,Book>();
9.    private Book initialBook = null;
10.   private List bookItems = null;
11.   private String book = null;
12.   private String selectedBook = null;
13.
14.   public Library() {
15.      Book peterpan = new Book();
16.      Book aliceInWonderland = new Book();
17.
18.      initialBook = peterpan;
19.
```

Listing 8–19   library/src/java/com/corejsf/Library.java (cont.)

```
20.      aliceInWonderland.setDirectory("books/aliceInWonderland");
21.      aliceInWonderland.setTitleKey("aliceInWonderland");
22.      aliceInWonderland.setImage("books/aliceInWonderland/cheshire.jpg");
23.      aliceInWonderland.setNumChapters(12);
24.
25.      peterpan.setDirectory("books/peterpan");
26.      peterpan.setTitleKey("peterpan");
27.      peterpan.setImage("books/peterpan/peterpan.jpg");
28.      peterpan.setNumChapters(15);
29.
30.      bookMap.put("aliceInWonderland", aliceInWonderland);
31.      bookMap.put("peterpan", peterpan);
32.   }
33.   public void setBook(String book) { this.book = book; }
34.   public String getBook() { return book; }
35.
36.   public Map<String,Book> getBooks() {
37.      return bookMap;
38.   }
39.   public void bookSelected(ValueChangeEvent e) {
40.      selectedBook = (String) e.getNewValue();
41.   }
42.   public Book getSelectedBook() {
43.      return selectedBook != null ? bookMap.get(selectedBook) : initialBook;
44.   }
45.   public List getBookItems() {
46.      if(bookItems == null) {
47.         bookItems = new LinkedList();
48.         Iterator<Book> it = bookMap.values().iterator();
49.         while(it.hasNext()) {
50.            Book book = it.next();
51.            bookItems.add(new SelectItem(book.getTitleKey(),
52.                                getBookTitle(book.getTitleKey())));
53.         }
54.      }
55.      return bookItems;
56.   }
57.   private String getBookTitle(String key) {
58.      return com.corejsf.util.Messages.
59.                 getString("com.corejsf.messages", key, null);
60.   }
61. }
```

Listing 8–20   library/src/java/com/corejsf/LibraryTileController.java

```
 1. package com.corejsf;
 2.
 3. import java.io.IOException;
 4. import javax.servlet.ServletContext;
 5. import javax.servlet.ServletException;
 6. import javax.servlet.http.HttpServletRequest;
 7. import javax.servlet.http.HttpServletResponse;
 8. import javax.servlet.http.HttpSession;
 9. import org.apache.tiles.ComponentContext;
10. import org.apache.tiles.Controller;
11.
12. public class LibraryTileController implements Controller {
13.    public void execute(ComponentContext tilesContext,
14.               HttpServletRequest request,
15.               HttpServletResponse response,
16.               ServletContext context)
17.               throws IOException, ServletException {
18.       HttpSession session = request.getSession();
19.
20.       String chapter = (String) request.getParameter("chapter");
21.       session.setAttribute("chapter", chapter == null || "".equals(chapter) ?
22.                     "chapter1" : chapter);
23.
24.       Library library = (Library) session.getAttribute("library");
25.
26.       if(library == null) {
27.          library = new Library();
28.          session.setAttribute("library", library);
29.       }
30.
31.       Book selectedBook = library.getSelectedBook();
32.       if(selectedBook != null) {
33.          session.setAttribute("book", selectedBook);
34.       }
35.    }
36.    public void perform(ComponentContext tilesContext,
37.               HttpServletRequest request,
38.               HttpServletResponse response,
39.               ServletContext context)
40.               throws IOException, ServletException {
41.       HttpSession session = request.getSession();
42.       execute(tilesContext, request, response, context);
43.    }
44. }
```

Listing 8–21 library/src/java/com/corejsf/Book.java

```java
1.  package com.corejsf;
2.
3.  import java.util.LinkedList;
4.  import java.util.List;
5.
6.  public class Book {
7.      private String titleKey;
8.      private String image;
9.      private String directory;
10.     private int numChapters;
11.     private List<String> chapterKeys = null;
12.
13.     // PROPERTY: titleKey
14.     public void setTitleKey(String titleKey) { this.titleKey = titleKey; }
15.     public String getTitleKey() { return titleKey; }
16.
17.     // PROPERTY: image
18.     public void setImage(String image) { this.image = image; }
19.     public String getImage() { return image; }
20.
21.     // PROPERTY: numChapters
22.     public void setNumChapters(int numChapters) { this.numChapters = numChapters;}
23.     public int getNumChapters() { return numChapters; }
24.
25.     // PROPERTY: directory
26.     public void setDirectory(String directory) { this.directory = directory;}
27.     public String getDirectory() { return directory; }
28.
29.     // PROPERTY: chapterKeys
30.     public List<String> getChapterKeys() {
31.         if(chapterKeys == null) {
32.             chapterKeys = new LinkedList<String>();
33.             for(int i=1; i <= numChapters; ++i)
34.                 chapterKeys.add("chapter" + i);
35.         }
36.         return chapterKeys;
37.     }
38. }
```

Listing 8–22   library/web/bookHeader.jsp

```
1. <%@ taglib uri="http://java.sun.com/jsf/core" prefix="f" %>
2. <%@ taglib uri="http://java.sun.com/jsf/html" prefix="h" %>
3.
4. <h:panelGrid columns="1" styleClass="bookHeader">
5.    <h:graphicImage value="#{book.image}"/>
6.    <h:outputText value="#{msgs[book.titleKey]}" styleClass="bookTitle"/>
7.    <hr>
8. </h:panelGrid>
```

Listing 8–23   library/web/bookMenu.jsp

```
1. <%@ taglib uri="http://java.sun.com/jsf/core" prefix="f" %>
2. <%@ taglib uri="http://java.sun.com/jsf/html" prefix="h" %>
3.
4. <h:dataTable value="#{book.chapterKeys}" var="chapterKey"
5.       styleClass="links" columnClasses="linksColumn">
6.    <h:column>
7.       <h:commandLink>
8.          <h:outputText value="#{msgs[chapterKey]}"/>
9.          <f:param name="chapter" value="#{chapterKey}"/>
10.      </h:commandLink>
11.   </h:column>
12. </h:dataTable>
```

Listing 8–24   library/web/bookContent.jsp

```
1. <%@ taglib uri="http://java.sun.com/jsp/jstl/core" prefix="c" %>
2.
3. <c:import url="${book.directory}/${chapter}.html"/>
```

Listing 8–25   library/web/styles.css

```
1. .library {
2.    vertical-align: top;
3.    width: 100%;
4.    height: 100%;
5. }
6. .libraryHeader {
7.    width: 100%;
8.    text-align: left;
```

Listing 8–25 `library/web/styles.css (cont.)`

```css
 9.     vertical-align: top;
10.     background-color: #ddd;
11.     font-weight: lighter;
12.     border: thin solid #777;
13. }
14. .bookHeader {
15.     width: 100%;
16.     text-align: center;
17.     background-color: #eee;
18.     border: thin solid CornflowerBlue;
19. }
20. .bookTitle {
21.     text-align: center;
22.     font-style: italic;
23.     font-size: 1.3em;
24.     font-family: Helvetica;
25. }
26. .menuColumn {
27.     vertical-align: top;
28.     background-color: #eee;
29.     border: thin solid #777;
30. }
31. .chapterColumn {
32.     vertical-align: top;
33.     text-align: left;
34.     width: *;
35.     padding: 3px;
36. }
37. .contentColumn {
38.     vertical-align: top;
39.     text-align: left;
40.     width: *;
41. }
42. .links {
43.     width: 85px;
44.     vertical-align: top;
45.     text-align: center;
46. }
47. .linksColumn {
48.     vertical-align: top;
49.     text-align: center;
50. }
```

Listing 8–26   library/web/WEB-INF/faces-config.xml

```
51. <?xml version="1.0"?>
52. <faces-config xmlns="http://java.sun.com/xml/ns/javaee"
53.    xmlns:xsi="http://www.w3.org/2001/XMLSchema-instance"
54.    xsi:schemaLocation="http://java.sun.com/xml/ns/javaee
55.       http://java.sun.com/xml/ns/javaee/web-facesconfig_1_2.xsd"
56.    version="1.2">
57. </faces-config>
```

Listing 8–27   library/web/WEB-INF/web.xml

```
 1. <?xml version="1.0"?>
 2. <web-app xmlns="http://java.sun.com/xml/ns/javaee"
 3.    xmlns:xsi="http://www.w3.org/2001/XMLSchema-instance"
 4.    xsi:schemaLocation="http://java.sun.com/xml/ns/javaee
 5.       http://java.sun.com/xml/ns/javaee/web-app_2_5.xsd"
 6.    version="2.5">
 7.    <servlet>
 8.       <servlet-name>Tiles Servlet</servlet-name>
 9.       <servlet-class>org.apache.tiles.servlets.TilesServlet</servlet-class>
10.       <init-param>
11.          <param-name>definitions-config</param-name>
12.          <param-value>/WEB-INF/tiles.xml</param-value>
13.       </init-param>
14.       <load-on-startup>2</load-on-startup>
15.    </servlet>
16.
17.    <servlet>
18.       <servlet-name>Faces Servlet</servlet-name>
19.       <servlet-class>javax.faces.webapp.FacesServlet</servlet-class>
20.       <load-on-startup>1</load-on-startup>
21.    </servlet>
22.
23.    <servlet-mapping>
24.       <servlet-name>Faces Servlet</servlet-name>
25.       <url-pattern>*.faces</url-pattern>
26.    </servlet-mapping>
27.
28.    <welcome-file-list>
29.       <welcome-file>index.html</welcome-file>
30.    </welcome-file-list>
31. </web-app>
```

Listing 8–28 `library/src/java/com/corejsf/messages.properties`

```
 1. libraryWindowTitle=Gutenberg Library
 2. aliceInWonderland=Alice in Wonderland
 3. peterpan=Peter Pan
 4. selectABookPrompt=Select a book
 5.
 6. chapter1=Chapter 1
 7. chapter2=Chapter 2
 8. chapter3=Chapter 3
 9. chapter4=Chapter 4
10. chapter5=Chapter 5
11. chapter6=Chapter 6
12. chapter7=Chapter 7
13. chapter8=Chapter 8
14. chapter9=Chapter 9
15. chapter10=Chapter 10
16. chapter11=Chapter 11
17. chapter12=Chapter 12
18. chapter13=Chapter 13
19. chapter14=Chapter 14
20. chapter15=Chapter 15
```

CUSTOM COMPONENTS, CONVERTERS, AND VALIDATORS

Chapter 9

JSF provides a basic set of components for building HTML-based web applications, such as text fields, checkboxes, buttons, and so on. However, most user interface designers want more advanced components, such as calendars, tabbed panes, or navigation trees, that are not part of the standard JSF component set. Fortunately, JSF makes it possible to build reusable JSF components with rich behavior.

This chapter shows you how to implement custom components. We use two custom components—a spinner and a tabbed pane, shown in Figure 9–1—to illustrate the various aspects of creating custom components.

The JSF API lets you implement custom components and associated tags with the same features as the JSF standard tags. For example, h:input uses a value expression to associate a text field's value with a bean property, so you could use value expressions to wire calendar cells to bean properties. JSF standard input components fire value change events when their value changes, so you could fire value change events when a different date is selected in the calendar.

The first part of this chapter uses the spinner component to illustrate basic issues that you encounter in all custom components. We then revisit the spinner to show more advanced issues:

- "Using an External Renderer" on page 387
- "Calling Converters from External Renderers" on page 393
- "Supporting Value Change Listeners" on page 394
- "Supporting Method Expressions" on page 396

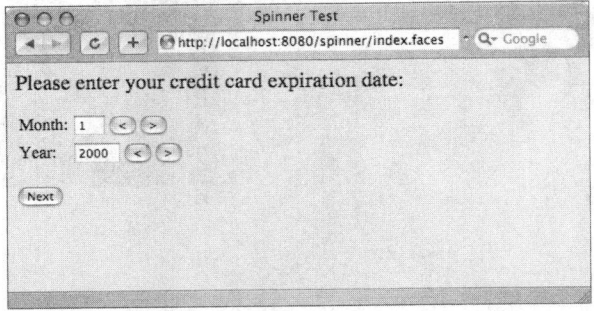

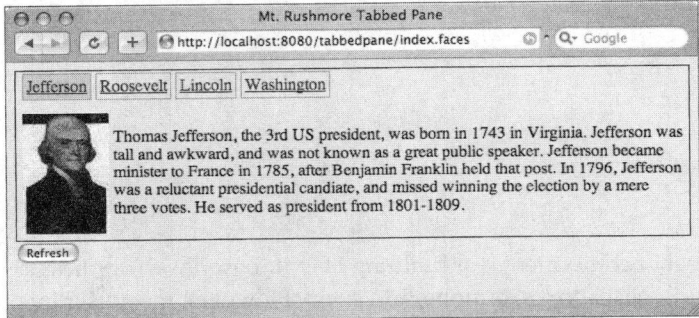

Figure 9–1   The spinner and the tabbed pane

The second half of the chapter examines a tabbed pane component that illustrates the following aspects of custom component development.

- "Processing SelectItem Children" page 411
- "Processing Facets" on page 412
- "Encoding CSS Styles" on page 413
- "Using Hidden Fields" on page 415
- "Saving and Restoring State" on page 415
- "Firing Action Events" on page 418

Classes for Implementing Custom Components

In the following sections, we discuss the classes that you need to implement custom components.

To motivate the discussion, we will develop a spinner component. A spinner lets you enter a number in a text field, either by typing it directly into the field or by activating an increment or decrement button. Figure 9–2 shows an application that uses two spinners for a credit card's expiration date, one for the month and another for the year.

In Figure 9–2, from top to bottom, all proceeds as expected. The user enters valid values, so navigation takes us to a designated JSF page that echoes those values.

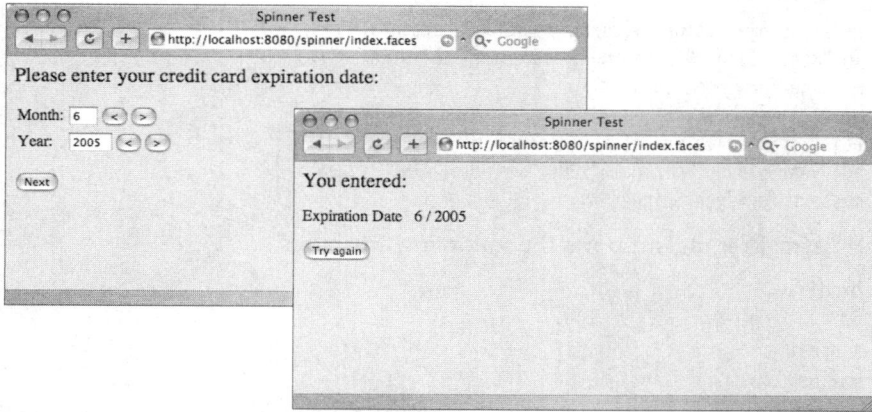

Figure 9–2   Using the spinner component

The spinner insists on integer values. Figure 9–3 shows an attempt to enter bad data. We let the standard integer converter handle conversion errors. You can see how we did it in "Using Converters" on page 369.

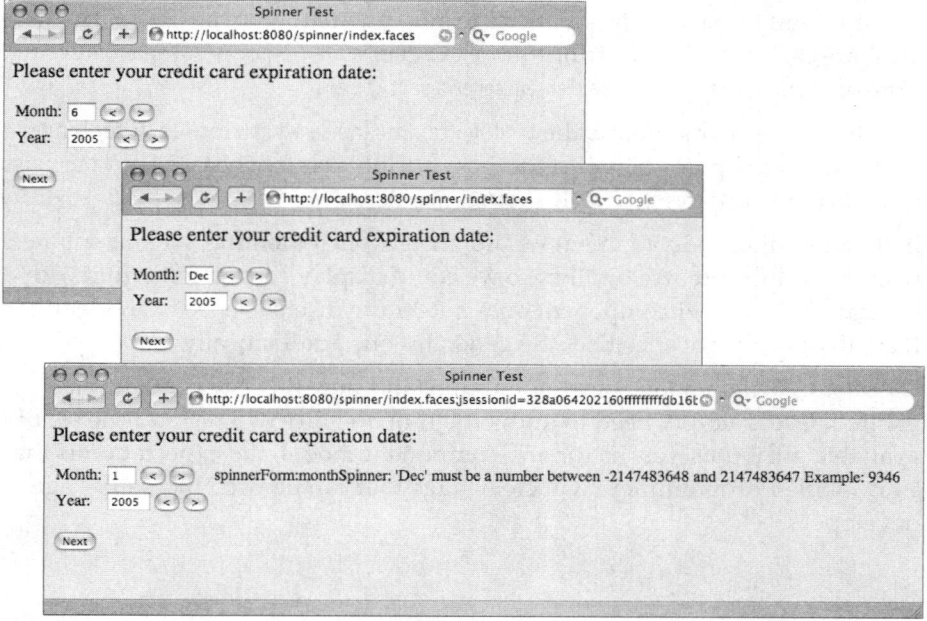

Figure 9–3   Handling conversion failures

Here is how you use corejsf:spinner:

```
<%@ taglib uri="http://corejsf.com/spinner" prefix="corejsf" %>
...
<corejsf:spinner value="#{cardExpirationDate.month}"
    id="monthSpinner" minimum="1" maximum="12" size="3"/>
<h:message for="monthSpinner"/>
...
<corejsf:spinner value="#{cardExpirationDate.year}"
    id="yearSpinner" minimum="1900" maximum="2100" size="5"/>
<h:message for="yearSpinner"/>
```

The corejsf:spinner tag supports the following attributes:

- binding
- id
- minimum
- maximum
- rendered
- size
- value

Only one of the attributes—value—is required.

The minimum and maximum attributes let you assign a range of valid values—for example, the month spinner has a minimum of 1 and a maximum of 12. You can also limit the size of the spinner's text field with the size attribute. The value attribute can take a literal string—for example, value="2"; or a value expression—for example, value="#{someBean.someProperty}".

Finally, the spinner supports the binding, id, and rendered attributes, which are discussed in Chapter 4. Support for those attributes is free because our tag class extends the javax.faces.webapp.UIComponentELTag class.

In the preceding code fragment we assigned explicit identifiers to our spinners with the id attribute. We did that so we could display conversion errors with h:message. The spinner component does not require users to specify an identifier. If an identifier is not specified, JSF generates one automatically.

Users of JSF custom tags need not understand how those tags are implemented. Users simply need to know the functionality of a tag and the set of available attributes. Just as for any component model, the expectation is that a few skilled programmers will create tags that can be used by many page developers.

Tags and Components

Minimally, a tag for a JSF custom component requires two classes:

- A class that processes tag attributes. By convention, the class name has a Tag suffix—for example, SpinnerTag.

- A component class that maintains state, renders a user interface, and processes input. By convention, the class name has a UI prefix—for example, UISpinner.

The tag class is part of the plumbing. It creates the component and transfers tag attribute values to component properties and attributes. The implementation of the tag class is largely mechanical. See "Implementing Custom Component Tags" on page 372 for more information on tag classes.

The UI class does the important work. It has two separate responsibilities:

- To *render* the user interface by encoding markup
- To *process user input* by decoding the current HTTP request

Component classes can delegate rendering and processing input to a separate renderer. By using different renderers, you can support multiple clients, such as web browsers and cell phones. Initially, our spinner component will render itself, but in "Using an External Renderer" on page 387, we show you how to implement a separate renderer for the spinner.

A component's UI class must extend the UIComponent class. That class defines over 40 abstract methods, so you will want to extend an existing class that implements them. You can choose from the classes shown in Figure 9–4.

Our UISpinner class will extend UIInput, which extends UIOutput and implements the EditableValueHolder interface. Our UITabbedPane will extend UICommand, which implements the ActionSource2 interface.

 NOTE: The ActionSource2 interface was added in JSF1.2. An ActionSource has methods to manage action listeners. An ActionSource2 additionally manages actions. In JSF 1.1, the ActionSource interface handled both actions and action listeners.

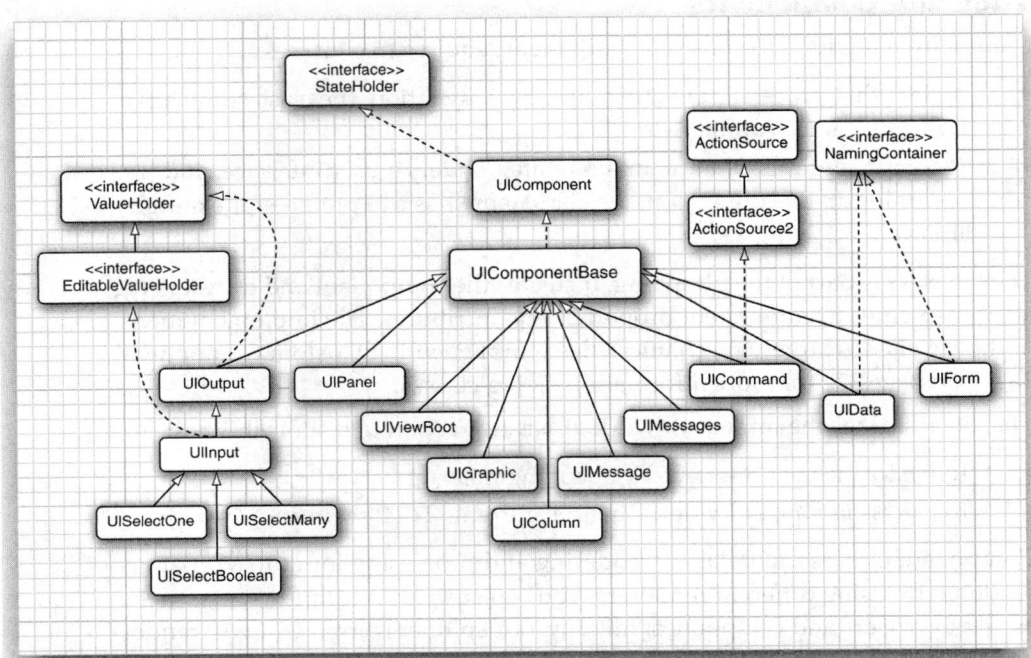

Figure 9–4 JSF component hierarchy (not all classes are shown)

The Custom Component Developer's Toolbox

When you implement custom components, you will become very familiar with a handful of JSF classes:

- `javax.faces.component.UIComponent`
- `javax.faces.webapp.UIComponentELTag`
- `javax.faces.context.FacesContext`
- `javax.faces.application.Application`
- `javax.faces.context.ResponseWriter`

`UIComponent` is an abstract class that defines what it means to be a component. Each component manages several important categories of data. These include:

- A list of *child components*. For example, the children of the `h:panelGrid` component are the components that are placed in the grid location. However, a component need not have any children.

- A map of *facet components*. Facets are similar to child components, but each facet has a key, not a position in a list. It is up to the component how to lay out its facets. For example, the h:dataTable component has header and footer facets.

- A map of *attributes*. This is a general-purpose map that you can use to store arbitrary key/value pairs.

- A map of *value expressions*. This is another general-purpose map that you can use to store arbitrary value expressions. For example, if a spinner tag has an attribute value="#{cardExpirationDate.month}", then the component stores a ValueExpression object for the given value expression under the key "value".

- A collection of *listeners*. This collection is maintained by the JSF framework.

When you define your own JSF components, you usually subclass one of the following three standard component classes:

- UICommand, if your component produces actions similar to a command button or link

- UIOutput, if your component displays a value but does not allow the user to edit it

- UIInput, if your component reads a value from the user (such as the spinner)

If you look at Figure 9–4, you will find that these three classes implement interfaces that specify these distinct responsibilities:

- ActionSource defines methods for managing action listeners.

- ActionSource2 defines methods for managing actions.

- ValueHolder defines methods for managing a component value, a local value, and a converter.

- EditableValueHolder extends ValueHolder and adds methods for managing validators and value change listeners.

 TIP: You often need to cast a generic UIComponent parameter to a subclass to access values, converters, and so on. Rather than casting to a specific class such as UISpinner, cast to an interface type, such as ValueHolder. That makes it easier to reuse your code.

The FacesContext class contains JSF-related request information. Among other things, you can access request parameters through FacesContext, get a reference to the Application object, get the current view root component, or get a reference to the response writer, which you use to encode markup.

The Application class keeps track of objects shared by a single application—for example, the set of supported locales, and available converters and validators. The Application class also serves as a factory, with factory methods for components, converters, and validators. In this chapter, we are mostly interested in using the Application class to create converters, and to obtain an expression factory for value and method expressions.

Nearly all custom components generate markup, so you will want to use the ResponseWriter class to ease that task. Response writers have methods for starting and ending HTML elements, and methods for writing element attributes.

We now return to the spinner implementation and view the spinner from a number of different perspectives. We start with every component's most basic tasks—generating markup and processing requests—and then turn to the more mundane issue of implementing the corresponding tag handler class.

Encoding: Generating Markup

JSF components generate markup for their user interfaces. By default, the standard JSF components generate HTML. Components can do their own encoding, or they can delegate encoding to a separate renderer. The latter is the more elegant approach because it lets you plug in different renderers—for example to encode markup in something other than HTML. However, for simplicity, we will start out with a spinner that renders itself.

Components encode markup with three methods:

- encodeBegin()
- encodeChildren()
- encodeEnd()

The methods are called by JSF at the end of the life cycle, in the order in which they are listed above. JSF invokes encodeChildren only if a component returns true from its getRendersChildren method. By default, getRendersChildren returns false for most components.

For simple components, like our spinner, that do not have children, you do not need to implement encodeChildren. Since we do not need to worry what gets encoded before or after the children, we do all our encoding in encodeBegin.

The spinner generates HTML for a text field and two buttons; that HTML looks like this:

```
<input type="text" name="..." value="current value"/>
<input type="submit" name="..." value="<"/>
<input type="submit" name="..." value=">"/>
```

Here is how that HTML is encoded in `UISpinner`:

```java
public class UISpinner extends UIInput {
   private static final String MORE = ".more";
   private static final String LESS = ".less";
   ...
   public void encodeBegin(FacesContext context) throws IOException {
      ResponseWriter writer = context.getResponseWriter();
      String clientId = getClientId(context);

      encodeInputField(writer, clientId);
      encodeDecrementButton(writer, clientId);
      encodeIncrementButton(writer, clientId);
   }
   private void encodeInputField(ResponseWriter writer, String clientId)
         throws IOException {
      writer.startElement("input", this);
      writer.writeAttribute("name", clientId, "clientId");

      Object v = getValue();
      if (v != null)
         writer.writeAttribute("value", v.toString(), "value");

      Integer size = (Integer) getAttributes().get("size");
      if (size != null) writer.writeAttribute("size", size, "size");

      writer.endElement("input");
   }
   private void encodeDecrementButton(ResponseWriter writer, String clientId)
         throws IOException {
      writer.startElement("input", this);
      writer.writeAttribute("type", "submit", null);
      writer.writeAttribute("name", clientId + LESS, null);
      writer.writeAttribute("value", "<", "value");
      writer.endElement("input");
   }
   private void encodeIncrementButton(ResponseWriter writer, String clientId)
         throws IOException {
      writer.startElement("input", this);
      writer.writeAttribute("type", "submit", null);
      writer.writeAttribute("name", clientId + MORE, null);
      writer.writeAttribute("value", ">", "value");
      writer.endElement("input");
   }
   ...
}
```

The ResponseWriter class has convenience methods for writing markup. The start-Element and endElement methods produce the element delimiters. They keep track of child elements, so you do not have to worry about the distinction between <input .../> and <input ...>...</input>. The writeAttribute method writes an attribute name/value pair with the appropriate escape characters.

The last parameter of the startElement and writeAttribute methods is intended for tool support, but it is currently unused. You are supposed to pass the rendered component object or attribute name, or null if the output does not directly correspond to a component or attribute.

UISpinner.encodeBegin faces two challenges. First, it must get the current state of the spinner. The numerical value is easily obtained with the getValue method that the spinner inherits from UIInput. The size is retrieved from the component's attribute map, using the getAttributes method.

(As you will see in the section "Implementing Custom Component Tags" on page 372, the SpinnerTag class stores the tag's size attribute in the component's value expression map, and the get method of the map returned by getAttributes evaluates the value expression.)

Second, the encoding method needs to come up with names for the HTML elements the spinner encodes. It calls the getClientId method to obtain the client ID of the component, which is composed of the ID of the enclosing form and the ID of this component, such as _id1:monthSpinner.

That identifier is created by the JSF implementation. The increment and decrement button names start with the client ID and end in .more and .less, respectively. Here is a complete example of the HTML generated by the spinner:

```
<input type="text" name="_id1:monthSpinner" value="1" size="3"/>
<input type="submit" name="_id1:monthSpinner.less" value="<"/>
<input type="submit" name="_id1:monthSpinner.more" value=">"/>
```

In the next section, we discuss how those names are used by the spinner's decode method.

 javax.faces.component.UIComponent

- void encodeBegin(FacesContext context) throws IOException
  The method called in the Render Response phase of the JSF life cycle, only if the component's renderer type is null. This signifies that the component renders itself.

- `String getClientId(FacesContext context)`
  Returns the client ID for this component. The JSF framework creates the client ID from the ID of the enclosing form (or, more generally, the enclosing *naming container*) and the ID of this component.

- `Map getAttributes()`
  Returns a mutable map of component attributes and properties. You use this method to view, add, update, or remove attributes from a component. You can also use this map to view or update properties. The map's get and put methods check whether the key matches a component property. If so, the property getter or setter is called.

  As of JSF 1.2, the map also gets attributes that are defined by value expressions. If get is called with a name that is not a property or attribute but a key in the component's value expression map, then the value of the associated expression is returned.

 NOTE: The spinner is a simple component with no children, so its encoding is rather basic. For a more complicated example, see how the tabbed pane renderer encodes markup. That renderer is shown in Listing 9–17 on page 419.

 NOTE: JSF invokes a component's encodeChildren method if the component returns true from getRendersChildren. Interestingly, it does not matter whether the component actually has children—as long as the component's getRendersChildren method returns true, JSF calls encodeChildren even if the component has no children.

`javax.faces.context.FacesContext`

- `ResponseWriter getResponseWriter()`
  Returns a reference to the response writer. You can plug your own response writer into JSF if you want. By default, JSF uses a response writer that can write HTML tags.

`javax.faces.context.ResponseWriter`

- `void startElement(String elementName, UIComponent component)`
  Writes the start tag for the specified element. The component parameter lets tools associate a component and its markup. The 1.0 version of the JSF reference implementation ignores this attribute.

- void endElement(String elementName)

  Writes the end tag for the specified element.

- void writeAttribute(String attributeName, String attributeValue,
  String componentProperty)

  Writes an attribute and its value. This method can only be called between calls to startElement() and endElement(). The componentProperty is the name of the component property that corresponds to the attribute. Its use is meant for tools. It is not supported by the 1.0 reference implementation.

Decoding: Processing Request Values

To understand the decoding process, keep in mind how a web application works. The server sends an HTML form to the browser. The browser sends back a POST request that consists of name/value pairs. That POST request is the only data that the server can use to interpret the user's actions inside the browser.

If the user clicks the increment or decrement button, the ensuing POST request includes the names and values of *all* text fields, but only the name and value of the *clicked* button. For example, if the user clicks the month spinner's increment button in the application shown in Figure 9–1 on page 356, the following request parameters are transferred to the server from the browser:

Name	Value
_id1:monthSpinner	1
_id1:yearSpinner	12
_id1:monthSpinner.more	>

When our spinner decodes an HTTP request, it looks for the request parameter names that match its client ID and processes the associated values. The spinner's decode method is listed below.

```
public void decode(FacesContext context) {
    Map requestMap = context.getExternalContext().getRequestParameterMap();
    String clientId = getClientId(context);

    int increment;
    if (requestMap.containsKey(clientId + MORE)) increment = 1;
    else if (requestMap.containsKey(clientId + LESS)) increment = -1;
    else increment = 0;

    try {
        int submittedValue
            = Integer.parseInt((String) requestMap.get(clientId));
```

```
        int newValue = getIncrementedValue(submittedValue, increment);
        setSubmittedValue("" + newValue);
        setValid(true);
    }
    catch(NumberFormatException ex) {
        // let the converter take care of bad input, but we still have
        // to set the submitted value or the converter won't have
        // any input to deal with
        setSubmittedValue((String) requestMap.get(clientId));
    }
}
```

The decode method looks at the request parameters to determine which of the spinner's buttons, if any, triggered the request. If a request parameter named *clientId*.less exists, where *clientId* is the client ID of the spinner we are decoding, then we know that the decrement button was activated. If the decode method finds a request parameter named *clientId*.more, then we know that the increment button was activated.

If neither parameter exists, we know that the request was not initiated by the spinner, so we set the increment to zero. We still need to update the value—the user might have typed a value into the text field and clicked the "Next" button.

Our naming convention works for multiple spinners in a page because each spinner is encoded with the spinner component's client ID, which is guaranteed to be unique. If you have multiple spinners in a single page, each spinner component decodes its own request.

Once the decode method determines that one of the spinner's buttons was clicked, it increments the spinner's value by 1 or –1, depending on which button the user activated. That incremented value is calculated by a private getIncrementedValue method:

```
private int getIncrementedValue(int submittedValue, int increment) {
    Integer minimum = (Integer) getAttributes().get("minimum");
    Integer maximum = (Integer) getAttributes().get("maximum");
    int newValue = submittedValue + increment;

    if ((minimum == null || newValue >= minimum.intValue()) &&
        (maximum == null || newValue <= maximum.intValue()))
        return newValue;
    else
        return submittedValue;
}
```

The getIncrementedValue method checks the value the user entered in the spinner against the spinner's minimum and maximum attributes. Those attributes are set by the spinner's tag handler class.

After it gets the incremented value, the decode method calls the spinner component's setSubmittedValue method. That method stores the submitted value in the component. Subsequently, in the JSF life cycle, that submitted value will be converted and validated by the JSF framework.

 CAUTION: You must call setValid(true) after setting the submitted value. Otherwise, the input is not considered valid, and the current page is redisplayed.

javax.faces.component.UIComponent

- void decode(FacesContext context)

  The method called by JSF at the beginning of the JSF life cycle—only if the component's renderer type is null, signifying that the component renders itself.

  The decode method decodes request parameters. Typically, components transfer request parameter values to component properties or attributes. Components that fire action events queue them in this method.

javax.faces.context.FacesContext

- ExternalContext getExternalContext()

  Returns a reference to a context proxy. Typically, the real context is a servlet or portlet context. If you use the external context instead of using the real context directly, your applications can work with servlets and portlets.

javax.faces.context.ExternalContext

- Map getRequestParameterMap()

  Returns a map of request parameters. Custom components typically call this method in decode() to see if they were the component that triggered the request.

javax.faces.component.EditableValueHolder

- void setSubmittedValue(Object submittedValue)

  Sets a component's submitted value—input components have editable values, so UIInput implements the EditableValueHolder interface. The submitted value is the value the user entered, presumably in a web page. For

HTML-based applications, that value is always a string, but the method accepts an Object reference in deference to other display technologies.

- void setValid(boolean valid)

  Custom components use this method to indicate their value's validity. If a component cannot convert its value, it sets the valid property to false.

Using Converters

The spinner component uses the standard JSF integer converter to convert strings to Integer objects, and vice versa. The UISpinner constructor simply calls setConverter, like this:

```java
public class UISpinner extends UIInput {
   ...
   public UISpinner() {
      setConverter(new IntegerConverter()); // to convert the submitted value
      setRendererType(null);                // this component renders itself
   }
```

The spinner's decode method traps invalid inputs in the NumberFormatException catch clause. However, instead of reporting the error, it sets the component's submitted value to the user input. Later on in the JSF life cycle, the standard integer converter will try to convert that value and will generate an appropriate error message for bad input.

Listing 9–1 contains the complete code for the UISpinner class.

Listing 9–1   spinner/src/java/com/corejsf/UISpinner.java

```java
1. package com.corejsf;
2.
3. import java.io.IOException;
4. import java.util.Map;
5. import javax.faces.component.UIInput;
6. import javax.faces.context.FacesContext;
7. import javax.faces.context.ResponseWriter;
8. import javax.faces.convert.IntegerConverter;
9.
10. public class UISpinner extends UIInput {
11.    private static final String MORE = ".more";
12.    private static final String LESS = ".less";
13.
14.    public UISpinner() {
15.       setConverter(new IntegerConverter()); // to convert the submitted value
16.       setRendererType(null); // this component renders itself
17.    }
```

Listing 9–1   spinner/src/java/com/corejsf/UISpinner.java (cont.)

```
18.
19.  public void encodeBegin(FacesContext context) throws IOException {
20.      ResponseWriter writer = context.getResponseWriter();
21.      String clientId = getClientId(context);
22.
23.      encodeInputField(writer, clientId);
24.      encodeDecrementButton(writer, clientId);
25.      encodeIncrementButton(writer, clientId);
26.  }
27.
28.  public void decode(FacesContext context) {
29.      Map<String, String> requestMap
30.          = context.getExternalContext().getRequestParameterMap();
31.      String clientId = getClientId(context);
32.
33.      int increment;
34.      if (requestMap.containsKey(clientId + MORE)) increment = 1;
35.      else if(requestMap.containsKey(clientId + LESS)) increment = -1;
36.      else increment = 0;
37.
38.      try {
39.          int submittedValue
40.              = Integer.parseInt((String) requestMap.get(clientId));
41.
42.          int newValue = getIncrementedValue(submittedValue, increment);
43.          setSubmittedValue("" + newValue);
44.          setValid(true);
45.      }
46.      catch(NumberFormatException ex) {
47.          // let the converter take care of bad input, but we still have
48.          // to set the submitted value, or the converter won't have
49.          // any input to deal with
50.          setSubmittedValue((String) requestMap.get(clientId));
51.      }
52.  }
53.
54.  private void encodeInputField(ResponseWriter writer, String clientId)
55.          throws IOException {
56.      writer.startElement("input", this);
57.      writer.writeAttribute("name", clientId, "clientId");
58.
59.      Object v = getValue();
60.      if (v != null)
61.          writer.writeAttribute("value", v.toString(), "value");
62.
```

| **Listing 9–1** | spinner/src/java/com/corejsf/UISpinner.java (cont.) |

```
63.        Integer size = (Integer)getAttributes().get("size");
64.        if(size != null)
65.           writer.writeAttribute("size", size, "size");
66.
67.        writer.endElement("input");
68.     }
69.
70.     private void encodeDecrementButton(ResponseWriter writer, String clientId)
71.           throws IOException {
72.        writer.startElement("input", this);
73.        writer.writeAttribute("type", "submit", null);
74.        writer.writeAttribute("name", clientId + LESS, null);
75.        writer.writeAttribute("value", "<", "value");
76.        writer.endElement("input");
77.     }
78.     private void encodeIncrementButton(ResponseWriter writer, String clientId)
79.           throws IOException {
80.        writer.startElement("input", this);
81.        writer.writeAttribute("type", "submit", null);
82.        writer.writeAttribute("name", clientId + MORE, null);
83.        writer.writeAttribute("value", ">", "value");
84.        writer.endElement("input");
85.     }
86.
87.     private int getIncrementedValue(int submittedValue, int increment) {
88.        Integer minimum = (Integer) getAttributes().get("minimum");
89.        Integer maximum = (Integer) getAttributes().get("maximum");
90.        int newValue = submittedValue + increment;
91.
92.        if ((minimum == null || newValue >= minimum.intValue()) &&
93.           (maximum == null || newValue <= maximum.intValue()))
94.           return newValue;
95.        else
96.           return submittedValue;
97.     }
98. }
```

---

javax.faces.component.ValueHolder

- void setConverter(Converter converter)

  Input and output components both have values and, therefore, both implement the ValueHolder interface. Values must be converted, so the ValueHolder interface defines a method for setting the converter. Custom components use this method to associate themselves with standard or custom converters.

Implementing Custom Component Tags

Now that you have seen how to implement the spinner component, there is one remaining chore: to supply a tag handler. The process is somewhat byzantine, and you may find it helpful to refer to Figure 9–5 as we discuss each step.

 NOTE: Custom tags use the JavaServer Pages tag library mechanism. For more information on JSP custom tags, see Chapter 7 of the Java EE 5 tutorial at `http://java.sun.com/javaee/5/docs/tutorial/doc/index.html`.

The TLD File

You need to produce a TLD (tag library descriptor) file that describes one or more tags and their attributes. Place that file into the WEB-INF directory. Listing 9–2 shows the TLD file that describes our spinner custom tag.

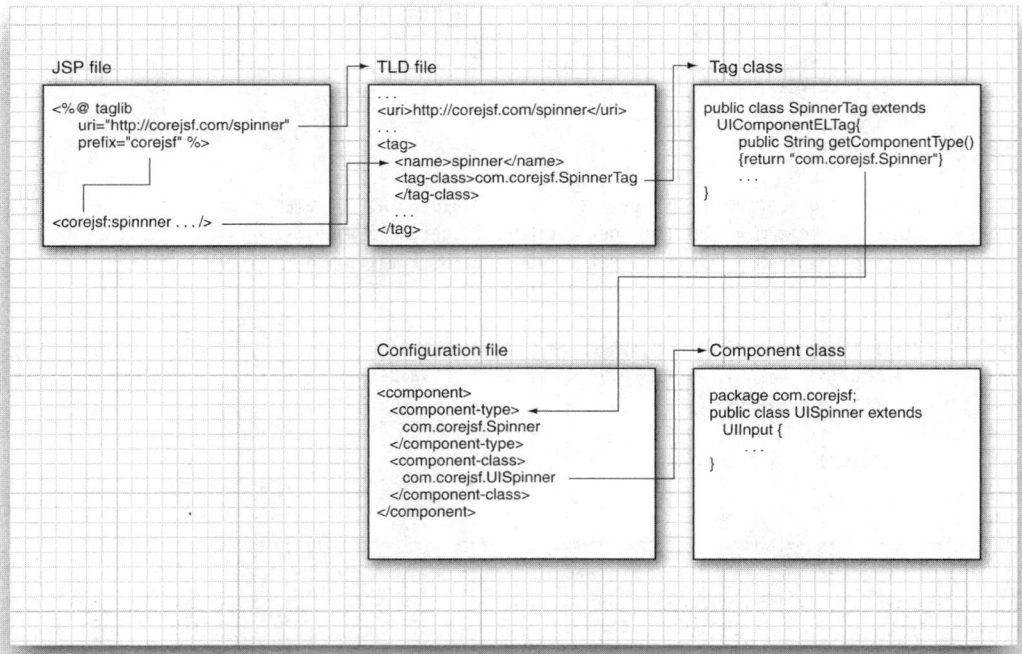

Figure 9–5   Locating a custom component

The purpose of the file is to specify the class name for the tag handler (`com.core-jsf.SpinnerTag`) and the permitted attributes of the tag (in our case, `id`, `rendered`, `minimum`, `maximum`, `size`, and `value`).

Note the `uri` tag that identifies the tag library:

```
<uri>http://corejsf.com/spinner</uri>
```

This is the URI that you reference in a `taglib` directive of the JSF page, such as

```
<%@ taglib uri="http://corejsf.com/spinner" prefix="corejsf" %>
```

This `taglib` directive is the analog to the directives that define the standard f and h prefixes in every JSF page.

 NOTE: You can choose arbitrary names for the TLD files—only the `.tld` extension matters. The JSF implementation searches for TLD files in the following locations:

- The `WEB-INF` directory or one of its subdirectories

- The `META-INF` directory or any JAR file in the `WEB-INF/lib` directory

The latter is useful if you want to package your converters as reusable JAR files.

 NOTE: In the following, we describe TLD files and tag handlers for JSF 1.2. The details are quite different for JSF 1.1. See page 383 for details.

Most attribute definitions in the TLD file contain a `deferred-value` child element, like this:

```
<attribute>
    <description>The spinner minimum value</description>
    <name>minimum</name>
    <deferred-value>
        <type>int</type>
    </deferred-value>
</attribute>
```

This syntax indicates that the attribute is defined by a value expression. The attribute value can be a constant string or a string that contains #{...} expressions. The `type` element specifies the Java type of the value expression. In our example, `minimum` is defined by a value expression of type `int`.

Some attributes are specified by method expressions instead of value expressions. For example, to define an action listener, you use the following tag:

```
<attribute>
    <name>actionListener</name>
    <deferred-method>
        <method-signature>
            void actionListener(javax.faces.event.ActionEvent)
        </method-signature>
    </deferred-method>
</attribute>
```

Generally, you want to allow value or method expressions for attributes. One exception is the id attribute that is defined as a *runtime expression value*—that is, a JSP expression but not a JSF value expression.

```
<attribute>
    <description>The client id of this component</description>
    <name>id</name>
    <rtexprvalue>true</rtexprvalue>
</attribute>
```

Listing 9–2   spinner/web/WEB-INF/spinner.tld

```
 1. <?xml version="1.0" encoding="UTF-8"?>
 2. <taglib xmlns="http://java.sun.com/xml/ns/javaee"
 3.     xmlns:xsi="http://www.w3.org/2001/XMLSchema-instance"
 4.     xsi:schemaLocation="http://java.sun.com/xml/ns/javaee
 5.         http://java.sun.com/xml/ns/javaee/web-jsptaglibrary_2_1.xsd"
 6.     version="2.1">
 7.     <tlib-version>1.1</tlib-version>
 8.     <short-name>spinner</short-name>
 9.     <uri>http://corejsf.com/spinner</uri>
10.
11.     <tag>
12.         <name>spinner</name>
13.         <tag-class>com.corejsf.SpinnerTag</tag-class>
14.         <body-content>empty</body-content>
15.         <attribute>
16.             <description>A value binding that points to a bean property</description>
17.             <name>binding</name>
18.             <deferred-value>
19.                 <type>javax.faces.component.UIComponent</type>
20.             </deferred-value>
21.         </attribute>
22.
23.         <attribute>
24.             <description>The client id of this component</description>
25.             <name>id</name>
```

Listing 9–2   spinner/web/WEB-INF/spinner.tld (cont.)

```
26.            <rtexprvalue>true</rtexprvalue>
27.        </attribute>
28.
29.        <attribute>
30.            <description>Is this component rendered?</description>
31.            <name>rendered</name>
32.            <deferred-value>
33.                <type>boolean</type>
34.            </deferred-value>
35.        </attribute>
36.
37.        <attribute>
38.            <description>The spinner minimum value</description>
39.            <name>minimum</name>
40.            <deferred-value>
41.                <type>int</type>
42.            </deferred-value>
43.        </attribute>
44.
45.        <attribute>
46.            <description>The spinner maximum value</description>
47.            <name>maximum</name>
48.            <deferred-value>
49.                <type>int</type>
50.            </deferred-value>
51.        </attribute>
52.
53.        <attribute>
54.            <description>The size of the input field</description>
55.            <name>size</name>
56.            <deferred-value>
57.                <type>int</type>
58.            </deferred-value>
59.        </attribute>
60.
61.        <attribute>
62.            <description>The value of the spinner</description>
63.            <name>value</name>
64.            <required>true</required>
65.            <deferred-value>
66.                <type>int</type>
67.            </deferred-value>
68.        </attribute>
69.    </tag>
70. </taglib>
```

The Tag Handler Class

Together with the TLD file, you need to supply a *tag handler class* for each custom tag. For a component tag, the tag handler class should be a subclass of UIComponentELTag. As you will see later, the tag handlers for custom converters need to subclass ComponentELTag, and custom validator tag handlers need to subclass ValidatorELTag.

Component tag classes have five responsibilities:

*   To identify a component type
*   To identify a renderer type
*   To provide setter methods for tag attributes
*   To store tag attribute values in the tag's component
*   To release resources

Now we look at the implementation of the SpinnerTag class:

```
public class SpinnerTag extends UIComponentELTag {
    private ValueExpression minimum;
    private ValueExpression maximum;
    private ValueExpression size;
    private ValueExpression value;

    ...
}
```

The spinner tag class has an instance field for each attribute. The tag class should keep all attributes as ValueExpression objects.

 NOTE: The id, binding, and rendered attributes are handled by the UIComponentELTag superclass.

The SpinnerTag class identifies its component type as com.corejsf.Spinner and its renderer type as null. A null renderer type means that a component renders itself or nominates its own renderer.

```
public String getComponentType() { return "com.corejsf.Spinner"; }
public String getRendererType()  { return null; }
```

 CAUTION: When the getRendererType method of the tag handler returns null, you must call setRendererType in the component constructor. If the component renders itself, call setRendererType(null).

SpinnerTag provides setter methods for the attributes it supports: minimum, maximum, value, and size, as follows:

```
public void setMinimum(ValueExpression newValue) { minimum = newValue; }
public void setMaximum(ValueExpression newValue) { maximum = newValue; }
public void setSize(ValueExpression newValue) { size = newValue; }
public void setValue(ValueExpression newValue) { value = newValue; }
```

When the tag is processed in the JSF page, the tag attribute value is converted to a ValueExpression object, and the setter method is called. Getter methods are not needed.

Tag handlers must override a setProperties method to copy tag attribute values to the component. The method name is somewhat of a misnomer because it usually sets component attributes or value expressions, not properties:

```
public void setProperties(UIComponent component) {
    // always call the superclass method
    super.setProperties(component);

    component.setValueExpression("size", size);
    component.setValueExpression("minimum", minimum);
    component.setValueExpression("maximum", maximum);
    component.setValueExpression("value", value);
}
```

Later, you can evaluate the value expression simply by using the attributes map. For example,

```
Integer minimum = (Integer) component.getAttributes().get("minimum");
```

The get method of the attributes map checks that the component has a value expression with the given key, and it evaluates it.

Finally, you need to define a release method that resets all instance fields to their defaults:

```
public void release() {
    // always call the superclass method
    super.release();

    minimum = null;
    maximum = null;
    size = null;
    value = null;
}
```

This method is necessary because the JSF implementation may cache tag handler objects and reuse them for parsing tags. If a tag handler is reused, it should not have leftover settings from a previous tag.

NOTE: Tag classes must call superclass methods when they override `setProperties` and `release`.

Listing 9–3 contains the complete code for the `SpinnerTag` tag handler.

Listing 9–3 spinner/src/java/com/corejsf/SpinnerTag.java

```
 1. package com.corejsf;
 2.
 3. import javax.el.ValueExpression;
 4. import javax.faces.component.UIComponent;
 5. import javax.faces.webapp.UIComponentELTag;
 6.
 7. public class SpinnerTag extends UIComponentELTag {
 8.     private ValueExpression minimum = null;
 9.     private ValueExpression maximum = null;
10.     private ValueExpression size = null;
11.     private ValueExpression value = null;
12.
13.     public String getRendererType() { return null; }
14.     public String getComponentType() { return "com.corejsf.Spinner"; }
15.
16.     public void setMinimum(ValueExpression newValue) { minimum = newValue; }
17.     public void setMaximum(ValueExpression newValue) { maximum = newValue; }
18.     public void setSize(ValueExpression newValue) { size = newValue; }
19.     public void setValue(ValueExpression newValue) { value = newValue; }
20.
21.     public void setProperties(UIComponent component) {
22.         // always call the superclass method
23.         super.setProperties(component);
24.
25.         component.setValueExpression("size", size);
26.         component.setValueExpression("minimum", minimum);
27.         component.setValueExpression("maximum", maximum);
28.         component.setValueExpression("value", value);
29.     }
30.
31.     public void release() {
32.         // always call the superclass method
33.         super.release();
34.
35.         minimum = null;
36.         maximum = null;
37.         size = null;
38.         value = null;
39.     }
40. }
```

API | `javax.faces.webapp.UIComponentELTag` JSF 1.2

- void setProperties(UIComponent component)

  Transfers tag attribute values to component properties, attributes, or both. Custom components must call the superclass setProperties method to make sure that properties are set for the attributes UIComponentELTag supports: binding, id, and rendered.

- void release()

  Clears the state of this tag so that it can be reused.

API | `javax.faces.component.UIComponent`

- void setValueExpression(String name, ValueExpression expr) JSF 1.2

  If the expression is a constant, without #{...} expressions, then it is evaluated and the (name, value) pair is put into the component's attribute map. Otherwise, the (name, expr) pair is put into the component's value expression map.

The Spinner Application

After a number of different perspectives of the spinner component, it is time to take a look at the spinner example in its entirety. This section lists the code for the spinner test application shown in Figure 9–1 on page 356. The directory structure is shown in Figure 9–6 and the code is shown in Listings 9–4 through 9–9.

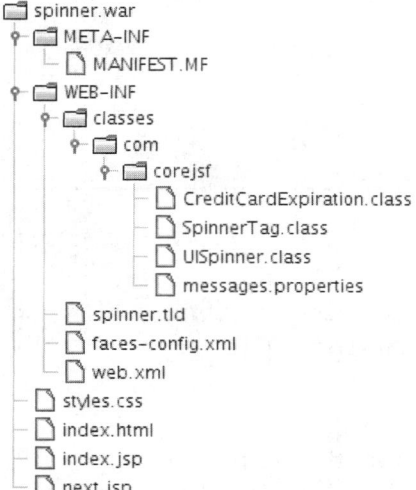

Figure 9–6   Directory structure for the spinner example

Listing 9–4   spinner/web/index.jsp

```
1.  <html>
2.  <%@ taglib uri="http://java.sun.com/jsf/core" prefix="f" %>
3.  <%@ taglib uri="http://java.sun.com/jsf/html" prefix="h" %>
4.  <%@ taglib uri="http://corejsf.com/spinner" prefix="corejsf" %>
5.  <f:view>
6.     <head>
7.        <link href="styles.css" rel="stylesheet" type="text/css"/>
8.        <title><h:outputText value="#{msgs.windowTitle}"/></title>
9.     </head>
10.
11.    <body>
12.       <h:form id="spinnerForm">
13.          <h:outputText value="#{msgs.creditCardExpirationPrompt}"
14.             styleClass="pageTitle"/>
15.          <p/>
16.          <h:panelGrid columns="3">
17.             <h:outputText value="#{msgs.monthPrompt}"/>
18.             <corejsf:spinner value="#{cardExpirationDate.month}"
19.                id="monthSpinner" minimum="1" maximum="12" size="3"/>
20.             <h:message for="monthSpinner"/>
21.             <h:outputText value="#{msgs.yearPrompt}"/>
22.             <corejsf:spinner value="#{cardExpirationDate.year}"
23.                id="yearSpinner" minimum="1900" maximum="2100" size="5"/>
24.             <h:message for="yearSpinner"/>
25.          </h:panelGrid>
26.          <p/>
27.          <h:commandButton value="#{msgs.nextButtonPrompt}" action="next"/>
28.       </h:form>
29.    </body>
30. </f:view>
31. </html>
```

Listing 9–5   spinner/web/next.jsp

```
1.  <html>
2.  <%@ taglib uri="http://java.sun.com/jsf/core" prefix="f" %>
3.  <%@ taglib uri="http://java.sun.com/jsf/html" prefix="h" %>
4.
5.  <f:view>
6.     <head>
7.        <link href="styles.css" rel="stylesheet" type="text/css"/>
8.        <title><h:outputText value="#{msgs.windowTitle}"/></title>
9.     </head>
```

Listing 9–5   `spinner/web/next.jsp (cont.)`

```
10.        <body>
11.          <h:form>
12.            <h:outputText value="#{msgs.youEnteredPrompt}" styleClass="pageTitle"/>
13.            <p>
14.            <h:outputText value="#{msgs.expirationDatePrompt}"/>
15.              <h:outputText value="#{cardExpirationDate.month}"/> /
16.              <h:outputText value="#{cardExpirationDate.year}"/>
17.            <p>
18.            <h:commandButton value="Try again" action="again"/>
19.          </h:form>
20.        </body>
21.      </f:view>
22. </html>
```

Listing 9–6   `spinner/src/java/com/corejsf/CreditCardExpiration.java`

```
1. package com.corejsf;
2.
3. public class CreditCardExpiration {
4.    private int month = 1;
5.    private int year = 2000;
6.
7.    // PROPERTY: month
8.    public int getMonth() { return month; }
9.    public void setMonth(int newValue) { month = newValue; }
10.
11.   // PROPERTY: year
12.   public int getYear() { return year; }
13.   public void setYear(int newValue) { year = newValue; }
14. }
```

Listing 9–7   `spinner/web/WEB-INF/faces-config.xml`

```
1. <?xml version="1.0"?>
2. <faces-config xmlns="http://java.sun.com/xml/ns/javaee"
3.    xmlns:xsi="http://www.w3.org/2001/XMLSchema-instance"
4.    xsi:schemaLocation="http://java.sun.com/xml/ns/javaee
5.        http://java.sun.com/xml/ns/javaee/web-facesconfig_1_2.xsd"
6.    version="1.2">
7.    <navigation-rule>
8.      <from-view-id>/index.jsp</from-view-id>
9.      <navigation-case>
```

Listing 9–7 spinner/web/WEB-INF/faces-config.xml (cont.)

```
10.          <from-outcome>next</from-outcome>
11.          <to-view-id>/next.jsp</to-view-id>
12.       </navigation-case>
13.    </navigation-rule>
14.
15.    <navigation-rule>
16.       <from-view-id>/next.jsp</from-view-id>
17.       <navigation-case>
18.          <from-outcome>again</from-outcome>
19.          <to-view-id>/index.jsp</to-view-id>
20.       </navigation-case>
21.    </navigation-rule>
22.
23.    <component>
24.       <component-type>com.corejsf.Spinner</component-type>
25.       <component-class>com.corejsf.UISpinner</component-class>
26.    </component>
27.
28.    <managed-bean>
29.       <managed-bean-name>cardExpirationDate</managed-bean-name>
30.       <managed-bean-class>com.corejsf.CreditCardExpiration</managed-bean-class>
31.       <managed-bean-scope>session</managed-bean-scope>
32.    </managed-bean>
33.
34.    <application>
35.       <resource-bundle>
36.          <base-name>com.corejsf.messages</base-name>
37.          <var>msgs</var>
38.       </resource-bundle>
39.    </application>
40. </faces-config>
```

Listing 9–8 spinner/src/java/com/corejsf/messages.properties

```
1. windowTitle=Spinner Test
2. creditCardExpirationPrompt=Please enter your credit card expiration date:
3. monthPrompt=Month:
4. yearPrompt=Year:
5. nextButtonPrompt=Next
6. youEnteredPrompt=You entered:
7. expirationDatePrompt=Expiration Date
8. changes=Changes:
```

| Listing 9–9 | spinner/web/styles.css |

```
1. body {
2.    background: #eee;
3. }
4. .pageTitle {
5.    font-size: 1.25em;
6. }
```

Defining Tag Handlers in JSF 1.1

In JSF 1.1, support for tag handlers was less elegant than in JSF 1.2. This section contains the details. Feel free to skip it if you do not have to write components that are backward compatible with JSF 1.1.

JSF 1.1 provides two separate tag superclasses, UIComponentTag and UIComponent-BodyTag. You extend the former if your component does not process its *body* (that is, the child tags and text between the start and end tag), and the latter if it does. Only four of the standard tags in JSF 1.1 extend UIComponentBodyTag: f:view, f:verbatim, h:commandLink, and h:outputLink. A spinner component does not process its body, so it would extend UIComponentTag.

 NOTE: A tag that implements UIComponentTag can *have* a body, provided that the tags inside the body know how to process themselves. For example, you can add an f:attribute child to a spinner.

Before JSF 1.2, TLD files used a DOCTYPE declaration instead of a schema declaration, like this:

```
<?xml version="1.0" encoding="ISO-8859-1" ?>
<!DOCTYPE taglib PUBLIC "-//Sun Microsystems, Inc.//DTD JSP Tag Library 1.2//EN"
   "http://java.sun.com/dtd/web-jsptaglibrary_1_2.dtd">
<taglib>
   <tlib-version>0.03</tlib-version>
   <jsp-version>1.2</jsp-version>
   ...
</taglib>
```

More important, you cannot use any deferred-value or deferred-method child elements for attributes. Instead, the tag handler class gets passed the expression strings. It must convert them to objects of type ValueBinding or MethodBinding. These are the JSF 1.1 analogs of the ValueExpression and MethodExpression classes.

Thus, the tag handler class must define setters for strings, like this:

```
public class SpinnerTag extends UIComponentTag {
   private String minimum;
   private String maximum;
   ...
   public void setMinimum(String newValue) { minimum = newValue; }
   public void setMaximum(String newValue) { maximum = newValue; }
   ...
}
```

In the setProperties method, you check whether the string is in fact a value binding. If so, you convert it to an object of type ValueBinding, the precursor to the ValueExpression class. Otherwise, you convert the string to the appropriate type and set it as a component attribute.

This conversion is rather tedious, and it is useful to define a helper method, such as the following:

```
public void setInteger(UIComponent component, String name, String expr) {
   if (expr == null) return null;
   else if (UIComponentTag.isValueReference(expr)) {
      FacesContext context = FacesContext.getCurrentInstance();
      Application app = context.getApplication();
      ValueBinding binding = app.createValueBinding(expr);
      component.setValueBinding(name, binding);
   }
   else
      component.getAttributes().put(name, new Integer(expr));
}
```

 NOTE: The map returned by the UIComponent.getAttributes method is smart: It accesses component properties and attributes. For example, if you call the map's get method with an attribute whose name is "value", the getValue method is called. If the attribute name is "minimum", and there is no getMinimum method, the component's attribute map is queried for the entry with key "minimum".

You call the helper method in the setProperties method, like this:

```
public void setProperties(UIComponent component) {
   super.setProperties(component);
   setInteger(component, "minimum", minimum);
   setInteger(component, "maximum", maximum);
   ...
}
```

Our helper method assumes that the expression evaluates to an integer. You would need other helper methods setString, setBoolean, and so on, for other types.

Attributes that define method bindings—such as the four commonly used attributes in Table 9–1—require additional work. You create a MethodBinding object by calling the createMethodBinding method of the Application class. That method has two parameters: the method binding expression and an array of Class objects that describe the method's parameter types. For example, this code creates a method binding for a value change listener:

```
FacesContext context = FacesContext.getCurrentInstance();
Application app = context.getApplication();
Class[] paramTypes = new Class[] { ValueChangeListener.class };
MethodBinding mb = app.createMethodBinding(attributeValue, paramTypes);
```

You then store the MethodBinding object with the component:

```
((EditableValueHolder) component).setValueChangeListener(mb);
```

Table 9–1   Method Binding Attributes

Attribute Name	Method Parameters	Method for Setting the Binding
valueChangeListener	ValueChangeEvent	EditableValueHolder.setValue-ChangeListener
validator	FacesContext, UIComponent, Object	EditableValueHolder.setValidator
actionListener	ActionEvent	ActionSource.setActionListener
action	*none*	ActionSource.setAction

Action listeners and validators follow exactly the same pattern. However, actions are slightly more complex. An action can be either a method binding or a fixed string, for example

```
<h:commandButton value="Login" action="#{loginController.verifyUser}"/>
```

or

```
<h:commandButton value="Login" action="login"/>
```

But the setAction method of the ActionSource interface requires a MethodBinding in all cases. If the action is a fixed string, you must construct a MethodBinding object whose getExpressionString method returns that string:

```
if (UIComponentTag.isValueReference(attributeValue))
    ((ActionSource) component).setMethodBinding(component, "action", attributeValue,
        new Class[] {});
else {
    FacesContext context = FacesContext.getCurrentInstance();
    Application app = context.getApplication();
```

```
    MethodBinding mb = new ActionMethodBinding(attributeValue);
    component.getAttributes().put("action", mb);
}
```

Here, ActionMethodBinding is the following class (which you must supply in your code):

```
public class ActionMethodBinding extends MethodBinding implements Serializable {
    private String result;

    public ActionMethodBinding(String result) { this.result = result; }
    public Object invoke(FacesContext context, Object params[]) { return result; }
    public String getExpressionString() { return result; }
    public Class getType(FacesContext context) { return String.class; }
}
```

Handling method expressions is much simpler in JSF 1.2 (see "Supporting Method Expressions" on page 396 for details).

API *javax.faces.context.FacesContext*

- `static FacesContext getCurrentInstance()`
  Returns a reference to the current FacesContext instance.

- `Application getApplication()`
  Returns the Application object associated with this web application.

 NOTE: The following methods are all deprecated. You should only use them to implement components that are backward compatible with JSF 1.1.

API `javax.faces.application.Application`

- `ValueBinding createValueBinding(String valueBindingExpression)`
  Creates a value binding and stores it in the application. The string must be a value binding expression of the form #{...}.

- `MethodBinding createMethodBinding(String methodBindingExpression, Class[] arguments)`
  Creates a method binding and stores it in the application. The methodBinding-Expression must be a method binding expression. The Class[] represents the types of the arguments passed to the method.

API `javax.faces.component.UIComponent`

- `void setValueBinding(String name, ValueBinding valueBinding)`
  Stores a value binding by name in the component.

`API` **javax.faces.webapp.UIComponentTag**

- static boolean isValueReference(String expression)
  Returns true if expression starts with "#{" and ends with "}".

`API` *javax.faces.component.EditableValueHolder*

- void setValueChangeListener(MethodBinding m)
  Sets a method binding for the value change listener of this component. The method must return void and is passed a ValueChangeEvent.

- void setValidator(MethodBinding m)
  Sets a method binding for the validator of this component. The method must return void and is passed a ValueChangeEvent.

`API` *javax.faces.component.ActionSource*

- void setActionListener(MethodBinding m)
  Sets a method binding for the action change listener of this component. The method must return void and is passed an ActionEvent.

- void setAction(MethodBinding m)
  Sets a method binding for the action of this component. The method can return an object of any type, and it has no parameters.

Revisiting the Spinner

Next, we revisit the spinner listed in the previous section. That spinner has two serious drawbacks. First, the spinner component renders itself, so you could not, for example, attach a separate renderer to the spinner when you migrate your application to cell phones.

Second, the spinner requires a roundtrip to the server every time a user clicks the increment or decrement button. Nobody would implement an industrial-strength spinner with those deficiencies. Now we see how to address them.

While we are at it, we will also add another feature to the spinner—the ability to attach value change listeners.

Using an External Renderer

In the preceding example, the UISpinner class was in charge of its own rendering. However, most UI classes delegate rendering to a separate class. Using separate renderers is a good idea: It becomes easy to replace renderers, to adapt to a different UI toolkit, or simply to achieve different HTML effects.

In "Encoding JavaScript to Avoid Server Roundtrips" on page 404 we see how to use an alternative renderer that uses JavaScript to keep track of the spinner's value on the client.

Using an external renderer requires these steps:

1.   Define an ID string for your renderer.
2.   Declare the renderer in a JSF configuration file.
3.   Modify your tag class to return the renderer's ID from the `getRendererType` method.
4.   Implement the renderer class.

The identifier—in our case, `com.corejsf.Spinner`—must be defined in a JSF configuration file, like this:

```
<faces-config>
    ...
    <component>
        <component-type>com.corejsf.Spinner</component-type>
        <component-class>com.corejsf.UISpinner</component-class>
    </component>

    <render-kit>
        <renderer>
            <component-family>javax.faces.Input</component-family>
            <renderer-type>com.corejsf.Spinner</renderer-type>
            <renderer-class>com.corejsf.SpinnerRenderer</renderer-class>
        </renderer>
    </render-kit>
</faces-config>
```

The `component-family` element serves to overcome a historical problem. The names of the standard HTML tags are meant to indicate the component type and the renderer type. For example, an `h:selectOneMenu` is a `UISelectOne` component whose renderer has type `javax.faces.Menu`. That same renderer can also be used for the `h:selectManyMenu` tag. But the scheme did not work so well. The renderer for `h:inputText` writes an HTML input text field. That renderer will not work for `h:outputText`—you do not want to use a text field for output.

So, instead of identifying renderers by individual components, renderers are determined by the renderer type and the *component family*. Table 9–2 shows the component families of all standard component classes. In our case, we use the component family `javax.faces.Input` because `UISpinner` is a subclass of `UIInput`.

The getRendererType of your tag class needs to return the renderer ID.

```
public class SpinnerTag extends UIComponentTag {
    ...
    public String getComponentType() { return "com.corejsf.Spinner"; }
    public String getRendererType()  { return "com.corejsf.Spinner"; }
    ...
}
```

 NOTE: Component IDs and renderer IDs have separate name spaces. It is okay to use the same string as a component ID and a renderer ID.

Table 9–2 Component Families of Standard Component Classes

Component Class	Component Family
UICommand	javax.faces.Command
UIData	javax.faces.Data
UIForm	javax.faces.Form
UIGraphic	javax.faces.Graphic
UIInput	javax.faces.Input
UIMessage	javax.faces.Message
UIMessages	javax.faces.Messages
UIOutput	javax.faces.Output
UIPanel	javax.faces.Panel
UISelectBoolean	javax.faces.SelectBoolean
UISelectMany	javax.faces.SelectMany
UISelectOne	javax.faces.SelectOne

It is also a good idea to set the renderer type in the component constructor:

```
public class UISpinner extends UIInput {
    public UISpinner() {
        setConverter(new IntegerConverter()); // to convert the submitted value
        setRendererType("com.corejsf.Spinner"); // this component has a renderer
    }
}
```

Then the renderer type is properly set if a component is used programmatically, without the use of tags.

The final step is implementing the renderer itself. Renderers extend the `javax.faces.render.Renderer` class. That class has seven methods, four of which are familiar:

- `void encodeBegin(FacesContext context, UIComponent component)`
- `void encodeChildren(FacesContext context, UIComponent component)`
- `void encodeEnd(FacesContext context, UIComponent component)`
- `void decode(FacesContext context, UIComponent component)`

The renderer methods listed above are almost identical to their component counterparts except that the renderer methods take an additional argument: a reference to the component being rendered. To implement those methods for the spinner renderer, we move the component methods to the renderer and apply code changes to compensate for the fact that the renderer is passed a reference to the component. That is easy to do.

Here are the remaining renderer methods:

- `Object getConvertedValue(FacesContext context, UIComponent component, Object submittedValue)`
- `boolean getRendersChildren()`
- `String convertClientId(FacesContext context, String clientId)`

The `getConvertedValue` method converts a component's submitted value from a string to an object. The default implementation in the `Renderer` class returns the value.

The `getRendersChildren` method specifies whether a renderer is responsible for rendering its component's children. If that method returns true, JSF will call the renderer's `encodeChildren` method; if it returns `false` (the default behavior), the JSF implementation will not call that method and the children will be encoded separately.

The `convertClientId` method converts an ID string (such as _id1:monthSpinner) so that it can be used on the client—some clients may place restrictions on IDs, such as disallowing special characters. However, the default implementation returns the ID string, unchanged.

If you have a component that renders itself, it is usually a simple task to move code from the component to the renderer. Listing 9–10 and Listing 9–11 show the code for the spinner component and the renderer, respectively.

Listing 9–10   spinner2/src/java/com/corejsf/UISpinner.java

```
 1. package com.corejsf;
 2.
 3. import javax.faces.component.UIInput;
 4. import javax.faces.convert.IntegerConverter;
 5.
 6. public class UISpinner extends UIInput {
 7.    public UISpinner() {
 8.       setConverter(new IntegerConverter()); // to convert the submitted value
 9.    }
10. }
```

Listing 9–11   spinner2/src/java/com/corejsf/SpinnerRenderer.java

```
 1. package com.corejsf;
 2.
 3. import java.io.IOException;
 4. import java.util.Map;
 5. import javax.faces.component.UIComponent;
 6. import javax.faces.component.EditableValueHolder;
 7. import javax.faces.component.UIInput;
 8. import javax.faces.context.FacesContext;
 9. import javax.faces.context.ResponseWriter;
10. import javax.faces.convert.ConverterException;
11. import javax.faces.render.Renderer;
12.
13. public class SpinnerRenderer extends Renderer {
14.    private static final String MORE = ".more";
15.    private static final String LESS = ".less";
16.
17.    public Object getConvertedValue(FacesContext context, UIComponent component,
18.          Object submittedValue) throws ConverterException {
19.       return com.corejsf.util.Renderers.getConvertedValue(context, component,
20.          submittedValue);
21.    }
22.
23.    public void encodeBegin(FacesContext context, UIComponent spinner)
24.          throws IOException {
25.       ResponseWriter writer = context.getResponseWriter();
26.       String clientId = spinner.getClientId(context);
27.
28.       encodeInputField(spinner, writer, clientId);
29.       encodeDecrementButton(spinner, writer, clientId);
30.       encodeIncrementButton(spinner, writer, clientId);
31.    }
```

Listing 9–11   spinner2/src/java/com/corejsf/SpinnerRenderer.java (cont.)

```
32.
33.   public void decode(FacesContext context, UIComponent component) {
34.      EditableValueHolder spinner = (EditableValueHolder) component;
35.      Map<String, String> requestMap
36.         = context.getExternalContext().getRequestParameterMap();
37.      String clientId = component.getClientId(context);
38.
39.      int increment;
40.      if (requestMap.containsKey(clientId + MORE)) increment = 1;
41.      else if (requestMap.containsKey(clientId + LESS)) increment = -1;
42.      else increment = 0;
43.
44.      try {
45.         int submittedValue
46.            = Integer.parseInt((String) requestMap.get(clientId));
47.
48.         int newValue = getIncrementedValue(component, submittedValue,
49.            increment);
50.         spinner.setSubmittedValue("" + newValue);
51.         spinner.setValid(true);
52.      }
53.      catch(NumberFormatException ex) {
54.         // let the converter take care of bad input, but we still have
55.         // to set the submitted value, or the converter won't have
56.         // any input to deal with
57.         spinner.setSubmittedValue((String) requestMap.get(clientId));
58.      }
59.   }
60.
61.   private void encodeInputField(UIComponent spinner, ResponseWriter writer,
62.         String clientId) throws IOException {
63.      writer.startElement("input", spinner);
64.      writer.writeAttribute("name", clientId, "clientId");
65.
66.      Object v = ((UIInput) spinner).getValue();
67.      if(v != null)
68.         writer.writeAttribute("value", v.toString(), "value");
69.
70.      Integer size = (Integer) spinner.getAttributes().get("size");
71.      if(size != null)
72.         writer.writeAttribute("size", size, "size");
73.
74.      writer.endElement("input");
75.   }
76.
```

Listing 9–11 spinner2/src/java/com/corejsf/SpinnerRenderer.java (cont.)

```
77.    private void encodeDecrementButton(UIComponent spinner,
78.       ResponseWriter writer, String clientId) throws IOException {
79.    writer.startElement("input", spinner);
80.    writer.writeAttribute("type", "submit", null);
81.    writer.writeAttribute("name", clientId + LESS, null);
82.    writer.writeAttribute("value", "<", "value");
83.    writer.endElement("input");
84.    }
85.
86.    private void encodeIncrementButton(UIComponent spinner,
87.       ResponseWriter writer, String clientId) throws IOException {
88.    writer.startElement("input", spinner);
89.    writer.writeAttribute("type", "submit", null);
90.    writer.writeAttribute("name", clientId + MORE, null);
91.    writer.writeAttribute("value", ">", "value");
92.    writer.endElement("input");
93.    }
94.
95.    private int getIncrementedValue(UIComponent spinner, int submittedValue,
96.       int increment) {
97.    Integer minimum = (Integer) spinner.getAttributes().get("minimum");
98.    Integer maximum = (Integer) spinner.getAttributes().get("maximum");
99.    int newValue = submittedValue + increment;
100.
101.   if ((minimum == null || newValue >= minimum.intValue()) &&
102.      (maximum == null || newValue <= maximum.intValue()))
103.      return newValue;
104.   else
105.      return submittedValue;
106.   }
107. }
```

Calling Converters from External Renderers

If you compare Listing 9–10 and Listing 9–11 with Listing 9–1, you will see that we moved most of the code from the original component class to a new renderer class.

However, there is a hitch. As you can see from Listing 9–10, the spinner handles conversions simply by invoking setConverter() in its constructor. Because the spinner is an input component, its superclass—UIInput—uses the specified converter during the Process Validations phase of the life cycle.

But when the spinner delegates to a renderer, it is the renderer's responsibility to convert the spinner's value by overriding `Renderer.getConvertedValue()`. So we must replicate the conversion code from `UIInput` in a custom renderer. We placed that code—which is required in all renderers that use a converter—in the static `getConvertedValue` method of the class `com.corejsf.util.Renderers` (see Listing 9–12 on page 398).

 NOTE: The `Renderers.getConvertedValue` method shown in Listing 9–12 is a necessary evil because `UIInput` does not make its conversion code publicly available. That code resides in the protected `UIInput.getConvertedValue` method, which looks like this in the JSF 1.2 Reference Implementation:

```
// This code is from the javax.faces.component.UIInput class:
public void getConvertedValue(FacesContext context, Object newSubmittedValue)
     throws ConverterException {
  Object newValue = newSubmittedValue;
  if (renderer != null) {
     newValue = renderer.getConvertedValue(context, this, newSubmittedValue);
  } else if (newSubmittedValue instanceof String) {
     Converter converter = getConverterWithType(context); // a private method
     if (converter != null)
       newValue = converter.getAsObject(
          context, this, (String) newSubmittedValue);
  }
  return newValue;
}
```

The private `getConverterWithType` method looks up the appropriate converter for the component value.

Because `UIInput`'s conversion code is buried in protected and private methods, it is not available for a renderer to reuse. Custom components that use converters must duplicate the code—see, for example, the implementation of `com.sun.faces.renderkit.html_basic.HtmlBasicInputRenderer` in the reference implementation. Our `com.corejsf.util.Renderers` class provides the code for use in your own classes.

Supporting Value Change Listeners

If your custom component is an input component, you can fire value change events to interested listeners. For example, in a calendar application, you may want to update another component whenever a month spinner value changes.

Fortunately, it is easy to support value change listeners. The UIInput class automatically generates value change events whenever the input value has changed. Recall that there are two ways of attaching a value change listener. You can add one or more listeners with f:valueChangeListener, like this:

```
<corejsf:spinner ...>
    <f:valueChangeListener type="com.corejsf.SpinnerListener"/>
    ...
</corejsf:spinner>
```

Or you can use a valueChangeListener attribute:

```
<corejsf:spinner value="#{cardExpirationDate.month}"
    id="monthSpinner" minimum="1" maximum="12" size="3"
    valueChangeListener="#{cardExpirationDate.changeListener}"/>
```

The first way doesn't require any effort on the part of the component implementor. The second way merely requires that your tag handler supports the valueChangeListener attribute. The attribute value is a method expression that requires special handling—the topic of the next section, "Supporting Method Expressions."

In the sample program, we demonstrate the value change listener by keeping a count of all value changes that we display on the form (see Figure 9–7).

```
public class CreditCardExpiration {
    private int changes = 0;
    // to demonstrate the value change listener
    public void changeListener(ValueChangeEvent e) {
        changes++;
    }
}
```

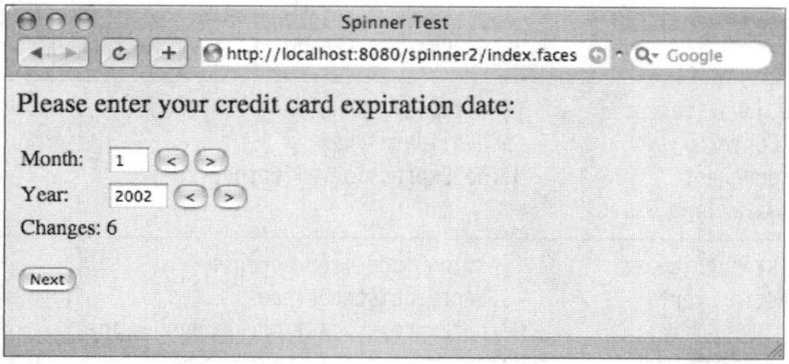

Figure 9–7   Counting the value changes

Supporting Method Expressions

Four commonly used attributes require method expressions (see Table 9–3).
You declare them in the TLD file with deferred-method elements, such as the
following:

```
<attribute>
    <name>valueChangeListener</name>
    <deferred-method>
        <method-signature>
            void valueChange(javax.faces.event.ValueChangeEvent)
        </method-signature>
    </deferred-method>
</attribute>
```

In the tag handler class, you provide setters for MethodExpression objects.

```
public class SpinnerTag extends UIComponentELTag {
    ...
    private MethodExpression valueChangeListener = null;

    public void setValueChangeListener(MethodExpression newValue) {
        valueChangeListener = newValue;
    }
    ...
}
```

Table 9–3   Processing Method Expressions

Attribute Name	method-signature Element in TLD	Code in setProperties Method
valueChangeListener	void valueChange(javax.faces. event.ValueChangeEvent)	((EditableValueHolder) component) .addValueChangeListener(new MethodExpressionValueChangeListener(expr));
validator	void validate(javax.faces. context.FacesContext, javax.faces.component. UIComponent, java.lang.Object)	((EditableValueHolder) component) .addValidator(new MethodExpressionValidator(expr));
actionListener	void actionListener(javax. faces.event.ActionEvent)	((ActionSource) component) .addActionListener(new MethodExpressionActionListener(expr));
action	java.lang.Object action()	((ActionSource2) component). addAction(expr);

In the setProperties method of the tag handler, you convert the MethodExpression object to an appropriate listener object and add it to the component:

```
public void setProperties(UIComponent component) {
   super.setProperties(component);
   ...
   if (valueChangeListener != null)
      ((EditableValueHolder) component).addValueChangeListener(
         new MethodExpressionValueChangeListener(valueChangeListener));
}
```

Table 9–3 shows how to handle the other method attributes.

 NOTE: The action attribute value can be either a method expression or a constant. In the latter case, a method is created that always returns the constant value.

The Sample Application

Figure 9–8 shows the directory structure of the sample application. As in the first example, we rely on the core JSF Renderers convenience class that contains the code for invoking the converter.

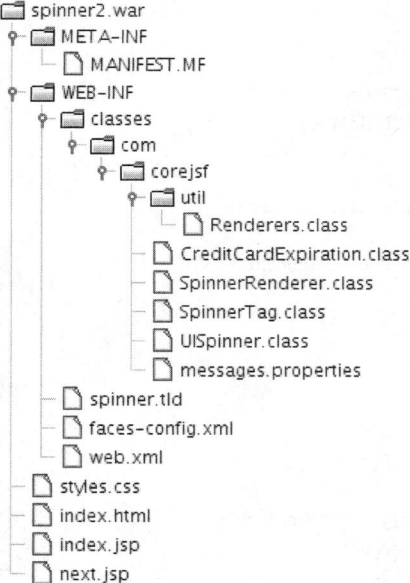

Figure 9–8   Directory structure of the revisited spinner example

(The Renderers class also contains a getSelectedItems method that we need later in this chapter—ignore it for now.) Listing 9–13 contains the revised SpinnerTag class, and Listing 9–14 shows the faces-config.xml file.

Listing 9–12   spinner2/src/java/com/corejsf/util/Renderers.java

```java
 1. package com.corejsf.util;
 2.
 3. import java.util.ArrayList;
 4. import java.util.Arrays;
 5. import java.util.Collection;
 6. import java.util.List;
 7. import java.util.Map;
 8.
 9. import javax.el.ValueExpression;
10. import javax.faces.application.Application;
11. import javax.faces.component.UIComponent;
12. import javax.faces.component.UIForm;
13. import javax.faces.component.UISelectItem;
14. import javax.faces.component.UISelectItems;
15. import javax.faces.component.ValueHolder;
16. import javax.faces.context.FacesContext;
17. import javax.faces.convert.Converter;
18. import javax.faces.convert.ConverterException;
19. import javax.faces.model.SelectItem;
20.
21. public class Renderers {
22.    public static Object getConvertedValue(FacesContext context,
23.        UIComponent component, Object submittedValue)
24.        throws ConverterException {
25.      if (submittedValue instanceof String) {
26.        Converter converter = getConverter(context, component);
27.        if (converter != null) {
28.            return converter.getAsObject(context, component,
29.                (String) submittedValue);
30.        }
31.      }
32.      return submittedValue;
33.    }
34.
35.    public static Converter getConverter(FacesContext context,
36.        UIComponent component) {
37.      if (!(component instanceof ValueHolder)) return null;
38.      ValueHolder holder = (ValueHolder) component;
39.
```

Listing 9–12   spinner2/src/java/com/corejsf/util/Renderers.java (cont.)

```
40.       Converter converter = holder.getConverter();
41.       if (converter != null)
42.          return converter;
43.
44.       ValueExpression expr = component.getValueExpression("value");
45.       if (expr == null) return null;
46.
47.       Class targetType = expr.getType(context.getELContext());
48.       if (targetType == null) return null;
49.       // Version 1.0 of the reference implementation will not apply a converter
50.       // if the target type is String or Object, but that is a bug.
51.
52.       Application app = context.getApplication();
53.       return app.createConverter(targetType);
54.    }
55.
56.    public static String getFormId(FacesContext context, UIComponent component) {
57.       UIComponent parent = component;
58.       while (!(parent instanceof UIForm))
59.          parent = parent.getParent();
60.       return parent.getClientId(context);
61.    }
62.
63.    @SuppressWarnings("unchecked")
64.    public static List<SelectItem> getSelectItems(UIComponent component) {
65.       ArrayList<SelectItem> list = new ArrayList<SelectItem>();
66.       for (UIComponent child : component.getChildren()) {
67.          if (child instanceof UISelectItem) {
68.             Object value = ((UISelectItem) child).getValue();
69.             if (value == null) {
70.                UISelectItem item = (UISelectItem) child;
71.                list.add(new SelectItem(item.getItemValue(),
72.                      item.getItemLabel(),
73.                      item.getItemDescription(),
74.                      item.isItemDisabled()));
75.             } else if (value instanceof SelectItem) {
76.                list.add((SelectItem) value);
77.             }
78.          } else if (child instanceof UISelectItems) {
79.             Object value = ((UISelectItems) child).getValue();
80.             if (value instanceof SelectItem)
81.                list.add((SelectItem) value);
82.             else if (value instanceof SelectItem[])
83.                list.addAll(Arrays.asList((SelectItem[]) value));
```

Listing 9–12 spinner2/src/java/com/corejsf/util/Renderers.java (cont.)

```
84.             else if (value instanceof Collection)
85.                 list.addAll((Collection<SelectItem>) value); // unavoidable
86.             // warning
87.             else if (value instanceof Map) {
88.                 for (Map.Entry<?, ?> entry : ((Map<?, ?>) value).entrySet())
89.                     list.add(new SelectItem(entry.getKey(),
90.                         "" + entry.getValue()));
91.             }
92.         }
93.     }
94.     return list;
95.     }
96. }
```

Listing 9–13 spinner2/src/java/com/corejsf/SpinnerTag.java

```
1. package com.corejsf;
2.
3. import javax.el.MethodExpression;
4. import javax.el.ValueExpression;
5. import javax.faces.component.EditableValueHolder;
6. import javax.faces.component.UIComponent;
7. import javax.faces.event.MethodExpressionValueChangeListener;
8. import javax.faces.webapp.UIComponentELTag;
9.
10. public class SpinnerTag extends UIComponentELTag {
11.     private ValueExpression minimum = null;
12.     private ValueExpression maximum = null;
13.     private ValueExpression size = null;
14.     private ValueExpression value = null;
15.     private MethodExpression valueChangeListener = null;
16.
17.     public String getRendererType() { return "com.corejsf.Spinner"; }
18.     public String getComponentType() { return "com.corejsf.Spinner"; }
19.
20.     public void setMinimum(ValueExpression newValue) { minimum = newValue; }
21.     public void setMaximum(ValueExpression newValue) { maximum = newValue; }
22.     public void setSize(ValueExpression newValue) { size = newValue; }
23.     public void setValue(ValueExpression newValue) { value = newValue; }
24.     public void setValueChangeListener(MethodExpression newValue) {
25.         valueChangeListener = newValue;
26.     }
27.
```

Listing 9–13   spinner2/src/java/com/corejsf/SpinnerTag.java (cont.)

```java
28.   public void setProperties(UIComponent component) {
29.      // always call the superclass method
30.      super.setProperties(component);
31.
32.      component.setValueExpression("size", size);
33.      component.setValueExpression("minimum", minimum);
34.      component.setValueExpression("maximum", maximum);
35.      component.setValueExpression("value", value);
36.      if (valueChangeListener != null)
37.         ((EditableValueHolder) component).addValueChangeListener(
38.               new MethodExpressionValueChangeListener(valueChangeListener));
39.   }
40.
41.   public void release() {
42.      // always call the superclass method
43.      super.release();
44.
45.      minimum = null;
46.      maximum = null;
47.      size = null;
48.      value = null;
49.      valueChangeListener = null;
50.   }
51. }
```

Listing 9–14   spinner2/web/WEB-INF/faces-config.xml

```xml
1. <?xml version="1.0"?>
2.
3. <faces-config xmlns="http://java.sun.com/xml/ns/javaee"
4.    xmlns:xsi="http://www.w3.org/2001/XMLSchema-instance"
5.    xsi:schemaLocation="http://java.sun.com/xml/ns/javaee
6.    http://java.sun.com/xml/ns/javaee/web-facesconfig_1_2.xsd"
7.    version="1.2">
8.
9.    <navigation-rule>
10.      <from-view-id>/index.jsp</from-view-id>
11.      <navigation-case>
12.         <from-outcome>next</from-outcome>
13.         <to-view-id>/next.jsp</to-view-id>
14.      </navigation-case>
15.   </navigation-rule>
16.
```

Listing 9–14 spinner2/web/WEB-INF/faces-config.xml (cont.)

```
17.    <navigation-rule>
18.       <from-view-id>/next.jsp</from-view-id>
19.       <navigation-case>
20.          <from-outcome>again</from-outcome>
21.          <to-view-id>/index.jsp</to-view-id>
22.       </navigation-case>
23.    </navigation-rule>
24.
25.    <managed-bean>
26.       <managed-bean-name>cardExpirationDate</managed-bean-name>
27.       <managed-bean-class>com.corejsf.CreditCardExpiration</managed-bean-class>
28.       <managed-bean-scope>session</managed-bean-scope>
29.    </managed-bean>
30.
31.    <component>
32.       <component-type>com.corejsf.Spinner</component-type>
33.       <component-class>com.corejsf.UISpinner</component-class>
34.    </component>
35.
36.    <render-kit>
37.       <renderer>
38.          <component-family>javax.faces.Input</component-family>
39.          <renderer-type>com.corejsf.Spinner</renderer-type>
40.          <renderer-class>com.corejsf.SpinnerRenderer</renderer-class>
41.       </renderer>
42.    </render-kit>
43.
44.    <application>
45.       <resource-bundle>
46.          <base-name>com.corejsf.messages</base-name>
47.          <var>msgs</var>
48.       </resource-bundle>
49.    </application>
50. </faces-config>
```

javax.faces.component.EditableValueHolder

- void addValueChangeListener(ValueChangeListener listener) **JSF 1.2**
  Adds a value change listener to this component.

- void addValidator(Validator val) **JSF 1.2**
  Adds a validator to this component.

API *javax.faces.component.ActionSource*

- void addActionListener(ActionListener listener) **JSF 1.2**
  Adds an action listener to this component.

API *javax.faces.component.ActionSource2* **JSF 1.2**

- void addAction(MethodExpression m)
  Adds an action to this component. The method has return type String and no parameters.

API *javax.faces.event.MethodExpressionValueChangeListener* **JSF 1.2**

- MethodExpressionValueChangeListener(MethodExpression m)
  Constructs a value change listener from a method expression. The method must return void and is passed a ValueChangeEvent.

API *javax.faces.validator.MethodExpressionValidator* **JSF 1.2**

- MethodExpressionValidator(MethodExpression m)
  Constructs a validator from a method expression. The method must return void and is passed a FacesContext, a UIComponent, and an Object.

API *javax.faces.event.MethodExpressionActionListener* **JSF 1.2**

- MethodExpressionActionListener(MethodExpression m)
  Constructs an action listener from a method expression. The method must return void and is passed an ActionEvent.

API *javax.faces.event.ValueChangeEvent*

- Object getOldValue()
  Returns the component's old value.

- Object getNewValue()
  Returns the component's new value.

API *javax.faces.component.ValueHolder*

- Converter getConverter()
  Returns the converter associated with a component. The ValueHolder interface is implemented by input and output components.

API `javax.faces.component.UIComponent`

- `ValueExpression getValueExpression(String name)` **JSF 1.2**
  Returns the value expression associated with the given name.

API `javax.faces.context.FacesContext`

- `ELContext getELContext()` **JSF 1.2**
  Returns the expression language context.

API `javax.el.ValueExpression` **JSF 1.2**

- `Class getType(ELContext context)`
  Returns the type of this value expression.

API `javax.faces.application.Application`

- `Converter createConverter(Class targetClass)`
  Creates a converter, given its target class. JSF implementations maintain a map of valid converter types, which are typically specified in a faces configuration file. If targetClass is a key in that map, this method creates an instance of the associated converter (specified as the value for the targetClass key) and returns it.

  If targetClass is not in the map, this method searches the map for a key that corresponds to targetClass's interfaces and superclasses, in that order, until it finds a matching class. Once a matching class is found, this method creates an associated converter and returns it. If no converter is found for the targetClass, its interfaces, or its superclasses, this method returns null.

Encoding JavaScript to Avoid Server Roundtrips

The spinner component performs a roundtrip to the server every time you click one of its buttons. That roundtrip updates the spinner's value on the server. Those roundtrips can take a severe bite out of the spinner's performance, so in almost all circumstances, it is better to store the spinner's value on the client and update the component's value only when the form in which the spinner resides is submitted. We can do that with JavaScript that looks like this:

```
<input type="text" name="_id1:monthSpinner" value="0"/>

<script language="JavaScript">
   document.forms['_id1']['_id1:monthSpinner'].spin = function (increment) {
```

```
      var v = parseInt(this.value) + increment;
      if (isNaN(v)) return;
      if ('min' in this && v < this.min) return;
      if ('max' in this && v > this.max) return;
          this.value = v;
   };
   document.forms['_id1']['_id1:monthSpinner'].min = 0;
</script>

<input type="button" value="<"
      onclick="document.forms['_id1']['_id1:monthSpinner'].spin(-1);"/>
<input type="button" value=">"
      onclick="document.forms['_id1']['_id1:monthSpinner'].spin(1);"/>
```

When you write JavaScript code that accesses fields in a form, you need to have access to the form ID, such as '_id1' in the expression

```
document.forms['_id1']['_id1:monthSpinner']
```

The second array index is the client ID of the component.

Obtaining the form ID is a common task, and we added a convenience method to the com.corejsf.util.Renderers class for this purpose:

```
public static String getFormId(FacesContext context, UIComponent component) {
   UIComponent parent = component;
   while (!(parent instanceof UIForm)) parent = parent.getParent();
   return parent.getClientId(context);
}
```

We will not go into the details of JavaScript programming here, but note that we are a bit paranoid about injecting global JavaScript functions into an unknown page. We do not want to risk name conflicts. Fortunately, JavaScript is a well-designed language with a flexible object model. Rather than writing a global spin function, we define spin to be a method of the text field object.

JavaScript lets you enhance the capabilities of objects on-the-fly by adding methods and fields. We use the same approach with the minimum and maximum values of the spinner, adding min and max fields if they are required.

The spinner renderer that encodes the preceding JavaScript is shown in Listing 9–15.

Note that the UISpinner component is completely unaffected by this change. Only the renderer has been updated, thus demonstrating the power of pluggable renderers.

Listing 9–15 spinner-js/src/java/com/corejsf/JSSpinnerRenderer.java

```
1. package com.corejsf;
2.
3. import java.io.IOException;
4. import java.text.MessageFormat;
5. import java.util.Map;
6. import javax.faces.component.EditableValueHolder;
7. import javax.faces.component.UIComponent;
8. import javax.faces.component.UIInput;
9. import javax.faces.context.FacesContext;
10. import javax.faces.context.ResponseWriter;
11. import javax.faces.convert.ConverterException;
12. import javax.faces.render.Renderer;
13.
14. public class JSSpinnerRenderer extends Renderer {
15.    public Object getConvertedValue(FacesContext context, UIComponent component,
16.        Object submittedValue) throws ConverterException {
17.      return com.corejsf.util.Renderers.getConvertedValue(context, component,
18.        submittedValue);
19.    }
20.
21.    public void encodeBegin(FacesContext context, UIComponent component)
22.        throws IOException {
23.      ResponseWriter writer = context.getResponseWriter();
24.      String clientId = component.getClientId(context);
25.      String formId = com.corejsf.util.Renderers.getFormId(context, component);
26.
27.      UIInput spinner = (UIInput)component;
28.      Integer min = (Integer) component.getAttributes().get("minimum");
29.      Integer max = (Integer) component.getAttributes().get("maximum");
30.      Integer size = (Integer) component.getAttributes().get("size");
31.
32.      writer.startElement("input", spinner);
33.      writer.writeAttribute("type", "text", null);
34.      writer.writeAttribute("name", clientId , null);
35.      writer.writeAttribute("value", spinner.getValue().toString(), "value");
36.      if (size != null)
37.        writer.writeAttribute("size", size , null);
38.      writer.endElement("input");
39.
40.      writer.write(MessageFormat.format(
41.        "<script language=\"JavaScript\">"
42.        + "document.forms[''{0}'']['''{1}''].spin = function (increment) '{'"
43.        + "var v = parseInt(this.value) + increment;"
44.        + "if (isNaN(v)) return;"
45.        + "if (\"min\" in this && v < this.min) return;"
```

Listing 9–15   spinner-js/src/java/com/corejsf/JSSpinnerRenderer.java (cont.)

```
46.          + "if (\"max\" in this && v > this.max) return;"
47.          + "this.value = v;"
48.          + "};",
49.          new Object[] { formId, clientId } ));
50.
51.       if (min != null) {
52.          writer.write(MessageFormat.format(
53.             "document.forms[''{0}''][''{1}''].min = {2};",
54.             new Object[] { formId, clientId, min }));
55.       }
56.       if (max != null) {
57.          writer.write(MessageFormat.format(
58.             "document.forms[''{0}''][''{1}''].max = {2};",
59.             new Object[] { formId, clientId, max }));
60.       }
61.       writer.write("</script>");
62.
63.       writer.startElement("input", spinner);
64.       writer.writeAttribute("type", "button", null);
65.       writer.writeAttribute("value", "<", null);
66.       writer.writeAttribute("onclick",
67.          MessageFormat.format(
68.             "document.forms[''{0}''][''{1}''].spin(-1);",
69.             new Object[] { formId, clientId }),
70.             null);
71.       writer.endElement("input");
72.
73.       writer.startElement("input", spinner);
74.       writer.writeAttribute("type", "button", null);
75.       writer.writeAttribute("value", ">", null);
76.       writer.writeAttribute("onclick",
77.          MessageFormat.format(
78.             "document.forms[''{0}''][''{1}''].spin(1);",
79.             new Object[] { formId, clientId }),
80.             null);
81.       writer.endElement("input");
82.    }
83.
84.    public void decode(FacesContext context, UIComponent component) {
85.       EditableValueHolder spinner = (EditableValueHolder) component;
86.       Map<String, String> requestMap
87.          = context.getExternalContext().getRequestParameterMap();
88.       String clientId = component.getClientId(context);
89.       spinner.setSubmittedValue((String) requestMap.get(clientId));
90.       spinner.setValid(true);
91.    }
92. }
```

Using Child Components and Facets

The spinner discussed in the first half of this chapter is a simple component that nonetheless illustrates a number of useful techniques for implementing custom components. To illustrate more advanced custom component techniques, we switch to a more complicated component: a tabbed pane, as shown in Figure 9–9.

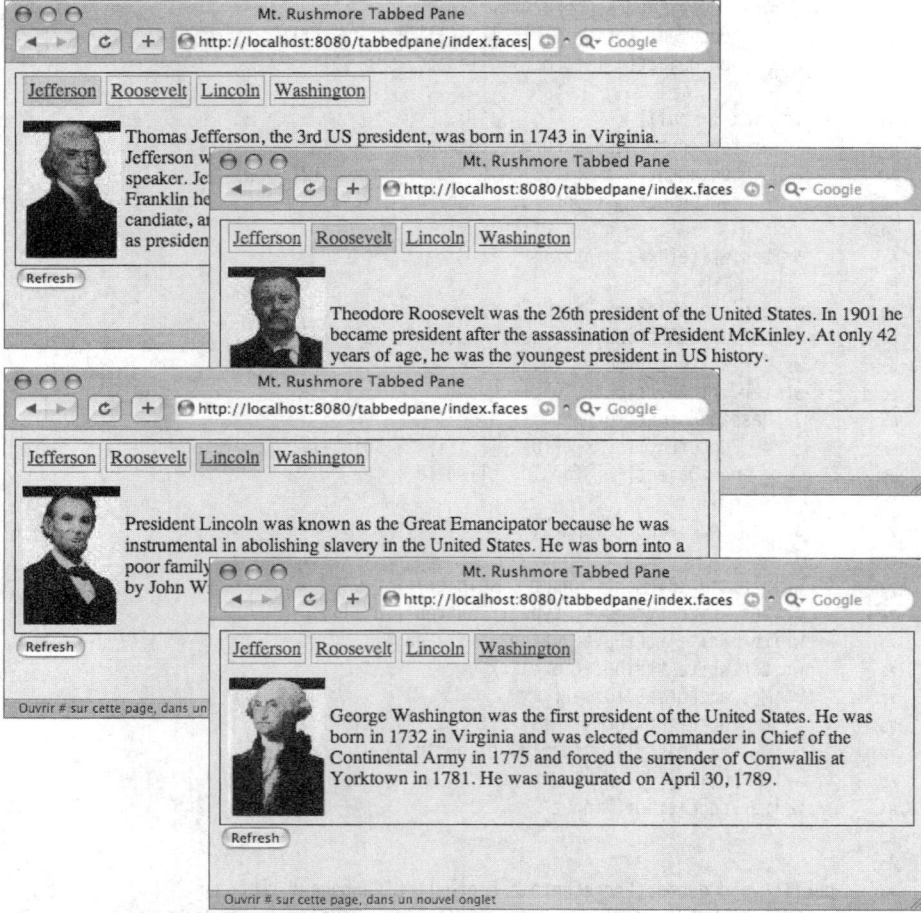

Figure 9–9   The tabbed pane component

The tabbed pane component differs from the tabbed pane implementation in Chapter 7 in an essential way. The implementation in Chapter 7 was ad hoc, composed of standard JSF tags such as h:graphicImage and h:commandLink. We will now develop a reusable component that page authors can simply drop into their pages.

The tabbed pane component has some interesting features:

- You can *use CSS classes* for the tabbed pane as a whole and also for selected and unselected tabs.

- You *specify tabs* with f:selectItem tags (or f:selectItems), the way the standard JSF menu and listbox tags specify menu or listbox items.

- You *specify tabbed pane content with a facet* (which the renderer renders). For example, you could specify the content for the "Washington" tab in Figure 9–9 as washington. Then the renderer looks for a facet of the tabbed pane named washington. This use of facets is similar to the use of header and footer facets in the h:dataTable tag.

- You can *add an action listener* to the tabbed pane. That listener is notified whenever a tab is selected.

- You can *localize tab text* by specifying keys from a resource bundle instead of the actual text displayed in the tab.

- The tabbed pane *uses hidden fields* to transmit the selected tab and its content from the client to the server.

Because the tabbed pane has so many features, there are several ways in which you can use it. Here is a simple use:

```
<corejsf:tabbedPane >
    <f:selectItem itemLabel="Jefferson"  itemValue="jefferson"/>
    <f:selectItem itemLabel="Roosevelt"  itemValue="roosevelt"/>
    <f:selectItem itemLabel="Lincoln"    itemValue="lincoln"/>
    <f:selectItem itemLabel="Washington" itemValue="washington"/>
    <f:facet name="jefferson">
        <h:panelGrid columns="2">
            <h:graphicImage value="/images/jefferson.jpg"/>
            <h:outputText value="#{msgs.jeffersonDiscussion}"/>
        </h:panelGrid>
    </f:facet>
    <!-- three more facets -->
    ...
</corejsf:tabbedPane>
```

The preceding code results in a rather plain-looking tabbed pane, as shown in Figure 9–10.

To get the effect shown in Figure 9–9, you can use CSS styles, like this:

```
<corejsf:tabbedPane styleClass="tabbedPane"
    tabClass="tab" selectedTabClass="selectedTab">
```

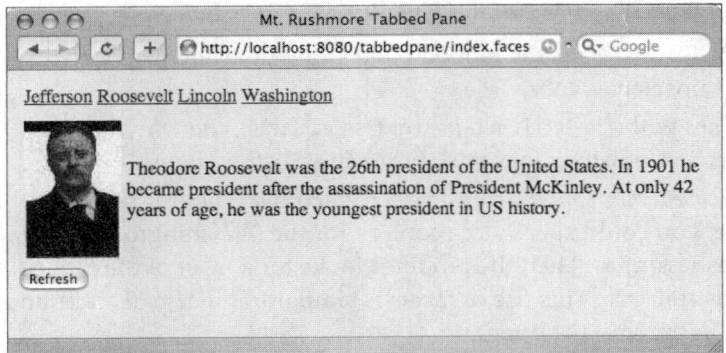

Figure 9–10   A plain tabbed pane

You can also use a single `f:selectItems` tag in lieu of multiple `f:selectitem` tags, like this:

```
<corejsf:tabbedPane styleClass="tabbedPane"
    tabClass="tab" selectedTabClass="selectedTab">
  <f:selectItems value="#{myBean.tabs}"/>
  ...
</corejsf:tabbedPane>
```

Here, the tabs are defined inside a bean.

In the previous example we directly specified the text displayed in each tab as select item labels: "Jefferson", "Roosevelt", etc. Before the tabbed pane renderer encodes a tab, it looks to see if those labels are keys in a resource bundle—if so, the renderer encodes the key's value. If the labels are not keys in a resource bundle, the renderer just encodes the labels as they are. You specify the resource bundle with the `resourceBundle` attribute, like this:

```
<corejsf:tabbedPane resourceBundle="com.corejsf.messages">
  <f:selectItem itemLabel="jeffersonTabText"  itemValue="jefferson"/>
  <f:selectItem itemLabel="rooseveltTabText"  itemValue="roosevelt"/>
  <f:selectItem itemLabel="lincolnTabText"    itemValue="lincoln"/>
  <f:selectItem itemLabel="washingtonTabText" itemValue="washington"/>
  ...
</corejsf:tabbedPane>
```

Notice the item labels—they are all keys in the messages resource bundle:

```
...
jeffersonTabText=Jefferson
rooseveltTabText=Roosevelt
lincolnTabText=Lincoln
washingtonTabText=Washington
...
```

Finally, the tabbed pane component fires an action event when a user selects a tab. You can use the f:actionListener tag to add one or more action listeners, or you can specify a method that handles action events with the tabbed pane's actionListener attribute, like this:

```
<corejsf:tabbedPane ... actionListener="#{tabbedPaneBean.presidentSelected}">
  <f:selectItems value="#{tabbedPaneBean.tabs}"/>
</corejsf:tabbedPane>
```

Now that we have an overview of the tabbed pane component, we take a closer look at how it implements advanced features. Here is what we cover in this section:

- "Processing SelectItem Children" on page 411
- "Processing Facets" on page 412
- "Encoding CSS Styles" on page 413
- "Using Hidden Fields" on page 415
- "Saving and Restoring State" on page 415
- "Firing Action Events" on page 418

Processing SelectItem *Children*

The tabbed pane lets you specify tabs with f:selectItem or f:selectItems. Those tags create UISelectItem components and add them to the tabbed pane as children. Because the tabbed pane renderer has children and because it renders those children, it overrides rendersChildren() and encodeChildren().

```
public boolean rendersChildren() {
   return true;
}
public void encodeChildren(FacesContext context, UIComponent component)
      throws java.io.IOException {
   // if the tabbedpane component has no children, this method is still called
   if (component.getChildCount() == 0) {
      return;
   }
   ...
   List items = com.corejsf.util.Renderers.getSelectItems(context, component);
   Iterator it = items.iterator();
   while (it.hasNext())
      encodeTab(context, writer, (SelectItem) it.next(), component);
      ...
   }
   ...
}
```

Generally, a component that processes its children contains code such as the following:

```
Iterator children = component.getChildren().iterator();
while (children.hasNext()) {
   UIComponent child = (UIComponent) children.next();
   processChild(context, writer, child, component);
}
```

However, our situation is more complex. Recall from Chapter 4 that you can specify a single select item, a collection of select items, an array of select items, or a map of Java objects as the value for the f:selectItems tag. Whenever your class processes children that are of type SelectItem or SelectItems, you need to deal with this mix of possibilities.

The com.corejsf.util.Renderers.getSelectItems method accounts for all those data types and synthesizes them into a list of SelectItem objects. You can find the code for the helper method in Listing 9–12 on page 398.

The encodeChildren method of the TabbedPaneRenderer calls this method and encodes each child into a tab. You will see the details in "Using Hidden Fields" on page 415.

Processing Facets

The tabbed pane uses facet names for the content associated with a particular tag. The encodeEnd method is responsible for rendering the selected facet:

```
public void encodeEnd(FacesContext context, UIComponent component)
      throws java.io.IOException {
   ResponseWriter writer = context.getResponseWriter();
   UITabbedPane tabbedPane = (UITabbedPane) component;
   String content = tabbedPane.getContent();
   ...
   if (content != null) {
      UIComponent facet = component.getFacet(content);
      if (facet != null) {
         if (facet.isRendered()) {
            facet.encodeBegin(context);
            if (facet.getRendersChildren())
               facet.encodeChildren(context);
            facet.encodeEnd(context);
         }
      }
   }
   ...
}
```

The UITabbedPane class has a field content that stores the facet name or URL of the currently displayed tab.

The encodeEnd method checks to see whether the content of the currently selected tab is the name of a facet of this component. If so, it encodes the facet by invoking its encodeBegin, encodeChildren, and encodeEnd methods. Whenever a renderer renders its own children, it needs to take over this responsibility.

API   `javax.faces.component.UIComponent`

- UIComponent getFacet(String facetName)

  Returns a reference to the facet if it exists. If the facet does not exist, the method returns null.

- boolean getRendersChildren()

  Returns a Boolean that is true if the component renders its children; otherwise, false. A component's encodeChildren method won't be called if this method does not return true. By default, getRendersChildren returns false.

- boolean isRendered()

  Returns the rendered property. The component is only rendered if the rendered property is true.

Encoding CSS Styles

You can support CSS styles in two steps:

1.   Add an attribute to the tag library descriptor.
2.   Encode the component's attribute in your renderer's encode methods.

First, we add attributes styleClass, tabClass, and selectedTabClass to the TLD:

```
<taglib>
    ...
    <tag>
        ...
      <attribute>
        <name>styleClass</name>
        <description>The CSS style for this component</description>
      </attribute>
        ...
    </tag>
</taglib>
```

Then we write attributes for the CSS classes:

```
public class TabbedPaneRenderer extends Renderer {
    ...
    public void encodeBegin(FacesContext context, UIComponent component)
            throws java.io.IOException {
        ResponseWriter writer = context.getResponseWriter();
        writer.startElement("table", component);

        String styleClass = (String) component.getAttributes().get("styleClass");
        if (styleClass != null)
            writer.writeAttribute("class", styleClass, "styleClass");

        writer.write("\n"); // to make generated HTML easier to read
    }
    public void encodeChildren(FacesContext context, UIComponent component)
            throws java.io.IOException {
        ...
        encodeTab(context, responseWriter, selectItem, component);
        ...
    }
    ...
    private void encodeTab(FacesContext context, ResponseWriter writer,
            SelectItem item, UIComponent component) throws java.io.IOException {
        ...
        String tabText = getLocalizedTabText(component, item.getLabel());
        ...
        String tabClass = null;
        if (content.equals(selectedContent))
            tabClass = (String) component.getAttributes().get("selectedTabClass");
        else
            tabClass = (String) component.getAttributes().get("tabClass");

        if (tabClass != null)
            writer.writeAttribute("class", tabClass, "tabClass");
        ...
    }
    ...
}
```

We encode the styleClass attribute for the tabbed pane's outer table and encode the tabClass and selectedTabClass attribute for each individual tag.

API   javax.faces.model.SelectItem

- Object getValue()

  Returns the select item's value.

Using Hidden Fields

Each tab in the tabbed pane is encoded as a hyperlink, like this:

```
<a href="#" onclick="document.forms[formId][clientId].value=content;
    document.forms[formId].submit();"/>
```

When a user clicks a particular hyperlink, the form is submitted (the href value corresponds to the current page). Of course, the server needs to know which tab was selected. This information is stored in a *hidden field* that is placed after all the tabs:

```
<input type="hidden" name="clientId"/>
```

When the form is submitted, the name and value of the hidden field are sent back to the server, allowing the decode method to activate the selected tab.

The renderer's encodeTab method produces the hyperlink tags. The encodeEnd method calls encodeHiddenFields(), which encodes the hidden field. You can see the details in Listing 9–17 on page 419.

When the tabbed pane renderer decodes the incoming request, it uses the request parameter, associated with the hidden field, to set the tabbed pane component's content:

```
public void decode(FacesContext context, UIComponent component) {
    Map requestParams = context.getExternalContext().getRequestParameterMap();
    String clientId = component.getClientId(context);
    String content = (String) (requestParams.get(clientId));
    if (content != null && !content.equals("")) {
        UITabbedPane tabbedPane = (UITabbedPane) component;
        tabbedPane.setContent(content);
    }
    ...
}
...
}
```

Saving and Restoring State

The JSF implementation saves and restores *all* objects in the current view between requests. This includes components, converters, validators, and event listeners. You need to implement state saving for your custom components.

When your application saves the state on the server, then the view objects are held in memory. However, when the state is saved on the client, then the view objects are encoded and stored in a hidden field, in a very long string that looks like this:

```
<input type="hidden" name="javax.faces.ViewState" id="javax.faces.ViewState"
    value="rO0ABXNyACBjb20uc3VuLmZhY2VzLnV0aWwuVHJlZVN0cnVjdHVyZRRmG0QclWAgAgAETAAI...
    ...4ANXBwcHBwcHBwcHBwcHBxAH4ANXEAfgA1cHBwcHQABnN1Ym1pdHVxAH4ALAAAAAA=" />
```

Saving state on the client is required to support users who turn off cookies, and it can improve scalability of a web application. Of course, there is a drawback: Voluminous state information is included in every request and response.

The UITabbedPane class has an instance field that stores the facet name of the currently displayed tab. Whenever your components have instance fields and there is a possibility that they are used in a web application that saves state on the client, then you need to implement the saveState and restoreState methods of the StateHolder interface.

These methods have the following form:

```
public Object saveState(FacesContext context) {
    Object values[] = new Object[n];
    values[0] = super.saveState(context);
    values[1] = instance field #1;
    values[2] = instance field #2;
    ...
    return values;
}

public void restoreState(FacesContext context, Object state) {
    Object values[] = (Object[]) state;
    super.restoreState(context, values[0]);
    instance field #1 = (Type) values[1];
    instance field #2 = (Type) values[2];
    ...
}
```

Here, we assume that the instance field values are serializable. If they are not, then you need to come up with a serializable representation of the component state. (For more information on Java serialization, see Horstmann and Cornell, 2004, 2005. *Core Java™ 2*, vol. 1, chap. 12.)

Listing 9–16 shows how the UITabbedPane class saves and restores its state.

 NOTE: You may wonder why the implementors did not simply use the standard Java serialization algorithm. However, Java serialization, while quite general, is not necessarily the most efficient format for encoding component state. The JSF architecture allows implementors of JSF containers to provide more efficient mechanisms.

To test why state saving is necessary, run this experiment:

- Comment out the saveState and restoreState methods.
- Activate client-side state saving by adding these lines to web.xml:

```
<context-param>
    <param-name>javax.faces.STATE_SAVING_METHOD</param-name>
    <param-value>client</param-value>
</context-param>
```

- Add a button `<h:commandButton value="Test State Saving"/>` to index.jsp.
- Run the application and click a tab.
- Click the "Test State Saving" button. The current page is redisplayed, but no tab is selected!

This problem occurs because the state of the page is saved on the client, encoded as the value of a hidden field. When the page is redisplayed, a new UITabbedPane object is constructed and its restoreState method is called. If the UITabbedPane class does not override the restoreState method, the content field is not restored.

 TIP: If you store all of your component state as *attributes*, you do not have to implement the saveState and restoreState methods because component attributes are automatically saved by the JSF implementation. For example, the tabbed pane can use a "content" attribute instead of the content field.

Then you do not need the UITabbedPane class at all. Use the UICommand superclass and declare the component class, like this:

```
<component>
    <component-type>com.corejsf.TabbedPane</component-type>
    <component-class>javax.faces.component.UICommand</component-class>
</component>
```

Listing 9–16   tabbedpane/src/java/com/corejsf/UITabbedPane.java

```
1. package com.corejsf;
2.
3. import javax.faces.component.UICommand;
4. import javax.faces.context.FacesContext;
5.
6. public class UITabbedPane extends UICommand {
7.     private String content;
8.
```

Listing 9–16 tabbedpane/src/java/com/corejsf/UITabbedPane.java (cont.)

```
9.   public String getContent() { return content; }
10.  public void setContent(String newValue) { content = newValue; }
11.
12.  // Comment out these two methods to see what happens
13.  // when a component does not properly save its state.
14.  public Object saveState(FacesContext context) {
15.     Object values[] = new Object[3];
16.     values[0] = super.saveState(context);
17.     values[1] = content;
18.     return values;
19.  }
20.
21.  public void restoreState(FacesContext context, Object state) {
22.     Object values[] = (Object[]) state;
23.     super.restoreState(context, values[0]);
24.     content = (String) values[1];
25.  }
26. }
```

javax.faces.component.StateHolder

- Object saveState(FacesContext context)
  Returns a Serializable object that saves the state of this object.

- void restoreState(FacesContext context, Object state)
  Restores the state of this object from the given state object, which is a copy of an object previously obtained from calling saveState.

- void setTransient(boolean newValue)
- boolean isTransient()
  Set and get the transient property. When this property is set, the state is not saved.

Firing Action Events

When your component handles action events or actions, you need to take the following steps:

- Your component should extend UICommmand.
- You need to queue an ActionEvent in the decode method of your renderer.

The tabbed pane component fires an action event when a user selects one of its tabs. That action is queued by TabbedPaneRenderer in the decode method.

```java
public void decode(FacesContext context, UIComponent component) {
   ...
   UITabbedPane tabbedPane = (UITabbedPane) component;
   ...
   component.queueEvent(new ActionEvent(tabbedPane));
}
```

This completes the discussion of the TabbedPaneRenderer class. You will find the complete code in Listing 9–17. The TabbedPaneTag class is as boring as ever, and we do not show it here.

Listing 9–17   tabbedpane/src/java/com/corejsf/TabbedPaneRenderer.java

```java
1.  package com.corejsf;
2.
3.  import java.io.IOException;
4.  import java.util.Map;
5.  import java.util.logging.Level;
6.  import java.util.logging.Logger;
7.  import javax.faces.component.UIComponent;
8.  import javax.faces.context.ExternalContext;
9.  import javax.faces.context.FacesContext;
10. import javax.faces.context.ResponseWriter;
11. import javax.faces.event.ActionEvent;
12. import javax.faces.model.SelectItem;
13. import javax.faces.render.Renderer;
14. import javax.servlet.ServletContext;
15. import javax.servlet.ServletException;
16. import javax.servlet.ServletRequest;
17. import javax.servlet.ServletResponse;
18.
19. // Renderer for the UITabbedPane component
20.
21. public class TabbedPaneRenderer extends Renderer {
22.    private static Logger logger = Logger.getLogger("com.corejsf.util");
23.
24.    // By default, getRendersChildren() returns false, so encodeChildren()
25.    // won't be invoked unless we override getRendersChildren() to return true
26.
27.    public boolean getRendersChildren() {
28.       return true;
29.    }
30.
31.    // The decode method gets the value of the request parameter whose name
32.    // is the client Id of the tabbedpane component. The request parameter
33.    // is encoded as a hidden field by encodeHiddenField, which is called by
```

```
34.  // encodeEnd. The value for the parameter is set by JavaScript generated
35.  // by the encodeTab method. It is the name of a facet or a JSP page.
36.
37.  // The decode method uses the request parameter value to set the
38.  // tabbedpane component's content attribute.
39.  // Finally, decode() queues an action event that's fired to registered
40.  // listeners in the Invoke Application phase of the JSF lifecycle. Action
41.  // listeners can be specified with the <corejsf:tabbedpane>'s actionListener
42.  // attribute or with <f:actionListener> tags in the body of the
43.  // <corejsf:tabbedpane> tag.
44.
45.  public void decode(FacesContext context, UIComponent component) {
46.     Map<String, String> requestParams
47.        = context.getExternalContext().getRequestParameterMap();
48.     String clientId = component.getClientId(context);
49.
50.     String content = (String) (requestParams.get(clientId));
51.     if (content != null && !content.equals("")) {
52.        UITabbedPane tabbedPane = (UITabbedPane) component;
53.        tabbedPane.setContent(content);
54.     }
55.
56.     component.queueEvent(new ActionEvent(component));
57.  }
58.
59.  // The encodeBegin method writes the starting <table> HTML element
60.  // with the CSS class specified by the <corejsf:tabbedpane>'s styleClass
61.  // attribute (if supplied)
62.
63.  public void encodeBegin(FacesContext context, UIComponent component)
64.        throws java.io.IOException {
65.     ResponseWriter writer = context.getResponseWriter();
66.     writer.startElement("table", component);
67.
68.     String styleClass = (String) component.getAttributes().get("styleClass");
69.     if (styleClass != null)
70.        writer.writeAttribute("class", styleClass, null);
71.
72.     writer.write("\n"); // to make generated HTML easier to read
73.  }
74.
75.  // encodeChildren() is invoked by the JSF implementation after encodeBegin().
76.  // The children of the <corejsf:tabbedpane> component are UISelectItem
77.  // components, set with one or more <f:selectItem> tags or a single
78.  // <f:selectItems> tag in the body of <corejsf:tabbedpane>
```

```
79.
80.  public void encodeChildren(FacesContext context, UIComponent component)
81.          throws java.io.IOException {
82.      // if the tabbedpane component has no children, this method is still
83.      // called
84.      if (component.getChildCount() == 0) {
85.          return;
86.      }
87.
88.      ResponseWriter writer = context.getResponseWriter();
89.      writer.startElement("thead", component);
90.      writer.startElement("tr", component);
91.      writer.startElement("th", component);
92.
93.      writer.startElement("table", component);
94.      writer.startElement("tbody", component);
95.      writer.startElement("tr", component);
96.
97.      for (SelectItem item : com.corejsf.util.Renderers.getSelectItems(component))
98.          encodeTab(context, writer, item, component);
99.
100.     writer.endElement("tr");
101.     writer.endElement("tbody");
102.     writer.endElement("table");
103.
104.     writer.endElement("th");
105.     writer.endElement("tr");
106.     writer.endElement("thead");
107.     writer.write("\n"); // to make generated HTML easier to read
108. }
109.
110. // encodeEnd() is invoked by the JSF implementation after encodeChildren().
111. // encodeEnd() writes the table body and encodes the tabbedpane's content
112. // in a single table row.
113.
114. // The content for the tabbed pane can be specified as either a URL for
115. // a JSP page or a facet name, so encodeEnd() checks to see if it's a facet;
116. // if so, it encodes it; if not, it includes the JSP page
117.
118. public void encodeEnd(FacesContext context, UIComponent component)
119.         throws java.io.IOException {
120.     ResponseWriter writer = context.getResponseWriter();
121.     UITabbedPane tabbedPane = (UITabbedPane) component;
122.     String content = tabbedPane.getContent();
```

Listing 9–17 tabbedpane/src/java/com/corejsf/TabbedPaneRenderer.java (cont.)

```
123.
124.        writer.startElement("tbody", component);
125.        writer.startElement("tr", component);
126.        writer.startElement("td", component);
127.
128.        if (content != null) {
129.           UIComponent facet = component.getFacet(content);
130.           if (facet != null) {
131.              if (facet.isRendered()) {
132.                 facet.encodeBegin(context);
133.                 if (facet.getRendersChildren())
134.                    facet.encodeChildren(context);
135.                 facet.encodeEnd(context);
136.              }
137.           } else
138.              includePage(context, component);
139.        }
140.
141.        writer.endElement("td");
142.        writer.endElement("tr");
143.        writer.endElement("tbody");
144.
145.        // Close off the column, row, and table elements
146.        writer.endElement("table");
147.
148.        encodeHiddenField(context, writer, component);
149.     }
150.
151.     // The encodeHiddenField method is called at the end of encodeEnd().
152.     // See the decode method for an explanation of the field and its value.
153.
154.     private void encodeHiddenField(FacesContext context, ResponseWriter writer,
155.           UIComponent component) throws java.io.IOException {
156.        // write hidden field whose name is the tabbedpane's client Id
157.        writer.startElement("input", component);
158.        writer.writeAttribute("type", "hidden", null);
159.        writer.writeAttribute("name", component.getClientId(context), null);
160.        writer.endElement("input");
161.     }
162.
163.     // encodeTab, which is called by encodeChildren, encodes an HTML anchor
164.     // element with an onclick attribute which sets the value of the hidden
165.     // field encoded by encodeHiddenField and submits the tabbedpane's enclosing
166.     // form. See the decode method for more information about the hidden field.
```

```
167.    // encodeTab also writes out a class attribute for each tab corresponding
168.    // to either the tabClass attribute (for unselected tabs) or the
169.    // selectedTabClass attribute (for the selected tab).
170.
171.    private void encodeTab(FacesContext context, ResponseWriter writer,
172.        SelectItem item, UIComponent component) throws java.io.IOException {
173.        String tabText = getLocalizedTabText(component, item.getLabel());
174.        String content = (String) item.getValue();
175.
176.        writer.startElement("td", component);
177.        writer.startElement("a", component);
178.        writer.writeAttribute("href", "#", "href");
179.
180.        String clientId = component.getClientId(context);
181.        String formId = com.corejsf.util.Renderers.getFormId(context, component);
182.
183.        writer.writeAttribute("onclick",
184.        // write value for hidden field whose name is the tabbedpane's client Id
185.
186.            "document.forms['" + formId + "']['" + clientId + "'].value='"
187.                + content + "'; " +
188.
189.                // submit form in which the tabbedpane resides
190.                "document.forms['" + formId + "'].submit(); ", null);
191.
192.        UITabbedPane tabbedPane = (UITabbedPane) component;
193.        String selectedContent = tabbedPane.getContent();
194.
195.        String tabClass = null;
196.        if (content.equals(selectedContent))
197.            tabClass = (String) component.getAttributes().get("selectedTabClass");
198.        else
199.            tabClass = (String) component.getAttributes().get("tabClass");
200.
201.        if (tabClass != null)
202.            writer.writeAttribute("class", tabClass, null);
203.
204.        writer.write(tabText);
205.
206.        writer.endElement("a");
207.        writer.endElement("td");
208.        writer.write("\n"); // to make generated HTML easier to read
209.    }
210.
```

Listing 9–17   tabbedpane/src/java/com/corejsf/TabbedPaneRenderer.java (cont.)

```
211.    // Text for the tabs in the tabbedpane component can be specified as
212.    // a key in a resource bundle, or as the actual text that's displayed
213.    // in the tab. Given that text, the getLocalizedTabText method tries to
214.    // retrieve a value from the resource bundle specified with the
215.    // <corejsf:tabbedpane>'s resourceBundle attribute. If no value is found,
216.    // getLocalizedTabText just returns the string it was passed.
217.
218.    private String getLocalizedTabText(UIComponent tabbedPane, String key) {
219.       String bundle = (String) tabbedPane.getAttributes().get("resourceBundle");
220.       String localizedText = null;
221.
222.       if (bundle != null) {
223.          localizedText = com.corejsf.util.Messages.getString(bundle, key, null);
224.       }
225.       if (localizedText == null)
226.          localizedText = key;
227.       // The key parameter was not really a key in the resource bundle,
228.       // so just return the string as is
229.       return localizedText;
230.    }
231.
232.    // includePage uses the servlet request dispatcher to include the page
233.    // corresponding to the selected tab.
234.
235.    private void includePage(FacesContext fc, UIComponent component) {
236.       ExternalContext ec = fc.getExternalContext();
237.       ServletContext sc = (ServletContext) ec.getContext();
238.       UITabbedPane tabbedPane = (UITabbedPane) component;
239.       String content = tabbedPane.getContent();
240.
241.       ServletRequest request = (ServletRequest) ec.getRequest();
242.       ServletResponse response = (ServletResponse) ec.getResponse();
243.       try {
244.          sc.getRequestDispatcher(content).include(request, response);
245.       } catch (ServletException ex) {
246.          logger.log(Level.WARNING, "Couldn't load page: " + content, ex);
247.       } catch (IOException ex) {
248.          logger.log(Level.WARNING, "Couldn't load page: " + content, ex);
249.       }
250.    }
251. }
```

Using the Tabbed Pane

Figure 9–9 on page 408 shows the tabbedpane application. The directory structure for the application is shown in Figure 9–11. Listing 9–18 shows the index.jsp page. Listing 9–19 through Listing 9–22 show the tag library descriptor, tag class, faces configuration file, and the style sheet for the tabbed pane application.

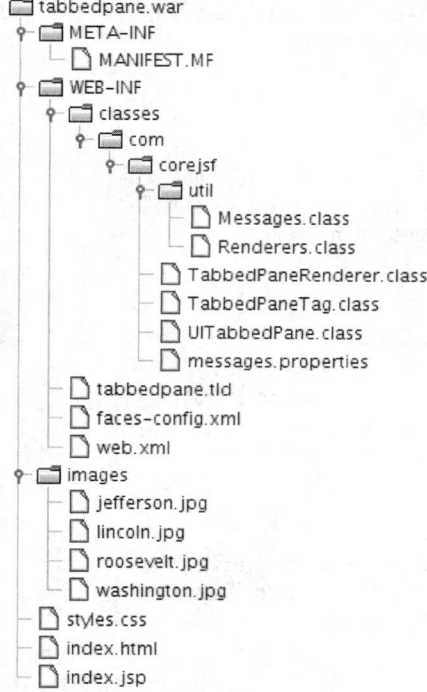

```
tabbedpane.war
  META-INF
    MANIFEST.MF
  WEB-INF
    classes
      com
        corejsf
          util
            Messages.class
            Renderers.class
          TabbedPaneRenderer.class
          TabbedPaneTag.class
          UITabbedPane.class
          messages.properties
    tabbedpane.tld
    faces-config.xml
    web.xml
  images
    jefferson.jpg
    lincoln.jpg
    roosevelt.jpg
    washington.jpg
  styles.css
  index.html
  index.jsp
```

Figure 9–11   Directory structure for the tabbed pane example

Listing 9–18   tabbedpane/web/index.jsp

```
1. <html>
2.    <%@ taglib uri="http://java.sun.com/jsf/core" prefix="f" %>
3.    <%@ taglib uri="http://java.sun.com/jsf/html" prefix="h" %>
4.    <%@ taglib uri="http://corejsf.com/tabbedpane" prefix="corejsf" %>
5.    <f:view>
6.       <head>
7.          <link href="styles.css" rel="stylesheet" type="text/css"/>
8.          <title><h:outputText value="#{msgs.windowTitle}"/></title>
9.       </head>
10.      <body>
11.         <h:form>
```

Listing 9–18   tabbedpane/web/index.jsp (cont.)

```
12.                <corejsf:tabbedPane styleClass="tabbedPane"
13.                                    tabClass="tab"
14.                           selectedTabClass="selectedTab">
15.                  <f:facet name="jefferson">
16.                    <h:panelGrid columns="2">
17.                      <h:graphicImage value="/images/jefferson.jpg"/>
18.                      <h:outputText value="#{msgs.jeffersonDiscussion}"
19.                        styleClass="tabbedPaneContent"/>
20.                    </h:panelGrid>
21.                  </f:facet>
22.                  <f:facet name="roosevelt">
23.                    <h:panelGrid columns="2">
24.                      <h:graphicImage value="/images/roosevelt.jpg"/>
25.                      <h:outputText value="#{msgs.rooseveltDiscussion}"
26.                        styleClass="tabbedPaneContent"/>
27.                    </h:panelGrid>
28.                  </f:facet>
29.                  <f:facet name="lincoln">
30.                    <h:panelGrid columns="2">
31.                      <h:graphicImage value="/images/lincoln.jpg"/>
32.                      <h:outputText value="#{msgs.lincolnDiscussion}"
33.                        styleClass="tabbedPaneContent"/>
34.                    </h:panelGrid>
35.                  </f:facet>
36.                  <f:facet name="washington">
37.                    <h:panelGrid columns="2">
38.                      <h:graphicImage value="/images/washington.jpg"/>
39.                      <h:outputText value="#{msgs.washingtonDiscussion}"
40.                        styleClass="tabbedPaneContent"/>
41.                    </h:panelGrid>
42.                  </f:facet>
43.
44.                  <f:selectItem itemLabel="#{msgs.jeffersonTabText}"
45.                    itemValue="jefferson"/>
46.                  <f:selectItem itemLabel="#{msgs.rooseveltTabText}"
47.                    itemValue="roosevelt"/>
48.                  <f:selectItem itemLabel="#{msgs.lincolnTabText}"
49.                    itemValue="lincoln"/>
50.                  <f:selectItem itemLabel="#{msgs.washingtonTabText}"
51.                    itemValue="washington"/>
52.                </corejsf:tabbedPane>
53.                <h:commandButton value="Refresh"/>
54.              </h:form>
55.          </body>
56.        </f:view>
57. </html>
```

Listing 9–19 tabbedpane/web/WEB-INF/tabbedpane.tld

```
1.  <?xml version="1.0" encoding="UTF-8"?>
2.  <taglib xmlns="http://java.sun.com/xml/ns/javaee"
3.     xmlns:xsi="http://www.w3.org/2001/XMLSchema-instance"
4.     xsi:schemaLocation="http://java.sun.com/xml/ns/javaee
5.     http://java.sun.com/xml/ns/javaee/web-jsptaglibrary_2_1.xsd"
6.     version="2.1">
7.     <description>A library containing a tabbed pane</description>
8.     <tlib-version>1.1</tlib-version>
9.     <short-name>tabbedpane</short-name>
10.    <uri>http://corejsf.com/tabbedpane</uri>
11.    <tag>
12.       <description>A tag for a tabbed pane component</description>
13.       <name>tabbedPane</name>
14.       <tag-class>com.corejsf.TabbedPaneTag</tag-class>
15.       <body-content>JSP</body-content>
16.       <attribute>
17.          <description>Component id of this component</description>
18.          <name>id</name>
19.          <rtexprvalue>true</rtexprvalue>
20.       </attribute>
21.       <attribute>
22.          <description>
23.             Component reference expression for this component
24.          </description>
25.          <name>binding</name>
26.          <deferred-value>
27.             <type>javax.faces.component.UIComponent</type>
28.          </deferred-value>
29.       </attribute>
30.       <attribute>
31.          <description>
32.             A flag indicating whether or not this component should
33.             be rendered. If not specified, the default value is true.
34.          </description>
35.          <name>rendered</name>
36.          <deferred-value>
37.             <type>boolean</type>
38.          </deferred-value>
39.       </attribute>
40.       <attribute>
41.          <description>The CSS style for this component</description>
42.          <name>style</name>
43.          <deferred-value>
44.             <type>java.lang.String</type>
45.          </deferred-value>
```

Listing 9–19 tabbedpane/web/WEB-INF/tabbedpane.tld (cont.)

```
46.        </attribute>
47.        <attribute>
48.            <description>The CSS class for this component</description>
49.            <name>styleClass</name>
50.            <deferred-value>
51.                <type>java.lang.String</type>
52.            </deferred-value>
53.        </attribute>
54.        <attribute>
55.            <description>The CSS class for unselected tabs</description>
56.            <name>tabClass</name>
57.            <deferred-value>
58.                <type>java.lang.String</type>
59.            </deferred-value>
60.        </attribute>
61.        <attribute>
62.            <description>The CSS class for the selected tab</description>
63.            <name>selectedTabClass</name>
64.            <deferred-value>
65.                <type>java.lang.String</type>
66.            </deferred-value>
67.        </attribute>
68.        <attribute>
69.            <description>
70.                The resource bundle used to localize select item labels
71.            </description>
72.            <name>resourceBundle</name>
73.            <deferred-value>
74.                <type>java.lang.String</type>
75.            </deferred-value>
76.        </attribute>
77.        <attribute>
78.            <description>
79.                A method expression that's called when a tab is selected
80.            </description>
81.            <name>actionListener</name>
82.            <deferred-method>
83.                <method-signature>
84.                    void actionListener(javax.faces.event.ActionEvent)
85.                </method-signature>
86.            </deferred-method>
87.        </attribute>
88.    </tag>
89. </taglib>
```

Listing 9–20   tabbedpane/src/java/com/corejsf/TabbedPaneTag.java

```
1. package com.corejsf;
2.
3. import javax.el.MethodExpression;
4. import javax.el.ValueExpression;
5. import javax.faces.component.ActionSource;
6. import javax.faces.component.UIComponent;
7. import javax.faces.event.MethodExpressionActionListener;
8. import javax.faces.webapp.UIComponentELTag;
9.
10. // This tag supports the following attributes
11. //
12. // binding (supported by UIComponentELTag)
13. // id (supported by UIComponentELTag)
14. // rendered (supported by UIComponentELTag)
15. // style
16. // styleClass
17. // tabClass
18. // selectedTabClass
19. // resourceBundle
20. // actionListener
21.
22. public class TabbedPaneTag extends UIComponentELTag {
23.     private ValueExpression style;
24.     private ValueExpression styleClass;
25.     private ValueExpression tabClass;
26.     private ValueExpression selectedTabClass;
27.     private ValueExpression resourceBundle;
28.     private MethodExpression actionListener;
29.
30.     public String getRendererType() { return "com.corejsf.TabbedPane"; }
31.     public String getComponentType() { return "com.corejsf.TabbedPane"; }
32.
33.     public void setTabClass(ValueExpression newValue) { tabClass = newValue; }
34.     public void setSelectedTabClass(ValueExpression newValue) {
35.         selectedTabClass = newValue;
36.     }
37.     public void setStyle(ValueExpression newValue) { style = newValue; }
38.     public void setStyleClass(ValueExpression newValue) {
39.         styleClass = newValue;
40.     }
41.     public void setResourceBundle(ValueExpression newValue) {
42.         resourceBundle = newValue;
43.     }
44.     public void setActionListener(MethodExpression newValue) {
```

Listing 9–20   tabbedpane/src/java/com/corejsf/TabbedPaneTag.java (cont.)

```
45.         actionListener = newValue;
46.     }
47.
48.     protected void setProperties(UIComponent component) {
49.         // make sure you always call the superclass
50.         super.setProperties(component);
51.
52.         component.setValueExpression("style", style);
53.         component.setValueExpression("styleClass", styleClass);
54.         component.setValueExpression("tabClass", tabClass);
55.         component.setValueExpression("selectedTabClass", selectedTabClass);
56.         component.setValueExpression("resourceBundle", resourceBundle);
57.         if (actionListener != null)
58.             ((ActionSource) component).addActionListener(
59.                 new MethodExpressionActionListener(actionListener));
60.     }
61.
62.     public void release() {
63.         // always call the superclass method
64.         super.release();
65.
66.         style = null;
67.         styleClass = null;
68.         tabClass = null;
69.         selectedTabClass = null;
70.         resourceBundle = null;
71.         actionListener = null;
72.     }
73. }
```

Listing 9–21   tabbedpane/web/WEB-INF/faces-config.xml

```
1.  <?xml version="1.0"?>
2.  <faces-config xmlns="http://java.sun.com/xml/ns/javaee"
3.     xmlns:xsi="http://www.w3.org/2001/XMLSchema-instance"
4.     xsi:schemaLocation="http://java.sun.com/xml/ns/javaee
5.         http://java.sun.com/xml/ns/javaee/web-facesconfig_1_2.xsd"
6.     version="1.2">
7.     <navigation-rule>
8.         <from-view-id>/index.jsp</from-view-id>
9.             <navigation-case>
10.                <to-view-id>/welcome.jsp</to-view-id>
11.            </navigation-case>
12.     </navigation-rule>
```

Listing 9–21 tabbedpane/web/WEB-INF/faces-config.xml (cont.)

```
13.
14.    <component>
15.      <description>A tabbed pane</description>
16.      <component-type>com.corejsf.TabbedPane</component-type>
17.      <component-class>com.corejsf.UITabbedPane</component-class>
18.    </component>
19.
20.    <render-kit>
21.      <renderer>
22.        <component-family>javax.faces.Command</component-family>
23.        <renderer-type>com.corejsf.TabbedPane</renderer-type>
24.        <renderer-class>com.corejsf.TabbedPaneRenderer</renderer-class>
25.      </renderer>
26.    </render-kit>
27.
28.    <application>
29.      <resource-bundle>
30.        <base-name>com.corejsf.messages</base-name>
31.        <var>msgs</var>
32.      </resource-bundle>
33.    </application>
34. </faces-config>
```

Listing 9–22 tabbedpane/web/styles.css

```
1.  body {
2.     background: #eee;
3.  }
4.  .tabbedPane {
5.     vertical-align: top;
6.     border: thin solid Blue;
7.  }
8.  .tab {
9.     padding: 3px;
10.    border: thin solid CornflowerBlue;
11.    color: Blue;
12. }
13. .selectedTab {
14.    padding: 3px;
15.    border: thin solid CornflowerBlue;
16.    color: Blue;
17.    background: PowderBlue;
18. }
```

Implementing Custom Converters and Validators

The custom converters and validators that you saw in Chapter 6 have a short-coming: They do not allow parameters. For example, we may want to specify a separator character for the credit card converter so that the page designer can choose whether to use dashes or spaces to separate the digit groups. In other words, custom converters should have the same capabilities as the standard f:convertNumber and f:convertDateTime tags. Specifically, we would like page designers to use tags, such as the following:

```
<h:outputText value="#{payment.card}">
   <corejsf:convertCreditcard separator="-"/>
</h:outputText>
```

To achieve this, we need to implement a custom converter tag. As with custom component tags, custom converter tags require a significant amount of programming, but the payback is a reusable tag that is convenient for page authors.

Custom Converter Tags

As with custom component tags, you need to put descriptions of custom converter tags into a TLD file. Place that file into the WEB-INF directory. Listing 9–23 shows the TLD file that describes a convertCreditcard custom tag.

Listing 9–23 custom-converter/web/WEB-INF/converter.tld

```
 1. <?xml version="1.0" encoding="UTF-8"?>
 2. <taglib xmlns="http://java.sun.com/xml/ns/javaee"
 3.    xmlns:xsi="http://www.w3.org/2001/XMLSchema-instance"
 4.    xsi:schemaLocation="http://java.sun.com/xml/ns/javaee
 5.       http://java.sun.com/xml/ns/javaee/web-jsptaglibrary_2_1.xsd"
 6.    version="2.1">
 7.    <tlib-version>1.1</tlib-version>
 8.    <tlib-version>1.1</tlib-version>
 9.    <short-name>converter</short-name>
10.    <uri>http://corejsf.com/converter</uri>
11.
12.    <tag>
13.       <name>convertCreditcard</name>
14.       <tag-class>com.corejsf.CreditCardConverterTag</tag-class>
15.       <body-content>empty</body-content>
16.       <attribute>
17.          <name>separator</name>
18.          <deferred-value>
19.             <type>java.lang.String</type>
20.          </deferred-value>
21.       </attribute>
22.    </tag>
23. </taglib>
```

The entries in this file should be mostly self-explanatory. The purpose of the file is to specify the class name for the tag handler (com.corejsf.CreditCardConverterTag) and the permitted attributes of the tag (in our case, separator). Note the uri tag that identifies the tag library.

The deferred-value child element inside the definition of the separator attribute indicates that the attribute is defined by a value expression that should yield a string. The attribute value can be a constant string or a string that contains #{...} expressions.

You reference the TLD identifier in a taglib directive of the JSF page, such as

```
<%@ taglib uri="http://corejsf.com/converter" prefix="corejsf" %>
```

You need to implement a tag handler class that fulfills three purposes:

1. To specify the converter class
2. To gather the tag attributes
3. To configure a converter object, using the gathered attributes

For a converter, the tag handler class should be a subclass of ConverterELTag. As you will see later, the handlers for custom validators need to subclass ValidatorELTag.

 NOTE: Before JSF 1.2, you needed to subclass ConverterTag or ValidatorTag. These classes are now deprecated.

Your tag handler class must specify a setter method for each tag attribute. For example,

```
public class ConvertCreditCardTag extends ConverterELTag {
    private ValueExpression separator;
    public void setSeparator(ValueExpression newValue) { separator = newValue; }
    ...
}
```

To configure a converter instance with the tag attributes, override the create-Converter method. Construct a converter object and set its properties from the tag attributes. For example,

```
public Converter createConverter() throws JspException {
    CreditCardConverter converter = new CreditCardConverter();
    ELContext elContext = FacesContext.getCurrentInstance().getELContext();
    converter.setSeparator((String) separator.getValue(elContext));
    return converter;
}
```

This method sets the separator property of the CreditCardConverter.

Finally, you need to define a release method for each tag handler class that resets all instance fields to their defaults:

```
public void release() {
    separator = null;
}
```

Listing 9–24 shows the complete tag class.

Listing 9–24   custom-converter/src/java/com/corejsf/
CreditCardConverterTag.java

```
1. package com.corejsf;
2.
3. import javax.el.ELContext;
4. import javax.el.ValueExpression;
5. import javax.faces.context.FacesContext;
6. import javax.faces.convert.Converter;
7. import javax.faces.webapp.ConverterELTag;
8. import javax.servlet.jsp.JspException;
9.
10. public class CreditCardConverterTag extends ConverterELTag {
11.    private ValueExpression separator;
12.
13.    public void setSeparator(ValueExpression newValue) {
14.        separator = newValue;
15.    }
16.
17.    public Converter createConverter() throws JspException {
18.        CreditCardConverter converter = new CreditCardConverter();
19.        ELContext elContext = FacesContext.getCurrentInstance().getELContext();
20.        converter.setSeparator((String) separator.getValue(elContext));
21.        return converter;
22.    }
23.
24.    public void release() {
25.        separator = null;
26.    }
27. }
```

API   **javax.faces.webapp.ConverterELTag**   JSF 1.2

- protected void createConverter()
  Override this method to create the converter and customize it by setting the properties specified by the tag attributes.

- `void release()`
  Clears the state of this tag so that it can be reused.

 javax.el.ValueExpression JSF 1.2

- `Object getValue(ELContext context)`
  Gets the current value of this value expression.

 javax.faces.context.FacesContext JSF 1.0

- `ELContext getELContext()` JSF 1.2
  Gets the context for evaluating expressions in the expression language.

Saving and Restoring State

When implementing converters or validators, you have two choices for state saving. The easy choice is to make your converter or validator class serializable. Implement the `Serializable` interface and follow the usual rules for Java serialization.

In the case of the credit card converter, we have a single instance field of type `String`, which is a serializable type. Therefore, we only need to implement the `Serializable` interface:

```
public class CreditCardConverter implements Converter, Serializable { ... }
```

The second choice is to supply a default constructor and implement the State-Holder interface. This is more work for the programmer, but it can yield a slightly more efficient encoding of the object state. Frankly, for small objects such as the credit card converter, this second choice is not worth the extra trouble.

In the interest of completeness, we describe the technique, using the standard `DateTimeConverter` as an example.

In the `saveState` method of the `StateHolder` interface, construct a serializable object that describes the instance fields. The obvious choice is an array of objects that holds the instance fields. In the `restoreState` method, restore the instance fields from that object.

```
public class DateTimeConverter implements Converter, StateHolder {
    public Object saveState(FacesContext context) {
        Object[] values = new Object[6];
        values[0] = dateStyle;
        values[1] = locale;
        values[2] = pattern;
        values[3] = timeStyle;
        values[4] = timeZone;
```

```
        values[5] = type;
        return values;
    }
    public void restoreState(FacesContext context, Object state) {
        Object[] values = (Object[]) state;
        dateStyle = (String) values[0];
        locale = (Locale) values[1];
        pattern = (String) values[2];
        timeStyle = (String) values[3];
        timeZone = (TimeZone) values[4];
        type = (String) values[5];
    }
    ...
}
```

Moreover, the StateHolder interface also requires you to add a transient property.
If the property is set, this particular object will not be saved. The property is the
analog of the transient keyword used in Java serialization.

```
public class DateTimeConverter implements Converter, StateHolder {
    private boolean transientFlag; // "transient" is a reserved word
    public boolean isTransient() { return transientFlag; }
    public void setTransient(boolean newValue) { transientFlag = newValue; }
    ...
}
```

 CAUTION: Converters, validators, and event listeners that implement
neither the Serializable nor the StateHolder interface are skipped when
the view is saved.

 NOTE: Here is an easy experiment to verify that converters must save their
state. Configure the custom-converter application to save state on the client
by adding this parameter to web.xml:

```
<context-param>
    <param-name>javax.faces.STATE_SAVING_METHOD</param-name>
    <param-value>client</param-value>
</context-param>
```

Comment out the Serializable interface of the CreditCardConverter class. To
the result.jsp page, add the button

```
<h:commandButton value="Test State Saving"/>
```

Enter a credit card number in index.jsp, click the "Process" button, and see
the number formatted with dashes: 4111-1111-1111-1111. Click the "Test
State Saving" button and see the dashes disappear.

The Sample Custom Converter Application

This completes the discussion of the custom converter example. Figure 9–12 shows the directory structure. Most files are unchanged from the preceding example. However, result.jsp calls the custom converter (see Listing 9–25).

The tag handler is in Listing 9–25. The modified converter and configuration file are in Listings 9–26 and 9–27.

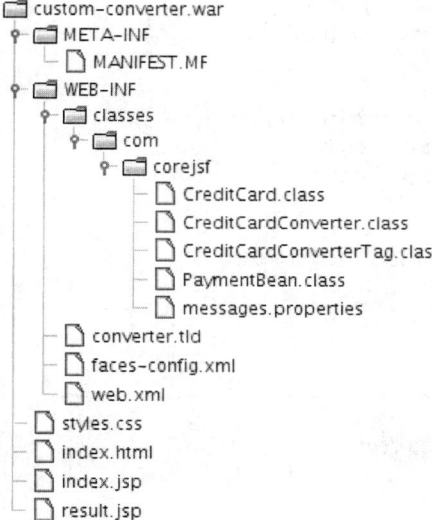

Figure 9–12   Directory structure of the custom converter program

---

Listing 9–25   custom-converter/web/result.jsp

```
 1. <html>
 2.    <%@ taglib uri="http://java.sun.com/jsf/core" prefix="f" %>
 3.    <%@ taglib uri="http://java.sun.com/jsf/html" prefix="h" %>
 4.    <%@ taglib uri="http://corejsf.com/converter" prefix="corejsf" %>
 5.    <f:view>
 6.       <head>
 7.          <link href="styles.css" rel="stylesheet" type="text/css"/>
 8.          <title><h:outputText value="#{msgs.title}"/></title>
 9.       </head>
10.       <body>
11.          <h:form>
12.             <h1><h:outputText value="#{msgs.paymentInformation}"/></h1>
```

Listing 9–25   custom-converter/web/result.jsp (cont.)

```
13.          <h:panelGrid columns="2">
14.            <h:outputText value="#{msgs.amount}"/>
15.            <h:outputText value="#{payment.amount}">
16.              <f:convertNumber type="currency"/>
17.            </h:outputText>
18.
19.            <h:outputText value="#{msgs.creditCard}"/>
20.            <h:outputText value="#{payment.card}">
21.              <corejsf:convertCreditcard separator="-"/>
22.            </h:outputText>
23.
24.            <h:outputText value="#{msgs.expirationDate}"/>
25.            <h:outputText value="#{payment.date}">
26.              <f:convertDateTime pattern="MM/yyyy"/>
27.            </h:outputText>
28.          </h:panelGrid>
29.          <h:commandButton value="#{msgs.back}" action="back"/>
30.        </h:form>
31.      </body>
32.    </f:view>
33. </html>
```

Listing 9–26   custom-converter/src/java/com/corejsf/
CreditCardConverter.java

```java
1. package com.corejsf;
2.
3. import java.io.Serializable;
4.
5. import javax.faces.component.UIComponent;
6. import javax.faces.context.FacesContext;
7. import javax.faces.convert.Converter;
8. import javax.faces.convert.ConverterException;
9.
10. public class CreditCardConverter implements Converter, Serializable {
11.    private String separator;
12.
13.    // PROPERTY: separator
14.    public void setSeparator(String newValue) { separator = newValue; }
15.
16.    public Object getAsObject(
17.       FacesContext context,
18.       UIComponent component,
19.       String newValue)
```

Listing 9–26 custom-converter/src/java/com/corejsf/
CreditCardConverter.java (cont.)

```
20.     throws ConverterException {
21.         StringBuilder builder = new StringBuilder(newValue);
22.         int i = 0;
23.         while (i < builder.length()) {
24.             if (Character.isDigit(builder.charAt(i)))
25.                 i++;
26.             else
27.                 builder.deleteCharAt(i);
28.         }
29.         return new CreditCard(builder.toString());
30.     }
31.
32.     public String getAsString(
33.         FacesContext context,
34.         UIComponent component,
35.         Object value)
36.         throws ConverterException {
37.         // length 13: xxxx xxx xxx xxx
38.         // length 14: xxxxx xxxx xxxxx
39.         // length 15: xxxx xxxxxx xxxxx
40.         // length 16: xxxx xxxx xxxx xxxx
41.         // length 22: xxxxxx xxxxxxxx xxxxxxxx
42.         if (!(value instanceof CreditCard))
43.             throw new ConverterException();
44.         String v = ((CreditCard) value).toString();
45.         String sep = separator;
46.         if (sep == null) sep = " ";
47.         int[] boundaries = null;
48.         int length = v.length();
49.         if (length == 13)
50.             boundaries = new int[] { 4, 7, 10 };
51.         else if (length == 14)
52.             boundaries = new int[] { 5, 9 };
53.         else if (length == 15)
54.             boundaries = new int[] { 4, 10 };
55.         else if (length == 16)
56.             boundaries = new int[] { 4, 8, 12 };
57.         else if (length == 22)
58.             boundaries = new int[] { 6, 14 };
59.         else
60.             return v;
61.         StringBuilder result = new StringBuilder();
62.         int start = 0;
```

Listing 9–26	custom-converter/src/java/com/corejsf/ CreditCardConverter.java (cont.)

```
63.        for (int i = 0; i < boundaries.length; i++) {
64.            int end = boundaries[i];
65.            result.append(v.substring(start, end));
66.            result.append(sep);
67.            start = end;
68.        }
69.        result.append(v.substring(start));
70.        return result.toString();
71.    }
72. }
```

Listing 9–27	custom-converter/web/WEB-INF/faces-config.xml

```
1. <?xml version="1.0"?>
2. <faces-config xmlns="http://java.sun.com/xml/ns/javaee"
3.     xmlns:xsi="http://www.w3.org/2001/XMLSchema-instance"
4.     xsi:schemaLocation="http://java.sun.com/xml/ns/javaee
5.         http://java.sun.com/xml/ns/javaee/web-facesconfig_1_2.xsd"
6.     version="1.2">
7.     <navigation-rule>
8.         <from-view-id>/index.jsp</from-view-id>
9.         <navigation-case>
10.            <from-outcome>process</from-outcome>
11.            <to-view-id>/result.jsp</to-view-id>
12.        </navigation-case>
13.    </navigation-rule>
14.
15.    <navigation-rule>
16.        <from-view-id>/result.jsp</from-view-id>
17.        <navigation-case>
18.            <from-outcome>back</from-outcome>
19.            <to-view-id>/index.jsp</to-view-id>
20.        </navigation-case>
21.    </navigation-rule>
22.
23.    <converter>
24.        <converter-id>com.corejsf.CreditCard</converter-id>
25.        <converter-class>com.corejsf.CreditCardConverter</converter-class>
26.    </converter>
27.
```

Listing 9–27 custom-converter/web/WEB-INF/faces-config.xml (cont.)

```
28.   <converter>
29.      <converter-for-class>com.corejsf.CreditCard</converter-for-class>
30.      <converter-class>com.corejsf.CreditCardConverter</converter-class>
31.   </converter>
32.
33.   <managed-bean>
34.      <managed-bean-name>payment</managed-bean-name>
35.      <managed-bean-class>com.corejsf.PaymentBean</managed-bean-class>
36.      <managed-bean-scope>session</managed-bean-scope>
37.   </managed-bean>
38.
39.   <application>
40.      <resource-bundle>
41.         <base-name>com.corejsf.messages</base-name>
42.         <var>msgs</var>
43.      </resource-bundle>
44.   </application>
45. </faces-config>
```

Custom Validator Tags

In the preceding sections, you saw how to implement a custom converter that offers page authors the same convenience as the standard JSF tags. In this section, you will see how to provide a custom validator.

The steps for providing a custom validator are almost the same as those for a custom converter:

1. Produce a TLD file and reference it in your JSF pages.
2. Implement a tag handler class that extends the ValidatorELTag class, gathers the attributes that the TLD file advertises, and passes them to a validator object.
3. Implement a validator class that implements the Validator interface. Supply the validate method in the usual way, by throwing a ValidatorException if an error is detected. Implement the Serializable or StateHolder interface to save and restore the state of validator objects.

As an example, let us do a thorough job validating credit card numbers (see Listing 9–27). We want to carry out three checks:

1. The user has supplied a value.
2. The number conforms to the Luhn formula.
3. The number starts with a valid prefix.

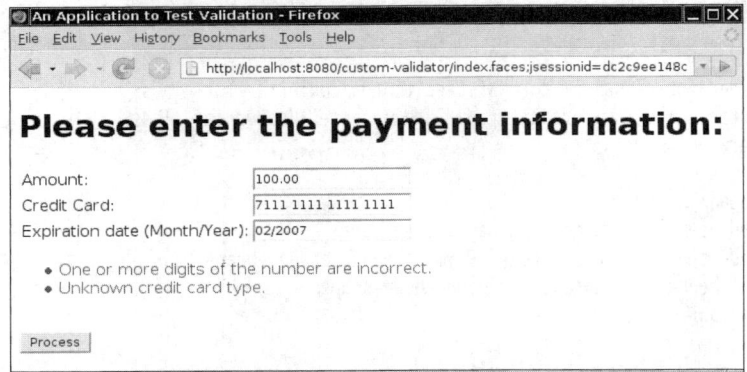

Figure 9–13   Thoroughly validating a credit card number

A credit card's prefix indicates card type—for example, a prefix between 51 and 55 is reserved for MasterCard, and a prefix of 4 indicates Visa. We could write custom code for this purpose, but instead we chose to implement a more general (and more useful) validator that validates arbitrary regular expressions.

We use that validator in the following way:

```
<corejsf:validateRegex expression="[3-6].*"
    errorDetail="#{msgs.unknownType}"/>
```

The regular expression [3-6].* denotes any string that starts with the digits 3 through 6. Of course, we could easily design a more elaborate regular expression that does a more careful check.

You will find the validator code in Listing 9–28. When reading through the code, keep in mind that the moral of the story here has nothing to do with regular expressions per se. Instead, the story is about what validators do when their component's data is invalid: They generate a faces message, wrap it inside a validator exception, and throw it.

By default, the validator displays an error message that complains about failing to match a regular expression. If your application's audience includes users who are unfamiliar with regular expressions, you will want to change the message. We give you attributes errorSummmary and errorDetail for this purpose.

We use a custom tag so that we can supply parameters to the validator. Implementing a custom tag for a validator is similar to creating a custom converter tag, which we described earlier in this chapter. However, the custom validator tag must extend the ValidatorTag class.

You can find the implementation of the `RegexValidatorTag` class in Listing 9–29.

Figure 9–14 shows the application's directory structure. Listing 9–32 shows the JSF page with the triple validation of the credit card field.

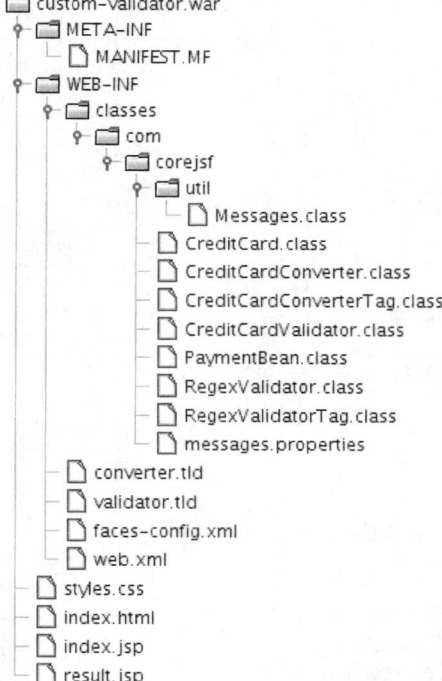

```
custom-validator.war
├── META-INF
│   └── MANIFEST.MF
├── WEB-INF
│   ├── classes
│   │   └── com
│   │       └── corejsf
│   │           ├── util
│   │           │   └── Messages.class
│   │           ├── CreditCard.class
│   │           ├── CreditCardConverter.class
│   │           ├── CreditCardConverterTag.class
│   │           ├── CreditCardValidator.class
│   │           ├── PaymentBean.class
│   │           ├── RegexValidator.class
│   │           ├── RegexValidatorTag.class
│   │           └── messages.properties
│   ├── converter.tld
│   ├── validator.tld
│   ├── faces-config.xml
│   └── web.xml
├── styles.css
├── index.html
├── index.jsp
└── result.jsp
```

Figure 9–14 Directory structure of the thoroughly validating application

Listing 9–30 shows `faces-config.xml`. Note the mapping of the validator ID to the validator class. The validator tag class is defined in the TLD file (Listing 9–31).

You have now seen how to implement custom tags for components, converters, and validators. We covered all essential issues that you will encounter as you develop custom tags. The code in this chapter should make a good starting point for your own implementations.

 *javax.faces.webapp.ValidatorTag*

- `void setValidatorId(String id)`
  Sets the ID of this validator. The ID is used to look up the validator class.

- `protected void createValidator()`

  Override this method to customize the validator by setting the properties specified by the tag attributes.

Listing 9–28   `custom-validator/src/java/com/corejsf/RegexValidator.java`

```
 1. package com.corejsf;
 2.
 3. import java.io.Serializable;
 4. import java.text.MessageFormat;
 5. import java.util.Locale;
 6. import java.util.regex.Pattern;
 7. import javax.faces.application.FacesMessage;
 8. import javax.faces.component.UIComponent;
 9. import javax.faces.context.FacesContext;
10. import javax.faces.validator.Validator;
11. import javax.faces.validator.ValidatorException;
12.
13. public class RegexValidator implements Validator, Serializable {
14.    private String expression;
15.    private Pattern pattern;
16.    private String errorSummary;
17.    private String errorDetail;
18.
19.    public void validate(FacesContext context, UIComponent component,
20.          Object value) {
21.       if (value == null) return;
22.       if (pattern == null) return;
23.       if(!pattern.matcher(value.toString()).matches()) {
24.          Object[] params = new Object[] { expression, value };
25.          Locale locale = context.getViewRoot().getLocale();
26.          FacesMessage message = com.corejsf.util.Messages.getMessage(
27.             "com.corejsf.messages", "badRegex", params);
28.          if (errorSummary != null)
29.            message.setSummary(
30.                new MessageFormat(errorSummary, locale).format(params));
31.          if (errorDetail != null)
32.            message.setDetail(
33.                new MessageFormat(errorDetail, locale).format(params));
34.          throw new ValidatorException(message);
35.       }
36.    }
37.
38.    // PROPERTY: expression
39.    public void setExpression(String newValue) {
40.       expression = newValue;
41.       pattern = Pattern.compile(expression);
42.    }
```

Listing 9–28 custom-validator/src/java/com/corejsf/RegexValidator.java (cont.)

```
43.
44.    // PROPERTY: errorSummary
45.    public void setErrorSummary(String newValue) {
46.        errorSummary = newValue;
47.    }
48.
49.    // PROPERTY: errorDetail
50.    public void setErrorDetail(String newValue) {
51.        errorDetail = newValue;
52.    }
53. }
```

Listing 9–29 custom-validator/src/java/com/corejsf/
RegexValidatorTag.java

```
1. package com.corejsf;
2.
3. import javax.el.ELContext;
4. import javax.el.ValueExpression;
5. import javax.faces.context.FacesContext;
6. import javax.faces.validator.Validator;
7. import javax.faces.webapp.ValidatorELTag;
8. import javax.servlet.jsp.JspException;
9.
10. public class RegexValidatorTag extends ValidatorELTag {
11.     private ValueExpression expression;
12.     private ValueExpression errorSummary;
13.     private ValueExpression errorDetail;
14.
15.     public void setExpression(ValueExpression newValue) {
16.         expression = newValue;
17.     }
18.
19.     public void setErrorSummary(ValueExpression newValue) {
20.         errorSummary = newValue;
21.     }
22.
23.     public void setErrorDetail(ValueExpression newValue) {
24.         errorDetail = newValue;
25.     }
26.
27.     public Validator createValidator() throws JspException {
28.         RegexValidator validator = new RegexValidator();
29.         ELContext elContext = FacesContext.getCurrentInstance().getELContext();
30.
```

Listing 9–29 custom-validator/src/java/com/corejsf/
RegexValidatorTag.java (cont.)

```
31.     validator.setExpression((String) expression.getValue(elContext));
32.     if (errorSummary != null)
33.        validator.setErrorSummary((String) errorSummary.getValue(elContext));
34.     if (errorDetail != null)
35.        validator.setErrorDetail((String) errorDetail.getValue(elContext));
36.
37.     return validator;
38.  }
39.
40.  public void release() {
41.     expression = null;
42.     errorSummary = null;
43.     errorDetail = null;
44.  }
45. }
```

Listing 9–30 custom-validator/web/WEB-INF/faces-config.xml

```
1. <?xml version="1.0"?>
2.
3. <faces-config xmlns="http://java.sun.com/xml/ns/javaee"
4.    xmlns:xsi="http://www.w3.org/2001/XMLSchema-instance"
5.    xsi:schemaLocation="http://java.sun.com/xml/ns/javaee
6.    http://java.sun.com/xml/ns/javaee/web-facesconfig_1_2.xsd"
7.    version="1.2">
8.    <navigation-rule>
9.       <from-view-id>/index.jsp</from-view-id>
10.      <navigation-case>
11.         <from-outcome>process</from-outcome>
12.         <to-view-id>/result.jsp</to-view-id>
13.      </navigation-case>
14.   </navigation-rule>
15.
16.   <navigation-rule>
17.      <from-view-id>/result.jsp</from-view-id>
18.      <navigation-case>
19.         <from-outcome>back</from-outcome>
20.         <to-view-id>/index.jsp</to-view-id>
21.      </navigation-case>
22.   </navigation-rule>
23.
```

Listing 9–30 custom-validator/web/WEB-INF/faces-config.xml (cont.)

```
24.    <converter>
25.        <converter-id>com.corejsf.CreditCard</converter-id>
26.        <converter-class>com.corejsf.CreditCardConverter</converter-class>
27.    </converter>
28.
29.    <converter>
30.        <converter-for-class>com.corejsf.CreditCard</converter-for-class>
31.        <converter-class>com.corejsf.CreditCardConverter</converter-class>
32.    </converter>
33.
34.    <validator>
35.        <validator-id>com.corejsf.CreditCard</validator-id>
36.        <validator-class>com.corejsf.CreditCardValidator</validator-class>
37.    </validator>
38.
39.    <validator>
40.        <validator-id>com.corejsf.Regex</validator-id>
41.        <validator-class>com.corejsf.RegexValidator</validator-class>
42.    </validator>
43.
44.    <managed-bean>
45.        <managed-bean-name>payment</managed-bean-name>
46.        <managed-bean-class>com.corejsf.PaymentBean</managed-bean-class>
47.        <managed-bean-scope>session</managed-bean-scope>
48.    </managed-bean>
49.
50.    <application>
51.        <resource-bundle>
52.            <base-name>com.corejsf.messages</base-name>
53.            <var>msgs</var>
54.        </resource-bundle>
55.    </application>
56. </faces-config>
```

Listing 9–31 custom-validator/web/WEB-INF/validator.tld

```
1. <?xml version="1.0" encoding="UTF-8"?>
2. <taglib xmlns="http://java.sun.com/xml/ns/javaee"
3.    xmlns:xsi="http://www.w3.org/2001/XMLSchema-instance"
4.    xsi:schemaLocation="http://java.sun.com/xml/ns/javaee
5.        http://java.sun.com/xml/ns/javaee/web-jsptaglibrary_2_1.xsd"
6.    version="2.1">
```

Listing 9–31 `custom-validator/web/WEB-INF/validator.tld (cont.)`

```
7.    <tlib-version>1.1</tlib-version>
8.    <short-name>validator</short-name>
9.    <uri>http://corejsf.com/validator</uri>
10.   <tag>
11.      <name>validateRegex</name>
12.      <tag-class>com.corejsf.RegexValidatorTag</tag-class>
13.      <body-content>empty</body-content>
14.      <attribute>
15.         <name>expression</name>
16.         <deferred-value>
17.            <type>java.lang.String</type>
18.         </deferred-value>
19.      </attribute>
20.      <attribute>
21.         <name>errorSummary</name>
22.         <deferred-value>
23.            <type>java.lang.String</type>
24.         </deferred-value>
25.      </attribute>
26.      <attribute>
27.         <name>errorDetail</name>
28.         <deferred-value>
29.            <type>java.lang.String</type>
30.         </deferred-value>
31.      </attribute>
32.   </tag>
33. </taglib>
```

Listing 9–32 `custom-validator/web/index.jsp`

```
1.  <html>
2.     <%@ taglib uri="http://java.sun.com/jsf/core" prefix="f" %>
3.     <%@ taglib uri="http://java.sun.com/jsf/html" prefix="h" %>
4.     <%@ taglib uri="http://corejsf.com/validator" prefix="corejsf" %>
5.     <f:view>
6.        <head>
7.           <link href="styles.css" rel="stylesheet" type="text/css"/>
8.           <title><h:outputText value="#{msgs.title}"/></title>
9.        </head>
10.       <body>
11.          <h:form>
12.             <h1><h:outputText value="#{msgs.enterPayment}"/></h1>
```

```
13.            <h:panelGrid columns="2">
14.               <h:outputText value="#{msgs.amount}"/>
15.               <h:inputText id="amount" value="#{payment.amount}">
16.                  <f:convertNumber minFractionDigits="2"/>
17.               </h:inputText>
18.
19.               <h:outputText value="#{msgs.creditCard}"/>
20.               <h:inputText id="card" value="#{payment.card}" required="true">
21.                  <f:validator validatorId="com.corejsf.CreditCard"/>
22.                  <corejsf:validateRegex expression="[3-6].*"
23.                     errorDetail="#{msgs.unknownType}"/>
24.               </h:inputText>
25.
26.               <h:outputText value="#{msgs.expirationDate}"/>
27.               <h:inputText id="date" value="#{payment.date}">
28.                  <f:convertDateTime pattern="MM/yyyy"/>
29.               </h:inputText>
30.            </h:panelGrid>
31.            <h:messages styleClass="errorMessage"
32.               showSummary="false" showDetail="true"/>
33.            <br/>
34.            <h:commandButton value="Process" action="process"/>
35.         </h:form>
36.      </body>
37.   </f:view>
38. </html>
```

EXTERNAL SERVICES

Topics in This Chapter

In this chapter, you learn how to access external services from your JSF application. We show you how to connect to databases, directory services, and web services. Our primary interest lies in the clean separation between the application logic and the configuration of resources.

Database Access with JDBC

In the following sections, we give you a brief refresher of the JDBC (Java Database Connectivity) API. We assume that you are familiar with basic SQL (Structured Query Language) commands. A more thorough introduction to these topics can be found in Horstmann and Cornell, 2004, 2005. *Core Java™ 2*, vol. 2, chap. 4. For your convenience, here is a brief refresher of the basics.

Issuing SQL Statements

To issue SQL statements to a database, you need a *connection* object. There are various methods of obtaining a connection. The most elegant one is to use a *data source*.

```
DataSource source = . . .
Connection conn = source.getConnection();
```

The section "Accessing a Container-Managed Resource" on page 462 describes how to obtain a data source in the GlassFish and Tomcat containers. For now, we assume that the data source is properly configured to connect to your favorite database.

Once you have the Connection object, you create a Statement object that you use to send SQL statements to the database. You use the executeUpdate method for SQL statements that update the database and the executeQuery method for queries that return a result set.

```
Statement stat = conn.createStatement();
stat.executeUpdate("INSERT INTO Users VALUES ('troosevelt', 'jabberwock')");
ResultSet result = stat.executeQuery("SELECT * FROM Users");
```

The ResultSet class has an unusual iteration protocol. First you call the next method to advance the cursor to the first row. (The next method returns false if no further rows are available.) Then you call the getString method to get a field value as a string. For example,

```
while (result.next()) {
    username = result.getString("username");
    password = result.getString("password");
    . . .
}
```

When you are done using the database, be certain that you close the connection. To ensure that the connection is closed under all circumstances, even when an exception occurs, wrap the query code inside a try/finally block, like this:

```
Connection conn = source.getConnection();
try {
    . . .
}
finally {
    conn.close();
}
```

Of course, there is much more to the JDBC API, but these simple concepts are sufficient to get you started.

 NOTE: Here we show you how to execute SQL statements from your web application. This approach is fine for lightweight applications that have modest storage requirements. For complex applications, you would want to use an object-relational mapping technology such as JPA (the Java Persistence Architecture) or Hibernate.

Connection Management

One of the more vexing issues for the web developer is the management of database connections. There are two conflicting concerns. First, opening a connection to a database can be time consuming. Several seconds may elapse for the processes of connecting, authenticating, and acquiring resources to be completed. Thus, you cannot simply open a new connection for every page request.

On the flip side, you cannot keep open a huge number of connections to the database. Connections consume resources, both in the client program and in the database server. Commonly, a database puts a limit on the maximum number of concurrent connections that it allows. Thus, your application cannot simply open a connection whenever a user logs on and leave it open until the user logs off. After all, your user might walk away and never log off.

One common mechanism for solving these concerns is to *pool* the database connections. A connection pool holds database connections that are already opened. Application programs obtain connections from the pool. When the connections are no longer needed, they are returned to the pool, but they are not closed. Thus, the pool minimizes the time lag of establishing database connections.

Implementing a database connection pool is not easy, and it certainly should not be the responsibility of the application programmer. As of version 2.0, JDBC supports pooling in a pleasantly transparent way. When you receive a pooled Connection object, it is actually instrumented so that its close method merely returns it to the pool. It is up to the application server to set up the pool and to give you a data source whose getConnection method yields pooled connections.

Each application server has its own way of configuring the database connection pool. The details are not part of any Java standard—the JDBC specification is completely silent on this issue. In the next section, we describe how to configure GlassFish and Tomcat for connection pooling. The basic principle is the same with other application servers, but of course the details may differ considerably.

To maintain the pool, it is still essential that you close every connection object when you are done using it. Otherwise the pool will run dry, and new physical connections to the database will need to be opened. Properly closing connections is the topic of the next section.

Plugging Connection Leaks

Consider this simple sequence of statements:

```
DataSource source = ...
Connection conn = source.getConnection();
Statement stat = conn.createStatement();
String command = "INSERT INTO Users VALUES ('troosevelt', 'jabberwock')";
stat.executeUpdate(command);
conn.close();
```

The code looks clean—we open a connection, issue a command, and immediately close the connection. But there is a fatal flaw. If one of the method calls throws an exception, the call to the close method never happens!

In that case, an irate user may resubmit the request many times in frustration, leaking another connection object with every click.

To overcome this issue, *always* place the call to close inside a finally block:

```
DataSource source = ...
Connection conn = source.getConnection();
try {
   Statement stat = conn.createStatement();
   String command = "INSERT INTO Users VALUES ('troosevelt', 'jabberwock')";
   stat.executeUpdate(command);
}
finally {
   conn.close();
}
```

This simple rule completely solves the problem of leaking connections.

The rule is most effective if you *do not combine* this try/finally construct with any other exception handling code. In particular, do not attempt to catch a SQLException in the same try block:

```
// we recommend that you do NOT do this
Connection conn = null;
try {
   conn = source.getConnection();
   Statement stat = conn.createStatement();
   String command = "INSERT INTO Users VALUES ('troosevelt', 'jabberwock')";
   stat.executeUpdate(command);
}
catch (SQLException) {
   // log error
}
finally {
   conn.close(); // ERROR
}
```

That code has two subtle mistakes. First, if the call to getConnection throws an exception, then conn is still null, and you can't call close. Moreover, the call to close can also throw a SQLException. You could clutter up the finally clause with more code, but the result is a mess. Instead, use two separate try blocks:

```
// we recommend that you use separate try blocks
try {
   Connection conn = source.getConnection();
   try {
      Statement stat = conn.createStatement();
      String command = "INSERT INTO Users VALUES ('troosevelt', 'jabberwock')";
      stat.executeUpdate(command);
   }
   finally {
      conn.close();
   }
}
catch (SQLException) {
   // log error
}
```

The inner try block ensures that the connection is closed. The outer try block ensures that the exception is logged.

 NOTE: Of course, you can also tag your method with throws SQLException and leave the outer try block to the caller. That is often the best solution.

Using Prepared Statements

A common optimization technique for JDBC programs is the use of the Prepared-Statement class. You use a *prepared statement* to speed up database operations if your code issues the same type of query multiple times. Consider the lookup of user passwords. You will repeatedly need to issue a query of the form

```
SELECT password FROM Users WHERE username=...
```

A prepared statement asks the database to precompile a query—that is, parse the SQL statement and compute a query strategy. That information is kept with the prepared statement and reused whenever the query is reissued.

You create a prepared statement with the prepareStatement method of the Connection class. Use a ? character for each parameter:

```
PreparedStatement stat = conn.prepareStatement(
   "SELECT password FROM Users WHERE username=?");
```

When you are ready to issue a prepared statement, first set the parameter values.

```
stat.setString(1, name);
```

(Note that the index value 1 denotes the first parameter.) Then issue the statement in the usual way:

```
ResultSet result = stat.executeQuery();
```

At first glance, it appears as if prepared statements would not be of much benefit in a web application. After all, you close the connection whenever you complete a user request. A prepared statement is tied to a database connection, and all the work of establishing it is lost when the physical connection to the database is terminated.

However, if the physical database connections are kept in a pool, then there is a good chance that the prepared statement is still usable when you retrieve a connection. Many connection pool implementations will cache prepared statements.

When you call prepareStatement, the pool will first look inside the statement cache, using the query string as a key. If the prepared statement is found, then it is reused. Otherwise, a new prepared statement is created and added to the cache.

All this activity is transparent to the application programmer. You request PreparedStatement objects and hope that, at least some of the time, the pool can retrieve an existing object for the given query.

 CAUTION: You cannot keep a PreparedStatement object and reuse it beyond a single request scope. Once you close a pooled connection, all associated PreparedStatement objects also revert to the pool. Thus, you should not hang on to PreparedStatement objects beyond the current request. Instead, keep calling the prepareStatement method with the same query string, and chances are good that you will get a cached statement object.

 NOTE: Even if you are not interested in performance, there is another good reason to use prepared statements: to guard against SQL injection attacks.

Configuring a Data Source

In the following sections, we show you how to configure a data source in your application server, such as GlassFish and Tomcat, and how to access the data source from a web application.

Configuring a Database Resource in GlassFish

GlassFish has a convenient web-based administration interface that you can use to configure a data source. Point your browser to http://localhost:4848 and log on. (The default username is admin and the default password is adminadmin.)

First, configure a database pool. Select "Connection Pools" and set up a new pool. Give a name to the pool, select a resource type (javax.sql.DataSource), and pick your database vendor (see Figure 10–1).

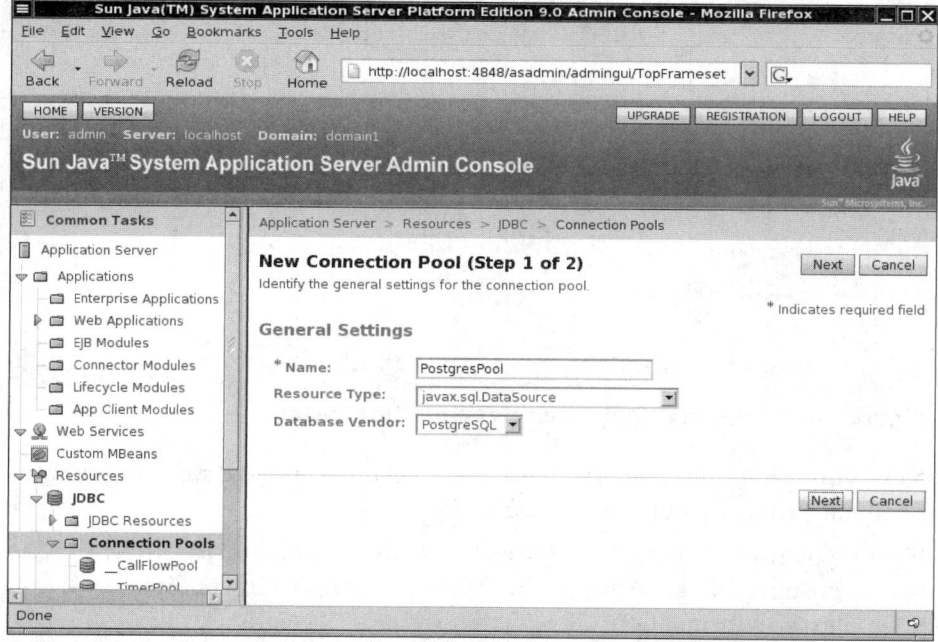

Figure 10–1   Configuring a connection pool in GlassFish

On the next screen, you specify database connection options such as username and password (see Figure 10–2).

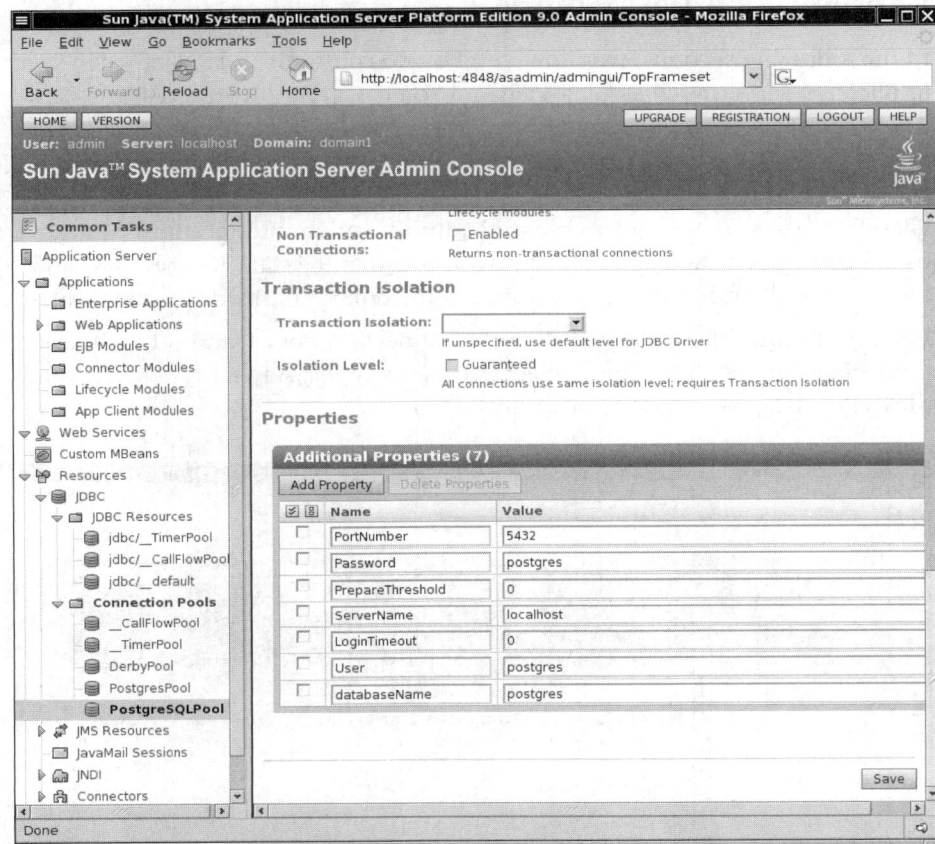

Figure 10–2   Specifying database connection options

Next, you configure a new data source. Give it the name jdbc/mydb and select the pool that you just set up (see Figure 10–3).

Finally, you need to place the database driver file (such as postgresql-8.2.jdbc3.jar for the PostgreSQL database) into the domains/domain1/lib/ext subdirectory of your GlassFish installation.

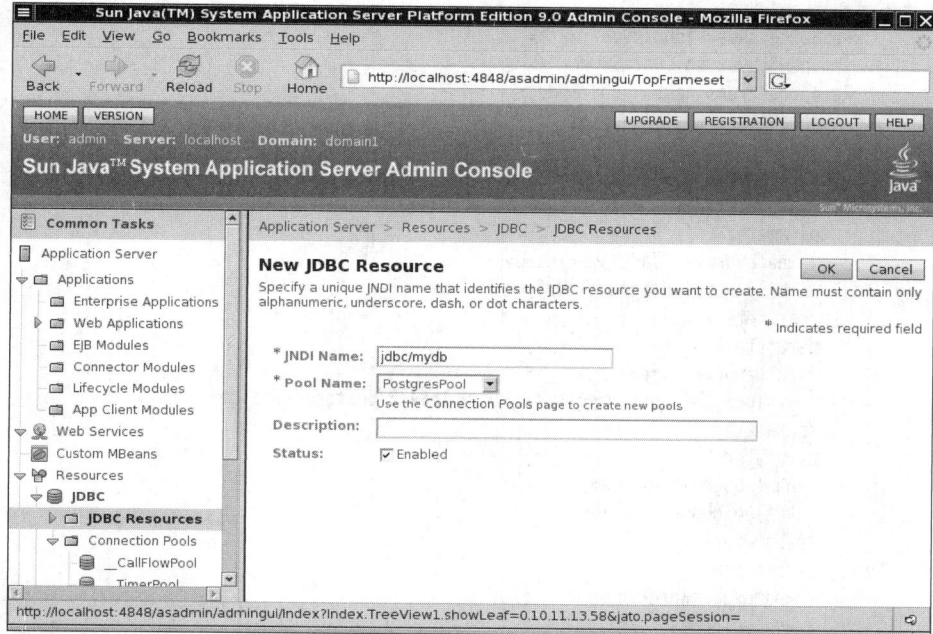

Figure 10–3   Configuring a data source

Configuring a Database Resource in Tomcat

In this section, we walk you through the steps of configuring a database resource pool in the Tomcat 5 container. If you do not use Tomcat, just skip this section.

Locate the `conf/server.xml` file and look for the element that describes the host that will contain your web application, such as

```
<!-- Define the default virtual host -->
<Host name="localhost" debug="0" appBase="webapps"
   unpackWARs="false" autoDeploy="true">
...
</Host>
```

Inside this element, place a `DefaultContext` element that specifies both the database details (driver, URL, username, and password) and the desired characteristics of the pool.

Here is a typical example, specifying a connection pool to a PostgreSQL database. The values that you need to customize are highlighted in bold.

```
<DefaultContext>
    <Resource name="jdbc/mydb" auth="Container"
      type="javax.sql.DataSource"/>
    <ResourceParams name="jdbc/mydb">
        <parameter>
            <name>factory</name>
            <value>org.apache.commons.dbcp.BasicDataSourceFactory</value>
        </parameter>
        <parameter>
            <name>driverClassName</name>
            <value>org.postgresql.Driver</value>
        </parameter>
        <parameter>
            <name>url</name>
            <value>jdbc:postgresql://127.0.0.1:5432/postgres</value>
        </parameter>
        <parameter>
            <name>username</name>
            <value>dbuser</value>
        </parameter>
        <parameter>
            <name>password</name>
            <value>dbpassword</value>
        </parameter>
        <parameter>
            <name>maxActive</name>
            <value>20</value>
        </parameter>
        <parameter>
            <name>maxIdle</name>
            <value>10</value>
        </parameter>
        <parameter>
            <name>poolPreparedStatements</name>
            <value>true</value>
        </parameter>
    </ResourceParams>
</DefaultContext>
```

 NOTE: You can also add the Resource and ResourceParams elements into the context of a specific web application. Then the data source is available only to that application.

To configure the pool, you specify a sequence of parameters (see Table 10–1 for the most common ones). A complete description of all valid parameters can be found at http://jakarta.apache.org/commons/dbcp/configuration.html.

Table 10–1   Common Tomcat Database Pool Parameters

Parameter Name	Description
driverClassName	The name of the JDBC driver, such as org.postgresql.Driver
url	The database URL, such as jdbc:postgresql:mydb
username	The database username
password	The password of the database user
maxActive	The maximum number of simultaneous active connections, or zero for no limit
maxIdle	The maximum number of active connections that can remain idle in the pool without extra ones being released, or zero for no limit
poolPreparedStatements	true if prepared statements are pooled (default: false)
removeAbandoned	true if the pool should remove connections that appear to be abandoned (default: false)
removeAbandonedTimeout	The number of seconds after which an unused connection is considered abandoned (default: 300)
logAbandoned	true to log a stack trace of the code that abandoned the connection (default: false)

To activate the pooling of prepared statements, be sure to set poolPreparedStatements to true.

The last three parameters in Table 10–1 refer to a useful feature of the Tomcat pool. The pool can be instructed to monitor and remove connections that appear to be abandoned. If a connection has not been used for some time, then it is likely that an application forgot to close it.

After all, a web application should always close its database connections after rendering the response to a user request. The pool can recycle unused connections and optionally log these events. The logging is useful for debugging because it allows the application programmer to plug connection leaks.

Place the database driver file into Tomcat's `common/lib` directory. If the database driver file has a `.zip` extension, you need to rename it to `.jar`, such as `classes12.jar` for the Oracle database.

 TIP: You can find detailed configuration instructions for a number of popular databases at `http://jakarta.apache.org/tomcat/tomcat-5.5-doc/jndi-datasource-examples-howto.html`.

Accessing a Container-Managed Resource

The Java EE specification requires that resources are declared in the `web.xml` file of your web application. For a data source, add the following entry to your `web.xml` file:

```
<resource-ref>
    <res-ref-name>jdbc/mydb</res-ref-name>
    <res-type>javax.sql.DataSource</res-type>
    <res-auth>Container</res-auth>
</resource-ref>
```

Note the name of the resource: `jdbc/mydb`. That name is used to look up the data source. There are two ways for doing the lookup. The most elegant one is *resource injection*. You declare a field in a managed bean and mark it with an annotation, like this:

```
@Resource(name="jdbc/mydb")
private DataSource source;
```

When the application server loads the managed bean, then the field is automatically initialized.

This feature works only in an application server that conforms to the Java EE 5 standard. If you use JSF 1.1 or the standalone Tomcat server, you have to work a little harder, and make a JNDI (Java Naming and Directory Interface) lookup yourself:

```
try {
    InitialContext ctx = new InitialContext();
    source = (DataSource) ctx.lookup("java:comp/env/jdbc/mydb");
}
catch (NamingException ex) {
    . . .
}
```

The java:comp/env prefix is the standard JNDI directory lookup path to the component environment in a Java EE container. By convention, you place JDBC resources in the jdbc subpath. It is up to you how to name the individual resources.

 CAUTION: GlassFish distinguishes beween "resource reference" names and JNDI names. For most resources, you need to specify a mapping in the sun-web.xml file (see page 489 for an example). However, for JDBC resources, no mapping is required.

Of course, for such a simple lookup, the @Resource annotation is only a minor convenience. However, other resource initializations are more complex. For another example of resource injection, see the section "Using Web Services" on page 516. There, we show you how to inject a web service port with a simple annotation. Without resource injection, we would need to access unsightly helper classes.

To be consistent, we like to use the annotation mechanism to initialize all resources. Table 10–2 lists the annotations that you can use to inject resources.

Table 10–2   Annotations for Resource Injection

Annotation	Resource Type
@Resource @Resources	Arbitrary JNDI Resource
@WebServiceRef @WebServiceRefs	Web service port
@EJB @EJBs	EJB Session Bean
@PersistenceContext @PersistenceContexts	Persistent Entity Manager
@PersistenceUnit @PersistenceUnits	Persistent Entity Manager Factory

A Complete Database Example

In this example, we show you how to verify a username/password combination. As with the example program in Chapter 1, we start with a simple login screen (Figure 10–4). If the username/password combination is correct, we show a welcome screen (Figure 10–5). Otherwise, we prompt the user to try again (Figure 10–6). Finally, if a database error occurred, we show an error screen (Figure 10–7).

Thus, we have four JSF pages, shown in Listing 10–1 through Listing 10–4. Listing 10–5 shows the faces-config.xml file with the navigation rules. The navigation rules use the loginAction and logoutAction properties of the UserBean class. Listing 10–6 gives the code for the UserBean.

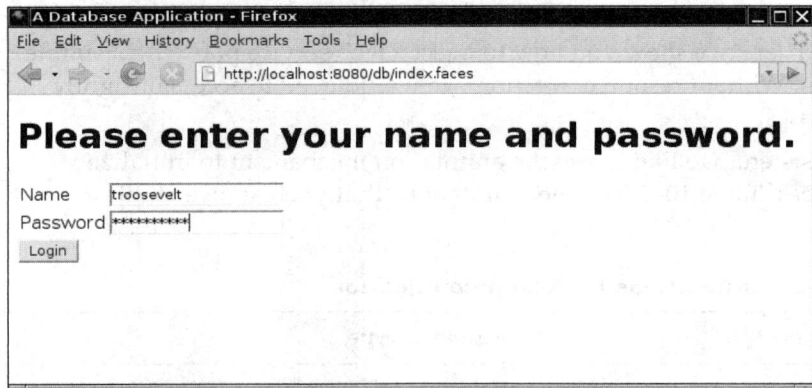

Figure 10–4   Login screen

Figure 10–5   Welcome screen

Figure 10–6   Authentication error screen

Figure 10–7   Internal error screen

In our simple example, we add the database code directly into the UserBean class. It would also be possible to have two layers of objects: beans for communication with the JSF pages, and data access objects that represent entities in the database.

We place the code for database access into the separate method:

```
public void doLogin() throws SQLException
```

That method queries the database for the username/password combination and sets the loggedIn field to true if the username and password match.

The button on the index.jsp page references the login method of the user bean. That method calls the doLogin method and returns a result string for the navigation handler. The login method also deals with exceptions that the doLogin method reports.

We assume that the doLogin method is focused on the database, not the user interface. If an exception occurs, doLogin should report it and take no further action. The login method, on the other hand, logs exceptions and returns a result string "internalError" to the navigation handler.

```java
public String login() {
    try {
        doLogin();
    }
    catch (SQLException ex) {
        logger.log(Level.SEVERE, "loginAction", ex);
        return "internalError";
    }
    if (loggedIn)
        return "loginSuccess";
    else
        return "loginFailure";
}
```

Before running this example, you need to start your database and create a table named Users and add one or more username/password entries:

```sql
CREATE TABLE Users (username CHAR(20), password CHAR(20))
INSERT INTO Users VALUES ('troosevelt', 'jabberwock')
```

You can then deploy and test your application.

Figure 10–8 shows the directory structure for this application, and Figure 10–9 shows the navigation map. The before mentioned application files follow in Listing 10–1 through Listing 10–6.

 NOTE: Lots of things can go wrong with database configurations. If the application has an internal error, look at the log file. In GlassFish, the default log file is domains/domain1/logs/server.log. In Tomcat, it is logs/catalina.out.

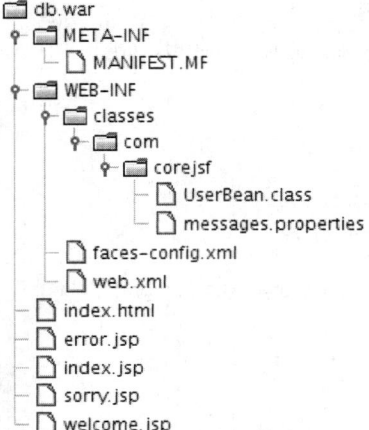

Figure 10–8   Directory structure of the database application

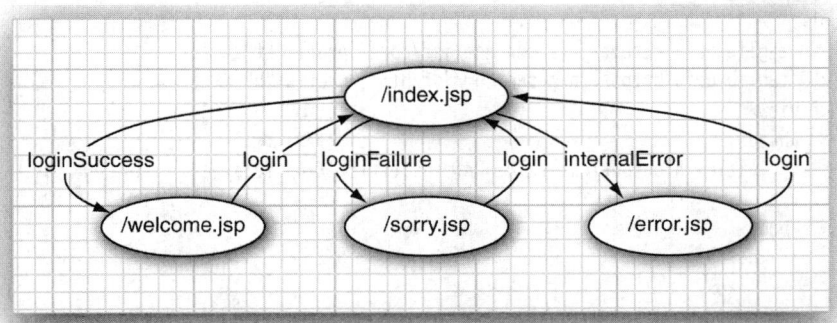

Figure 10–9   Navigation map of the database application

Listing 10–1   `db/web/index.jsp`

```
1.  <html>
2.      <%@ taglib uri="http://java.sun.com/jsf/core" prefix="f" %>
3.      <%@ taglib uri="http://java.sun.com/jsf/html" prefix="h" %>
4.      <f:view>
5.        <head>
6.          <title><h:outputText value="#{msgs.title}"/></title>
7.        </head>
8.        <body>
9.          <h:form>
```

Listing 10–1   db/web/index.jsp (cont.)

```
10.             <h1><h:outputText value="#{msgs.enterNameAndPassword}"/></h1>
11.             <h:panelGrid columns="2">
12.                 <h:outputText value="#{msgs.name}"/>
13.                 <h:inputText value="#{user.name}"/>
14.
15.                 <h:outputText value="#{msgs.password}"/>
16.                 <h:inputSecret value="#{user.password}"/>
17.             </h:panelGrid>
18.             <h:commandButton value="#{msgs.login}" action="#{user.login}"/>
19.         </h:form>
20.     </body>
21.     </f:view>
22. </html>
```

Listing 10–2   db/web/welcome.jsp

```
1. <html>
2.     <%@ taglib uri="http://java.sun.com/jsf/core" prefix="f" %>
3.     <%@ taglib uri="http://java.sun.com/jsf/html" prefix="h" %>
4.     <f:view>
5.         <head>
6.             <title><h:outputText value="#{msgs.title}"/></title>
7.         </head>
8.         <body>
9.             <h:form>
10.                 <p>
11.                 <h:outputText value="#{msgs.welcome}"/>
12.                 <h:outputText value="#{user.name}"/>!
13.                 </p>
14.                 <p>
15.                 <h:commandButton value="#{msgs.logout}" action="#{user.logout}"/>
16.                 </p>
17.             </h:form>
18.         </body>
19.     </f:view>
20. </html>
```

Listing 10–3   db/web/sorry.jsp

```
1. <html>
2.   <%@ taglib uri="http://java.sun.com/jsf/core" prefix="f" %>
3.   <%@ taglib uri="http://java.sun.com/jsf/html" prefix="h" %>
4.   <f:view>
5.     <head>
6.       <title><h:outputText value="#{msgs.title}"/></title>
7.     </head>
8.     <body>
9.       <h:form>
10.        <h1><h:outputText value="#{msgs.authError}"/></h1>
11.        <p>
12.          <h:outputText value="#{msgs.authError_detail}"/>!
13.        </p>
14.        <p>
15.          <h:commandButton value="#{msgs.continue}" action="login"/>
16.        </p>
17.      </h:form>
18.    </body>
19.  </f:view>
20. </html>
```

Listing 10–4   db/web/error.jsp

```
1. <html>
2.   <%@ taglib uri="http://java.sun.com/jsf/core" prefix="f" %>
3.   <%@ taglib uri="http://java.sun.com/jsf/html" prefix="h" %>
4.   <f:view>
5.     <head>
6.       <title><h:outputText value="#{msgs.title}"/></title>
7.     </head>
8.     <body>
9.       <h:form>
10.        <h1><h:outputText value="#{msgs.internalError}"/></h1>
11.        <p><h:outputText value="#{msgs.internalError_detail}"/></p>
12.        <p>
13.          <h:commandButton value="#{msgs.continue}" action="login"/>
14.        </p>
15.      </h:form>
16.    </body>
17.  </f:view>
18. </html>
```

Listing 10–5 db/web/WEB-INF/faces-config.xml

```
1.  <?xml version="1.0"?>
2.  <faces-config xmlns="http://java.sun.com/xml/ns/javaee"
3.    xmlns:xsi="http://www.w3.org/2001/XMLSchema-instance"
4.    xsi:schemaLocation="http://java.sun.com/xml/ns/javaee
5.      http://java.sun.com/xml/ns/javaee/web-facesconfig_1_2.xsd"
6.    version="1.2">
7.    <navigation-rule>
8.      <from-view-id>/index.jsp</from-view-id>
9.      <navigation-case>
10.       <from-outcome>loginSuccess</from-outcome>
11.       <to-view-id>/welcome.jsp</to-view-id>
12.     </navigation-case>
13.     <navigation-case>
14.       <from-outcome>loginFailure</from-outcome>
15.       <to-view-id>/sorry.jsp</to-view-id>
16.     </navigation-case>
17.     <navigation-case>
18.       <from-outcome>internalError</from-outcome>
19.       <to-view-id>/error.jsp</to-view-id>
20.     </navigation-case>
21.   </navigation-rule>
22.   <navigation-rule>
23.     <from-view-id>/welcome.jsp</from-view-id>
24.     <navigation-case>
25.       <from-outcome>login</from-outcome>
26.       <to-view-id>/index.jsp</to-view-id>
27.     </navigation-case>
28.   </navigation-rule>
29.   <navigation-rule>
30.     <from-view-id>/sorry.jsp</from-view-id>
31.     <navigation-case>
32.       <from-outcome>login</from-outcome>
33.       <to-view-id>/index.jsp</to-view-id>
34.     </navigation-case>
35.   </navigation-rule>
36.   <navigation-rule>
37.     <from-view-id>/error.jsp</from-view-id>
38.     <navigation-case>
39.       <from-outcome>login</from-outcome>
40.       <to-view-id>/index.jsp</to-view-id>
41.     </navigation-case>
42.   </navigation-rule>
43.
```

Listing 10-5   db/web/WEB-INF/faces-config.xml (cont.)

```
44.    <managed-bean>
45.        <managed-bean-name>user</managed-bean-name>
46.        <managed-bean-class>com.corejsf.UserBean</managed-bean-class>
47.        <managed-bean-scope>session</managed-bean-scope>
48.    </managed-bean>
49.
50.    <application>
51.        <resource-bundle>
52.            <base-name>com.corejsf.messages</base-name>
53.            <var>msgs</var>
54.        </resource-bundle>
55.    </application>
56. </faces-config>
```

Listing 10-6   db/src/java/com/corejsf/UserBean.java

```
1. package com.corejsf;
2.
3. import java.sql.Connection;
4. import java.sql.PreparedStatement;
5. import java.sql.ResultSet;
6. import java.sql.SQLException;
7. import java.util.logging.Level;
8. import java.util.logging.Logger;
9.
10. import javax.annotation.Resource;
11. import javax.sql.DataSource;
12.
13. public class UserBean {
14.     private String name;
15.     private String password;
16.     private boolean loggedIn;
17.     private Logger logger = Logger.getLogger("com.corejsf");
18.
19.     @Resource(name="jdbc/mydb")
20.     private DataSource ds;
21.
22.     /*
23.     If you use Tomcat or JSF 1.1, remove the @Resource line and add this constructor:
24.     public UserBean()
25.     {
26.         try {
27.             Context ctx = new InitialContext();
28.             ds = (DataSource) ctx.lookup("java:comp/env/jdbc/mydb");
```

Listing 10–6 db/src/java/com/corejsf/UserBean.java (cont.)

```
29.        } catch (NamingException ex) {
30.            logger.log(Level.SEVERE, "DataSource lookup failed", ex);
31.        }
32.    }
33.    */
34.
35.    public String getName() { return name; }
36.    public void setName(String newValue) { name = newValue; }
37.
38.    public String getPassword() { return password; }
39.    public void setPassword(String newValue) { password = newValue; }
40.
41.    public String login() {
42.        try {
43.            doLogin();
44.        }
45.        catch (SQLException ex) {
46.            logger.log(Level.SEVERE, "login failed", ex);
47.            return "internalError";
48.        }
49.        if (loggedIn)
50.            return "loginSuccess";
51.        else
52.            return "loginFailure";
53.    }
54.
55.    public String logout() {
56.        loggedIn = false;
57.        return "login";
58.    }
59.
60.    public void doLogin() throws SQLException {
61.        if (ds == null) throw new SQLException("No data source");
62.        Connection conn = ds.getConnection();
63.        if (conn == null) throw new SQLException("No connection");
64.
65.        try {
66.            PreparedStatement passwordQuery = conn.prepareStatement(
67.                "SELECT password from Users WHERE username = ?");
68.
69.            passwordQuery.setString(1, name);
70.
71.            ResultSet result = passwordQuery.executeQuery();
72.
```

Listing 10–6	db/src/java/com/corejsf/UserBean.java (cont.)

```
73.          if (!result.next()) return;
74.          String storedPassword = result.getString("password");
75.          loggedIn = password.equals(storedPassword.trim());
76.        }
77.        finally {
78.          conn.close();
79.        }
80.      }
81. }
```

An Introduction to LDAP

In the preceding section, you have seen how to read a username and password from a database. In this section, we look at LDAP (Lightweight Directory Access Protocol). LDAP servers are more flexible and efficient for managing user information than are database servers. Particularly in large organizations, in which data replication is an issue, LDAP is preferred over relational databases for storing directory information.

Because LDAP is less commonly used than relational database technology, we briefly introduce it here. For an in-depth discussion of LDAP, we recommend the "LDAP bible": Howes, Timothy et al, 2003. *Understanding and Deploying LDAP Directory Services,* (2nd ed.). Addison-Wesley Professional.

LDAP Directories

LDAP uses a *hierarchical* database. It keeps all data in a tree structure, not in a set of tables as a relational database would. Each entry in the tree has:

- Zero or more *attributes*. An attribute has a key and a value. An example attribute is cn=John Q. Smith. The key cn stores the "common name." (See Table 10–3 for the meaning of commonly used LDAP attributes.)

- One or more *object classes*. An object class defines the set of required and optional attributes for this element. For example, the object class person defines a required attribute cn and an optional attribute telephoneNumber. Of course, the object classes are different than Java classes, but they also support a notion of inheritance. For example, inetOrgPerson is a subclass of person with additional attributes.

- A *distinguished name* (for example, uid=troosevelt,ou=people,dc=corejsf,dc=com). The distinguished name is a sequence of attributes that trace a path joining the entry with the root of the tree. There may be alternate paths, but one of them must be specified as distinguished.

Table 10–3 Commonly Used LDAP Attributes

Attribute Name	Meaning
dc	Domain component
cn	Common name
sn	Surname
dn	Distinguished name
o	Organization
ou	Organizational unit
uid	Unique identifier

Figure 10–10 shows an example of a directory tree.

How to organize the directory tree and what information to put in it can be a matter of intense debate. We do not discuss the issues here. Instead, we assume that an organizational scheme has been established and that the directory has been populated with the relevant user data.

Configuring an LDAP Server

You have several options for running an LDAP server to try out the programs in this section. Here are the most popular choices:

- The free OpenLDAP server (http://openldap.org), available for Linux and Windows, and built into Mac OS X
- A high-performance server such as the Sun Java System Directory Server (http://www.sun.com/software/products/directory_srvr/home_directory.html), which is available on a variety of platforms
- Microsoft Active Directory

We give you brief instructions for configuring OpenLDAP. If you use another directory server, the basic steps are similar.

Our sample directory uses the standard object class inetOrgPerson. (We use that class because it has useful attributes such as uid and mail.) You should make sure that your LDAP server recognizes this object class.

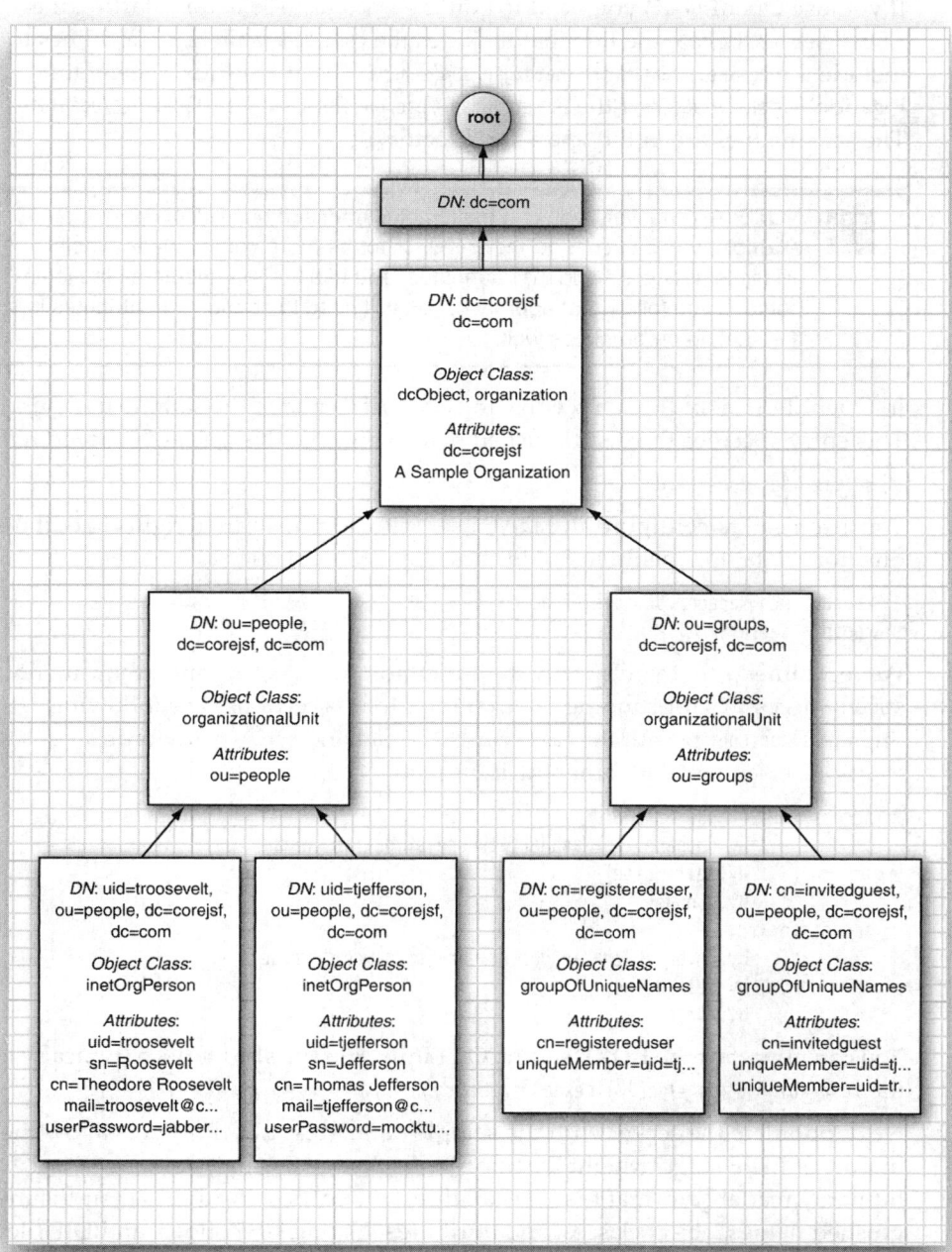

Figure 10–10 A directory tree

If you use OpenLDAP, you need to edit the slapd.conf file before starting the LDAP server. Locate the line that includes the core.schema file, and add lines to include the cosine.schema and inetorgperson.schema files. (On Linux, the default location for the slapd.conf file is /etc/ldap, /etc/openldap, or /usr/local/etc/openldap. The schema files are in the schema subdirectory.)

 NOTE: Alternatively, you can make adjustments to our sample data. For example, you can change inetOrgPerson to the more commonly available person, omit the uid and mail attributes, and use the sn attribute as the login name. If you follow that approach, you will need to change the attributes in the sample programs as well.

In OpenLDAP, edit the suffix entry in slapd.conf to match the sample data set. This entry specifies the distinguished name suffix for this server. It should read

```
suffix  "dc=corejsf,dc=com"
```

You also need to configure an LDAP user with administrative rights to edit the directory data. In OpenLDAP, add these lines to slapd.conf:

```
rootdn  "cn=Manager,dc=corejsf,dc=com"
rootpw  secret
```

We recommend that you specify authorization settings, although they are not strictly necessary for running the examples in this sections. The following settings in slapd.conf permit the Manager user to read and write passwords, and everyone else to read all other attributes.

```
access to attr=userPassword
            by dn.base="cn=Manager,dc=corejsf,dc=com" write
            by self write
            by * none
access to *
            by dn.base="cn=Manager,dc=corejsf,dc=com" write
            by self write
            by * read
```

You can now start the LDAP server. On Linux, run the slapd service (typically in the /usr/sbin or /usr/local/libexec directory).

Next, populate the server with the sample data. Most LDAP servers allow the import of LDIF (Lightweight Directory Interchange Format) data. LDIF is a humanly readable format that lists all directory entries, including their distinguished names, object classes, and attributes. Listing 10–7 shows an LDIF file that describes our sample data:

```
. ldap/misc/sample.ldif
```

For example, with OpenLDAP, you use the `ldapadd` tool to add the data to the directory:

```
ldapadd -f sample.ldif -x -D "cn=Manager,dc=corejsf,dc=com" -w secret
```

Before proceeding, it is a good idea to double-check that the directory contains the data that you need. We suggest that you use an LDAP browser such as JXplorer (`http://sourceforge.net/projects/jxplorer/`) or Jarek Gawor's LDAP Browser/Editor (`http://www.mcs.anl.gov/~gawor/ldap/`). Both are convenient Java programs that let you browse the contents of any LDAP server. Launch the program and configure it with the following options:

- Host: `localhost`
- Port: `389`
- Base DN: `dc=corejsf,dc=com`
- User DN: `cn=Manager,dc=corejsf,dc=com`
- Password: `secret`

Make sure that the LDAP server has started, then connect. If everything is in order, you should see a directory tree similar to the one shown in Figure 10–11.

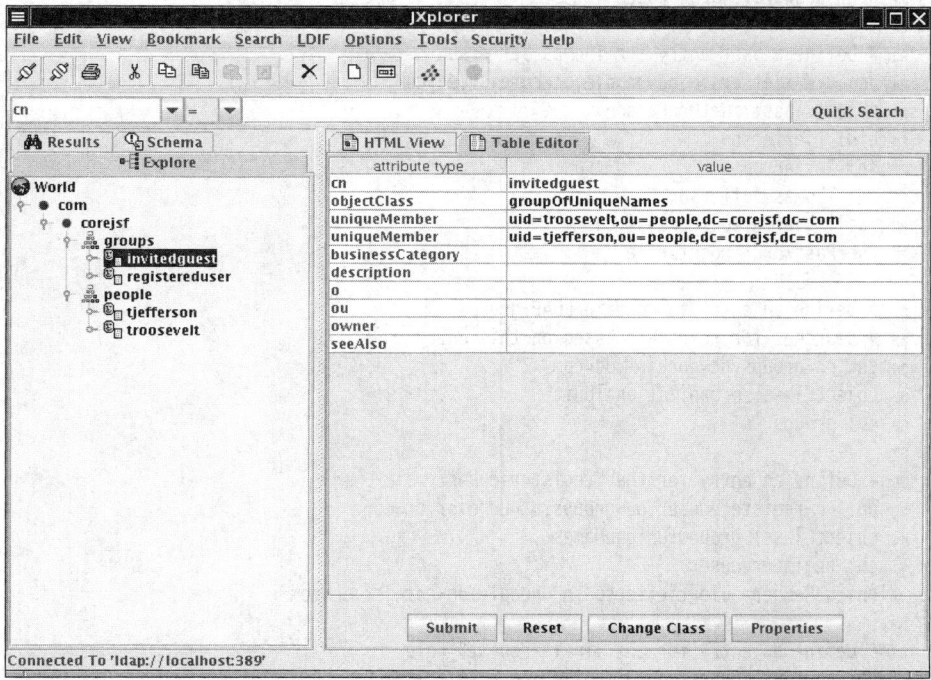

Figure 10–11 Inspecting an LDAP directory tree

Listing 10–7 `ldap/setup/sample.ldif`

```
 1. # Define top-level entry
 2. dn: dc=corejsf,dc=com
 3. objectClass: dcObject
 4. objectClass: organization
 5. dc: corejsf
 6. o: A Sample Organization
 7.
 8. # Define an entry to contain people
 9. # searches for users are based on this entry
10. dn: ou=people,dc=corejsf,dc=com
11. objectClass: organizationalUnit
12. ou: people
13.
14. # Define a user entry for Theodore Roosevelt
15. dn: uid=troosevelt,ou=people,dc=corejsf,dc=com
16. objectClass: inetOrgPerson
17. uid: troosevelt
18. sn: Roosevelt
19. cn: Theodore Roosevelt
20. mail: troosevelt@corejsf.com
21. userPassword: jabberwock
22.
23. # Define a user entry for Thomas Jefferson
24. dn: uid=tjefferson,ou=people,dc=corejsf,dc=com
25. objectClass: inetOrgPerson
26. uid: tjefferson
27. sn: Jefferson
28. cn: Thomas Jefferson
29. mail: tjefferson@corejsf.com
30. userPassword: mockturtle
31.
32. # Define an entry to contain LDAP groups
33. # searches for roles are based on this entry
34. dn: ou=groups,dc=corejsf,dc=com
35. objectClass: organizationalUnit
36. ou: groups
37.
38. # Define an entry for the "registereduser" role
39. dn: cn=registereduser,ou=groups,dc=corejsf,dc=com
40. objectClass: groupOfUniqueNames
41. cn: registereduser
42. uniqueMember: uid=tjefferson,ou=people,dc=corejsf,dc=com
43.
44. # Define an entry for the "invitedguest" role
45. dn: cn=invitedguest,ou=groups,dc=corejsf,dc=com
```

Listing 10–7 `ldap/setup/sample.ldif (cont.)`

```
46. objectClass: groupOfUniqueNames
47. cn: invitedguest
48. uniqueMember: uid=troosevelt,ou=people,dc=corejsf,dc=com
49. uniqueMember: uid=tjefferson,ou=people,dc=corejsf,dc=com
```

Accessing LDAP Directory Information

Once you have your LDAP database populated, it is time to connect to it with a Java program. You use JNDI, an interface that unifies various directory protocols.

Start by getting a *directory context* to the LDAP directory, with the following incantation:

```
Hashtable env = new Hashtable();
env.put(Context.SECURITY_PRINCIPAL, userDN);
env.put(Context.SECURITY_CREDENTIALS, password);
DirContext initial = new InitialDirContext(env);
DirContext context = (DirContext) initial.lookup("ldap://localhost:389");
```

Here, we connect to the LDAP server at the local host. The port number 389 is the default LDAP port.

If you connect to the LDAP database with an invalid username/password combination, an `AuthenticationException` is thrown.

 NOTE: Sun's JNDI tutorial suggests an alternative way to connect to the server:

```
Hashtable env = new Hashtable();
env.put(Context.INITIAL_CONTEXT_FACTORY, "com.sun.jndi.ldap.LdapCtxFactory");
env.put(Context.PROVIDER_URL, "ldap://localhost:389");
env.put(Context.SECURITY_PRINCIPAL, userDN);
env.put(Context.SECURITY_CREDENTIALS, password);
DirContext context = new InitialDirContext(env);
```

However, it seems undesirable to hardwire the Sun LDAP provider into your code. JNDI has an elaborate mechanism for configuring providers, and you should not lightly bypass it.

To list the attributes of a given entry, specify its distinguished name and then use the `getAttributes` method:

```
Attributes answer
  = context.getAttributes("uid=troosevelt,ou=people,dc=corejsf,dc=com");
```

You can get a specific attribute with the get method—for example:

```
Attribute commonNameAttribute = answer.get("cn");
```

To enumerate all attributes, you use the NamingEnumeration class. The designers of this class felt that they too could improve on the standard Java iteration protocol, and they gave us this usage pattern:

```
NamingEnumeration attrEnum = answer.getAll();
while (attrEnum.hasMore()) {
    Attribute attr = (Attribute) attrEnum.next();
    String id = attr.getID();
    ...
}
```

Note the use of hasMore instead of hasNext.

Since an attribute can have multiple values, you need to use another Naming-Enumeration to list them all:

```
NamingEnumeration valueEnum = attr.getAll();
while (valueEnum.hasMore()) {
    Object value = valueEnum.next();
    ...
}
```

However, if you know that the attribute has a single value, you can call the get method to retrieve it:

```
String commonName = (String) commonNameAttribute.get();
```

You now know how to query the directory for user data. Next, we take up operations for modifying the directory contents.

To add a new entry, gather the set of attributes in a BasicAttributes object. (The BasicAttributes class implements the Attributes interface.)

```
Attributes attrs = new BasicAttributes();
attrs.put("objectClass", "inetOrgPerson");
attrs.put("uid", "alincoln");
attrs.put("sn", "Lincoln");
attrs.put("cn", "Abraham Lincoln");
attrs.put("mail", "alincoln@corejsf.com");
String pw = "redqueen";
attrs.put("userPassword", pw.getBytes());
```

Then call the createSubcontext method. Provide the distinguished name of the new entry and the attribute set.

```
context.createSubcontext("uid=alincoln,ou=people,dc=corejsf,dc=com", attrs);
```

CAUTION: When assembling the attributes, remember that the attributes are checked against the schema. Do not supply unknown attributes and be sure to supply all attributes that are required by the object class. For example, if you omit the sn of person, the createSubcontext method will fail.

To remove an entry, call destroySubcontext:

```
context.destroySubcontext("uid=alincoln,ou=people,dc=corejsf,dc=com");
```

Finally, you may want to edit the attributes of an existing entry. You call the method

```
context.modifyAttributes(distinguishedName, flag, attrs);
```

Here, flag is one of

```
DirContext.ADD_ATTRIBUTE
DirContext.REMOVE_ATTRIBUTE
DirContext.REPLACE_ATTRIBUTE
```

The attrs parameter contains a set of the attributes to be added, removed, or replaced.

Conveniently, the BasicAttributes(String, Object) constructor constructs an attribute set with a single attribute. For example,

```
context.modifyAttributes(
    "uid=alincoln,ou=people,dc=corejsf,dc=com",
    DirContext.ADD_ATTRIBUTE,
    new BasicAttributes("telephonenumber", "+18005551212"));

context.modifyAttributes(
    "uid=alincoln,ou=people,dc=corejsf,dc=com",
    DirContext.REMOVE_ATTRIBUTE,
    new BasicAttributes("mail", "alincoln@coresjf.com"));

context.modifyAttributes(
    "uid=alincoln,ou=people,dc=corejsf,dc=com",
    DirContext.REPLACE_ATTRIBUTE,
    new BasicAttributes("userPassword", newpw.getBytes()));
```

Finally, when you are done with a context, you should close it:

```
context.close();
```

You now know enough about directory operations to carry out the tasks that you will commonly need when working with LDAP directories. A good source for more advanced information is the JNDI tutorial at http://java.sun.com/products/jndi/tutorial.

However, we are not quite ready to put together a JSF application that uses LDAP. It would be extremely unprofessional to hardcode the directory URL and the manager password into a program. Instead, these values should be specified in a configuration file.

The next section discusses various options for the management of configuration parameters. We put the alternatives to work with an application that allows users to self-register on a web site; we use LDAP to store the user information.

API   `javax.naming.directory.InitialDirContext`   Java SE 1.3

- `InitialDirContext(Hashtable env)`

  Constructs a directory context, using the given environment settings. The hash table can contain bindings for `Context.SECURITY_PRINCIPAL`, `Context.SECURITY_CREDENTIALS`, and other keys (see the API documentation for the `javax.naming.Context` interface for details).

API   *javax.naming.Context*   Java SE 1.3

- `Object lookup(String name)`

  Looks up the object with the given name. The return value depends on the nature of this context. It commonly is a subtree context or a leaf object.

- `Context createSubcontext(String name)`

  Creates a subcontext with the given name. The subcontext becomes a child of this context. All path components of the name, except for the last one, must exist.

- `void destroySubcontext(String name)`

  Destroys the subcontext with the given name. All path components of the name, except for the last one, must exist.

- `void close()`

  Closes this context.

API   *javax.naming.directory.DirContext*   Java SE 1.3

- `Attributes getAttributes(String name)`

  Gets the attributes of the entry with the given name.

- `void modifyAttributes(String name, int flag, Attributes modes)`

  Modifies the attributes of the entry with the given name. The value flag is one of `DirContext.ADD_ATTRIBUTE`, `DirContext.REMOVE_ATTRIBUTE`, or `DirContext.REPLACE_ATTRIBUTE`

javax.naming.directory.Attributes Java SE 1.3

- `Attribute get(String id)`
  Gets the attribute with the given ID.

- `NamingEnumeration getAll()`
  Yields an enumeration that iterates through all attributes in this attribute set.

- `void put(String id, Object value)`
  Adds an attribute to this attribute set.

`javax.naming.directory.BasicAttributes` Java SE 1.3

- `BasicAttributes(String id, Object value)`
  Constructs an attribute set that contains a single attribute with the given ID and value.

javax.naming.directory.Attribute Java SE 1.3

- `String getID()`
  Gets the ID of this attribute.

- `Object get()`
  Gets the first attribute value of this attribute if the values are ordered or an arbitrary value if they are unordered.

- `NamingEnumeration getAll()`
  Yields an enumeration that iterates through all values of this attribute.

javax.naming.NamingEnumeration Java SE 1.3

- `boolean hasMore()`
  Returns true if this enumeration object has more elements.

- `Object next()`
  Returns the next element of this enumeration.

Managing Configuration Information

Whenever your application interfaces with external services, you need to specify configuration parameters: URLs, usernames, passwords, and so on. You should never hardcode these parameters inside your application classes—doing so would make it difficult to update passwords, switch to alternative servers, and so on.

In the section on database services, you saw a reasonable approach for managing the database configuration. The configuration information is placed inside server.xml. The servlet container uses this information to construct a data source and bind it to a well-known name. The classes that need to access the database use JNDI look up the data source.

Placing configuration information into server.xml is appropriate for a *global* resource such as a database. This resource be used by all web applications inside the container. On the other hand, application-specific configuration information should be placed inside web.xml or faces-config.xml. Using the example of an LDAP connection, we explore all three possibilities.

Configuring a Bean

Whenever you define a bean in faces-config.xml, you can provide initialization parameters by using the managed-property element. Here is how we can initialize a bean that connects to an LDAP directory:

```
<managed-bean>
    <managed-bean-name>userdir</managed-bean-name>
    <managed-bean-class>com.corejsf.UserDirectoryBean</managed-bean-class>
    <managed-bean-scope>application</managed-bean-scope>
    <managed-property>
        <property-name>URL</property-name>
        <value>ldap://localhost:389</value>
    </managed-property>
    <managed-property>
        <property-name>managerDN</property-name>
        <value>cn=Manager,dc=corejsf,dc=com</value>
    </managed-property>
    <managed-property>
        <property-name>managerPassword</property-name>
        <value>secret</value>
    </managed-property>
</managed-bean>
```

You see the familiar managed-bean-name and managed-bean-class elements. However, this bean is given *application scope*. The bean object stays alive for the duration of the entire application, and it can serve multiple sessions. Finally, we used the managed-property settings to initialize the bean. Thus, we achieved our goal of placing these initialization parameters inside a configuration file rather than hardwiring them into the bean code.

Of course, our bean needs setters for these properties:

```
public class UserDirectoryBean {
    private String url;
    private String managerDN;
    private String managerPW;

    public void setManagerDN(String newValue) { managerDN = newValue; }
    public void setManagerPassword(String newValue) { managerPW = newValue; }
    public void setURL(String newValue) { url = newValue; }

    public DirContext getRootContext() throws NamingException { ... }
}
```

When the bean is constructed, the setters are invoked with the values specified in faces-config.xml.

Finally, client code needs to have access to the bean object. For example, suppose the UserBean class wants to connect to the directory:

```
UserDirectoryBean userdir = ... // how?
DirContext context = userdir.connect(dn, pw);
```

To look up a JSF bean, you use its value binding of its name, as in the following statements:

```
FacesContext context = FacesContext.getCurrentInstance();
Application app = context.getApplication();
ValueBinding binding = app.createValueBinding("#{userdir}");
UserDirectoryBean dir = (UserDirectoryBean) binding.getValue(context);
```

In summary, here are the steps for configuring a JSF bean:

1. Place the configuration parameters inside managed-property elements in the faces-config.xml file.
2. Provide property setters for these properties in the bean class.
3. Look up the bean object through its value binding.

This configuration method is straightforward and convenient. However, it is not suitable for configuring objects that should be available to multiple web applications. Moreover, purists might argue that faces-config.xml is intended to describe the logic of a web application, not its interface with external resources, and that web.xml would be more appropriate for the latter. Read on if either of these objections matters to you.

Configuring the External Context

In this section, we assume that your JSF application is launched as a servlet. You can supply parameters in web.xml by providing a set of context-param elements inside the web-app element:

```
<web-app>
   <context-param>
      <param-name>URL</param-name>
      <param-value>ldap://localhost:389</param-value>
   </context-param>
   <context-param>
      <param-name>managerDN</param-name>
      <param-value>cn=Manager,dc=corejsf,dc=com</param-value>
   </context-param>
   <context-param>
      <param-name>managerPassword</param-name>
      <param-value>secret</param-value>
   </context-param>
   ...
</web-app>
```

To read a parameter, get the *external context* object. That object describes the execution environment that launched your JSF application. If you use a servlet container, then the external context is a wrapper around the ServletContext object. The ExternalContext class has a number of convenience methods to access properties of the underlying servlet context. The getInitParameter method retrieves a context parameter value with a given name.

 CAUTION: Do not confuse context-param with init-param. The latter tag is used for parameters that a servlet can process at startup. It is unfortunate that the method for reading a context parameter is called getInitParameter.

Here is the code for getting an LDAP context from configuration parameters in web.xml:

```
public DirContext getRootContext() throws NamingException {
   ExternalContext external
      = FacesContext.getCurrentInstance().getExternalContext();

   String managerDN = external.getInitParameter("managerDN");
   String managerPW = external.getInitParameter("managerPassword");
   String url = external.getInitParameter("URL");
```

```
Hashtable env = new Hashtable();
env.put(Context.SECURITY_PRINCIPAL, managerDN);
env.put(Context.SECURITY_CREDENTIALS, managerPW);
DirContext initial = new InitialDirContext(env);

Object obj = initial.lookup(url);
if (!(obj instanceof DirContext))
    throw new NamingException("No directory context");
return (DirContext) obj;
}
```

Follow these steps for accessing resources through the external context:

1. Place the configuration parameters inside context-param elements in the web.xml file.

2. Use the ExternalContext to look up the parameter values.

3. Turn the parameters into objects for your application.

As you can see, this configuration method works at a lower level than the configuration of a JSF bean. The web.xml file contains an unstructured list of parameters. It is up to you to construct objects that make use of these parameters.

 javax.faces.context.FacesContext

*   ExternalContext getExternalContext()
    Gets the external context, a wrapper such as a servlet or portlet context around the execution environment of this JSF application.

 javax.faces.context.ExternalContext

*   String getInitParameter(String name)
    Gets the initialization parameter with the given name.

Configuring a Container-Managed Resource

We now discuss how to specify container-wide resources. The information in this section is specific to GlassFish and Tomcat. Other containers will have similar mechanisms, but the details will differ.

Earlier in this chapter, we showed you how to configure a JDBC data source so that you can locate it through resource injection or with a JNDI lookup. This is an attractive method for specifying systemwide resources. Fortunately, Glass-Fish and Tomcat let you fit your own resources into the same mechanism.

In GlassFish, you use the administration interface to add a custom JNDI resource (see Figure 10–12). In our sample application, the custom resource is an LDAP directory. Supply the name ldap/mydir and type javax.naming.directory.DirContext. Unfortunately, there is no standard factory for LDAP directory contexts, and we will implement a custom factory of type com.corejsf.DirContextFactory. Finally, specify the following connection parameters as additional properties:

```
URL=ldap://localhost:389
java.naming.security.principal=cn=Manager,dc=corejsf,dc=com
java.naming.security.credentials=secret
```

 NOTE: We use the standard JNDI environment names for the principal and credentials. The Context interface constants that we used previously are merely shortcuts for the environment names. For example, Context.SECURITY_PRINCIPAL is the string "java.naming.security.principal".

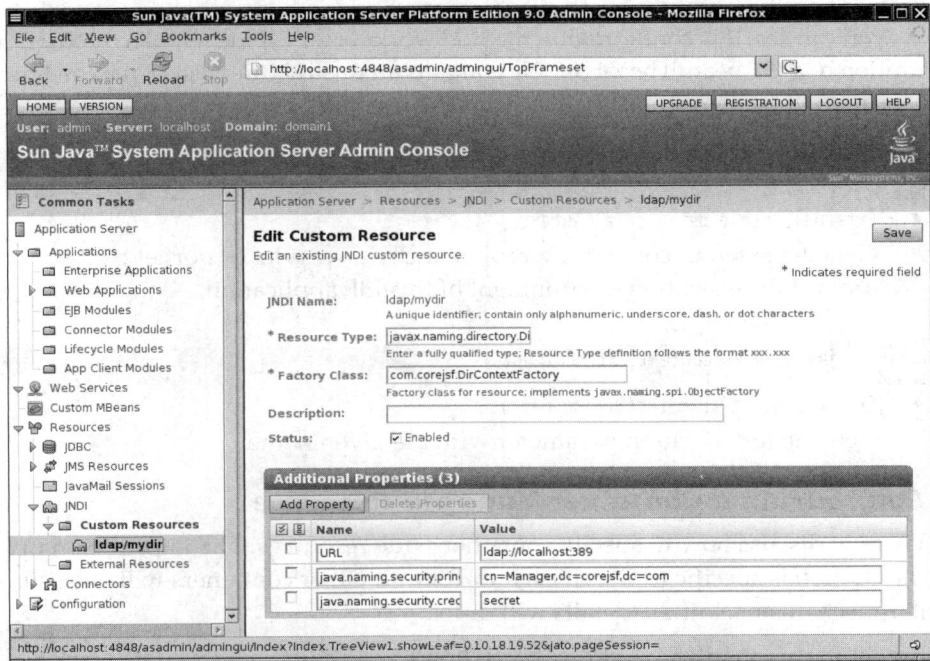

Figure 10–12   Configuring an LDAP resource in GlassFish

You also need to supply a file WEB-INF/sun-web.xml, as shown in Listing 10–8. This file maps the application server's resource name to the JNDI name. We use the same name for both.

Listing 10–8   ldap3/web/WEB-INF/sun-web.xml (GlassFish only)

```
1. <!DOCTYPE sun-web-app PUBLIC
2.    "-//Sun Microsystems, Inc.//DTD Application Server 9.0 Servlet 2.5//EN"
3.    "http://www.sun.com/software/appserver/dtds/sun-web-app_2_5-0.dtd">
4. <sun-web-app>
5.    <resource-ref>
6.       <res-ref-name>ldap/mydir</res-ref-name>
7.       <jndi-name>ldap/mydir</jndi-name>
8.    </resource-ref>
9. </sun-web-app>
```

Now we need to implement the factory class. All factories need to implement the ObjectFactory interface type and implement the getObjectInstance method.

```
public class DirContextFactory implements ObjectFactory {

   public Object getObjectInstance(Object obj,
      Name n, Context nameCtx, Hashtable environment)
      throws NamingException {
      ...
   }
}
```

This method, defined in glorious generality, can be used to produce any object from arbitrary configuration information. There is quite a bit of variability in how the parameters are used, but fortunately we need only to understand what parameters the application server supplies when requesting a resource.

The configuration parameters are placed into a Reference object, a kind of hash table on a megadose of steroids. Our factory places the parameters into a plain hash table and then gets the directory context (see Listing 10–9 for the complete source code).

 NOTE: The class com.sun.jndi.ldap.LdapCtxFactory (which is used in Sun's JNDI tutorial) also implements the ObjectFactory interface. Unfortunately, you cannot use that class as a factory for LDAP connections in an application server. The getObjectInstance method of com.sun.jndi.ldap.LdapCtxFactory expects an Object parameter that is either a URL string, an array of URL strings, or a Reference object containing a value with key "URL". The other environment settings must be provided in the Hashtable parameter. That is not what the application server supplies.

Listing 10–9 ldap3/setup/java/com/corejsf/DirContextFactory.java

```java
1. package com.corejsf;
2.
3. import java.util.Enumeration;
4. import java.util.Hashtable;
5.
6. import javax.naming.Context;
7. import javax.naming.Name;
8. import javax.naming.NamingException;
9. import javax.naming.RefAddr;
10. import javax.naming.Reference;
11. import javax.naming.directory.DirContext;
12. import javax.naming.directory.InitialDirContext;
13. import javax.naming.spi.ObjectFactory;
14.
15. public class DirContextFactory implements ObjectFactory {
16.     public Object getObjectInstance(Object obj,
17.        Name n, Context nameCtx, Hashtable environment)
18.        throws NamingException {
19.
20.        Hashtable<String, String> env = new Hashtable<String, String>();
21.        String url = null;
22.        Reference ref = (Reference) obj;
23.        Enumeration addrs = ref.getAll();
24.        while (addrs.hasMoreElements()) {
25.            RefAddr addr = (RefAddr) addrs.nextElement();
26.            String name = addr.getType();
27.            String value = (String) addr.getContent();
28.            if (name.equals("URL")) url = value;
29.            else env.put(name, value);
30.        }
31.        DirContext initial = new InitialDirContext(env);
32.        if (url == null) return initial;
33.        else return initial.lookup(url);
34.     }
35. }
```

 NOTE: Compile this file and place it inside a JAR file.

```
cd corejsf-examples/ch10/ldap3/setup/java
javac com/corejsf/DirContextFactory.java
jar cvf dirctxfactory.jar com/corejsf/*.class
```

Then move the JAR file into the *glassfish*/domains/domain1/lib/ext directory.

With Tomcat, the steps are similar. You specify a `Resource` and its `ResourceParams` in `server.xml`.

```
<Resource name="ldap/mydir" auth="Container"
    type="javax.naming.directory.DirContext"/>

<ResourceParams name="ldap/mydir">
    <parameter>
        <name>factory</name>
        <value>com.corejsf.DirContextFactory</value>
    </parameter>
    <parameter>
        <name>URL</name>
        <value>ldap://localhost:389</value>
    </parameter>
    <parameter>
        <name>java.naming.security.principal</name>
        <value>cn=Manager,dc=corejsf,dc=com</value>
    </parameter>
    <parameter>
        <name>java.naming.security.credentials</name>
        <value>secret</value>
    </parameter>
</ResourceParams>
```

Place the JAR file with the `DirContextFactory` into the `common/lib` directory of Tomcat and restart the server. You do not need a `sun-web.xml` file.

Creating an LDAP Application

We will now put together a complete application that stores user information in an LDAP directory.

The application simulates a news web site that gives users free access to news as long as they provide some information about themselves. We do not actually provide any news. We simply provide a screen to log in (Figure 10–13) and a separate screen to register for the service (Figure 10–14). Upon successful login, users can read news and update their personal information (Figure 10–15).

The update screen is similar to the registration screen, and we do not show it. Figure 10–16 shows the directory structure, and Figure 10–17 shows the page flow between the news service pages.

We provide three versions of this application, with configuration information in `faces-config.xml`, `web.xml`, and the application server, respectively.

All three versions have identical web pages (see Listing 10–10 through Listing 10–13). (We omit the listings of repetitive pages.) The primary difference between the versions is the implementation of the getRootContext method in the UserBean class (Listing 10–14).

The first application has a UserDirectoryBean class (Listing 10–15) that is configured in faces-config.xml (Listing 10–16). The second application makes an ad hoc lookup of servlet initialization parameters. The third version uses resource injection, using the class of Listing 10–9. See the preceding sections for details. Finally, for completeness, Listing 10–17 contains the code for the Name class that is used in the UserBean class.

Figure 10–13   Logging in to the news service

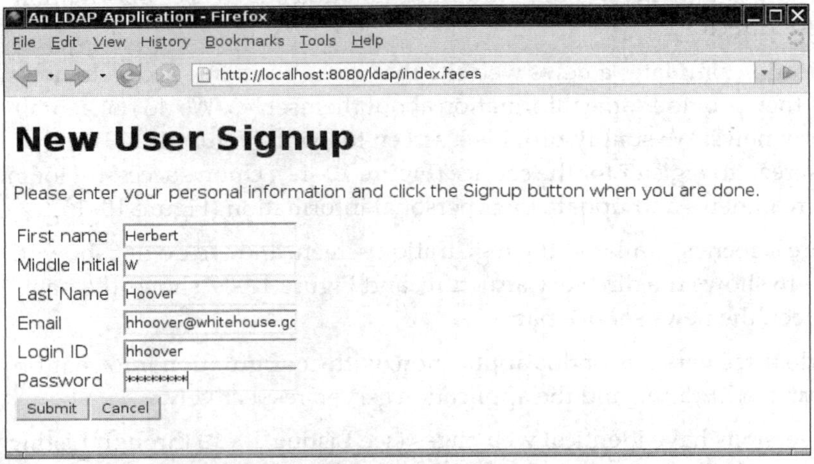

An LDAP Application - Firefox

File Edit View History Bookmarks Tools Help

http://localhost:8080/ldap/index.faces

New User Signup

Please enter your personal information and click the Signup button when you are done.

First name   Herbert
Middle Initial W
Last Name   Hoover
Email   hhoover@whitehouse.go
Login ID   hhoover
Password   ********
Submit   Cancel

Figure 10–14   Registering for the news service

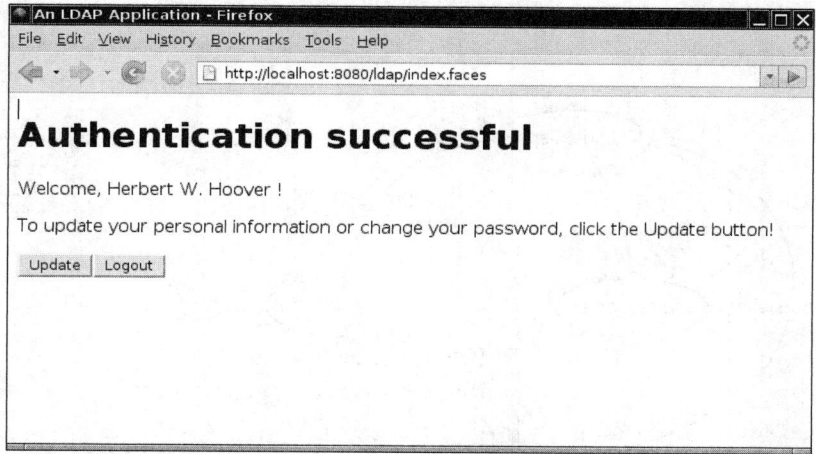

Figure 10–15   Main screen of the news service

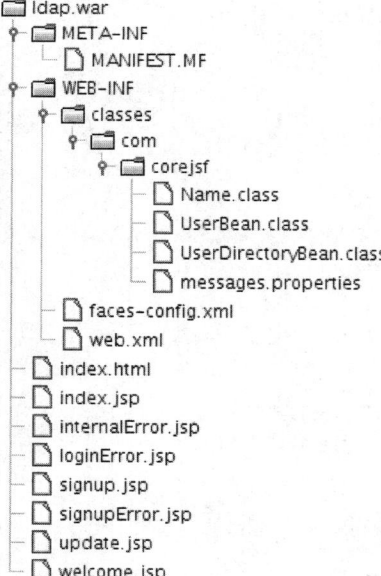

Figure 10–16   The directory structure of the LDAP example

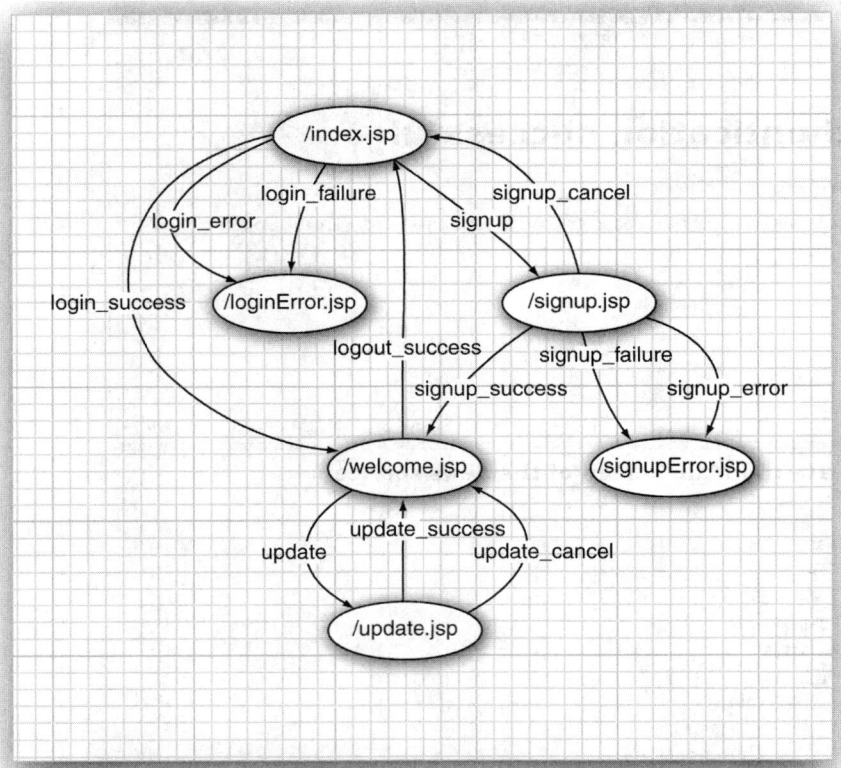

Figure 10–17 Page flow of the news service

Listing 10–10   `ldap/web/index.jsp`

```
1.  <html>
2.    <%@ taglib uri="http://java.sun.com/jsf/core" prefix="f" %>
3.    <%@ taglib uri="http://java.sun.com/jsf/html" prefix="h" %>
4.    <f:view>
5.      <head>
6.        <title><h:outputText value="#{msgs.title}"/></title>
7.      </head>
8.      <body>
9.        <h:form>
10.         <h1><h:outputText value="#{msgs.enterNameAndPassword}"/></h1>
11.         <h:panelGrid columns="2">
12.           <h:outputText value="#{msgs.loginID}"/>
13.           <h:inputText value="#{user.id}"/>
```

Listing 10–10 `ldap/web/index.jsp (cont.)`

```
14.
15.                <h:outputText value="#{msgs.password}"/>
16.                <h:inputSecret value="#{user.password}"/>
17.           </h:panelGrid>
18.           <h:commandButton value="#{msgs.login}" action="#{user.login}"/>
19.           <br/>
20.           <h:outputText value="#{msgs.signupNow}"/>
21.           <h:commandButton value="#{msgs.signup}" action="signup"/>
22.        </h:form>
23.      </body>
24.    </f:view>
25. </html>
```

Listing 10–11 `ldap/web/signup.jsp`

```
1. <html>
2.    <%@ taglib uri="http://java.sun.com/jsf/core" prefix="f" %>
3.    <%@ taglib uri="http://java.sun.com/jsf/html" prefix="h" %>
4.    <f:view>
5.      <head>
6.        <title><h:outputText value="#{msgs.title}"/></title>
7.      </head>
8.      <body>
9.        <h:form>
10.          <h1><h:outputText value="#{msgs.newUserSignup}"/></h1>
11.          <p><h:outputText value="#{msgs.newUserSignup_detail}"/></p>
12.          <h:panelGrid columns="2">
13.            <h:outputText value="#{msgs.firstName}"/>
14.            <h:inputText value="#{user.name.first}"/>
15.
16.            <h:outputText value="#{msgs.middleInitial}"/>
17.            <h:inputText value="#{user.name.middle}"/>
18.
19.            <h:outputText value="#{msgs.lastName}"/>
20.            <h:inputText value="#{user.name.last}"/>
21.
22.            <h:outputText value="#{msgs.email}"/>
23.            <h:inputText value="#{user.email}"/>
24.
25.            <h:outputText value="#{msgs.loginID}"/>
26.            <h:inputText value="#{user.id}"/>
27.
```

Listing 10–11   ldap/web/signup.jsp (cont.)

```
28.                <h:outputText value="#{msgs.password}"/>
29.                <h:inputSecret value="#{user.password}"/>
30.             </h:panelGrid>
31.             <h:commandButton value="#{msgs.submit}" action="#{user.signup}"/>
32.             <h:commandButton value="#{msgs.cancel}" action="signup_cancel"/>
33.          </h:form>
34.       </body>
35.    </f:view>
36. </html>
```

Listing 10–12   ldap/web/welcome.jsp

```
1. <html>
2.    <%@ taglib uri="http://java.sun.com/jsf/core" prefix="f" %>
3.    <%@ taglib uri="http://java.sun.com/jsf/html" prefix="h" %>
4.    <f:view>
5.       <head>
6.          <title><h:outputText value="#{msgs.title}"/></title>
7.       </head>
8.       <body>
9.          <h:form>
10.            <h1><h:outputText value="#{msgs.success}"/></h1>
11.            <p>
12.               <h:outputText value="#{msgs.welcome}"/>
13.               <h:outputText value="#{user.name}"/>!
14.            </p>
15.            <p>
16.               <h:outputText value="#{msgs.success_detail}"/>
17.            </p>
18.            <h:commandButton value="#{msgs.update}" action="update"/>
19.            <h:commandButton value="#{msgs.logout}" action="#{user.logout}"/>
20.         </h:form>
21.      </body>
22.   </f:view>
23. </html>
```

Listing 10–13   ldap/web/loginError.jsp

```
 1. <html>
 2.    <%@ taglib uri="http://java.sun.com/jsf/core" prefix="f" %>
 3.    <%@ taglib uri="http://java.sun.com/jsf/html" prefix="h" %>
 4.    <f:view>
 5.       <head>
 6.          <title><h:outputText value="#{msgs.title}"/></title>
 7.       </head>
 8.       <body>
 9.          <h:form>
10.             <h1><h:outputText value="#{msgs.loginError}"/></h1>
11.             <p>
12.                <h:outputText value="#{msgs.loginError_detail}"/>
13.             </p>
14.             <p>
15.                <h:commandButton value="#{msgs.tryAgain}" action="login"/>
16.                <h:commandButton value="#{msgs.signup}" action="signup"/>
17.             </p>
18.          </h:form>
19.       </body>
20.    </f:view>
21. </html>
```

Listing 10–14   ldap/src/java/com/corejsf/UserBean.java

```
 1. package com.corejsf;
 2.
 3. import java.util.logging.Level;
 4. import java.util.logging.Logger;
 5.
 6. import javax.el.ELContext;
 7. import javax.el.ExpressionFactory;
 8. import javax.el.ValueExpression;
 9. import javax.faces.application.Application;
10. import javax.faces.context.FacesContext;
11. import javax.naming.NameNotFoundException;
12. import javax.naming.NamingException;
13. import javax.naming.directory.Attributes;
14. import javax.naming.directory.BasicAttributes;
15. import javax.naming.directory.DirContext;
16.
```

Listing 10–14 ldap/src/java/com/corejsf/UserBean.java (cont.)

```
17. public class UserBean {
18.    private Name name;
19.    private String id;
20.    private String email;
21.    private String password;
22.    private Logger logger = Logger.getLogger("com.corejava");
23.
24.    public UserBean() { name = new Name(); }
25.
26.    public DirContext getRootContext() throws NamingException {
27.       FacesContext context = FacesContext.getCurrentInstance();
28.       ELContext elContext = context.getELContext();
29.       Application app = context.getApplication();
30.       ExpressionFactory factory = app.getExpressionFactory();
31.       ValueExpression ex = factory.createValueExpression(elContext,
32.          "#{userdir}", UserDirectoryBean.class);
33.       UserDirectoryBean dir =
34.          (UserDirectoryBean) ex.getValue(elContext);
35.       return dir.getRootContext();
36.    }
37.
38.    public Name getName() { return name; }
39.    public void setName(Name newValue) { name = newValue; }
40.
41.    public String getEmail() { return email; }
42.    public void setEmail(String newValue) { email = newValue; }
43.
44.    public String getId() { return id; }
45.    public void setId(String newValue) { id = newValue; }
46.
47.    public String getPassword() { return password; }
48.    public void setPassword(String newValue) { password = newValue; }
49.
50.    public String login() {
51.       try {
52.          DirContext context = getRootContext();
53.          try {
54.             String dn = "uid=" + id + ",ou=people,dc=corejsf,dc=com";
55.             Attributes userAttributes = context.getAttributes(dn);
56.             String cn = (String) userAttributes.get("cn").get();
57.             name.parse(cn);
58.             email = (String) userAttributes.get("mail").get();
59.             byte[] pw = (byte[])
60.                userAttributes.get("userPassword").get();
```

Listing 10–14 ldap/src/java/com/corejsf/UserBean.java (cont.)

```
61.              if (password.equals(new String(pw)))
62.                  return "login_success";
63.              else
64.                  return "login_failure";
65.          } finally {
66.              context.close();
67.          }
68.      }
69.      catch (NamingException ex) {
70.          logger.log(Level.SEVERE, "loginAction", ex);
71.          return "login_error";
72.      }
73.  }
74.
75.  public String signup() {
76.      try {
77.          DirContext context = getRootContext();
78.          try {
79.              String dn = "uid=" + id + ",ou=people,dc=corejsf,dc=com";
80.
81.              try {
82.                  context.lookup(dn);
83.                  return "signup_failure";
84.              }
85.              catch (NameNotFoundException ex) {}
86.
87.              Attributes attrs = new BasicAttributes();
88.              attrs.put("objectClass", "inetOrgPerson");
89.              attrs.put("uid", id);
90.              attrs.put("sn", name.getLast());
91.              attrs.put("cn", name.toString());
92.              attrs.put("mail", email);
93.              attrs.put("userPassword", password.getBytes());
94.              context.createSubcontext(dn, attrs);
95.          } finally {
96.              context.close();
97.          }
98.      }
99.      catch (NamingException ex) {
100.         logger.log(Level.SEVERE, "loginAction", ex);
101.         return "signup_error";
102.     }
103.
104.     return "signup_success";
105. }
```

Listing 10–14   ldap/src/java/com/corejsf/UserBean.java (cont.)

```
106.
107.   public String update() {
108.      try {
109.         DirContext context = getRootContext();
110.         try {
111.            String dn = "uid=" + id + ",ou=people,dc=corejsf,dc=com";
112.            Attributes attrs = new BasicAttributes();
113.            attrs.put("sn", name.getLast());
114.            attrs.put("cn", name.toString());
115.            attrs.put("mail", email);
116.            attrs.put("userPassword", password.getBytes());
117.            context.modifyAttributes(dn,
118.               DirContext.REPLACE_ATTRIBUTE, attrs);
119.         } finally {
120.            context.close();
121.         }
122.      }
123.      catch (NamingException ex) {
124.         logger.log(Level.SEVERE, "updateAction", ex);
125.         return "internal_error";
126.      }
127.
128.      return "update_success";
129.   }
130.
131.   public String logout() {
132.      password = "";
133.      return "logout_success";
134.   }
135. }
```

Listing 10–15   ldap/src/java/com/corejsf/UserDirectoryBean.java

```
1. package com.corejsf;
2.
3. import java.util.Hashtable;
4. import javax.naming.Context;
5. import javax.naming.NamingException;
6. import javax.naming.directory.DirContext;
7. import javax.naming.directory.InitialDirContext;
8.
9. public class UserDirectoryBean {
10.    private String url;
11.    private String managerDN;
12.    private String managerPW;
```

Listing 10–15   ldap/src/java/com/corejsf/UserDirectoryBean.java (cont.)

```
13.
14.    public void setManagerDN(String newValue) { managerDN = newValue; }
15.    public void setManagerPassword(String newValue) {
16.        managerPW = newValue; }
17.    public void setURL(String newValue) { url = newValue; }
18.
19.    public DirContext getRootContext() throws NamingException {
20.        Hashtable<String, String> env = new Hashtable<String, String>();
21.        env.put(Context.SECURITY_PRINCIPAL, managerDN);
22.        env.put(Context.SECURITY_CREDENTIALS, managerPW);
23.        DirContext initial = new InitialDirContext(env);
24.
25.        Object obj = initial.lookup(url);
26.        if (!(obj instanceof DirContext))
27.            throw new NamingException("No directory context");
28.        return (DirContext) obj;
29.    }
30. }
```

Listing 10–16   ldap/web/WEB-INF/faces-config.xml

```
1.  <?xml version="1.0"?>
2.  <faces-config xmlns="http://java.sun.com/xml/ns/javaee"
3.      xmlns:xsi="http://www.w3.org/2001/XMLSchema-instance"
4.      xsi:schemaLocation="http://java.sun.com/xml/ns/javaee
5.          http://java.sun.com/xml/ns/javaee/web-facesconfig_1_2.xsd"
6.      version="1.2">
7.      <navigation-rule>
8.          <from-view-id>/index.jsp</from-view-id>
9.          <navigation-case>
10.             <from-outcome>login_success</from-outcome>
11.             <to-view-id>/welcome.jsp</to-view-id>
12.         </navigation-case>
13.         <navigation-case>
14.             <from-outcome>login_error</from-outcome>
15.             <to-view-id>/loginError.jsp</to-view-id>
16.         </navigation-case>
17.         <navigation-case>
18.             <from-outcome>login_failure</from-outcome>
19.             <to-view-id>/loginError.jsp</to-view-id>
20.         </navigation-case>
21.     </navigation-rule>
```

Listing 10–16 `ldap/web/WEB-INF/faces-config.xml (cont.)`

```
22.    <navigation-rule>
23.      <from-view-id>/signup.jsp</from-view-id>
24.      <navigation-case>
25.        <from-outcome>signup_success</from-outcome>
26.        <to-view-id>/welcome.jsp</to-view-id>
27.      </navigation-case>
28.      <navigation-case>
29.        <from-outcome>signup_failure</from-outcome>
30.        <to-view-id>/signupError.jsp</to-view-id>
31.      </navigation-case>
32.      <navigation-case>
33.        <from-outcome>signup_error</from-outcome>
34.        <to-view-id>/signupError.jsp</to-view-id>
35.      </navigation-case>
36.      <navigation-case>
37.        <from-outcome>signup_cancel</from-outcome>
38.        <to-view-id>/index.jsp</to-view-id>
39.      </navigation-case>
40.    </navigation-rule>
41.    <navigation-rule>
42.      <from-view-id>/welcome.jsp</from-view-id>
43.      <navigation-case>
44.        <from-outcome>update</from-outcome>
45.        <to-view-id>/update.jsp</to-view-id>
46.      </navigation-case>
47.      <navigation-case>
48.        <from-outcome>logout_success</from-outcome>
49.        <to-view-id>/index.jsp</to-view-id>
50.      </navigation-case>
51.    </navigation-rule>
52.    <navigation-rule>
53.      <from-view-id>/update.jsp</from-view-id>
54.      <navigation-case>
55.        <from-outcome>update_success</from-outcome>
56.        <to-view-id>/welcome.jsp</to-view-id>
57.      </navigation-case>
58.      <navigation-case>
59.        <from-outcome>update_cancel</from-outcome>
60.        <to-view-id>/welcome.jsp</to-view-id>
61.      </navigation-case>
62.    </navigation-rule>
63.    <navigation-rule>
64.      <navigation-case>
65.        <from-outcome>login</from-outcome>
```

Listing 10–16 `ldap/web/WEB-INF/faces-config.xml (cont.)`

```
66.            <to-view-id>/index.jsp</to-view-id>
67.         </navigation-case>
68.         <navigation-case>
69.            <from-outcome>signup</from-outcome>
70.            <to-view-id>/signup.jsp</to-view-id>
71.         </navigation-case>
72.         <navigation-case>
73.            <from-outcome>internal_error</from-outcome>
74.            <to-view-id>/internalError.jsp</to-view-id>
75.         </navigation-case>
76.      </navigation-rule>
77.
78.      <managed-bean>
79.         <managed-bean-name>user</managed-bean-name>
80.         <managed-bean-class>com.corejsf.UserBean</managed-bean-class>
81.         <managed-bean-scope>session</managed-bean-scope>
82.      </managed-bean>
83.
84.      <managed-bean>
85.         <managed-bean-name>userdir</managed-bean-name>
86.         <managed-bean-class>com.corejsf.UserDirectoryBean</managed-bean-class>
87.         <managed-bean-scope>application</managed-bean-scope>
88.         <managed-property>
89.            <property-name>URL</property-name>
90.            <value>ldap://localhost:389</value>
91.         </managed-property>
92.         <managed-property>
93.            <property-name>managerDN</property-name>
94.            <value>cn=Manager,dc=corejsf,dc=com</value>
95.         </managed-property>
96.         <managed-property>
97.            <property-name>managerPassword</property-name>
98.            <value>secret</value>
99.         </managed-property>
100.      </managed-bean>
101.
102.      <application>
103.         <resource-bundle>
104.            <base-name>com.corejsf.messages</base-name>
105.            <var>msgs</var>
106.         </resource-bundle>
107.      </application>
108.   </faces-config>
```

Listing 10–17 ldap/src/java/com/corejsf/Name.java

```java
1. package com.corejsf;
2.
3. public class Name {
4.    private String first;
5.    private String middle;
6.    private String last;
7.
8.    public Name() { first = ""; middle = ""; last = ""; }
9.
10.   public String getFirst() { return first; }
11.   public void setFirst(String newValue) { first = newValue; }
12.   public String getMiddle() { return middle; }
13.   public void setMiddle(String newValue) { middle = newValue; }
14.   public String getLast() { return last; }
15.   public void setLast(String newValue) { last = newValue; }
16.
17.   public void parse(String fullName) {
18.      int firstSpace = fullName.indexOf(' ');
19.      int lastSpace = fullName.lastIndexOf(' ');
20.      if (firstSpace == -1) {
21.         first = "";
22.         middle = "";
23.         last = fullName;
24.      }
25.      else {
26.         first = fullName.substring(0, firstSpace);
27.         if (firstSpace < lastSpace)
28.            middle = fullName.substring(firstSpace + 1, lastSpace);
29.         else
30.            middle = "";
31.         last = fullName.substring(lastSpace + 1, fullName.length());
32.      }
33.   }
34.
35.   public String toString() {
36.      StringBuilder builder = new StringBuilder();
37.      builder.append(first);
38.      builder.append(' ');
39.      if (middle.length() > 0) {
40.         builder.append(middle.charAt(0));
41.         builder.append(". ");
42.      }
43.      builder.append(last);
44.      return builder.toString();
45.   }
46. }
```

Container-Managed Authentication and Authorization

In the preceding sections, you saw how a web application can use an LDAP directory to look up user information. It is up to the application to use that information appropriately, to allow or deny users access to certain resources. In this section, we discuss an alternative approach: *container-managed authentication*. This mechanism puts the burden of authenticating users on the application server.

It is much easier to ensure that security is handled consistently for an entire web application if the container manages authentication and authorization. The application programmer can then focus on the flow of the web application without worrying about user privileges.

Most of the configuration details in this chapter are specific to GlassFish and Tomcat, but other application servers have similar mechanisms.

To protect a set of pages, you specify access control information in the web.xml file. For example, the following security constraint restricts all pages in the protected subdirectory to authenticated users who have the role of registereduser or invitedguest.

```
<security-constraint>
   <web-resource-collection>
      <url-pattern>/protected/*</url-pattern>
   </web-resource-collection>
   <auth-constraint>
      <role-name>registereduser</role-name>
      <role-name>invitedguest</role-name>
   </auth-constraint>
</security-constraint>
```

The role of a user is assigned during authentication. Roles are stored in the user directory, together with usernames and passwords.

 NOTE: If JSF is configured to use a /faces prefix for JSF pages, then you must add a corresponding URL pattern to the security constraint, such as /faces/protected/* as in the preceding example.

Next, you need to specify how users authenticate themselves. The most flexible approach is form-based authentication. Add the following entry to web.xml:

```
<login-config>
    <auth-method>FORM</auth-method>
    <form-login-config>
        <form-login-page>/login.html</form-login-page>
        <form-error-page>/noauth.html</form-error-page>
    </form-login-config>
</login-config>
```

The form login configuration specifies a web page into which the user types the username and password. You are free to design any desired appearance for the login page, but you must include a mechanism to submit a request to j_security_check with request parameters named j_username and j_password. The following form will do the job:

```
<form method="POST" action="j_security_check">
    User name: <input type="text" name="j_username"/>
    Password:  <input type="password" name="j_password"/>
    <input type="submit" value="Login"/>
</form>
```

The error page can be any page at all.

When the user requests a protected resource, the login page is displayed (see Figure 10–18). If the user supplies a valid username and password, then the requested page appears. Otherwise, the error page is shown.

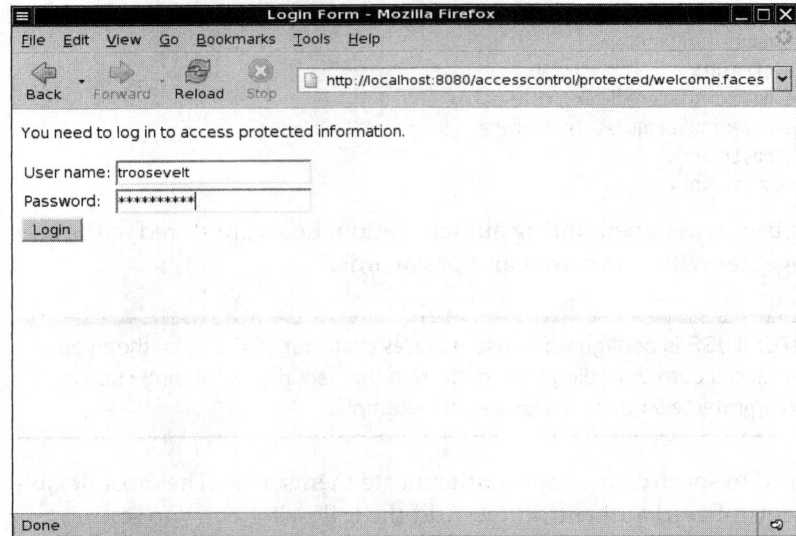

Figure 10–18   Requesting a protected resource

NOTE: To securely transmit the login information from the client to the server, you should use SSL (Secure Sockets Layer). Configuring a server for SSL is beyond the scope of this book. For more information, turn to http://java.sun.com/developer/technicalArticles/WebServices/appserv8-1.html (GlassFish) or http://jakarta.apache.org/tomcat/tomcat-5.5-doc/ssl-howto.html (Tomcat).

You can also specify "basic" authentication by placing the following login configuration into web.xml:

```
<login-conf>
  <auth-method>BASIC</auth-method>
  <realm-name>This string shows up in the dialog</realm-name>
</login-conf>
```

In that case, the browser pops up a password dialog (see Figure 10–19). However, a professionally designed web site will probably use form-based authentication.

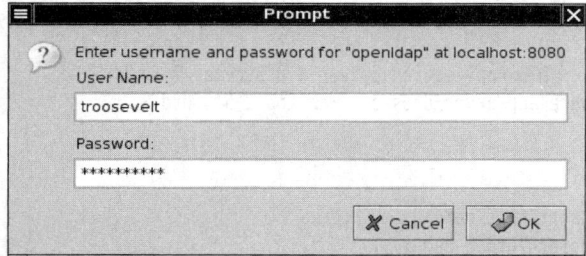

Figure 10–19   Basic authentication

The web.xml file describes only which resources have access restrictions and which roles are allowed access. It is silent on how users, passwords, and roles are stored. You configure that information by specifying a *realm* for the web application. A realm is any mechanism for looking up usernames, passwords, and roles. Application servers commonly supports several standard realms that access user information from one of the following sources:

- An LDAP directory
- A relational database
- A file (such as Tomcat's conf/tomcat-users.xml)

In GlassFish, you use the administration interface to configure a realm. In the Configuration -> Security -> Realms menu, create a new realm called openldap. Use the default class name and specify the following connection parameters as "additional properties":

```
directory: ldap://localhost:389
base-dn: ou=people,dc=corejsf,dc=com
jaas-context: ldapRealm
search-bind-dn: cn=Manager,dc=corejsf,dc=com
search-bind-password: secret
search-filter: uid=%s
group-base-dn: ou=groups,dc=corejsf,dc=com
group-target: cn
group-search-filter: uniqueMember=%d
```

You also need to supply a file WEB-INF/sun-web.xml, as shown in Listing 10–18. This file maps role names to group names. We use the same names for both.

Listing 10–18 accesscontrol/web/WEB-INF/sun-web.xml (GlassFish only)

```
1. <?xml version="1.0" encoding="UTF-8"?>
2.
3. <!DOCTYPE sun-web-app PUBLIC
4.    "-//Sun Microsystems, Inc.//DTD Application Server 9.0 Servlet 2.5//EN"
5.    "http://www.sun.com/software/appserver/dtds/sun-web-app_2_5-0.dtd">
6. <sun-web-app>
7.
8.    <security-role-mapping>
9.        <role-name>registereduser</role-name>
10.        <group-name>registereduser</group-name>
11.    </security-role-mapping>
12.    <security-role-mapping>
13.        <role-name>invitedguest</role-name>
14.        <group-name>invitedguest</group-name>
15.    </security-role-mapping>
16.
17. </sun-web-app>
```

To configure a realm in Tomcat, you supply a Realm element. Listing 10–19 shows a typical example, a JNDI realm for an LDAP server.

Listing 10–19	accesscontrol/src/conf/context.xml (Tomcat only)

```
 1. <Context path="/accesscontrol" docbase="webapps/accesscontrol.war">
 2. <Realm className="org.apache.catalina.realm.JNDIRealm"
 3.   debug="99"
 4.   connectionURL="ldap://localhost:389"
 5.   connectionName="cn=Manager,dc=corejsf,dc=com"
 6.   connectionPassword="secret"
 7.   userPattern="uid={0},ou=people,dc=corejsf,dc=com"
 8.   userPassword="userPassword"
 9.   roleBase="ou=groups,dc=corejsf,dc=com"
10.   roleName="cn"
11.   roleSearch="(uniqueMember={0})"/>
12. </Context>
```

The configuration lists the URL and login information, and describes how to look up users and roles. The Realm element is placed inside a Context element in the file context.xml. This is the preferred mechanism for supplying an application-specific realm in Tomcat.

 CAUTION: You can also configure a realm in the Engine or Host element of the server.xml file. However, that realm is then used by the manager application in addition to your regular web application. If you want to use the manager application to install your web applications, then you must make sure that the username and password that you use for installation is included in the realm, with a role of manager.

Since the application server is in charge of authentication and authorization, there is nothing for you to program. Nevertheless, you may want to have programmatic access to the user information. The HttpServletRequest yields a small amount of information, in particular, the name of the user who logged in. You get the request object from the external context:

```
ExternalContext external
   = FacesContext.getCurrentInstance().getExternalContext();
HttpServletRequest request
   = (HttpServletRequest) external.getRequest();
String user = request.getRemoteUser();
```

You can also test whether the current user belongs to a given role. For example,

```
String role = "admin";
boolean isAdmin = request.isUserInRole(role);
```

NOTE: Currently, there is no specification for logging off or for switching identities when using container-managed security. This is a problem, particularly for testing web applications. GlassFish and Tomcat use cookies to represent the current user. You need to quit and restart your browser (or at least clear personal data) whenever you want to switch your identity. We resorted to using Lynx for testing because it starts up much faster than a graphical web browser (see Figure 10–20).

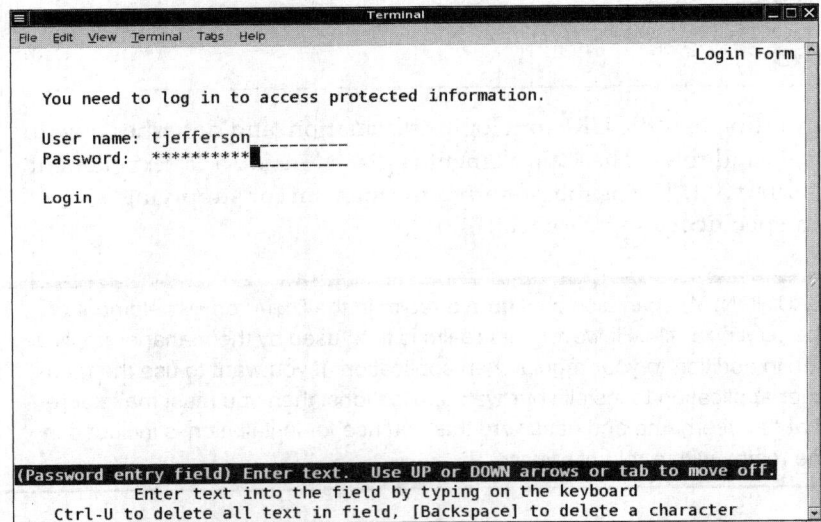

Figure 10–20 Using Lynx for testing a web application

We give you a skeleton application that shows container-managed security at work. When you access the protected resource protected/welcome.jsp (Listing 10–20), then the authentication dialog of Listing 10–21 is displayed. You can proceed only if you enter a username and password of a user belonging to the registereduser or invitedguest role.

Upon successful authentication, the page shown in Figure 10–21 is displayed. The welcome page shows the name of the registered user and lets you test for role membership.

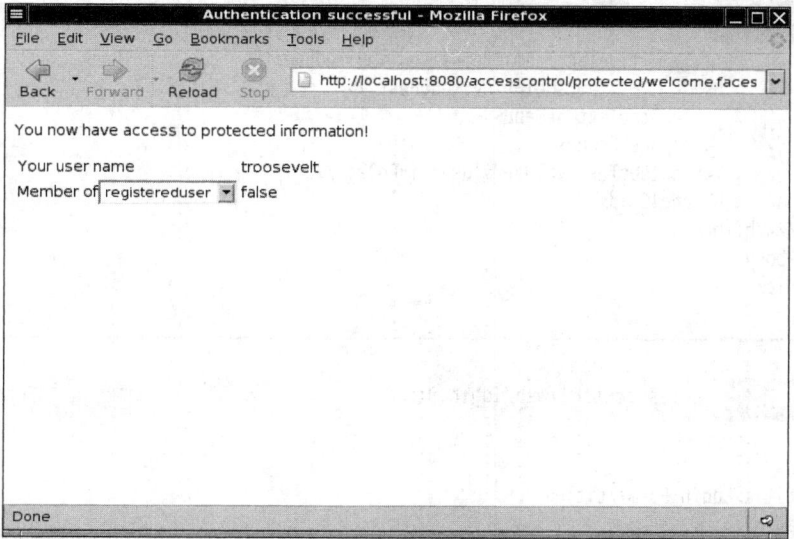

Figure 10–21 Welcome page of the authentication test application

---

Listing 10–20 accesscontrol/web/protected/welcome.jsp

```
 1. <html>
 2.    <%@ taglib uri="http://java.sun.com/jsf/core" prefix="f" %>
 3.    <%@ taglib uri="http://java.sun.com/jsf/html" prefix="h" %>
 4.    <f:view>
 5.       <head>
 6.          <title><h:outputText value="#{msgs.title}"/></title>
 7.       </head>
 8.       <body>
 9.          <h:form>
10.             <p><h:outputText value="#{msgs.youHaveAccess}"/></p>
11.             <h:panelGrid columns="2">
12.                <h:outputText value="#{msgs.yourUserName}"/>
13.                <h:outputText value="#{user.name}"/>
14.
15.                <h:panelGroup>
16.                   <h:outputText value="#{msgs.memberOf}"/>
17.                   <h:selectOneMenu onchange="submit()" value="#{user.role}">
18.                      <f:selectItem itemValue="" itemLabel="Select a role"/>
19.                      <f:selectItem itemValue="admin" itemLabel="admin"/>
20.                      <f:selectItem itemValue="manager" itemLabel="manager"/>
21.                      <f:selectItem itemValue="registereduser"
22.                         itemLabel="registereduser"/>
```

Listing 10–20   accesscontrol/web/protected/welcome.jsp (cont.)

```
23.                        <f:selectItem itemValue="invitedguest"
24.                            itemLabel="invitedguest"/>
25.                    </h:selectOneMenu>
26.                </h:panelGroup>
27.                <h:outputText value="#{user.inRole}"/>
28.            </h:panelGrid>
29.        </h:form>
30.    </body>
31.  </f:view>
32. </html>
```

Listing 10–21   accesscontrol/web/login.html

```
1. <html>
2.    <head>
3.       <title>Login Form</title>
4.    </head>
5.
6.    <body>
7.       <form method="post" action="j_security_check">
8.          <p>You need to log in to access protected information.</p>
9.          <table>
10.            <tr>
11.               <td>User name:</td>
12.               <td>
13.                  <input type="text" name="j_username"/>
14.               </td>
15.            </tr>
16.            <tr>
17.               <td>Password:</td>
18.               <td>
19.                  <input type="password" name="j_password"/>
20.               </td>
21.            </tr>
22.         </table>
23.         <input type="submit" value="Login"/>
24.      </form>
25.   </body>
26. </html>
```

Figure 10–22 shows the directory structure of the application. The web.xml file in Listing 10–22 restricts access to the protected directory. Listing 10–23 contains the page that is displayed when authorization fails. Listing 10–20 contains the protected page. You can find the code for the user bean in Listing 10–24 and the message strings in Listing 10–25.

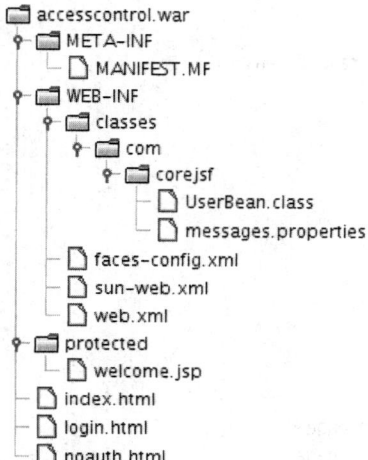

```
accesscontrol.war
├── META-INF
│   └── MANIFEST.MF
├── WEB-INF
│   ├── classes
│   │   └── com
│   │       └── corejsf
│   │           ├── UserBean.class
│   │           └── messages.properties
│   ├── faces-config.xml
│   ├── sun-web.xml
│   └── web.xml
├── protected
│   └── welcome.jsp
├── index.html
├── login.html
└── noauth.html
```

Figure 10–22   Directory structure of the access control application

Listing 10–22   accesscontrol/web/WEB-INF/web.xml

```xml
 1. <?xml version="1.0"?>
 2. <web-app xmlns="http://java.sun.com/xml/ns/javaee"
 3.    xmlns:xsi="http://www.w3.org/2001/XMLSchema-instance"
 4.    xsi:schemaLocation="http://java.sun.com/xml/ns/javaee
 5.       http://java.sun.com/xml/ns/javaee/web-app_2_5.xsd"
 6.    version="2.5">
 7.    <servlet>
 8.       <servlet-name>Faces Servlet</servlet-name>
 9.       <servlet-class>javax.faces.webapp.FacesServlet</servlet-class>
10.       <load-on-startup>1</load-on-startup>
11.    </servlet>
12.
13.    <servlet-mapping>
14.       <servlet-name>Faces Servlet</servlet-name>
15.       <url-pattern>*.faces</url-pattern>
16.    </servlet-mapping>
17.
18.    <welcome-file-list>
19.       <welcome-file>index.html</welcome-file>
20.    </welcome-file-list>
```

Listing 10–22 accesscontrol/web/WEB-INF/web.xml (cont.)

```
21.
22.    <security-constraint>
23.       <web-resource-collection>
24.          <web-resource-name>Protected Pages</web-resource-name>
25.          <url-pattern>/protected/*</url-pattern>
26.       </web-resource-collection>
27.       <auth-constraint>
28.          <role-name>registereduser</role-name>
29.          <role-name>invitedguest</role-name>
30.       </auth-constraint>
31.    </security-constraint>
32.
33.    <login-config>
34.       <auth-method>FORM</auth-method>
35.       <realm-name>openldap</realm-name>
36.       <form-login-config>
37.          <form-login-page>/login.html</form-login-page>
38.          <form-error-page>/noauth.html</form-error-page>
39.       </form-login-config>
40.    </login-config>
41.
42.    <security-role>
43.       <role-name>registereduser</role-name>
44.    </security-role>
45.    <security-role>
46.       <role-name>invitedguest</role-name>
47.    </security-role>
48. </web-app>
```

Listing 10–23 accesscontrol/web/noauth.html

```
1. <html>
2.    <head>
3.       <title>Authentication failed</title>
4.    </head>
5.
6.    <body>
7.       <p>Sorry--authentication failed. Please try again.</p>
8.    </body>
9. </html>
```

Listing 10–24 accesscontrol/src/java/com/corejsf/UserBean.java

```java
1. package com.corejsf;
2.
3. import java.util.logging.Logger;
4. import javax.faces.context.ExternalContext;
5. import javax.faces.context.FacesContext;
6. import javax.servlet.http.HttpServletRequest;
7.
8. public class UserBean {
9.     private String name;
10.    private String role;
11.    private Logger logger = Logger.getLogger("com.corejsf");
12.
13.    public String getName() {
14.        if (name == null) getUserData();
15.        return name == null ? "" : name;
16.    }
17.
18.    public String getRole() { return role == null ? "" : role; }
19.    public void setRole(String newValue) { role = newValue; }
20.
21.    public boolean isInRole() {
22.        ExternalContext context
23.            = FacesContext.getCurrentInstance().getExternalContext();
24.        Object requestObject = context.getRequest();
25.        if (!(requestObject instanceof HttpServletRequest)) {
26.            logger.severe("request object has type " + requestObject.getClass());
27.            return false;
28.        }
29.        HttpServletRequest request = (HttpServletRequest) requestObject;
30.        return request.isUserInRole(role);
31.    }
32.
33.    private void getUserData() {
34.        ExternalContext context
35.            = FacesContext.getCurrentInstance().getExternalContext();
36.        Object requestObject = context.getRequest();
37.        if (!(requestObject instanceof HttpServletRequest)) {
38.            logger.severe("request object has type " + requestObject.getClass());
39.            return;
40.        }
41.        HttpServletRequest request = (HttpServletRequest) requestObject;
42.        name = request.getRemoteUser();
43.    }
44. }
```

Listing 10–25   accesscontrol/src/java/com/corejsf/messages.properties

```
1. title=Authentication successful
2. youHaveAccess=You now have access to protected information!
3. yourUserName=Your user name
4. memberOf=Member of
```

API   *javax.servlet.HttpServletRequest*

- String getRemoteUser() **Servlet 2.2**

  Gets the name of the user who is currently logged in, or null if there is no such user.

- boolean isUserInRole(String role) **Servlet 2.2**

  Tests whether the current user belongs to the given role.

Using Web Services

When a web application needs to get information from an external source, it typically uses a remote procedure call mechanism. In recent years, *web services* have emerged as a popular technology for this purpose.

Technically, a web service has two components:

- A server that can be accessed with a transport protocol such as SOAP (Simple Object Access Protocol)
- A description of the service in the WSDL (Web Service Description Language) format

Fortunately, you can use web services, even if you know nothing at all about SOAP and just a little about WSDL.

To make web services easy to understand, we look at a concrete example: the Amazon Web Services, described at http://www.amazon.com/gp/aws/landing.html. The Amazon Web Services allow a programmer to interact with the Amazon system for a wide variety of purposes. For example, you can get listings of all books with a given author or title, or you can fill shopping carts and place orders.

Amazon makes these services available for use by companies that want to sell items to their customers, using the Amazon system as a fulfillment backend. To run our example program, you will need to sign up with Amazon and get a free accessKey that lets you connect to the service.

A primary attraction of web services is that they are language-neutral. We will access the Amazon Web Services by using the Java programming language, but other developers can equally well use C++ or PHP. The WSDL descriptor describes the services in a language-independent manner. For example, the WSDL for the Amazon E-Commerce Service (located at http://webservices.amazon.com/AWSECommerceService/AWSECommerceService.wsdl) describes an ItemSearch operation as follows:

```
<operation name="ItemSearch">
   <input message="tns:ItemSearchRequestMsg"/>
   <output message="tns:ItemSearchResponseMsg"/>
</operation>
...
<message name="ItemSearchRequestMsg">
   <part name="body" element="tns:ItemSearch"/>
</message>
<message name="ItemSearchResponseMsg">
   <part name="body" element="tns:ItemSearchResponse"/>
</message>
```

Here are the definitions of the ItemSearch and ItemSearchResponse types:

```
<xs:element name="ItemSearch">
   <xs:complexType>
      <xs:sequence>
         <xs:element name="MarketplaceDomain" type="xs:string" minOccurs="0"/>
         <xs:element name="AWSAccessKeyId" type="xs:string" minOccurs="0"/>
         <xs:element name="SubscriptionId" type="xs:string" minOccurs="0"/>
         <xs:element name="AssociateTag" type="xs:string" minOccurs="0"/>
         <xs:element name="XMLEscaping" type="xs:string" minOccurs="0"/>
         <xs:element name="Validate" type="xs:string" minOccurs="0"/>
         <xs:element name="Shared" type="tns:ItemSearchRequest" minOccurs="0"/>
         <xs:element name="Request" type="tns:ItemSearchRequest" minOccurs="0"
            maxOccurs="unbounded"/>
      </xs:sequence>
   </xs:complexType>
</xs:element>

<xs:element name="ItemSearchResponse">
   <xs:complexType>
      <xs:sequence>
         <xs:element ref="tns:OperationRequest" minOccurs="0"/>
         <xs:element ref="tns:Items" minOccurs="0" maxOccurs="unbounded"/>
      </xs:sequence>
   </xs:complexType>
</xs:element>
```

Several technologies provide a Java programming layer over the SOAP protocol. Using the JAX-WS technology, the ItemSearch operation becomes a method call

```
void itemSearch(String marketPlaceDomain, String awsAccessKeyId,
    String subscriptionId, String associateTag, String xmlEscaping, String validate,
    ItemSearchRequest shared, List<ItemSearchRequest> request,
    Holder<OperationRequest> opHolder, Holder<List<Items>> responseHolder)
```

 NOTE: The WSDL file does not specify *what* the service does. It specifies only the parameter and return types.

The ItemSearchRequest parameter type is defined as

```
<xs:complexType name="ItemSearchRequest">
    <xs:sequence>
        <xs:element name="Actor" type="xs:string" minOccurs="0"/>
        <xs:element name="Artist" type="xs:string" minOccurs="0"/>
        . . .
        <xs:element name="Author" type="xs:string" minOccurs="0"/>
        . . .
        <xs:element name="ResponseGroup" type="xs:string" minOccurs="0"
            maxOccurs="unbounded"/>
        . . .
        <xs:element name="SearchIndex" type="xs:string" minOccurs="0"/>
        . . .
</xs:complexType>
```

This description is translated into a class:

```
public class ItemSearchRequest {
    public ItemSearchRequest() { ... }
    public String getActor() { ... }
    public void setActor(String newValue) { ... }
    public String getArtist() { ... }
    public void setArtist(String newValue) { ... }
    ...
    public String getAuthor() { ... }
    public void setAuthor(String newValue) { ... }
    ...
    public List<String> getResponseGroup() { ... }
    ...
    public void setSearchIndex(String newValue) { ... }
    ...
}
```

To invoke the search service, construct an `ItemSearchRequest` object and call the `itemSearch` method of a "port" object:

```
ItemSearchRequest request = new ItemSearchRequest();
request.getResponseGroup().add("ItemAttributes");
request.setSearchIndex("Books");

Holder<List<Items>> responseHolder = new Holder<List<Items>>();
request.setAuthor(name);
port.itemSearch("", accessKey, "", "", "", "", request, null, null, responseHolder);
```

The port object translates the Java object into a SOAP message, passes it to the Amazon server, translates the returned message into a `ItemSearchResponse` object, and places the response in the "holder" object.

 NOTE: The Amazon documentation about the parameters and return values is extremely sketchy. However, you can fill out forms at `http://awszone.com/scratchpads/index.aws` to see the SOAP requests and responses. Those help you guess what parameter values you need to supply and what return values you can expect.

You obtain the port object through dependency injection. Annotate a field with the `@WebServiceRef` annotation:

```
@WebServiceRef(wsdlLocation=
    "http://webservices.amazon.com/AWSECommerceService/AWSECommerceService.wsdl")
private AWSECommerceService service;
```

Then call:

```
AWSECommerceServicePortType port = service.getAWSECommerceServicePort();
```

To generate a JAR file with the required "client-side artifact" classes, run these commands:

```
glassfish/bin/wsimport -p com.corejsf.amazon
    http://webservices.amazon.com/AWSECommerceService/AWSECommerceService.wsdl
jar cvf aws.jar com/corejsf/amazon/*.class
```

Place the resulting JAR file into the `WEB-INF/lib` directory of your JSF application.

To compile the `AuthorSearchBean` class, include *glassfish*/lib/appserv-ws.jar, *glassfish*/lib/appserv-ws.jar, and aws.jar in the class path.

NOTE: If you use Tomcat instead of GlassFish, you need to download and install the Java Web Services Developer Pack (JWSDP) from http://java.sun.com/webservices/jwsdp. Refer to the JWSDP documentation for more information.

Our sample application is straightforward. The user specifies an author name and clicks the "Search" button (see Figure 10–23).

Figure 10–23 Searching for books with a given author

We show the first page of the response in a data table (see Figure 10–24). This shows that the web service is successful. We leave it as the proverbial exercise for the reader to extend the functionality of the application.

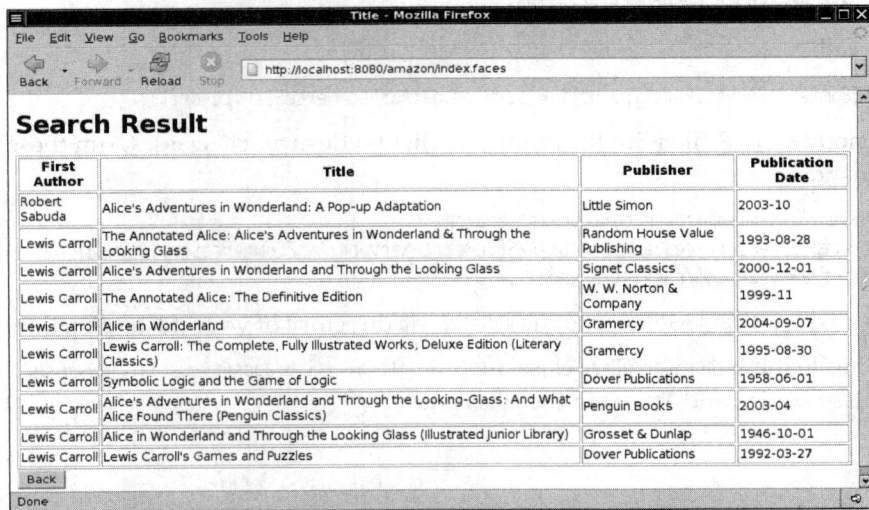

Figure 10–24 A search result

Figure 10–25 shows the directory structure of the application. Note the JAR file in the WEB-INF/lib directory.

The bean class in Listing 10–26 contains the call to the web service. The call returns an object of type ItemSearchResponse. We stash away that object so that the result.jsp page can display its contents.

Note how the access key is set in faces-config.xml (Listing 10–27). Be sure to supply your own key in that file.

Listing 10–28 through Listing 10–30 show the JSF pages. The result.jsp page contains a data table that displays information from the response object that was returned by the search service.

Finally, Listing 10–31 is the message bundle.

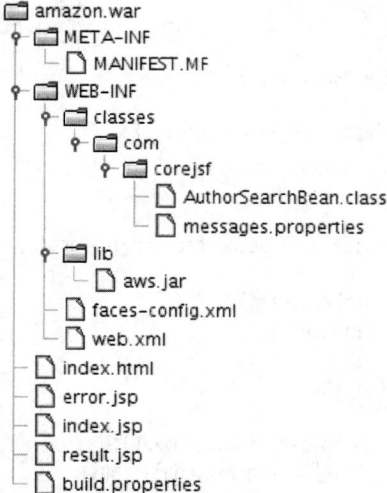

Figure 10–25   Directory structure of the web service test application

Listing 10–26   amazon/src/java/com/corejsf/AuthorSearchBean.java

```
1. package com.corejsf;
2.
3. import java.util.List;
4.
5. import javax.xml.ws.Holder;
6. import javax.xml.ws.WebServiceRef;
7.
```

Listing 10–26 amazon/src/java/com/corejsf/AuthorSearchBean.java (cont.)

```
 8. import com.corejsf.amazon.AWSECommerceService;
 9. import com.corejsf.amazon.AWSECommerceServicePortType;
10. import com.corejsf.amazon.Item;
11. import com.corejsf.amazon.ItemSearchRequest;
12. import com.corejsf.amazon.Items;
13.
14. public class AuthorSearchBean {
15.    @WebServiceRef(wsdlLocation="http://webservices.amazon.com/
16.       AWSECommerceService/AWSECommerceService.wsdl")
17.    private AWSECommerceService service;
18.
19.    private String name;
20.    private List<Item> response;
21.    private String accessKey;
22.
23.    public String getName() { return name; }
24.    public void setName(String newValue) { name = newValue; }
25.
26.    public void setAccessKey(String newValue) { accessKey = newValue; }
27.
28.    public String search() {
29.       try {
30.          AWSECommerceServicePortType port = service.getAWSECommerceServicePort();
31.
32.          ItemSearchRequest request = new ItemSearchRequest();
33.          request.getResponseGroup().add("ItemAttributes");
34.          request.setSearchIndex("Books");
35.          request.setAuthor(name);
36.
37.          Holder<List<Items>> responseHolder = new Holder<List<Items>>();
38.          port.itemSearch("", accessKey, "", "", "", "", request, null, null,
39.             responseHolder);
40.          response=responseHolder.value.get(0).getItem();
41.
42.          return "success";
43.       } catch(Exception e) {
44.          e.printStackTrace();
45.          return "failure";
46.       }
47.    }
48.
49.    public List<Item> getResponse() { return response; }
50. }
```

Listing 10–27 amazon/web/WEB-INF/faces-config.xml

```
1.  <?xml version="1.0"?>
2.  <faces-config xmlns="http://java.sun.com/xml/ns/javaee"
3.     xmlns:xsi="http://www.w3.org/2001/XMLSchema-instance"
4.     xsi:schemaLocation="http://java.sun.com/xml/ns/javaee
5.        http://java.sun.com/xml/ns/javaee/web-facesconfig_1_2.xsd"
6.     version="1.2">
7.     <navigation-rule>
8.        <from-view-id>/index.jsp</from-view-id>
9.        <navigation-case>
10.          <from-outcome>success</from-outcome>
11.          <to-view-id>/result.jsp</to-view-id>
12.       </navigation-case>
13.       <navigation-case>
14.          <from-outcome>failure</from-outcome>
15.          <to-view-id>/error.jsp</to-view-id>
16.       </navigation-case>
17.    </navigation-rule>
18.    <navigation-rule>
19.       <from-view-id>/result.jsp</from-view-id>
20.       <navigation-case>
21.          <from-outcome>back</from-outcome>
22.          <to-view-id>/index.jsp</to-view-id>
23.       </navigation-case>
24.    </navigation-rule>
25.    <navigation-rule>
26.       <from-view-id>/error.jsp</from-view-id>
27.       <navigation-case>
28.          <from-outcome>continue</from-outcome>
29.          <to-view-id>/index.jsp</to-view-id>
30.       </navigation-case>
31.    </navigation-rule>
32.
33.    <managed-bean>
34.       <managed-bean-name>authorSearch</managed-bean-name>
35.       <managed-bean-class>com.corejsf.AuthorSearchBean</managed-bean-class>
36.       <managed-bean-scope>session</managed-bean-scope>
37.       <managed-property>
38.          <property-name>accessKey</property-name>
39.          <value>XXXXXXXXXXXXXXXXXXXX</value>
40.       </managed-property>
41.    </managed-bean>
42.
```

Listing 10–27   amazon/web/WEB-INF/faces-config.xml (cont.)

```
43.    <application>
44.       <resource-bundle>
45.          <base-name>com.corejsf.messages</base-name>
46.          <var>msgs</var>
47.       </resource-bundle>
48.    </application>
49. </faces-config>
```

Listing 10–28   amazon/web/index.jsp

```
1. <html>
2.    <%@ taglib uri="http://java.sun.com/jsf/core" prefix="f" %>
3.    <%@ taglib uri="http://java.sun.com/jsf/html" prefix="h" %>
4.    <f:view>
5.       <head>
6.          <link href="styles.css" rel="stylesheet" type="text/css"/>
7.          <title><h:outputText value="#{msgs.title}"/></title>
8.       </head>
9.       <body>
10.         <h:form>
11.            <h1><h:outputText value="#{msgs.authorSearch}"/></h1>
12.            <h:outputText value="#{msgs.author}"/>
13.            <h:inputText value="#{authorSearch.name}"/>
14.            <h:commandButton value="#{msgs.search}"
15.               action="#{authorSearch.search}"/>
16.         </h:form>
17.      </body>
18.   </f:view>
19. </html>
```

Listing 10–29   amazon/web/result.jsp

```
1. <html>
2.    <%@ taglib uri="http://java.sun.com/jsf/core" prefix="f" %>
3.    <%@ taglib uri="http://java.sun.com/jsf/html" prefix="h" %>
4.    <f:view>
5.       <head>
6.          <title><h:outputText value="#{msgs.title}"/></title>
7.       </head>
8.       <body>
9.          <h:form>
```

Listing 10-29   amazon/web/result.jsp (cont.)

```
10.              <h1><h:outputText value="#{msgs.searchResult}"/></h1>
11.              <h:dataTable value="#{authorSearch.response}" var="item"
12.                  border="1">
13.                  <h:column>
14.                    <f:facet name="header">
15.                        <h:outputText value="#{msgs.author1}"/>
16.                    </f:facet>
17.                    <h:outputText value="#{item.itemAttributes.author[0]}"/>
18.                  </h:column>
19.                  <h:column>
20.                    <f:facet name="header">
21.                        <h:outputText value="#{msgs.title}"/>
22.                    </f:facet>
23.                    <h:outputText value="#{item.itemAttributes.title}"/>
24.                  </h:column>
25.                  <h:column>
26.                    <f:facet name="header">
27.                        <h:outputText value="#{msgs.publisher}"/>
28.                    </f:facet>
29.                    <h:outputText value="#{item.itemAttributes.publisher}"/>
30.                  </h:column>
31.                  <h:column>
32.                    <f:facet name="header">
33.                        <h:outputText value="#{msgs.pubdate}"/>
34.                    </f:facet>
35.                    <h:outputText value="#{item.itemAttributes.publicationDate}"/>
36.                  </h:column>
37.              </h:dataTable>
38.              <h:commandButton value="#{msgs.back}" action="back"/>
39.            </h:form>
40.        </body>
41.    </f:view>
42. </html>
```

Listing 10-30   amazon/web/error.jsp

```
1. <html>
2.    <%@ taglib uri="http://java.sun.com/jsf/core" prefix="f" %>
3.    <%@ taglib uri="http://java.sun.com/jsf/html" prefix="h" %>
4.    <f:view>
5.      <head>
6.        <title><h:outputText value="#{msgs.title}"/></title>
7.      </head>
```

Listing 10–30   amazon/web/error.jsp (cont.)

```
 8.      <body>
 9.        <h:form>
10.            <h1><h:outputText value="#{msgs.internalError}"/></h1>
11.            <p><h:outputText value="#{msgs.internalError_detail}"/></p>
12.            <p>
13.                <h:commandButton value="#{msgs.continue}" action="login"/>
14.            </p>
15.        </h:form>
16.      </body>
17.    </f:view>
18. </html>
```

Listing 10–31   amazon/src/java/com/corejsf/messages.properties

```
 1. title=A Faces Application that Invokes a Web Service
 2. authorSearch=Author Search at Amazon
 3. author=Author
 4. format=Format
 5. search=Search
 6. searchResult=Search Result
 7. internalError=Internal Error
 8. internalError_detail=To our chagrin, an internal error has occurred. \
 9.    Please report this problem to our technical staff.
10. continue=Continue
11. author1=First Author
12. title=Title
13. publisher=Publisher
14. pubdate=Publication Date
15. back=Back
```

You have now seen how your web applications can connect to external services, such as databases, directories, and web services. Here are some general considerations to keep in mind.

- JAR files are placed either in the WEB-INF/lib directory of the web application or in a library directory of the application server. You would do the latter only for libraries that are used by many applications, such as JDBC drivers.

- Application servers typically provide common services for database connection pooling, authentication realms, and so on. Dependency injection provides a convenient and portable mechanism for locating the classes that are needed to access these services.

- Configuration parameters can be placed into `faces-config.xml` or `web.xml`. The former is more appropriate for parameters that are intrinsic to the web application; the latter should be used for parameters that are determined at deployment time.

AJAX

Topics in This Chapter

Chapter 11

Web developers have long been mired in the mundane business of form processing without the means to acheive the high level of interactivity common in desktop applications. Or so we thought. When Google unveiled Google Maps, they proved that web applications can provide rich user interfaces that are just as compelling as desktop applications.

Google Maps also set in motion an incredible wave of innovation whose effects will be felt in the software development community for some time to come. In this chapter we will see some of that innovation in action as we explore using JSF and Ajax (Asynchronous JavaScript with XMLHttpRequest) together to create rich user interfaces. Along the way, we will discuss the following topics:

- Ajax fundamentals (page 530)
- Implementing Ajax with a servlet in a JSF application (page 532)
- Using JSF phase listeners for more complex Ajax scenarios (page 537)
- Form completion (page 534) and realtime validation (page 537)
- Accessing UI view state from an Ajax call (page 542)
- Dealing with client-side state saving and Ajax (page 542)
- Direct Web Remoting (page 543)
- Wrapping Ajax in JSF components (page 546)
- Using the Ajax4jsf framework (page 554)

Ajax Fundamentals

Ajax is a simple three-step process:

1.   Invoke a URL from JavaScript code on the client.
2.   Handle the URL on the server and write to the response.
3.   After the response is complete, integrate the response into the DOM (Document Object Model).

These steps are almost identical to what JSF does when you click a link, which illicits a request. JSF handles that request on the server by ultimately writing to the response, which overwrites the previous response.

The same applies for Ajax requests, except for the last step. In an Ajax request, we don't refresh the entire page; instead, we update only part of the page. That subtle difference lets us perform all kinds of interesting interactions that were heretofore unheard of in web applications.

To illustrate the steps in an Ajax request, we now take a look at the application shown in Figure 11-1.

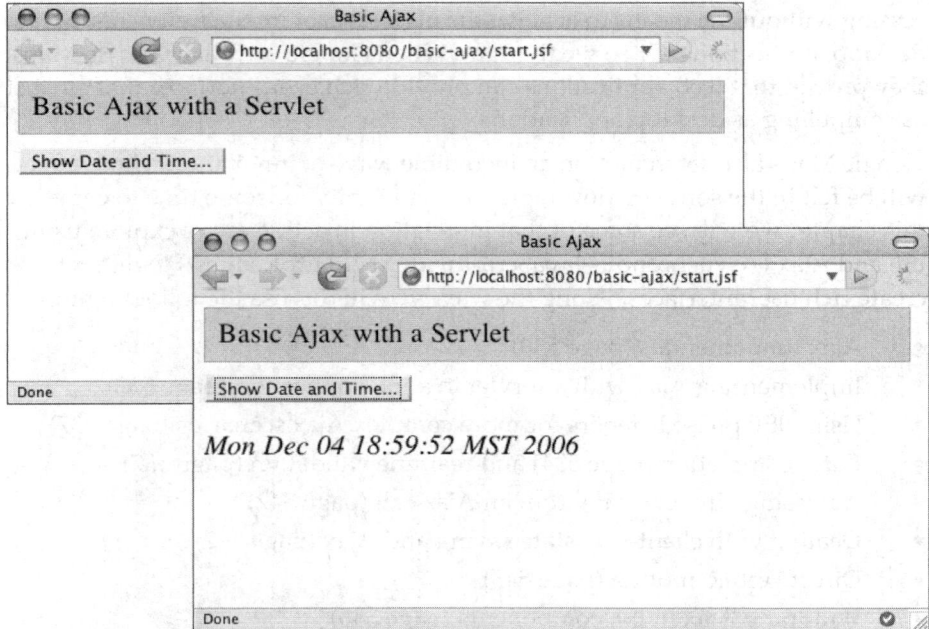

Figure 11-1   Basic Ajax with an XHR object and a servlet

The application shown in Figure 11–1 performs an Ajax request to obtain the current date and time from the server. Subsequently, on the client, the application integrates that response into the web page's DOM. That causes the date to update without refreshing the entire page.

Here is how it works. First, we have a DIV, which is initially empty. After the request, we update that DIV's inner HTML. Here is the DIV and the button that sets everything in motion:

```
<h:commandButton type="button"
   value="#{msgs.buttonPrompt}"
   onclick="showDateAndTime();"
   styleClass="button"/>

<div id="dateDIV" class="dateDiv"/>
```

Notice the button's type is button, which means it is a push button and not a submit button. When a user activates that button, JSF does not submit the surrounding form; instead, it calls the JavaScript showDateAndTime function, which looks like this:

```
<script type="text/javascript" language="Javascript1.1">
<!--
var xhr;

function showDateAndTime() {
   sendRequest("dateAndTime.ajax", // the URL
      processAjaxCall);    // the callback function
}

function sendRequest(url, handler) {
   initXHR();
   xhr.onreadystatechange = handler; // set callback function
   xhr.open("GET", url, true); // open asynchronous GET request
   xhr.send(null); // send the request without params
}

function initXHR() {
   if(window.XMLHttpRequest) {  // Not a Microsoft browser
      xhr = new XMLHttpRequest();
   }
   else if(window.ActiveXObject) { // Microsoft browser
      xhr = new ActiveXObject("Microsoft.XMLHTTP");
   }
}
```

```
function processAjaxCall() {
  if(xhr.readyState == 4) {  // if the request is finished...
    if(xhr.status == 200) { // ...and everything's okay
      // Get the dateDiv DIV and configure it
      // with the response text
      var dateDiv = window.document.getElementById("dateDIV")
      dateDiv.innerHTML = xhr.responseText;
    }
  }
}
```

The showDateAndTime function calls sendRequest(), which locates the XMLHttpRequest object—otherwise known as the XHR (XMLHttpRequest) object—with the initXHR function.

Once we have the XHR object, we are ready to go. First, we set the XHR object's callback function to our own processAjaxCall() and then we open and send the request. As the Ajax call progresses, the XHR object will repeatedly invoke our callback function with news concerning the request's progress.

As it turns out in practice, folks are mostly concerned with reacting to an Ajax request after it has successfully completed, as is the case for our example. In our callback function, we check for a successful request code, named readystate == 4 and status == 200. That status code corresponds to the HTTP status, meaning that the request was handled successfully.

Once the Ajax call has successfully completed, we set the inner HTML of our DIV to the response text. That response is generated by a servlet:

```
public class AjaxServlet extends HttpServlet {
  public void doGet(HttpServletRequest request, HttpServletResponse response)
          throws ServletException, IOException {
    response.setContentType("text/plain");
    response.setHeader("Cache-Control", "no-cache");
    response.setStatus(HttpServletResponse.SC_OK);
    response.getWriter().write(((new java.util.Date()).toString()));
  }
}
```

The preceding servlet is associated with the URL dateAndTime.ajax in the deployment descriptor, which associates all URLs that end in .ajax with the AjaxServlet.

NOTE: Ajax newcomers sometimes mistakenly believe that Ajax, because it provides a more responsive user interface, reduces server-side traffic. In fact, Ajax applications typically have more server-side traffic because each Ajax request involves a trip to the server. Because those requests are asynchronous, however, Ajax creates the perception of a more responsive UI, though it typically does not reduce the load on the server.

JavaScript Libraries

On page 531, we implemented about 30 lines of JavaScript code to execute the simplest of Ajax use cases. And there are undoubtedly browser-specific issues that our simplistic Ajax code does not account for.

To reduce the amount of JavaScript code you need to write for Ajax requests, and to make sure that those requests succeed across multiple browsers, you should use a JavaScript library that neatly encapsulates those boring details and sharp edges in convenient JavaScript objects.

The Prototype Library

For the rest of this chapter, we use the Prototype JavaScript library to take care of our Ajax calls. Prototype is a popular library that has Ajax support, among other things, built in. For example, here is the JavaScript from page 531, rewritten with Prototype:

```
function showDateAndTime() {
    new Ajax.Updater("dateDIV", // DIV to update
        "dateAndTime.ajax",     // URL
        { method: "get" });     // HTTP method
    }
}
```

In the preceding code fragment, we are using the Prototype Ajax.Updater object to perform the Ajax call and to update the dateDIV's inner HTML when the Ajax call is done. Note the reduction of code from the listing on page 531: We reduced about 30 lines of JavaScript to two lines. That is a whopping 94 percent reduction in code, and as an added bonus, we are guaranteed that our code will run on every significant browser. Not a bad return on investment.

For more information about Prototype, visit the Prototype homepage at http://prototype.conio.net.

The Fade Anything Technique Library

It is a good practice to provide visual cues for regions of a web page that you update with Ajax. One of the most popular visual cues is a slow fade from one color to another, typically from yellow to the default background color.

The Fade Anything Technique library is a scant 91 lines of JavaScript that lets you fade elements in a page. You can also control the fade's animation rate, starting and ending colors, and duration. We use the Fade Anything Technique library in the remaining examples in this chapter whenever we use Ajax to update elements in a page. For more information about the Fade Anything Technique library, see http://www.axentric.com.

Form Completion

One of the prototypical Ajax use cases is form completion, in which a user enters information in a field that causes other fields on the page to change. For example, we can use Ajax to react to the value entered into a zip code field, as shown in Figure 11–2.

When the user leaves the zip code text field, we send an Ajax request to the server, passing the current value of the zip code field as a request parameter. We associate the zip code field with the event handler, like this:

```
<h:inputText id="zip"
    size="5"
    value="#{bb.zip}"
    onblur="zipChanged(this.value);"/>
```

The zipChanged function uses Prototype to send the Ajax request:

```
<script type="text/javascript" language="Javascript1.1">
<!--
    function zipChanged(zip) {
        if(zip.length != 5) {
            clearCityAndStateFields();
        }
        else {
            new Ajax.Request(
                "zipChanged.ajax",    // URL
                {     method: "get", // HTTP method
                    parameters: "zip=" + zip, // Request params
                    onComplete: processZipCodeSelection, // callback
                });
        }
        ...
```

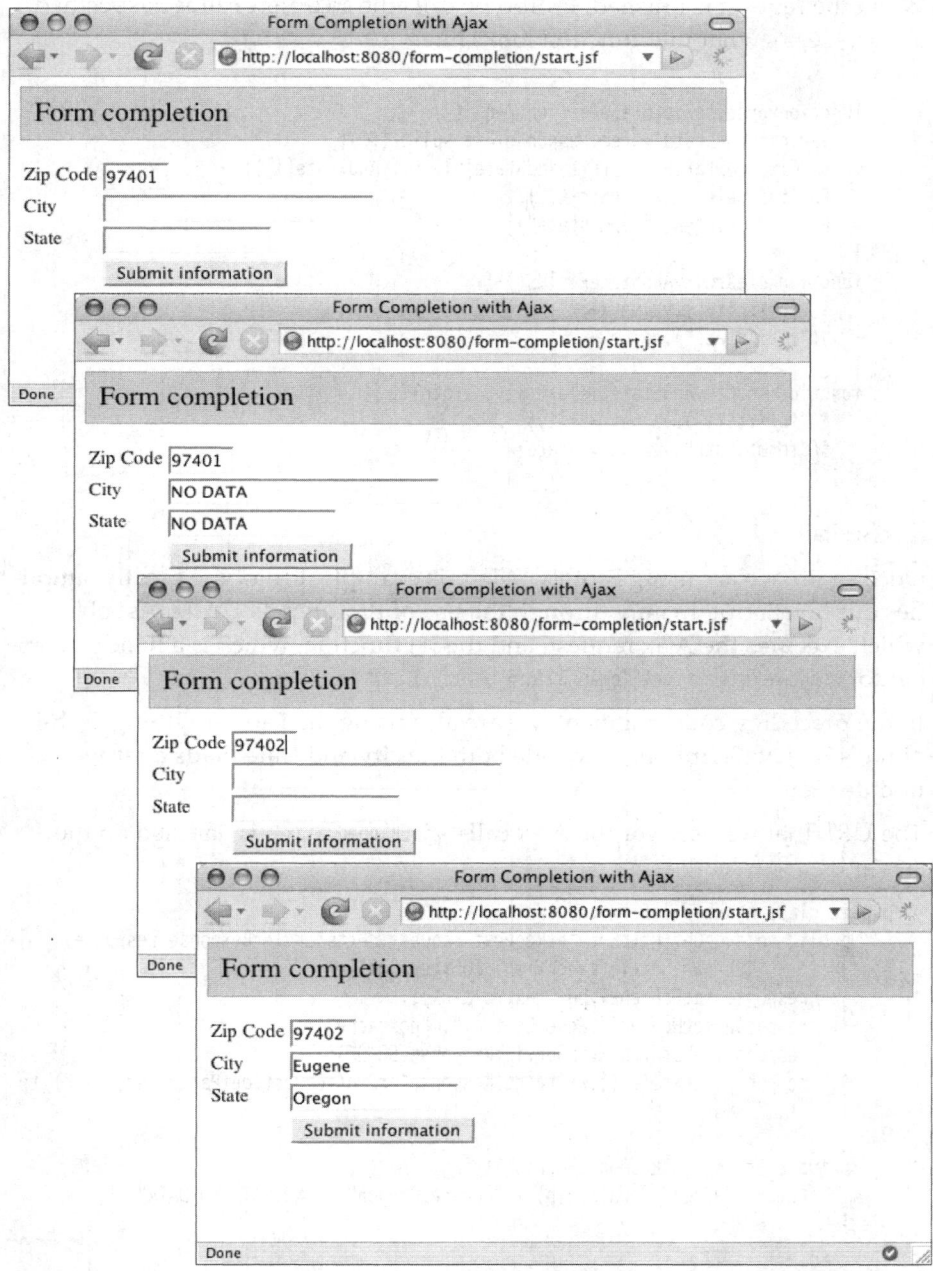

Figure 11–2 Form completion. Top: User enters an unknown zip code; Bottom: User enters a known zip code.

When the request is finished, Prototype calls the `onComplete` callback specified above. Here's what that function looks like:

```
...
function processZipCodeSelection(req) {
    var cityAndState = req.responseText.split(',');
    setCityAndStateFields(cityAndState[0], cityAndState[1]);
    Fat.fade_element("form:city");
    Fat.fade_element("form:state");
}
function clearCityAndStateFields() {
    $("form:city").value  = "";
    $("form:state").value = "";
}
function setCityAndStateFields(city, state) {
    $("form:city").value  = city;
    $("form:state").value = state;
}
-->
</script>
```

Once again, we are using Prototype in this example. Prototype greatly simplifies our JavaScript, mainly through the use of Prototype's `Ajax.Request` object, which executes the Ajax request, and the `$()` function, which is a handy shortcut for `window.document.getElementById()`.

In the preceding code fragment, we are also using the Fade Anything Technique's Fat JavaScript object to fade both the city and state fields after we update them.

The URL that we used for the Ajax call—`zipChanged.ajax`—is handled on the server by a servlet:

```
public class AjaxServlet extends HttpServlet {
    public void doGet(HttpServletRequest request, HttpServletResponse response)
            throws ServletException, IOException {
        response.setContentType("text/plain");
        response.setHeader("Cache-Control", "no-cache");
        response.setStatus(HttpServletResponse.SC_OK);
        response.getWriter().write(getResponseForZip(request.getParameter("zip")));
    }

    private String getResponseForZip(String zip) {
        return "97402".equals(zip) ? "Eugene,Oregon" : "NO DATA,NO DATA";
    }
}
```

If the servlet finds the zip code in our database, it writes a simple string to the response with this format: *City,State*. If we do not find a match, we return this instead: *NO DATA,NO DATA*. When the request is finished, we parse that response string and set the inner HTML of the city and state text fields to their respective values. Of course, in a real application, you might opt for a more robust database of zip codes.

 NOTE: The preceding form completion example requires very little knowledge of JSF, other than attaching JavaScript event handlers to JSF components (with DHTML attributes provided by the tags in the HTML tag library) and knowing how JSF creates client identifiers from component IDs. As that example illustrates, simple Ajax interactions can be easily implemented in a JSF application without much knowledge of JSF itself.

Realtime Validation

As we saw in "Form Completion" on page 534, you can implement basic Ajax in a JSF application with little more than a servlet and a few lines of JavaScript. In this example, we will implement realtime validation, which will give us the opportunity to explore some of the more complex interactions between Ajax and JSF.

The application shown in Figure 11–3 performs realtime validation. When the user enters the fifth character of the zip code, we execute an Ajax request to validate those five digits.

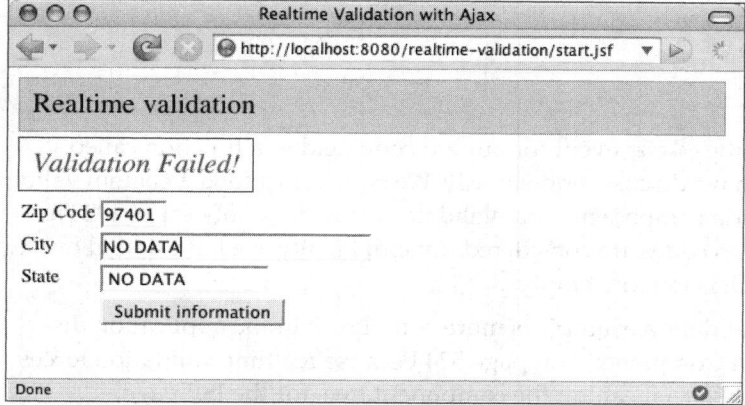

Figure 11–3   Realtime validation

On the server, we obtain a reference to the component that represents the zip code field, and iterate over that component's validators, invoking each in turn. If any of the validators attached to the component throws an exception, we catch the exception, write an error to the response, and terminate the request.

Subsequently, back on the client, we display that error response in a DIV. That scenario is shown in Figure 11–3, where the user has entered an invalid zip code.

Here is the pertinent JSP:

```
<html>
    <f:view>
        <body>
            ...
            <p><div id="errors" class="errors"></div></p>

            <h:form id="form">
                <h:panelGrid columns="2">
                    ...
                    <h:inputText id="zip"
                            size="5"
                            value="#{bb.zip}"
                            onfocus="clearCityAndStateFields();"
                            onblur="zipBlurred(this.value);"
                            onkeyup="zipChanged(this.value);">
                        <f:validator
                            validatorId="com.clarity.ZipCodeValidator"/>
                    </h:inputText>
                    ...
                </h:panelGrid>
            </h:form>
        </body>
    </f:view>
</html>
```

We have wired the onkeyup event for our zip code field to a function called zipChanged, which we discuss momentarily. We have also added a custom validator to the zip code component. That validator recognizes only the 97402 zip code; all other zip codes are considered invalid. Finally, we have added our errors DIV, which is initially empty.

This realtime validation example is more complex than the application discussed in "Form Completion" on page 534 because realtime validation forces us to access *view state*, meaning the component tree, for the JSP page.

Remember that we need to get a reference to the zip code component and iterate over its validators. To do that, we need access to the view state, *which is only available to POST requests*. Because of that restriction, we issue a POST request:

```
<script type="text/javascript" language="Javascript1.1">
<!--
function zipChanged(zip) {
   if(zip.length != 5) {
      hideErrorsDiv();
      return;
   }

   new Ajax.Request(window.document.forms[0].action,
      {      method: "post",
         parameters: "ajax=true&zip=" + zip,
         onComplete: processRealtimeValidation
   });
}
```

Notice the URL that we are using for this request: window.document.forms[0].action. That URL represents the action for the lone form in the page; in effect, we are tricking JSF into thinking that the user submitted the form. We are doing that because we want to access the view state for the current page, which JSF makes available—after the Restore View phase of the life cycle—when the form is submitted.

The preceding code shows how we invoke the URL from the client, but how do we handle the URL on the server? In this case, because we need access to view state, we cannot use a servlet. Servlets know nothing about JSF, so they cannot access view state. Instead, we use a phase listener and handle the request after the Restore View phase, when JSF has restored the component tree for us. Figure 11–4 shows the JSF life cycle when our phase listener handles the request.

After the Restore View phase, JSF invokes our phase listener, which checks to see if this is an Ajax request, signified by a request parameter; if so, the phase listener validates the component, generates a response, and short-circuits the life cycle. Here is a truncated listing of that phase listener:

```
public class AjaxPhaseListener implements PhaseListener {
    ...
    public PhaseId getPhaseId() {
        return PhaseId.RESTORE_VIEW; // interested in RESTORE VIEW phase only
    }
    public void beforePhase(PhaseEvent phaseEvent {
        // not interested because view state hasn't been restored yet
    }
```

```java
public void afterPhase(PhaseEvent phaseEvent) {
    FacesContext   fc = FacesContext.getCurrentInstance();
    Map requestParams = fc.getExternalContext()
                          .getRequestParameterMap();
    String ajaxParam = (String)requestParams.get("ajax");

    if("true".equals(ajaxParam)) {
        // Get a reference to the zip code component
        ...
        if(zip != null) {
            // Get the servlet response and the zip code
            // component's validators
            ...
            for (int i = 0; i < validators.length; i++) {
                // Invoke each validator and catch exceptions
            }
        }
        fc.responseComplete(); // that's all for this response
    }
  }
}
```

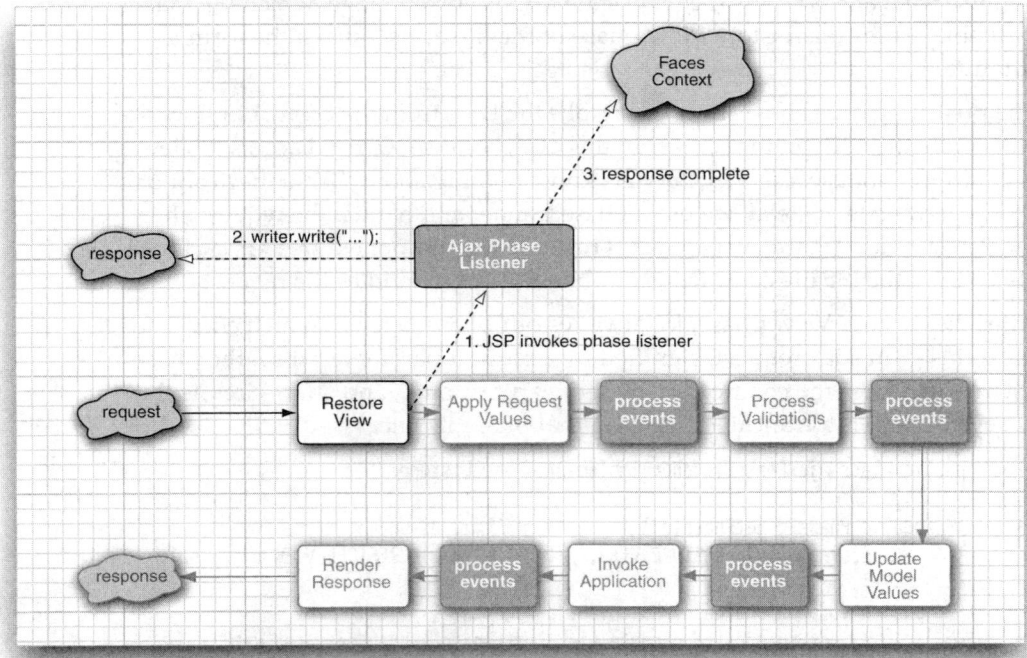

Figure 11–4 The JSF life cycle with an Ajax phase listener

The preceding code fragment leaves out the majority of the details of the method. Here, we emphasize that the phase listener goes into action after the Restore View phase of the life cycle, and after JSF has prepped the view state for us. If the current request is an Ajax request—signified by a request parameter named ajax whose value must be true—the phase listener locates the zip code component and its validators, iterates over the validators, and generates a response. Finally, it calls the responseComplete method on the Faces context to short-circuit the rest of the life cycle.

Notice that the phase listener only short-circuits the life cycle when we explicitly qualify a request as an Ajax request. That qualification is necessary because we must distinguish between Ajax requests and non-Ajax requests: We cannot short-circuit the life cycle on every request, or our application would not work at all.

Finally, back on the client, we process the response:

```
function processRealtimeValidation(xhr) {
    var rt = xhr.responseText;
    if(xhr.responseText == "okay") {
        hideErrorsDiv();
    }
    else {
        showErrorsDiv(rt);
    }
}
```

If the response text is okay, we know the zip code was valid, so we hide the errors DIV. If the response text is anything other than okay, we display the response text in the errors DIV.

API | **javax.faces.context.FacesContext**

- void responseComplete()

    Forces JSF to short-circuit the life cycle. After this method is called, JSF will not execute the next phase in the life cycle.

API | **javax.faces.event.EditableValueHolder**

- Validator[] getValidators()

    Returns an array of validators associated with an input component. All input components implement the EditableValueHolder interface.

NOTE: POST requests are meant to change state on the server, whereas GET requests are for obtaining information only. Because of that distinction, JSF makes view state available to only to POST requests, which allows modifications to view state. If you're implementing functionality that requires access to view state, then you must send a POST request.

Propagating Client-Side View State

If your application stores view state on the client and you need access to view state, then you must propagate that state with your Ajax calls.

If you look carefully at the phase listener from the previous example, you will see that we have taken client-side state saving into account. Notice that we invoke a JavaScript function called getJSFState:

```
<script type="text/javascript" language="Javascript1.1">
<!--
   function zipChanged(zip) {
       var jsfState = getJSFState();
       new Ajax.Request(
          window.document.forms[0].action,
          {method: "post",
           parameters: "ajax=true&zip=" + zip + "&javax.faces.ViewState=" + jsfState,
           onComplete: processRealtimeValidation
           });
       }
       ...
```

The getJSFState function returns a string that we pass through to the request as a request parameter named javax.faces.ViewState. That string is the serialized version of the current component tree, which was previously stored by JSF in a hidden field, named javax.faces.ViewState component.

```
   ...
   function getJSFState() {
      var state = window.document.getElementsByName("javax.faces.ViewState");
      var value = null;

      if(null != state && 0 < state.length) {
          value = state[0].value;
          var encodedValue = encodeURI(value);
          var re = new RegExp("\\+", "g");
          return encodedValue.replace(re, "\%2B");
      }
   }
```

To get the serialized view state, we access the value of the hidden field with the special name javax.faces.ViewState. Then we escape all plus signs in the string and return it to the zipChanged function, which propagates the state.

If you are saving state on the server, none of this section applies to your application. Still, in general, you should account for client-side state saving so that your application works in both cases.

 NOTE: When you store view state on the client, JSF serializes the view, optionally compresses it, and stores the resulting string in a hidden field. The name of the field, javax.faces.ViewState, is specified in the JSF 1.2 specification, so you can write code, such as the preceding JavaScript, that accesses the view state. However, earlier versions of the JSF specification did not explicitly define the name of that hidden field. As a result, if you've written code for JSF 1.1 that relies on that name, you may have to update your code for JSF 1.2.

Direct Web Remoting

We've seen how JavaScript libraries can greatly reduce the amount of JavaScript code you need to write to implement Ajax functionality in your applications. For example, earlier in this chapter, we replaced approximately 30 lines of handcrafted JavaScript with a single call to the Prototype library:

```
function showDateAndTime() {
    new Ajax.Updater("dateDIV",  // DIV to update
        "dateAndTime.ajax",      // URL
        { method: "get" });      // HTTP method
    }
}
```

In the preceding code fragment, we execute an Ajax GET request with the URL dateAndTime.ajax. When the request is complete, Prototype updates the inner HTML of the dateDIV with the response text. Can things possibly get easier than that?

In fact, they can. Remember that although the JavaScript in the preceding code fragment is simple enough, you still have to implement server-side logic to handle the Ajax request. That means you have to implement a servlet, phase listener, or some other special, Ajax-savvy object that knows how to handle your Ajax requests. That Ajax-savvy object is a middleman of sorts that typically calls JavaBean methods of one kind or another.

It would be nice if we could dispense with the middleman and just invoke JavaBean methods directly from JavaScript. For example, what if we could transform the preceding JavaScript into a simple function invocation, like this:

```
$("dateDIV").innerHTML = ZipCodes.getCityAndStateForZip(zip);
```

Now we have really simplified our Ajax call, down to a single function invocation. All of this is possible with the open-source Direct Web Remoting (DWR), which aims to make remote method calls as simple as possible.

DWR is a simple, yet powerful, framework that has a good deal of mind share in the Java community. The homepage for DWR is shown in Figure 11–5.

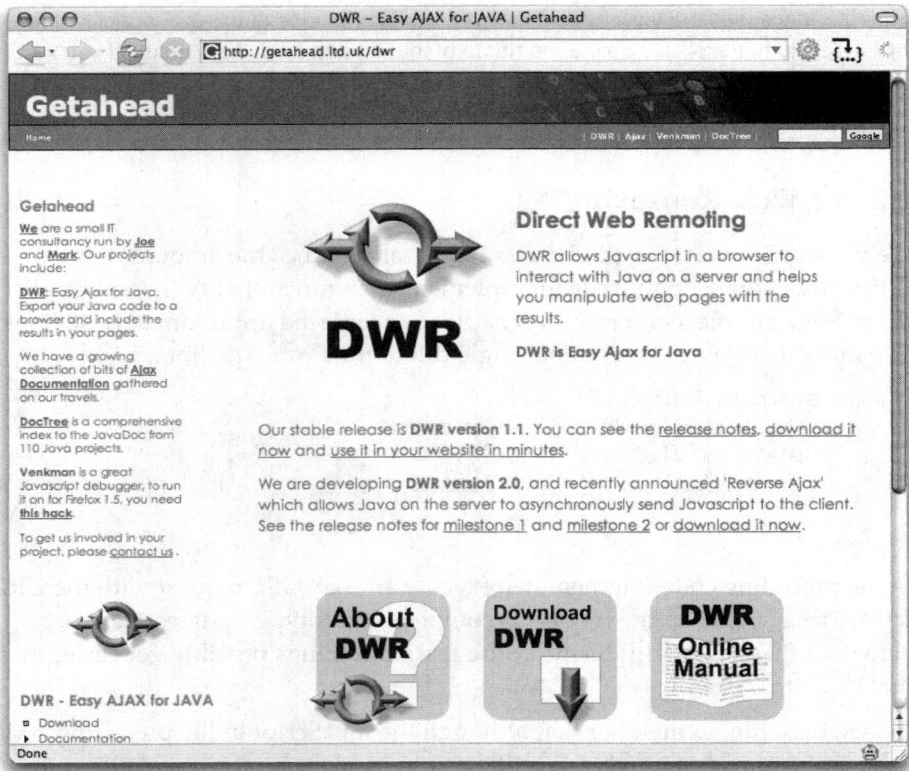

Figure 11–5   The DWR homepage

To illustrate the usefulness of DWR, we rewrite the application discussed in "Form Completion" on page 534 to use DWR. The DWR version of the application is shown in Figure 11–6.

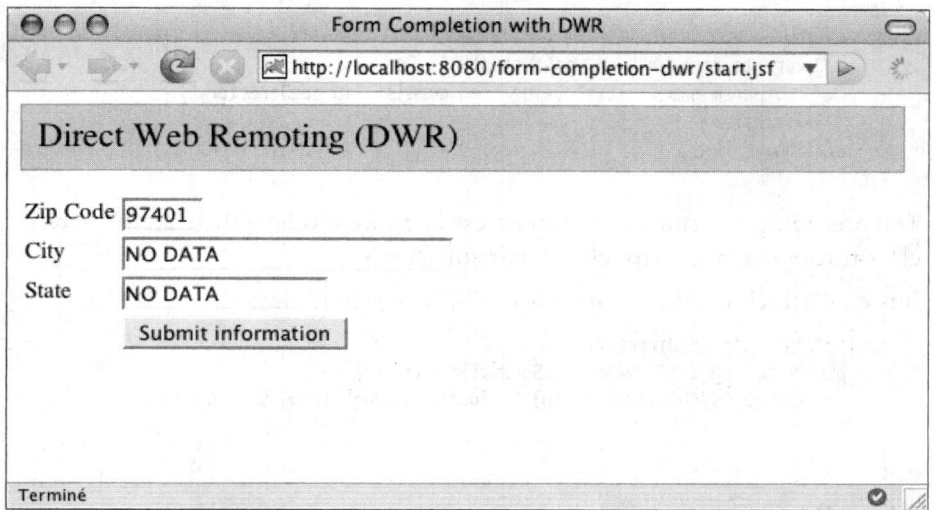

Figure 11–6   Using DWR

The application shown in Figure 11–6 uses a DWR call to a server-side bean method:

```
<script type='text/javascript'
        src='/form-completion-dwr/dwr/interface/ZipCodes.js'></script>
...
function zipChanged(zip) {
   if(zip.length != 5) {
      clearCityAndStateFields();
   }
   else {
      // A DWR call. See /WEB-INF/dwr.xml
      ZipCodes.getCityAndStateForZip(zip, processZipCodeSelection);
   }
}
```

In the preceding code, we invoke the getCityAndStateForZip method on a Java-Script object named ZipCodes. That JavaScript object is available to us by virtue of the formulaic script element in the preceding code.

We associate the ZipCodes JavaScript object with a JavaBean on the server in an XML configuration file, like this:

```
<!DOCTYPE dwr PUBLIC
    "-//GetAhead Limited//DTD Direct Web Remoting 1.0//EN"
    "http://www.getahead.ltd.uk/dwr/dwr10.dtd">
```

```
<dwr>
    <allow>
        <create creator="new" javascript="ZipCodes">
            <param name="class" value="com.corejsf.ZipCodeDirectory"/>
        </create>
    </allow>
</dwr>
```

The preceding incantation allows access to all methods of the ZipCodeDirectory class through a JavaScript object named ZipCodes.

It is a bit anticlimactic, but here is the ZipCodeDirectory class:

```
public class ZipCodeDirectory {
    public String getCityAndStateForZip(String zip) {
        return "97402".equals(zip) ? "Eugene,Oregon" : "NO DATA,NO DATA";
    }
}
```

Ajax Components

Ajax is cool, but implementing—and especially reimplementing and debugging—low-level Ajax code is not cool. To rid ourselves of that burden entirely, we now turn to JSF custom components, which happen to be an excellent vehicle for encapsulating Ajax code. Once encapsulated, our custom components can be used via JSP tags to create compelling user experiences.

Hybrid Components

It should be fairly obvious that the road to Ajax bliss can be paved by implementing custom renderers that emit JavaScript code.

Even more interesting, however, are JSF components that wrap existing JavaScript components. After all, why would you want to implement components, such as accordions or drag-and-drop, from scratch when you have a wide variety of existing components to choose from: Prototype, Scriptaculous, Dojo, and Rico? Wrapping those components with JSF components, so that you can use them in your JSF applications, is a straightforward task.

The Rico Accordion

Rico is a one of a number of frameworks based on Prototype. Rico provides amenities such as drag-and-drop and a handful of useful components. One of those components is an accordion, in the Flash tradition, shown in Figure 11–7.

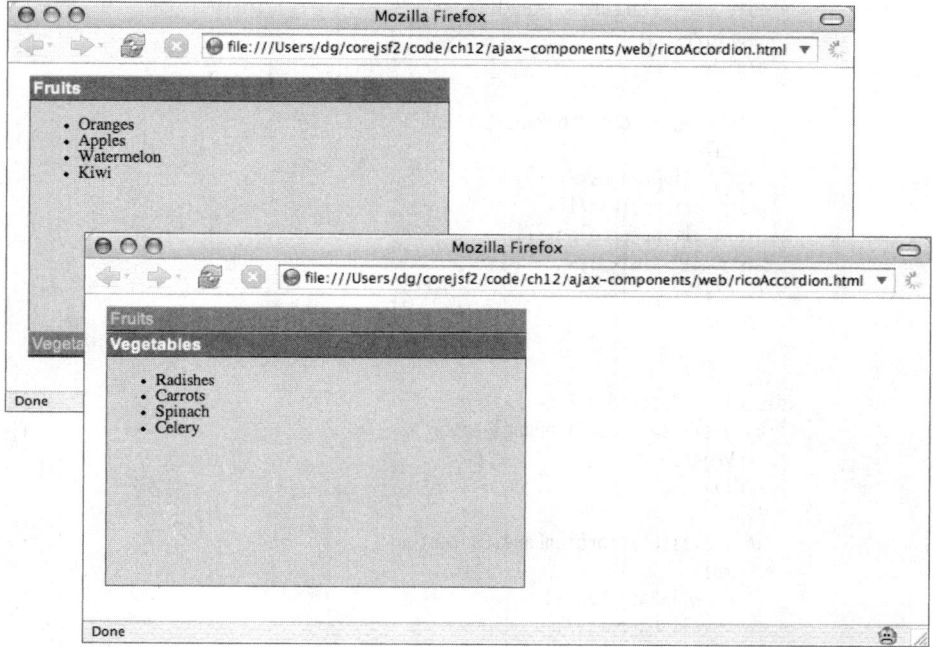

Figure 11–7   The Rico accordion

The Rico accordion component is similar to a tabbed pane with fancy transitions—when you click the header of an accordion panel, the header animates either up or down to reveal its associated panel. Here is how you implement the accordion, shown in Figure 11–7, using HTML:

```html
<html>
   <head>
      <link href="styles.css" rel="stylesheet" type="text/css"/>
      <script type='text/javascript' src='prototype.js'></script>
      <script type='text/javascript' src='rico-1.1.2.js'></script>
      <script type='text/javascript'>
         function createAccordion() {
            new Rico.Accordion($("theDiv"));
         }
      </script>
   </head>

   <body onload="createAccordion();">
      <div id="theDiv" class="accordion">
         <div class="accordionPanel">
```

```
          <div class="accordionPanelHeader">
              Fruits
          </div>

          <div class="accordionPanelContent">
            <ul>
                <li>Oranges</li>
                <li>Apples</li>
                <li>Watermelon</li>
                <li>Kiwi</li>
            </ul>
          </div>
      </div>

      <div class="accordionPanel">
          <div class="accordionPanelHeader">
              Vegetables
          </div>

          <div class="accordionPanelContent">
            <ul>
                <li>Radishes</li>
                <li>Carrots</li>
                <li>Spinach</li>
                <li>Celery</li>
            </ul>
          </div>
        </div>
      </div>
  </body>
</html>
```

When the preceding page loads, Rico creates an instance of Rico.Accordion, which adds behaviors to the DIV that it's passed. In this case, Rico endows the DIV with JavaScript event handlers that react to mouse clicks in the header of each panel.

In the next section, we see how to wrap the Rico accordion in a JSF component.

The JSF-Rico Accordion Hybrid

The application shown in Figure 11–8 is a hybrid component, meaning a JSF component that wraps a JavaScript component. In this case, that JavaScript component is a Rico accordion component.

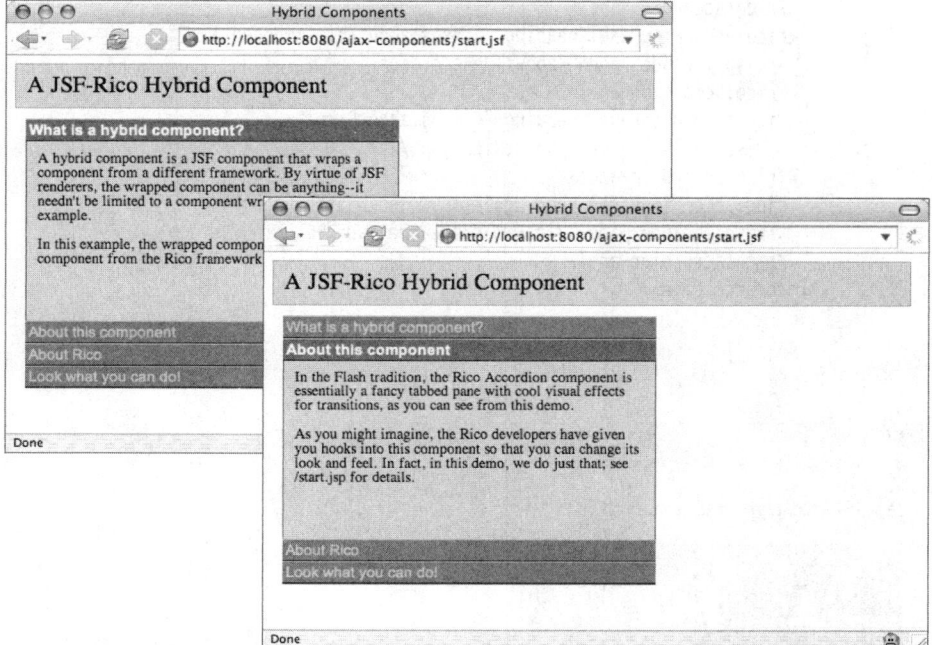

Figure 11–8   A JSF component that wraps a Rico accordion component

The Rico component automatically adds a scrollbar if the content of a panel overflows the size of the panel, so we get that functionality for free. As Figure 11–9 illustrates, you can put anything you want in an accordion panel, including forms.

Using the accordion component is simple:

```
<html>
   <%@ taglib uri="http://java.sun.com/jsf/html" prefix="h" %>
   <%@ taglib uri="http://java.sun.com/jsf/core" prefix="f"%>
   <%@ taglib uri="http://corejsf/rico" prefix="rico"%>
   <f:view>
      ...
      <rico:accordion name="bookAccordion"
            panelHeight="175"
            styleClass="accordion"
            panelClass="accordionPanel"
            headerClass="accordionPanelHeader"
            contentClass="accordionPanelContent">
         <rico:accordionPanel heading="#{msgs.whatIsAHybrid}">
               <jsp:include page="/whatIsAHybrid.jsp"/>
```

```
        </rico:accordionPanel>
        <rico:accordionPanel heading="#{msgs.aboutThisComponent}">
           <jsp:include page="/aboutTheAccordion.jsp"/>
        </rico:accordionPanel>
        <rico:accordionPanel heading="#{msgs.aboutRico}">
           <jsp:include page="/aboutRico.jsp"/>
        </rico:accordionPanel>
        <rico:accordionPanel heading="#{msgs.lookWhatYouCanDo}">
           <jsp:include page="/lookWhatYouCanDo.jsp"/>
        </rico:accordionPanel>
     </rico:accordion>
     ...
   </f:view>
</html>
```

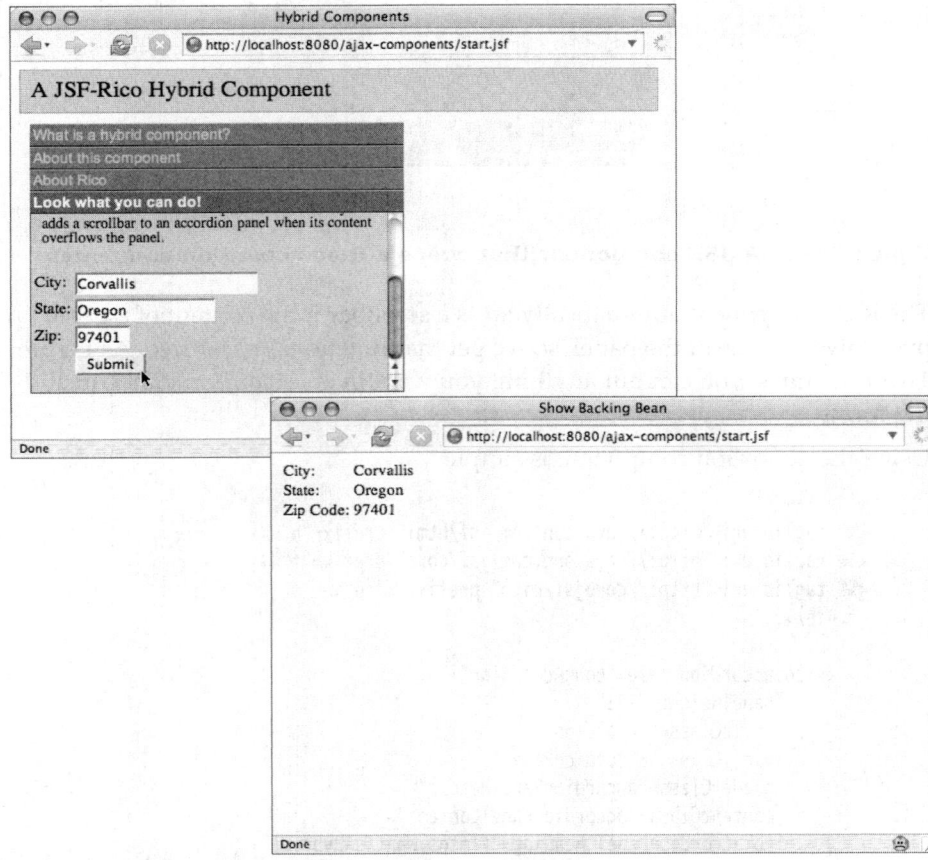

Figure 11–9   Putting forms inside accordion panels

The `rico:accordion` and `rico:accordionPanel` tags represent custom renderers that we pair with `UICommand` components. Those renderers generate the Rico-aware Java-Script that creates the Rico accordion.

The Rico-aware renderers do two things you may find useful if you decide to implement JSF components with Ajax capabilities of your own: keeping your JavaScript separate from your renderers and transmitting JSP tag attributes to that JavaScript code.

Keeping JavaScript Out of Renderers

One thing quickly becomes apparent if you start implementing Ajax-enabled custom components: You do not want to generate JavaScript with `PrintWriter.write` statements. It is much easier to maintain JavaScript if it is in a file of its own. Finally, it is convenient to colocate JavaScript files with the Java classes that use them. Let's see how we can do those things.

The `AccordionRenderer` class generates a script element whose src attribute's value is `rico-script.jsf`:

```
public class AccordionRenderer extends Renderer {
    public void encodeBegin(FacesContext fc,
            UIComponent component)
            throws IOException {
        ResponseWriter writer = fc.getResponseWriter();
        // write the script for loading the Rico JS file
        writer.write("<script type='text/javascript'"
            + "src='rico-script.jsf'>"
            + "</script>");
        ...
    }
}
```

That src attribute—`rico-script.jsf`—results in a call to the server with the URL `rico-script.jsf`. That URL is handled by a phase listener:

```
public class AjaxPhaseListener implements PhaseListener {
    private static final String RICO_SCRIPT_REQUEST = "rico-script";
    private static final String PROTOTYPE_SCRIPT_FILE = "prototype.js";
    private static final String SCRIPTACULOUS_SCRIPT_FILE = "scriptaculous.js";
    private static final String RICO_SCRIPT_FILE = "rico-1.1.2.js";

    public PhaseId getPhaseId() {    // We need access to the view state
        return PhaseId.RESTORE_VIEW; // in afterPhase()
    }
    public void beforePhase(PhaseEvent phaseEvent) { // not interested
    }
```

```
        public void afterPhase(PhaseEvent phaseEvent) { // After the RESTORE VIEW phase
            FacesContext fc = FacesContext.getCurrentInstance();
            if(((HttpServletRequest)fc.getExternalContext()
                                .getRequest()).getRequestURI()
                                .contains(RICO_SCRIPT_REQUEST)) {
                try {
                    readAndWriteFiles(fc, phaseEvent, new String[] {
                            PROTOTYPE_SCRIPT_FILE,
                            SCRIPTACULOUS_SCRIPT_FILE,
                            RICO_SCRIPT_FILE
                    });
                }
                catch(java.io.IOException ex) {
                    ex.printStackTrace();
                }
                phaseEvent.getFacesContext().responseComplete();
            }
        }
        private void readAndWriteFiles(FacesContext fc, PhaseEvent pe, STring[] files) {
            // Read files and write them to the response
        }
    }
```

If the request URI contains the string rico-script, the phase listener reads three files and writes them to the response: prototype.js, scriptaculous.js, and rico-1.1.2.js.

Realize that this roundabout way of reading JavaScript files could be avoided by simply specifying the files themselves in the script element generated by the accordion renderer; however, that would require us to hardcode the location of that file. Because we have used a phase listener to load the JavaScript files, we can colocate those JavaScript files with the phase listener, without having to explicitly specify the JavaScript file locations in the JSP pages.

Transmitting JSP Tag Attributes to JavaScript Code

If you implement Ajax-enabled JSF components, you will most likely need to transfer tag attributes, specified in a JSP page, to JavaScript that is stored in a file of its own, as described in "Keeping JavaScript Out of Renderers" on page 551. Let's see how that is done with the accordion component.

First, the accordion tag class provides setters and getters, which are called by JSP, for its tag attribute values. After JSP transmits tag attribute values to tag properties, JSF calls the tag's setProperties method, which passes those attribute values through to the component.

```java
public class AccordionTag extends UIComponentELTag {
    private ValueExpression name = null;
    ...
    public void setName(ValueExpression name) { // Called by JSP
        this.name = name;
    }
    ...
    protected void setProperties(UIComponent component) { // Called by JSF
        ...
        component.setValueExpression("name", name);
        ...
    }
}
```

When the component is rendered, the accordion renderer obtains the tag values from the component and generates a small snippet of JavaScript that passes the component values through to the JavaScript; in this case, we are passing the name of the DIV that Rico will endow with accordion functionality. That DIV was originally specified as the name attribute of the rico:accordion tag.

```java
public class AccordionRenderer extends Renderer {
    ...
    public void encodeEnd(FacesContext fc,
            UIComponent component)
            throws IOException {
        ResponseWriter writer = fc.getResponseWriter();
        // Finish enclosing DIV started in encodeBegin()
        writer.write("</div>");
        // Write the JS that creates the Rico Accordian component
        Map accordionAttributes = component.getAttributes();
        String div = (String)accordionAttributes.get("name");
        writer.write("<script type='text/javascript'>");
        writer.write("new Rico.Accordion( $('" + div + "'), ");
        writeAccordionAttributes(writer, accordionAttributes);
        writer.write(");");
        writer.write("</script>");
    }
    public boolean getRendersChildren() {
        return false;
    }
    private void writeAccordionAttributes(ResponseWriter writer, Map attrs) {
        try {
            // Add the rest of the Accordion's properties here.
            // See rico-1.1.2.js, line 179.
            writer.write(" { ");
            writer.write("   panelHeight: " + attrs.get("panelHeight"));
            writer.write(" } ");
```

```
        } catch (IOException e) {
            e.printStackTrace();
        }
    }
}
```

Ajax4jsf

Now that we have discussed the particulars of both implementing and encapsulating Ajax with JSF, we turn our attention to a framework that takes care of many of those details for you: Ajax4jsf.

Ajax4jsf is a java.net project, whose homepage (https://ajax4jsf.dev.java.net/ajax/ajax-jsf) is shown in Figure 11–10. Ajax4jsf provides 18 handy JSP tags that you can use to seamlessly integrate Ajax into your JSF applications. You can find a list of all the tags and their corresponding descriptions at the Ajax4jsf homepage. In our brief exploration of Ajax4jsf, we will discuss two of those tags: a4j:support, which lets you attach Ajax functionality to a component, typically an input component; and a4j:status, which renders JSF components at the start and end of each Ajax4jsf Ajax call.

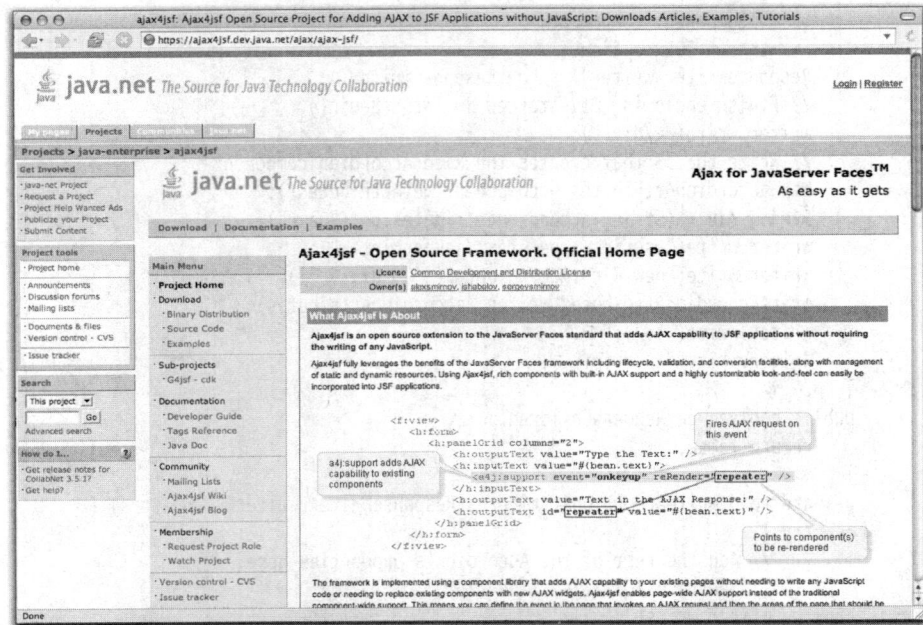

Figure 11–10   The Ajax4jsf homepage

To illustrate both the power and pitfalls of using Ajax4jsf, we revisit the form completion and realtime validation examples from earlier in this chapter.

Implementing Form Completion with Ajax4jsf

Figure 11–11 and Figure 11–12 show the form completion example implemented with Ajax4jsf. The top picture in Figure 11–11 shows the result of entering an unrecognized zip code (the only zip code the application recognizes is 97402), and subsequently tabbing out of the zip code field. In that case, we use Ajax4jsf to make an Ajax call that determines that 97401 is unrecognized and updates the city and state text fields accordingly.

The bottom picture in Figure 11–11 shows the result of shift-tabbing back into the zip code field after entering an unrecognized zip code. In that case, we clear out the city and state fields in preparation for a new zip code entry, again by using Ajax4jsf to make an Ajax call.

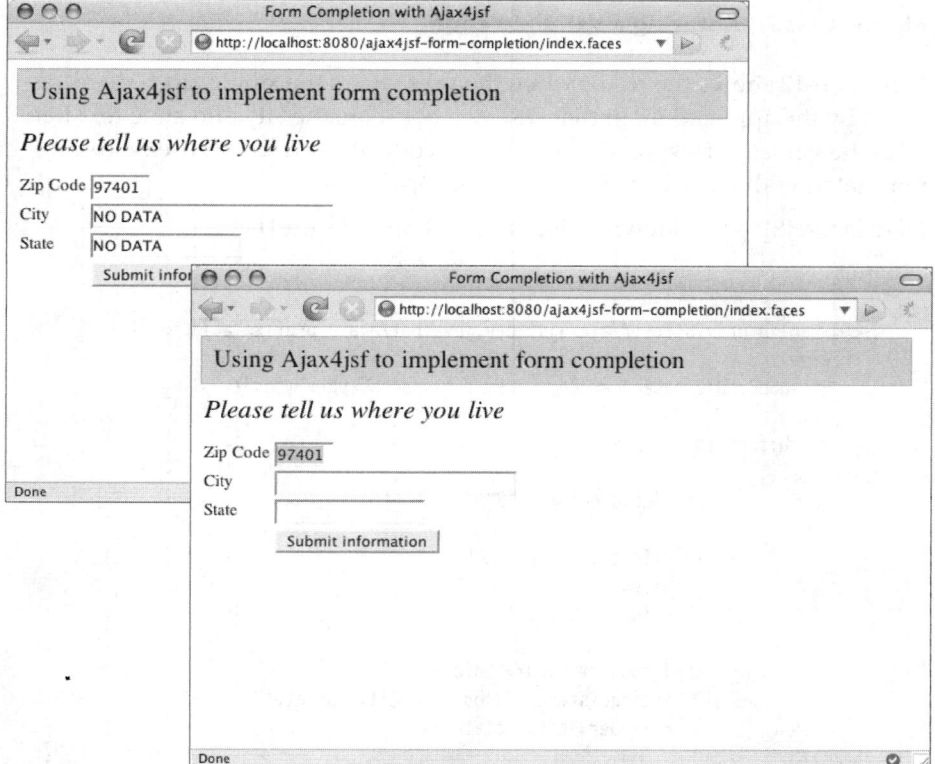

Figure 11–11   Entering an unrecognized zip code

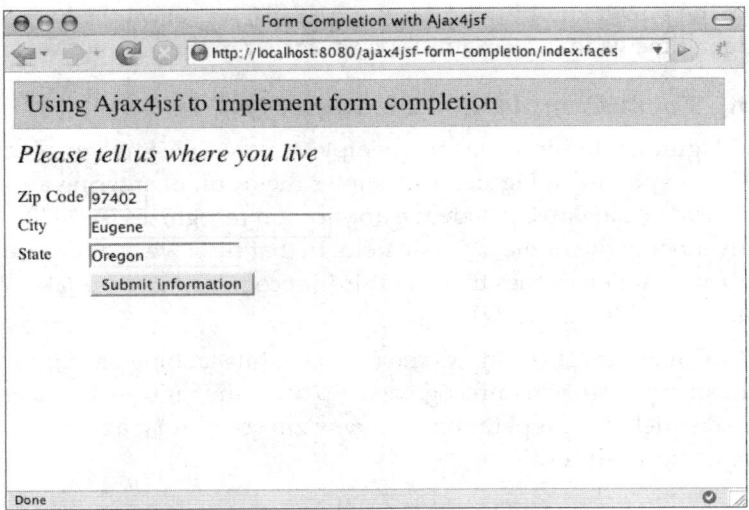

Figure 11–12   Entering a valid zip code

Figure 11–12 shows the result when the user enters the single zip code recognized by the application. In that case, we populate the city and state text fields with the values corresponding to that zip code. Once again, those fields are populated with an Ajax call made by Ajax4jsf.

Here is the JSP page shown in Figure 11–11 and Figure 11–12:

```
<html>
...
<%@ taglib uri="https://ajax4jsf.dev.java.net/ajax" prefix="a4j" %>
<f:view>
    <f:loadBundle basename="com.corejsf.messages" var="msgs"/>
    ...
        <h:form id="form">
        ...
            <h:panelGrid columns="2">
            ...
            <h:inputText id="zip"
                size="5"
                value="#{bb.zip}">

                <a4j:support event="onfocus"
                    actionListener="#{bb.clearCityAndState}"
                    reRender="city, state"/>
```

```
                    <a4j:support event="onblur"
                        actionListener="#{bb.setCityAndStateForZip}"
                        reRender="city, state"
                        oncomplete="Fat.fade_element('form:city');
                        Fat.fade_element('form:state');"/>
                </h:inputText>

                <h:outputLabel for="city"
                        value="#{msgs.cityPrompt}"/>
                <h:inputText id="city"
                        size="25"
                        value="#{bb.city}"/>

                <h:outputLabel for="state"
                        value="#{msgs.statePrompt}"/>
                <h:inputText id="state"
                        size="15"
                        value="#{bb.state}"/>
                    ...
            </h:panelGrid>
        </h:form>
    </body>
  </f:view>
</html>
```

The preceding JSP page uses two a4j:support tags to implement the Ajax calls. Both tags are enclosed in the zip code input component; one of those tags is triggered by an onblur event, whereas the other is triggered by an onFocus event.

When the zip code field receives focus, Ajax4jsf makes an Ajax call to the server, which invokes the JSF life cycle. Ajax4jsf intervenes in the life cycle and adds an action listener to the call. That action listener is our backing bean's setCityAndStateForZip method.

When the zip code field loses focus, Ajax4jsf makes another Ajax call to the server, which again invokes the JSF life cycle, and once again Ajax4jsf adds an action listener to the call. That action listener is our backing bean's clearCityAndState method. The backing bean's implementation is shown below:

```
package com.corejsf;

import javax.faces.event.ActionEvent;

public class BackingBean {
    private String zip;
    private String city;
    private String state;
```

```
public String getState() { return state; }
public void setState(String state) { this.state = state; }
public String getCity() { return city; }
public void setCity(String city) { this.city = city; }
public String getZip() { return zip; }
public void setZip(String zip) { this.zip = zip; }

public void clearCityAndState(ActionEvent e) {
    setCity("");
    setState("");
}

public void setCityAndStateForZip(ActionEvent e) {
    if (zip.equals("97402")) {
        setCity("Eugene");
        setState("Oregon");
    }
    else if(zip.equals("80132")) {
        setCity("Monument");
        setState("Colorado");
    }
    else {
        setCity("NO DATA");
        setState("NO DATA");
    }
}
}
```

Notice the reRender attributes for the a4j:support tags. When the Ajax calls initiated by Ajax4jsf return, Ajax4jsf *rerenders only the city and state fields*, which causes those fields to fetch their appropriate values from our backing bean. That is the fundamental magic of Ajax4jsf—*it can rerender part of a JSF tree of components instead of the entire tree.*

Because Ajax4jsf rerenders the city and state fields, all our backing bean has to do is make sure that the city and state properties, to which the fields are wired, have been appropriately updated.

Implementing Realtime Validation with Ajax4jsf

In the preceding example, we saw that Ajax4jsf can be easy and quite natural to use for JSF developers. In fact, the last example was so simple that you might be wondering why we took the time to show you how to do the same thing by hand, and why we have gone to such great lengths in this chapter to illustrate the low-level details of implementing Ajax from scratch. Why not just start with Ajax4jsf and leave out the rest of that stuff, if you will never need to know those low-level details?

The truth is that although Ajax4jsf can be drop-dead simple to use for simple applications, you must understand the low-level details of using Ajax with JSF for more complex applications to use Ajax4jsf effectively. In fact, our realtime validation example that we discussed earlier in this chapter, which is just a conceptual step above the form completion example, is complex enough to throw a monkey wrench into using Ajax4jsf. In that case, you must have a solid understanding of the JSF life cycle and how Ajax works with JSF. So now we take a look at the realtime validation example implemented with Ajax4jsf and, more imporantly, divulge the monkey wrench.

Figure 11–13, Figure 11–14, and Figure 11–15 all show the Ajax4jsf version of our realtime validation example in action.

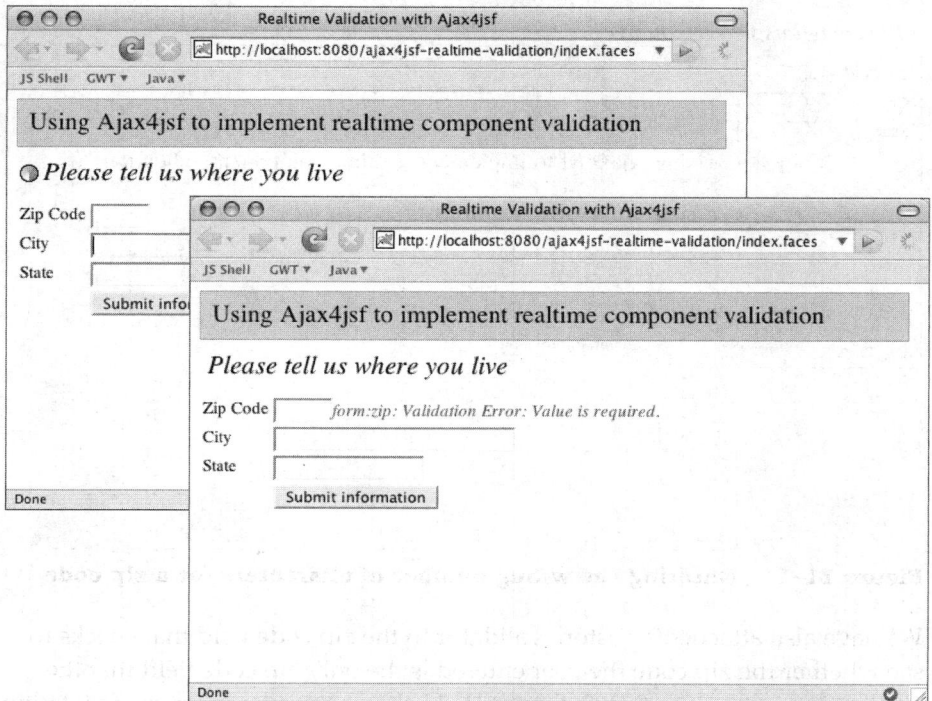

Figure 11–13   Leaving the zip code field blank

Figure 11–13 shows what happens when you leave the zip code field blank and tab out of the field. Notice that we display a busy indicator during the Ajax call, and subsequently hide it when the call is complete. The zip code field is a required field. So the Ajax call generates an appropriate error message, which we display using an h:outputText tag that shows an errorMessage property contained in our backing bean. As you will see momentarily, we set that errorMessage property when validation fails as a result of the Ajax call.

We have also attached a length validator to the zip code field, which requires the user to enter exactly five characters in the field. Once again, we use Ajax4jsf to make an Ajax call to validate the field and display an appropriate error message when validation fails, as shown in Figure 11–14.

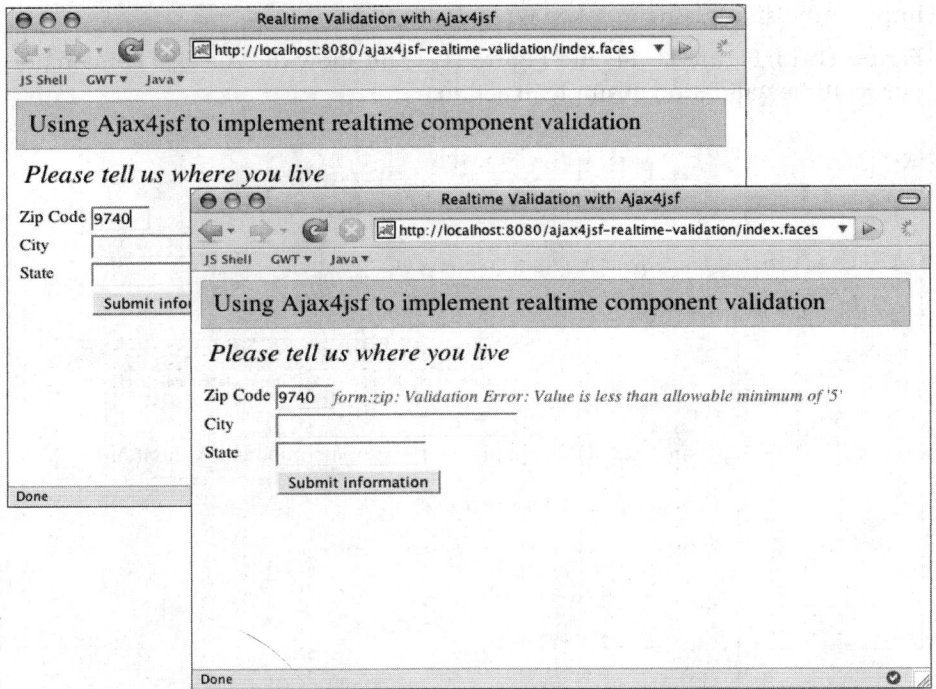

Figure 11–14 Entering the wrong number of characters for a zip code

We have also attached a custom validator to the zip code field that checks to see whether the zip code the user entered is the only zip code field that the application recognizes: 97402. Figure 11–15 shows the consequence of violating that constraint, which is yet another error message that lets the poor user know that the zip code was invalid, but provides no clue as to what the only valid zip code is. We trust that if you ever implement such a zip code field that you will be more conscientious than we have been in that regard.

Finally, if the user enters the correct zip code, he is rewarded with city and state fields that are populated with the appropriate values for the 97402 zip code, as was the case in the form completion example.

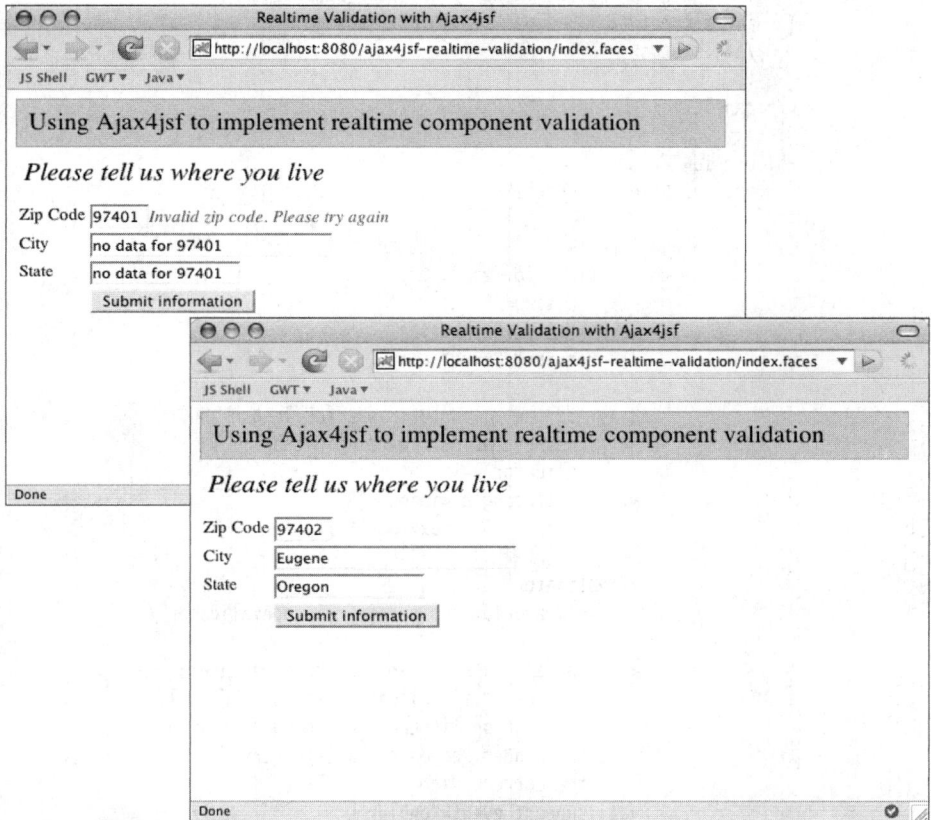

Figure 11–15 Using five digits for the zip code

Now that we have seen how the example works, we look at how it is implemented. Here is the JSP page:

```
<html>
   ...
   <%@ taglib uri="https://ajax4jsf.dev.java.net/ajax" prefix="a4j" %>

   <f:view locale="en">
      <f:loadBundle basename="com.corejsf.messages" var="msgs"/>
      ...
      <body>
```

```
...
<h:panelGrid columns="2" styleClass="heading">
   <a4j:status id="status">
      <f:facet name="start">
         <h:graphicImage value="/indicator_radar.gif"/>
      </f:facet>
   </a4j:status>
   ...
</h:panelGrid>

<h:form id="form">
   <h:panelGrid columns="2">
      ...
      <h:panelGroup>
         <h:inputText id="zip"
                   size="5"
                   value="#{bb.zip}"
                required="true">

               <!-- Add two validators: one for length and
                    another for our custom zip code
                    validator -->
               <f:validateLength minimum="5"
                                 maximum="5"/>

               <f:validator
                  validatorId="com.corejsf.ZipcodeValidator"/>

               <!-- The a4j:support tag must be immediate;
                    otherwise, if validation fails, JSF will
                    skip action listeners and go directly to
                    the Render Response phase to rerender
                    the current view. -->
               <a4j:support event="onblur"
                     immediate="true"
                  actionListener="#{bb.validateZip}"
                     reRender="city, state, errorMessage"/>

         </h:inputText>

         <h:outputText id="errorMessage"
                   value="#{bb.errorMessage}"
                   style="color: red; font-style: italic;"/>
      </h:panelGroup>

      <h:outputLabel for="city"
                 value="#{msgs.cityPrompt}"/>
```

```
                <h:inputText id="city" binding="#{bb.cityInput}"
                        size="25"
                        value="#{bb.city}"/>

                <h:outputLabel for="state"
                        value="#{msgs.statePrompt}"/>
                <h:inputText id="state" binding="#{bb.stateInput}"
                        size="15"
                        value="#{bb.state}"/>
                ...
            </h:panelGroup>
        </h:panelGrid>
    </h:form>
    </body>
  </f:view>
</html>
```

The first thing to notice is that we have used the a4j:status tag to display the busy indicator. You can specify start and stop facets for that tag, and when any Ajax call initiated by Ajax4jsf occurs, Ajax4jsf will display the start facet's component. When the call completes, Ajax4jsf will display the stop facet's component.

In our case, we did not specify a stop facet, and so Ajax4jsf will simply remove the start facet's component from the page when the call is complete.

Second, notice that the zip code field is required, and that we have added a length validator and our custom validator to that input component.

Third—and here is part one of the monkey wrench—is the fact the we have made the a4j:support tag inside the zip code component immediate. If we neglect to do that, our example will no longer work. To find out why, other than reading the comment in the preceding JSP page, we take a look at our backing bean's implementation:

```
package com.corejsf;

import javax.faces.event.ActionEvent;
import javax.faces.context.FacesContext;
import javax.faces.component.UIInput;
import javax.faces.application.FacesMessage;
import java.util.Iterator;

public class BackingBean {
    private String zip;
    private String city;
    private String state;
```

```java
private String errorMessage = null;

public String getState() { return state; }
public void setState(String state) { this.state = state; }
public String getCity() { return city; }
public void setCity(String city) { this.city = city; }
public String getZip() { return zip; }
public void setZip(String zip) { this.zip = zip; }

// Error message setter & getter, plus a clear error msg method
public String getErrorMessage() {
    return errorMessage;
}
public void setErrorMessage(String errorMessage) {
    this.errorMessage = errorMessage;
}
public void clearErrorMessage(ActionEvent e) {
    errorMessage = null;
}

// AJAX

/* cityInput and stateInput are set by component
 * bindings in the view:
 *
 * <h:inputText id="city" binding="#{bb.cityInput}"
 *          size="25"
 *          value="#{bb.city}"/>
 *
 * <h:inputText id="state" binding="#{bb.stateInput}"
 *          size="15"
 *          value="#{bb.state}"/>
 *
 */
private UIInput cityInput = null; // cityInput
public UIInput getCityInput() {
    return cityInput;
}
public void setCityInput(UIInput cityInput) {
    this.cityInput = cityInput;
}

private UIInput stateInput = null; // stateInput
public UIInput getStateInput() {
    return stateInput;
}
public void setStateInput(UIInput stateInput) {
```

```java
        this.stateInput = stateInput;
}


/* validateZip is called by Ajax4jsf in response to
 * an onblur in the zip code textfield:
 *
 * <a4j:support event="onblur"
 *         immediate="true"
 *      actionListener="#{bb.validateZip}"
 *         reRender="city, state, errorMessage"/>
 */
public void validateZip(ActionEvent e) {
    // This executes too fast to see the busy indicator in
    // the view, so we slow it down
    try {
        Thread.sleep(250);
    }
    catch (InterruptedException e1) {
        e1.printStackTrace();
    }

    UIInput input = (UIInput)e.getComponent() // Ajax4jsf comp
                            .getParent();   // input comp
    if (input != null) {
        String zip = (String)input.getSubmittedValue();
        if (zip != null) {
            // set city and state properties according
            // to the zip field's submitted value
            setCityAndState(zip);

            // validate the zip field
            FacesContext fc = FacesContext.getCurrentInstance();
            input.validate(fc); // iterates over input's validators
            if ( ! input.isValid())
                setErrorMessage(fc, input);

            // Force JSF to refresh city and state input fields.
            // If an input component's submitted value is not null,
            // JSF will not refresh the field.
            cityInput.setSubmittedValue(null);
            stateInput.setSubmittedValue(null);
        }
    }
}
private void setErrorMessage(FacesContext fc, UIInput input) {
    // set errorMessage to the first message for the zip field
```

```
            Iterator it = fc.getMessages(input.getClientId(fc));
            if (it.hasNext()) {
                FacesMessage facesMessage = (FacesMessage)it.next();
                errorMessage = facesMessage.getSummary();
            }
        }
        private void setCityAndState(String zip) {
            String cityAndState = ZipcodeDatabase.getCityAndState(zip);
            if (cityAndState != null) { // zip recognized
                String[] cityStateArray = cityAndState.split(",");
                setCity(cityStateArray[0]);
                setState(cityStateArray[1]);
            }
            else { // unknown zip with 5 chars
                if (zip.length() == 5) {
                    setCity ("no data for " + zip);
                    setState("no data for " + zip);
                }
                else { // unknown zip without 5 chars
                    setCity(null);
                    setState(null);
                }
            }
        }
    }
```

Remember that the a4j:support tag adds an action listener to the JSF life cycle. That is pretty evident considering that the name of the tag's corresponding attribute is actionListener. But the consequences of that listener may not be so readily apparent.

As the Ajax call goes through the JSF life cycle, JSF will validate our zip code component about halfway through the life cycle in the Process Validations phase. If validation fails, JSF immediately proceeds to the Render Response phase of the life cycle to redisplay the page, which is standard JSF behavior whenever validation fails. Realize that JSF itself has no idea that this is an Ajax call, so it cycles through the life cycle as though we had submitted the form in which the zip code component is contained.

If validation fails in the Process Validations phase and JSF proceeds to the Render Response phase as a result, it will skip any action listeners associated with the call, because action listeners are invoked just *before* the Render Response phase. So, we make the action listener immediate, which means JSF will invoke the listener at the front of the life cycle (after the Apply Request Values phase), and subsequently proceed to the Render Response phase. Therefore, *if we don't make our action listener immediate*, by specifying immediate=true for our a4j:status component, *our action listener will never be invoked.*

Now for part two of the monkey wrench, which is more insidious than part one. Notice that our action listener invokes the validate method on our zip code component. If the component is invalid after that call, we know that validation failed, and we set the errorMessage property of the backing bean accordingly, which is what we display in the view.

To recap so far: We use the a4j:support tag to add an action listener to the JSF life cycle when Ajax4jsf makes its Ajax call after we leave the zip code field. Our action listener manually validates the input field, and it must be immediate to keep JSF from performing validation and skipping our listener when validation fails.

One more part to the monkey wrench puzzle: When JSF performs validation, and validation succeeds for all input components, JSF sets all the input component's submitted values (which is what the user typed into the fields) to null. On the other hand, if validation fails for one or more inputs, JSF leaves the submitted values as they were.

When JSF subsequently rerenders the page, either because validation failed or because there was no navigation specified for the form submit, JSF checks the input components to see if their submitted values are null; if so, it refetches the component's values. However, if the submitted values are not null, meaning that validation failed, JSF does *not* repopulate the fields by fetching their associated values; instead, it redisplays those submitted values. That is how JSF retains erroneous values in input components when validation fails, which is desired behavior.

Because we are invoking validation manually, our input component's submitted values are never set to null when validation succeeds, as would be the case if JSF were invoking validation. So we must do that manually for the city and state fields to display Eugene and Oregon, respectively, when validation succeeds. To do that, we use component bindings and call setSubmittedValue(null) on the city and state components.

This exercise should convince you that using Ajax4jsf is not as simple as our form completion with Ajax4jsf example in the preceding section might lead you to believe. You *must* have a solid grasp of the JSF life cycle and what JSF does during that life cycle. For that, you will probably need a good book on JSF, and thankfully, you have one. You must also understand how Ajax4jsf implements Ajax. For example, Ajax4jsf's a4j:support tag does not pull the rug out from under JSF by invoking responseComplete on the Faces context, as we did early on in this chapter. Instead, the life cycle proceeds as it normally would with the addition of an action listener, and it is vital that you understand the ramifications of that design choice.

For completeness, we offer listings of our custom zip code validator, and a zip code database used by our backing bean. Here is the validator:

```java
package com.corejsf;

import com.corejsf.util.Messages;

import javax.faces.context.FacesContext;
import javax.faces.component.UIComponent;
import javax.faces.validator.ValidatorException;
import javax.faces.validator.Validator;

public class ZipcodeValidator implements Validator {
    public void validate(FacesContext fc,
                         UIComponent c,
                         Object zip)
        throws ValidatorException {
        String cityAndState = ZipcodeDatabase
                            .getCityAndState((String)zip);

        if (cityAndState == null) {
            throw new ValidatorException(
                Messages.getMessage("com.corejsf.messages",
                                    "badZip"));
        }
    }
}
```

And here is the database:

```java
package com.corejsf;

public class ZipcodeDatabase {
    public static String getCityAndState(String zip) {
        if ("97402".equals(zip))
            return "Eugene,Oregon";
        else
            return null;
    }
}
```

OPEN SOURCE

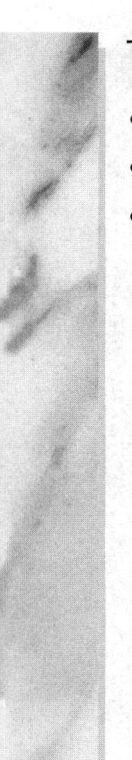

Chapter 12

When Sun first conceived of JSF, it counted on a vibrant open source community to help drive innovation. Although it took longer than expected, that is exactly what happened with the advent of projects such as Apache Shale, JBoss Seam, and Facelets. Those open source projects—along with other projects based on JSF, such as AjaxFaces—not only provide immediate benefit for JSF developers, but are also shaping JSF's future.

In this chapter, we take a look at three significant innovations:

- Web flow
- Alternate view technologies
- EJB (Enterprise JavaBeans) integration

Web flow is an industrial-strength version of JSF's default navigation mechanism. With web flow you can easily define complicated user interactions.

Starting with JSF 1.2 and JSP 2.1, the differences that caused incompatibilities between the two have now been banished to the dustbin, and you should be able to use them together without difficulty. However, even with that idyllic scenario, there is still a considerable segment of the JSF developer community that would like to replace JSP altogether with a lightweight templating mechanism. Luckily, JSF was built to accomodate just such a scenario.

If you have not taken a look at EJB 3.0, you may be surprised at just how much this most-maligned of specifications has matured to become a viable solution for many developers. Alas, the EJB and JSF component models are incompatible, which opens the door for frameworks that provide a unified component model.

Next, we take a look at these three innovations through the lens of three open source frameworks that implement them: Shale, Facelets, and Seam.

Web Flow—Shale

From the folks that brought you Struts comes Shale, a set of services layered on top of JSF. Shale has lots of features that make everyday JSF development much easier:

- Web flow
- Remote method calls for Ajax
- Templating and Tapestry-like views
- Client- and server-side validation with Apache Commons Validator
- Testing framework with support for unit and integration testing
- Spring, JNDI, and Tiles integration
- View controllers (concrete implementation of the JSF backing bean concept)

Shale web flow lets you implement a series of interactions between a user and your application. That set of interactions is more commonly called a *user conversation*, *dialog*, or *wizard*. Shale uses the term *dialog*, so that is the term we will use here.

A Shale dialog consists of one or more states. These states have transitions that define how control is transferred from one state to another. Dialogs also have a special state, called the *end state*, that exits the dialog and releases dialog state. Here is an example of a Shale dialog definition:

```
<dialogs>
    <dialog name="Example Dialog"
        start="Starting State">
        ...
        <view name="Starting State"
            viewId="/viewForThisState.jsp">
            <transition outcome="next"
                target="The Next State"/>
            <transition outcome="cancel"
                target="Exit"/>
        </view>
```

```
<view name="The Next State"
    viewId="/nextView.jsp">
    <transition outcome="next"
        target="Yet Another State"/>
    <transition outcome="cancel"
        target="Exit"/>
</view>
...
<end name="Exit"/>
</dialog>
</dialogs>
```

In the preceding code fragment, we defined—in an XML configuration file—a dialog named Example Dialog with three states: Starting State, The Next State, and Exit. The transitions define how Shale navigates from one state to another—for example, in a JSP page, you can do this:

```
<h:commandButton id="next"
    value="#{msgs.nextButtonText}"
    action="next"/>
```

If the preceding dialog's state is The Next State and you click the button, Shale uses that outcome—next—to send you to the next state, in this case named Yet Another State. Because of The Next State's second transition, clicking a button whose action is cancel will end the dialog.

That contrived example shows the basics of Shale dialogs, but Figure 12–1 illustrates a more realistic example of a bill pay wizard. The wizard lets you make an online payment and is composed of four steps: Payee Information, Payment Method, Payment Schedule, and Summary. Each of those steps is shown in Figure 12–1, from top to bottom, respectively.

But the bill pay wizard has a twist. If you select "Wire Transfer" for your payment method and click the "Next" button, you do not go directly to the "Payment Schedule" panel, as Figure 12–1 leads you to believe. Instead, a subdialog intervenes that collects the wire transfer information.

That sequence of events is shown in Figure 12–2. Notice that the top and bottom pictures in that figure are from the surrounding dialog, whereas the middle pictures are from the wire transfer subdialog.

So there is our finished application, with two dialogs, one nested in the other. Now we take a look at the key steps in implementing those dialogs.

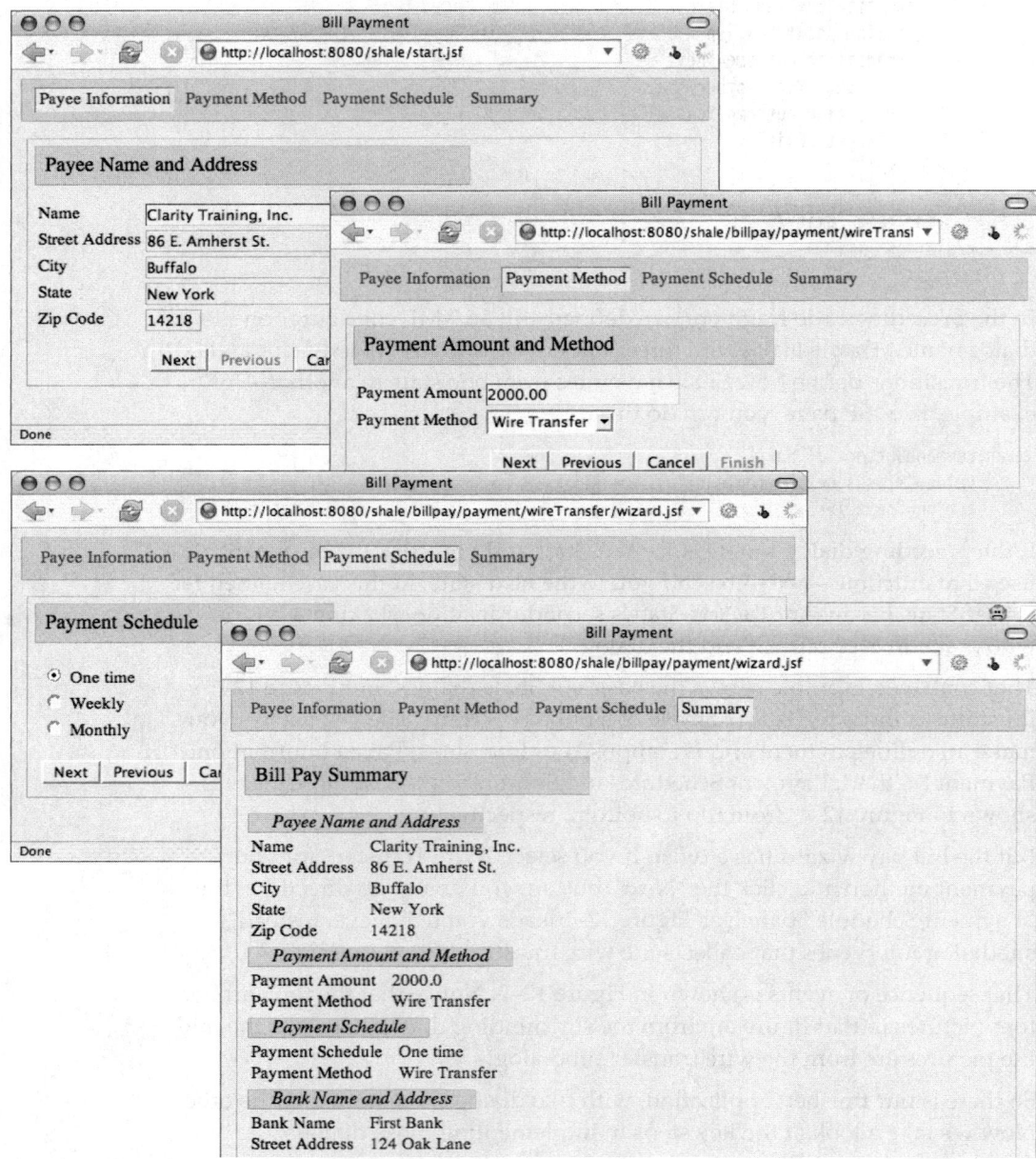

Figure 12–1   The bill pay wizard

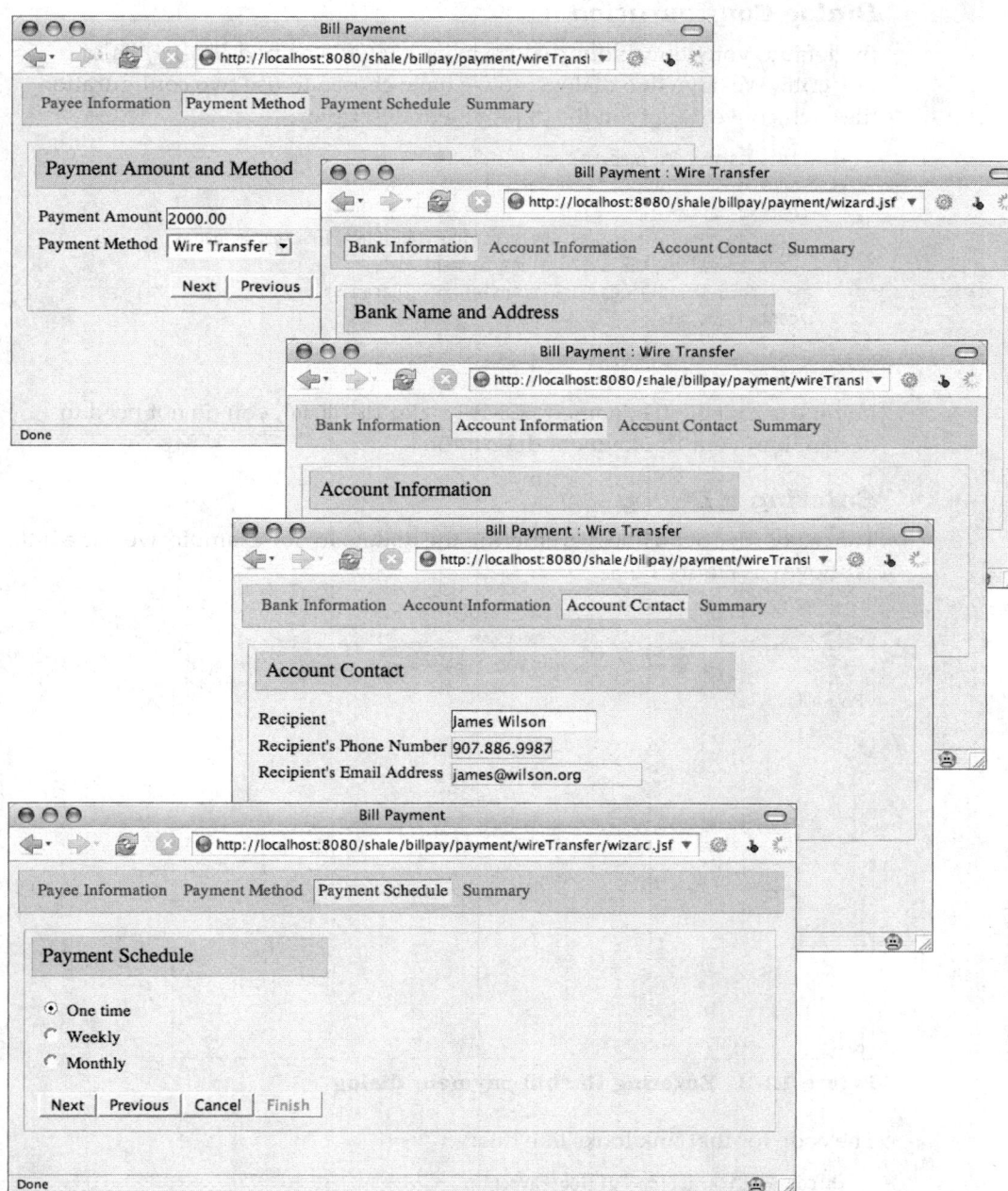

Figure 12–2   Wire transfer subdialog (summary panel not shown)

Dialog Configuration

By default, you define your dialogs in an XML file named /WEB-INF/dialog-config.xml. We have two dialogs, so we have chosen to use two configuration files, which we declare in the deployment descriptor:

```
<!-- this is WEB-INF/web.xml -->
<web-app>
   <context-param>
      <param-name>org.apache.shale.dialog.CONFIGURATION</param-name>
      <param-value>/WEB-INF/dialogs/payment.xml,
         /WEB-INF/dialogs/wire-transfer.xml</param-value>
   </context-param>
   ...
</web-app>
```

If you use a single file, named /WEB-INF/dialog-config.xml, you do not need to declare it in your deployment descriptor.

Entering a Dialog

The next order of business is entering the dialog. In our example, we use a link, as shown in Figure 12–3.

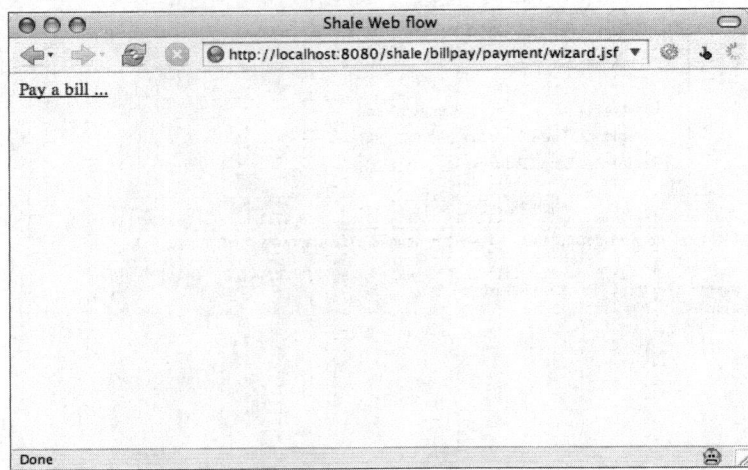

Figure 12–3 Entering the bill payment dialog

The code for that link looks like this:

```
<h:commandLink action="dialog:Payment">
   <h:outputText value="#{msgs.billpayPrompt}"/>
</h:commandLink>
```

As you might suspect, Shale places special meaning on any action that starts with the string dialog:. The name that follows the colon represents the name of a dialog, which Shale subsequently enters when a user clicks the link.

Dialog Navigation

By default, Shale dialogs are defined in XML. Here is how the Payment dialog, referenced in the preceding code fragment, is defined:

```xml
<?xml version="1.0" encoding="UTF-8"?>

<!DOCTYPE dialogs PUBLIC
    "-//Apache Software Foundation//DTD Shale Dialog Configuration 1.0//EN"
    "http://struts.apache.org/dtds/shale-dialog-config-1_0.dtd">

<dialogs>
    <dialog name="Payment"
        start="Setup">
        ...
        <action name="Setup"
            method="#{dialogLauncher.setupPaymentDialog}">
            <transition outcome="success"
                target="Payee Information"/>
        </action>

        <!-- Payee Information -->
        <view name="Payee Information"
            viewId="/billpay/payment/wizard.jsp">
            <transition outcome="next"
                target="Payment Method"/>
        </view>
        ...
```

When you enter a dialog, Shale loads the state specified with the dialog element's start attribute. In our case, that state is Setup, which is an *action state*. Action states execute a method and immediately transition to another state, depending upon the string returned from the method (the action's outcome).

When Shale enters our dialog's Setup state, it invokes the setupPaymentDialog method on a managed bean named dialogLauncher. That method stores some objects in dialog scope (see "Dialog Scope" on page 578 for more information about that method) and returns the string success.

That success outcome causes Shale to load the Payee Information state, which is a *view state*. View states load a view, specified with the viewId attribute, and wait for the user to click a button or a link, which generates an outcome that Shale uses to navigate to the next state.

So, to summarize, when you click the link to enter the dialog, Shale loads the
Setup action state, which invokes dialogLauncher.setupPaymentDialog(). That method
returns success, which causes Shale to load /billpay/payment/wizard.jsp and wait for
the next outcome.

At some point, our dialog ends with the end state:

```
    ...
    <end  name="Exit" viewId="/start.jsp"/>
  </dialog>
</dialogs>
```

The end state is a special view state that exits the current dialog and subsequently loads the view specified with the viewId attribute.

Dialog Scope

Throughout the JSP pages in our wizards, we have input fields wired to an
object that is stored as the current dialog's data object—for example:

```
<h:inputText id="name"
    size="30"
    value="#{dialog.data.name}"
    ...
    styleClass="input"/>
```

When you enter a dialog, Shale puts an object, named dialog, in session scope
and when you exit the dialog, Shale removes the dialog object from the session,
thereby effectively creating a dialog scope.

You can store an object of your choosing in the dialog object by setting the dialog's data property. In the preceding code, we access that data object to wire a
text field to the data object's name property. As is often the case, our data object is
a simple collection of properties representing the fields in the wizard's panels.

This all begs a question: How does our data object get associated with the dialog's data property? Like the Payment dialog discussed in "Dialog Navigation" on
page 577, the Wire Transfer dialog also has a Setup action state that Shale executes
when you enter the dialog. That method stores the data object in the dialog's
data property. Here is how we declare the Setup method:

```
<dialogs>
  <dialog name="Wire Transfer Dialog"
      start="Setup">
      ...
      <action name="Setup"
        method="#{dialogLauncher.setupWireTransferDialog}">
```

```
          <transition outcome="success"
              target="Bank Information"/>
        </action>
        ...
        <end name="Exit"/>
      </dialog>
    </dialogs>
```

Shale executes dialogLauncher.setupWireTransferDialog() when you enter the Wire Transfer dialog. So we have two methods, setupPaymentDialog and setupWireTransfer-Dialog, that Shale executes immediately after entering the Payment and Wire Transfer dialogs, respectively. Those methods look like this:

```
public class DialogLauncher extends AbstractFacesBean {
    private BillpayData billpayData = null;

    // Called just afer entering the payment dialog
    public String setupPaymentDialog() {
        billpayData = new BillpayData();
        billpayData.setTransfer(new WireTransferData());

        setValue("#{dialog.data}", billpayData);
        return "success";
    }

    // Called just afer entering the wire transfer dialog
    public String setupWireTransferDialog() {
        setValue("#{dialog.data}", billpayData.getTransfer());
        return "success";
    }
}
```

The setupPaymentDialog method creates two objects, that combined, contain all the properties on all the panels for the Payment and Wire Transfer dialogs. Because the Wire Transfer dialog is a subdialog of the Payment dialog, we likewise store the wire transfer data object in the payment data object.

While a dialog is active, the dialog object and its associated data object, are available via JSF expressions like #{dialog.data.someProperty}. When the dialog exits, Shale removes the dialog object from "dialog" scope and it is no longer accessible via JSF expressions. It is interesting to note that the data object for a dialog could easily be a map, which effectively gives you a bona fide new scope.

NOTE: Notice that the `DialogLauncher` class in the preceding code extends Shale's `AbstractFacesBean`. That class has a number of handy methods, some of which are listed below, that you will find useful for JSF development in general. For example, `DialogLauncher` uses `AbstractFacesBean.setValue()`, which sets a bean property's value to a given string, which can be a value expression.

API   `org.apache.shale.faces.AbstractFacesBean`

- `Object getBean(String beanName)`

  Returns a managed bean with the specified `beanName`, if one exists. This method delegates to the JSF variable resolver, which, by default, searches request, session, and application scope—in that order—for managed beans. If no managed bean is found with the given name, the variable resolver looks for a managed bean definition for the bean in question; if the definition exists, JSF creates the bean. If the bean does not exist and has no definition, this method returns `null`.

- `Object getValue(String expr)`

  Given a value expression, this method returns the corresponding object. For example: `LoginPage page = (LoginPage)getValue("#{loginPage}");`

- `void setValue(String expr, Object value)`

  This method is the inverse of `getValue`; it sets a value, given a value expression; for example: `setValue("#{loginPage}", new LoginPage());`

Dialog Context Sensitivity

Look closely at the tabs and buttons for the dialog panels in Figure 12–1 on page 574 and Figure 12–2 on page 575, and you will see that they are context sensitive. That sensitivity is implemented in a page object and accessed in JSF expressions. Here is how the sensitivity of the wizard buttons is controlled:

```
<h:commandButton id="next"
    value="#{msgs.nextButtonText}"
    action="next"
    styleClass="wizardButton"
    disabled="#{not dialog.data.page.nextButtonEnabled}"/>
```

If the page object stored in the dialog's data returns `true` from `isNextButtonEnabled()`, JSF enables the button. Similar properties, such as `previousButtonEnabled`, are contained in the page object and accessed in `wizardButtons.jsp`. Here is how the CSS styles for the tabs at the top of each wizard panel are set:

```
<h:panelGrid columns="5">
   <h:outputText value="#{msgs.payeeTabPrompt}"
      styleClass="#{dialog.data.page.payeeStyle}"/>
</h:panelGrid>
```

The page object accesses dialog state programatically. In our application, we implemented a base class that encapsulates the basics:

```
public class BaseDialogPage {
   protected BaseDialogPage() {
      // Base class only...
   }
   protected Status getDialogStatus() {
      Map sessionMap = FacesContext.getCurrentInstance()
         .getExternalContext()
         .getSessionMap();
      return(Status)sessionMap.get(org.apache.shale.dialog.Globals.STATUS);
   }
   protected boolean stateEquals(String stateName) {
      return stateName.equals(getDialogStatus().getStateName());
   }
   protected boolean isStateOneOf(String[] these) {
      String state = getDialogStatus().getStateName();
      for (int i=0; i < these.length; ++i) {
         if(state.equals(these[i]))
         return true;
      }
      return false;
   }
}
```

Shale stores a status object in session scope, which we retrieve in the preceding code. From that status object we can determine the current state. We subsequently put those base class methods to good use in subclasses. Here is the page class for the Payment dialog:

```
public class BillpayPage extends BaseDialogPage {
   // State constants
   private static final String PAYEE_INFORMATION = "Payee Information";
   private static final String PAYMENT_METHOD = "Payment Method";
   private static final String PAYMENT_SCHEDULE = "Payment Schedule";
   private static final String SUMMARY = "Summary";

   public String enterPaymentDialog() {
      return "dialog:Payment";
   }

   // View logic for panels:
```

```java
public boolean isPayeeRendered() {
    return stateEquals(PAYEE_INFORMATION);
}
public boolean isPaymentMethodRendered() {
    return stateEquals(PAYMENT_METHOD);
}
public boolean isPaymentScheduleRendered() {
    return stateEquals(PAYMENT_SCHEDULE);
}
public boolean isSummaryRendered() {
    return stateEquals(SUMMARY);
}

// View logic for buttons:

public boolean isNextButtonEnabled() {
    return isStateOneOf(new String[] {
        PAYEE_INFORMATION, PAYMENT_METHOD, PAYMENT_SCHEDULE });
}
public boolean isPreviousButtonEnabled() {
    return isStateOneOf(new String[] {
        PAYMENT_METHOD, PAYMENT_SCHEDULE, SUMMARY });
}
public boolean isCancelButtonEnabled() {
    return true;
}
public boolean isFinishButtonEnabled() {
    return stateEquals(SUMMARY);
}

// View logic for CSS style names

public String getPayeeStyle() {
    return isPayeeRendered() ?
        "selectedHeading" : "unselectedHeading";
}

public String getPaymentMethodStyle() {
    return isPaymentMethodRendered() ?
        "selectedHeading" : "unselectedHeading";
}

public String getPaymentScheduleStyle() {
    return isPaymentScheduleRendered() ?
        "selectedHeading" : "unselectedHeading";
}
```

```
public String getSummaryStyle() {
    return isSummaryRendered() ?
        "selectedHeading" : "unselectedHeading";
}
}
```

The preceding class controls the visibility of panels, enabled state of buttons, and CSS tab styles, all by programatically determining the current dialog state.

Subdialogs

In our example, the Wire Transfer dialog is a subdialog of the Payment dialog. Here is how that is defined:

```
<dialogs>
    <dialog name="Payment"
        start="Setup">
        ...
        <!-- The following action navigates from the Payment
            Method page depending upon the payment method
            that the user selected from a drop-down list.
            The action simply returns that value. -->
        <action name="Navigate Based on Transfer Mechanism"
            method="#{dialog.data.navigateTransfer}">
            <transition outcome="Wire Transfer"
                target="Wire Transfer"/>
        </action>

        <subdialog name="Wire Transfer"
            dialogName="Wire Transfer Dialog">
            <transition outcome="cancel"
                target="Payment Method"/>
            <transition outcome="success"
                target="Payment Schedule"/>
        </subdialog>
        ...
    </dialog>
</dialogs>
```

Inside the Payment dialog we declare a Wire Transfer subdialog. We navigate to that subdialog through an action state named Navigate Based on Transfer Mechanism that returns the string selected from a drop-down list of transfer types. If that string is Wire Transfer, Shale navigates to the Wire Transfer subdialog.

Notice the transitions for that subdialog: If those outcomes (cancel and success) are not handled in the subdialog, Shale associates them with the states Payment Method and Payment Schedule, respectively.

The Wire Transfer subdialog is a dialog, defined like any other:

```xml
<dialogs>
  <dialog name="Wire Transfer Dialog"
    start="Setup">

    <action name="Setup"
      method="#{dialogLauncher.setupWireTransferDialog}">
      <transition outcome="success"
        target="Bank Information"/>
    </action>

    <view name="Bank Information"
      viewId="/billpay/payment/wireTransfer/wizard.jsp">
      <transition outcome="next"
        target="Account Information"/>
      <transition outcome="cancel"
        target="Exit"/>
    </view>

    <view name="Account Information"
      viewId="/billpay/payment/wireTransfer/wizard.jsp">
      <transition outcome="previous"
        target="Bank Information"/>
      <transition outcome="next"
        target="Account Contact"/>
      <transition outcome="cancel"
        target="Exit"/>
    </view>

    <view name="Account Contact"
      viewId="/billpay/payment/wireTransfer/wizard.jsp">
      <transition outcome="previous"
        target="Account Information"/>
      <transition outcome="next"
        target="Summary"/>
      <transition outcome="cancel"
        target="Exit"/>
    </view>

    <view name="Summary"
      viewId="/billpay/payment/wireTransfer/wizard.jsp">
      <transition outcome="previous"
        target="Account Contact"/>
      <transition outcome="finish"
        target="Finish"/>
      <transition outcome="cancel"
```

```
                target="Exit"/>
        </view>

        <action name="Finish"
            method="#{dialog.data.finish}">
            <transition outcome="success"
                target="Exit"/>
        </action>

        <end name="Exit"/>
    </dialog>
</dialogs>
```

Shale's dialog support is a powerful upgrade to JSF's built-in navigation capabilities. By itself, it is a compelling inducement to add Shale to your tool chest.

Alternate View Technologies—Facelets

In the early days of enterprise Java, developers dealt in HTML directly, by emitting HTML from servlets. Over the years, we have moved to eradicate HTML from our views with the advent of JSP and, especially, JSP custom tags, which do a neat job of encapsulating Java code and removing it from JSP pages.

Everything is a trade-off, but overall the trend toward JSP tags has made JSP pages more readable, maintainable, and extensible.

However, JSP has a dark side: When software developers and graphic designers work independently, the JSP model breaks down badly. Graphic designers are typically not familiar with JSP or the set of custom JSP tags that software developers use on any given project.

Software developers, on the other hand, can have a devil of a time incorporating a look and feel into a web application laden with custom tags that ultimately generate HTML, as is the case for a typical JSF application. If JSP is used on a project in which software developers and graphic designers work separately, only rigid discipline provides any hope of success. Fortunately, there is an alternative.

XHTML Views

Now we cut to the chase. We are going to use Facelets, an open source display technology for JSF, to implement our views in XHTML (Extensible HTML) instead of JSP. In our XHTML files, we will have mock-up HTML that is edited by a graphic designer, *but at runtime, Facelets will swap out that mock-up HTML with JSF components*. This will allow graphic designers to create a look and feel with mock-up markup that developers can replace with JSF components at runtime. And here is the clincher: *The JSF components absorb the mock-up's look and feel.*

Feel free to take a moment to ponder the ramifications.

This sort of chicanery, first pioneered in the Java web application space by Tapestry, truly borders on magic. Now we see how it works. First, an XHTML page, shown in Figure 12–4.

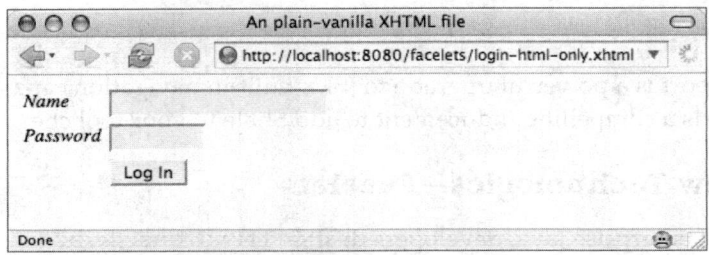

Figure 12–4   A simple XHTML page

Here is the listing for that page:

```
<!DOCTYPE html PUBLIC "-//W3C//DTD XHTML 1.0 Transitional//EN"
        "http://www.w3.org/TR/xhtml1/DTD/xhtml1-transitional.dtd">

<html xmlns="http://www.w3.org/1999/xhtml">
   <head>
        <link href="styles.css" rel="stylesheet" type="text/css"/>
        <title>An plain-vanilla XHTML file</title>
   </head>

   <body>
      <form id="login">
         <table cellpadding="2px;">
            <tr>
               <td>
                  <label for="name" class="label">
                     Name
                  </label>
               </td>
               <td>
                  <input type="text"
                     id="name"
                     style="background: #ffa"/>
               </td>
            </tr>
```

```
    <tr>
        <td>
            <label for="password" class="label">
                Password
            </label>
        </td>
        <td>
            <input type="password"
                id="password"
                size="8"
                class="input"/>
        </td>
    </tr>
    <tr>
        <td></td>
        <td>
            <input type="submit"
                value="Log In"/>
        </td>
    </tr>
    </table>
    </form>
    </body>
</html>
```

You cannot get much more vanilla than that. Next we wire those HTML elements to JSF components.

Replacing Markup with JSF Components: The jsfc Attribute

We are going to use JSF components to turn our nonfunctional markup into a thriving web page, as shown in Figure 12–5.

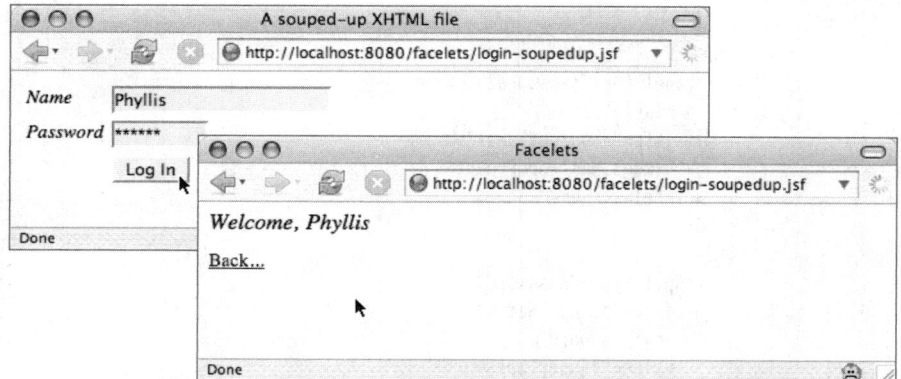

Figure 12–5 Replacing XHTML markup at runtime with JSF components

Here is the transformation of our XHTML file:

```
<!DOCTYPE html PUBLIC "-//W3C//DTD XHTML 1.0 Transitional//EN"
    "http://www.w3.org/TR/xhtml1/DTD/xhtml1-transitional.dtd">

<html xmlns="http://www.w3.org/1999/xhtml"
    xmlns:f="http://java.sun.com/jsf/core">

<head>
    <link href="styles.css" rel="stylesheet" type="text/css"/>
    <f:loadBundle basename="com.corejsf.messages" var="msgs"/>
    <title>#{msgs.windowTitle}</title>
</head>

<body>
    <form jsfc="h:form" id="login">
        <table cellpadding="2px;">
            <tr>
                <td>
                    <label for="name"
                        class="label"
                        jsfc="h:outputLabel">
                        #{msgs.namePrompt}
                    </label>
                </td>
                <td>
                    <input type="text"
                        id="name"
                        value="#{user.name}"
                        style="background: #ffa;"
                        jsfc="h:inputText"/>
                </td>
            </tr>
            <tr>
                <td>
                    <label for="password"
                        class="label"
                        jsfc="h:outputLabel">
                        #{msgs.passwordPrompt}
                    </label>
                </td>
                <td>
                    <input type="password"
                        jsfc="h:inputSecret"
                        id="password"
                        value="#{user.password}"
                        size="8"
                        class="input"/>
```

```
                        </td>
                    </tr>
                    <tr>
                        <td> </td>
                        <td>
                            <input type="submit"
                                jsfc="h:commandButton"
                                value="#{msgs.loginButtonText}"
                                action="login"/>
                        </td>
                    </tr>
                </table>
            </form>
        </body>
</html>
```

Three things about this example:

- Notice the address bar URLs in Figure 12–4 on page 586 and Figure 12–5 on page 587. The former URLs end in .xhtml, whereas the latter end in .jsf. This means that Figure 12–4 shows what the graphic designer sees and Figure 12–5 shows what software developers, and ultimately end users, see.

- We use an XML namespace to enable Facelet tags that mimic the JSF core tag library. Subsequently, we use the f:loadBundle tag from that namespace to load a resource bundle. Finally, we use value expressions, such as #{msgs.namePrompt}, directly in the page—no h:outputText is required—to access keys in the resource bundle.

- We have added jsfc attributes to our form, labels, text fields, and button. When you run this souped-up XHTML page through Facelets, it swaps the markup for components of the specified type.

You might wonder what the graphic designer sees when she views this souped-up XHTML file. Figure 12–6 provides the answer.

The browser does not know what to do with JSF value expressions. So it just uses them as is, which is convenient for translators, who can glean the context of a translation just by looking at the XHTML.

 NOTE: What does the browser, or any other tool that lets you view XHTML, do with those jsfc attributes? Nothing! So graphic designers can continue to iterate over your XHTML files to refine the look and feel, while you work on the components that will ultimately be used at runtime.

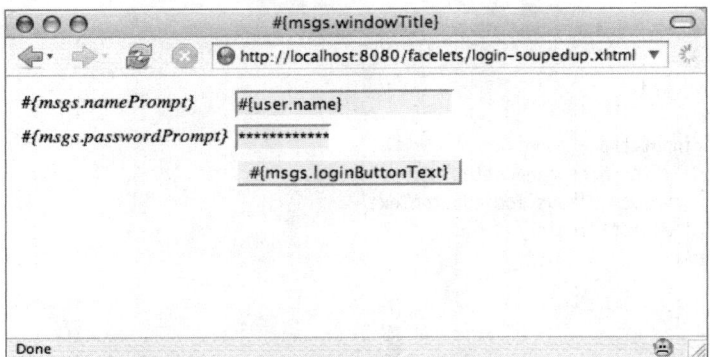

Figure 12–6   What the graphic designer sees

 NOTE: Shale has something similar to Facelets, called Clay. Like Facelets, Clay gives you clean separation of graphic design and software development concerns with HTML views. One advantage Clay has over Facelets is that it works with ill-formed HTML, whereas Facelets requires XHTML.

Using JSF Tags

Fundamentally, Facelets, like Tapestry, cleanly separates graphic design from software development. But if you are both a graphic designer and a software developer, there are still viable reasons to prefer the more traditional JSP-based approach. For example, XHTML is more verbose than JSP and therefore can be harder to maintain over the long run. If you yearn for the more traditional approach with JSP tags, Facelets can easily accomodate. It's just that you are not really using JSP at all.

Facelets recognizes tags that look identical to their JSP counterparts, but it is Facelets, not JSP, that processes the tags. As Facelets parses the XHTML, it creates the resulting component tree.

Figure 12–7 shows the login application from page 587 with Facelet JSF tags.

Now our XHTML page looks like this:

```
<!DOCTYPE html PUBLIC "-//W3C//DTD XHTML 1.0 Transitional//EN"
    "http://www.w3.org/TR/xhtml11/DTD/xhtml11-transitional.dtd">

<html xmlns="http://www.w3.org/1999/xhtml"
    xmlns:ui="http://java.sun.com/jsf/facelets"
    xmlns:f="http://java.sun.com/jsf/core"
    xmlns:h="http://java.sun.com/jsf/html">
```

```
<head>
    <link href="styles.css" rel="stylesheet" type="text/css"/>
    <f:loadBundle basename="com.corejsf.messages" var="msgs"/>
    <title>#{msgs.facesTagsWindowTitle}</title>
</head>

<body>
    <h:form id="login">
        <h:panelGrid columns="2" cellpadding="3px">
            <h:outputLabel for="name"
                value="#{msgs.namePrompt}"/>
            <h:inputText type="text"
                id="name"
                value="#{user.name}"
                class="input"/>

            <h:outputLabel for="password"
                class="label"
                value="#{msgs.passwordPrompt}"/>
            <h:inputSecret
                id="password"
                value="#{user.password}"
                size="8"
                class="input"/>

            <h:outputText value=""/>
            <h:commandButton value="#{msgs.loginButtonText}"
                action="login"/>
        </h:panelGrid>
    </h:form>
</body>
</html>
```

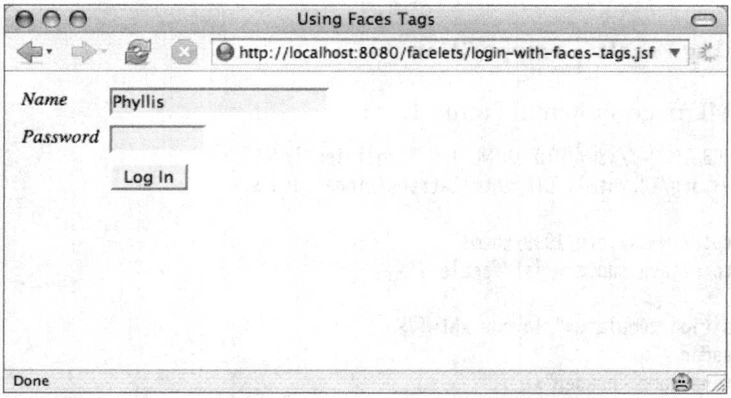

Figure 12–7   A Facelets view that uses JSF tags

Notice that with the preceding code, we have purposely chosen to forego the
jsfc approach, which, as we have seen, lets software developers and graphic
designers work separately, in parallel.

In the end of course, it is your call whether to separate graphic design and software development. Either way, Facelets adds some very appealing features to
this fundamental replacement of JSF's default display technology.

Page Composition with Templates

Facelets lets you compose web pages from individual XHTML fragments,
similar to the popular Tiles framework. Figure 12–8 shows such a web page.

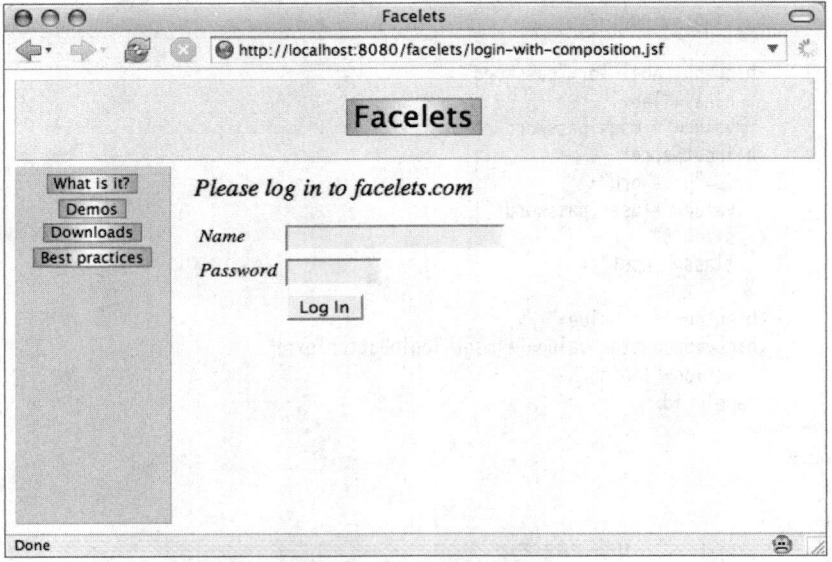

Figure 12–8   Using Facelets composition

Here is the XHTML page shown in Figure 12–8:

```
<!DOCTYPE html PUBLIC "-//W3C//DTD XHTML 1.0 Transitional//EN"
    "http://www.w3.org/TR/xhtml1/DTD/xhtml1-transitional.dtd">

<html xmlns="http://www.w3.org/1999/xhtml"
    xmlns:ui="http://java.sun.com/jsf/facelets">
    <body>
        <ui:composition template="/layout.xhtml">
            <!-- Header -->
            <ui:define name="header">
```

```
                <img src="images/facelets.jpg"/>
            </ui:define>

            <!-- Menu -->
            <ui:define name="menu">
                <img src="images/whatisit.jpg"/>
                <img src="images/demos.jpg"/>
                <img src="images/downloads.jpg"/>
                <img src="images/bestpractices.jpg"/>
            </ui:define>

            <!-- Content -->
            <ui:define name="content">
            <ui:include src="login-composition.xhtml"/>
          </ui:define>
        </ui:composition>
      </body>
    </html>
```

In the preceding code, we define a page *composition* that has a *template*, and we define *content* that is displayed by the template. Since the word "template" is so overloaded, it might help to think of the template as a layout instead. Here is the template for the preceding composition.

```
<!DOCTYPE html PUBLIC "-//W3C//DTD XHTML 1.0 Transitional//EN"
    "http://www.w3.org/TR/xhtml1/DTD/xhtml1-transitional.dtd">

<html xmlns="http://www.w3.org/1999/xhtml"
    xmlns:ui="http://java.sun.com/jsf/facelets"
    xmlns:f="http://java.sun.com/jsf/core"
    xmlns:h="http://java.sun.com/jsf/html"
    xmlns:c="http://java.sun.com/jstl/core">

<link href="styles.css" rel="stylesheet" type="text/css"/>
<f:loadBundle basename="com.corejsf.messages" var="msgs"/>

<head>
    <title>Facelets</title>
</head>

<body>
    <div class="header">
        <ui:insert name="header"/>
    </div>

    <div class="menu">
        <ui:insert name="menu"/>
    </div>
```

```
        <div class="content">
            <ui:insert name="content"/>
        </div>
    </body>
</html>
```

Admittedly, there is not much layout there, other than three DIVs. The rest of the layout is encapsulated in CSS for a further separation of concerns. But the result is the same: the template, in this case an XHTML file and its stylesheet, represent the layout for the composition.

Notice the three `ui:define` tags in the code beginning on page 592. The first `ui:define` tag, representing the header of the page, contains a lone image. The next tag, representing the menu, contains four images. The most interesting tag is the third `ui:define` tag, which includes content from another XHTML file with the `ui:include` tag. That XHTML file looks like this:

```
<ui:composition xmlns:ui="http://java.sun.com/jsf/facelets"
    xmlns:h="http://java.sun.com/jsf/html"
    xmlns:c="http://java.sun.com/jstl/core">
    <!-- the contents of this tag are the same as the body of the
        listing on page 586 -->
</ui:composition>
```

The body of the preceding `ui:composition` is the same as the body of the XHTML file that begins on page 586.

NOTE: Why bother to use Facelets composition, when we can just neatly encapsulate the layout and its content in one file? Because if we have multiple views that share layout, we want to define that layout in only one place and reuse it for multiple views, much the same as you include content with JSP's `jsp:include`, or Facelets' `ui:include`. Realize that in the preceding example, any composition that defines `header`, `menu`, and `content` regions can reuse the same layout. That is pretty powerful.

Facelets Custom Tags

Facelets has many more features than we have covered here, so at this point we refer you to the Faclets documentation, but before we do, we will show you one more feature: Facelets custom tags.

You can easily create your own XHTML tags and use them in your Facelets views. For example, Figure 12–9 shows the application discussed in "Page Composition with Templates" on page 592, equipped with a custom tag that

shows the HTTP headers for the current request, but only when there is a
request parameter named debug whose value is true.

A severely abbreviated listing of Figure 12–9 follows:

```
<html xmlns="http://www.w3.org/1999/xhtml"
    xmlns:ui="http://java.sun.com/jsf/facelets"
    xmlns:debug="http://corejsf/facelets/debug">
    ...
        <debug:headers/>
    ...
</html>
```

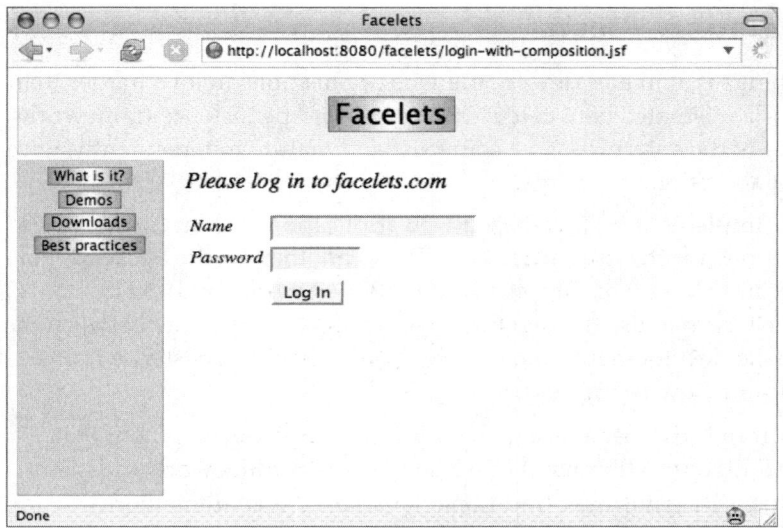

Figure 12–9   A debug tag that is triggered by a request attribute

We must include our namespace declaration and then we are free to use the
tag. The tag is defined in an XML file:

```
<facelet-taglib>
    <namespace>http://corejsf/facelets/debug</namespace>
    <tag>
        <tag-name>headers</tag-name>
        <source>tags/corejsf/debug/headers.xhtml</source>
    </tag>
</facelet-taglib>
```

We specify the name of the tag, headers, and the file it represents: tags/corejsf/
debug/headers.xhtml. Here is that file:

```
<ui:composition xmlns:ui="http://java.sun.com/jsf/facelets"
    xmlns:h="http://java.sun.com/jsf/html"
    xmlns:c="http://java.sun.com/jstl/core">
    <c:choose>
        <c:when test="#{not empty param.debug and param.debug == 'true'}">
            <h:outputText value="#{msgs.debugHeaders}"/>
            <p><h:outputText value="#{header}" style="color: red;"/></p>
        </c:when>
    </c:choose>
</ui:composition>
```

That's it. A Facelets custom tag in three easy steps.

EJB Integration—Seam

One of the things that makes developing web applications in Java harder than it should be is a mismatch between user interface and persistence frameworks. The two sides of the enterprise Java coin exist and mature independently, without much collaboration or synergy.

Traditionally, implementing Java-based web applications meant learning two frameworks—one for the user interface (UI) and another for the backend. For example: JSF and Hibernate; Tapestry and EJB3; Webwork and IBATIS, etc. Then you must learn to use the two frameworks together. Synergy between the two could make development much easier, if only UI and persistence frameworks could somehow be united.

Enter Seam, from JBoss. Seam is a new approach to web development that unites JSF and EJB3 (or Hibernate) into a single potent framework with compelling productivity gains over traditional Java-based web frameworks. Seam works with either Hibernate or EJB3, and you can run it either in the JBoss server or Tomcat 5.5. Next, we see how it works.

An Address Book

To illustrate Seam fundamentals, let's explore the implementation of a Seam address book application, which maintains a list of contacts in a database. The address book is a typical create-read-update-delete application. Figure 12–10 shows how to add contacts to the database. Figure 12–11 on page 599 and Figure 12–12 on page 600 show how to delete and edit contacts, respectively.

The address book has three JSP pages: the address book page, which lists all the contacts in the address book, a page to add a contact, and a page to edit a contact. From looking at those JSP pages, you cannot discern that this is a Seam application.

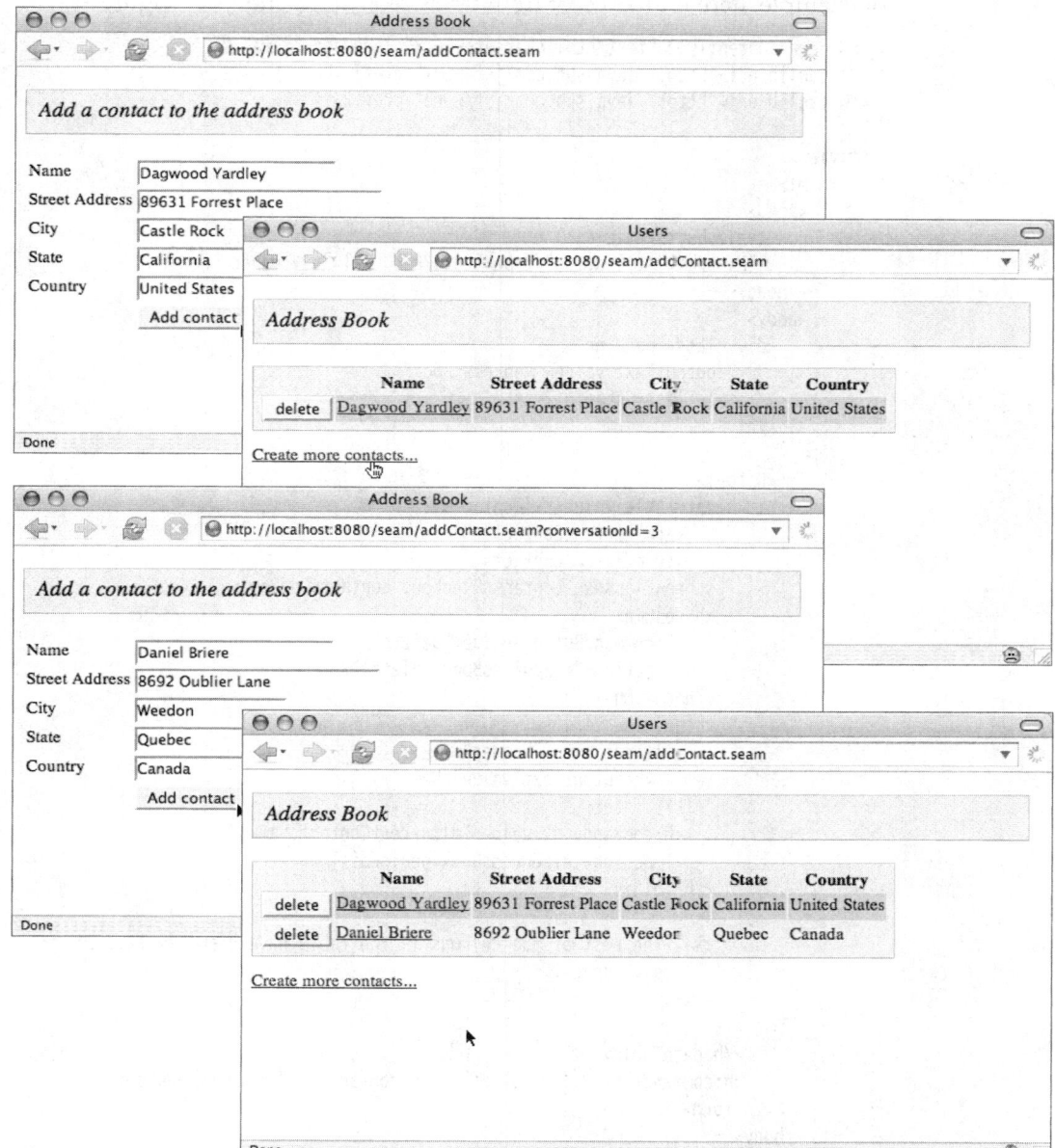

Figure 12–10 Adding two contacts to an empty address book

For example, here is an excerpt from addressBook.jsp, as shown in Figure 12–10:

```jsp
<%@ page contentType="text/html;charset=UTF-8" language="java" %>
<%@ taglib uri="http://java.sun.com/jsf/html" prefix="h" %>
<%@ taglib uri="http://java.sun.com/jsf/core" prefix="f" %>

<f:view>
   <html>
      <head>
         <title>Users</title>
         <link href="styles.css" type="text/css" rel="stylesheet"/>
      </head>
      <body>
         <div class="heading">
            <h:outputText value="Address Book"
            styleClass="headingText"/>
         </div>

         <h:form>
            <h:dataTable value="#{contacts}"
                var="currentContact"
                styleClass="contacts"
                rowClasses="contactsEvenRow, contactsOddRow">
               <h:column>
                  <h:commandButton value="delete"
                     action="#{addressBook.delete}"/>
               </h:column>
               <h:column>
                  <f:facet name="header">
                     <h:outputText value="Name"/>
                  </f:facet>
                  <h:commandLink value="#{currentContact.name}"
                     action="#{addressBook.beginEdit}"/>
               </h:column>

               <%-- The rest of the columns in the table have been ommitted to
                  save space.
               --%>

            </h:dataTable>
            <h:commandLink value="Create more contacts..." action="addContact"/>
         </h:form>
      </body>
   </html>
</f:view>
```

As you might expect, the contacts table is implemented with an h:dataTable tag. The value attribute for that tag points to a managed bean named contacts, and in the body of the h:dataTable tag we access another managed bean named address-Book. We use this bean to wire buttons and links to JSF action methods.

The application's other two JSP pages, addContact.jsp and editContact.jsp, are equally innocuous, plain-vanilla JSF views without the slightest hint of any framework other than JSF.

The interesting part of this application lies in its managed beans. You would never know it from the JSP page alone, but the contacts and addressBook beans from the preceding code are both EJBs. The former is an entity bean, whereas the latter is a stateful session bean. Now we see how it all fits together.

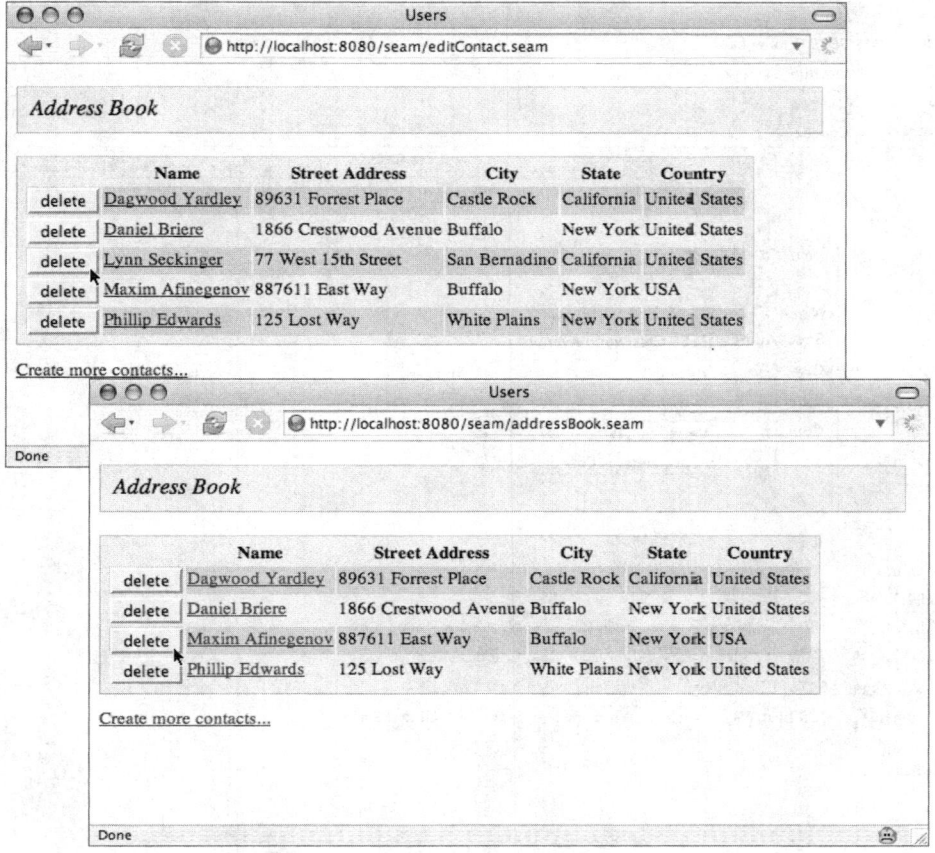

Figure 12–11   Deleting a contact in the address book

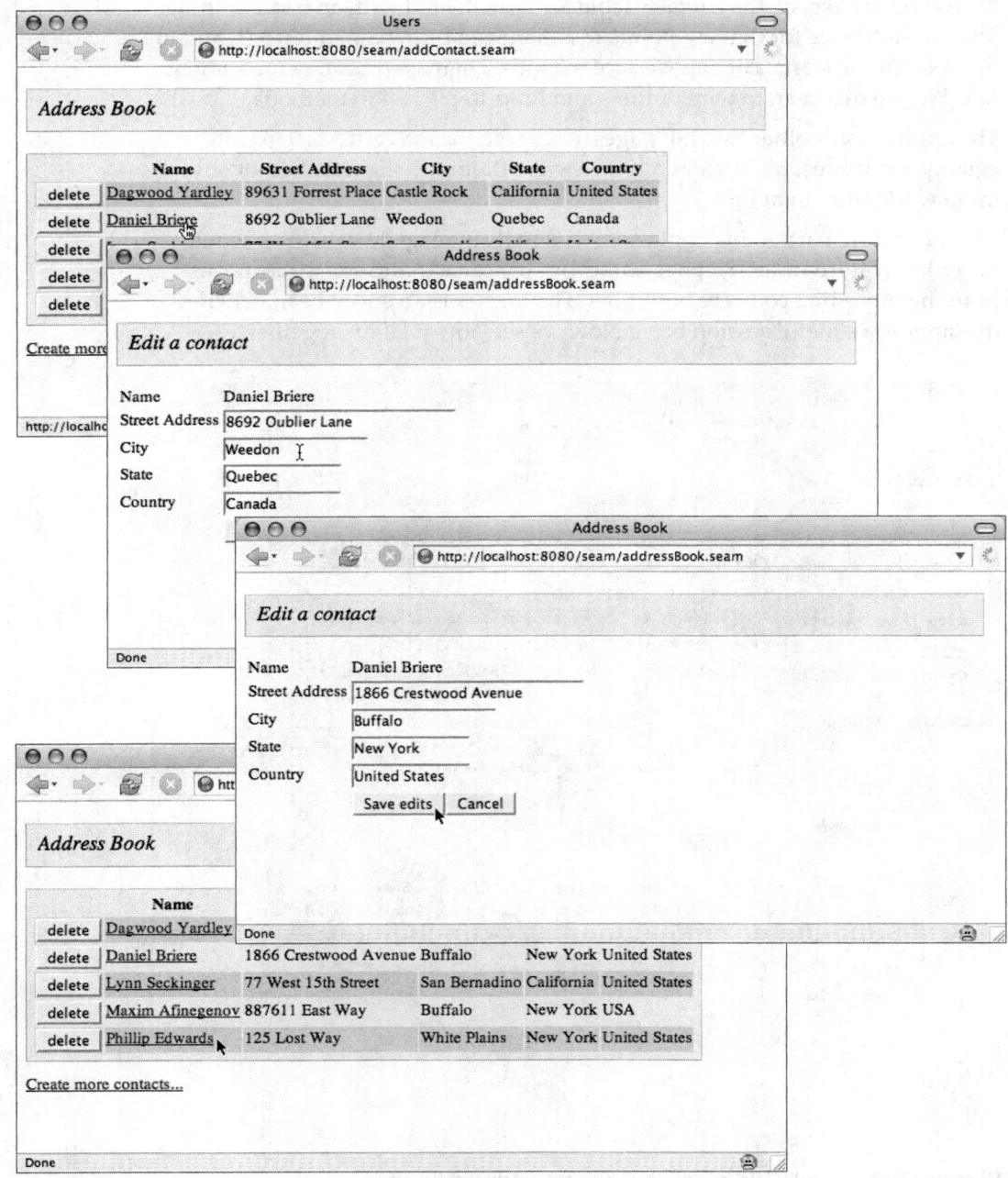

Figure 12–12   Editing a contact in the address book

Configuration

Our application's configuration consists of two XML files: one for JSF and another for persistence. As is typical for Seam applications, our JSF configuration file contains no managed bean declarations—those have been transformed into annotations. In fact, our JSF configuration file consists almost entirely of navigation rules for navigating from one web page to another. The JSF configuration file is so unremarkable that it deserves no further mention.

The persistence XML file is marginally more interesting:

```
<persistence>
    <persistence-unit name="userDatabase">
        <provider>org.hibernate.ejb.HibernatePersistence</provider>
        <jta-data-source>java:/DefaultDS</jta-data-source>
        <properties>
            <property name="hibernate.dialect"
                value="org.hibernate.dialect.HSQLDialect"/>
            <property name="hibernate.hbm2ddl.auto" value="create-drop"/>
        </properties>
    </persistence-unit>
</persistence>
```

In the preceding XML file, we declare our database intentions, including the database name, data source, and Hibernate SQL dialect.

That is essentially all there is for configuration. For our implementation, we used the JBoss embedded EJB server with Tomcat 5.5.

To understand the address book implementation, we start on the ground floor: the database.

Entity Beans

We are storing contacts in a database, so we need an entity bean:

```
@Entity
@Name("contact")
@Scope(ScopeType.EVENT)
@Table(name="contacts")
public class Contact implements Serializable {
    private static final long serialVersionUID = 48L;
    private String name, streetAddress, city;
    private String state, country;
    ...
    public Contact(String name) {
        this.name = name;
    }
```

```java
public Contact() {}

@Id @NotNull @Length(min=5, max=25)
public String getName() {
   return name;
}

public void setName(String name) {
   this.name = name;
}

// Standard JavaBeans setters and getters for the
// remaining variables are ommitted.

public String toString() {
   return "Contact(" + name + ")";
}
}
```

The annotations before the class declaration state that the Contact class represents an entity bean. We access that bean, named contact, in addContact.jsp:

```html
<h:panelGrid columns="2">
   <h:outputText value="Name"/>
   <h:panelGroup>
      <h:inputText id="name"
         value="#{contact.name}"
         size="20"/>
      <h:message for="name"/>
   </h:panelGroup>

   <h:outputText value="Street Address"/>
   <h:panelGroup>
      <h:inputText id="streetAddress"
         value="#{contact.streetAddress}"
         size="25"/>
      <h:message for="streetAddress"/>
   </h:panelGroup>

   ...

   <h:outputText value=""/>
   <h:commandButton value="Add contact"
      action="#{addressBook.addToBook}"/>
   <h:commandButton value="Cancel"
      action="#{addressBook.cancel}"/>
</h:panelGrid>
```

By virtue of the annotations in the Contact class, when Seam first encounters the name contact in a value expression, it creates an instance of com.corejsf.Contact and places it in request scope (Seam refers to request scope as *event scope*). We also specify the name of the database table—contacts—that corresponds to our entity bean.

The @Id annotation designates the name property as the primary key for the contacts table. The @NotNull and @Length annotations specify that the name property cannot be null and must contain between five and 25 characters.

 NOTE: In the preceding code fragment, we used a total of seven annotations to add persistence to a plain old Java object (POJO) and to transform it into a JSF managed bean. In fact, we used three distinct types of annotations:

- EJB3
- JSF
- Hibernate validator framework

The @Entity, @Table, and @Id annotations are EJB3 annotations, whereas the @Name and @Scope annotations are JSF-related. Finally, the @NotNull and @Length annotations are for the Hibernate validator framework, which can be used with either Hibernate or EJB3.

 NOTE: Seam performs validation at the model level, not the view level, as is typical for JSF applications.

Stateful Session Beans

Now we have a relatively simple-minded entity bean that we can persist to the database, so it is time to look at the class where the real action is: the stateful session bean that harbors JSF action methods called from JSP pages. First, we declare a local interface:

```
package com.corejsf;

import javax.ejb.Local;

@Local
public interface AddressBook {
    public String addToBook();
    public String delete();
    public String beginEdit();
```

```
    public String edit();
    public void findContacts();
}
```

Next, we implement the stateful session bean:

```
// NOTE: this is not a complete listing. Parts of this class are purposely ommitted
// pending further discussion.

@Stateful
@Scope(ScopeType.SESSION)
@Name("addressBook")
public class AddressBookAction implements Serializable, AddressBook {
    @In(required=false) private Contact contact;
    ...
    @PersistenceContext(type= PersistenceContextType.EXTENDED)
    private EntityManager em;
    ...

    @IfInvalid(outcome=Outcome.REDISPLAY)
    public String addToBook() {
        List existing = em.createQuery("select name from Contact where name=:name")
            .setParameter("name", contact.getName())
            .getResultList();

        if (existing.size()==0) {
            // save to the database if the contact doesn't
            // already exist
            em.persist(contact);
            ...
            return "success";
        }
        else {
            facesContext.addMessage(null,
                new FacesMessage("contact already exists"));
            return null;
        }
    }
    ...

    @Remove @Destroy
    public void destroy() {}
}
```

The @Name annotation specifies the name of a managed bean. We referenced that addressBook bean from addressBook.jsp, listed on page 598. We use the @Scope annotation to specify the addressBook bean's scope.

With the @In annotation, we *inject* the contact instance, which means that Seam will intercept all AddressBookAction method calls, and if a scoped variable named contact exists, Seam will inject it into AddressBookAction's contact property before invoking the method. For the contact property, injection is not required; otherwise, Seam would throw an exception for any method called when there was no contact scoped variable for Seam to inject.

In the addToBook method, we use the EJB entity manager to save the contact to the database. The addToBook method is called from addContact.jsp

```
<h:form>
    <h:panelGrid columns="2">
        <h:outputText value="Name"/>
        <h:panelGroup>
            <h:inputText id="name"
                value="#{contact.name}"
                size="20"/>
            <h:message for="name"/>
        </h:panelGroup>
        ...

        <h:outputText value=""/>
        <h:commandButton value="Add contact"
            action="#{addressBook.addToBook}"/>
    </h:panelGrid>
</h:form>
    </body>
</html>
</f:view>
```

Here is how the scenario unfolds: When you load addContact.jsp, Seam encounters the expression #{contact.name}. Since the contact bean is request-scoped (or event-scoped in Seam-speak), Seam creates an instance of com.corejsf.Contact and stores it in request scope under the name contact. Then Seam calls contact.getName() to populate the name text field as the page loads. Subsequently, the contact bean is available throughout the rest of the page.

When the user submits the form, assuming all submitted values pass validation, Seam invokes the corresponding setter methods for the contact object's properties and invokes addressBook.addToBook().

When Seam intercepts the call to addressBook.addToBook(), it first injects the value of the request-scoped contact variable into the addressBook's contact property; thus, addToBook() has access to the contact entity bean, and from there it uses the EJB entity manager to drive the changes home to the database.

NOTE: The address book has two EJBs: an entity bean representing a contact and a stateful session bean. The contact entity beans are stored in the database, whereas the stateful session bean contains JSF action methods and maintains the list of contacts in the database. The stateful session bean could just as easily have been implemented as a JavaBean. But we wanted the convenience of database access in our JSF actions, so we opted for a session bean, as is often the case for Seam applications.

JSF DataModel *Integration*

Seam has built-in support for JSF tables. Once again, take a look at a severely truncated listing of the contacts table in addressBook.jsp:

```
<h:dataTable value="#{contacts}"
   var="currentContact"
   styleClass="contacts"
   rowClasses="contactsEvenRow, contactsOddRow">
   ...
</h:dataTable>
```

Now we revisit the stateful session bean, AddressBookAction, that we discussed in "Stateful Session Beans" on page 603. In that discussion, we ommitted some details, which we explore in the next couple of sections. Here, we look at the @DataModel and @DataModelSelection annotations and their corresponding properties. First, we discuss @DataModel:

```
public class AddressBookAction implements Serializable, AddressBook {
   @DataModel
   @Out(required=false)
   private List<Contact> contacts;
   ...

   @Factory("contacts")
   public void findContacts() {
      contacts = em.createQuery("from Contact")
         .getResultList();
   }
   ...
}
```

When Seam comes across <h:dataTable value="#{contacts}"...>...</h:dataTable> in addressBook.jsp, it looks for a scoped variable named contacts. If the contacts variable does not exist, Seam creates it with a call to the variable's *factory* method: AddressBookAction.findContacts(). That method performs a database query to ensare

all the contacts in the database and stores the resulting list in the contacts variable. At the end of the factory method call, Seam exports the contacts variable to
page scope, at the behest of the @Out annotation.

As you can see from this example, Seam factory methods let you wire a JSF
component to a persistent object; in the preceding example, we wired a list of
contacts from the database to a JSF table.

Seam also has special support for handling table selections. In AddressBookAction,
we add a @DataModelSelection annotation:

```java
public class AddressBookAction implements Serializable, AddressBook {
    @DataModel
    @Out(required=false)
    private List<Contact> contacts;

    @DataModelSelection
    @Out(required=false, scope=ScopeType.CONVERSATION)
    private Contact selectedContact;
    ...

    @End
    public String edit() {
        em.persist(selectedContact);
        contacts = em.createQuery("from Contact").getResultList();
        return "edited";
    }
    ...

    // This method is called from addressBook.jsp.
    public String delete() {
        // Deletes the selected contact from the database
        contacts.remove(selectedContact);
        em.remove(selectedContact);
        return "deleted";
    }
    ...
}
```

When the user clicks a button or link from the contacts table, Seam injects
the selected contact into the AddressBookAction's selectedContact variable before
entering the action method associated with the button or link. For example,
when the user clicks a "delete" button on the address book page, Seam invokes
AddressBookAction.delete(). But before it does, it injects the selected contact into
the AddressBookAction's selectedContact variable. Interestingly, setter and getter

methods are not required for the selectedContact variable—it is enough to declare the variable and its annotation, and Seam takes care of the rest.

In addition to injecting the selectedContact variable, we also export (or outject, if you must) it to *conversation* scope, so we can access it in editContact.jsp. Next, we see what conversation scope is all about.

Conversation Scope

In web applications, we have request scope, which spans a single HTTP request, and session scope, which sticks around indefinitely. Often, when implementing a series of interactions, such as a wizard, for example, it would be nice to have a scope in between request and session. In Seam, that's conversation scope.

When we delete a contact from the address book, it is a one-step process. The user clicks a "delete" button, and Seam invokes AddressBookAction.delete(), as outlined in the previous section. Seam takes care to inject the selected contact before making the call (this is discussed in "JSF DataModel Integration" on page 606). The delete method deletes the contact from the database and updates the list of contacts.

However, editing a contact is a two-step process. It starts when the user clicks the link representing the contact's name:

```
<h:dataTable value="#{contacts}" var="currentContact"
        styleClass="contacts"
        rowClasses="contactsEvenRow, contactsOddRow">
    <h:column>
        <h:commandButton value="delete"
            action="#{addressBook.delete}"/>
    </h:column>
    <h:column>
        <f:facet name="header">
            <h:outputText value="Name"/>
        </f:facet>
        <h:commandLink value="#{currentContact.name}"
            action="#{addressBook.beginEdit}"/>
    </h:column>
</h:dataTable>
```

Seam invokes AddressBookAction.beginEdit(), once again injecting the selected contact into the selectedContact variable before making the call. Here is how beginEdit() is implemented:

```
public class AddressBookAction implements Serializable, AddressBook {
    ...

    @DataModelSelection
    @In(required=false)
    @Out(required=false, scope=ScopeType.CONVERSATION)
    private Contact selectedContact;
    ...

    @Begin public String beginEdit() {
        return "edit";
    }

    @End public String edit() {
        em.persist(selectedContact);
        contacts = em.createQuery("from Contact").getResultList();
        return "edited";
    }

}
```

The beginEdit method is a JSF action method that returns a string outcome used by JSF to navigate to the next view. That is unremarkable. What is remarkable is the @Begin annotation, which signifies that beginEdit() starts a conversation. When we leave beginEdit(), Seam exports the selectedContact to conversation scope, where we subsequently access it in editContact.jsp.

The @End annotation, attached to the edit method, signifies the end of the conversation. When we exit that method, Seam removes the selectedContact from conversation scope.

 NOTE: We could have eschewed conversations and instead stored the selected contact in session scope. In the edit method, we could have manually removed the selected contact from session scope, thereby creating a psuedo-conversation scope. In fact, many developers have done just that sort of thing; however, it is tedious and error prone. It is much more convenient to let the framework take care of that bookeeping so you can concentrate on higher-level concerns.

How Do I . . .

Chapter 13

The preceding chapters covered the JSF technology in a systematic manner, organized by core concepts. However, every technology has certain aspects that defy systematic exposure, and JSF is no exception. At times, you will ask yourself "How do I . . ." and not find an answer, perhaps because JSF does not really offer support for the feature or because the solution is unintuitive. This chapter was designed to help out. We answer, in somewhat random order, common questions that we found in discussion groups or that we received from readers.

Web User Interface Design

In this section, we show you how to use features such as pop-ups, applets, and file upload dialogs in your web pages. We hope that future versions of JSF will include ready-made components for these tasks. Here, we show you how to implement and configure the required components.

How do I find more components?

The JSF standard defines a minimal set of components. The only standard component that goes beyond basic HTML is the data table. This comes as a disappointment to anyone who is lured by the promise of JSF to be "Swing for the web."

You may well wonder why the JSF specification developers did not include a set of professionally designed components such as trees, date and time pickers, and the like. However, it takes tremendous skill to do this, and it is a skill that is entirely different from being able to produce a technology specification.

To see just how difficult it is to implement a coherent component library, have a look at the open source Apache MyFaces components (`http://myfaces.apache.org/tomahawk/index.html`). In isolation, the components are perfectly functional and some are even nice to look at (see Figure 13–1). However, there is little commonality in visual design or the programming interface between the Tomahawk components.

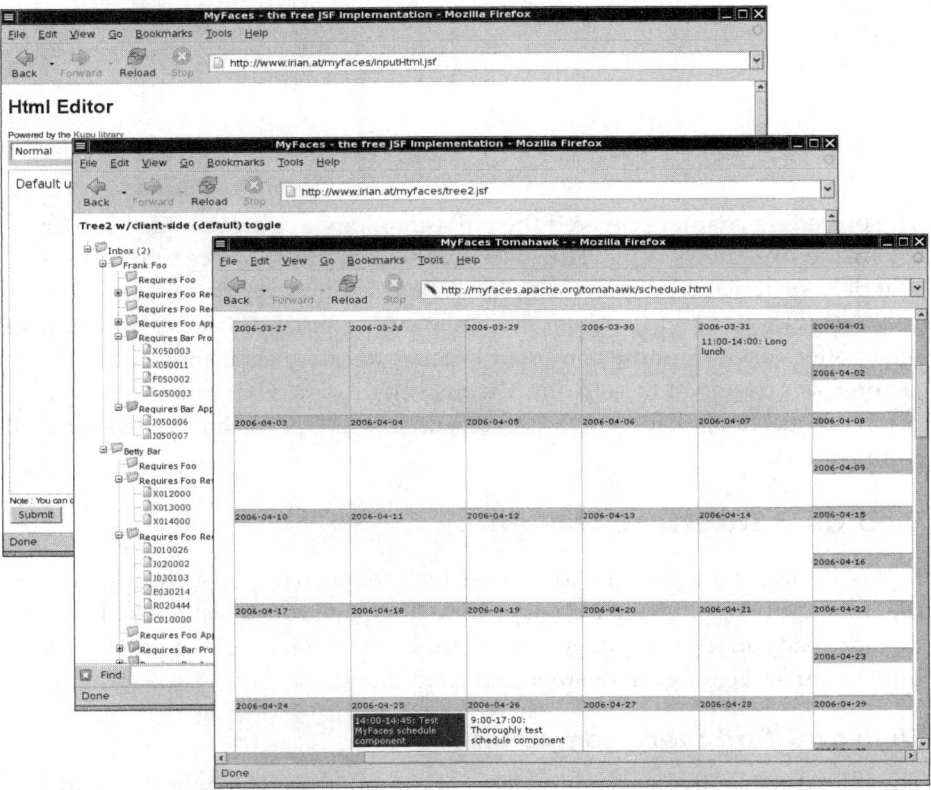

Figure 13–1   MyFaces components

You will have to wait for a rich set of standard JSF components, at least until JSF 2.0. In the meantime, here are several component libraries that are worth investigating.

1. The Apache MyFaces components may not be ideal, but they have two great advantages: They are freely available, and they are available right now. Table 13–1 shows some of the most interesting components.

2. The ADF Faces components set by Oracle (http://www.cle.com/technology/products/jdev/htdocs/partners/addins/exchange/jsf/index.html) has a professionally designed look. It contains advanced components for trees, tabbed panes, tables, and so on, as well as stylish analogs to the basic HTML buttons and input fields. These components were donated to the Apache organization in 2006 and should be freely available to the general public after some time in the Apache incubator.

3. ICEfaces (http://icefaces.org) is an open source library of components with Ajax support.

4. Java Studio Creator (http://developers.sun.com/prodtech/javatools/jscreator) is a tool for visually designing JSF components. Creator also includes a set of professionally designed components. At the 2006 Java One conference, Sun announced that it will open-source these components.

5. The Java BluePrints project has developed a set of Ajax components (https://blueprints.dev.java.net/ajaxcomponents.html). These include autocompletion, Google map interfaces, pop-up balloons, a file upload with a progress indicator, and several other pretty and useful components.

You can find additional component listings at http://jsfcentral.com/products/components and http://www.jamesholmes.com/JavaServerFaces/#software-comp.

Table 13–1 MyFaces Components

Tag	Description
tree	A tree component
treeColumn	A table in which one column is a tree
tree2	Another tree component
jscookMenu	A JavaScript-based menu
panelNavigation	A vertical hierarchical menu
panelNavigation2	The successor to panelNavigation
calendar	A calendar input component
inputDate	A date/time input component
schedule	A schedule with day, week, and month views of tasks
inputHtml	A JavaScript-based input component for HTML text

Table 13–1   MyFaces Components (cont.)

Tag	Description
fileUpload	A file upload component
rssTicker	Retrieves an RSS feed
tabbedPane	A tabbed pane, similar to the one in Chapter 9
panelStack	Displays one panel from multiple choices
popup	A pop-up that is rendered when the mouse is moved over a target
dataTable	An extension of the standard dataTable, with support for clickable sort headers and model state saving
dataScroller	A component for scrolling a table
newspaperTable	Wraps a long table into newspaper columns
dataList	Displays data as numbered lists, bulleted lists, or comma-separated lists
saveState	Saves arbitrary state with the client
aliasBean	Defines an alias for a bean that is included in a subview
buffer	Renders part of a page into a buffer for later use
stylesheet	Loads a style sheet from a location relative to the base of the web application
jsValueChangeListener	A client-side value change listener

How do I support file uploads?

The users of your application may want to upload files, such as photos or documents (see Figure 13–2 and Figure 13–3).

Unfortunately, there is no standard file upload component in JSF. However, it turns out that it is fairly straightforward to implement one. The hard work has already been done by the folks at the Apache organization in the Commons file upload library (see http://jakarta.apache.org/commons/fileupload). We will show you how to incorporate the library into a JSF component.

 NOTE: The MyFaces project contains a file upload component with slightly different attributes from ours (see http://myfaces.apache.org/tomahawk/fileUpload.html).

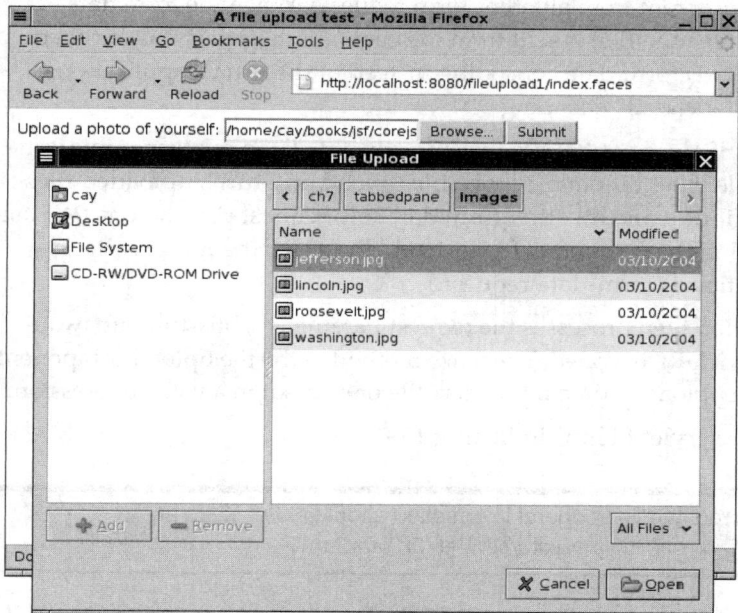

Figure 13–2   Uploading an image file

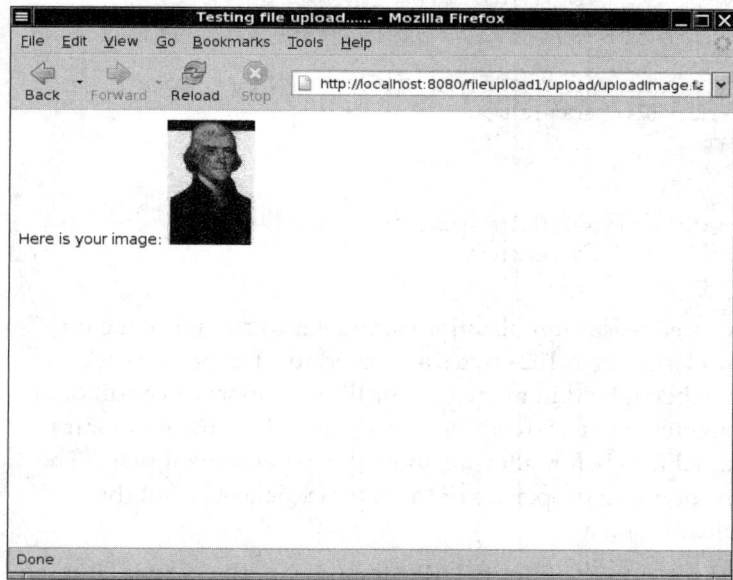

Figure 13–3   Uploaded image

A file upload is different from all other form requests. When the form data (including the uploaded file) is sent from the client to the server, it is encoded with the "multipart/form-data" encoding instead of the usual "application x-www-form-urlencoded" encoding.

Unfortunately, JSF does not handle this encoding at all. To overcome this issue, we install a *servlet filter* that intercepts a file upload and turns uploaded files into request attributes and all other form data into request parameters. (We use a utility method in the Commons file upload library for the dirty work of decoding a multipart/form-data request.)

The JSF application then processes the request parameters, blissfully unaware that they were not URL encoded. The decode method of the file upload component either places the uploaded data into a disk file or stores it in a value expression.

The code for the servlet filter is in Listing 13–1.

 NOTE: You can find general information about servlet filters at http://java.sun.com/products/servlet/Filters.html.

You need to install the filter in the web-inf.xml file, using this syntax:

```
<filter>
    <filter-name>Upload Filter</filter-name>
    <filter-class>com.corejsf.UploadFilter</filter-class>
    <init-param>
        <param-name>com.corejsf.UploadFilter.sizeThreshold</param-name>
        <param-value>1024</param-value>
    </init-param>
</filter>
<filter-mapping>
    <filter-name>Upload Filter</filter-name>
    <url-pattern>/upload/*</url-pattern>
</filter-mapping>
```

The filter uses the sizeThreshold initialization parameter to configure the file upload object. Files larger than 1024 bytes are saved to a temporary disk location rather than being held in memory. Our filter supports an additional initialization parameter, com.corejsf.UploadFilter.repositoryPath, the temporary location for uploaded files before they are moved to a permanent place. The filter sets the corresponding properties of the DiskFileUpload object of the Commons file upload library.

The filter mapping restricts the filter to URLs that start with /upload/. Thus, we avoid unnecessary filtering of other requests.

Figure 13–4 shows the directory structure of the sample application.

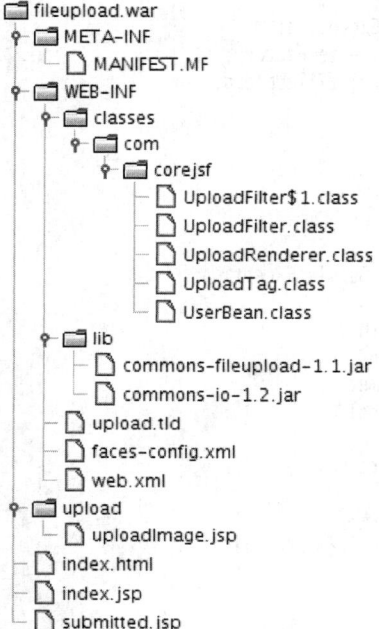

Figure 13–4   The directory structure of the file upload application

Listing 13–1   `fileupload/src/java/com/corejsf/UploadFilter.java`

```
 1. package com.corejsf;
 2.
 3. import java.io.File;
 4. import java.io.IOException;
 5. import java.util.Collections;
 6. import java.util.Enumeration;
 7. import java.util.HashMap;
 8. import java.util.List;
 9. import java.util.Map;
10. import javax.servlet.Filter;
11. import javax.servlet.FilterChain;
12. import javax.servlet.FilterConfig;
13. import javax.servlet.ServletException;
14. import javax.servlet.ServletRequest;
15. import javax.servlet.ServletResponse;
16. import javax.servlet.http.HttpServletRequest;
17. import javax.servlet.http.HttpServletRequestWrapper;
```

Listing 13–1 `fileupload/src/java/com/corejsf/UploadFilter.java` (cont.)

```
18. import org.apache.commons.fileupload.FileItem;
19. import org.apache.commons.fileupload.FileUploadException;
20. import org.apache.commons.fileupload.disk.DiskFileItemFactory;
21. import org.apache.commons.fileupload.servlet.ServletFileUpload;
22.
23.
24. public class UploadFilter implements Filter {
25.    private int sizeThreshold = -1;
26.    private String repositoryPath;
27.
28.    public void init(FilterConfig config) throws ServletException {
29.       repositoryPath = config.getInitParameter(
30.         "com.corejsf.UploadFilter.repositoryPath");
31.       try {
32.          String paramValue = config.getInitParameter(
33.            "com.corejsf.UploadFilter.sizeThreshold");
34.          if (paramValue != null)
35.             sizeThreshold = Integer.parseInt(paramValue);
36.       }
37.       catch (NumberFormatException ex) {
38.          ServletException servletEx = new ServletException();
39.          servletEx.initCause(ex);
40.          throw servletEx;
41.       }
42.    }
43.
44.    public void destroy() {
45.    }
46.
47.    public void doFilter(ServletRequest request,
48.       ServletResponse response, FilterChain chain)
49.       throws IOException, ServletException {
50.
51.       if (!(request instanceof HttpServletRequest)) {
52.          chain.doFilter(request, response);
53.          return;
54.       }
55.
56.       HttpServletRequest httpRequest = (HttpServletRequest) request;
57.
58.       boolean isMultipartContent
59.          = ServletFileUpload.isMultipartContent(httpRequest);
60.       if (!isMultipartContent) {
61.          chain.doFilter(request, response);
62.          return;
63.       }
```

Listing 13-1 fileupload/src/java/com/corejsf/UploadFilter.java (cont.)

```
64.
65.        DiskFileItemFactory factory = new DiskFileItemFactory();
66.        if (sizeThreshold >= 0)
67.           factory.setSizeThreshold(sizeThreshold);
68.        if (repositoryPath != null)
69.           factory.setRepository(new File(repositoryPath));
70.        ServletFileUpload upload = new ServletFileUpload(factory);
71.
72.        try {
73.           List<FileItem> items = (List<FileItem>) upload.parseRequest(httpRequest);
74.           final Map<String, String[]> map = new HashMap<String, String[]>();
75.           for (FileItem item : items) {
76.              String str = item.getString();
77.              if (item.isFormField())
78.                 map.put(item.getFieldName(), new String[] { str });
79.              else
80.                 httpRequest.setAttribute(item.getFieldName(), item);
81.           }
82.
83.           chain.doFilter(new
84.              HttpServletRequestWrapper(httpRequest) {
85.                 public Map<String, String[]> getParameterMap() {
86.                    return map;
87.                 }
88.                 // busywork follows ... should have been part of the wrapper
89.                 public String[] getParameterValues(String name) {
90.                    Map<String, String[]> map = getParameterMap();
91.                    return (String[]) map.get(name);
92.                 }
93.                 public String getParameter(String name) {
94.                    String[] params = getParameterValues(name);
95.                    if (params == null) return null;
96.                    return params[0];
97.                 }
98.                 public Enumeration<String> getParameterNames() {
99.                    Map<String, String[]> map = getParameterMap();
100.                   return Collections.enumeration(map.keySet());
101.                }
102.           }, response);
103.        } catch (FileUploadException ex) {
104.           ServletException servletEx = new ServletException();
105.           servletEx.initCause(ex);
106.           throw servletEx;
107.        }
108.     }
109. }
```

Now we move on to the upload component. It supports two attributes: value and target. The value denotes a value expression into which the file contents are stored. This makes sense for short files. More commonly, you will use the target attribute to specify the target location of the file.

The implementation of the FileUploadRenderer class in Listing 13–2 is straightforward. The encodeBegin method renders the HTML element. The decode method retrieves the file items that the servlet filter placed into the request attributes and disposes of them as directed by the tag attributes. The target attribute denotes a file relative to the server directory containing the root of the web application.

The associated tag handler class, in Listing 13–3, is as dull as ever.

Finally, when using the file upload tag, you need to remember to set the form encoding to "multipart/form-data" (see Listing 13–4).

Listing 13–2   fileupload/src/java/com/corejsf/UploadRenderer.java

```
 1. package com.corejsf;
 2.
 3. import java.io.File;
 4. import java.io.IOException;
 5. import java.io.InputStream;
 6. import java.io.UnsupportedEncodingException;
 7. import javax.el.ValueExpression;
 8. import javax.faces.FacesException;
 9. import javax.faces.component.EditableValueHolder;
10. import javax.faces.component.UIComponent;
11. import javax.faces.context.ExternalContext;
12. import javax.faces.context.FacesContext;
13. import javax.faces.context.ResponseWriter;
14. import javax.faces.render.Renderer;
15. import javax.servlet.ServletContext;
16. import javax.servlet.http.HttpServletRequest;
17. import org.apache.commons.fileupload.FileItem;
18.
19. public class UploadRenderer extends Renderer {
20.    public void encodeBegin(FacesContext context, UIComponent component)
21.       throws IOException {
22.       if (!component.isRendered()) return;
23.       ResponseWriter writer = context.getResponseWriter();
24.
25.       String clientId = component.getClientId(context);
26.
```

Listing 13–2 fileupload/src/java/com/corejsf/UploadRenderer.java (cont.)

```
27.      writer.startElement("input", component);
28.      writer.writeAttribute("type", "file", "type");
29.      writer.writeAttribute("name", clientId, "clientId");
30.      writer.endElement("input");
31.      writer.flush();
32.   }
33.
34.   public void decode(FacesContext context, UIComponent component) {
35.      ExternalContext external = context.getExternalContext();
36.      HttpServletRequest request = (HttpServletRequest) external.getRequest();
37.      String clientId = component.getClientId(context);
38.      FileItem item = (FileItem) request.getAttribute(clientId);
39.
40.      Object newValue;
41.      ValueExpression valueExpr = component.getValueExpression("value");
42.      if (valueExpr != null) {
43.         Class valueType = valueExpr.getType(context.getELContext());
44.         if (valueType == byte[].class) {
45.            newValue = item.get();
46.         }
47.         else if (valueType == InputStream.class) {
48.            try {
49.               newValue = item.getInputStream();
50.            } catch (IOException ex) {
51.               throw new FacesException(ex);
52.            }
53.         }
54.         else {
55.            String encoding = request.getCharacterEncoding();
56.            if (encoding != null)
57.               try {
58.                  newValue = item.getString(encoding);
59.               } catch (UnsupportedEncodingException ex) {
60.                  newValue = item.getString();
61.               }
62.            else
63.               newValue = item.getString();
64.         }
65.         ((EditableValueHolder) component).setSubmittedValue(newValue);
66.         ((EditableValueHolder) component).setValid(true);
67.      }
68.
69.      Object target = component.getAttributes().get("target");
70.
```

Listing 13–2   fileupload/src/java/com/corejsf/UploadRenderer.java (cont.)

```
71.        if (target != null) {
72.           File file;
73.           if (target instanceof File)
74.              file = (File) target;
75.           else {
76.              ServletContext servletContext
77.                 = (ServletContext) external.getContext();
78.              String realPath = servletContext.getRealPath(target.toString());
79.              file = new File(realPath);
80.           }
81.
82.           try { // ugh--write is declared with "throws Exception"
83.              item.write(file);
84.           } catch (Exception ex) {
85.              throw new FacesException(ex);
86.           }
87.        }
88.     }
89. }
```

Listing 13–3   fileupload/src/java/com/corejsf/UploadTag.java

```
1. package com.corejsf;
2.
3. import javax.el.ValueExpression;
4. import javax.faces.component.UIComponent;
5. import javax.faces.webapp.UIComponentELTag;
6.
7. public class UploadTag extends UIComponentELTag {
8.     private ValueExpression value;
9.     private ValueExpression target;
10.
11.    public String getRendererType() { return "com.corejsf.Upload"; }
12.    public String getComponentType() { return "com.corejsf.Upload"; }
13.
14.    public void setValue(ValueExpression newValue) { value = newValue; }
15.    public void setTarget(ValueExpression newValue) { target = newValue; }
16.
17.    public void setProperties(UIComponent component) {
18.       super.setProperties(component);
19.       component.setValueExpression("target", target);
20.       component.setValueExpression("value", value);
21.    }
```

Listing 13–3   fileupload/src/java/com/corejsf/UploadTag.java (cont.)

```
22.
23.    public void release() {
24.        super.release();
25.        value = null;
26.        target = null;
27.    }
28. }
```

Listing 13–4   fileupload/web/upload/uploadImage.jsp

```
 1. <html>
 2.    <%@ taglib uri="http://java.sun.com/jsf/core" prefix="f" %>
 3.    <%@ taglib uri="http://java.sun.com/jsf/html" prefix="h" %>
 4.    <%@ taglib uri="http://corejsf.com/upload" prefix="corejsf" %>
 5.
 6.    <f:view>
 7.        <head>
 8.            <title>A file upload test</title>
 9.        </head>
10.        <body>
11.            <h:form enctype="multipart/form-data">
12.                Upload a photo of yourself:
13.                <corejsf:upload target="upload/#{user.id}_image.jpg"/>
14.                <h:commandButton value="Submit" action="submit"/>
15.            </h:form>
16.        </body>
17.    </f:view>
18. </html>
```

How do I show an image map?

To implement a client-side image map, supply the usemap attribute with the
h:outputImage element:

```
<h:outputImage value="image location" usemap="#aLabel"/>
```

You can then specify the map in HTML in the JSF page:

```
<map name="aLabel">
   <area shape="polygon" coords="..." href="...">
   <area shape="rect" coords="..." href="...">
   ...
</map>
```

However, this approach does not integrate well with JSF navigation. It would be nicer if the map areas acted like command buttons or links.

Chapter 12 of the Java EE 5 tutorial (http://java.sun.com/javaee/5/docs/tutorial/doc) includes sample map and area tags that overcome this limitation.

To see the image map in action, load the bookstore6 web application that is included with the tutorial (see Figure 13–5). Here is how the tags are used in the tutorial application:

```
<h:graphicImage id="mapImage" url="/template/world.jpg" alt="#{bundle.ChooseLocale}"
    usemap="#worldMap" />
<b:map id="worldMap" current="NAmericas" immediate="true" action="bookstore"
    actionListener="#{localeBean.chocseLocaleFromMap}"  >
  <b:area id="NAmerica" value="#{NA}" onmouseover="/template/world_namer.jpg"
      onmouseout="/template/world.jpg" targetImage="mapImage" />
  <b:area id="SAmerica" value="#{SA}" onmouseover="/template/world_samer.jpg"
      onmouseout="/template/world.jpg" targetImage="mapImage" />
    . . .
</b:map>
```

The area values are defined in faces-config.xml, such as

```
<managed-bean>
    <managed-bean-name> NA </managed-bean-name>
    <managed-bean-class> com.sun.bookstore6.model.ImageArea </managed-bean-class>
    <managed-bean-scope> application </managed-bean-scope>
    <managed-property>
        <property-name>coords</property-name>
        <value>
53,109,1,110,2,167,19,168,52,149,67,164,67,165,68,167,70,168,72,170,74,172,75,174,77,
175,79,177,81,179,80,179,77,179,81,179,81,178,80,178,82,211,28,238,15,233,15,242,31,
252,36,247,36,246,32,239,89,209,92,216,93,216,100,216,103,218,113,217,116,224,124,221,
128,230,163,234,185,189,178,177,162,188,143,173,79,173,73,163,79,157,64,142,54,139,53,
109
        </value>
    </managed-property>
</managed-bean>
```

Alternatively, you can use a technique that we showed in Chapter 7. Put the image inside a command button, and process the x and y coordinates on the server side:

```
<h:commandButton image="..." actionListener="..."/>
```

Attach an action listener that gets the client ID of the button, attaches the suffixes .x and .y, and looks up the coordinate values in the request map. Process the values in any desired way. With this technique, the server application needs to know the geometry of the image.

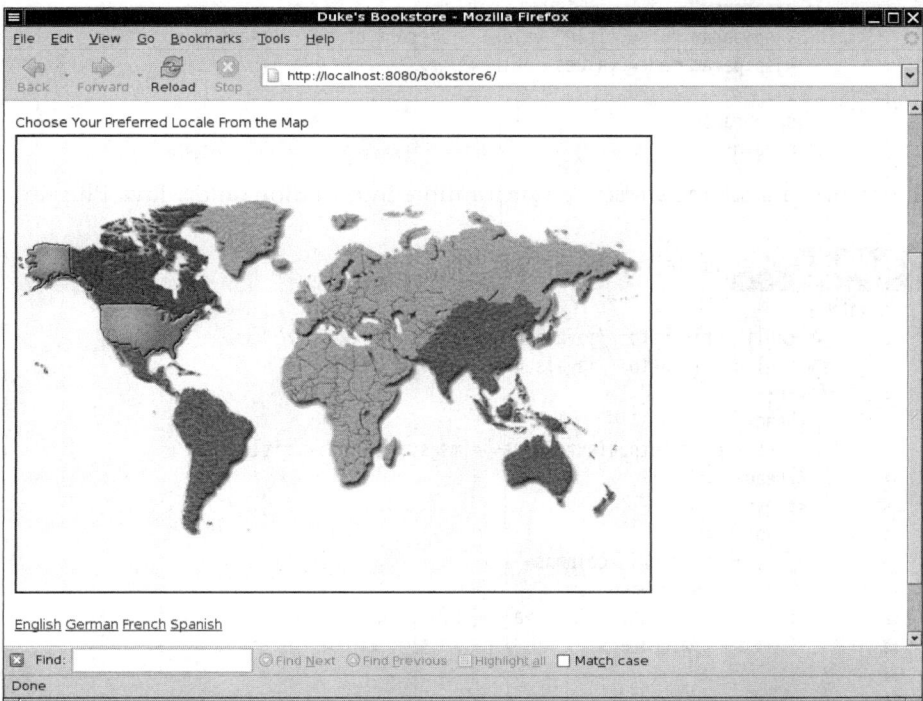

Figure 13–5   Image map sample component

How do I include an applet in my page?

Include the applet tag in the usual way (see, for example, Listing 13–5). This page displays the chart applet from Horstmann and Cornell, 2004, 2005. *Core Java™ 2*, vol. 1, chap. 10 (see Figure 13–6).

Just keep a couple of points in mind:

- If you use JSF 1.1 and you include the applet tag inside a JSF component that renders its children (such as a panel grid), then you need to enclose it inside

  ```
  <f:verbatim>...</f:verbatim>
  ```

- You may want to consider using the jsp:plugin tag instead of the applet tag. That tag generates the appropriate markup for the Java Plug-in. For example,

  ```
  <jsp:plugin type="applet" code="Chart.class"
      width="400" height="300">
  ```

```
        <jsp:params>
            <jsp:param name="title" value="Diameters of the Planets"/>
            <jsp:param name="values" value="9"/>
            ...
        </jsp:params>
    </jsp:plugin>
```

See http://java.sun.com/products/plugin for more information on the Java Plug-in.

Listing 13–5   applet/web/index.jsp

```
1.  <html>
2.      <%@ taglib uri="http://java.sun.com/jsf/core" prefix="f" %>
3.      <%@ taglib uri="http://java.sun.com/jsf/html" prefix="h" %>
4.      <f:view>
5.          <head>
6.            <title><h:outputText value="#{msgs.title}"/></title>
7.          </head>
8.          <body>
9.            <h:form>
10.              <h:panelGrid columns="1">
11.                  <h:column>
12.                      <h:outputText value="#{msgs.header}"/>
13.                  </h:column>
14.
15.                  <h:column>
16.                      <applet code="Chart.class" width="400" height="300">
17.                          <param name="title" value="Diameters of the Planets"/>
18.                          <param name="values" value="9"/>
19.                          <param name="name.1" value="Mercury"/>
20.                          <param name="name.2" value="Venus"/>
21.                          <param name="name.3" value="Earth"/>
22.                          <param name="name.4" value="Mars"/>
23.                          <param name="name.5" value="Jupiter"/>
24.                          <param name="name.6" value="Saturn"/>
25.                          <param name="name.7" value="Uranus"/>
26.                          <param name="name.8" value="Neptune"/>
27.                          <param name="name.9" value="Pluto"/>
28.                          <param name="value.1" value="3100"/>
29.                          <param name="value.2" value="7500"/>
30.                          <param name="value.3" value="8000"/>
31.                          <param name="value.4" value="4200"/>
32.                          <param name="value.5" value="88000"/>
33.                          <param name="value.6" value="71000"/>
34.                          <param name="value.7" value="32000"/>
35.                          <param name="value.8" value="30600"/>
```

Listing 13–5	applet/web/index.jsp (cont.)

```
36.                          <param name="value.9" value="1430"/>
37.                      </applet>
38.                  </h:column>
39.              </h:panelGrid>
40.          </h:form>
41.      </body>
42.  </f:view>
43. </html>
```

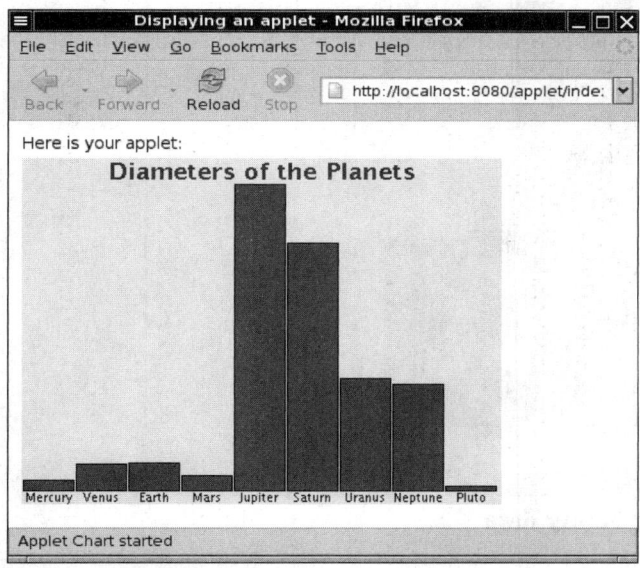

Figure 13–6   The chart applet

How do I produce binary data in a JSF page?

Sometimes you will want to dynamically produce binary data, such as an image or a PDF file. It is difficult to do this in JSF because the default view handler sends text output to a writer, not a stream. It would theoretically be possible to replace the view handler, but it is far easier to use a helper servlet for producing the binary data. Of course, you still want to use the comforts of JSF—in particular, value expressions—to customize the output. Therefore, you want to provide a JSF tag that gathers the customization data and sends it to a servlet.

As an example, we implement a JSF tag that creates a chart image (see Figure 13–7). The image contains JPEG-formatted data that was dynamically generated.

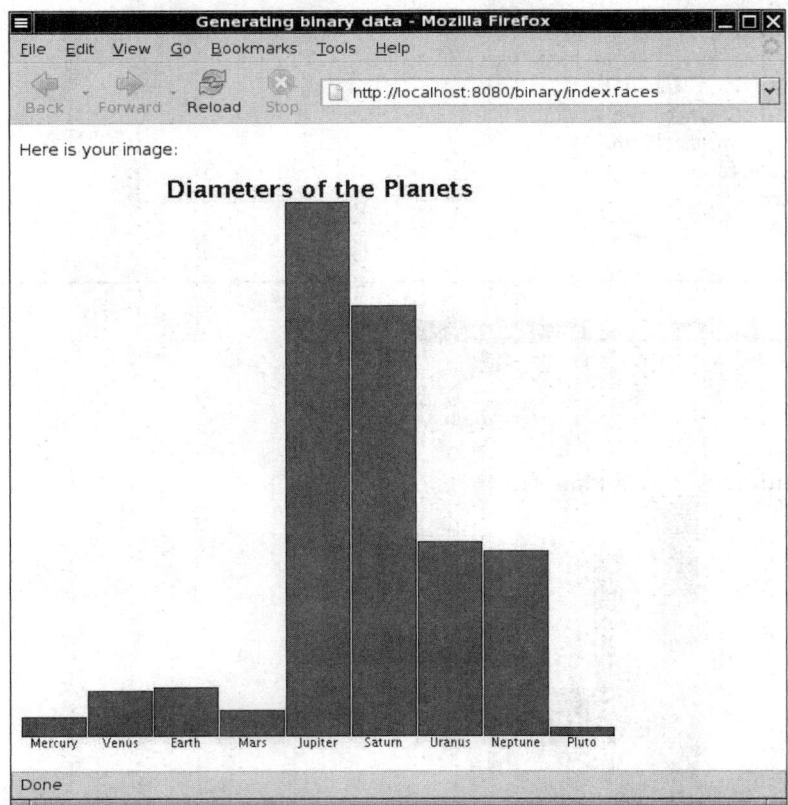

Figure 13–7   Producing binary data

 NOTE: We use the chart as an example for the binary data technique. If you want to display sophisticated graphs in your web application, check out the ChartCreator component at http://jsf-comp.sourceforge.net/components/chartcreator.

Listing 13–6 includes the chart with the following tag:

```
<corejsf:chart width="500" height="500"
    title="Diameters of the Planets"
    names="#{planets.names}" values="#{planets.values}"/>
```

Here, names and values are value expression of type String[] and double[]. The renderer, whose code is shown in Listing 13–7, produces an image tag:

```
<img width="500" height="500" src="/binary/BinaryServlet?id=a unique ID" />
```

The image is produced by the BinaryServlet (see Listing 13–8). Of course, the servlet needs to know the customization data. The renderer gathers the data from the component attributes in the usual way, bundles them into a transfer object (see Listing 13–10), and places the transfer object into the session map.

```
Map<String, Object> attributes = component.getAttributes();
Integer width = (Integer) attributes.get("width");
if (width == null) width = DEFAULT_WIDTH;
Integer height = (Integer) attributes.get("height");
if (height == null) height = DEFAULT_HEIGHT;
String title = (String) attributes.get("title");
if (title == null) title = "";
String[] names = (String[]) attributes.get("names");
double[] values = (double[]) attributes.get("values");

ChartData data = new ChartData();
data.setWidth(width);
data.setHeight(height);
data.setTitle(title);
data.setNames(names);
data.setValues(values);

String id = component.getClientId(context);
ExternalContext external = FacesContext.getCurrentInstance().getExternalContext();
Map<String, Object> session = external.getSessionMap();
session.put(id, data);
```

The servlet retrieves the transfer object from the session map and calls the transfer object's write method, which renders the image into the response stream.

```
HttpSession session = request.getSession();
String id = request.getParameter("id");
BinaryData data = (BinaryData) session.getAttribute(id);

response.setContentType(data.getContentType());
OutputStream out = response.getOutputStream();
data.write(out);
out.close();
```

To keep the servlet code general, we require that the transfer class implements an interface BinaryData (see Listing 13–9).

You use the same approach to generate any kind of binary data. The only difference is the code for writing data to the output stream.

Listing 13–6   binary1/web/index.jsp

```
 1. <html>
 2.    <%@ taglib uri="http://java.sun.com/jsf/core" prefix="f" %>
 3.    <%@ taglib uri="http://java.sun.com/jsf/html" prefix="h" %>
 4.    <%@ taglib uri="http://corejsf.com/chart" prefix="corejsf" %>
 5.    <f:view>
 6.       <head>
 7.          <title>Generating binary data</title>
 8.       </head>
 9.       <body>
10.          <h:form>
11.             <p>Here is your image:</p>
12.             <corejsf:chart width="500" height="500"
13.                title="Diameters of the Planets"
14.                names="#{planets.names}" values="#{planets.values}"/>
15.          </h:form>
16.       </body>
17.    </f:view>
18. </html>
```

Listing 13–7   binary1/src/java/com/corejsf/ChartRenderer.java

```
 1. package com.corejsf;
 2.
 3. import java.io.IOException;
 4. import java.util.Map;
 5. import javax.faces.component.UIComponent;
 6. import javax.faces.context.ExternalContext;
 7. import javax.faces.context.FacesContext;
 8. import javax.faces.context.ResponseWriter;
 9. import javax.faces.render.Renderer;
10.
11. public class ChartRenderer extends Renderer {
12.    private static final int DEFAULT_WIDTH = 200;
13.    private static final int DEFAULT_HEIGHT = 200;
14.
15.    public void encodeBegin(FacesContext context, UIComponent component)
16.       throws IOException {
17.       if (!component.isRendered()) return;
18.
19.       Map<String, Object> attributes = component.getAttributes();
20.       Integer width = (Integer) attributes.get("width");
21.       if (width == null) width = DEFAULT_WIDTH;
22.       Integer height = (Integer) attributes.get("height");
```

```
23.      if (height == null) height = DEFAULT_HEIGHT;
24.      String title = (String) attributes.get("title");
25.      if (title == null) title = "";
26.      String[] names = (String[]) attributes.get("names");
27.      double[] values = (double[]) attributes.get("values");
28.      if (names == null || values == null) return;
29.
30.      ChartData data = new ChartData();
31.      data.setWidth(width);
32.      data.setHeight(height);
33.      data.setTitle(title);
34.      data.setNames(names);
35.      data.setValues(values);
36.
37.      String id = component.getClientId(context);
38.      ExternalContext external
39.          = FacesContext.getCurrentInstance().getExternalContext();
40.      Map<String, Object> session = external.getSessionMap();
41.      session.put(id, data);
42.
43.      ResponseWriter writer = context.getResponseWriter();
44.      writer.startElement("img", component);
45.
46.      writer.writeAttribute("width", width, null);
47.      writer.writeAttribute("height", height, null);
48.      String path = external.getRequestContextPath();
49.      writer.writeAttribute("src", path + "/BinaryServlet?id=" + id, null);
50.      writer.endElement("img");
51.
52.      context.responseComplete();
53.   }
54. }
```

```
1. package com.corejsf;
2.
3. import java.io.IOException;
4. import java.io.OutputStream;
5.
6. import javax.servlet.ServletException;
7. import javax.servlet.http.HttpServlet;
8. import javax.servlet.http.HttpServletRequest;
```

Listing 13–8 binary1/src/java/com/corejsf/BinaryServlet.java (cont.)

```
 9. import javax.servlet.http.HttpServletResponse;
10. import javax.servlet.http.HttpSession;
11.
12. public class BinaryServlet extends HttpServlet {
13.    protected void processRequest(HttpServletRequest request,
14.          HttpServletResponse response)
15.       throws ServletException, IOException {
16.
17.       HttpSession session = request.getSession();
18.       String id = request.getParameter("id");
19.       BinaryData data = (BinaryData) session.getAttribute(id);
20.
21.       response.setContentType(data.getContentType());
22.       OutputStream out = response.getOutputStream();
23.       data.write(out);
24.       out.close();
25.    }
26.
27.    protected void doGet(HttpServletRequest request, HttpServletResponse response)
28.    throws ServletException, IOException {
29.       processRequest(request, response);
30.    }
31.
32.    protected void doPost(HttpServletRequest request, HttpServletResponse response)
33.    throws ServletException, IOException {
34.       processRequest(request, response);
35.    }
36. }
```

Listing 13–9 binary1/src/java/com/corejsf/BinaryData.java

```
1. package com.corejsf;
2.
3. import java.io.IOException;
4. import java.io.OutputStream;
5.
6. public interface BinaryData {
7.    String getContentType();
8.    void write(OutputStream out) throws IOException;
9. }
```

Listing 13–10   binary1/src/java/com/corejsf/ChartData.java

```
1.  package com.corejsf;
2.
3.  import java.awt.Color;
4.  import java.awt.Font;
5.  import java.awt.Graphics2D;
6.  import java.awt.font.FontRenderContext;
7.  import java.awt.font.LineMetrics;
8.  import java.awt.geom.Rectangle2D;
9.  import java.awt.image.BufferedImage;
10. import java.io.IOException;
11. import java.io.OutputStream;
12. import java.util.Iterator;
13. import javax.imageio.ImageIO;
14. import javax.imageio.ImageWriter;
15.
16. public class ChartData implements BinaryData {
17.
18.     private int width, height;
19.     private String title;
20.     private String[] names;
21.     private double[] values;
22.
23.     private static final int DEFAULT_WIDTH = 200;
24.     private static final int DEFAULT_HEIGHT = 200;
25.
26.     public ChartData() {
27.         width = DEFAULT_WIDTH;
28.         height = DEFAULT_HEIGHT;
29.     }
30.
31.     public void setWidth(int width) {
32.         this.width = width;
33.     }
34.
35.     public void setHeight(int height) {
36.         this.height = height;
37.     }
38.
39.     public void setTitle(String title) {
40.         this.title = title;
41.     }
42.
43.     public void setNames(String[] names) {
44.         this.names = names;
45.     }
```

Listing 13–10   binary1/src/java/com/corejsf/ChartData.java (cont.)

```
46.
47.    public void setValues(double[] values) {
48.        this.values = values;
49.    }
50.
51.    public String getContentType() {
52.        return "image/jpeg";
53.    }
54.
55.    public void write(OutputStream out) throws IOException {
56.        BufferedImage image = new BufferedImage(width, height,
57.            BufferedImage.TYPE_INT_RGB);
58.        Graphics2D g2 = (Graphics2D) image.getGraphics();
59.        drawChart(g2, width, height, title, names, values);
60.
61.        Iterator<ImageWriter> iter = ImageIO.getImageWritersByFormatName("jpeg");
62.        ImageWriter writer = iter.next();
63.        writer.setOutput(ImageIO.createImageOutputStream(out));
64.        writer.write(image);
65.    }
66.
67.    private static void drawChart(Graphics2D g2, int width, int height,
68.        String title, String[] names, double[] values)
69.    {
70.        // clear the background
71.        g2.setPaint(Color.WHITE);
72.        g2.fill(new Rectangle2D.Double(0, 0, width, height));
73.        g2.setPaint(Color.BLACK);
74.
75.        if (names == null || values == null || names.length != values.length)
76.            return;
77.
78.        // compute the minimum and maximum values
79.        if (values == null) return;
80.        double minValue = 0;
81.        double maxValue = 0;
82.        for (double v : values) {
83.            if (minValue > v) minValue = v;
84.            if (maxValue < v) maxValue = v;
85.        }
86.        if (maxValue == minValue) return;
87.
88.        Font titleFont = new Font("SansSerif", Font.BOLD, 20);
89.        Font labelFont = new Font("SansSerif", Font.PLAIN, 10);
90.
```

Listing 13–10 binary1/src/java/com/corejsf/ChartData.java (cont.)

```
91.    // compute the extent of the title
92.    FontRenderContext context = g2.getFontRenderContext();
93.    Rectangle2D titleBounds
94.       = titleFont.getStringBounds(title, context);
95.    double titleWidth = titleBounds.getWidth();
96.    double top = titleBounds.getHeight();
97.
98.    // draw the title
99.    double y = -titleBounds.getY(); // ascent
100.   double x = (width - titleWidth) / 2;
101.   g2.setFont(titleFont);
102.   g2.drawString(title, (float)x, (float)y);
103.
104.   // compute the extent of the bar labels
105.   LineMetrics labelMetrics
106.      = labelFont.getLineMetrics("", context);
107.   double bottom = labelMetrics.getHeight();
108.
109.   y = height - labelMetrics.getDescent();
110.   g2.setFont(labelFont);
111.
112.   // get the scale factor and width for the bars
113.   double scale = (height - top - bottom)
114.      / (maxValue - minValue);
115.   int barWidth = width / values.length;
116.
117.   // draw the bars
118.   for (int i = 0; i < values.length; i++) {
119.      // get the coordinates of the bar rectangle
120.      double x1 = i * barWidth + 1;
121.      double y1 = top;
122.      double barHeight = values[i] * scale;
123.      if (values[i] >= 0)
124.         y1 += (maxValue - values[i]) * scale;
125.      else {
126.         y1 += maxValue * scale;
127.         barHeight = -barHeight;
128.      }
129.
130.      // fill the bar and draw the bar outline
131.      Rectangle2D rect = new Rectangle2D.Double(x1, y1,
132.         barWidth - 2, barHeight);
133.      g2.setPaint(Color.RED);
134.      g2.fill(rect);
```

| Listing 13–10 | binary1/src/java/com/corejsf/ChartData.java (cont.) |

```
135.        g2.setPaint(Color.BLACK);
136.        g2.draw(rect);
137.
138.        // draw the centered label below the bar
139.        Rectangle2D labelBounds
140.           = labelFont.getStringBounds(names[i], context);
141.
142.        double labelWidth = labelBounds.getWidth();
143.        x = i * barWidth + (barWidth - labelWidth) / 2;
144.        g2.drawString(names[i], (float)x, (float)y);
145.      }
146.   }
147. }
```

It is also possible to generate binary data directly from JSF, without a servlet. However, you must be very careful with the timing and grab the servlet output stream before the JSF implementation starts writing the response. Grabbing the servlet output stream cannot happen in a component renderer. A JSF component contributes to the page output, but it does not replace it.

Instead, we install a phase listener that is activated after the Restore View phase. It writes the binary data and then calls the responseComplete method to skip the other phases.

```
public class BinaryPhaseListener implements PhaseListener {
   public PhaseId getPhaseId() {
      return PhaseId.RESTORE_VIEW;
   }
   ...
   public void afterPhase(PhaseEvent event) {
      if (!event.getFacesContext().getViewRoot().getViewId()
            .startsWith("/binary")) return;
      HttpServletResponse servletResponse
         = (HttpServletResponse) external.getResponse();
      servletResponse.setContentType(data.getContentType());
      OutputStream out = servletResponse.getOutputStream();
      write data to out
      context.responseComplete();
   }
}
```

The filter action happens only with view IDs that start with /binary. As with the servlet solution, the key for the data transfer object is included as a GET parameter.

To trigger the filter, the image URL needs to be a valid JSF URL such as *appname*/binary.faces?id=*key* or *appname*/faces/binary?id=*key*. The exact type depends on the mapping of the Faces servlet. The renderer obtains the correct format from the view handler's getActionURL method:

```
ViewHandler handler = context.getApplication().getViewHandler();
String url = handler.getActionURL(context, "/binary");
```

Listing 13–11 shows the phase listener. The following element is required in faces-config.xml to install the listener:

```
<lifecycle>
   <phase-listener>com.corejsf.BinaryPhaseListener</phase-listener>
</lifecycle>
```

Listing 13–11 binary2/src/java/com/corejsf/BinaryPhaseListener.java

```
1. package com.corejsf;
2.
3. import java.io.IOException;
4. import java.io.OutputStream;
5. import java.util.Map;
6. import javax.faces.FacesException;
7. import javax.faces.context.ExternalContext;
8. import javax.faces.context.FacesContext;
9. import javax.faces.event.PhaseEvent;
10. import javax.faces.event.PhaseId;
11. import javax.faces.event.PhaseListener;
12. import javax.servlet.http.HttpServletResponse;
13.
14. public class BinaryPhaseListener implements PhaseListener {
15.    public static final String BINARY_PREFIX = "/binary";
16.
17.    public static final String DATA_ID_PARAM = "id";
18.
19.    public PhaseId getPhaseId() {
20.       return PhaseId.RESTORE_VIEW;
21.    }
22.
23.    public void beforePhase(PhaseEvent event) {
24.    }
25.
26.    public void afterPhase(PhaseEvent event) {
27.       if (!event.getFacesContext().getViewRoot().getViewId().startsWith(
28.          BINARY_PREFIX))
29.          return;
```

| Listing 13–11 | binary2/src/java/com/corejsf/BinaryPhaseListener.java (cont.) |

```
30.
31.        FacesContext context = event.getFacesContext();
32.        ExternalContext external = context.getExternalContext();
33.
34.        String id = (String) external.getRequestParameterMap().get(DATA_ID_PARAM);
35.        HttpServletResponse servletResponse =
36.            (HttpServletResponse) external.getResponse();
37.        try {
38.          Map<String, Object> session = external.getSessionMap();
39.          BinaryData data = (BinaryData) session.get(id);
40.          if (data != null) {
41.            servletResponse.setContentType(data.getContentType());
42.            OutputStream out = servletResponse.getOutputStream();
43.            data.write(out);
44.          }
45.        } catch (IOException ex) {
46.          throw new FacesException(ex);
47.        }
48.        context.responseComplete();
49.    }
50. }
```

How do I show a large data set, one page at a time?

As you saw in Chapter 5, you can add scrollbars to a table. But if the table is truly large, you don't want it sent to the client in its entirety. Downloading the table takes a long time, and chances are that the application user wants to see only the first few rows anyway.

The standard user interface for navigating a large table is a *pager,* a set of links to each page of the table, to the next and previous pages, and if there are a great number of pages, to the next and previous batch of pages. Figure 13–8 shows a pager that scrolls through a large data set—the predefined time zones, obtained by a call to java.util.TimeZone.getAvailableIDs().

Unfortunately, JSF does not include a pager component. However, it is fairly easy to write one, and we give you the code to use or modify in your own applications.

The pager is a companion to a data table. You specify the ID of the data table, the number of pages that the pager displays, and the styles for the selected and unselected links. For example,

```
<h:dataTable id="timezones" value="#{bb.data}" var="row" rows="10">
   ...
</h:dataTable>
<corejsf:pager dataTableId="timezones" showpages="20"
selectedStyleClass="currentPage"/>
```

Suppose the user clicks the ">" link to move to the next page. The pager locates the data table and updates its first property, adding the value of the rows property. You will find that code in the decode method of the PagerRenderer in Listing 13–12.

The encode method is a bit more involved. It generates a set of links. Similar to a commandLink, clicking the link activates JavaScript code that sets a value in a hidden field and submits the form.

Listing 13–13 shows the index.jsp page that generates the table and the pager. Listing 13–14 shows the trivial backing bean.

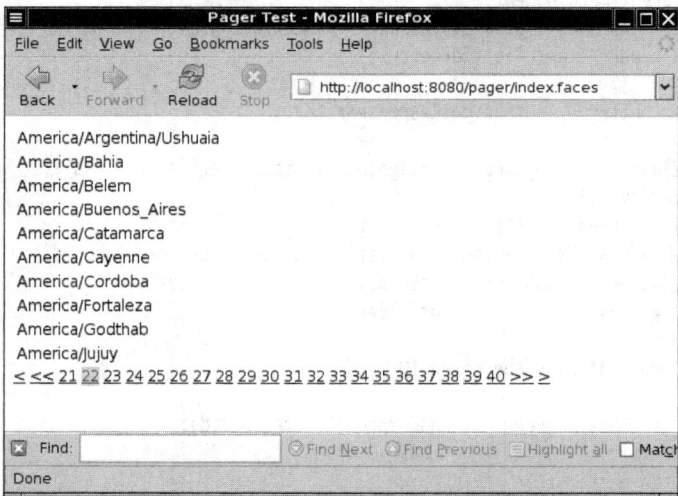

Figure 13–8   Table with a pager

 NOTE: The MyFaces data scroller component (http://myfaces.apache.org/tomahawk/dataScroller.html) offers similar functionality.

Listing 13–12 pager/src/java/com/corejsf/PagerRenderer.java

```
1. package com.corejsf;
2.
3. import java.io.IOException;
4. import java.util.Map;
5. import javax.faces.component.UIComponent;
6. import javax.faces.component.UIData;
7. import javax.faces.component.UIForm;
8. import javax.faces.context.FacesContext;
9. import javax.faces.context.ResponseWriter;
10. import javax.faces.render.Renderer;
11.
12. public class PagerRenderer extends Renderer {
13.     public void encodeBegin(FacesContext context, UIComponent component)
14.         throws IOException {
15.         String id = component.getClientId(context);
16.         UIComponent parent = component;
17.         while (!(parent instanceof UIForm)) parent = parent.getParent();
18.         String formId = parent.getClientId(context);
19.
20.         ResponseWriter writer = context.getResponseWriter();
21.
22.         String styleClass = (String) component.getAttributes().get("styleClass");
23.         String selectedStyleClass
24.             = (String) component.getAttributes().get("selectedStyleClass");
25.         String dataTableId = (String) component.getAttributes().get("dataTableId");
26.         Integer a = (Integer) component.getAttributes().get("showpages");
27.         int showpages = a == null ? 0 : a.intValue();
28.
29.         // find the component with the given ID
30.
31.         UIData data = (UIData) component.findComponent(dataTableId);
32.
33.         int first = data.getFirst();
34.         int itemcount = data.getRowCount();
35.         int pagesize = data.getRows();
36.         if (pagesize <= 0) pagesize = itemcount;
37.
38.         int pages = itemcount / pagesize;
39.         if (itemcount % pagesize != 0) pages++;
40.
41.         int currentPage = first / pagesize;
42.         if (first >= itemcount - pagesize) currentPage = pages - 1;
43.         int startPage = 0;
44.         int endPage = pages;
```

Listing 13–12 pager/src/java/com/corejsf/PagerRenderer.java (cont.)

```
45.        if (showpages > 0) {
46.           startPage = (currentPage / showpages) * showpages;
47.           endPage = Math.min(startPage + showpages, pages);
48.        }
49.
50.        if (currentPage > 0)
51.           writeLink(writer, component, formId, id, "<", styleClass);
52.
53.        if (startPage > 0)
54.           writeLink(writer, component, formId, id, "<<", styleClass);
55.
56.        for (int i = startPage; i < endPage; i++) {
57.           writeLink(writer, component, formId, id, "" + (i + 1),
58.              i == currentPage ? selectedStyleClass : styleClass);
59.        }
60.
61.        if (endPage < pages)
62.           writeLink(writer, component, formId, id, ">>", styleClass);
63.
64.        if (first < itemcount - pagesize)
65.           writeLink(writer, component, formId, id, ">", styleClass);
66.
67.        // hidden field to hold result
68.        writeHiddenField(writer, component, id);
69.     }
70.
71.     private void writeLink(ResponseWriter writer, UIComponent component,
72.        String formId, String id, String value, String styleClass)
73.        throws IOException {
74.        writer.writeText(" ", null);
75.        writer.startElement("a", component);
76.        writer.writeAttribute("href", "#", null);
77.        writer.writeAttribute("onclick", onclickCode(formId, id, value), null);
78.        if (styleClass != null)
79.           writer.writeAttribute("class", styleClass, "styleClass");
80.        writer.writeText(value, null);
81.        writer.endElement("a");
82.     }
83.
84.     private String onclickCode(String formId, String id, String value) {
85.        StringBuilder builder = new StringBuilder();
86.        builder.append("document.forms[");
87.        builder.append("'");
88.        builder.append(formId);
89.        builder.append("'");
```

Listing 13-12   pager/src/java/com/corejsf/PagerRenderer.java (cont.)

```
 90.        builder.append("]['");
 91.        builder.append(id);
 92.        builder.append("'].value='");
 93.        builder.append(value);
 94.        builder.append("';");
 95.        builder.append(" document.forms[");
 96.        builder.append("'");
 97.        builder.append(formId);
 98.        builder.append("'");
 99.        builder.append("].submit()");
100.        builder.append("; return false;");
101.        return builder.toString();
102.     }
103.
104.     private void writeHiddenField(ResponseWriter writer, UIComponent component,
105.        String id) throws IOException {
106.        writer.startElement("input", component);
107.        writer.writeAttribute("type", "hidden", null);
108.        writer.writeAttribute("name", id, null);
109.        writer.endElement("input");
110.     }
111.
112.     public void decode(FacesContext context, UIComponent component) {
113.        String id = component.getClientId(context);
114.        Map<String, String> parameters
115.           = context.getExternalContext().getRequestParameterMap();
116.
117.        String response = (String) parameters.get(id);
118.        if (response == null || response.equals("")) return;
119.
120.        String dataTableId = (String) component.getAttributes().get("dataTableId");
121.        Integer a = (Integer) component.getAttributes().get("showpages");
122.        int showpages = a == null ? 0 : a.intValue();
123.
124.        UIData data = (UIData) component.findComponent(dataTableId);
125.
126.        int first = data.getFirst();
127.        int itemcount = data.getRowCount();
128.        int pagesize = data.getRows();
129.        if (pagesize <= 0) pagesize = itemcount;
130.
131.        if (response.equals("<")) first -= pagesize;
132.        else if (response.equals(">")) first += pagesize;
133.        else if (response.equals("<<")) first -= pagesize * showpages;
134.        else if (response.equals(">>")) first += pagesize * showpages;
```

Listing 13–12   pager/src/java/com/corejsf/PagerRenderer.java (cont.)

```
135.        else {
136.            int page = Integer.parseInt(response);
137.            first = (page - 1) * pagesize;
138.        }
139.        if (first + pagesize > itemcount) first = itemcount - pagesize;
140.        if (first < 0) first = 0;
141.        data.setFirst(first);
142.    }
143. }
```

Listing 13–13   pager/web/index.jsp

```
1. <html>
2.    <%@ taglib uri="http://java.sun.com/jsf/core" prefix="f" %>
3.    <%@ taglib uri="http://java.sun.com/jsf/html" prefix="h" %>
4.    <%@ taglib uri="http://corejsf.com/pager" prefix="corejsf" %>
5.
6.    <f:view>
7.        <head>
8.            <link href="styles.css" rel="stylesheet" type="text/css"/>
9.            <title>Pager Test</title>
10.       </head>
11.       <body>
12.          <h:form>
13.             <h:dataTable id="timezones" value="#{bb.data}" var="row" rows="10">
14.                <h:column>
15.                   <h:selectBooleanCheckbox value="{bb.dummy}" onchange="submit()"/>
16.                </h:column>
17.                <h:column>
18.                    <h:outputText value="#{row}" />
19.                </h:column>
20.             </h:dataTable>
21.             <corejsf:pager dataTableId="timezones"
22.                showpages="20" selectedStyleClass="currentPage"/>
23.                <h:commandButton value="foo"/>
24.          </h:form>
25.       </body>
26.    </f:view>
27. </html>
```

| **Listing 13–14** | pager/src/java/com/corejsf/BackingBean.java |

```
1. package com.corejsf;
2.
3. public class BackingBean {
4.     private String[] data = java.util.TimeZone.getAvailableIDs();
5.     public String[] getData() { return data; }
6.
7.     public boolean getDummy() { return false; }
8.     public void setDummy(boolean b) {}
9. }
```

How do I generate a pop-up window?

The basic method for a pop-up window is simple. Use the JavaScript calls

```
popup = window.open(url, name, features);
popup.focus();
```

The features parameter is a string, such as

```
"height=300,width=200,toolbar=no,menubar=no"
```

The pop-up window should be displayed when the user clicks a button or link. Attach a function to the onclick handler of the button or link, and have the function return false so that the browser does not submit the form or follow the link. For example,

```
<h:commandButton value="..." onclick="doPopup(this); return false;"/>
```

The doPopup function contains the JavaScript instructions for popping up the window. It is contained in a script tag inside the page header.

However, challenges arise when you need to transfer data between the main window and the pop-up.

Now we look at a specific example. Figure 13–9 shows a page with a pop-up window that lists the states of the USA or the provinces of Canada, depending on the setting of the radio buttons. The list is generated by a backing bean on the server.

How does the backing bean know which state was selected? After all, the form has not yet been posted back to the server when the user requests the pop-up. We show you two solutions—each of them is interesting in its own right and may give you ideas for solving similar problems.

In the first solution, we pass the selection parameter to the pop-up URL, like this:

```
window.open("popup.faces?country=" + country[i].value, "popup', features);
```

The popup.faces page retrieves the value of the country request parameter as param.country:

```
<h:dataTable value="#{bb.states[param.country]}" var="state">
```

Here, the states property of the backing bean bb yields a map whose index is the country name.

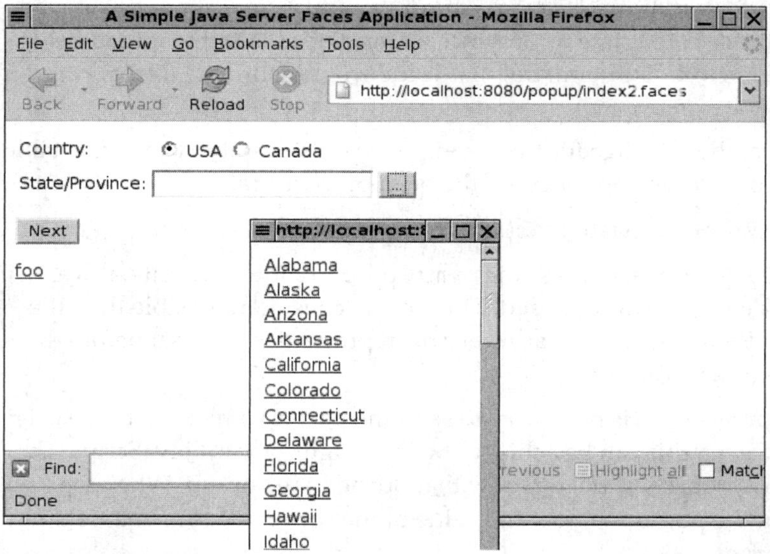

Figure 13–9 Popping up a window to select a state or province

The second solution (suggested by Marion Bass and Sergey Smirnov) is more involved but also more powerful. In this technique, the pop-up window is first created as a blank window and then filled with the response to a JSF command.

The JSF command is issued by a form that contains a hidden field and an invisible link, like this:

```
<h:form id="hidden" target="popup">
   <h:inputHidden id="country" value="#{bb.country}"/>
   <h:commandLink id="go" action="showStates"/>
</h:form>
```

Note the following details:

- The target of the form has the same name as the pop-up window. Therefore, the browser will show the result of the action inside the pop-up.

- The hidden country field will be populated before the form is submitted. It sets the bb.country value expression. This enables the backing bean to return the appropriate set of states or provinces.
- The action attribute of the command link is used by the navigation handler to select the JSF page that generates the pop-up contents.

The doPopup function initializes the hidden field and fires the link action:

```
document.getElementById("hidden:country").value = country[i].value;
document.getElementById("hidden:go").onclick(null);
```

The value of the selected state or province is transferred into the hidden field. When the hidden form is submitted, that value will be stored in the backing bean.

In this solution, the JSF page for the pop-up is more straightforward. The table of states or provinces is populated by the bean property call

```
<h:dataTable value="#{bb.statesForCountry}" var="state">
```

The statesForCountry property takes the country property into account—it was set when the hidden form was decoded. This approach is more flexible than the first approach because it allows arbitrary bean properties to be set before the pop-up contents are computed.

With both approaches, it is necessary to send the pop-up data back to the original page. However, this can be achieved with straightforward JavaScript. The pop-up's opener property is the window that opened the pop-up. When the user clicks a link in the pop-up, we set the value of the corresponding text field in the original page:

```
opener.document.forms[formId][formId + ":state"].value = value;
```

How does the pop-up know the form ID of the original form? Here we take advantage of the flexibility of JavaScript. You can add instance fields to any object on-the-fly. We set an openerFormId field in the pop-up window when it is constructed:

```
popup = window.open(...);
popup.openerFormId = source.form.id;
```

When we are ready to modify the form variables, we retrieve it from the pop-up window, like this:

```
var formId = window.openerFormId;
```

These are the tricks that you need to know to deal with pop-up windows. The following example shows the two approaches that we discussed. The index.jsp and popup.jsp files in Listing 13–15 and Listing 13–16 show the first approach, using a request parameter to configure the pop-up page.

The index2.jsp and popup2.jsp files in Listing 13–17 and Listing 13–18 show the second approach, filling the pop-up page with the result of a JSF action. Listing 13–19 shows the backing bean, and Listing 13–20 shows the configuration file. Note how the showStates action leads to the popup2.jsp page.

Listing 13–15   popup/web/index.jsp

```
1.  <html>
2.    <%@ taglib uri="http://java.sun.com/jsf/core" prefix="f" %>
3.    <%@ taglib uri="http://java.sun.com/jsf/html" prefix="h" %>
4.
5.    <f:view>
6.      <head>
7.        <script language="JavaScript1.1">
8.          function doPopup(source) {
9.            country = source.form[source.form.id + ":country"];
10.           for (var i = 0; i < country.length; i++) {
11.             if (country[i].checked) {
12.               popup = window.open("popup.faces?country="
13.                 + country[i].value, "popup",
14.                 "height=300,width=200,toolbar=no,menubar=no,"
15.                 + "scrollbars=yes");
16.               popup.openerFormId = source.form.id;
17.               popup.focus();
18.             }
19.           }
20.         }
21.       </script>
22.       <title>A Simple Java Server Faces Application</title>
23.     </head>
24.     <body>
25.       <h:form>
26.         <table>
27.           <tr>
28.             <td>Country:</td>
29.             <td>
30.               <h:selectOneRadio id="country" value="#{ob.country}">
31.                 <f:selectItem itemLabel="USA"  itemValue="USA"/>
32.                 <f:selectItem itemLabel="Canada"  itemValue="Canada"/>
33.               </h:selectOneRadio>
34.             </td>
35.           </tr>
```

```
36.              <tr>
37.                <td>State/Province:</td>
38.                <td>
39.                  <h:inputText id="state" value="#{bb.state}"/>
40.                </td>
41.                <td>
42.                  <h:commandButton value="..."
43.                      onclick="doPopup(this); return false;"/>
44.                </td>
45.              </tr>
46.            </table>
47.            <p>
48.              <h:commandButton value="Next" action="next"/>
49.            </p>
50.          </h:form>
51.        </body>
52.      </f:view>
53.  </html>
```

```
1.  <html>
2.    <%@ taglib uri="http://java.sun.com/jsf/core" prefix="f" %>
3.    <%@ taglib uri="http://java.sun.com/jsf/html" prefix="h" %>
4.
5.    <f:view>
6.      <head>
7.        <script type="text/javascript" language="JavaScript1.2">
8.          function doSave(value) {
9.            var formId = window.openerFormId;
10.           opener.document.forms[formId][formId + ":state"].value = value;
11.           window.close();
12.          }
13.        </script>
14.        <title>Select a state/province</title>
15.      </head>
16.      <body>
17.        <h:form>
18.          <h:dataTable value="#{bb.states[param.country]}" var="state">
19.            <h:column>
20.              <h:outputLink value="#"
21.                onclick="doSave('#{state}');">
22.                <h:outputText value="#{state}" />
23.              </h:outputLink>
```

Listing 13–16 popup/web/popup.jsp (cont.)

```
24.                </h:column>
25.              </h:dataTable>
26.            </h:form>
27.          </body>
28.        </f:view>
29. </html>
```

Listing 13–17 popup/web/index2.jsp

```
1. <html>
2.    <%@ taglib uri="http://java.sun.com/jsf/core" prefix="f" %>
3.    <%@ taglib uri="http://java.sun.com/jsf/html" prefix="h" %>
4.
5.    <f:view>
6.       <head>
7.          <script language="JavaScript1.1">
8.             function doPopup(source) {
9.                country = source.form[source.form.id + ":country"];
10.               for (var i = 0; i < country.length; i++) {
11.                  if (country[i].checked) {
12.                     popup = window.open("",
13.                        "popup",
14.                        "height=300,width=200,toolbar=no,menubar=no,"
15.                        + "scrollbars=yes");
16.                     popup.openerFormId = source.form.id;
17.                     popup.focus();
18.                     document.getElementById("hidden:country").value
19.                        = country[i].value;
20.                     document.getElementById("hidden:go").onclick(null);
21.                  }
22.               }
23.            }
24.         </script>
25.         <title>A Simple Java Server Faces Application</title>
26.      </head>
27.      <body>
28.         <h:form>
29.            <table>
30.               <tr>
31.                  <td>Country:</td>
32.                  <td>
33.                     <h:selectOneRadio id="country" value="#{ob.country}">
34.                        <f:selectItem itemLabel="USA"  itemValue="USA"/>
35.                        <f:selectItem itemLabel="Canada"  itemValue="Canada"/>
```

```
36.              </h:selectOneRadio>
37.          </td>
38.        </tr>
39.        <tr>
40.          <td>State/Province:</td>
41.          <td>
42.            <h:inputText id="state" value="#{bb.state}"/>
43.          </td>
44.          <td>
45.            <h:commandButton value="..."
46.                onclick="doPopup(this); return false;"/>
47.          </td>
48.        </tr>
49.      </table>
50.      <p>
51.        <h:commandButton value="Next" action="next"/>
52.      </p>
53.    </h:form>
54.
55.    <%-- This hidden form sends a request to a popup window. --%>
56.    <h:form id="hidden" target="popup">
57.      <h:inputHidden id="country" value="#{bb.country}"/>
58.      <h:commandLink id="go" action="showStates"/>
59.    </h:form>
60.  </body>
61. </f:view>
62. </html>
```

```
1. <html>
2. <%@ taglib uri="http://java.sun.com/jsf/core" prefix="f" %>
3. <%@ taglib uri="http://java.sun.com/jsf/html" prefix="h" %>
4.
5. <f:view>
6.    <head>
7.      <script language="JavaScript1.1">
8.        function doSave(value) {
9.          var formId = window.openerFormId;
10.          opener.document.forms[formId][formId + ":state"].value = value;
11.          window.close();
12.        }
13.      </script>
```

Listing 13–18 popup/web/popup2.jsp (cont.)

```
14.          <title>Select a state/province</title>
15.        </head>
16.        <body>
17.          <h:form>
18.            <h:dataTable value="#{bb.statesForCountry}" var="state">
19.              <h:column>
20.                <h:outputLink value="#"
21.                  onclick="doSave('#{state}');">
22.                  <h:outputText value="#{state}" />
23.                </h:outputLink>
24.              </h:column>
25.            </h:dataTable>
26.          </h:form>
27.        </body>
28.      </f:view>
29. </html>
```

Listing 13–19 popup/src/java/com/corejsf/BackingBean.java

```
1. package com.corejsf;
2.
3. import java.util.HashMap;
4. import java.util.Map;
5.
6. public class BackingBean {
7.    private String country = "USA";
8.    private String state = "";
9.    private static Map<String, String[]> states;
10.
11.   // PROPERTY: country
12.   public String getCountry() { return country; }
13.   public void setCountry(String newValue) { country = newValue; }
14.
15.   // PROPERTY: state
16.   public String getState() { return state; }
17.   public void setState(String newValue) { state = newValue; }
18.
19.   public Map<String, String[]> getStates() { return states; }
20.
21.   public String[] getStatesForCountry() { return (String[]) states.get(country); }
22.
```

Listing 13–19 popup/src/java/com/corejsf/BackingBean.java (cont.)

```
23.    static {
24.        states = new HashMap<String, String[]>();
25.        states.put("USA",
26.            new String[] {
27.                "Alabama", "Alaska", "Arizona", "Arkansas", "California",
28.                "Colorado", "Connecticut", "Delaware", "Florida", "Georgia",
29.                "Hawaii", "Idaho", "Illinois", "Indiana", "Iowa", "Kansas",
30.                "Kentucky", "Louisiana", "Maine", "Maryland", "Massachusetts",
31.                "Michigan", "Minnesota", "Mississippi", "Missouri", "Montana",
32.                "Nebraska", "Nevada", "New Hampshire", "New Jersey", "New Mexico",
33.                "New York", "North Carolina", "North Dakota", "Ohio", "Oklahoma",
34.                "Oregon", "Pennsylvania", "Rhode Island", "South Carolina",
35.                "South Dakota", "Tennessee", "Texas", "Utah", "Vermont",
36.                "Virginia", "Washington", "West Virginia", "Wisconsin", "Wyoming"
37.            });
38.
39.        states.put("Canada",
40.            new String[] {
41.                "Alberta", "British Columbia", "Manitoba", "New Brunswick",
42.                "Newfoundland and Labrador", "Northwest Territories",
43.                "Nova Scotia", "Nunavut", "Ontario", "Prince Edward Island",
44.                "Quebec", "Saskatchewan", "Yukon"
45.            });
46.    }
47. }
```

Listing 13–20 popup/web/WEB-INF/faces-config.xml

```
1. <?xml version="1.0"?>
2.
3. <faces-config xmlns="http://java.sun.com/xml/ns/javaee"
4.    xmlns:xsi="http://www.w3.org/2001/XMLSchema-instance"
5.    xsi:schemaLocation="http://java.sun.com/xml/ns/javaee
6.        http://java.sun.com/xml/ns/javaee/web-facesconfig_1_2.xsd"
7.    version="1.2">
8.    <navigation-rule>
9.        <navigation-case>
10.            <from-outcome>next</from-outcome>
11.            <to-view-id>/welcome.jsp</to-view-id>
12.        </navigation-case>
13.        <navigation-case>
14.            <from-outcome>showStates</from-outcome>
15.            <to-view-id>/popup2.jsp</to-view-id>
16.        </navigation-case>
```

Listing 13–20 popup/web/WEB-INF/faces-config.xml (cont.)

```
17.        <navigation-case>
18.            <from-outcome>technique1</from-outcome>
19.            <to-view-id>/index.jsp</to-view-id>
20.        </navigation-case>
21.        <navigation-case>
22.            <from-outcome>technique2</from-outcome>
23.            <to-view-id>/index2.jsp</to-view-id>
24.        </navigation-case>
25.    </navigation-rule>
26.
27.    <managed-bean>
28.        <managed-bean-name>bb</managed-bean-name>
29.        <managed-bean-class>com.corejsf.BackingBean</managed-bean-class>
30.        <managed-bean-scope>session</managed-bean-scope>
31.    </managed-bean>
32. </faces-config>
```

How do I selectively show and hide components?

It is very common to show or hide parts of a page, depending on some condition. For example, when a user is not logged on, you may want to show input fields for the username and password. But if a user is logged on, you would want to show the username and a logout button.

It would be wasteful to design two separate pages that differ in this small detail. Instead, we want to include all components in our page and selectively display them.

You can solve this issue with the JSTL c:if construct. However, mixing JSF and JSTL tags is unsightly. It is easy to achieve the same effect with JSF alone.

If you want to enable or disable one component (or a container like a panel group), use the rendered property, such as

```
<h:panelGroup rendered="#{userBean.loggedIn}">...</h:panelGroup>
```

If you want to switch between two component sets, you can use complementary rendered attributes:

```
<h:panelGroup rendered="#{!userBean.loggedIn}">...</h:panelGroup>
<h:panelGroup rendered="#{userBean.loggedIn}">...</h:panelGroup>
```

For more than two choices, it is best to use a component, such as panelStack in the Apache MyFaces components library (http://myfaces.apache.org/tomahawk/panel-Stack.html). A panel stack is similar to the tabbed pane that you saw in Chapter 9, except that there are no tabs. Instead, one of the child components is selected programmatically.

With the `panelStack`, each child component must have an ID. The `selectedPanel` attribute specifies the ID of the child that is rendered:

```
<t:panelStack selectedPanel="#{userBean.status}">
    <h:panelGroup id="new">...</h:panelGroup>
    <h:panelGroup id="loggedIn">...</h:panelGroup>
    <h:panelGroup id="loggedOut">...</h:panelGroup>
</t:panelStack>
```

The `getStatus` method of the user bean should return a string `"new"`, `"loggedIn`, or `"loggedOut"`.

How do I customize error pages?

You probably do not want your users to see scary stack traces when they run into an error in your web application. There are two mechanisms for customizing the display of errors.

You can specify an error page for a specific JSF page with the following JSP directive:

```
<%@ page errorPage="error.jsp" %>
```

When an error occurs during execution of the Java code of the compiled page, the `error.jsp` page is displayed. However, this mechanism is not often useful for JSF programmers. Errors that happen during page compilation or during execution of deferred expressions do not trigger the JSP error page.

It is better to use the `error-page` tag in the `web.xml` file. Specify either a Java exception class or an HTTP error code. For example,

```
<error-page>
    <exception-type>java.lang.Exception</exception-type>
    <location>/exception.jsp</location>
</error-page>
<error-page>
    <error-code>500</error-code>
    <location>/error.jsp</location>
</error-page>
<error-page>
    <error-code>404</error-code>
    <location>/notfound.jsp</location>
</error-page>
```

If an exception occurs and an error page matches its type, then the matching error page is displayed. Otherwise, an HTTP error 500 is generated.

If an HTTP error occurs and there is a matching error page, it is displayed. Otherwise, the default error page is displayed.

CAUTION: If an error occurs while your application is trying to display a custom error page, the default error page is displayed instead. If your custom error page stubbornly refuses to appear, check the log files for messages relating to your error page.

If you use the JSP errorPage directive, the exception object is available in the request map with the key "javax.servlet.jsp.jspException". If you use the servlet error-page mechanism, several objects related to the error are placed in the request map (see Table 13–2). You can use these values to display information that describes the error.

Table 13–2   Servlet Exception Attributes

Key	Value	Type
javax.servlet.error.status_code	The HTTP error code	Integer
javax.servlet.error.message	A description of the error	String
javax.servlet.error.exception_type	The class of the exception	Class
javax.servlet.error.exception	The exception object	Throwable
javax.servlet.error.request_uri	The path to the application resource that encountered the error	String
javax.servlet.error.servlet_name	The name of the servlet that encountered the error	String

The following sample application uses this technique. We purposely produce a null pointer exception in the password property of the UserBean, resulting in the error report shown in Figure 13–10. Listing 13–21 shows the web.xml file that sets the error page to errorDisplay.jsp (Listing 13–22).

Listing 13–23 shows the ErrorBean class. Its getStackTrace method assembles a complete stack trace that contains all nested exceptions.

 NOTE: The errorDisplay.jsp page uses an f:subview tag. This is a workaround for an anomaly in the JSF reference implementation—using f:view in an error page causes an assertion error in the framework code.

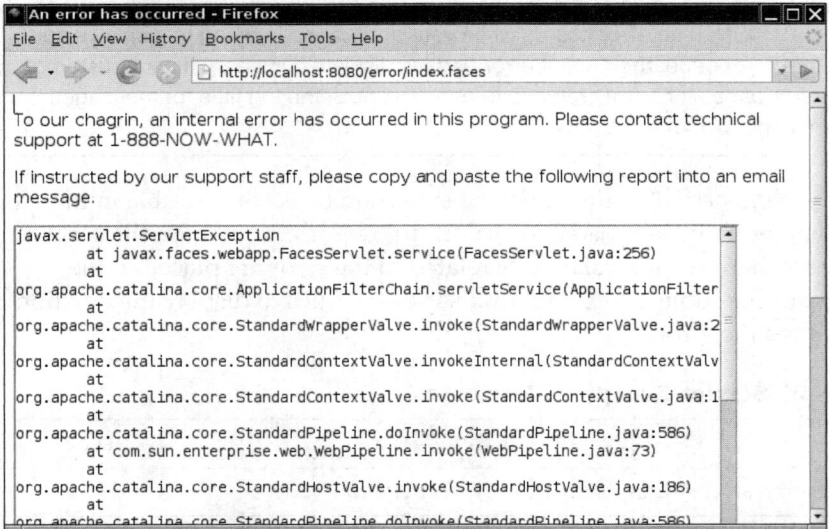

Figure 13–10   A customized error display

Listing 13–21   error/web/WEB-INF/web.xml

```
1. <?xml version="1.0"?>
2. <web-app xmlns="http://java.sun.com/xml/ns/javaee"
3.     xmlns:xsi="http://www.w3.org/2001/XMLSchema-instance"
4.     xsi:schemaLocation="http://java.sun.com/xml/ns/javaee
5.         http://java.sun.com/xml/ns/javaee/web-app_2_5.xsd"
6.     version="2.5">
7.     <servlet>
8.         <servlet-name>Faces Servlet</servlet-name>
9.         <servlet-class>javax.faces.webapp.FacesServlet</servlet-class>
10.         <load-on-startup>1</load-on-startup>
11.     </servlet>
12.
13.     <servlet-mapping>
14.         <servlet-name>Faces Servlet</servlet-name>
15.         <url-pattern>*.faces</url-pattern>
16.     </servlet-mapping>
17.
18.     <welcome-file-list>
19.         <welcome-file>/index.html</welcome-file>
20.     </welcome-file-list>
```

Listing 13–21   error/web/WEB-INF/web.xml (cont.)

```
21.
22.     <error-page>
23.         <error-code>500</error-code>
24.         <location>/errorDisplay.faces</location>
25.     </error-page>
26.  </web-app>
```

Listing 13–22   error/web/errorDisplay.jsp

```
1.  <html>
2.     <%@ taglib uri="http://java.sun.com/jsf/core" prefix="f" %>
3.     <%@ taglib uri="http://java.sun.com/jsf/html" prefix="h" %>
4.
5.     <f:subview id="dummy">
6.        <head>
7.           <title><h:outputText value="#{msgs.title}"/></title>
8.        </head>
9.        <body>
10.          <h:form>
11.             <p><h:outputText value="#{msgs.errorOccurred}"/></p>
12.             <p><h:outputText value="#{msgs.copyReport}"/></p>
13.             <h:inputTextarea value="#{error.stackTrace}"
14.                rows="40" cols="80" readonly="true"/>
15.          </h:form>
16.        </body>
17.     </f:subview>
18.  </html>
```

Listing 13–23   error/src/java/com/corejsf/ErrorBean.java

```
1.  package com.corejsf;
2.
3.  import java.io.PrintWriter;
4.  import java.io.StringWriter;
5.  import java.sql.SQLException;
6.  import java.util.Map;
7.  import javax.faces.context.FacesContext;
8.  import javax.servlet.ServletException;
9.
10. public class ErrorBean {
11.    public String getStackTrace() {
12.       FacesContext context = FacesContext.getCurrentInstance();
13.       Map<String, Object> request
14.          = context.getExternalContext().getRequestMap();
```

Listing 13–23   error/src/java/com/corejsf/ErrorBean.java (cont.)

```
15.        Throwable ex = (Throwable) request.get("javax.servlet.error.exception");
16.        StringWriter sw = new StringWriter();
17.        PrintWriter pw = new PrintWriter(sw);
18.        fillStackTrace(ex, pw);
19.        return sw.toString();
20.     }
21.
22.     private static void fillStackTrace(Throwable t, PrintWriter w) {
23.        if (t == null) return;
24.        t.printStackTrace(w);
25.        if (t instanceof ServletException) {
26.           Throwable cause = ((ServletException) t).getRootCause();
27.           if (cause != null) {
28.              w.println("Root cause:");
29.              fillStackTrace(cause, w);
30.           }
31.        } else if (t instanceof SQLException) {
32.           Throwable cause = ((SQLException) t).getNextException();
33.           if (cause != null) {
34.              w.println("Next exception:");
35.              fillStackTrace(cause, w);
36.           }
37.        } else {
38.           Throwable cause = t.getCause();
39.           if (cause != null) {
40.              w.println("Cause:");
41.              fillStackTrace(cause, w);
42.           }
43.        }
44.     }
45. }
```

Validation

JSF has strong support for server-side validation of a single component. However, if you want to carry out client-side validation or to validate relationships among components, you are on your own. The following sections tell you how you can overcome these issues.

How do I write my own client-side validation tag?

Suppose you have developed a JavaScript function for validation and tested it on multiple browsers. Now you would like to use it in your JSF applications. You need two tags:

1. A validator tag that is attached to each component that requires validation.
2. A component tag that generates the JavaScript code for validating all components on the form. The component tag must be added to the end of the form. Note that you cannot use a validator tag for this purpose. Only components can render output.

As an example, we show you how to make use of the credit card validation code in the Apache Commons Validator project. You can download the code from `http://jakarta.apache.org/commons/validator`.

We produce two tags: a `creditCardValidator` tag that can be added to any JSF input component and a component tag `validatorScript` that generates the required JavaScript code.

The `creditCardValidator` tag has two attributes. The `message` attribute specifies the error message template, such as

```
{0} is not a valid credit card number
```

The `arg` attribute is the value that should be filled in for {0}, usually the field name. For example,

```
<corejsf:creditCardValidator
   message="#{msgs.invalidCard}" arg="#{msgs.primaryCard}"/>
```

The code for the validator is in Listing 13–24 on page 661. The validator class has two unrelated purposes: validation and error message formatting.

The class carries out a traditional server-side validation, independent of the client-side JavaScript code. After all, it is not a good idea to rely solely on client-side validation. Users may have deactivated JavaScript in their browsers. Also, automated scripts or web-savvy hackers may send unvalidated HTTP requests to your web application.

The `getErrorMessage` method formats an error message that will be included in the client-side JavaScript code. The error message is constructed from the `message` and `arg` attributes.

The `validatorScript` component is far more interesting (see Listing 13–25 on page 663). Its `encodeBegin` method calls the recursive `findCreditCardValidators` method, which walks the component tree, locates all components, enumerates their validators, checks which ones are credit card validators, and gathers them in a map object. The `writeValidationFunctions` method writes the JavaScript code that invokes the validation function on all fields with credit card validators.

You must place the `validatorScript` tag at the *end* of the form, like this:

```
<h:form id="paymentForm" onsubmit="return validatePaymentForm(this);">
   ...
   <corejsf:validatorScript functionName="validatePaymentForm"/>
</h:form>
```

 CAUTION: If you place the validatorScript tag before the tags for the components that need to be validated, then the code that traverses the form component may not find the validators! This unintuitive and annoying behavior is a consequence of the JSP mechanism on which the JSF reference implementation is based. When a JSP-based implementation renders a JSF page *for the first time*, the component tree does not yet exist. Instead, it intermingles rendering and construction of the component tree.

Listing 13–26 on page 665 shows a sample JSF page. Figure 13–11 shows the error that is generated when a user tries to submit an invalid number.

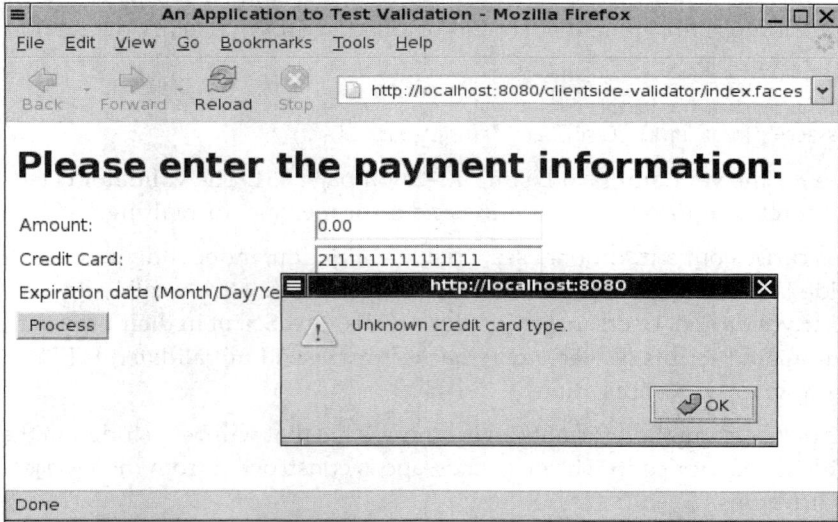

Figure 13–11   Client-side credit card validation

The details of the writeValidationFunctions method depend on the intricacies of the JavaScript code in the Commons Validator project.

First, the writeValidationFunctions method produces the validation function that is called in the onsubmit handler of the form:

```
var bCancel = false;
function functionName(form) { return bCancel || validateCreditCard(form); }
```

If a form contains "Cancel" or "Back" buttons, their onclick handlers should set the bCancel variable to true, to bypass validation.

The validateCreditCard function is the entry point into the Commons Validator code. It expects to find a function named *formName_*creditCard that constructs a configuration object. The writeValidationFunctions method generates the code for the creditCard function.

Unfortunately, the details are rather convoluted. The *formName_*creditCard function returns an object with one instance field for each validated form element. Each instance field contains an array with three values: the ID of the form element, the error message to display when validation fails, and a validator-specific customization value. The credit card validator does not use this value; we supply the empty string.

The instance field names do not matter. In the writeValidationFunctions method, we take advantage of the flexibility of JavaScript and call the fields 0, 1, 2, and so on. For example,

```
function paymentForm_creditCard() {
    this[0] = new Array("paymentForm:primary",
        "Primary Credit Card is not a valid card number", "");
    this[1] = new Array("paymentForm:backup",
        "Backup Credit Card is not a valid card number", "");
}
```

If you design your own JavaScript functions, you can provide a saner mechanism for bundling up the parameters.

Listing 13–24 clientside-validator/src/java/com/corejsf/
CreditCardValidator.java

```
 1. package com.corejsf;
 2.
 3. import java.io.Serializable;
 4. import java.text.MessageFormat;
 5. import java.util.Locale;
 6. import javax.faces.application.FacesMessage;
 7. import javax.faces.component.UIComponent;
 8. import javax.faces.context.FacesContext;
 9. import javax.faces.validator.Validator;
10. import javax.faces.validator.ValidatorException;
11.
12. public class CreditCardValidator implements Validator, Serializable {
13.     private String message;
14.     private String arg;
```

```
15.
16.  // PROPERTY: message
17.  public void setMessage(String newValue) { message = newValue; }
18.
19.  // PROPERTY: arg
20.  public void setArg(String newValue) { arg = newValue; }
21.  public String getArg() { return arg; }
22.
23.  public void validate(FacesContext context, UIComponent component,
24.      Object value) {
25.    if(value == null) return;
26.    String cardNumber;
27.    if (value instanceof CreditCard)
28.      cardNumber = value.toString();
29.    else
30.      cardNumber = getDigitsOnly(value.toString());
31.    if(!luhnCheck(cardNumber)) {
32.      FacesMessage message = new FacesMessage(FacesMessage.SEVERITY_ERROR,
33.        getErrorMessage(value, context), null);
34.      throw new ValidatorException(message);
35.    }
36.  }
37.
38.  public String getErrorMessage(Object value, FacesContext context) {
39.    Object[] params = new Object[] { value };
40.    if (message == null)
41.      return com.corejsf.util.Messages.getString(
42.        "com.corejsf.messages", "badLuhnCheck", params);
43.    else {
44.      Locale locale = context.getViewRoot().getLocale();
45.      MessageFormat formatter = new MessageFormat(message, locale);
46.      return formatter.format(params);
47.    }
48.  }
49.
50.  private static boolean luhnCheck(String cardNumber) {
51.    int sum = 0;
52.
53.    for(int i = cardNumber.length() - 1; i >= 0; i -= 2) {
54.      sum += Integer.parseInt(cardNumber.substring(i, i + 1));
55.      if(i > 0) {
56.        int d = 2 * Integer.parseInt(cardNumber.substring(i - 1, i));
57.        if(d > 9) d -= 9;
58.        sum += d;
```

```
59.        }
60.      }
61.
62.      return sum % 10 == 0;
63.    }
64.
65.    private static String getDigitsOnly(String s) {
66.      StringBuilder digitsOnly = new StringBuilder ();
67.      char c;
68.      for(int i = 0; i < s.length (); i++) {
69.        c = s.charAt (i);
70.        if (Character.isDigit(c)) {
71.          digitsOnly.append(c);
72.        }
73.      }
74.      return digitsOnly.toString ();
75.    }
76.  }
```

```
1. package com.corejsf;
2.
3. import java.io.IOException;
4. import java.util.Map;
5. import java.util.LinkedHashMap;
6. import javax.faces.component.EditableValueHolder;
7. import javax.faces.component.UIComponent;
8. import javax.faces.component.UIComponentBase;
9. import javax.faces.context.FacesContext;
10. import javax.faces.context.ResponseWriter;
11. import javax.faces.validator.Validator;
12.
13. public class UIValidatorScript extends UIComponentBase {
14.    private Map<String, Validator> validators
15.      = new LinkedHashMap<String, Validator>();
16.
17.    public String getRendererType() { return null; }
18.    public String getFamily() { return null; }
19.
```

Listing 13-25	clientside-validator/src/java/com/corejsf/ UIValidatorScript.java (cont.)

```java
20.   private void findCreditCardValidators(UIComponent c, FacesContext context) {
21.      if (c instanceof EditableValueHolder) {
22.         EditableValueHolder h = (EditableValueHolder) c;
23.         for (Validator v : h.getValidators()) {
24.            if (v instanceof CreditCardValidator) {
25.               String id = c.getClientId(context);
26.               validators.put(id, v);
27.            }
28.         }
29.      }
30.
31.      for (UIComponent child : c.getChildren())
32.         findCreditCardValidators(child, context);
33.   }
34.
35.   private void writeScriptStart(ResponseWriter writer) throws IOException {
36.      writer.startElement("script", this);
37.      writer.writeAttribute("type", "text/javascript", null);
38.      writer.writeAttribute("language", "Javascript1.1", null);
39.      writer.write("\n<!--\n");
40.   }
41.
42.   private void writeScriptEnd(ResponseWriter writer) throws IOException {
43.      writer.write("\n-->\n");
44.      writer.endElement("script");
45.   }
46.
47.   private void writeValidationFunctions(ResponseWriter writer,
48.      FacesContext context) throws IOException {
49.      writer.write("var bCancel = false;\n");
50.      writer.write("function " );
51.      writer.write(getAttributes().get("functionName").toString());
52.      writer.write("(form) { return bCancel || validateCreditCard(form); }\n");
53.
54.      writer.write("function ");
55.      String formId = getParent().getClientId(context);
56.      writer.write(formId);
57.      writer.write("_creditCard() { \n");
58.      // for each field validated by this type, add configuration object
59.      int k = 0;
60.      for (String id : validators.keySet()) {
61.         CreditCardValidator v = (CreditCardValidator) validators.get(id);
62.         writer.write("this[" + k + "] = ");
63.         k++;
```

Listing 13–25	clientside-validator/src/java/com/corejsf/UIValidatorScript.java (cont.)

```
64.
65.        writer.write("new Array('");
66.        writer.write(id);
67.        writer.write("', '");
68.        writer.write(v.getErrorMessage(v.getArg(), context));
69.        writer.write("', '');\n"); // Third element unused for credit card valida-
tor
70.    }
71.    writer.write("}\n");
72. }
73.
74. public void encodeBegin(FacesContext context) throws IOException {
75.    ResponseWriter writer = context.getResponseWriter();
76.
77.    validators.clear();
78.    findCreditCardValidators(context.getViewRoot(), context);
79.
80.    writeScriptStart(writer);
81.    writeValidationFunctions(writer, context);
82.    writeScriptEnd(writer);
83. }
84. }
```

Listing 13–26	clientside-validator/web/index.jsp

```
1. <html>
2.    <%@ taglib uri="http://java.sun.com/jsf/core" prefix="f" %>
3.    <%@ taglib uri="http://java.sun.com/jsf/html" prefix="h" %>
4.    <%@ taglib uri="http://corejsf.com/creditcard" prefix="corejsf" %>
5.    <f:view>
6.       <head>
7.          <link href="styles.css" rel="stylesheet" type="text/css"/>
8.          <script src="scripts/validateCreditCard.js"
9.             type="text/javascript" language="JavaScript1.1">
10.         </script>
11.         <title><h:outputText value="#{msgs.title}"/></title>
12.      </head>
13.      <body>
14.         <h:form id="paymentForm" onsubmit="return validatePaymentForm(this);">
15.            <h1><h:outputText value="#{msgs.enterPayment}"/></h1>
16.            <h:panelGrid columns="3">
17.               <h:outputText value="#{msgs.amount}"/>
```

| **Listing 13–26** | clientside-validator/web/index.jsp (cont.) |

```
18.              <h:inputText id="amount" value="#{payment.amount}">
19.                 <f:convertNumber minFractionDigits="2"/>
20.              </h:inputText>
21.              <h:message for="amount" styleClass="errorMessage"/>
22.
23.              <h:outputText value="#{msgs.creditCard}"/>
24.              <h:inputText id="card" value="#{payment.card}" required="true">
25.                 <corejsf:creditCardValidator
26.                     message="#{msgs.unknownType}"arg="#{msgs.creditCard}"/>
27.              </h:inputText>
28.              <h:message for="card" styleClass="errorMessage"/>
29.
30.              <h:outputText value="#{msgs.expirationDate}"/>
31.              <h:inputText id="date" value="#{payment.date}">
32.                 <f:convertDateTime pattern="MM/dd/yyyy"/>
33.              </h:inputText>
34.              <h:message for="date" styleClass="errorMessage"/>
35.           </h:panelGrid>
36.           <h:commandButton value="Process" action="process"/>
37.           <corejsf:validatorScript functionName="validatePaymentForm"/>
38.        </h:form>
39.     </body>
40.  </f:view>
41. </html>
```

How do I use the Shale Validator for client-side validation?

In the preceding section, you saw how to write your own validator tag that puts a validation script from the Commons Validator project to work. If you like that approach, there is no need to get busy and replicate that work for all of the other validators.

The Apache Shale project (http://struts.apache.org/struts-shale) has provided a custom tag library for this purpose. (We originally wrote that tag library for the first edition of this book and then contributed it to the Shale project.)

To use the Shale Validator, follow these instructions:

1. Place the library files shale-core.jar and commons-validator.jar into the WEB-INF/lib directory of your web application, together with the libraries that are needed to support them. At the time of this writing, the following additional JAR files are required: commons.logging.jar, commons.digester.jar, commons-beanutils.jar, commons-collections.jar, and jakarta-oro.jar. To get the

correct version of these files, download the shale-dependencies-*date*.zip file that matches your Shale distribution.

2. Include a tag library declaration, such as

    ```
    <%@ taglib uri="http://struts.apache.org/shale/core" prefix="s" %>
    ```

    Here, we use s as a prefix. As always, you can use any prefix of your choice.

3. Include a call to the validation method in the onsubmit handler of your form, like this:

    ```
    <h:form id="paymentForm" onsubmit="return validatePaymentForm(this);">
    ```

    Just before the </h:form> tag, add an s:validatorScript tag:

    ```
    <s:validatorScript functionName="validatePaymentForm"/>
    ```

    The function name must match the function in the onsubmit handler.

4. Add validators to your components, for example:

    ```
    <h:inputText id="amount" value="#{payment.amount}">
        <s:commonsValidator type="floatRange"arg="#{msgs.amount}"
            client="true" server="true">
            <s:validatorVar name="min" value="10"/>
            <s:validatorVar name="max" value="10000"/>
        </s:commonsValidator>
    </h:inputText>
    ```

    The type argument is the validator type. It should be one of the types listed in Table 13–3. Supply the argument for the error message in the arg attribute. Typically, this is the name of the field.

    Supply parameters min, max, minlength, maxlength, mask, and datePatternStrict as required by the validation method that you choose.

5. If you want to tweak the validation behavior, or add new validator rules, read http://wiki.apache.org/struts/Shale/Validation.

Table 13–3   Struts Client-Side Validators

Validator Name	Parameters	Purpose
required	none	Checks that the field has characters other than white space.
maxlength	maxlength	Checks that the field length is at most the value of the maxlength parameter.

Table 13–3   Struts Client-Side Validators (cont.)

Validator Name	Parameters	Purpose
minlength	minlength	Checks that the field length is at least the value of the minlength parameter.
byte	none	Checks that the field contains an integer between –128 and 127.
short	none	Checks that the field contains an integer between –32768 and 32767.
integer	none	Checks that the field contains an integer between –2147483648 and 2147483647.
float	none	Checks that the field contains a floating-point number.
intRange	min, max	Checks that the field contains an integer between min and max. Both must be specified.
floatRange	min, max	Checks that the field contains a floating-point number between min and max. Both must be specified.
date	datePatternStrict	Checks that the field contains a date with the given pattern.
email	none	Checks that the field contains a syntactically correct email address.
creditCard	none	Checks that the field contains a credit card number that passes the Luhn check.
mask	mask	Checks that the field matches the regular expression given in the mask parameter.

 NOTE: Unfortunately, the Commons Validator displays a pop-up when it finds a validation error. It would be nicer to place an error message next to the offending field. This feature is supported in Cagatay Civici's client-side validation package at http://jsf-comp.sourceforge.net/components/clientvalidators/index.html.

How do I validate relationships between components?

In JSF, validators are intended to check the validity of a single component. However, you often need to test relationships between components. For example, it is common to ask users to reenter a password. You would like to show a validation error if the two passwords are not identical.

The sophisticated approach is to design a custom component that renders two input fields, one for the password and one for the confirmed password. That is quite elegant, but of course it is a lot of work.

The other approach is to let the *last* of the related components do the validation. The preceding components will have their local values set, and your validator code can read them. For the last component only, you need to use the value that was passed by the validation method.

The validation method is most conveniently placed in a backing bean that also holds the components of the form. For example,

```
public class BackingBean
{
   private UIInput passwordField;
   private UIInput confirmField;
   ...
   public void validateConfirmField(FacesContext context, UIComponent component,
      Object value) {
      if (!passwordField.getLocalValue().equals(value))
         throw new ValidatorException(...);
}
```

You then attach the validator to the confirmation field:

```
<h:inputText binding="#{bb.confirmField}" required="true"
   validator="#{bb.validateConfirmField}"/>
```

For a more complete example of this technique, see Chapter 6.

Programming

In the following sections, we discuss issues that are of interest to JSF programmers. We show you how to use Eclipse with JSF, how to reduce the drudgery of common implementation tasks, how to initialize your application, and how to package components into a reusable JAR file.

How do I use JSF with Eclipse?

You can use Eclipse to edit JSF pages and to compile the code for beans, converters, validators, and components. We assume that you are familiar with the basic operation of Eclipse, and so we cover only the special configuration details for JSF programming.

The principal issue is the installation of JSF and Ant libraries. It would be tedious to install the libraries separately for each project.

First, we consider the JSF libraries. The trick is to make a project that contains the libraries, and to use it as a base for all JSF projects. Here is how you set up the base project (which we will call jsflibs).

1. Select File -> New -> Project from the menu and supply the project name, jsflibs.
2. In the "Java Settings" screen of the project wizard, click the "Libraries" tab, then click the "Add External JARs..." button. If you use GlassFish, simply add the javaee.jar file from the *glassfish*/lib directory. If you use another JSF implementation, add all required JAR files.

Figure 13–12   Adding libraries to the jsflibs **project**

3. Click the "Order and Export" button and check the libraries that you just added (see Figure 13–13).
4. Click the "Finish" button.

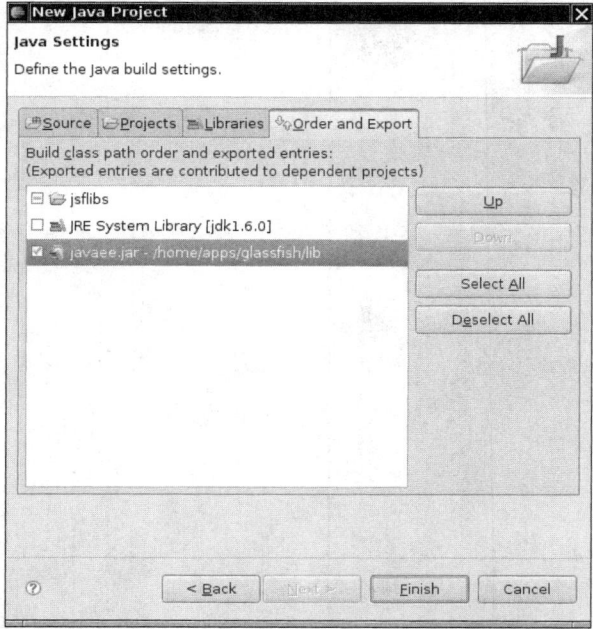

Figure 13–13   Exporting libraries in the `jsflibs` **project**

Whenever you set up your JSF projects, start with the "New Java Project" wizard in the usual way. However, when you get to the "Java Settings" screen, click the "Projects" tab and check the `jsflibs` project (see Figure 13–14). Now all the required libraries are automatically included in your project.

For easy invocation of Ant, the `build.xml` file must be included in the project directory. This differs from the setup of our sample applications, for which we use a single `build.xml` file for all applications. If you like our setup, add the following `build.xml` file into each Eclipse project directory:

```
<project default="build.war">
    <basename property="app" file="${basedir}"/>
    <property file="../build.properties"/>
    <property name="appdir" value="${basedir}"/>
    <import file="../build.xml"/>
</project>
```

Figure 13–14 **Including the** jsflibs **project**

Or, if you prefer, copy the build.xml and build.properties files into each project.

To run Ant, right-click the build.xml file and select "Run Ant...". The Ant messages show up in the console.

 TIP: We recommend that you install the XMLBuddy plugin and make it the default editor for JSF pages. You can download it from http://xmlbuddy.com. Of course, since XML Buddy is a real XML editor, it will frown upon <%...%> delimiters. We suggest that you use proper XML syntax (see the note on page 15 of Chapter 1).

With this configuration, Eclipse becomes a bare bones development environment for JSF. Of course, you would like more, such as autocompletion in JSF pages, wiggly underlines when you make errors in JSF or XML files, visual editing of page navigation, debugging, and so on. All this will be supplied by the JSF extensions to the Web Tools Platform (WTP), which itself is based on several other Eclipse extensions. At the time of this writing, the installation procedure and feature set are still quite preliminary. In particular, the JSF Tools project is only approaching version 0.5.

If you want to experiment with these upcoming features, we suggest that you make a separate installation of Eclipse and use the Software Update feature to download the extensions. Select the JSF Tools and have the installer find all required extensions.

How do I locate a configuration file?

Some applications prefer to process their own configuration files rather than using faces-config.xml or web.xml. The challenge is to locate the file because you do not know where the web container stores the files of your web application. In fact, the web container need not physically store your files at all—it can choose to read them out of the WAR file.

Instead, use the getResourceAsStream method of the ExternalContext class. For example, suppose you want to read app.properties in the WEB-INF directory of your application. Here is the required code:

```
FacesContext context = FacesContext.getCurrentInstance();
ExternalContext external = context.getExternalContext();
InputStream in = external.getResourceAsStream("/WEB-INF/app.properties");
```

How can a JSF component access resources from a JAR file?

Suppose you provide a component library and deliver it to your customers in a file mycomponent.jar. Some of the renderers need to generate links to images or JavaScript code that are stored inside the JAR file. You could ask your customers to extract a file with resources into a specific location, but that is error-prone and less attractive than just telling them to drop a JAR file into WEB-INF/lib.

As an example, consider a spinner with graphical increment and decrement buttons (see Figure 13–15). The renderer will want to generate HTML of the form

```
<input type="image" url="image URL" .../>
```

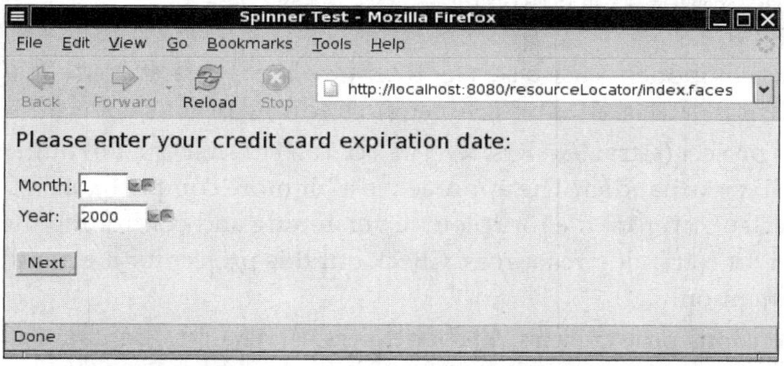

Figure 13–15   The spinner component with image buttons

The challenge is to specify an image URL that activates some mechanism for fetching the image from the component JAR file.

There is no standard solution to this problem, perhaps because the basic HTML render kit does not require images or lengthy JavaScript. However, four approaches have been proposed:

1.   The simplest approach is to use a servlet to locate resources:

```
public class ResourceServlet extends HttpServlet {
    public void doGet(HttpServletRequest req, HttpServletResponse resp)
          throws ServletException, IOException {
        String resourcePath = req.getPathInfo();
        if (resourcePath == null) return;
        InputStream in = getClass().getResourceAsStream(resourcePath);
        if (in == null) return;
        OutputStream out = resp.getOutputStream();
        int ch;
        while ((ch = in.read()) != -1) out.write(ch);
    }
}
```

Place the servlet code in the same JAR file as the component renderer and the image resources. Render URLs of the form resource/*resourcePath*.

Unfortunately, this approach requires the user of your component to edit the web.xml of their application. They need to add these elements:

```
<servlet>
    <servlet-name>Resource Servlet</servlet-name>
    <servlet-class>com.corejsf.ResourceServlet</servlet-class>
</servlet>

<servlet-mapping>
    <servlet-name>Resource Servlet</servlet-name>
    <url-pattern>/resource/*</url-pattern>
</servlet-mapping>
```

2.   The MyFaces components use a servlet filter (see http://myfaces.apache.org/tomahawk/extensionsFilter.html). This also requires editing of web.xml.

3.   The Weblets project (https://weblets.dev.java.net/doc/introduction.html) augments the JSF view handler. The approach is a bit more complex and requires a weblet-config.xml file for resource versioning and controlling the URL pattern for retrieving resources. Check out this project for a generic and robust solution.

4.   The JSF Extensions project (https://jsf-extensions.dev.java.net/) contains a phase listener for fetching resources. This approach is attractive because

the listener can be specified in the META-INF/faces-config.xml file of the component JAR file. We implemented a slight variation of this approach.

Listing 13–27 shows the phase listener implementation. The spinnerLib project in the companion code builds a component file spinnerLib.jar that contains a spinner with graphical buttons. (We leave it as an exercise to the reader to arrange the buttons more nicely.) The resourceLocatorTest application in the companion code contains an application that uses the spinner. Note that the application needs to do nothing about resource loading; it simply contains spinnerLib.jar in the WEB-INF/lib directory.

Listing 13–27 spinnerLib/src/java/com/corejsf/ResourcePhaseListener.java

```
1.  package com.corejsf;
2.
3.  import java.io.IOException;
4.  import java.io.InputStream;
5.  import java.io.OutputStream;
6.  import java.util.HashMap;
7.  import java.util.Map;
8.  import javax.faces.FacesException;
9.  import javax.faces.application.ViewHandler;
10. import javax.faces.context.ExternalContext;
11. import javax.faces.context.FacesContext;
12. import javax.faces.event.PhaseEvent;
13. import javax.faces.event.PhaseId;
14. import javax.faces.event.PhaseListener;
15. import javax.servlet.http.HttpServletResponse;
16.
17. public class ResourcePhaseListener implements PhaseListener {
18.
19.     public static final String RESOURCE_PREFIX = "/resource";
20.
21.     public static final String RESOURCE_LOCATION_PARAM = "r";
22.
23.     public static final String CONTENT_TYPE_PARAM = "ct";
24.
25.     public static final String DEFAULT_CONTENT_TYPE = "application/octet-stream";
26.
27.     private Map<String, String> extensionToContentType = null;
28.
29.     public ResourcePhaseListener() {
30.         extensionToContentType = new HashMap<String, String>();
31.         extensionToContentType.put(".js", "text/javascript");
32.         extensionToContentType.put(".gif", "image/gif");
33.         extensionToContentType.put(".jpg", "image/jpeg");
34.         extensionToContentType.put(".jpeg", "image/jpeg");
```

```
35.       extensionToContentType.put(".png", "image/png");
36.   }
37.
38.   public PhaseId getPhaseId() {
39.       return PhaseId.RESTORE_VIEW;
40.   }
41.
42.   public void beforePhase(PhaseEvent phaseEvent) {
43.   }
44.
45.   public void afterPhase(PhaseEvent event) {
46.       if (event.getFacesContext().getViewRoot().getViewId().startsWith(
47.           RESOURCE_PREFIX)) {
48.         FacesContext context = event.getFacesContext();
49.         ExternalContext external = context.getExternalContext();
50.
51.         String resourcePath =
52.             (String) external.getRequestParameterMap().get(
53.                 RESOURCE_LOCATION_PARAM);
54.         if (resourcePath == null)
55.           return;
56.
57.         String contentType =
58.             (String) external.getRequestParameterMap().get(
59.                 CONTENT_TYPE_PARAM);
60.         if (contentType == null) {
61.           int extensionIndex = resourcePath.lastIndexOf(".");
62.           if (extensionIndex != -1)
63.             contentType =
64.                 extensionToContentType.get(resourcePath
65.                     .substring(extensionIndex));
66.           if (contentType == null)
67.             contentType = DEFAULT_CONTENT_TYPE;
68.         }
69.
70.         InputStream in = getClass().getResourceAsStream(resourcePath);
71.         HttpServletResponse servletResponse =
72.             (HttpServletResponse) external.getResponse();
73.         try {
74.           OutputStream out = servletResponse.getOutputStream();
75.           servletResponse.setContentType(contentType);
76.           int ch;
77.           while ((ch = in.read()) != -1)
78.             out.write(ch);
79.         } catch (IOException ex) {
80.           throw new FacesException(ex);
```

```
81.          }
82.        context.responseComplete();
83.      }
84.    }
85.
86.    /**
87.     * Returns a URL for fetching a resource through this listener
88.     *
89.     * @param context the faces context
90.     * @param String resourcePath the path to the resource
91.     * @param String contentType the content type to include in the URL, or null
92.     *              if no content type should be included
93.     * @return the URL of the form
94.     *          /appname/resource.faces?r=resourcePath,ct=contentType or
95.     *          /appname/faces/resource?r=resourcePath,ct=contentType
96.     */
97.    public static String getURL(FacesContext context, String resourcePath,
98.          String contentType) {
99.      ViewHandler handler = context.getApplication().getViewHandler();
100.
101.      String url = handler.getActionURL(context, RESOURCE_PREFIX);
102.      StringBuilder r = new StringBuilder(url);
103.      r.append("?" + RESOURCE_LOCATION_PARAM + "=").append(resourcePath);
104.      if (contentType != null)
105.        r.append("," + CONTENT_TYPE_PARAM + "=").append(contentType);
106.      return r.toString();
107.    }
108. }
```

How do I package a set of tags into a JAR file?

If you designed components, validators, or converters that are reusable across multiple projects, you will want to package them into JAR files so that they can be added to the WEB-INF/lib directory of any web application.

You will want to make the JAR file self-contained so that users do not have to worry about editing tag library descriptor or configuration files. Follow these steps:

1. Place a TLD file into the META-INF directory. The TLD file should contain a uri element that users of your library can reference in their JSF pages.

2. Place a file named faces-config.xml into the META-INF directory that contains the required component, validator, and converter elements.

3. Place any resource bundles and configuration files together with your classes. Load them with ResourceBundle.getBundle or Class.getResourceAsStream.

4. Avoid name clashes by using an appropriate prefix for the global names, such as component names, message keys, or loggers, used by your implementation.

For example, Figure 13–16 shows the directory structure of the spinner component library that was discussed on page 673.

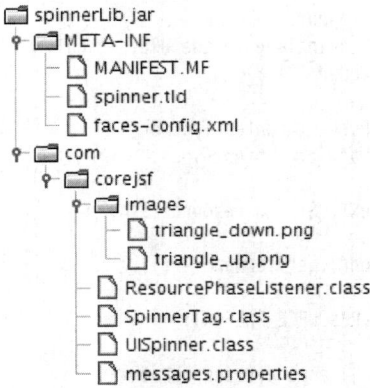

Figure 13–16   The directory structure of a spinner component library

How do I get the form ID for generating document.forms[id] in JavaScript?

Some components will need to generate JavaScript code to access the current form, either to submit it or to access fields contained in the form.

The JSF API has no convenience method for finding the form ID. Use the following code:

```
UIComponent parent = component;
while (!(parent instanceof UIForm)) parent = parent.getParent();
String formId = parent.getClientId(context);
```

(We supply this code in the getFormId method of the com.corejsf.util.Renderers class.)

You can now render JavaScript commands, like this:

```
String command = "document.forms['" + formId + "'].submit()";
```

How do I make a JavaScript function appear only once per page?

Some components require substantial amounts of client-side JavaScript. If you have multiple instances of such a component in your page, you do not want to render multiple copies of the function.

To suppress multiple copies of the same code, your renderer can get the request map (facesContext.getExternalContext().getRequestMap()) and put a value of Boolean.TRUE with a key that indicates the component type. Next time the renderer is called, it can retrieve the key to find out if it has run previously in the same request.

How do I carry out initialization or cleanup work?

JSF 1.2 takes advantage of the @PostConstruct and @PreDestroy annotations that are part of Java SE 6/EE 5 Common Annotations, as defined in JSR 250. If a managed bean is loaded in a Java EE 5-compliant container, methods that are annotated with @PostConstruct will be automatically called.

When a request, session, or application scope ends, the methods of all managed beans in the scope that are annotated with @PostConstruct will be invoked. Put your initialization and cleanup work into methods of your managed beans and provide the @PostConstruct and @PreDestroy annotations.

In the future, standalone web containers such as Tomcat may also choose to support these annotations.

If you use JSF 1.1 or you do not want to rely on the annotation support, you must attach listeners that carry out your initialization and cleanup work.

- To manage application scope objects, attach a ServletContextListener. Implement the contextInitialized and contextDestroyed methods. Add the listener class to the web.xml file like this:

```
<listener>
    <listener-class>mypackage.MyListener</listener-class>
</listener>
```

- To manage session scope objects, attach an HttpSessionListener. Implement the sessionCreated and sessionDestroyed methods. Add the listener class to the web.xml file as in the preceding case.

- To manage request scope objects, attach a PhaseListener. (Phase listeners are discussed in Chapter 7.) You can initialize objects in the beforePhase method when the phase ID is APPLY_REQUEST_VALUES. You can clean up in the afterPhase method when the phase ID is RENDER_RESPONSE.

How do I store a managed bean longer than request scope but shorter than session scope?

Obviously, most web applications need to store data beyond a single page request, but the session scope is too long. Disadvantages of session scope include:

- Excessive memory consumption
- Risk of stale data
- Problems with multiple windows that refer to different states

The last issue is particularly vexing. A user might browse for information, then open another window and continue along another path in the other window to compare the results.

Ideally, an application would like to keep state for a conversation that involves a sequence of related screens.

A number of approaches have been proposed to solve this problem.

1. The Apache MyFaces components library contains a nonvisual saveState component (`http://myfaces.apache.org/tomahawk/uiSaveState.html`). You use the component to add beans or bean properties to the view state when it is saved, and to restore them when the view is restored. Combine this with client-side state saving, and you have a simple ad hoc solution. Place components such as the following onto some of your pages:

    ```
    <t:saveState id="save1" value="#{myBean1}"/>
    <t:saveState id="save2" value="#{myBean2.myproperty}"/>
    ```

    The state is carried between pages with matching components, and it is discarded when a page is reached that does not have a matching component.

2. The JSF Extensions project (`https://jsf-extensions.dev.java.net`) imitates the "flash" scope of Ruby on Rails. The flash is a map whose entries have a limited lifetime. When you place an entry into the flash, it available in the next page and discarded when the user moves to a subsequent page. The JSF Extensions project defines a top-level variable flash in the expression language for accessing the flash.

3. With the dialog manager in the Apache Shale project (`http://struts.apache.org/struts-shale/features-dialog-manager.html`), you define a sequence of pages that make up a "dialog." The dialog manager allows you to consider the page sequence as a reusable unit. One of the features is a dialog scope that holds entries while the dialog is in progress and removes them when the dialog is complete.

4. The Seam framework (http://www.jboss.com/products/seam) allows you to group related pages into a "conversation." Through the use of annotations, beans can be scoped to live in a conversation. It is possible to have multiple conversations, involving the same pages, in separate browser windows. These concepts are likely to find their way into a future version of JSF via JSR 299 (http://jcp.org/en/jsr/detail?id=299). For more information on the Seam framework, see Chapter 12.

How do I extend the JSF expression language?

Sometimes it is useful to extend the expression language. For example, the JNDI integration in Shale allows you to use expressions such as #{jndi['jdbc/CustomerDB']} for making JNDI lookups. (See http://struts.apache.org/struts-shale/features-jndi-integration.html for more information.) This was achieved by adding a *resolver* that processes an expression base.property (or the equivalent base[property]), where base is the string "jndi" and property is the JNDI name.

In JSF 1.2, you extend the ELResolver class to implement a resolver. The key method is

```
public Object getValue(ELContext context, Object base, Object property)
```

If your resolver knows how to resolve the expression base.property, then you call

```
context.setPropertyResolved(true);
```

and return the value of the expression.

There are several other methods for type inquiry and builder tool support; see the API documentation for details.

Next, we view a concrete example: looking up components by ID. Consider, for example, the expression

```
view.loginForm.password.value
```

We want to find the component with the ID loginForm inside the view root, then the component with the ID password inside the form, and then call its getValue method. Our resolver will handle expressions of the form *component.name*:

```
public class ComponentIdResolver extends ELResolver {
   public Object getValue(ELContext context, Object base, Object property) {
      if (base instanceof UIComponent && property instanceof String) {
         UIComponent r = ((UIComponent) base).findComponent((String) property);
         if (r != null) {
            context.setPropertyResolved(true);
            return r;
         }
      }
```

```
      }
      return null;
   }
   ...
}
```

Note that our resolver is called to resolve the first two subexpressions (view.log-inForm and view.loginForm.password). The last expression is resolved by the managed bean resolver that is part of the JSF implementation.

The initial expression view is a special case. Resolvers are called with base set to null and property set to the initial expression string. The JSF implicit object resolver resolves that expression, returning the UIViewRoot object of the page.

As another example, we build a resolver for system properties. For example, the expression

```
sysprop['java.version']
```

should return the result of calling

```
System.getProperty("java.version");
```

To make matters more interesting, the expression

```
sysprop.java.version
```

should also work. This custom resolver must handle the special case in which the base is null and the property is "sysprop". It must also deal with partially complete subexpressions such as sysprop.java.

We collect the list of expressions in a nested class SystemPropertyResolver.PartialResolution. Our resolver distinguishes two cases:

1.   If base is null and property is "sysprop", return an empty PartialResolution object.

2.   If base is a PartialResolution object and property is a string, add the property to the end of the list. Then try to look up the system property whose key is the dot-separated concatenation of the list entries. If the system property exists, return it. Otherwise, return the augmented list.

The following code excerpt illustrates these cases:

```
public class SystemPropertyResolver extends ELResolver {
   public Object getValue(ELContext context, Object base, Object property) {
      if (base == null && "sysprop".equals(property)) {
         context.setPropertyResolved(true);
         return new PartialResolution();
      }
```

```
      if (base instanceof PartialResolution && property instanceof String) {
         ((PartialResolution) base).add((String) property);
         Object r = System.getProperty(base.toString());
         context.setPropertyResolved(true);
         if (r == null) return base;
         else return r;
      }
      return null;
   }
   ...
   public static class PartialResolution extends ArrayList<String> {
      public String toString() {
         StringBuilder r = new StringBuilder();
         for (String s : this)
         {
            if (r.length() > 0) r.append('.');
            r.append(s);
         }
         return r.toString();
      }
   }
}
```

To add the custom resolver to your JSF application, add elements such as the following to faces-config.xml (or another application configuration file):

```
<application>
   <el-resolver>com.corejsf.ComponentIdResolver</el-resolver>
   ...
</application>
```

You will find the complete implementation for the two sample resolvers in the ch12/resolver example of the companion code.

 NOTE: In JSF 1.1, modifying the expression language is a bit more cumbersome. The JSF 1.1 implementation provides concrete subclasses of the abstract classes VariableResolver and PropertyResolver. A VariableResolver resolves the initial subexpression, and the PropertyResolver is in charge of evaluating the dot or bracket operator.

If you want to introduce your own variables, you supply your own variable resolver and specified it in the application configuration file, like this:

```
<application>
   <variable-resolver>
      com.corejsf.CustomVariableResolver
   </variable-resolver>
   ...
</application>
```

In your resolver class, supply a constructor with a single parameter of type VariableResolver. Then the JSF implementation passes you its default variable resolver. This makes it straightforward to use the decorator pattern. Here is an example of a variable resolver that recognizes the variable name sysprop:

```
public class CustomVariableResolver extends VariableResolver {
   private VariableResolver original;

   public CustomVariableResolver(VariableResolver original) {
      this.original = original;
   }

   public Object resolveVariable(FacesContext context, String name) {
      if (name.equals("sysprop")) return System.getProperties();
      return original.resolveVariable(context, name);
   }
}
```

The implementation of a PropertyResolver is similar.

The JSF implementation applies resolvers in the following order:

1. Resolve JSP implict objects.
2. Resolve JSF implicit objects facesContext and view.
3. Resolve names of managed beans.
4. Resolve names of resource bundles.
5. Process resolvers in application configuration resources (such as faces-config.xml).
6. Process legacy variable resolvers.
7. Process legacy property resolvers.
8. Process resolvers added by calling Application.addELResolver.

Debugging and Logging

Troubleshooting a JSF application can be painful. So many minor details must be just right or your application will not work. Error messages can be hard to find or nonexistent. Minor typos can give rise to an application that simply does not start or that seems to get stuck. This section contains some tips to help you out.

How do I decipher a stack trace?

When you see a screen, such as the one in Figure 13–17, count yourself lucky.

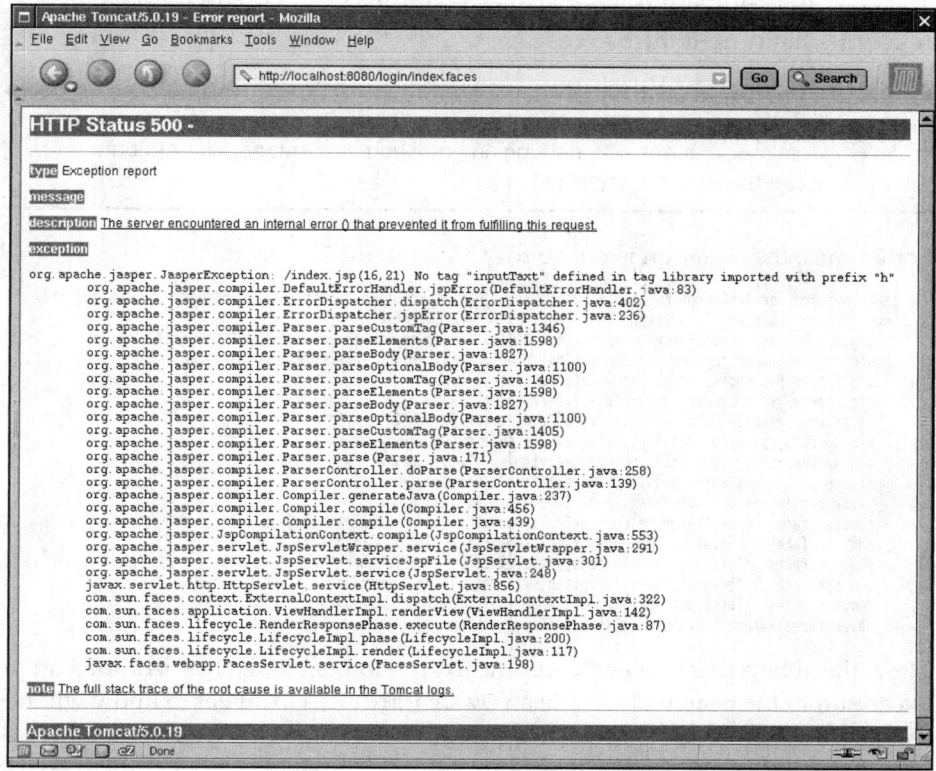

Figure 13–17   Error page

Read the first line (or the first line that seems to make some sense), and correlate it with your JSF file. In this case, there is an illegal tag (inputTaxt instead of inputText) in line 16, column 21, or, we hope, somewhere near there.

The error report may also indicate a problem with your code. For example,

```
java.lang.ClassCastException
    com.corejsf.UploadRenderer.decode(UploadRenderer.java:73)
    javax.faces.component.UIComponentBase.decode(UIComponentBase.java:658)
    javax.faces.component.UIInput.decode(UIInput.java:464)
    javax.faces.component.UIComponentBase.processDecodes(UIComponentBase.java:878)
    javax.faces.component.UIInput.processDecodes(UIInput.java:380)
    javax.faces.component.UIForm.processDecodes(UIForm.java:139)
    javax.faces.component.UIComponentBase.processDecodes(UIComponentBase.java:873)
    javax.faces.component.UIViewRoot.processDecodes(UIViewRoot.java:305)
    com.sun.faces.lifecycle.ApplyRequestValuesPhase.execute(ApplyRequestValuesPhase.java:79)
    com.sun.faces.lifecycle.LifecycleImpl.phase(LifecycleImpl.java:200)
    com.sun.faces.lifecycle.LifecycleImpl.execute(LifecycleImpl.java:90)
    javax.faces.webapp.FacesServlet.service(FacesServlet.java:197)
    com.corejsf.UploadFilter.doFilter(UploadFilter.java:68)
```

The remedy is straightforward. Have a look at line 73 of `UploadRenderer.java` and find out what caused the bad cast.

 TIP: If your stack trace states that errors in your code are in unknown source locations, compile with debugging on. If you use Ant, add the attribute debug="true" to the javac task.

Sometimes, the situation is not so rosy. Consider this report:

```
javax.servlet.ServletException: javax.faces.el.EvaluationException: Error getting property 'password' from
bean of type com.corejsf.UserBean: java.lang.NullPointerException
   org.apache.jasper.runtime.PageContextImpl.doHandlePageException(PageContextImpl.java:864)
   org.apache.jasper.runtime.PageContextImpl.handlePageException(PageContextImpl.java:800)
   org.apache.jsp.index_jsp._jspService(index_jsp.java:78)
   org.apache.jasper.runtime.HttpJspBase.service(HttpJspBase.java:133)
   javax.servlet.http.HttpServlet.service(HttpServlet.java:856)
   org.apache.jasper.servlet.JspServletWrapper.service(JspServletWrapper.java:311)
   org.apache.jasper.servlet.JspServlet.serviceJspFile(JspServlet.java:301)
   org.apache.jasper.servlet.JspServlet.service(JspServlet.java:248)
   javax.servlet.http.HttpServlet.service(HttpServlet.java:856)
   com.sun.faces.context.ExternalContextImpl.dispatch(ExternalContextImpl.java:322)
   com.sun.faces.application.ViewHandlerImpl.renderView(ViewHandlerImpl.java:142)
   com.sun.faces.lifecycle.RenderResponsePhase.execute(RenderResponsePhase.java:87)
   com.sun.faces.lifecycle.LifecycleImpl.phase(LifecycleImpl.java:200)
   com.sun.faces.lifecycle.LifecycleImpl.render(LifecycleImpl.java:117)
   javax.faces.webapp.FacesServlet.service(FacesServlet.java:198)
```

Here, the subsystem that evaluates the expression language has wrapped an exception in the bean code inside an `EvaluationException`. You get to know where the `EvaluationException` is thrown, but that does not help you—you need the location of the `NullPointerException` that caused it.

Your next step is to inspect the log files. In this case, the log contains a more detailed report:

```
Caused by: javax.faces.el.EvaluationException: Error getting property 'password' from bean of type
com.corejsf.UserBean: java.lang.NullPointerException
       at com.sun.faces.el.PropertyResolverImpl.getValue(PropertyResolverImpl.java:89)
       at com.sun.faces.el.impl.ArraySuffix.evaluate(ArraySuffix.java:162)
       at com.sun.faces.el.impl.ComplexValue.evaluate(ComplexValue.java:146)
       at com.sun.faces.el.impl.ExpressionEvaluatorImpl.evaluate(ExpressionEvaluatorImpl.java:238)
       at com.sun.faces.el.ValueBindingImpl.getValue(ValueBindingImpl.java:155)        ... 55 more
Caused by: java.lang.NullPointerException
       at com.corejsf.UserBean.getPassword(UserBean.java:12)
       at sun.reflect.NativeMethodAccessorImpl.invoke0(Native Method)
       at sun.reflect.NativeMethodAccessorImpl.invoke(NativeMethodAccessorImpl.java:39)
       at sun.reflect.DelegatingMethodAccessorImpl.invoke(DelegatingMethodAccessorImpl.java:25)
       at java.lang.reflect.Method.invoke(Method.java:324)
       at com.sun.faces.el.PropertyResolverImpl.getValue(PropertyResolverImpl.java:79)
       ... 59 more
```

Finally, information you can use: Line 12 of `UserBean.java` caused the problem.

Unfortunately, sometimes the stack trace gives you no useful information at all. Here is an example of a bad case:

```
javax.servlet.ServletException: Cannot find FacesContext
    org.apache.jasper.runtime.PageContextImpl.doHandlePageException(PageContextImpl.java:867)
    org.apache.jasper.runtime.PageContextImpl.handlePageException(PageContextImpl.java:800)
    org.apache.jsp.index_jsp._jspService(index_jsp.java:78)
    org.apache.jasper.runtime.HttpJspBase.service(HttpJspBase.java:133)
    javax.servlet.http.HttpServlet.service(HttpServlet.java:856)
    org.apache.jasper.servlet.JspServletWrapper.service(JspServletWrapper.java:311)
    org.apache.jasper.servlet.JspServlet.serviceJspFile(JspServlet.java:301)
    org.apache.jasper.servlet.JspServlet.service(JspServlet.java:248)
    javax.servlet.http.HttpServlet.service(HttpServlet.java:856)
```

What caused this error? Misalignment of the planets? No—the problem was a bad URL: `http://localhost:8080/login/index.`**`jsp`** instead of `http://localhost:8080/login/index.`**`faces`**.

How do I avoid the "stack trace from hell"?

Most Java programmers expect that the compiler finds their syntax errors. Unfortunately, when you develop a JSF application, the compiler only checks your Java source code. Mismatches between the JSF pages, managed beans, and configuration files are only detected at runtime. Slow turnaround time and undecipherable stack traces can be a serious drag on programmer productivity.

Here are some suggestions for detecting errors before you are faced with the "stack trace from hell."

1. Use a validating XML editor for JSF pages and configuration files. The editor should alert you when you misspell element or attribute names, or do not nest elements properly. The default JSP and XML editors in Net-Beans do a fine job. In Eclipse, XMLBuddy is a reasonable choice. If you use a standalone text editor, find a plug-in, such as nXML for Emacs.

2. Use a JSF development environment that understands managed beans and the expression language. If your IDE supports autocompletion, you will not make typos in the first place. If your IDE checks consistency between your JSF pages, managed beans, and `faces-config.xml`, many errors can be detected before deployment.

3. Run the verifier. Most application servers can verify a WAR file before deployment. The verifier can find a variety of errors, such as missing classes and syntax errors in your JSF pages. With GlassFish, run the command

    glassfish/bin/`verifier` *appname*.war

    If you use NetBeans, right-click the project and choose "Verify Project" from the menu.

4. If you use the Sun JSF implementation, force validation of the syntax of `faces-config.xml` and the managed objects that it defines. Add these lines to your `web.xml` file:

```
<context-param>
    <param-name>com.sun.faces.validateXml</param-name>
    <param-value>true</param-value>
</context-param>
<context-param>
    <param-name>com.sun.faces.verifyObjects</param-name>
    <param-value>true</param-value>
</context-param>
```

5.   Use a debugger. Most IDEs support remote debugging of the application server. You can set breakpoints in managed beans and renderers and, with some IDEs, even in JSF pages. The setup can be complex if your IDE does not have predefined support for your application server, but it is well worth the effort.

How do I "hot deploy" my application?

Deploying an application takes time. The application server needs to shut down the old version of the application and then unpack, verify, and initialize the new version. This can be extremely distracting to the developer.

In hot deployment mode, you copy changed files to a deployment directory. The application server senses the change in the file time stamp and incrementally updates the application to use the new file. The result is much faster turn-around and increased developer productivity.

If you use an IDE such as NetBeans, it automatically uses hot deployment. But if you use your own build process, you need to understand how to enable hot deployment in your application server. Here are the rules for GlassFish:

1.   Do not create a WAR file. Instead, you use *directory deployment*. The layout of your build directory needs to be exactly what it would have been in the WAR file. This is sometimes called an *exploded* directory.

2.   Execute the command

     glassfish/bin/asadmin deploydir *buildDirectoryPath*

     to set the directory for your web app and to perform initial deployment. (The last component of the build directory path needs to have the same name as your web application.)

3.   By default, GlassFish uses *dynamic reloading*. When the files in your build directory change, wait two seconds and refresh the browser. This works well when you change a JSF page. However, other changes (such as changes in classes or configuration files) require redeployment. You can trigger redeployment by changing the time stamp of the file *buildDirectoryPath*/.reload (for example, with the Unix touch command).

How do I comment out a part of a JSF page?

Sometimes, to find out which part of a JSF page causes a stack trace, you may want to use the time-honored, divide-and-conquer strategy of commenting out parts of the page to isolate the offending component.

You may find, to your surprise, that the XML comments <!-- ... --> do *not* prevent the enclosed components from being processed. Instead, the components are processed, and they are rendered, enclosed inside <!-- ... -->, so that the rendered markup does not show up in the HTML document. However, this does not help you with debugging since the same exceptions are still thrown.

This behavior seems odd, but keep in mind that most JSF pages are not real XML. They may contain non-XML constructs in JSP syntax, such as <%@ taglib ... %> directives. The JSP processor valiantly tries to parse this mess, and it leaves the XML comment delimiters alone.

There are two remedies. You can use JSP comments <%-- ... --%>. Any components inside these delimiters are not processed.

Alternatively, you can use strict XML for your JSF pages, as described in Chapter 2. If you enclose your JSF pages in a jsp:root tag, then the XML comments will work as expected.

```
<?xml version="1.0"?>
<jsp:root version="2.0"
    xmlns:jsp="http://java.sun.com/JSP/Page"
    xmlns:f="http://java.sun.com/jsf/core"
    xmlns:h="http://java.sun.com/jsf/html">
    <!-- Ok to use XML comments to comment out tags -->
</jsp:root>
```

How do I find the logs?

The details depend on your web container. GlassFish logs all messages in the file *glassfish*/domains/domain1/logs/server.log. You can inspect this file in a text editor, or you can use the GlassFish administration interface.

Log onto http://localhost:4848/asadmin. The default username is admin and the default password is adminadmin. After logging on, you will see a screen similar to the one in Figure 13–18.

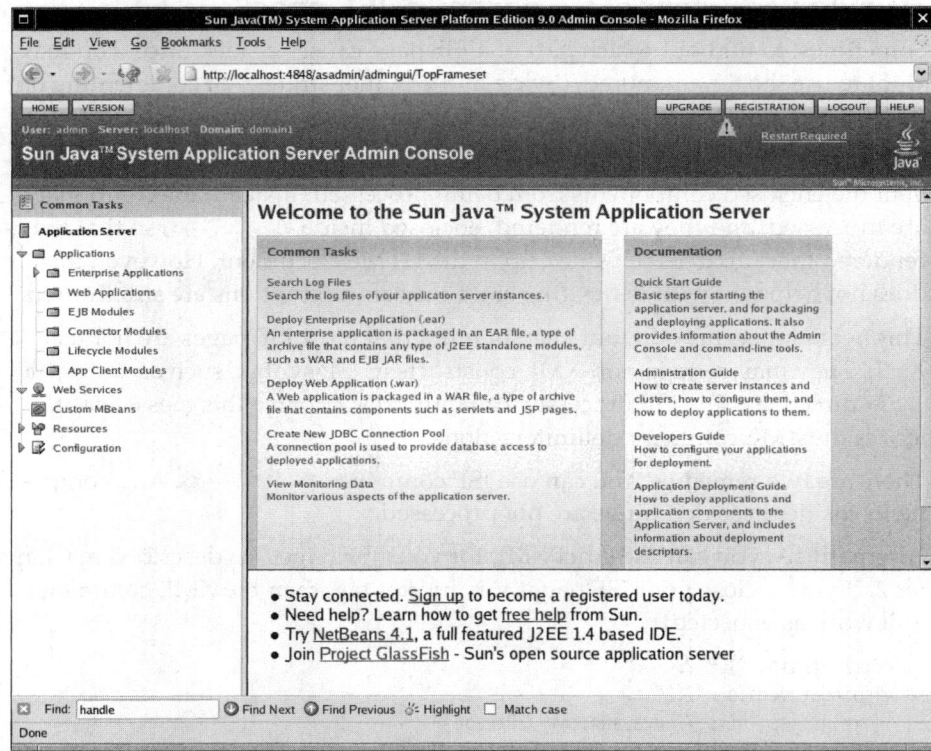

Figure 13–18   The GlassFish administration interface

The first task in the "Common Tasks" window is "Search Log Files". Click this link to get to the log viewer (see Figure 13–19).

Tomcat 5 keeps logs in the *tomcat*/logs directory. The standard Tomcat log files are as follows:

*   catalina.out
*   localhost_log.*date*.log

Here *date* is a date stamp, such as 2003-06-30. The catalina.out file contains all output that was sent to System.out and System.err. In the default configuration, that includes all logging messages with level INFO or higher. The localhost_log.*date*.log files contain the logging messages that were generated by the servlet context.

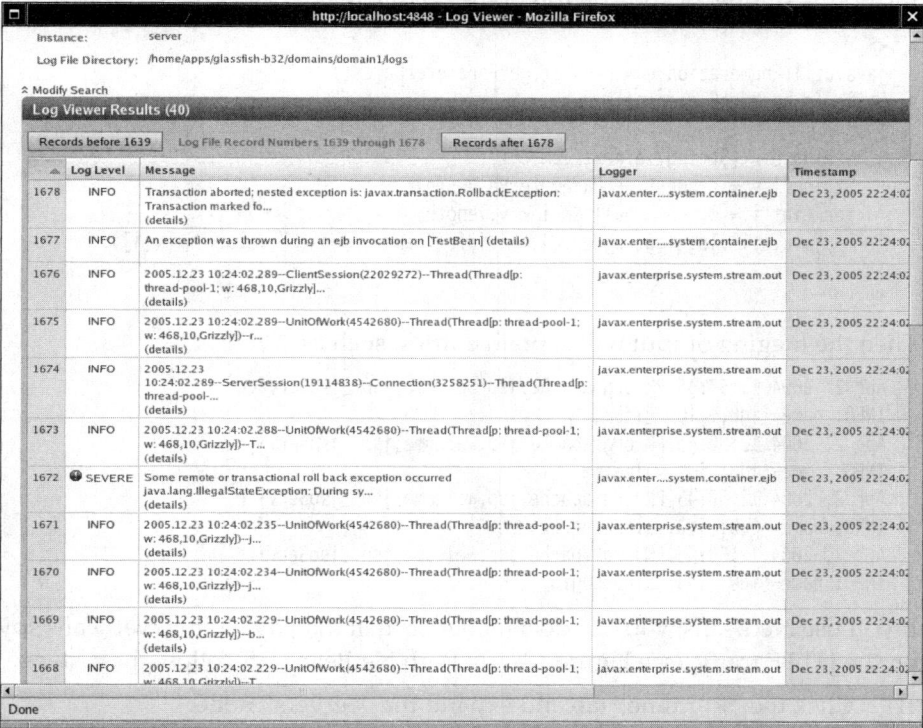

Figure 13–19   The GlassFish log viewer

 NOTE: Both Tomcat and the JSF reference implementation use Apache Commons logging (see `http://jakarta.apache.org/commons/logging.html`). This logging library is a bridge to various logging libraries, in particular the `java.util.logging` library that was introduced in JDK 1.4 and the Apache Log4J library (`http://logging.apache.org/log4j/docs/`). There are religious wars over which logging library is better and whether Commons logging is a good idea (see, for example, `http://www.qos.ch/logging/thinkAgain.html`). We must admit to a slight preference for `java.util.logging`. It may not be perfect, but it is good enough, and it is a standard part of Java.

How do I find out what parameters my page received?

It is often helpful to know what parameters the client sent back to the server when a form was submitted. Here is a quick and dirty method for logging the request parameters.

Insert this snippet of code on top of the JSF file that receives the request:

```
<%
java.util.Enumeration e = request.getParameterNames();
while (e.hasMoreElements())
{
    String n = (String) e.nextElement();
    String[] v = request.getParameterValues(n);
    for (int i = 0; v != null && i < v.length; i++)
        java.util.logging.Logger.global.info("name=" + n + ",value=" + v[i]);
}
%>
```

Then the logging output will contain entries, such as:

```
Apr 2, 2004 12:50:45 PM org.apache.jsp.welcome_jsp _jspService
INFO: name=_id0,value=_id0
Apr 2, 2004 12:50:45 PM org.apache.jsp.welcome_jsp _jspService
INFO: name=_id0:_id1,value=me
Apr 2, 2004 12:50:45 PM org.apache.jsp.welcome_jsp _jspService
INFO: name=_id0:_id2,value=secret
Apr 2, 2004 12:50:45 PM org.apache.jsp.welcome_jsp _jspService
INFO: name=_id0:_id3,value=Login
```

If you use NetBeans, you can do a lot better than that, by having NetBeans spy on the HTTP traffic (see Figure 13–20). With NetBeans 5.5, follow these steps:

1. Click the "Runtime" tab and expand the "Servers" node.
2. Right-click the GlassFish entry and select "Properties".
3. Check "Use HTTP monitor".
4. After you run your application, select the Window -> HTTP Monitor menu option.

The HTTP monitor displays all traffic between the browser and the web server, and conveniently decodes the requests. This is particularly valuable when you develop your own custom components.

How do I turn on logging of the JSF container?

The JSF reference implementation contains copious logging statements whose output can be very helpful in tracking down problems with your applications.

With GlassFish, you can conveniently control logging through the administration user interface. Log onto http://localhost:4848/asadmin. The default username is admin and the default password is adminadmin.

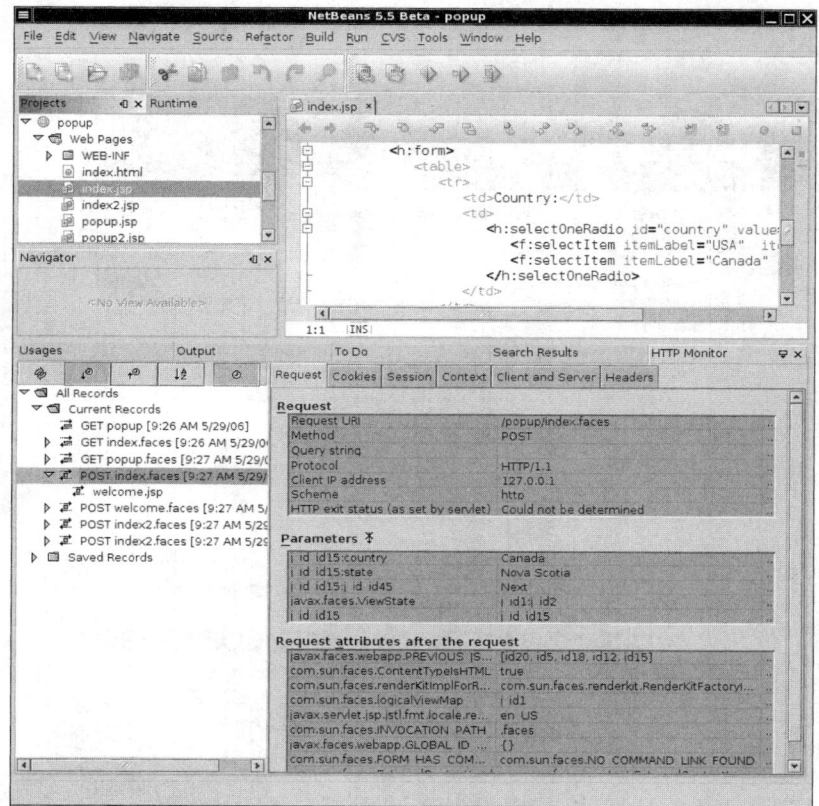

Figure 13–20   The NetBeans HTTP monitor

Then click the "Application Server" node, then the "Logging" tab and then the "Log Levels child" tab. At the bottom of the screen, you will find a table with the title "Additional Module Log Level Properties". Into that table, add an entry with name javax.enterprise.resource.webcontainer.jsf and level FINEST (see Figure 13–21).

When you search the logs, be sure to set the logging level to a value finer than the default level of INFO (see Figure 13–22).

These settings produce a huge amount of logging information. You can fine-tune it by selecting logging for only those children that interest you. The child loggers have suffixes

```
.application    .context      .renderkit
.config         .lifecycle    .taglib
```

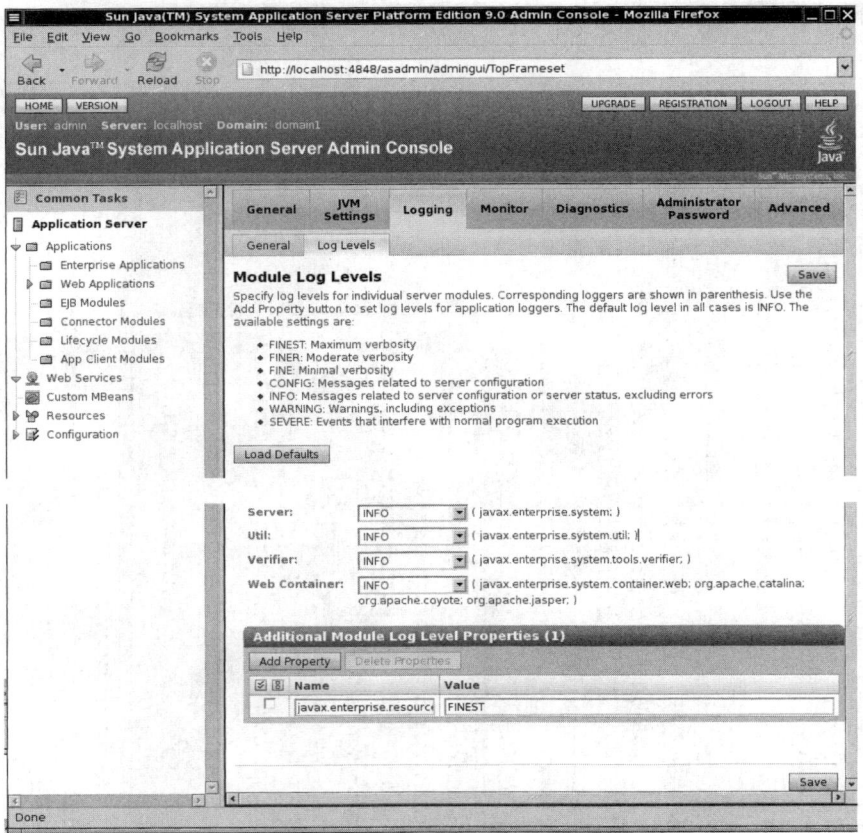

Figure 13–21   Activating JSF container logging in GlassFish

For example, if you are interested in monitoring the life cycle phases, then set only javax.enterprise.resource.webcontainer.jsf.lifecycle to FINEST.

In Tomcat, you use the standard mechanism of the java.util.logging library to configure logging output.

1. Edit the startup script catalina.sh or catalina.bat in the *tomcat*/bin directory. At the top, add a line that sets the variable CATALINA_OPTS to the following parameter definition:

    -Djava.util.logging.config.file=*tomcat*/conf/logging.properties

    In Unix/Linux, use this syntax:

    CATALINA_OPTS="-Djava.util.logging.config.file=*tomcat*/conf/logging.properties"

In Windows, use this syntax:

```
set CATALINA_OPTS=-Djava.util.logging.config.file=tomcat\conf\logging.properties
```

(As always, *tomcat* denotes the name of the Tomcat installation such as /usr/local/jakarta-tomcat-5.5.19 or c:\jakarta-tomcat-5.5.19.)

2. Copy the file logging.properties from the subdirectory jre/lib inside your Java SDK to the *tomcat*/conf directory.

3. Edit the file *tomcat*/conf/logging.properties. Locate the line

    ```
    java.util.logging.ConsoleHandler.level = INFO
    ```

    and change INFO to FINEST. At the end of the file, add a line

    ```
    javax.enterprise.resource.webcontainer.jsf=FINEST
    ```

    (If you use JSF 1.1, set com.sun.faces.level=FINEST instead.)

4. Restart Tomcat and run a JSF application. Then inspect the file *tomcat*/logs/catalina.out.

To turn off JSF container logging, edit *tomcat*/conf/logging.properties and change com.sun.faces.level to INFO.

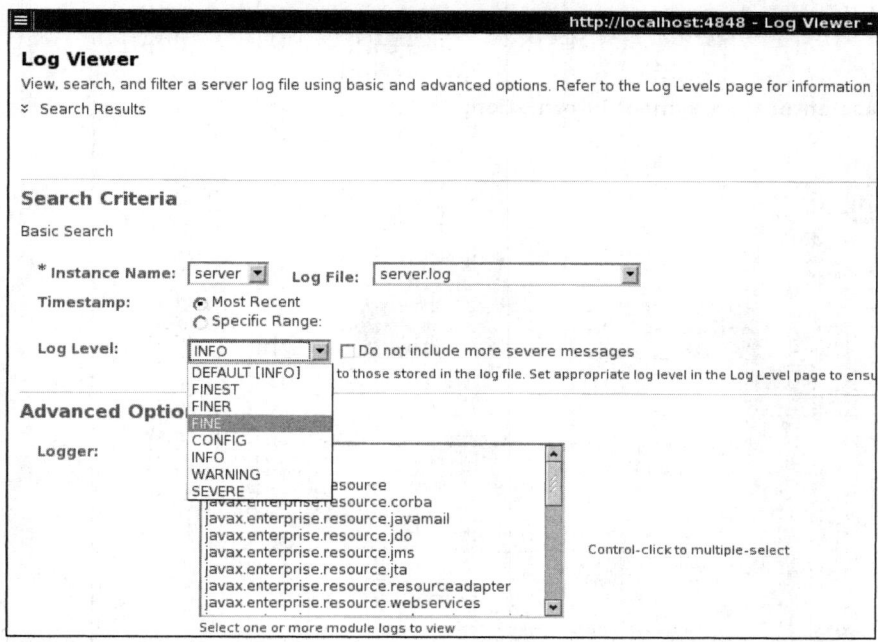

Figure 13–22   Setting the logging level in the GlassFish log viewer

CAUTION: If Tomcat finds the Apache Log4J library on the class path, then it will use that logging library unless you specifically add the following definition to `CATALINA_OPTS`:

`-Dorg.apache.commons.logging.Log=org.apache.commons.logging.impl.Jdk14Logger`

How do I debug a stuck page?

Sometimes, a JSF page seems "stuck." When you click the submit button, the page is redisplayed. Here is what you can do to debug such a page:

- First, double-check the navigation rules to make sure that the page navigation is indeed set up properly.
- The most common reason for a stuck page is a validation or conversion error. This is easy to check by placing a `<h:messages/>` tag on the page.
- If you still do not spot the error, install a phase tracker. You saw a simple implementation in Chapter 7, but for industrial-strength spying, check out FacesTrace from `http://facestrace.sourceforge.net`. It gives you a visual display of the phases (see Figure 13–23).

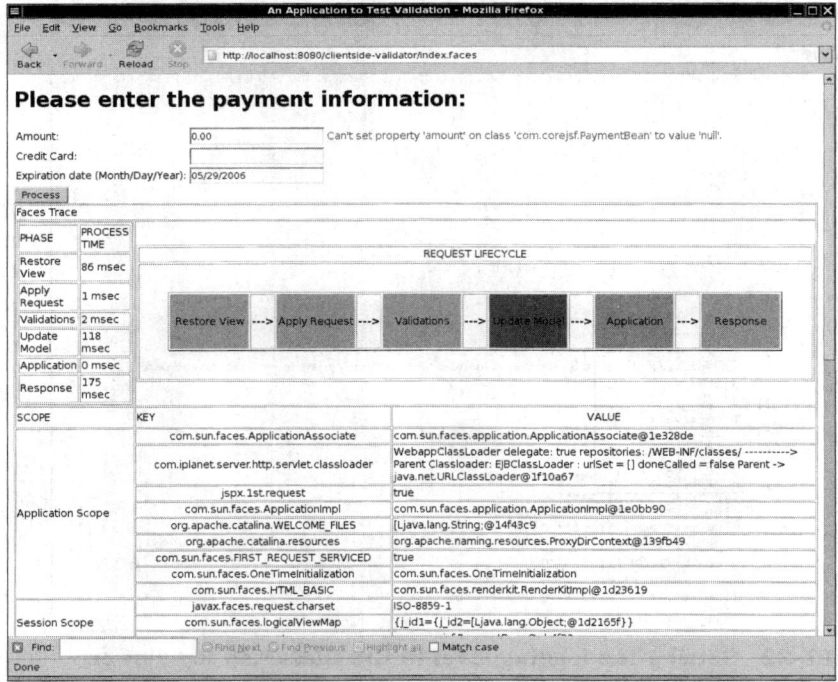

Figure 13–23   FacesTrace in action

FacesTrace is easy to use. Add its JAR file and the Commons Logging JAR file to your web application's `WEB-INF/lib` directory. Import the tag library:

`<%@ taglib uri="http://sourceforge.net/projects/facestrace" prefix="ft"%>`

Then add a tag

`<ft:trace/>`

at the end of your JSF page.

How do I find the library source?

You can download the library source from `http://javaserverfaces.dev.java.net`. The library source can be very helpful for troubleshooting, and to clarify opaque points of the specification.

The library code is organized in three directories:

- `jsf-api`, the documented API classes whose package names start with `javax.faces`
- `jsf-ri`, the reference implementation classes whose package names start with `com.sun.faces`
- `jsf-tools`, the tools that mechanically generate tag handlers and renderers

To get a complete set of source files, you must run the Ant script in the `jsf-tools` directory.

1. Copy the file `build.properties.template` to `build.properties`. Edit the following entries:

   `jsf.build.home=`*path to the* `javaserverfaces_sources` *directory*
   `container.name=glassfish`
   `container.home=`*path to the GlassFish installation*

2. Run ant `main`.

3. The missing source code is produced in the `jsf-ri/build/generate` directory.

Finally, it is sometimes useful to find configuration details of the JSF implementation, such as the JSF names or class names of the standard components, renderers, converters, and validators. Look inside the files `jsf-ri/src/com/sun/faces/jsf-ri-config.xml` and `jsf-ri/build/classes/com/sun/faces/standard-xml-renderkit.xml`.

Index

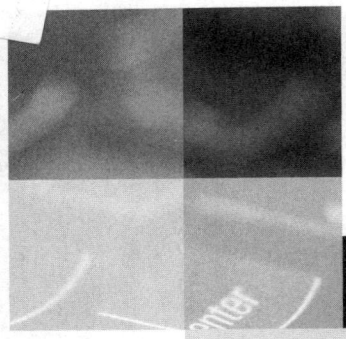

inform IT

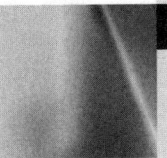